Dominant Powers and Subordinate States

Dominant Powers and Subordinate States

The United States in Latin America
and the Soviet Union in Eastern Europe

Edited by Jan F. Triska

Duke Press Policy Studies   Duke University Press

Durham 1986

Like the other authors in this volume, Jeffrey L. Hughes
contributed one essay to this symposium. But because his
study dealt with issues discussed in different sections of
the book, he agreed to split his contribution into three
segments. As a consequence, Hughes's original chapter
now appears in three different parts of this volume.

Printed in the United States of America on acid-free paper ∞
Library of Congress Cataloging-in-Publication Data
Dominant powers and subordinate states.
(Duke Press policy studies)
Bibliography: p.
Includes index.
1. United States—Foreign relations—Latin America.
2. Latin America—Foreign relations—United States.
3. Soviet Union—Foreign relations—Europe, Eastern.
4. Europe, Eastern—Foreign relations—Soviet Union.
I. Triska, Jan F.   II. Series.
JX1391.D66   1986   327.1'4   86-16718
ISBN 0-8223-0686-7
ISBN 0-8223-0748-0 (paper)

Contents

Preface   ix

Acknowledgements   xiii

Introduction: About This Volume *Jan F. Triska*   1

Part I   History of the Two Regions

1   Historical Comparability *Jeffrey L. Hughes*   25
2   Historical Overview and Comparative Analysis
     Robert Wesson   47
3   Economic Change and State Development *James R. Kurth*   85

Part II   Concepts and Theories

4   Dominant-Subordinate Relationships: How Shall We Define
     Them? How Do We Compare Them? *David B. Abernethy*   103
5   On Influence and Spheres of Influence *Paul Keal*   124
6   Sphere-of-Interest Behavior: A Literature Search and
     Methodological Reflections *Gabriel A. Almond*   145
7   On Bargaining *Jeffrey L. Hughes*   168

Part III   Dominant Powers

8   The Dominant Powers and Their Strategies *David D. Finley*   201

9 The Logics of Hegemony: The United States as a Superpower in Central America *Terry Karl and Richard R. Fagen* 218

10 The Military as an Instrument of Influence and Control *Condoleezza Rice* 239

11 Military Interventions: Doctrines, Motives, Goals, and Outcomes *Jiri Valenta* 261

Part IV Subordinate States

12 The Subordinate States and Their Strategies *Paul M. Johnson* 285

13 Capitalist Dependency and Socialist Dependency: The Case of Cuba *Robert A. Packenham* 310

14 The Politics of Dependence in Poland and Mexico *Jeffrey L. Hughes* 342

Part V Evolution of Spheres of Influence

15 Costs of Domination, Benefits of Subordination *Paul Marer and Kazimierz Z. Poznanski* 371

16 Dominant Powers and Subordinate Regions: 1914 and Today *Richard Ned Lebow* 400

17 The Future of Dominant-Subordinate Systems *Michael I. Handel* 423

Summary and Conclusion *Jan F. Triska* 440

Sources 471

Index 499

Contributors 505

without comparisons to make

the mind does not know how to proceed

—Alexis de Tocqueville

Preface

During the 1980–81 academic year I was a Fellow at the Kennan Institute of the Wilson Center for Scholars in Washington, D.C. In February 1981, with the assistance of the Director of the Center, Jim Billington; his Deputy, Pross Gifford; the Secretary of the Kennan Institute, Tom Gleason; and Chuck Bergquist, a Fellow at the Center and a Latin Americanist from Duke University, I organized and chaired a seminar designed to compare Latin America and Eastern Europe as subordinate regions in international relations.

This was at the height of the Polish crisis, some six weeks after General Wojciech Jaruzelski declared martial law in order to crush the Solidarity movement. New developments were unfolding daily in the El Salvador and Nicaragua crises, and Soviet troops were battling insurgent forces in Afghanistan after a year of Soviet occupation. Zbigniew Brzezinski, the former National Security Advisor, in a speech before the French Institute of International Relations in Paris on January 12, 1981, argued that "if the workers of Gdansk have the right to demand a decent wage and decent weekly hours, the peasants of El Salvador and Nicaragua have a right to demand their land." The events breaking in Eastern Europe and in Latin America were dramatic, and public interest was high. My friends and I were ready for some experimental comparison of the United States and the USSR as regional powers. Perhaps it might lead to something useful, we thought.

Fellows at the Center, scholars in the Washington area, government officials, and others interested in the topic came to the seminar. The room was crowded. The seminar started in an orderly manner and stayed on an even keel for a while but ended in bedlam. The shouting match between those who argued for systematic comparison ("Let's do it!") and those who were against it ("How dare you compare the United States and the USSR!" or "*Dependencia* in Latin America has nothing in common with Soviet hegemony in Eastern Europe!") was beyond control. The seminar was a huge success. I became inspired.

On my return to Stanford, I managed to persuade two creative but busy scholars to join forces with me. Robert Packenham, a distinguished student of Latin American politics, and Jeffrey L. Hughes, an imaginative international relations scholar, patiently listened to my arguments for starting at Stanford a comparative study of the United States and the USSR as dominant powers. They kindly let me talk them into a full-fledged collaboration. After two years of preparatory work, Jeff and I offered a graduate seminar on "The United States and the USSR as Regional Powers." We combined intensive reading of theoretical as well as empirical literature on international regions, useful in conceptualizing Latin America and Eastern Europe as subsystems to be compared, with research papers by both students and instructors. The next academic year Robert Packenham joined Jeff and me, and we offered the seminar this time for two quarters, separating one quarter of reading from the other quarter of research. The three of us offered the two-quarter seminar again in 1985–86.

In addition, I organized two panels on the subject in 1985, one at the American Political Science Association meeting in New Orleans in September and the other in November at the Third World Congress of the American Association for the Advancement of Slavic Studies in Washington, D.C. In addition to Bob Packenham, Jeff Hughes, and myself, the panelists included David Finley of Colorado College, Cole Blasier of the University of Pittsburgh, William Zimmerman of the University of Michigan, Paul Johnson of Florida State University, André Liebich of Université du Québec à Montréal, and Robert Wesson of the Hoover Institution.

When the conference on "Dominant Powers and the Subordinate States: the United States in Latin America and the USSR in Eastern Europe" finally took place at Stanford in January 1986, we were well prepared. Our four years of study paid off. The conference participants were authors of books or articles we had read and discussed in the seminars. Meeting them at the conference was like greeting old friends. They had all had a year to research and write their papers. To assist them in this task, I had mailed to them the bibliographies we had collected for our Stanford seminars, as well as an essay I had written defining the subject, posing the central questions to which I sought answers, and discussing the implications of the problem. This essay is now part of the introduction.

At the conference, drafts of the papers were presented, discussed, and revised. The papers now appear as chapters in this volume.

Jan F. Triska
Stanford University
May 1986

Acknowledgments

The contributors to this symposium and I wish to express our gratitude to several important individuals at Stanford who helped to bring this volume to a successful completion: Rachelle Marshall, copy editor and our principal mentor; Elizabeth Rafferty, undergraduate assistant in the Department of Political Science; Lewis Shepherd, coordinator of people, services, and manuscripts; Barbara Burwick and Susan Sullivan of the International Relations Program; Dr. Barbara Voytek, program coordinator of the Center for Russian and East European Studies; Arlee R. Ellis, department administrator in Political Science; and Eliska Ryznar, head catalog law librarian and our index compositor. We also benefited from the suggestions of the two book reviewers for Duke University Press, Professors Karen Dawisha of the University of Maryland and Jack Donnelly of the University of North Carolina at Chapel Hill.

I have been fortunate in obtaining able assistance from Zdenek L. Suda, Professor of Sociology at the University of Pittsburgh; Charles Drekmeier, Professor of Political Science at Stanford; Yuri Yoshizawa, my Stanford research assistant; Carmel, my wife and severest critic; and, last but not least, the students in P.S. 228, a graduate political science seminar, on whom Robert A. Packenham, Jeffrey L. Hughes, and I tested our ideas.

I wish to acknowledge my intellectual debt to Professor Edy Kaufman of the University of Edinburgh for his book *The Superpowers and Their Spheres of Influence: The United States and the Soviet Union in*

Eastern Europe and Latin America, published by St. Martin's Press in New York in 1977. I reviewed the book favorably in the Spring 1978 issue of *Political Science Quarterly*, vol. 93, no. 1, pp. 135–36. At that time I praised the study, pointing out that it was an important, novel undertaking that answered many significant questions. I also agreed with the author that much remained to be done. This symposium is an attempt to answer some of the remaining questions. It is our tribute to Edy Kaufman, continuing collectively what he successfully initiated as a one-man research effort.

Finally, I am pleased to acknowledge the generous support of the Center for Latin American Studies, the Center for Research in International Studies, the Center for Russian and East European Studies, the Koret Public Policy Symposium Fund, and the Program on International Relations, all of Stanford University, and the Berkeley-Stanford Program on Soviet International Behavior.

Jan F. Triska

Introduction: About This Volume

Jan F. Triska

Investigators who had paid careful attention to more than one country or area soon discovered the intellectual power that is inherent in such comparison.—Karl W. Deutsch

The purpose of this introduction is twofold. First, I wish to show why, after a lifelong study of Soviet–East European relations, I felt the need to broaden the inquiry by comparing those relations with another dominant-subordinate relationship, namely that of the United States with Latin America.* The second purpose is to describe, concisely but conscientiously, the organization and contents of this book.

The Genesis of This Volume

I have been concerned for a long time now with the relationship between the Soviet Union and what is commonly called in the literature —though not very precisely—"Eastern Europe." (Suda, 1984.) This relationship in its strong hegemonic cast is now forty years old; its implications and consequences for international relations, in their East-West setting but also in their North-South dimension, are enormous. And yet how much do we know with accuracy, insight, and clarity about the developmental dynamics of those relations, their uniqueness as a historical phenomenon, the bargaining process they represent, the power excesses and restraints they contain, the modalities of

*The first part of this introduction appeared in *Kosmas* 2 (1984), no. 2: 11–24.

conflict and cooperation they display, the ideological constructs they affect, and the future dilemmas and options they imply?

After World War II, to fill the power vacuum in Central and Eastern Europe, the Soviet Union emerged as the dominant power in the region, the result of American-Soviet collusion at Yalta that divided Europe into Western-American and Eastern-Soviet halves. The Soviets proceeded to use their superior capabilities as leverage in making excessive demands on the adjacent areas along their western border.

Composed of eight relatively small countries — East Germany, Poland, Czechoslovakia, Hungary, Romania, Yugoslavia, Bulgaria, and Albania — this region included about one-fourth of the population of Europe (some 120 million people) living on almost one-fourth of Europe's territory (about a half-million square miles). These "East Europeans" shared very little in common except, of course, their newly imposed iron bond with the USSR.

At Soviet insistence the eight political systems changed their political structures and institutions, their values relevant to politics, their social and economic formations, and their policies. The transformation of the region was rapid, profound, and all-encompassing. The Soviet-dominated area was formed by consent when possible and by force when necessary.

Since the postwar period, the give-and-take between the subordinate political units and the superordinate dominant power have been constant, steady, and sustained. The Soviet Union has tried to maximize its power monopoly and hegemony over the region in order to maximize its own power in the international system. To that end, it has minimized national autonomy in the subordinate East European area. The states in Eastern Europe, on the other hand, have tried to elicit benefits from the USSR as payment for their dependent status while trying to reduce the Soviet power over them by increasing their own autonomy of action. Being excluded from the benefits of membership in the international system to the extent of their subordination to the USSR, some East European states have tried to pursue their interests within the constraints of dependency; others have tried to break out.

The history of Eastern Europe offers irrefutable evidence that while the benefits of domination are high for the dominant power, so are the costs of subordination for the dependent states. The defection of Yugoslavia in 1948, followed by Stalinist repression and terror in Eastern Europe; the Soviet suppression of the East German uprising in 1953; the concession by the 1956 Twentieth Congress of the CPSU that East European countries should be permitted to build "their own roads to socialism," followed by the crisis in Poland and the Soviet-suppressed revolution in Hungary in 1956; the defection of Albania in 1960; the assertion of autonomy by Romania in 1963; the East European economic reforms induced by Soviet neglect in the early 1960s; the Soviet occupation of Czechoslovakia in 1968; the suppression of the Solidarity movement in Poland from 1981 on; and the Soviet cooling of West German–East German relations in 1984—a study of these events reveals that subordination leads to isolation from the international system and results in economic stagnation, maintenance of unpopular regimes, and general demoralization. The cost of deviation, on the other hand, is even higher, as is the risk: deviants and would-be defectors tend to put the security of the region into question, and their behavior could be contagious. Retaliation and reprisal may be expected to be swift. But the rewards for successful deviation and/or defection are very high indeed, and thus attractive to the desperate.

The major problem of Soviet–East European relations is thus the issue of social change. East Europe reveals a deep, progressive alienation between frustrated and restive social forces and obsolete political structures and ideas. This has been the dilemma of the USSR all along: how to deal with social change in Eastern Europe, without, on the one hand, pushing the dependent people into desperate situations or, on the other, harming the Soviets' own dominant interests in Eastern Europe. The national communist elites ruling in Eastern Europe, installed and protected by the USSR, have been embarrassing economically, retrogressive socially, and reactionary politically. These local elites have denied meaningful social participation to the majority of the people while being unable to cope significantly with the negative consequences of Soviet domination. Their response over the years to any unfriendly domestic reaction has been simple: repress the troublemakers, give the rest of the population what you can, but do not rock the boat—preserve the status quo by all means.

This uninspired management of social change has not been a good practice: it has bottled up social pressures and led to periodic explosions. Should these explosions become chronic and cumulative, the whole regional system could backfire.

The Utility of Comparison
But having said all that, we are not much closer to answering the several pointed questions posed at the outset. As long as much of the data and hard evidence, due to government and party secrecy, are hidden from view, a more precise evaluation and more accurate judg-

ment as to the exact nature of Soviet–East European relations will remain elusive. We will have to wait for detailed, objective evidence to come in. In the meantime, however, it may be helpful and even enlightening to look at comparative theoretical and empirical literature—on dominant powers–dependent states relations, on spheres of influence, on bargaining, on the international political economy, on the power of weak states, and on imperialism—in conceptualizing with greater precision East European–Soviet relations. There is also a body of comparative literature that should prove a useful source of hypotheses as to the strategies dependent states may pursue to enhance their autonomy and welfare, the success with which these are employed in highly constraining situations, and the similarities and differences they exhibit across dependent subsystems.

The utility of comparison, both *synchronic* (over space) and *diachronic* (over time), cannot be exaggerated:

> Comparison is the engine of knowledge. Because the comprehension of a single case is linked to the understanding of many cases, because we perceive the particular better in the light of generalities, international comparison increases tenfold the possibility of explaining political phenomena. The observer who studies just one country could interpret as normal what in fact appears to the comparativist as abnormal. Even that which is most familiar can escape perception. *Was ist bekannt, ist nicht erkannt*, underlined Hegel. . . . The juxtaposition of cases is useful not only to situate each one in relation to others but also because it calls for generalizations, those wide melting pots that turn each particular experience into an exemplar, a deviant or a clinical "case," allowing in return a better understanding even of what is specific. (Dogan and Pelassy, 1984.)

There are many historical examples of dominant powers–dependent states relations, from ancient Greece to nineteenth-century Europe and Africa. In the post-World War II period and especially since the early 1970s, several studies have appeared that, in attempting to understand and explain concepts such as spheres of influence, subordinate regions, dependencies, and patron-client relationships, compared the U.S.–Latin American regional system with that of the USSR–Eastern Europe. (Marer, 1974a; Kaufman, 1976; Zimmerman, 1978; Ray, 1981; Clark and Bahry, 1983a; Lebow, 1984.) These studies not only helped to transcend limited historical comparisons but often led to an insightful and more accurate assessment of contemporary Soviet behavior in Eastern

Europe, especially in affording a better sense of the range of possible evolutionary trends there. Comparing contemporary regional systems may thus be a way to organize inquiry that avoids the narrow single focus while offering advantages over the static treatment by a priori assumptions at a high level of abstraction. A comparative analysis should, moreover, permit exploration both within regional systems as well as across such systems. This type of inquiry should also enhance the rigor of East European studies while broadening the analysis. For example, the concept of dependency and corporatism, widely used in Latin American studies, was given theoretical prominence by a Romanian theorist who applied it earlier in this century in Eastern Europe. (Schmitter, 1978.) Similarly, "bureaucratic authoritarianism," the subject of important recent Latin American studies, manifests significant similarities to the East European experience. (Collier, 1979.)

The subject of this volume is thus a cumulative, in-depth comparison of two dominant powers, the United States and the USSR, and their dependencies, Eastern Europe and Latin America, over a span of time. The major issues the volume will address are the principal differences and similarities between a democracy, on the one hand, and an authoritarian system, on the other, in terms of their roles as dominant regional powers. How similar or different are the two superpowers' objectives and strategies in their subordinate regions? What are their opportunities and their constraints? And what are the goals and strategies of the dependent states? Why are there differences in penetration/compliance between them?

If it is true that all nations act to maximize their satisfaction within the constraints of their international environment, then regional powers such as the United States and the USSR, because of their superior capabilities, are less constrained in adjacent areas characterized by inferior capabilities than they are elsewhere in the international environment. Using their superior capabilities as leverages in making demands on their weak adjacent regions, they enhance the probability that their demands, greater than elsewhere, will be met. Leverages of others within as well as outside the regions are limited to the extent of the leverage of the regional powers (although countries with inferior capabilities in a region can often exercise considerable leverage through "nuisance power"). In that sense the will and the capability of the regional powers are decisive, and their power in their regions tends to be hegemonic.

The corollary of the regional powers' will to make substantive demands and to use their superior capability as leverage in their regions is the receptivity of the weak states to the regional powers' demands and their willingness and ability to meet them. There are leaders, elites, movements, groups, etc., in the regions willing and able to engage in the bargaining process and to accommodate the regional powers' demands. While the cost of a regional power's leverage is part of the price of achieving the meeting of a demand, the cost of accommodation to the regional power's demand in the region often results in the deprivation of local domestic satisfaction with a consequent increase in the constraints imposed by the international environment.

Leverage takes many forms — economic, military, ideological, political, etc. It may be positive or negative or a combination of both. The demands are negotiated by the regional powers' agents through various international channels and are directed at national (or regional) targets within the region willing and able to meet the demands. The targets evaluate the capability of the regional power in terms of its performance, in the region as well as at large. Their willingness (and sometimes ability) to accommodate the regional powers' demands depends on their performance in the region — their ability to deliver. The regional powers' agents evaluate the regional response in terms of the regional powers' return on investment — the payoff.

The two regional powers, the United States and the USSR, claim and enforce vis-à-vis each other exclusive control in their respective regions. As a consequence of their East-West zero-sum game, they push their respective clients into the same kind of prisoners' dilemma they themselves are locked into. Because of the regional powers' superior leverage, noncompliance with that strategy or opposition to it, though not impossible, tends to be risky and costly within the region.

Spheres of Influence
There is a broad general agreement in the literature that spheres of influence are geographical areas where one power has exclusive liberty of action (by agreement, by fiat, by restraint of others); where other powers abstain from interfering so that one power can interfere alone; where one power dominates, other powers accept the domination, and the locals acquiesce or resign themselves to subordinate status; or where one power penetrates an adjacent geographical region to the exclusion of other powers. (Keal, 1983b.) A sphere of influence differs from a *dependence*, which is an asymmetric form of interdependence, an external reliance of one state on another that connotes a nonexploitative, symbiotic relationship. A dependence differs from a

dependency, which suggests lack of actor autonomy, a complex of constraints on an actor's behavior, displaced domestic groups, a gap between unpopular elites and masses, economic stagnation, etc. (Caporaso, 1978.) A sphere of influence differs also from an outright *annexation*. In spheres of influence the dominant powers exercise effective control over an area without at the same time claiming formal authority. Annexation, on the other hand, includes both extension of effective control *and* formal authority of the dominant power (Lasswell, 1958), a physical incorporation. On the part of the United States, examples of annexations include parts of Mexico, Puerto Rico, Hawaii, and Alaska; on the part of the USSR, the Baltic Republics, Kurile Islands, parts of Czechoslovakia, Poland, and Romania.

Influence

Influence is a troublesome concept. It is used loosely in the literature, and many attribute to it different meanings and different properties. It has to do with causality—A causing B to do, or refrain from doing, something A desires—and linkage, a conversion process whereby A translates *resources* (diplomatic, economic, ideological, scientific, cultural, military, or other assets), or *skills* (e.g., perseverance), or other means into desired change in B's policies.

Or, to put it differently, influence is a process in which A seeks to change or sustain the behavior of B at acceptable cost and risk. To do so, A offers B a carrot, a stick, or both. A may offer B an asset desired by B in exchange for B's compliance. Or it may threaten B with a sanction. Or A may use both approaches sequentially or simultaneously. B then either changes or sustains its behavior or suffers the consequences.

In a recent study, Rensselaer W. Lee (1983) suggests four separate conversion mechanisms: sanctions (positive or negative, i.e., embargoes, invasions, credits); explicit contingency statements (threats or promises); diffuse contingency statements (advice, encouragement, warning); and more subtle conditioning or "invisible control" (impact without signals). But in one way or another all the conversion processes amount to a simple "If you do X, I will do Y," or "If you don't do X, I will do Y." Because influence is a constant operative in all international relations, it is accepted as a specific part of the general rules of the game among nations.

Simply put, the dominant power's military power, supported by nonmilitary assets and unchallenged by others, does translate into political power and influence.

The Dominant Powers' Strategies

Given their objectives, the dominant powers' attempt to (1) minimize dangers—political, economic, and military—to themselves in the region; (2) discourage states in the region from acting independently; and (3) use regional capabilities—political, economic, and military —for their own purposes. Having established this dominant relationship, the dominant powers view any autonomous relational changes in the subordinate region with suspicion: would such changes harm or aid the established status quo? If they would harm it, they are viewed with apprehension, whatever their local merit. If they would aid it, they are viewed as worthy of support, whatever their local harm. (But the two interests, regional and local, may also coincide, creating at times a symbiotic relationship.) The gravest perceived dangers to the established status quo may range from the subordinate states becoming neutral rather than dependent, to the defection of states in the region to rival dominant powers, to direct challenge in the region by rival dominant powers.

The dominant powers' policies toward their dependent areas are not identical. They differ because the superpowers are different and the penetrated regions are different. The *similarities* stem from the superpowers' principal objective—to maximize their own power and, to that extent, minimize regional autonomy. The *differences* stem from the different, distinctive political systems, cultures, and ideologies that the dominant powers export to the subordinate areas, the types of strategies and instruments used to sustain local dependence, and the way they are implemented.

Differences Between the Subordinate Regions

The differences are both (1) inherent in the region and (2) superimposed by the dominant powers. (1) Latin America is more of a community than Eastern Europe. Regional cohesion in Latin America is relatively high; states in Latin America resemble and complement each other because of their Indo-Iberic cultural background, their common anticolonial history, their shared feelings on the subject of self-determination and regional interaction; their common religious affiliation (90 percent of them are Roman Catholics, the largest Catholic community in the world); and their excellent system of communication. The level of Latin American interaction—personal, professional, functional, economic, and political—is considerable. Regional organizations and institutions, many of which exclude U.S. participation, blossom. In Eastern Europe, on the other hand, there is little regional community. Except for Soviet penetration, the people in Eastern Europe have not much in common; diversity is high. All regional organizations in Eastern Europe are Soviet-led, and most interaction is Soviet-sponsored. Unlike Latin America in relation to the United States, Eastern Europe has a higher standard of living than the USSR; its population is about one-half that of Latin America, its geographical size much smaller than Latin America, its economic development higher than Latin America, and its economic capability lower. (Kaufman, 1976.) (See table A.)

(2) At the same time the two regions are arenas for different kinds of domination. Latin American societies tend to be relatively more open, less directly regimented by the United States, more openly critical of the United States, and with greater freedoms of press and speech. In Eastern Europe the USSR values greater discipline, docility, and emulation of its own values and institutions than does the United States in Latin America. The unequal relationships within the two regions are perceived differently: Latin Americans claim mainly economic exploitation (in terms of national resources, short-term investments, cheap labor, large U.S. assets in Latin America), while Soviet exploitation of Eastern Europe is principally political and security-oriented.

Regional Similarities: Eastern Europe and Latin America
As a consequence of the many differences between the two regions as well as between the two kinds of domination, the list of regional simi-

Table A. Regional Differences: Latin America and Eastern Europe

	Inherent		Superimposed	
	LA	EE	LA	EE
Community	high	low	low	high
Interaction	high	low	low	high
Organizations	high	low (none)	medium (low)	high
Societal openness			encouraged	discouraged
Democratic values			encouraged	discouraged
Discipline, docility			minimal	maximal
Exploitation			economic	political and security

larities is not very long. There are no inherent regional similarities except for a common resentment against domination. The regional powers are blamed for:

the relative isolation of the two regions from the benefits of the international system;

economic slowdown, retardation, and stagnation;

maintenance of unpopular political regimes;

gaps between elites serving the dominant powers' interests and the masses;

denial of meaningful political participation;

high emphasis on bipolarity; and

suppression of legitimate social change.

Superimposed regional similarities stem from the dominant powers' objectives and strategies as superpowers rather than from their tactics, means, tools, choices, and restraints. As contenders on the world scene, the dominant powers wish to use subordinate regions to their own advantage. For that reason they must deny their own subordinate region and its assets to the rival power. They value stability in their regions, and for that reason they try to control both interstate as well as intrastate conflicts. They prefer the status quo and therefore discourage social change that could harm their interests. The regional states, in turn, attempt to use the rival power as a counterbalance to the superimposed domination.

Constraints on the Dominant Powers
The constraints are both domestic and foreign. Domestic constraints stem from the dominant powers' political systems and ideologies. In the case of the United States, these constraints are the product of constitutionalism, separation of powers, checks and balances, pluralism, political culture, public opinion, concern for human rights, and democratic values. The Soviet Union is constrained by domestic claimants for scarce resources such as the military, the police, the economic planners, and the CP bureaucrats. Foreign constraints are based on the nature of the subordinate region (the type, level, character, and intensity of its cohesion, interaction, communication capability, and cooperation); views of other powers (most of the industrialized states as well as the Third World) that share the subordinate peoples' goals, primarily the attainment and maintenance of national and regional independence; policies of international organizations (the United Nations, World Bank, IMF, UNESCO, UNIDO, etc.); international pressure

groups (the World Council of Churches, the Vatican, Amnesty International, etc.); and international public opinion. (Kaufman, 1976.)

Strategies of Dependent Areas
"If men have insufficient resources," wrote Blau, "if no satisfactory alternatives are available to them, if they cannot use coercive force, and if their needs are pressing, [those] who can supply benefits that meet these needs attain power over them." (1964: 149.) In turn, "their compliance with orders ... discharges their obligations" (14). In pursuit of their objectives, then, the dependent states' strategies are to find resources, alternatives, benefits, and forces that would reduce or eliminate their dependency. In the process they bargain, trying to minimize their compliance in exchange for maximum benefits.

The dominant power's military intervention, which makes deviation difficult, is an indicator of the failure of other influence strategies but is relatively easy for the dominant power to carry out. It is also justified on ideological grounds. (Some call the Soviet defense of socialism the "Soviet Johnson doctrine"; both doctrines stress the dominant powers' right to protect their subordinate areas. Poland, 1956, Hungary, 1956, Czechoslovakia, 1968, and Poland, 1981, may be compared with Guatemala, 1954, Cuba, 1961, Dominican Republic, 1965, and El Salvador, Grenada, and Nicaragua, 1983. The USSR stresses the inviolability of socialism; the United States wishes to "safeguard American property," "bring order," "protect the lives of American citizens," and "prevent communism from taking hold in Latin America."

Some left-wing forces in Latin America and all dissidents in Eastern Europe have little hope of bringing about substantive changes, either peacefully or through violence. To achieve meaningful change is difficult, and to maintain it is even more difficult. The margin of superpower security, whether U.S. or Soviet, mostly permits only safe, moderate changes in local social structures and dependency relations. Local dissenters tend to have only gradualist strategies open to them. In addition to differences in the degree of regional penetration by the dominant powers, there are also differences in the degree of state penetration within the subordinate regions. Not all East European or Latin American states are penetrated equally. Poland's agriculture is very little collectivized; Hungary's economy has capitalist ("free enterprise") features; Romania's foreign policy is out of harmony with Soviet foreign policy; Mexican presidents habitually lecture and put down American presidents; Panama successfully pressed for the return of the Canal; Ecuador and Peru periodically arrest American tuna fishermen. It seems that when constraints on the superpowers are operative, when compliance of the locals is satisfactory, and when geopolitics is not a factor, dependency (parasitism) may acquire attributes of dependence (symbiosis) or may even pass for interdependence.

The Organization of This Volume

This volume is a collective attempt to compare the U.S.–Latin American and Soviet–East European regional systems in order to better understand: (1) international influence on those systems, (2) change in subordinate regions, (3) evolutionary tendencies, trends, conditions, and developments in the relations between the dominant states and their dependencies, (4) the implications of sphere-of-influence building for East-West as well as for North-South relations, and (5) differences between democratic and authoritarian foreign policy behavior and between socialist and capitalist developmental frames of reference.

Still, the two overarching concerns of this symposium are (1) the difference between a liberal democracy, the United States, on the one hand, and an authoritarian communist party state, the Soviet Union, on the other; and (2) the problem of social change in subordinate states and regions. (1) The distinction between democratic and authoritarian foreign policies has been a major concern of political theorists for over two millenia. Focusing on limited, issue-specific areas of regional foreign policy behavior of the United States and the Soviet Union will permit us, we hope, to generate sharper and more comprehensive insights and comparisons. (2) How to deal with social change in dependent states has been the major dilemma of all dominant powers: arresting social change may lead to desperation and explosion in the area, costly to the dominant power; but permitting social change to take place may harm the dominant power's interests even more. What can, and should, the dominant powers do? And what can, and should, the subordinate states do?

The seventeen chapters that follow are arranged according to their central themes. Part I is a historical overview of the two regional systems, a systematic comparison of the developments of the two regions as spheres of influence, as well as of the evolution of the Monroe Doctrine and the Soviet defense of socialism (often not entirely correctly called the Brezhnev doctrine).

Like all the other authors in this volume, Jeffrey L. Hughes contributed one essay to the symposium. But because his study dealt with issues discussed in three different sections of the book, he agreed to split his contribution into segments. Here, in the first segment of his original chapter, Hughes writes about "Historical Comparability." He begins by affirming the usefulness of comparing Soviet–East European and U.S.–Latin American spheres of influence. He then addresses the normative and analytical complexities involved in such a comparative analysis, giving special weight to the perspective of the weaker states. Next he puts the problem in perspective by sketching out a long-standing European tradition comparing U.S. and Russian power in their adjacent regions up through the early twentieth century. Finally, he shows how the post-World War II literature comparing the superpowers' roles and spheres of influence developed, and how it illustrates not only the complexities of analysis noted earlier, but also the benefits of specific comparisons between the regions.

Robert Wesson in "Historical Overview and Comparative Analysis" maintains that the spheres of influence of the two dominant powers are similar as a result of power relations and dissimilar because of their different systems and methods. Both spheres are outgrowths of nation-building, have a fundamental geographic basis, and are security-oriented. But the Soviet sphere, Wesson contends, is much more important for the Soviet Union than the American sphere is for the United States, and its binding is primarily military; the looser American sphere is tied mostly by economic bonds. The principle behind the Soviet sphere is organization and politicization in the Leninist mode; the American practice has been political interference or armed intervention only as needed to protect the market economy and fend off intrusions.

Also in Part I, James R. Kurth in "Economic Change and State Development" examines the relationship between economic change and political regimes in the states of subordinate regions. His focus is on Latin America and Eastern Europe, but comparative references are also made to the Middle East.

In subordinate regions, Kurth argues, different levels of industrialization are associated with different kinds or "central tendencies" of political regimes. For example, in agricultural economies it is normal for the political regime to be a traditional monarchy (e.g., Eastern Europe before World War II, the Middle East until the 1950s–1960s). Deviations from this norm are likely to be relatively unstable or especially brutal (e.g., caudillo dictatorships in Latin America until the 1960s). Conversely, in the early import-substitution or consumer-goods stage of industrialization, the political regime is likely to be a national-populist one, usually a dictatorship but sometimes a democratic system (e.g., the Southern Cone of Latin America in the 1930s–1960s, the Middle East since the 1960s). During the later, capital-goods stage of industrialization, it is normal for the political regime to be a bureaucratic-authoritarian one such as the Southern Cone of Latin America in the 1960s–1970s and Eastern Europe in the 1950s–1970s. Finally, in the stage of advanced or mature industrialization, the norm for the political regime is to be social-democratic (e.g., Western Europe since the 1950s).

But the dominant powers in subordinate regions, Kurth concludes, often cannot accept these central tendencies in the politics of their client states, and they intervene to impose or support a different mode of regime, usually one that represents a political formula that is growing obsolete. The Soviets have done so in contemporary Eastern Europe, the United States frequently in Latin America. The methods of intervention also vary according to the levels of economic development. And the author further discusses the impact of economic crises on subordinate regimes.

Part II (Concepts and Theories) focuses on strengths and weaknesses as a comparative lens for studying the two regional systems, as well as on the dilemmas and paradoxes of unequal interactions. The relevance of data comparison and cases for theory formation are also discussed. The chapters included here examine concepts such as empires and colonies; influence, power, and bargaining; relations between patrons and clients; dependence and dependency; and penetration and integration.

In particular, David B. Abernethy in "Dominant-Subordinate Relationships: How Shall We Define Them? How Do We Compare Them?" tries to do four things: (1) define the characteristics of a dominant state–subordinate state relationship; (2) indicate how two or more such relationships might be compared: initially by identifying similarities, then by identifying differences; (3) begin the comparison process by noting similar features in the U.S.–Latin American and the Soviet Union–East European cases; and (4) identify these similar features by comparing the two cases with yet another set of cases: the formal empires established by Western European states over territories and peoples in the Americas, Africa, and Asia.

Abernethy defines the relationship between a dominant and a subordinate state as possessing the following characteristics: the interaction between the two states has a certain degree of functional breadth and historical depth; consequences of the interaction are significant for the subordinate state; the two states are markedly unequal in "compliance capacity"; the dominant state has demonstrated the will successfully to use its greater compliance capacity; the domestic and foreign policy autonomy of the subordinate state is seriously constrained by its awareness of the compliance capacity and interests of the dominant state; institutions based within the dominant state penetrate the subordinate state's territory, becoming simultaneously domestic political actors within the subordinate state *and* external influences upon it.

Comparison of the two dominant-subordinate cases discussed in this volume with European colonial empires highlights several additional features that the U.S.–Latin American and Soviet–East European cases have in common. Subordinate states are legally sovereign; the two dominant states articulate an anticolonial ideology; sphere-of-influence boundaries are not clearly defined; dominant and subordinate states are connected by land; the two dominant states are physically distant from one another, as are their respective spheres of influence; cultural penetration by the dominant states is limited; the dominant states lack the will to use the most destructive features of their compliance capacity (i.e., nuclear weapons) on each other or on their subordinate states.

Paul Keal in his chapter "On Influence and Spheres of Influence" claims that states in spheres of influence are of only two kinds: influencing powers and the states influenced by them. A sphere of influence brings into focus the relationship between an influencing power and the states influenced by it. The importance of spheres of influence in international politics, however, has been chiefly their use as a device for regulating relations between two or more influencing powers.

When compared in this light, the Soviet Union and the United States are guided by the imperatives of their position as great powers in the international hierarchy. Their behavior is comparable and interrelated through the influence they exercise on each other. In turn, what they allow each other shapes the relationship between each of them and the states in their respective spheres. Thus the possibilities for change within a sphere are linked to the relationship between influencing powers.

Generally spheres of influence promote order in relations between influencing powers but disorder and injustice in relations between those powers and the states they influence. Keal concludes that as a framework for analysis the concept of spheres of influence is limited. It is useful for comparative or quantitative analysis of influence and spheres of influence. But it does not illuminate the spectrum of qualitative differences in the degrees and kinds of influence that dominant powers exert within either the same or different spheres.

In his chapter "Sphere-of-Interest Behavior: A Literature Search and Methodological Reflections," Gabriel A. Almond does two things: (1) he searches the literature from classical political theory to contemporary foreign policy studies for propositions about the importance of regime characteristics for foreign, defense, and sphere-of-interest-policy; and (2) he discusses the methodological issues that arise in efforts to compare Soviet and U.S. behavior in Eastern Europe and Latin America. After considering *dependencia* approaches to these methodological issues, Almond discusses three kinds of comparison of Soviet and U.S. sphere-of-interest-behavior: descriptive, evaluative, and explanatory. And he presents the logical structure of an explanatory theory of sphere-of-interest comparison, which generates four sets of hypotheses — strategic, political, ideological, and economic.

In "On Bargaining" Jeffrey L. Hughes argues that superpower motivations and mechanisms of influence differ in their spheres of influence in Latin America and Eastern Europe but remain comparable in terms of their bargaining relations with weaker states. First, both dominant powers obtain benefits and incur costs in their relations with weaker states in ways similar to previous historical systems of predominance-dependency relations. Second, a bargaining model helps capture the similar dynamics and variations in influence strategies within each sphere; it outlines the conditions for greater power control, on the one hand, and weak state autonomy, on the other. Third, Hughes analyzes declines in U.S. and Soviet predominance in their spheres in the post-World War II period in terms of the model, as well as the concomitant variations in patterns of weak state diplomacy, which vary systematically according to a typology of bargaining profiles drawn from the model. Finally, the author uses the implications of the analysis to reflect on the costs and vulnerabilities of the superpowers' positions and the evolving nature of their influence in Eastern Europe and Latin America.

Part III deals with the two dominant powers — their interactions in the international system, their strategies in their regions, their militaries as instruments of influence and control, and their responses to changes in subordinate states. In particular, David D. Finley in "The Dominant Powers and Their Strategies" compares the strategies that the United States and the Soviet Union have pursued as the dominant powers in their respective regions. The first part of his chapter presents the thesis that their de facto strategies have been the product of tensions between their declared strategies and the events that have been perceived to frustrate them. Thereafter he establishes a conceptual and theoretical framework for regional comparisons. Then he identifies similarities and differences between the dominant powers' strategies, in the contexts of East-West and North-South relations and with reference to pressures for change in the domestic order of the subordinate states. Finally, he assesses implications of present trends for U.S. and Soviet strategies in the future.

In "U.S. Imperialism in Central America and Soviet Hegemony in Eastern Europe" Terry Karl and Richard R. Fagen argue that despite important similarities in behavior (U.S. troops in Vietnam and Soviet troops in Afghanistan, U.S. use of local client militaries in Central America and Soviet use of a client military in Poland), the U.S. and Soviet spheres of influence are not, at root, equivalent systems of dominant-subordinate relationships. The authors do not, however, set out to prove this assertion through parallel case materials. Rather, they examine four separate but interrelated systemic logics: (1) superpowers in conflict, (2) the United States as the dominant power in the capitalist world system, (3) antirevolutionary politics in a regional context, and (4) the specificity of regime type (democracy) in the United States. Karl and Fagen argue that important similarities between the United States and the Soviet Union are found in the first domain, where in reciprocal and mutually reinforcing fashion each superpower acts to consolidate its global position at the expense of the other within a Cold War context of semi-zero-sum calculations. In contrast, the other analytical categories serve to differentiate between the two superpowers in terms of their hegemonic systems and their behavior. From this perspective, the authors maintain, logic one, although critically important, actually explains the least. Thus they concentrate on the other three logics, suggesting that an understanding of the sources, instrumentalities, and constraints on U.S. attempts to exercise hegemony in Central America will not be found primarily in an abstract consideration of superpower behavior in a (militarily) bipolar world.

In "The Military as an Instrument of Influence and Control" Condoleezza Rice first examines the way in which the United States and the Soviet Union pursue their normative and functional objectives in structuring their relations with the indigenous military in their respective spheres of influence. Second, she compares the mechanisms employed. Third, she constructs a rough set of indicators that allow comparison of the use of the military instrument by the United States and the Soviet Union. The index has three elements: penetration, multiplicity of layers, and sustainability, and she draws empirical evidence from a number of cases in which the dominant power is known to have objected, at some critical juncture, to the course of a subordinate state's development and turned to military intervention as a remedy. In sum, Rice tries to assess the strengths and weaknesses of the military as an instrument for influence-building and/or control in subordinate states.

In "Military Interventions: Doctrines, Motives, Goals, and Outcomes," Jiri Valenta compares interventions by the dominant powers in countries within their spheres of influence. Both the United States and the Soviet Union have far-reaching interventionist capabilities that they have used directly or indirectly to affect the domestic affairs of subordinate states. Some symmetry between U.S. and Soviet interventionist strategy is undeniable, especially in attempts to legitimize and justify interventions. A degree of similarity is also manifest in the doctrines they use to support their actions; however, interventions are not usually a response to clear-cut doctrines. The motives of both dominant powers have often been multifaceted and changing, reflecting evolving images of national security. Nevertheless, in spite of such similarities, Valenta argues, the interventionist outcomes have been asymmetrical, primarily because the motives, conditions, and political-ideological approaches that facilitate the Soviet structural interventionist continuity in Eastern Europe have been lacking on the part of the United States. Unlike Soviet interventions, most U.S. interventions were not means of establishing or maintaining permanent U.S. control.

Part IV contains three chapters focusing on subordinate states in Eastern Europe and Latin America—their autonomy strategies, their chances for either symbiotic relations with dominant powers or for defection from the domination, and the difference between capitalist and socialist domination. Here Paul M. Johnson in "The Subordinate States and Their Strategies" examines the structure and the process of the two regional systems from the vantage point of the dependent states. While the leaders of these states see the attainment of greater autonomy as desirable, in practice the active pursuit of this value is apt to involve unpleasant trade-offs. Ideological preconceptions, the desire for great power protection against aggressive third powers or domestic insurgents, and the belief that continuing economic interaction with the hegemon is (on net) beneficial to the country's economic development frequently stand in the way of more assertive policies by the smaller states.

Johnson's analysis of the principal interests of the United States and the USSR in their respective regions points out several parallels but on balance suggests a larger asymmetry. The salience of the East European region to the Soviet foreign policymakers has been much greater than the salience of Latin America to United States leaders. The Soviet leaders' closer attention to the region may account for their greater success in maintaining consistent compliance with their preferences by their smaller allies, but Johnson's explication of the differences in the two superpowers' capabilities for exerting influence through specific, institutionalized mechanisms of penetration (military-coercive, political, economic, and normative) suggests other reasons as well. The concentration of bureaucratic power over both economic decision-making and the media of communication/socialization in the hands of the political leadership provides the Soviet leaders with significant advantages in comparison with the more decentralized and mutually autonomous structures of power characteristics of U.S. political, economic, and cultural life.

Despite the extensive mechanisms encouraging or compelling small state conformity in both Eastern Europe and Latin America, Johnson maintains, conflicts of interest between the superpowers and the subordinate states nevertheless come to the surface with regularity. Because of their significance to the regional hegemon, the smaller states have always enjoyed some bargaining power, if only because consistent rigid neglect of their most basic interests threatens the very survival of institutions on which the hegemon relies for control. The "threat of collapse" may be a potent bargaining tool. The most spectacular confrontations, however, take place when small states come to perceive progress toward one or more of their vital and pressing objectives as being blocked by constraints imposed by the hegemon. In such circumstances the hegemon is apt to resort to the full range of military, political and economic sanctions available to it, and successful assertion of independence by the small state requires strategies tailored to deterring or counteracting each of the specific mechanisms of control.

Robert A. Packenham in "Capitalist Dependency and Socialist Dependency: The Case of Cuba" asks whether socialism makes a difference so far as structural dependency and its alleged internal and policy concomitants are concerned. Recent interpretations of Latin American and Third World development answer in the affirmative. However, although these authors have done studies of concrete situations of capitalist dependency, they have seldom done studies of concrete situations of socialist dependency, especially as regards the internal and policy aspects that are central in the approach.

The study of Cuba before and after 1959 provides an especially good opportunity to address this question—really several questions—and thus to contribute to the comparative analysis of capitalist and socialist dependency. The analysis suggests both affirmative and negative answers. Based on the Cuban case one can say that the specific features, forms, and mechanisms of dependency under socialism are indeed often quite different from those under capitalism. However, Packenham also suggests, contrary to the dominant view, that domination and exploitation of popular classes by an alliance of external actors and the internal elites they are linked with continue under socialism no less than, and in some ways more than, they did under capitalism. The context and forms are different, but the facts of domination and exploitation continue.

In "The Politics of Dependence in Poland and Mexico" Jeffrey L. Hughes maintains that spheres of influence are fashioned to forestall *external* threats at acceptable cost. Yet a comparison of Soviet-Polish and U.S.-Mexican relations illustrates the nature of challenges that can arise *within* each sphere. Comparison of Poland and Mexico is justified, Hughes argues, by reason of their strategic location, size, culture, and unfolding of severe internal crises—crises that in some sense threaten the political or economic mainstays of each sphere system. There are also important similarities, as well as differences, in their bargaining relations with the superpowers. While both Poland and Mexico have become more dependent upon their superpower patron in the 1980s, this has been accompanied by their increased challenges to superpower preferences and the latter's decreased ability to effectively cope with the sources of challenge at low cost. The bargaining model outlined in chapter 7 is used to examine this paradox; it helps explain why there are fewer ways the superpowers can threaten their key neighbors without also harming themselves. Whether the incentives for repression and austerity will predominate over adjustment and cooperation is unclear. In either case, the meaning of security takes on problematic dimensions.

Part V (Evolution of Spheres of Influence) attempts to assess the meaning and value of change from the past to the future. How is the domination/subordination relationship changing—in scope, content, intensity, direction, and instruments? Why is it changing? How do both parties manipulate each other? With what results?

Paul Marer and Kazimierz Z. Poznanski in "Costs of Domination,

Benefits of Subordination" present a sweeping overview of postwar economic developments in Eastern Europe, a general discussion of the evolution of Soviet–Eastern European economic relations during the last four decades, and a detailed analysis of "who subsidizes whom and by how much?" in those relations. Throughout this chapter they compare Soviet–Eastern European relations with U.S.–Latin American relations, focusing particularly on the economies of the Southern Cone and Mexico in Central America. The intersystem comparisons deal primarily with three forms of superpower influence on subordinate states: the promotion or imposition of an "appropriate" economic system; the structural dependence arising from the superpower's dominant role as supplier or market; and the net transfer of wealth between the superpower and its dependent states.

Marer and Poznanski conclude that because the East European countries have by and large exhausted the resources that could be mobilized from domestic, Soviet, or Western sources under their Soviet-imposed economic and political system, they face not temporary but fundamental economic difficulties. No obvious or likely solutions are in prospect, a fact of fundamental, long-term importance for the USSR. This contrasts with the situation of the developing Latin American countries within the U.S. sphere of influence, where constraints on development are less severe and can be traced more to domestic than to external factors.

In the chapter entitled "Dominant Powers and Subordinate Regions: 1914 and Today" Richard Ned Lebow argues that to understand the full range of possible interactions and to better assess the efficacy of specific national strategies, it is useful to examine relations between dominant powers and subordinate regions in historical perspective. His chapter explores some of the similarities and differences between contemporary dominant power–subordinate region interactions and those in the decade before 1914. He shows why these interactions were an important cause of World War I and delineates the conditions in which they could become a source of grave superpower tensions in the future.

Using the concepts "dominant" and "subordinate" to describe the relationship between states implies that the more powerful states can translate their military and economic strength into political and economic gains; that they can, at least up to a point, control the behavior of weaker states. This, however, is often not the case, maintains Michael I. Handel in "The Future of Dominant-Subordinate Systems."

The United States was unable to win the war in Vietnam despite its military superiority and had to ignominiously withdraw its troops from Lebanon; nor can the United States readily influence, let alone control, the policies of countries such as Egypt or Israel, which it heavily supports. Possession of superior military strength did not prompt the United States to undertake any major military action against Iran during the hostage crisis and has not enabled the United States to significantly muzzle or restrain Libya's strongman, Colonel Muammar Qaddafi. Similarly, the Soviet Union cannot impose its will on Afghanistan or control the policies of Ghana, Syria, Vietnam, or Romania. In short, the powerful frequently do not dominate and the weak are not necessarily submissive. This disparity between the concepts we employ and the reality of international relations has led Handel to identify some possible causes for the decline in the utility of power in relations between the great nations and weaker states. In his essay Handel identifies five interrelated trends that first emerged in the aftermath of World War II and have become far more pronounced since the 1950s:

(1) The rise of democratic values and their influence on hegemonic policies; (2) the gradual change, recognized belatedly and reluctantly, from the primacy of foreign policy to the primacy of domestic politics in the concerns of the great powers; (3) the nuclear revolution and the emergence of a new shared interest between the superpowers—that is, the need to avoid direct confrontation and the risk of a nuclear war; (4) the much higher cost of using conventional military power; (5) the recognition on the part of the great powers that they can enjoy just as great (or perhaps greater) economic benefits by means of trade and the mechanisms of free trade than they can achieve through direct dominance.

Handel concludes that the costs of direct dominance and intervention have become unacceptably high and that indirect control is not only cheaper and more effective but also comes without the responsibilities that direct dominance involves.

The authors in this volume represent a spectrum of fields of scholarship, a mix of modes and levels of analysis, as well as an assortment of points of view. This is both useful and, given the nature of the subject, inevitable. But there is one important common denominator, one thing that all the authors share, and that is their appreciation of the usefulness of comparing the two regional systems. They all agree that if social scientists do not search for similarities and differences in phenomena and classes of phenomena across space and over time, their observations are bound to be time-bound, ahistorical, and inaccurate. And, what is even more important, the authors agree that in addition to significant differences between the two spheres of influence, there are significant similarities as well.

I History of the Two Regions

1

Historical Comparability

Jeffrey L. Hughes

The same phenomenon will occasionally be found to recur with startling exactitude in times and places far remote from each other, though in very different guise.—Jacob Burckhardt, *Reflections on History*, 1871.

This chapter addresses the problems and benefits of comparing the Soviet–East European and U.S.–Latin American spheres of influence.* The appropriateness of comparing these regions and social systems has been questioned from different standpoints. But even a rejection of the comparison indirectly affirms it. So the comparison is unavoidable and is best done explicitly and systematically. There are also real theoretical and practical benefits to be gained from weighing the similarities and differences between the regional systems. It is surprising, therefore, to find that there is a comparatively small amount of literature on this topic and that, until recently, the work that has been done

*I would like to acknowledge the support of the MacArthur Foundation and the Ford Foundation Dual Competence Fellowship in Soviet/East European and International Security Studies.

has been only sporadically developed by individual scholars. Accounting for the logic of the development of this literature highlights both the complexities and the usefulness of comparing the superpower spheres.

First, I outline several potential benefits of systematically comparing superpower policies in their spheres of influence. Second, I address the normative and analytical complexities involved in comparing the contemporary spheres. These point to reasons why the literature on this topic has developed so fitfully. Third, I identify several conditions that favored scholarly objectivity or that raised questions requiring comparative analysis of these regions. Initial post-World War II scholarship in this area, for example, almost never involved U.S. or Soviet nationals, comparisons came from outside the spheres or from the weaker states. The relevance of these conditions is illustrated in an examination of (a) a long-standing European intellectual tradition comparing the development of U.S. and Russian power and its implications for adjacent regions up through the early part of this century, an account that also helps put the contemporary comparison in perspective, and (b) the pattern of development of the post-World War II literature comparing the regions. The pattern by which this work initially developed reflects the conditions of objectivity and testifies to the normative and analytical complexities noted earlier. But it also reflects an evolution toward a more coherent field of study that raises and focuses on questions requiring more specific comparisons.

The Potential Benefits of Comparing U.S. and Soviet Spheres of Influence

There are clear benefits to be had from making rigorous comparisons between U.S. policy in Latin America and that of the Soviet Union in Eastern Europe. Therefore it is surprising to find that "the researcher in spheres of influence has an unsurveyed forest to explore into which some faint pathways have been trod by a few pioneers and by others on their way to different destinations." (Vloyantes, 1975: 31.) After briefly outlining the analytical and practical benefits of comparison, the chapter will explain why these benefits have been incompletely realized and describe the logic by which these faint pathways have developed to define an area of study.

The argument for comparing the two spheres of influence does not simplistically imply that the USSR is "as good" as the United States or that the latter is "as bad" as the former. First, it addresses the commonalities of great power that cannot be ignored. Although some treat the United States as having a unique approach to foreign relations, others recognize a consistent and inevitable tradition of realpolitik. This combination of unique worldview and traditional pursuit of power is amply evident in the Soviet case. Second, the comparison sharpens theoretical claims. It challenges explanations constructed for one region to account for outcomes in the other region: either similar outcomes one would not expect or could not account for from one's theory, or different, unanticipated outcomes resulting from the effects of a key variable in the other region. Third, it addresses the reasons why even a nobly motivated U.S. policy may occasionally founder from the standpoint of the weaker states. It therefore may foster corrective action and a more differentiated analysis of threats to regional stability. Fourth, comparison systematically addresses fundamental difficulties of perception. These affect both theory and practice and are not limited to the great powers alone. There is an account of a Turkish diplomat lauding the good fortune of his Mexican hosts to live next to a benign superpower. From the Turkish standpoint, having waged centuries of conflict with Russia, this comparative advantage was self-evident. The embarrassed silence of the Mexican diplomats to the toast, however, was followed by their interpretation of Mexican history indicating that they perceived their burden to be as great as that of the Turks. Comparison capitalizes on and tests the limits of the notion that "our enemies are nearer the truth in their opinion of us than we are ourselves" (La Rochefoucauld, 1665; cited in 1959: 90), and nearer, perhaps, than even our sympathetic friends.

Finally, in the light of historical change, comparison may offer a more balanced assessment of the prospects for democracy. Some argue that totalitarianism is irreversible, that, in Kundera's words, the Soviet empire in central Europe is a "tunnel without end," attributing a majestic staying power to this form of social organization that potentially outlasts all others. On this view any comparison risks blurring the issues, weakening resistance. But left unchallenged this morally unassailable position risks myopia. It attempts to establish a general principle from the comparatively short post-World War II period, a principle that is held to override previous historical experience of social movements and empires. It fails to distinguish forms of domination that were present in Russian expansionism and antedate communism. It underemphasizes how Soviet ideology has little staying power in Eastern Europe but for Soviet power, and how assertive the underlying cultural traditions remain. It neglects changes in China over only a decade. The argument cautioning about the unique qualities of the effectiveness of communist control in Third World states is based primarily on the short experience of the ruling life-spans of particular charismatic leaders, and inadequately distinguishes the causal role of indigenous nationalism from the use of ideological shibboleths to curry favor and bolster precarious legitimacy. It fails to adequately distinguish between the verbal pronouncements of communism and the underlying diversity of practices (e.g., Maoism) that may be endorsed for reasons independent of Soviet power or for tactical reasons rather than inherently irreversible ideological appeal. Therefore comparison helps put the contest between social systems in perspective. Marxism-Leninism as a secular religion is no less subject to a diminished role as an organizing principle than other doctrines have been in imperial China, the Holy Roman Empire, or colonial Spain. Comparison exposes the pretenses of Soviet justification for empire; analysis of it in traditional great power terms shows its prospects to be less favorable in the long run compared to those of the U.S. sphere that requires less coercion and more rewards to sustain it.

Normative and Analytical Complexities of Comparison of the Spheres

Given the theoretical and practical value of comparing the roles of the United States and the USSR in their spheres, what accounts for the dearth of sustained work in this field? Although no one objects to comparison per se, many would object to finding any significant similarities in the ways both superpowers exercise their influence or in the dilemmas posed to weaker states in their responses. Most Soviet and U.S. policymakers would reject the notion of any comparability between the motivation or effects of their policy and their adversary's; with each assured of their own reasonable intentions, guile and intransigence can be attributed to the other. Similarly, those analysts who attribute U.S. foreign policy to the dictates of capitalism, or Soviet policy to messianic communism, would see only fundamental contrasts, since their explanation of behavior follows from the unique nature attributed to the superpower, making comparisons impossible. Comparison of U.S. and Soviet policy, therefore, challenges the analyst's objectivity and requires clarification of standards of comparison. It is possible that neither the strongest partisans nor the severest critics of American and Soviet policy, respectively, see their own state's policy or its adversary's in all its complexity or view it as impartially as some others do. Two perspectives, one from each sphere, illustrate both the insights and complexities of even the most objective attempts at comparative analysis.

Octavio Paz of Mexico, a leading Latin American intellectual and former diplomat, provides an excellent example of both the complexities and potentials inherent in comparing superpower rules in spheres of influence. For example, in one passage he states his basic normative position:

> Not a few European and Latin American intellectuals attempt to equate the policy of the United States with that of the Soviet Union, as though they were twin monsters. Hypocrisy, naivete, or cynicism? It seems to me that what is monstrous is the comparison itself. The errors, the failures, and the sins of the United States are enormous, and I'm not trying to absolve that nation. [One can observe many shortcomings over the years in their policies toward Third World states.] All this having been said, however, it must be added that the capitalist democracies have preserved fundamental freedoms within their own borders [and the possible though tenuous "seeds of freedom" in those countries within their influence]. On the other hand, ideological war abroad and totalitarian despotism at home are the two constituent features of the Soviet regime and of its vassal countries. (1985: 72–73.)

Yet in a subsequent paragraph Paz compares both the U.S. and USSR as hegemonic powers. He sprinkles his analyses with precisely the parallel that he rejected above. For example, when discussing the central role "the program of 'modernization'" came to play in Mexico, he writes: "What happened later is a familiar story: the Mexican Revolution was taken over by a political bureaucracy not without similarities to the communist bureaucracies of Eastern Europe, and by a capitalist class made in the image and likeness of U.S. capitalism and dependent upon it." (1985: 152–53; see similar parallels in Paz, 1972: 11, 27, 37, 41.) In his summary survey of the situation in Latin America he notes that it

> would not be complete unless mention were made of a foreign element that both precipitated disintegration and fortified tyrannies: U.S. imperialism. The fragmentation of our countries, the civil wars, their militarism and dictatorships were, naturally, not invented by the United States. Yet that nation bears a primordial responsibility, since it seized upon this state of affairs in order to

turn a profit, to further its own interests, and to dominate. It has fostered divisions between countries, parties, and leaders; it has threatened to use force, and has not hesitated to use force every time it has seen its interests endangered; when this was to its advantage, it has backed rebellions or strengthened tyrannies.... Because of all the foregoing, the United States has been one of the greatest stumbling blocks that we have encountered in our determined effort to modernize our countries.... A historical Nemesis: the United States has been, in Latin America, the protector of tyrants and the ally of the enemies of democracy. (1985: 168–69.)

But Paz is also very critical of both Cuba and Nicaragua. Paz's normative preference is in tension with his efforts at detached analysis. He makes the comparisons he rejects. The result is far from a black-and-white picture of the world, but rather a nuanced and contradictory one.

George Konrad of Hungary, a major East European writer, provides a similar independent perspective. He is publicly critical of the Soviet Union in his recent book, at some risk to his personal well-being. There is no mistaking his normative preferences. Konrad has a clear preference for pluralist democracy and West European culture. He finds the United States "rather attractive" and Western Europe more so. He laconically notes: "No one emigrates eastward. In our tutelage, we have not done so well with the Eastern empire." (1984: 22, 35.) Yet his parallels regarding the exertion of power are even more explicit than Paz's:

According to an ideology still widely accepted today (though not always articulated), great nation states have a right to try to maintain or expand their spheres of influence. The Soviet Union calls the United States an imperialist power and the United States calls the Soviet Union an imperialist power, and their propaganda makes a strong case for both sides being right. Perhaps the European states are no better, but they are less dangerous because they have less power. . . . Like the Soviet Union in Eastern Europe, the United States cannot make itself loved in Latin America. In both places, crude national interest and great power arrogance show through only too clearly. Nationalism in Eastern Europe is anti-Soviet, and in Latin America anti-American. The arrogance of power so blinds the Soviet and American elites that they can only take offense at this without being able to do anything about it. They are incapable of dealing with small nations in the way they should and the way those nations expect: on a footing of equality. (1984: 33, 21.)

Even more specifically he avers: "To their Central American neighbors [the United States] sends the same goods as the Russians, it seems: weapons and police experts. There are and will be pro-Soviet societies in the Third World to whom America can offer no better alternative than competition on the open world market—a competition in which those societies, unless they are unusually rich in natural resources, have a very small chance of coming out ahead." (20.) Konrad argues that U.S. indignation over events in Poland is mirrored in Soviet indignation over death squads in El Salvador, chastising both powers for their "all-too-evident selectivity." (23–24.) Interestingly, when Konrad addresses Poland again in the context of Soviet policing of Eastern Europe he notes that "now another means of implementing Yalta has made its appearance. Armed domestic authority can carry out a Latin American-style coup against the majority of society." (70–71.)

Some of Paz's characterizations of the monolithic nature of the Soviet "ideocracy" and the unanimity of purpose and malevolence of its policies in Eastern Europe may be overstated. Konrad's characterization of U.S. policy and his critique of its justifications under the delusive rubrics of "God and democracy" as being the functional equivalent of Marxism-Leninism for the Soviets is similarly overstated, although he reserves his harshest words for the latter. The point is that independent thinkers within the two spheres of influence have regularly made comparisons between superpower roles and their direct or indirect effects in Latin America and Eastern Europe—even when the comparison conflicts with their normative preferences or personal security. Furthermore, Paz's use of the East European experience as a benchmark for comparison with domestic outcomes in Latin America is mirrored in Konrad's invocation of Latin America to evaluate the possibility of achieving autonomy *even under the best of circumstances*.

Paz affirms the comparison he rejects, while Konrad would like to reject the comparison he affirms. The purpose of each man's analysis is exhortative, to improve the position and well-being of weaker states. In contrast to proscribers of comparison initially referred to, Paz and Konrad broaden the range of our perceptions. They are profoundly moral in intent. The comparisons they make and the questions they raise about results in dependent regions cannot simply be deflected by complaints that this mistakenly establishes moral equivalence (U.S. critics) or that it is doctrinally inconsistent and thus a historically unconscionable comparison (Soviet critics). The ambiguities of their analyses call for further close comparison to determine similarities and differences, not a prohibition of comparison by fiat.*

Conditions of Impartiality: The Historical Bases of Comparison and the Development of the Contemporary Literature

Having noted the benefits and need for comparison of the superpowers and their spheres of influence, as well as the complexity and resulting lack of focused attention on this issue, we now need to examine the development of U.S. and Russian spheres and the literature treating them. Paz and Konrad are illustrative of some tendencies of many post-World War II comparisons of U.S. and Soviet policy in Latin America and Eastern Europe.** The parallels they drew are

---

*Similar ambiguity appears in striking fashion in recent writings and remarks of Czeslaw Milosz. On the one hand, he rejects comparability between dilemmas faced by Eastern Europeans and Latin Americans; the latter in a world of contesting totalitarian and democratic states can only be "unconcerned with things of which inhabitants of Poland or Czechoslovakia have firsthand knowledge." (1983: 106.) He seems to maintain there is a fundamental "nonparallelism" not only at the regional level but at the level of the superpowers: "A basic difference between the various social structures shouldn't be underestimated. You shouldn't put on the same balancing scale organisms that are completely different. You cannot compare a lemon and a triangle. They don't belong to the same realm." Thus, "to compare the two systems on a purely moral basis, that is completely wrong!" On the other hand, in the next breath, when focusing specifically on the weaker states, he notes: "Unfortunately, the horrors of the war against the Nazi regime, the experience of Poland before the war and before the Communist regime, and then subsequent decades of Communist rule, give an insight into a general pattern which, when we observe Latin America, repeats itself." He continues: "They have agricultural problems, the problem of the peasants and the problem of unemployment in the cities. We've had our share of all these problems in Poland. Of course, there are specific historical factors in every country and those factors should not be underestimated. But there is a general pattern which repeats itself in many countries. . . . Based upon our own [Polish] experience, it is with a certain boredom that we look at the repetition of the pattern in Latin America. For instance, an economy dictated not by economic reasons but by ideological ones." (1986: 34–35.) Even if we interpret this last remark to apply only to Cuba and Nicaragua, an interpretation at variance with his use of the general term "Latin America," it would still argue for comparing the regions, while if we interpret his evocation of similarities to Latin America more generally, his observations are directly at variance with his notions of "nonparallelism." This would lead to the question of why one observes similar patterns in the weaker states despite the fact that they face different pressures. As with Paz and Konrad, one admires the honest ambiguity of the position rather than its logical, Procrustean consistency.

**There are ambiguities involved in using the terms "Eastern Europe" and "Latin America." Milan Kundera, for example, objects to the ready acceptance of the term "Eastern

sporadic, dispersed in diverse places in their work, and not sufficiently developed. They are also examples of the fact that much of the literature was fundamentally developed and carried on by scholars living outside of America and Russia, or who emigrated from or live in one of the affected weaker states. This is particularly true up to about 1970. Even since that time the few U.S. scholars making the comparison tended to have a background in international law, with its penchant for definition and comparative exegesis, or to use rigorous, well-defined social scientific models and methods. Often at least two of these conditions were present: (1) geographical and psychological distance; (2) the use of definitional comparison built into the structure of the field; or (3) the key directing role of a social science model or method. These may have been the necessary conditions for impartial analysis. Only in recent years have comparisons of superpower influence and behavior become more frequent and systematic. As islands of literature have emerged on this topic, the role of these three preconditions becomes less necessary in fostering research in this area.

Historical Bases of Comparison of U.S. and Russian Spheres
There is a long-standing European tradition comparing Russian/Soviet and American policy as it pertains to their spheres of influence. This sets the comparison in historical perspective. It provides the background for an overview of some contemporary comparisons that, while not comprehensive, illustrates how the literature comparing these regions developed and defined a scholarly issue. The historical account illustrates how even then geographical and psychological distance from the two regions fostered comparison, while the additional two

Europe" because it denigrates its historical connections to Western Europe and seems to imply continuing subservience of those regimes. He prefers the term "Central Europe." However, we will stick with conventional usage, including Yugoslavia and Albania in our analyses. Similar analytical challenges could be posed to using the term "Latin America." Important regional distinctions could be made. Some would argue that the comparison with Eastern Europe should be limited to Central America. However, it is also possible to argue that "the United States generally had a Latin American policy, rather than either a Central American, a Caribbean and a South American policy or a special policy towards each of the major countries in the region. It was inclined to pursue its strategic, commercial and ideological interests within a general set of ideas about relations with Latin America," though it behaved more intensely nearby in that "it used force only in Mexico, the Caribbean and Central America, where its concerns were most pressing and its capability for action greatest." (Holbraad, 1984: 99.) Therefore, while we will use the term "Latin America" and examine examples of the U.S. approach throughout the region, it is also understood that its behavior is more geographically defined.

conditions take on more importance in our more ideological twentieth century.*

The early nineteenth century was the reverse image of mid-twentieth-century U.S.-Russian relations. In the beginning of the nineteenth century the United States was the new and isolated revolutionary power, while Russia was the premier status quo power fearing revolutionary contagion. The tsar's armies had marched across Europe and taken Paris, taking up the role as the gendarme of Europe. America was consolidating its position, warding off opposing great powers as in 1812, and issuing doctrinal pronouncements about the proper principles that its adjacent regions should adopt. Russia opposed radicalism in Latin America and feared expanding liberalism in Europe, both of which it partly attributed to the American example. The twentieth century, in contrast, has seen the rise of the Soviet revolutionary specter; after the Bolsheviks survived great power challenges and intervention in their revolution, they turned outward after a period of consolidating isolationism, seeking to prescribe the proper ways to order social relations in their adjacent regions. The mantle of premier status quo power passed to the United States after World War II. It came to fear radicalism in Latin America and expanding communism in Europe. And just as the United States sought to insulate Latin America from its cultural and historical ties with the Old World in the nineteenth century, so did the Soviets seek to insulate Eastern Europe from its traditional European orientation. Thus these states have long been comparable in their uniqueness and the roles they play. In recent decades they have become even more directly comparable in their phasing, as *both* are arguably now status quo powers while both Latin America and Eastern Europe are tending to reassert their older ties.

Europeans have always readily compared American and Russian development and power. As early as 1790 a German diplomat anticipated the rise of America and Russia to empire, outstripping Europe and leaving it with only the shards of its traditions (Dukes, 1970: 1, 33.) The U.S. issuance of the Monroe Doctrine in 1823 hinted of contestation to come: "The fact is often overlooked that the Doctrine had two barrels, the first of which was aimed ostensibly at Russia, and the second largely at Russia.... No one seems to have given Alexander I his due. If he had not made such extravagant claims [around Alaska in]

---

*The focus of this subsection is on nineteenth- and early twentieth-century European thinkers comparing the two regions. While citations are made to more contemporary authors regarding historical detail to place the thinkers in context, these should not obscure the focus on the intellectual development of this tradition.

1821 and if he had not assumed leadership of the European autocrats in repressing liberal stirrings, the Monroe Doctrine . . . would not have been issued at the time it was and in the form it was." (Bailey, 1950: 32, 33.) In 1822 the tsar "expressed regret that the United States had seen fit to recognize revolutionary governments" in Latin America that had just won their independence. Two weeks later the Monroe Doctrine was issued. (Dallin, 1945: 240.) The United States sought to sustain the separation of the New from the tainted Old World in its hemisphere. "Americans believed as firmly in the eventual triumph of their system as Lenin and Trotsky did in theirs a century later." (Gaddis, 1978: 14.) It is difficult not to appreciate the irony today of Russian opposition to U.S. recognition of revolutionary regimes in Latin America. At the same time, however, the United States came to oppose Simón Bolívar's efforts to band together Latin American states as an independent actor, and thus was on its way to founding a sphere of influence (Cuevas Cancino, 1977.)

Russia felt it "had reason to fear the ideological precedent the Americans had set" by their Revolution, the tsar noting in 1823 that "too many examples demonstrate that the contagion of revolutionary principles is arrested neither by distance nor by physical obstacles." Interestingly, the tsar had greater concern about the influence of America's example in other regions than he did about the existence of the United States itself. He attributed the violent Latin American revolutions of this period to this revolutionary contagion, but felt the outcomes were even more suspect, asking "Where are the Franklins, the Washingtons, and the Jeffersons of southern [Latin] America?" (Gaddis, 1978: 13–16.) The tsar was also concerned over the inspiration and demonstration effects in Europe—and the sources of inspiration of the Decembrist revolt of 1825 and the Revolutions of 1830 indicate his fears were not totally imaginary. A similar ideological antagonism was expressed by Americans about Russian influence. Subsequently "a serious conflict over the Polish question arose between St. Petersburg and Washington" as the United States "reacted with strong indignation to the Russian methods of suppressing the Polish uprising in 1832," leading one analyst to reflect that "it is interesting to note how frequently the Polish question has played an important role in Russian-American relations." (Dallin, 1945: 242.) Even at this early stage in their relations, America and Russia were exploring the extent and nature of their interests, influence, and ideological alignments in Latin America and Central Europe.

Tocqueville's oft-quoted remarks of 1835 forecasting the rise of America and Russia to positions of predominance was not, therefore, entirely without contemporary reference points: "Their starting point is different, and their courses are not the same; yet each of them seems to be marked out by the will of Heaven to sway the destinies of half the globe." (In Roberts, 1962.) In 1863 the *London Times* "did betray fear as to the expansionist ambitions of the American and Russian giants." (Bailey, 1950: 86–91.) The comment was occasioned, interestingly enough, by a period of Russo-American friendship. The possibility of American-Russian collaboration had even been anticipated in the decision of the United States to issue the Monroe Doctrine independently of Britain and France, reflecting not only an opposition in principle to their involvement in the New World, but also a desire to refrain from presenting a united front against Russia and to leave open the prospect of future agreements with Russia. In the 1850s the Crimean War tied down Britain and France in a war with Russia at a time when "prospects for their intervention in the Caribbean appeared considerable." The war also resulted in expanded U.S.-Russian trade. In 1862 Russia effectively torpedoed British and French efforts to mediate an end to the Civil War that would have confirmed the South's independence (Gaddis, 1978: 11, 20, 21), but also by fracturing the Union reduced its potential as a commercial counterpoise to Russia's rivals. In 1863 some perceived that Russian naval visits to both U.S. coasts helped restrain British intervention in the Civil War on behalf of the South and the French expedition in Mexico by threatening their commerce, though the Russians' prime motive was a safer haven for their fleets. Conversely, European attention to the situation in the Americas limited British and French threats against Russian repression in Poland that same year (Bailey, 1950: 86–91), particularly because the United States declined to join an anti-Russian coalition that might benefit the Poles but allow unfavorable foreign focus on her own war position (Dallin, 1945: 245–47.) An underlying rivalry remained, however, as Russia hoped that the North would have trouble subduing the South and have to resort to "military occupation" to keep it in the Union. A Russian envoy, perhaps in partial reference to the Polish crisis, reported that "the revolutionaries and demagogues of the old continent have always found moral support and often also material help in the American democracy. With the downfall of the democratic system in the United States they now lose one of their main supporters . . . let us hope this will serve as an instructive lesson to the European anarchists and phrasemongers." The tsar was less sanguine, however. (Dallin, 1945: 245.) Again, from the standpoint of today it is difficult not to appreciate an ironic role reversal:

the nineteenth-century Russian hope for internal American decay to limit perceived revolutionary subversion in its adjacent areas such as Greece and Poland is mirrored in hopes of those that internal economic decay in the USSR makes it susceptible to economic pressure and constrains its expansionism, though neither represents a modal view.

In the later nineteenth century Henry Adams, by birth an American but with his heart in the European tradition, had grave forebodings about U.S. and Russian competition. He journeyed

> to Russia across the Polish plain, and . . . brought enough of America with him to see a division in the order of social nature that seemed, as it grew, to halve the world. To Adams it seemed that the major political conflicts of the future would occur between these forms of social energy. [America and Russia were treated as polar] cases of different kinds of attention and different susceptibility to the forces of nature. America *reacted* because her organization was less committed, more sensitive, and perhaps more superficial than Russia's. Russia *resisted* because, fully committed to herself, her organization was profound and obliterated at the edges. Both reaction and resistance were forms of movement to some extent outside intelligent control. . . . Both could be understood only in contradiction; each was perhaps the outside force that affected change in intensity (or inertia) in the other. (Blackmur, 1980: 153, 155, 154.)

Thus Adams set Russia up "at one pole of conflict in foreign affairs." "American foreign policy vis-à-vis Russia" was "the struggle between intensity that had to be intelligent and inertia that merely had to roll." It was the steady expansion of the Russian mass versus the intensity of American technology. Anticipating later containment policy, Adams looked "at Russia as the force that demanded action in American foreign policy [and] concluded that Russian expansion would continue . . . until its mass met a force equal to or superior to it by reason of its greater intensity," marking out Germany as a key issue, since it "stood on the exposed European edge of expansion" and thus had "to decide whether to ally with the West or merge into Russia." In the long run, however, Adams expected coal power would transform the Russian behemoth along a dynamic similar to the United States "that would, at the end of a generation, leave the gap between east and west relatively the same." (Blackmur, 1980: 244–46, 157.) At the same time Sir John Seeley made similar observations about these "enormous political aggregations" that once technologically transformed would "completely dwarf ... European states ... and depress them into a second class." (Barraclough, 1964: 100.) In the early twentieth century Max Weber associated Russia and America with "continental imperialism" in contrast to the "overseas' imperialism" of the British, also noting that "at present, the United States and Russia are the best examples" of how "big decisions in foreign policy are made by a small number of persons." (Weber, 1978; vol. 2: 914, 1439–40.)

Thus by the beginning of this century the United States and Russia had long been envisioned by European observers as comparable dominant powers, imperial empires, and competing social systems. America had a head start and greater leeway in consolidating its sphere of influence in Latin America in its own image. In the 1890s Britain effectively withdrew from the Caribbean and "admitted the regional dominance of the United States" when it acceded to the secretary of state's statement that "today the United States is practically sovereign on this continent, and its fiat is law upon the subjects to which it confines its interposition." (Fox, 1944: 14.) In effect, it "carved out the Caribbean area (if not the whole hemisphere) as a U.S. 'sphere of influence' in which it was to U.S. interests to dominate its trade and to keep peace for the well-being and furtherance of commercial intercourse." (Schmitt, 1968: 35.)

U.S. dominance was particularly evident in the period of frequent interventions from 1900 to 1930. The United States was now powerful enough to actively apply the Monroe Doctrine on its own. And while the Good Neighbor Policy was a turn toward restraint, the Latin American states remained skeptical, since "our so-called painless imperialism has seemed painless only to us. The Central American republics, who played host to our marines, custom directors, and bank supervisors, found the bayonet supported lessons in modern accounting very painful indeed. It looked at the time as if our respect for frontiers and territorial integrity was merely the outcome of our preference for custom houses and central banks," though in fact control of the "American Mediterranean," or Gulf of Mexico, was also a key motive. (Spykman, 1942: 64, 46–49.) Thus "the U.S. system was not designed accidentally or without well-considered policies.... It was based on principles that had worked, indeed on principles that made the United States the globe's greatest power: a confidence in capitalism, a willingness to use military force, a fear of foreign influence, and a dread of revolutionary instability." (LaFeber, 1983: 18.) Over the same time, however, one could also point to Russia's systematic policing of social change in Poland and Hungary, and Pan-Slavist impulses in the Balkans and the Near East, interrupted only by Germany's quest for primacy in Europe.

The Pattern of Development of the Contemporary Literature
World War I and World War II brought U.S. and Soviet Russian interests into closer interaction than ever before. In the nineteenth century they were able to sustain at least cordial relations, not being much in contact and united in their wariness of the British. They were also able to cooperate despite the ideological gulf they recognized between them. But domestic politics played an important part in making ideological issues more important to U.S. diplomacy "as the cautious noninterventionist tradition of the nineteenth century had given way to the belief that American institutions could be made secure only through their maximum possible diffusion in the world." (Gaddis, 1978: 55.) Russia's approach to the world focused on conventional security concerns until the Russian Revolution introduced a pronounced ideological bent. By 1917 both Woodrow Wilson and Lenin were proclaiming incompatible world-embracing visions. They clashed directly for the first time in the ill-fated allied intervention in Russia. Prior to World War II the "annexation of the Baltic countries by the Soviet Union marked the height of political antagonism between Russia and the United States." The United States stated its opposition to such "predatory activities" as intervention into these weak states, while the Soviet press responded that "American control of Cuba and the Philippines" served as proof that America was not absolved of charges of "predatory activities." (Dallin, 1945: 258–59.)

After the Allied defeat of Germany in World War II, U.S. and Soviet interests came increasingly into direct opposition, and, in the absence of any common foe, they became each other's prime adversary. The terms "superpower" and "bipolarity" were coined in 1944, and while Britain was analytically granted an important role, its fortunes were recognized as linked to U.S. power. It was also recognized that "Britain and America can no more prevent the Soviet Union from being its own judge as to what constitutes a friendly, anti-fascist regime in Eastern Europe than Britain or the Soviet Union could prevent the United States from making a fresh landing of marines in Nicaragua," but that "the United States would pay a heavy penalty for unprovoked intervention in a Latin American state, since its good neighbor policy would be destroyed and its moral authority throughout the world lessened. Similarly, the Soviet Union will be judged at the bar of democratic world opinion; and if its influence in Eastern Europe is misused, it too will pay a high price." For a variety of reasons, however, it was predicted that the Soviets might well incur such costs and opprobrium at this stage of their history, particularly in regard to Poland. (Fox, 1944; 97–98, 57, 69, 74, 82–83, 92–96.) Indeed, in differing manners soon each had come to "sway the destinies of half the globe."

Some of the most prescient scholars comparing the developing U.S. and Russian positions before 1945, such as Tocqueville or Adams, used the European great powers as their vantage point. The literature in the post-World War II period shows important continuity in this respect, though many more analysts from weaker states join the issue. The vantage points of important comparative analyses of the spheres, and the methodological approaches of those making the comparisons, illustrate the virtues of these conditions for balanced analyses. However, this overview not only points out the similarities that have been recognized, but also the differences between the spheres that are at issue theoretically.

The Cold War accented the differences between the United States and the USSR. In 1946 Stalin's "first major postwar foreign policy speech stressed the incompatibility between communism and capitalism, implying that future wars were inevitable until the world economic system was restructured along Soviet lines," while Truman stated that "at the present moment in world history nearly every nation must choose between alternative ways of life." (Gaddis, 1978; 182, 185.) Europeans, however, continued to keep their historical perspective. In 1947 the British historian E. H. Carr compared the Soviet role in Eastern Europe with long-standing U.S. security concerns in Latin America as manifested in the Monroe Doctrine (1947: 110.) At this point, however, it was the contest over and contrast between Eastern and Western Europe that commanded attention in the superpower competition; Latin America was very much in the background because it seemed secure. In the United States the totalitarian model of Soviet society gained special prominence in the 1950s, making Soviet politics and policy axiomatically different from those of the United States (a tendency mirrored in Soviet thinking about America). In contrast, in France in the mid-1950s Raymond Aron was comparing capitalist and so-called socialist societies with a common ideal type of industrial society, going back to the nineteenth century. (Aron, 1963.) While Aron himself stressed the differences more than the similarities, a point made more clearly in his book *Democracy and Totalitarianism* (1969), he continued the tradition of impartial comparison. Nor did his strong preference for democracy prevent him from writing *The Imperial Republic* (1974) about American policy in the postwar period.

As Europe recovered economically and reasserted itself politically, and as the Berlin situation stabilized, instability in Latin America was thrust more to the fore. The United States intervened there more or less "successfully" in 1954 and 1965 in anticipation of a communist threat, but unsuccessfully in Cuba in 1961, though it compelled a change of Soviet policy there in 1962. The Soviets had of course intervened in Eastern Europe: the two most prominent interventions in Hungary in 1956 and Czechoslovakia in 1968. By the end of the 1960s the behavior of the two superpowers over two decades could be compared. They had each accumulated huge nuclear stockpiles that linked their mutual security more tightly than ever. The Soviets maintained that peaceful coexistence was possible, while U.S. leaders envisioned détente. In fact, in 1969 Bertrand Russell, Jean-Paul Sartre, and others warned of a superpower condominium at the expense of the rest of the world through division of the globe into spheres of influence. The Chinese were perhaps the most outspoken of all in expressing such apprehensions and accusations.

In the early 1970s two British analysts published new comparative historical analyses of superpower development and policy. (Dukes, 1970; Parker, 1972.) Barraclough (1964), the British historian, had preceded this with a seminal analysis of the rise of the United States and the USSR to primacy in world politics, while Brzezinski (1970), formerly of Poland, essentially forecasted developmental trends of the superpowers into the future. This tradition was carried on in the 1980s by Jonsson (1984) of Norway, who devoted more attention to systematically comparing their foreign policies. The logic of empire and hegemony was also addressed in comparative terms. Galtung, also of Norway, developed his structural theory of imperialism in the late 1960s and early 1970s, applying the appellations of "topdogs" and "underdogs" to states in both the East and West. (1971, 1980.) Liska, formerly of Czechoslovakia, examined both U.S. and Soviet policies, applying the metaphor of imperial empires to both powers. (E.g., 1967, 1978.) Akzin (1971), an Israeli scholar, compared the two superpowers' roles in adjacent areas in the contemporary period and with imperial precursors. In Australia and later in Britain, Bull analyzed the comparative forms of superpower dominance, hegemony, and primacy in historical and political-legal terms, applying them to the United States and the USSR in their spheres of influence. (1971, 1977.) Bull's general distinctions were designed to apply over history and across power systems.

They addressed the type and degree of imperial coercion of the great power in its sphere considered as a whole, as well as the degree of willing acceptance on the part of the lesser states. Pure domination involved systematic high coercion and low acceptance and respect for the dependencies' sovereignty; primacy involved the reverse; and hegemony was an intermediate level of influence involving sporadic intervention and grudging but superficial acceptance of the sovereignty of weak states. Bull treated the contemporary Soviet and U.S. presence in Eastern Europe and Latin America as hegemony (a term applied to the U.S. role as early as 1942 by Spykman of Holland).

Similarly, Vloyantes's (1975) study of Finland and "The Theory of the Soft Sphere of Influence" in the postwar period also made comparisons between the East European and Latin American experience. A state in a "hard sphere" chafed under what was but a disguise for imperialism, whereas in a "soft sphere" imperialism was diluted as well as disguised. His distinctions applied in time to different dependent states. When he initiated research on this project in Finland in the 1960s as part of "a broader study of the subject as a phenomenon in international relations," he "soon learned that almost nothing had been done on the systematic analysis of these relationships" within spheres of influence. (1975: vii.) Kaufman (1976) of Israel developed the first comprehensive, comparative treatment of superpower policy solely in reference to their spheres of influence in Eastern Europe and Latin America.

The drama and impact of superpower interventions led to analysis of conditions of intervention. The analogy of the superpower role in crisis situations and interventions aided a cross-fertilization of concepts. Approaches developed to account for one superpower's behavior came to be applied to the other. For example, Blaiser (1976), who is a scholar of both Latin America and the USSR, in his examination of the role of bureaucratic politics and decision-making perceptions in explaining U.S. responses to social change in Latin America, noted parallels between U.S. behavior there and Soviet behavior in Eastern Europe. The "bureaucratic politics" approach that informs his work was developed by Allison for foreign policy analysis in his (1971) studies of U.S. decision-making in the Cuban missile crisis, particularly in regard to whether to use an air strike in Cuba. The same approach was used by Valenta, originally of Czechoslovakia, in his analyses of the Soviet decision to intervene in Czechoslovakia in 1968. (1979a, 1979b.) Decision-making models pertaining to foreign policy were also applied across regions. The "operational code" conception, for example, had been originally developed with the explanation of Soviet behavior in mind. However, George (1969) distilled out more general aspects that were applicable to systematic analysis of decisionmakers of all states. The approach was later applied to U.S. presidents and statesmen, and even in as distant a realm as Mexican foreign policy. (Poitras, 1981: 105–6).* By 1982 Scott was developing an explicit theoretical model of constraint systems that applied to both spheres of influence at the outset (1982a: 69–125, 213–320), representing the logical extension of this trend.

A counterpart to analyzing and comparing the dynamics of each superpower in respect to its own sphere was to examine how each superpower behaved toward its adversary. International law scholars joined the issue at this point, stimulated by the issue of great power intervention and its justification. Students of international law Weisband and Frank (1972) and Falk (1972) examined the process of mutual tacit recognition by the superpowers of the others' spheres in Eastern Europe and Latin America. (See also Scott, 1982b, reprinting relevant work of his from this period.) They explored the tension that exists between superpowers' stabilizing their relations by tacitly abiding by their respective spheres, on the one hand, and their lack of respect for sovereignty, rights of self-determination, and progressive social change of the weaker states, on the other. Agreement is tacit because it violates international norms. However, tacit agreement is subject to misinterpretation by superpowers in regard to what demesne they feel the adversary accepts, and by dependent states regarding the limits of permissible deviant behavior within the sphere. Klein (1974: 143–68) of Geneva compared the similarities in how the Monroe and Brezhnev doctrines attempted to reconcile the international norm of equality of states with the factual realities of power. Analysis in this tradition has been developed in greater detail in the 1980s by Keal of Australia (1983a, 1983b) and international law student Dore (1984).

Policies of the weaker states received increasing attention within theoretical frameworks. As socialist polycentrism increased, it became

---

*We may also note how deductive coalition maintenance theory, often applied to Western decision-making since the 1960s, was by the 1970s applied to East European elite and Politburo decision-making patterns since Khrushchev. This cross-fertilization at the decision-making level was accompanied by a more general process of conceptual interpenetration, using interest-group models, integration theory, leadership change spending cycles, and more recently, corporatism. This piecemeal interpenetration of models indicates their useful role in helping to impartially bring about comparisons that would otherwise have languished.

possible to see East European state policies as more than an extension of Moscow's. It became possible to compare them to Latin American states. A Scandinavian volume (Schou and Brundtland, 1971) juxtaposed articles about Latin American and East European state policies. Singer (1972), completing his analytical study in Malaysia, explicitly compared states from these regions within his larger comprehensive study of weak states. Zimmerman (1972), using social science concepts, drew a parallel between Warsaw Pact and CMEA states and OAS states, and showed how some East European states sought to enhance their autonomy by increasing their alternatives outside the Soviet-controlled socialist system. Similarly, Hirschman (1978) drew some parallels between the Latin American and East European regions in his remarks on dependency theory and argued that the weaker states were not necessarily passively consigned to forms of dependency but enjoyed the relative advantage of concentrated attention on bargaining for advantage that could not systematically be matched by the superpowers, whose attention was necessarily spread more widely. This theme is reflected in Rosenau's examinations of the range of strategies pursued by states seeking enhanced autonomy as part of his "adaptation theory" of international relations (1981). Handel (1982) of Israel, in his comprehensive study of weak states, including specific comparisons of the two spheres, examines the interplay of the capabilities and strategies of weak states and the character of the larger international system within which they find themselves (also 1981).

Once a general acceptance of the comparability of the two spheres was sufficiently widespread, scholars logically took to examining theses that were held to explain the political and economic outcomes in the weaker states from one region and testing them in the other. The conflicting positions of Cohen (1973: 83–97), D. Ray (1973), and Gilbert (1974) anticipated the contrasting theses of this debate. Cohen and Ray basically focused on political dynamics and argued that dependency was not a function of capitalism but of power discrepancies, and that it therefore existed in Eastern Europe as well. Gilbert countered with a focus on economics and argued that Eastern Europe was better off economically than Latin America and that U.S. imperialism explained the key differences.

Research efforts addressing these theses have been rigorous, analytic efforts, both conceptually and statistically. Paul Marer (1974a) argued that up to about 1960 there were parallels between the Soviets' experience in Eastern Europe and the classic meaning of Western imperialism, whereas thereafter the economic benefits also started flowing the other way; he consequently adopted a model that bridged both periods and took into account the political results of this trade linkage irrespective of the economic gain or even losses. Zimmerman, with more of a political focus (1978), questioned whether the claims of dependency theory were uniquely upheld in Latin America and basically concluded that Eastern Europe manifested many of the expectations of capitalist dependency in at least as great a degree. His (1981) analysis sustained his (1972) conceptualization of both regions as political, hierarchical regional systems. Goochman and J. Lee Ray (1979) noted the similarities of the constraints the Eastern European and Latin American states faced in their bargaining, while later Ray's analysis (1981) emphasized more the differences in results in each sphere, with Eastern Europe tending to be better off economically, while Latin America had more political latitude. Bahry and Clark (1980) argued that Latin American conceptions of economic dependency did not alone suffice to explain patterns of East European political compliance, but nonetheless argued (Clark and Bahry, 1983a, 1983b) that Eastern Europe manifested dependent development, a concept usually applied to Latin America. The outcomes were similar, though the path dependency took was more economic in the latter region and political in the former. In another conceptual regional comparison Reisinger (1983) used a collective goods model often applied to NATO (and which could also be applied to the OAS) that shows these states benefiting from free riding in terms of military expenditures. Reisinger applied the model to an analysis of Eastern Europe, which turned out not to benefit in that fashion.

Even the most recent conceptual studies and rigorous research, therefore, leaves us with many questions: Is political power predominant in both regions, or are there basic differences in political and economic control? In comparative terms, which regions benefit more economically or politically? Are there central economic and developmental differences or similarities between the weak states? When is capitalism a boon or a burden to the weaker states? Research at this general level is provocative, but inconclusive; it focuses on differing issues and at different levels of analysis. It tries to take existing general theories and affirm or reject them. To what extent are the differing views reconcilable or not? Answers may not be forthcoming at this level of debate. This problem is not confined to Western scholarship. For example, starting in the early 1970s "several leading [Soviet] Latin Americanists . . . concluded that the major countries of Latin America were so advanced economically that they should be compared to the countries of southern Europe [and by implication parts of Eastern Europe] rather than to Africa or Asia.'' (Hough, 1985: 666.) However, by the 1980s, after several symposia on Latin America and the questioning of trends in U.S. influence and economic ties, the Soviets could only conclude among themselves that "there is still a great deal of disagreement over the topic of Latin American dependence." (Rothenberg, 1983: 16.) Thus the analytical complexities do not simply stem from ideological differences. Approaches are also needed that are tailored to a comparison of the regions at the outset as well as more specific case comparisons.*

In sum, the study of this subject was developed by scholars over time according to an explainable logic. There were important normative, perceptual, and political disincentives for making the comparisons. However, a separate area of study is now crystallizing. Descriptive comparisons and juxtaposition of empirical material from each sphere have been followed by explicit testing of hypotheses and theories. Attention to simply the most gripping parallels, such as interventions and defections, is being followed by attention to the more lackluster but persistent day-to-day politics of dependence. There have long been general studies that treat the United States and USSR as analytically similar actors with blocs that follow similar dynamics (e.g., Herbert Butterfield, John Herz, Morton Kaplan, William Riker, and Kenneth Waltz). Other studies apply arms race models or game theory symmetrically. But these remain at a high level of generality. They address the effects of policy in sustaining a coalition vis-à-vis the adversary, not in respect to the weaker countries of the bloc. They do not engage the emotions or conflicting theories in the same fashion.

This brief account of the pattern of the development of the literature explicitly comparing or applying conceptual models across regions is intended to put my arguments and others in this volume in perspective. It justifies the comparisons normatively and analytically. It argues that this enterprise is much more than the fanciful or idiosyncratic effort that Kingsley Amis' protagonist savages his own scholarly treatment of another "strangely neglected topic" for being: a "funeral parade of yawn-enforcing facts," notable for "the pseudo-light it threw upon nonproblems." (1953: 16.) The facts are only starting to be brought together, the problems are very real, and the systematic confrontation of the explanatory challenge only beginning.

*The other sections of my essay included in this volume attempt to do both these things.

2

Historical Overview and Comparative Analysis

Robert Wesson

Most of the earth could reasonably be considered in the sphere of influence of either the United States or the Soviet Union; only a few countries, notably the Asian giants, China and India, and a number of African and Near Eastern countries can be said to stand independent of the two leaders.

A large number of nations around the world are subject to the political and economic influence of the United States; that is, their foreign policy choices are swayed by preferences of the United States, at least in regard to matters of concern to the United States. This category includes over a hundred countries with which the United States carries on friendly relations. On the other hand, there are at least twenty countries subject to the Soviet sway, including Mongolia, which is practically a part of the Soviet Union; Finland, which is ideologically alien but bound in foreign affairs; and several Marxist-Leninist-aligned states of Africa.

Within these broad spheres, there are all manner of economic, cultural, and political relations between the leading and the subordinate or dependent powers; and they well deserve the attention of students of international affairs. They are, however, excessively complex, diverse, and multiform. It is consequently logical to concentrate attention, in studying how superpowers deal with dependents, on limited regions in which relations are especially intense and unequal. For the Soviet Union this means the six East European countries belonging to the Warsaw Pact (WTO). For the United States this means Latin America, especially the Caribbean–Central American area. For both, the narrowly defined sphere of influence is the region in which the superpower feels special responsibility and is most sensitive to intrusions.

Only in modern times have superpowers possessed zones from which the opposing superpower is excluded. The Soviet sphere originated only after World War II, when Soviet armies turned military victory into political dominance nearly everywhere that they advanced. On the American side neither the time of establishing the sphere nor its outlines can be definitely fixed, but a recognizable U.S. sphere began taking shape in the 1890s.

There have been other spheres of influence, of course, but the prevalent idea in the empire-building of the late nineteenth century was rather different; namely, to bring some order into the scramble for colonies by conceding parts of Africa or Asia to certain powers. By contrast, the American and Soviet spheres of influence were carved out without the consent of other great powers and are based on proximity and dominance or primacy. They exist de facto, and domination is not formally claimed by the hegemonic power or recognized by its rival. Whereas European powers hungry for colonies in the last decades of the nineteenth century frankly laid stake to their spheres, from which others were to abstain, the contemporary hegemonic powers maintain universalist pretensions and regard the idea of a division of the world as theoretically reprehensible. Most important, the spheres of the superpowers are organic continuations or outgrowths of the construction of the continental states as they expanded into areas of weakness and then reached beyond.

There are basic parallels between American and Soviet zones. Both were built on a combination of economic interest, strategic or defensive needs, and messianism. Both are accepted as natural and inviolable by the dominant power, part of its standing in the world. Both expect the weaker states to conform politically and ideologically, rather strictly in the Soviet case, loosely in the American; and both rest fundamentally on a monopoly of force in the area.

This implies that membership is compulsory. The Soviet sphere consists of the countries that have no choice, because of Soviet forces on the ground or in the vicinity, in Central, Eastern, and Southeastern Europe, plus Mongolia and potentially Afghanistan. Vietnam is not regarded as part of the Soviet zone because its adherence is apparently voluntary—in return for military support—and presumably could be terminated by a Vietnamese decision. The American sphere similarly does not include Australia and the Netherlands, although their association with the United States is very close. Strictly delimited, it comprises the small countries of the Central American–Caribbean region, in which the United States could intervene forcefully if it desired without excessive costs. U.S. influence in South America is on a different level. Although it has a much closer relationship with such countries as Brazil and Argentina than with, for example, Nigeria or Zaire, the United States would consider intervening in those countries only under the most extreme circumstances; and the possibility of invasion from the north probably figures very little in their calculations. Whereas the United States has intervened politically or militarily in the affairs of eight countries of the Caribbean–Central American region, in South America it has never gone beyond what may be called intrigue, as in assisting the downfall of the leftist Allende government in Chile in 1973.

The American Sphere

The original expression of the American claim to a special role in Latin America is the Monroe Doctrine of 1823. This statement in President James Monroe's address to Congress declared the New World closed to further colonization and warned European powers against any effort to seek to retake the Spanish possessions that by this date had made good their independence or "to extend their [monarchic] political system to any part of this hemisphere." This declaration, quite bold for a power without naval strength to enforce it, was an expression of idealism arising from the vision of the Americas as a New World, with a superior political system, in contrast to the feudalistic Old World, ideas that came from the Declaration of Independence and the Constitution. It also expressed the isolationist impulse classically stated in George Washington's Farewell Address. (Perkins, 1955: 4–9.) The Spanish colonies, throwing off the colonial yoke as the British colonies had done, were welcomed as fellow republics in a monarchic world. There was no hint of general hemispheric domination by the United States, a possibility not realizable for decades.

The United States was the first non-Latin American state to recognize the new nations of the hemisphere (Kryzanek, 1985: 7), but interest in them flagged after Monroe's pronouncement. Several offers of alliance by Latin American governments were scorned (Perkins, 1961: 47), and it was noted with regret that Latin American governments were anything but democratic. For most of the nineteenth century contacts were not intense. Latin American intellectuals looked to Europe, especially France, and Britain was economically dominant in the area. The United States even declined to participate in inter-American conferences in 1846, 1856, and 1865. (Perkins, 1966: 52.)

The young United States was, however, engaged in expansion. From the time settlers landed on the Atlantic coast and began the westward march, territorial growth was the order of the day; and it nourished the feeling that the hemisphere belonged by right to the vibrant young republic. Acquisitions such as Jefferson's Louisiana purchase and the Florida purchase multiplied the national territory, and there was interest in lands to the south as well. In the 1840s the U.S. government, especially President James K. Polk, revived the Monroe Doctrine in dealing not with the entire hemisphere but with North America, particularly Texas and Oregon. Texas, breaking away from Mexico, had applied in 1837 to join the Union, but President Martin Van Buren refused. Polk saw signs of British and French interest in Texas as a threat to U.S. security (Merk, 1966: 279); it was annexed, and in the resultant war with Mexico, the United States acquired huge additional territories.

Toward the end of the nineteenth century, expansionism entered a new phase of imperialism in the classic sense. A variety of reasons may be suggested. Settlement having crossed the continent and reached the Pacific Ocean, there was a certain restless momentum for looking overseas. The importance of a canal across the Central American isthmus was becoming apparent, and there was a growing feeling that it should be an enterprise of the United States alone; Central America, and by extension the Caribbean, hence assumed a new importance. The economy was growing, foreign trade was increasingly important, and expanding industry was looking to foreign as well as domestic markets, although the bulk of U.S. exports was still agricultural. British trade and investment in Latin America were much larger than American —indeed until World War I—but Yankee traders and entrepreneurs were increasingly active, especially in Central America, following in the footsteps of William Walker, who ruled Nicaragua from 1855 to 1857.

Probably most important, however, was the imperialist fever of Europe. The idea had taken hold that national greatness required overseas colonies and politically protected markets. The old imperial powers, Britain and France, sought to add to their already huge holdings by staking out unclaimed parts of the globe, especially in Africa; and they were joined by newly powerful and ambitious Germany, trying to catch up in Africa, the Pacific islands, and Asia. Italy undertook to conquer Ethiopia; Japan felt sufficiently modernized to take Formosa (Taiwan) and lay claim to Korea; even Belgium appropriated the Congo. (May, 1968: 177.)

Admiral Alfred Thayer contributed to this mentality in the United States with his very influential work on the importance of seapower for national destiny and the consequent necessity for overseas bases and coaling stations. Taking his advice, the United States began in 1884 a rapid buildup of its decrepit navy, which rose in a mere fifteen years to the first rank. (Plesur, 1971: 99–100.)

Nationalism was also rising with the rapid growth of the nation, which by 1890 was the world's leading economic power. Swelling pride nourished feelings of destiny and the duty to give the peoples of the world the benefit of American freedom and democracy. This was mixed with a strain of racism, whereby the Anglo-Saxon was deemed responsible for most of the advance of civilization. In the words of a prominent pastor-publicist, Josiah Strong, "This race of unequalled energy, with all the majesty of wealth and numbers behind it—representative, let us hope, of the largest liberty, the highest civilization—having developed peculiarly aggressive traits calculated to impress its institutions upon mankind, will spread itself over the earth." (Dulles, 1962: 160.) Such sentiments, however, were those of a small minority; up to the 1890s a large majority of Americans doubted the value of colonies, viewed the conquest of alien peoples as morally wrong, and doubted that American institutions were for export. (May, 1968: 166; Walter LaFeber, 1963: 408.)

In 1889 Secretary of State James G. Blaine sponsored an inter-American meeting in Washington with the unrealistic purpose of setting up a customs union. (It talked of peace and established a Commercial Bureau of the American Republics that in 1910 turned into the Pan-American Union, precursor of the Organization of American States.) In 1893, however, President Grover Cleveland refused to annex Hawaii, where American settlers had dethroned the native queen, on grounds that the population was opposed. In 1895 national self-confidence led to some lofty language, as Secretary of State Richard Olney used a minor boundary dispute between Britain and Venezuela to tell the former, "Today the United States is practically sovereign on this continent, and its fiat is law upon the subjects to which it confines its interposition." (Walter, 1972: 51–52.)

The issue that brought the United States into the imperial arena was Cuba. The Cubans rose against unenlightened Spanish rule in 1868–78 and again in 1895. The colonial authorities treated the insurgents with considerable brutality, which was played up emotionally by the U.S. press. Cleveland wanted to keep out of the affair, as did President William McKinley; but in the atmosphere of excitement after the sinking of the battleship Maine (by cause unknown), in April 1898 McKinley asked Congress to intervene for humane and business reasons, that is to go to war. That the weak Spanish government was prepared to concede almost everything demanded was hardly noticed. However, McKinley declared himself opposed to any annexation of territory; and Congress, upon declaring war, passed a self-denying resolution against annexation or control of Cuba.

The brief easy war, with few casualties from enemy action (many more from disease) and shining victories, encouraged foreign adventurism and confirmed the nation's good opinion of itself. The harvest of the war caused problems, however. Cuba, in keeping with the Teller Amendment, was not annexed but occupied for a few years and required to include in its constitution an authorization (the Platt Amendment) for the United States to intervene at its discretion. Puerto Rico, by contrast, was placed under U.S. jurisdiction, in large part for its strategic value, and has remained in a somewhat ambiguous relationship to the federal union since. The big question was what to do with the Philippines, much farther away and with a very much larger and quite alien population. The country debated the question, and it was a major issue in the electoral campaign of 1900, the Democrats opposing and the Republicans leaning toward acquisition. Church groups and apparently a majority of vocal opinion favored fulfilling the American duty of civilizing the archipelago. (May, 1968: 6.) But the Republicans won the election mostly on economic grounds. Meanwhile, Philippine nationalists had begun fighting American occupiers as they had fought the Spanish. (O'Toole, 1984: 383–96.)

McKinley saw no acceptable alternatives: the Philippines could not be returned to Spain nor could they be set adrift to be seized by Germany or Japan. Hence he opted to protect, educate, and uplift the

Philippine peoples. The administration also accepted Hawaii as a way station to the Philippines and the Orient.

The burst of territorial acquisitions came to an end, however, as quickly as it had begun. The chief of the imperialists, Theodore Roosevelt, became president in 1901 by the assassination of McKinley, but he added only the Panama Canal Zone to American possessions. The experience of guerrilla war in the Philippines and complications of dealing with colonies, which the Constitution did not provide for, discouraged more acquisitions.

While eschewing the responsibility of administering additional peoples, however, the nation undertook to intervene more freely for mostly strategic, partly commercial purposes in the zone it saw as its backyard. Near the top of the list was the long-mooted Panama Canal. In 1900 Britain ceded to the United States its treaty right of participation. Roosevelt dickered with Colombian authorities for authorization to build a canal across Panama, but when they proved difficult he supported a Panamanian uprising in 1903. The infant Panamanian republic immediately granted American wishes, including a strip of land along the canal route and a right of intervention to defend it. President Roosevelt boasted of "taking" the Canal Zone, (Kryzanek, 1985: 28), but eventually the United States paid Colombia $25 million to recognize the independence of its former province.

Bad debts caused problems as European powers tried to collect from delinquent borrowers in the Caribbean, especially the Dominican Republic and Haiti. Their use of force being forbidden by the Monroe Doctrine as interpreted, the interests of civilized order and sanctity of contracts required that the United States take a hand. In 1904 Roosevelt, irked by instability, pronounced his corollary to the Monroe Doctrine: conditions "may finally require intervention by some civilized state, and in the Western Hemisphere the United States cannot ignore this duty." (Perkins, 1966: 103.) This position seemed necessary also to protect the canal then abuilding, and it answered general urges to spread U.S. influence. In the following Taft administration emphasis shifted from intervention to "Dollar Diplomacy." This did not mean using political or military means to support American financial interests but financial means to strengthen political positions. (Perkins, 1966: 108.)

The assumption of stewardship in the Caribbean area led to prolonged intervention in both the Dominican Republic and Haiti. An American official was placed in charge of Dominican customs in 1905 to meet demands of European creditors; the Dominicans were encouraged to agree by the presence of a U.S. warship. U.S. authorities oversaw elections in 1913, but disorders continued, and the Marines entered to subdue a revolt in 1916. They stayed until 1924, and customs receivership lasted until 1941. At one time U.S. authorities partially replaced the Dominican government.

Next door Haiti was also occupied and partly governed by U.S. officials in this period. After disturbances in 1915 the Wilson administration, fearful of loss of U.S. property and complications with European powers, sent a force into Port-au-Prince despite refusal of Haitian authorities to invite them. Although the occupying administration built roads and schools and tried to remake the country, it was bitterly resented. The occupiers took over most of the functions of government, and a small guerrilla conflict developed. A treaty was drafted in 1915 to make Haiti a protectorate, but the Senate refused it. (Kryzanek, 1985: 341.) U.S. forces were finally withdrawn only in 1934.

Political disturbances plus concern for U.S. interests, especially in relation to the potential canal route, likewise brought the Marines to Nicaragua. They were several times in and out, helping one party to power, leaving only to come back when the favored president was threatened or overthrown. President Woodrow Wilson wanted a naval base on Nicaragua's west coast. In 1916 it was proposed that the United States establish a protectorate over Nicaragua, but the Senate refused to ratify the corresponding treaty. (LaFeber, 1983: 53.) Marines stood guard, with a brief break, from 1912 to 1933, usually only a few hundred strong but an affront to the national feeling. In the interest of law and order Nicaraguans organized what was intended to be a nonpolitical constabulary or National Guard, which became the instrument of dictatorship of Anastasio Somoza (whom the United States left in command of the Guard) and of his heirs from 1936 to 1979.

It is seldom remembered that U.S. Marines went into Honduras in 1907, 1911, 1919, and 1925 in disturbed situations. They remained each time only a few weeks and never became deeply involved in local politics, perhaps mostly because Honduras was of slight strategic importance. Intervention in Cuba meanwhile was a discouraging failure. After reorganizing the Cuban judiciary and administration, sanitation and education departments, and giving the country a constitution, U.S. forces withdrew in 1902 (except for the base at Guantanamo). They were drawn back by disorders, in which one party or another would try to use the United States against its enemies, from 1906 to 1909 and again in 1912. In 1920–23 American officers were not only arranging elections but managing Cuban finances. (Kryzanek, 1985:35.) Thereafter, despite considerable turmoil, there was no further application of the Platt Amendment, which was renounced in 1934. But Cuba remained economically closely tied to the United States by the preferential quota for Cuban sugar, in return for which U.S. manufactures had easy access to Cuba.

In 1914 Wilson ordered the occupation of Mexico's chief port, Vera Cruz, to protect American investments in the nearby oil fields according to some, to prevent President Victoriano Huerta from receiving an arms shipment according to others. (Huerta's government had murdered his predecessor, Francisco Madero.) The effect in either case was to hasten Huerta's downfall and the victory of forces ancestral to the present government of Mexico.

U.S. influence peaked around 1920, when it was assumed that a frown or smile from Washington decided the fate of governments of the Central American–Caribbean area. The inclination to intervene declined, and the feeling grew that it was futile to try to force weak and backward countries to behave as the United States desired. The idea of Marines fighting Haitians or chasing guerrillas led by Augusto César Sandino in the jungles of Nicaragua was unpopular. Fears of German advances were ended by World War I, attitudes were changing, and no more incursions were undertaken. The presence of the Marines in foreign countries was also becoming embarrassing. Thus it was harder for the United States to condemn the Japanese invasion of Manchuria "to keep order" in 1931 because the Marines were doing that in Nicaragua. (Connell-Smith, 1974: 152.) At a meeting of the previously nonpolitical Pan-American Union in 1923, Latin American resentment came to the fore: thirteen of twenty-one states represented supported a resolution against intervention. (Perkins, 1961: 70.) The United States sidestepped the demand but seemed to hear the message. The Roosevelt Corollary was disavowed under Herbert Hoover in 1930, and Marines began pulling out of Haiti.

Strong change of direction and the inauguration of a new period of U.S. relations with its area of primacy or hegemony came with the administration of Franklin Roosevelt, who promised a "New Deal" not only to the United States but to the hemisphere. In his inaugural address he announced the "Good Neighbor" policy, and he proceeded rapidly to put it into effect.

In 1933 near-anarchy in Cuba invited intervention, but instead Roosevelt revoked the Platt Amendment. The Marines were withdrawn from Nicaragua in 1933 and from Haiti the next year. In 1933 a bill was passed for the gradual separation of the Philippines, whose eventual independence had been promised in 1916. In 1936 U.S. treaty rights of intervention in Panama were renounced.

The United States also accepted the principle of nonintervention, which the Latins had been advocating for many years. By an agreement adopted at Montevideo in 1933, "No state has a right to intervene in the internal or external affairs of another"; and this was ratified by the U.S. Senate without dissent. A 1936 conference at Buenos Aires reaffirmed and strengthened the commitment to nonintervention, and the Senate again approved it unanimously. At the same time the Latin American states, aware of growing Nazi power, agreed to consult in case of an external threat.

The Monroe Doctrine seemed thereby converted into a collective security agreement, and the U.S. sphere of influence entered a new era in which the use of force by the hegemonic power was no longer permissible—and was no longer undertaken except when Washington perceived a threat to the political integrity of the hemisphere. Thus in 1938 Roosevelt resisted pressures to punish Mexico for nationalizing important U.S. oil interests. There was some movement to penalize Mexico economically, but President Lázaro Cárdenas promised compensation and was basically friendly, and the Axis threat made settlement imperative. (Blasier, 1976: 122–23.) If there had been a possibility of the Nazis gaining a foothold in the Central American–Caribbean region, the United States would doubtless have reacted as forcefully as seemed necessary.

In the later 1930s the United States became concerned with Nazi influence in Argentina, Chile, Bolivia, and Brazil—the countries of the hemisphere in which it was most difficult for the United States to make itself felt. The United States reacted partly by trying to increase its influence through various cooperative programs, and partly by trying to bind the American republics closer. A Lima conference in 1938 strengthened provisions for consultation in the event of a threat, and one seemed to loom in 1940 as German armies overran most of Western Europe. By the Declaration of Havana (1940) an attack on any American state was to be regarded as an attack on all, and it was resolved to permit no transfer of European colonies in the hemisphere to another nonhemispheric power, i.e., Germany. Prior to Pearl Harbor, Mexico, Brazil, and several other countries agreed to permit U.S. use of naval and air bases (Perkins, 1961: 30), and most of Latin America followed the United States into war with Germany and Japan immediately after Pearl Harbor. Only Chile and Argentina held out for a long time, the latter until near the end of the war. This cooperation was in marked contrast to the failure of the United States to enlist its southern neighbors in World War I, when Mexico, Argentina, Chile, and Venezuela remained neutral.

World War II brought hemispheric unity and U.S. influence to their height. American war aims, however, were somewhat ambiguously contrary to the general idea of spheres of influence. The Atlantic Charter (1941) by implication opposed exclusive geographic spheres, as it promised world cooperation for the freedom of peoples. The universalist American vision of general collective security, free trade, and no exploitation of one nation by another saw spheres of influence as obsolete and harmful, like colonial empires. Yet this vision clashed with the realities of power, and Roosevelt's idea of the four great powers (including Britain and China) acting as world policemen implied a beat for each. In any event, the Monroe Doctrine was accepted by the Charter of the United Nations, as it had been by the Covenant of the League of Nations.

As it became apparent that the Soviet Union was not to be a friendly fellow policeman but the adversary against which the United States saw itself doing police duty, the United States sought to turn the hemispheric association into an alliance, nominally for general security, in practice against communist movements allied or potentially allied with the Soviet Union. By the Act of Rio (1947) and the Inter-American Treaty of Reciprocal Assistance, any attack on an American state was to be considered an attack on all; and measures short of war (such as breaking relations) were to be obligatory if supported by two-thirds of the states. (Stuart and Tigner, 1975: 138.) The following year at Bogota, against a backdrop of exceptionally violent leftist rioting, the American ministers established the Organization of American States to expand and deepen the old Pan-American Union.

The OAS was widely regarded as a means of pacifically assuring U.S. hemispheric domination, because it seemed easy enough for this country to mobilize a two-thirds majority of more or less docile states, especially in Central America and the Caribbean. This condition was not to endure long, however, because the United States found it difficult to cope with ideological-subversive threats and to secure the cooperation it desired from states wary of anything suggestive of interference in internal politics—which combating subversion inevitably entailed.

The problem came to the fore in Guatemala in 1954. (Blasier, 1976: 151–77.) The United States was troubled by the Arbenz government's nationalization of American properties (especially holdings of United

Fruit), hospitality to communist organizations, and receipt of arms from Eastern Europe—the classic entanglement of material, ideological, and strategic concerns. The chief proponent of action, Secretary of State John Foster Dulles, may have felt compelled to act to secure U.S. influence in Central America in compensation for the Eisenhower administration's inability to fulfill campaign talk of reducing Soviet control of Eastern Europe. (For a detailed account, see Schlesinger and Kinzer, 1983.)

The United States sought OAS backing for action against the Guatemalan government, but at a Caracas conclave it was able to push through only a mild resolution, adopted under pressure and without enthusiasm. Participation of the CIA working out of Honduras and Nicaragua in the subsequent overthrow of Arbenz was denied at the time, and the ambassador to Guatemala was publicly uncommitted. The ouster of Arbenz was chiefly the work of conservative officers who feared the establishment of worker-peasant militias. The CIA's candidate "invaded" Guatemala with fewer than two hundred men. But Ambassador John Peurifoy practically took charge upon the removal of Arbenz, and the victory was much celebrated in Washington. It was widely reprobated in Latin America, and it may have been on balance negative for the cohesion of the OAS. The episode doubtless contributed to the outpouring of anti-U.S. feeling Vice President Richard Nixon encountered on his South American tour in 1958, when mobs stoned his motorcade in Lima and Caracas.

A much more serious problem was the defection of Fidel Castro's Cuba to the Soviet camp, 1960–61. This occurred through a series of hostile actions and retaliations, seasoned by Castro's anti-U.S. rhetoric. The Eisenhower administration, thinking in terms of times past, thought economic and political measures would easily bring Castro down. But he sought Soviet aid and protection; and Nikita Khrushchev promised it, celebrating the demise of the Monroe Doctrine.

The desertion of Cuba, strategically the most important country of Latin America after Mexico, was unacceptable; and the CIA tried to repeat its Guatemalan success by organizing and arming Cuban exiles. But the Bay of Pigs landing was a total failure because, unlike the Castillo Armas invasion of Guatemala, it lacked support within the target country and its armed forces, and President John F. Kennedy refused to use U.S. personnel. The result was to admit a permanent breach in the American system.

Following the fiasco, Kennedy declared in effect that the United States would tolerate no more Cubas. (Keal, 1983b: 113.) But only nonviolent, that is, ineffective and possibly counterproductive measures were taken against Cuban communism, principally expulsion from the OAS and more or less effective diplomatic and commercial isolation from the rest of the hemisphere. Although Cuba was permitted to be communist, it was not fully free to turn away from U.S. suzerainty, as was shown by the missile crisis of 1962, when the Soviets were found to have installed nuclear weapons in Cuba. At U.S. insistence the missiles were withdrawn. In return, the United States pledged not to invade Cuba again. The outcome of Khrushchev's effort to obtain an easy strategic advantage was a demonstration that the United States would not permit offensive Soviet weapons in its zone. A notable fact of the crisis was the full support of the rest of Latin America for the U.S. position.

A more positive reaction to Castro's threat to revolutionize the hemisphere was Kennedy's Alliance for Progress. This envisioned a capital investment from various sources of $80 billion over ten years, in return for which Latin American countries were to carry out social and economic reforms. (Levinson and de Onis, 1970.) It was proposed to put the hemisphere community on a sounder basis, mixing reform with economic progress to defeat subversion with freedom and democracy. The Alliance did not achieve enough to impress anyone, and it was nearly forgotten well before the end of its decade because neither radicals nor conservatives welcomed U.S.-sponsored reform, there was no consistent direction, and U.S. support dropped away after the death of Kennedy in 1963. To some extent the faltering Alliance for Progress was replaced by an expanded program of military assistance to Latin America, specializing in antisubversive training.

By this time Latin Americans were feeling decidedly independent, even in the area of closest U.S. influence. In January 1964 Panama broke diplomatic relations over an incident that involved flying the U.S. flag in the Canal Zone. President Lyndon Johnson was unable either to get the Panamanians to back down or to get the backing of the OAS but had to agree to revisions of the 1903 treaty. (Steward, 1980: 210–11.) It is also significant that in the 1960s Latin American nations, led by Ecuador and Peru, were able to impose a 200-mile limit in territorial waters, despite vigorous opposition of the United States.

The United States was still able to muster considerable Latin American support for its intervention in the Dominican Republic in 1965. When leftist forces seemed about to defeat the conservative army, the Johnson administration, foreseeing another Cuba, took up positions favoring the conservative side. A reluctant two-thirds majority (mostly

of states of the Caribbean region) was mustered to sponsor the operation and relieve the United States of some of the onus; a Brazilian
general was placed nominally in command. U.S. and OAS forces were
withdrawn after little more than a year, leaving behind a friendly elected
president. It was one of the most successful or least unsuccessful of
interventions. The Soviet Union denounced it all but took no action, in
effect recognizing the American sphere. President Johnson used the
occasion to reiterate the basic American interest: "The American nations
must not, cannot, and will not permit the establishment of another
Communist government in the Western Hemisphere." (Stuart and Tigner,
1975: 448.)

After the Alliance for Progress and until 1980 the idea of a "special
relation" with Latin America declined, and the United States turned
from a regional to a global confrontation of problems. The United
States rejected the idea of special trade arrangements with Latin America in favor of a general system (Pastor, 1982: 1045), and official aid to
Latin America was much reduced, while the Latins ran up large debts
in international financial markets. The U.S. share of Latin American
imports shrank from 50 percent in 1960 to 30 percent in 1980, although
Latin America's gross product rose in the same period from 13 percent
to 26 percent of that of the United States. (Bitar, 1984: 5–15.)

Latin America returned to the forefront of U.S. policy concerns with
the overthrow of Nicaraguan dictator Anastasio Somoza in 1979, the
victory of a Marxist-Leninist-led revolution and the installation of a
government about as hostile to the United States as any in the world.
The situation was almost a replay of the overthrow of Batista by Fidel
Castro in 1958–59. As at various times in the past the United States
found no means of handling a friendly dictator who had lost political
capacity and popular support. The Carter administration tried to disso-
ciate itself from the Somoza regime when it was teetering and thereby
assured its fall without earning credit for it. It was impossible to muster the cooperation of the OAS to support the moderates of the anti-
Somocista coalition; and the Sandinistas, whose official song damned
the United States as "the enemy of humanity," gradually gained complete power.

The Reagan administration was resolved to restore the American
presence in the world, and this appeared especially urgent and at the
same time practicable in Central America, where Nicaragua seemed to
be pulling El Salvador with it into the Soviet orbit. However, despite the
weakness and poverty of Nicaragua and its nearness to the United
States, the Reagan administration found no policy with which to halt

its drift toward dependence on or de facto alliance with Cuba and indirectly the Soviet Union. U.S. emphasis was on the military approach, and American maneuvers in Honduras hinted at possible intervention. But there was little support among the public or in Congress for this, although the provocation was far greater than when the Marines had entered Nicaragua earlier in the century. It was possible, however, to give support to anti-Sandinista forces, originally consisting of Somoza followers who had fled the country in 1979 but bolstered increasingly by refugees from the Sandinista government. This help had to be given covertly at first, then was limited to nonmilitary or "humanitarian" suppliers. But this policy offered no promise of either overcoming the Sandinistas or bringing them to major concessions. The administration was unwilling to accept the permanence of a Marxist-Leninist Nicaragua but unable to undo it.

The guerrilla movement in El Salvador, which took shape soon after the victory of the Sandinistas in Nicaragua, proved more manageable. In El Salvador the United States had the advantage of supporting a recognized government instead of trying to overthrow one as in Nicaragua, but it labored under the handicap that the firmest anticommunists were a military-oligarchic clique that had held power by force—including murder—for many decades. The administration sought with some success to combine military assistance against the Marxist-Leninist guerrillas with a reshaping of Salvadoran politics and the establishment, through a series of elections, of a more or less democratic government, or at least a responsible and legitimate one under a centrist civilian, José Napoleón Duarte.

Whatever the Reagan administration's desire to restore U.S. preeminence over the hemispheric sphere, it lacked means of doing so. The OAS was no longer useful, and it may have served to brake U.S. actions as much as to support them; there was no other important organizational framework for U.S. influence, which was largely unofficial and uncoordinated. Trade and financial ties, made more crucial by the overwhelming foreign debt of nearly all Latin American countries, helped to keep Latin America in the general Western framework but did not make the republics especially amenable to U.S. wishes. Cultural influence was likewise large, especially in television programming; it was denounced at times as "cultural imperialism," but its political effect was doubtful. Economic aid was significant only in regard to small countries, especially of the Caribbean Basin. Military assistance and arms sales continued to be important, but there were many suppliers—including France, Israel, and even Brazil for many items.

The United States by siding with Britain in the 1982 Falklands/Malvinas War weakened security ties, at least for some years, and even led to talk of a Latin American system excluding the United States. The principal intervention the United States could essay in most of the hemisphere was the granting of some economic favors to approved governments, plus the mostly moral encouragement of the trend to democratic government.

There was an increasing differentiation between the narrower sphere of the Caribbean Basin and South America, which includes the bulk of the population and resources of Latin America. While U.S. aid to South America shrank, it increased to the Caribbean area (including Central America), which was enlarged to include former non-Latin European colonies, Jamaica, Trinidad, Guyana, and smaller islands. In recent years the bulk of U.S. aid to Latin America has gone to Central America, which has less than a tenth of the population of the region.

This has occurred in part because of the more direct impact of the closer area on the United States; communist influence in Central America, by the domino analogy, has been viewed by some as a threat to the U.S. southern border. In a sense this region was united by shared problems, especially of unemployment, resource and land shortages, and monoculture. (Pastor, 1982: 1041.) It was all the more tied to the United States since 10 to 20 percent of the population of many countries —the Dominican Republic, Nicaragua, Haiti, El Salvador, and others —were living in the United States.

Reasons for past U.S. intervention are difficult to disentangle. To some extent they have been economic, but this has certainly not been true in the sense of seeking added wealth for the United States through fairly costly undertakings in lands of trivial economic importance to this country. On the contrary, it would appear that American presidents have seen business relations as a good means of extending U.S. influence. They have felt that U.S. business was beneficial and so was to be helped and encouraged to improve backward countries.

There has also, of course, been a large streak of noblesse oblige in U.S. policy, the sense that the United States has been peculiarly blessed in its politics and civilization, and has some duty to spread them. (Bemis, 1943: 384–85.) There is no reason to doubt that McKinley believed he was acting for the welfare of the benighted people of the Philippines. It is striking that the most interventionist of American presidents was Wilson, who was especially legal-minded and an idealist of freedom—and correspondingly inclined to do good in the world as he understood it.

Probably the greatest factor in shaping U.S. policy toward Latin America, however, has been security concerns. Despite problems such as trade, debt, migration, and narcotics traffic, fear of communism was decisive in triggering sharp reactions. The uncomfortable feeling that the southern flank could not be taken for granted (Marcella, 1985: 5) was the chief impetus for measures of economic and social improvement. The essence of the Monroe Doctrine, the exclusion of competing powers, remains unchanged. Defense against outside attack is much simpler than defense against subversion, which appears to be defense of the status quo or identification with the interests of the rich and powerful. This becomes a problem if popular or radical movements arise and identify the United States with the oppressive order. If the United States then seeks to support its friends, the opposition looks to the other superpower for assistance and a political model, and the United States sees its suspicions confirmed.

If the United States felt no threat, much less attention would doubtless go to its sphere of influence. In any case, the United States is unsystematic in the application of power. Latin America can hardly be defined as an area of hegemonic sway. Even Mexico, economically dependent as it is, has continued to demonstrate independence in foreign policy, especially regarding Central America, to the discomfort of Washington. The ability of the United States to influence such countries as Brazil or Argentina, or even weaker powers such as Colombia or Peru, is limited; U.S. military coercion of these countries is hardly more feasible than in regard to Syria or Thailand.

The limited ability of the United States to get South America to follow its lead becomes apparent when Washington tries to impose a policy. For example, President Jimmy Carter was unable to secure significant cooperation in the grain embargo to chastise the Soviet Union for the invasion of Afghanistan; Brazil and Argentina used the occasion to increase sales. The boycott of the 1980 Moscow Olympics was heeded only by dictatorial or military-ruled countries, doubtless for their own purposes. (Wesson, 1982b: 18.) Similarly, the Reagan administration was able to secure practically no backing in South America for its Central American policies.

Yet the U.S. sphere is an important reality, both for the Caribbean and Central America and for Latin America as a whole. The Latin Americans are very much aware of the presence of the United States; indeed, they still attribute to it exaggerated powers over their affairs, although habits of deference have been reduced by the Vietnam War, the Falklands/Malvinas War, the broadening of economic relations, and the lessened dependency on U.S. armaments. The United States is the focus of foreign relations of all Latin American countries, where intellectuals seek delivery from U.S. power. (For advocacy of an independent foreign policy line, see, for example, Ferreira, 1985: 70–95 and Wesson, 1986.)

The U.S. sphere is perhaps better defined as the area of special concern and responsibility for the United States, a psychological as well as a geographical concept. Carter made an energetic effort to derail the Brazilian nuclear program (Wesson, 1981), whereas he would hardly have noticed a similar program in Asia. The United States is not indifferent to political and ideological developments anywhere, but the threshold of alarm is far higher in Africa or South Asia than in Latin America. It is no great matter if a half-dozen African countries claim to be Marxist-Leninist. But today, as when the Monroe Doctrine was enunciated, the United States has its area of pride, responsibility, and relatively large influence and freedom of action. In this zone it will above all oppose however it can any extension of an alien political system—at one time monarchy, now Marxist-Leninist party rule.

The Soviet Sphere

The Soviet zone of hegemony must be considered the successor of that of tsarist Russia, just as the Soviet Union is heir to most of the territory of the Romanov empire. Like the American, the Russian sphere is a continuation of expansion when it became unsuitable, for one reason or another, to incorporate new areas of domination into the imperial state. There was a reversal or hiatus with the Leninist revolution, but old patterns were brought back by Stalin.

A peculiarity of Russian empire-building was that it began within the decadent Tatar realm and continued as a process of taking over the heritage of that empire. The princes of Muscovy first prospered as favorites of the Tatar overlords, then proceeded to make good their independence, and went on to conquer former Tatar lands, especially to the East, through Kazan, across the Urals, and eventually to the Pacific. They also pressed south and southeast, to the Black and Caspian seas, through a series of wars with the Turks. They met much more difficulty in pushing to the West, but they profited from the decay and breakup of once-great Poland to acquire the Ukraine and other territories. (Parker, 1969.)

In part, Russian expansion followed emigration into sparsely populated areas, as did that of the United States. But whereas American expansion engulfed no important preexisting states, Russian growth (except in thinly populated Siberia) mostly meant incorporation of weaker states, some of them rather large and populous, such as Georgia, the Ukraine, most of Poland in the eighteenth century, and the Central Asian Khanates. Religion was one motivation of the Russian outreach, to protect Orthodoxy on the other side of the border, especially toward the Balkans. More important was security. The frontier was always to be made safer by pushing it farther away and obtaining strong points to defend previous acquisitions. Russia became "the greatest absorber of other peoples" (Beveridge, 1903: 211), a multinational state very different from the United States, whose multiethnicity derives almost entirely from immigration.

There was a special urge to move southward to Constantinople (Istanbul) and the Straits, partly to control the exit from the Black Sea, partly to move toward the Holy Land, partly to assert Russia's destiny as heir of the Byzantine empire and Third Rome. But Russia was not finical; it pushed anywhere it perceived weakness. Having expanded approximately to its 1914 frontiers early in the nineteenth century, it went on to swallow the Transcaucasus and Central Asia with large racially and culturally alien populations.

The Russian practice was not to maintain weaker states as permanent vassals but, in the logic of contiguity, to incorporate them into the body of the autocratic empire. States that came under the Russian wing as more or less separate entities, such as the Ukraine, Georgia, and Poland were step by step placed under the general administrative control of the Russian capital. The fact that their populations were non-Russian made no difference in theory for the catholic empire. Indeed, their discontents and consequent occasional efforts to secure independence made it necessary to deprive them of autonomy.

Consequently, Russia in 1914 possessed an empire but only a modest sphere of influence, including northern Persia (Iran) and perhaps Serbia. Nevertheless, the tsarist state empire went into a war it knew might endanger its political system lest Austria rob it of its influence in the Balkans, where it had a "historic mission." (Harcave, 1968: 409–12.)

Lenin denounced the Russian empire as a "prisonhouse of nationalities," and much of his support came from aggrieved minorities, especially Jews, Caucasians, Poles, and Balts. But these ethnic revolutionaries did not so much wish to break up the empire as to secure justice within it in the name of universal principles. The new Soviet state turned away from tsarist imperialism to embrace the universalism of world socialist revolution and class struggle. This was expected to come, as predicted by Marx, in the most advanced capitalist countries, headed by Germany.

It soon appeared, however, that the tsarist and Soviet outlook differed less in practice than in theory. In the telegram in which Lenin recognized the independence of the Ukraine he demanded that it conform to the discipline of the Bolshevik party, that is, in effect, to subordinate itself to the centralized Russian-dominated state. (Wesson, 1969: 47–48.) Soviet armies restored Russian power across nearly all the former tsarist dominions, including Georgia, where they overthrew a socialist republic, and Central Asia, where Russian settlers had a role not unlike that of capitalistic colonialists. Outer Mongolia was made into a satellite, although it was not annexed out of deference to Chinese feelings. In the west the fortunes of war and the ability of smaller peoples to obtain support from Europe caused the loss of a strip from Finland along the Baltic through eastern Poland to Bessarabia. But the drive to revolutionize Poland in the Russo-Polish War of 1920 was virtually a replay of the contests between Poland and Russia in previous centuries.

In its weakness the young Soviet state had to reconcile itself to the loss of western territories. But it recovered economically and built up military strength under Stalin until by 1939 it was able to take advantage of the conflict between Nazi-Fascist and democratic powers of Western Europe. Stalin dickered with both Hitler and Britain and France. But the latter powers were not in a position to reward him with coveted lands. Because of Stalin's beneficent neutrality Hitler gave him a hunting license for the Baltic states, a large part of Poland (inhabited mostly by White Russians and Ukrainians), and Bessarabia (which became Moldavia). Stalin had difficulties only with Finland; the resistance of the Finns was so fierce that he settled for minor territorial gains in 1940.

In October 1940, when Stalin was considering joining the German-Japanese alliance, he sought German agreement for a Soviet sphere of expansion in the direction of Iran and India. Hitler was prepared to concede this, but the further Soviet demand for an opening in the southern Balkans and control of the Straits conflicted with Nazi ambitions. Hitler halted the negotiations and instead began preparations for invasion.

The idea of a Soviet sphere of influence was unspoken as long as Soviet troops were fighting on their own ground, but Stalin never indicated a loss of interest in Eastern Europe. The question of extension of Soviet power came to the fore as Soviet soldiers crossed the

1941 boundaries. Eastern Europe was effectively conceded to the Soviets at the Teheran Conference of Roosevelt, Winston Churchill, and Stalin in November–December 1943. The Yalta Conference of February 1944 tried to keep up some hope for democracy in Eastern Europe, but the vagueness of the agreements may have encouraged the Soviets to believe they had a free hand in the occupied territories. (Brzezinski, 1984–85: 279–80.) The Potsdam Conference (July–August 1945) likewise failed to clearly define the future condition of Europe.

At no time did the Soviets overtly claim an exclusive right in the countries occupied by their forces, nor did they admit to creating a sphere of influence, an imperialistic concept they rejected. On the contrary, Stalin in the latter part of the war specifically reassured the Western powers on that score. Stalin did not, however, admit any interference or accept outside advice regarding the territories he de facto controlled. He did not mind going back to historical motifs suggestive of tsarist ideas; most prominently, he resurrected the old concept of Slavic unity, Pan-Slavism, to lay a basis for closer relations between Russia and Slavic nations of Eastern and Southern Europe. (This effort climaxed at a Pan-Slavic Congress in Belgrade in December 1946, but it rapidly receded and was dropped after Yugoslavia's Josip Broz Tito broke with Stalin.)

The American concept, or at least the Rooseveltian concept, was universalist, a world order without power politics and hence without spheres of influence. But Roosevelt also conceived of the big powers acting as world policemen, presumably over zones pertaining to them. Others advocated some kind of delimitation as the means of avoiding conflict. For example, Walter Lippmann proposed dividing the world into U.S., British, Russian, Chinese, and possibly Indian regions. (Bull, 1977: 222.) George Kennan concluded that the Soviet Union would not put much trust in any world organization, could not be expected to cooperate in a liberal-democratic global order, and would insist on holding its sphere of hegemony. Vice President Henry Wallace, from a different ideological standpoint, also proposed mutual recognition of Soviet and American spheres. (Keal, 1983b: 72–73.)

The British, experienced in balance-of-power politics, took the lead in seeking a demarcation of spheres with the Soviets. Thus Churchill and Stalin in 1944 came to a quick informal agreement parceling up the Balkans, assigning most countries to Soviet dominance but leaving Greece under the British aegis. Churchill was eager for American-British forces to get onto as much ground as possible in Europe, especially the Balkans, on the realistic basis that military presence meant political predominance and that it was more reasonable to try to limit the Soviet advance than to pretend that it did not entail hegemony.

There were many reasons for Soviet determination to keep control over Eastern Europe: desire to control the traditional route for invasion of Russia, traditional expansionist aims, Pan-Slavism, desire to profit from reparations and confiscation of German assets, awareness that the Soviet Union could not compete economically in a free Eastern Europe, ideas of Russian and revolutionary-proletarian destiny, and a sense of right because of war losses in the liberation of Eastern Europe. As General Secretary Leonid Brezhnev told a Czech in 1968, "Your country is in the region occupied by Soviet soldiers in World War II. We paid for this with great sacrifices, and we will never leave." (Johnson, 1985: 256.) The fact that several countries, especially Hungary and Romania, had supported the Hitlerite cause, together with the hostility of Eastern Europe (except Czechoslovakia) toward the Soviet Union between the wars, also contributed. Such reasons applied especially to Germany, which the Soviets were resolved to hold or neutralize so far as possible. Former tsarist territories (except central Poland) were simply taken into the Soviet state.

The United States and Britain excluded the Soviet Union from sharing in the administration of Germany, Italy, and Japan but did not contest Soviet priority in East Europe. (Brzezinski, 1984–85: 285.) They did question the Soviet Union's right to security guarantees and to "friendly" governments on its western borders, across which the Nazi invasion had come. But the Declaration of Liberated Europe, agreed to by Great Britain, the United States, and the Soviet Union in 1944, called for democratic governments in all occupied territories (Keal, 1983b: 87), and in American eyes the right to have "friendly" neighbors did not mean the right to Sovietize them.

But Stalin did not trust anything less than complete domination, aware that East Europeans allowed to choose for themselves would probably be anti-Russian and anticommunist.

The agents of Sovietization were the Red Army, national communist parties, and the police. Professionals of the old Comintern, officially dissolved in August 1943 as a gesture to the Western allies but kept organizationally in place for future use, entered along with Soviet army units and began their work of organizing the conquered populations. The Soviet zone seemed based on the old Russian principle that where the Russian army went, there it stayed. The few exceptions included Yugoslavia and Romania, from which Khrushchev felt able to withdraw Soviet forces in 1958.

Procedures varied according to circumstances. Typically there was formed, with Soviet officers looking on, a coalition regime led by communists, who also controlled the police. In due course there were increasingly formalistic elections, and the new states were certified as "people's democracies." Soviet agents and advisors helped along the way, and joint companies based on German assets gave the Soviet Union a stake in the economy. (Zimmerman, 1984: 129.) Many anti-communists made the task of Sovietization easier by fleeing to the West. Romania and Bulgaria were fully communist by the spring of 1945; the process was completed in Hungary and Czechoslovakia only early in 1948.

A turning point was the Soviet Union's rejection of the Marshall Plan in 1947 and its refusal to permit Czechoslovakia and Poland (and by implication Finland) to participate, as those countries had moved to do when the plan was first announced. Soviet management of the Polish elections in that year also made plain that everything necessary would be done to assure completely subservient governments in Eastern Europe.

The Truman Doctrine (1947), declaring the U.S. intention to protect Greece and Turkey from communist subversion or Soviet pressure, was another step toward demarcation of spheres. The Soviets responded by tightening bonds where they were in control. The Truman Doctrine did not seek to roll back communist power, only to prevent its extension. The U.S. Joint Chiefs of Staff wrote off Czechoslovakia even before it was Sovietized in February 1948. (Keal, 1983b: 100.) There was some fear that acknowledging the Soviet sphere might invite its enlargement, so this satisfaction was refused; but the United States conspicuously failed to take any serious measures — such as economic sanctions — to raise the cost of imposing Stalinist regimes on former enemy and allied countries.

Despite the secular principles of Russian imperialism, the dictates of Marxist-Leninist ideology, and the express universalism of the first Soviet constitution, the Sovietized territories were not incorporated into the Soviet Union but were kept as an area of hegemony with separate administrations and inevitably some aspirations to autonomy. Only former tsarist lands were annexed, plus a small stretch of former East Prussia. This restraint may be considered a concession to world opinion and an indication of some acceptance of the international system and its traditional rules. It was also probably motivated by Soviet weakness in the aftermath of the war and fear of complications with the United States (sole possessor of nuclear weapons).

The chief instruments of the American effort to draw a line against further communist expansion were the Truman Doctrine, which served as the rationale for aid to Greece and Turkey, and the Marshall Plan, a program to strengthen dangerously weak Western Europe. In 1948 Stalin tested the American will by the Berlin blockade, but the United States responded with a successful airlift. In 1949 the NATO alliance was put in place to bind the Western powers militarily. A year later the United States went to war in Korea to check a communist thrust in Asia.

The Cold War was essentially a duel over the boundaries of American and Soviet spheres in the broadest sense. In late 1947, in answer to the Truman Doctrine, the Cominform was established as a successor to the Comintern. It joined together the communist parties of Eastern Europe and the Soviet Union, plus the two main communist parties of Western Europe, the French and Italian. Its chief function, however, was to publish a paper and to organize the anti-Tito campaign after he fell from grace; after Stalin's death the Cominform was discarded.

In 1948 the Soviets consolidated their grip on Czechoslovakia. (Korbel, 1959.) The Soviet army had withdrawn, leaving in charge a coalition headed by communists but touted as a bridge between East and West. The reason for the takeover was that the communist-dominated government was losing popularity and was expected to suffer in scheduled elections. Such a loss would confirm Stalin's belief that he could not count on any country's loyalty unless it were run in Soviet fashion. A few months later Titoist Yugoslavia rebelled against Soviet interference and asserted its independence.

Tito's rebellion was a challenge to the coherence of the Soviet zone, and it was deemed necessary to extirpate his influence by a series of purges, show trials, and executions. Stalin ruled Eastern Europe as a wartime leader and chief of the world communist movement, and the region was organized as satrapies under little Stalins — Klement Gottwald in Czechoslovakia, Mátyás Rákosi in Hungary, Boleslaw Bierut in Poland, Gheorghe Gheorghiu-Dej in Romania, and Georgi Dimitrov in Bulgaria. Each country had its Stalinist police and Stalinist economic plan for heavy industrialization and collectivization of agriculture, while the Soviet Union conducted overall foreign policy. The Council for Mutual Economic Assistance (CMEA) was formed in January 1949 in response to the Marshall Plan, but it remained inactive while Stalin lived because of his dislike for any multilateral forum. Relations were carried on mostly informally, through party contacts and Soviet advisors;

the chief formal ties were treaties pledging friendship and cooperation. (Hutchings, 1983: 15.)

This system functioned fairly well while Eastern Europe was recuperating from the war, but tensions grew beneath the surface and came out after Stalin's death in March 1953. After May 1953 there was some relaxation in Eastern Europe as well as in the Soviet Union; under the "New Course," there was a slackening of collectivization of agriculture, loosening of police controls and censorship, and the termination of joint Soviet–East European enterprises. In June there were riots in Plzeň, Czechoslovakia, and soon afterward more serious disturbances in East Berlin, which were put down by the Soviet army.

Bigger troubles arose after Nikita Khrushchev gained control and undertook to restore something of Leninism by relaxing strictures on the economy and literature, and by trying to bring back some of the idealism of the revolution. He also sought to replace the Stalinist command of Eastern Europe with an ostensibly equal union of states dedicated to socialism. (Kux, 1980: 23.) Most dramatically, in February 1956 he attacked Stalin as not only a murderer of good party people but a bungler and incompetent war leader.

Eastern Europe was already infected with hopes of much more liberalization, if not freedom, when Khrushchev went to Belgrade in May 1955 to apologize to Tito for Stalin's maltreatment, apparently with hopes of luring him back into the bloc. This Soviet backdown further encouraged flux in Eastern Europe, and the blackening of Stalin's image by Khrushchev increased the ferment. In October 1956, after workers' riots in Poznan, Poland, the Polish party all but rebelled and chose as its new leader a man imprisoned under Stalin, Władysław Gomułka. Khrushchev blustered, but the Poles stood firm, and Khrushchev compromised rather than risk a bloody encounter. The Poles obtained some autonomy, including a modus vivendi with the Roman Catholic Church, remission of collectivization, and a little latitude for private enterprise. Polish privileges were subsequently whittled down, but Poland has enjoyed special status among the bloc nations ever since.

In Hungary, where the authority of the party had been dissolving for many months, the success of the Poles found a strong echo. In the face of this, the government fell apart, and the new regime was so bold as to ask for the withdrawal of Soviet troops and release from the alliance. After some indecision, Soviet forces reentered, put a bloody end to the regime of Imre Nagy, and installed a non-Stalinist, János Kádár. The

Soviet intervention was facilitated by the fact that Soviet units had been in Hungary since the end of the war and also by the fortuitous circumstance that the West was preoccupied and badly divided by the Anglo-French-Israeli invasion of Egypt to recover the Suez Canal, against the firm opposition of the United States.

The Soviets reacted to their problems in Hungary by reimposing discipline on the bloc. Hungary, however, was permitted under Kádár to lighten somewhat the control over the economy and expression of opinion. Khrushchev, who called the bloc a *sodruzhestvo*, or "comradeship," of nations, permitted some latitude under the Soviet aegis. Romania, relieved of Soviet military occupation in 1958, deviated most of all, opposing the Soviets in many small matters of economics and foreign and military policy. (Zimmerman, 1984: 134–35.)

Lacking a godlike leader, the Soviet bloc was increasingly institutionalized. The CMEA was brought to life and provided with a large staff to coordinate the economies of members. In 1956 the five-year plans of Eastern European states were synchronized with those of the Soviet Union, and in 1959 the CMEA received a charter and a council in which members were theoretically equal. The Warsaw Treaty Organization (WTO), was formed in 1955 after West Germany entered NATO, to bring the national forces into a single framework under a Soviet commander; it was specifically designed to defend not only territories but "socialism." (Zimmerman, 1984: 136.) In 1961 it began holding joint maneuvers.

The lines of the Soviet sphere were drawn tighter. The Sino-Soviet split, maturing since Stalin's death, became definite with the pullout of Soviet advisors from China in 1960. It was followed in 1961 by the defiant defection of Albania, which the Soviets had no means of hindering. The Chinese alternative model gave a little more latitude for ideological diversity in Eastern Europe; Romania especially cultivated relations with Beijing.

On the other hand, the German Democratic Republic was fully integrated after the Berlin Wall, built in 1961, stopped the exodus to West Germany. East Germany was occupied by a larger Soviet force than any other East European country, and the East German army, unlike the forces of other bloc countries, was wholly subordinated to WTO (that is, Soviet) command in peacetime. (Stent, 1985: 48.) A divided Germany, however, continued to represent a sore spot in the division of Europe.

In the 1960s the nations of Eastern Europe graduated from "people's democracies" to "socialist nations." Under Brezhnev there was less emphasis on the viability of East European societies and their economic systems, and more on their cohesion. Nonetheless, the next major challenge to Soviet dominion came in Czechoslovakia in 1968, not from workers or intellectuals acting against the party but from within the ruling circles of the party itself, as repressed democratic urges bubbled up under the stimulus of economic stagnation. (Hutchings, 1983: 36.) Creeping reformism led to a remarkable effervescence in the spring and summer, when nearly everyone seemed to agree on the need for change. Censorship collapsed, and Czechs suddenly found themselves enjoying a great deal of freedom—sponsored by the communist party itself. The Soviet Union seems to have been afraid most of all of the bad example, not only on East Europeans but on peoples of the western part of the Soviet Union. There were echoes in several East European countries, even some sympathetic movements in Moscow and the Ukraine.

The Soviet invasion of Czechoslovakia in August 1968 was assisted by small contingents from satellites, the East Germans, Poles, and Bulgarians joining with some eagerness, and the Hungarians rather reluctantly; Romania sharply criticized the invasion. (Hutchings, 1983: 44–45.)

The action was rationalized as defense of socialism in a *Pravda* article of September 28, stating the superiority of "proletarian internationalism" to bourgeois concepts of international law: "Every communist party is responsible not only to its own people but to the entire communist movement"; they must take a "class approach to the question of sovereignty"; and socialist countries owed their independence to the Soviet armed forces. Brezhnev gave a slightly softer expression to the same ideas in a speech in Warsaw on November 12, 1968: "And when internal and external forces hostile to socialism try to turn the development of socialism backwards to a capitalist restoration, when a threat arises to the cause of socialism in that country, a threat to the security of the socialist community as a whole, this is no longer an issue only for the people of that country in question but a general issue which is the concern of all the socialist countries." (Steele, 1974: 179, 182.)

Czechoslovakia was brought to passivity and into as much conformity as its neighbors under the government of Gustav Husák, which was considerably more repressive than that of Kádár in Hungary. Episodes like 1956 and 1968 reasserted Soviet hegemony over the bloc at a cost of the loss of many adherents of the Soviet-led movement abroad, especially in Western Europe.

The near-breakdown of communist rule in Poland, 1980–81, was largely the doing of the workers, who founded a powerful free union movement, Solidarity. For a time Solidarity seemed stronger than the demoralized government and the largely dissolved party. As Solidarity pressed for political freedom as well as workers' rights, the Soviets sabotaged agreements between the workers and the regime (Korbonski, 1984b: 82) and seemed on the verge of invasion. The Polish military under General Wojciech Jaruzelski came to the rescue of party rule in December 1981 and declared martial law. With considerable difficulty Jaruzelski repressed anti-Soviet forces, but for years Soviet authority was seriously compromised. With private farming and a powerful independent Church, Poland seemed immune to a pro-Russian ideology and was economically and politically a loss for the bloc. (Milewski, Pomian, and Zielonka, 1985–86: 337–59.)

The Soviet Union has thus shown the ability to meet recurring threats to the stability of the bloc, which becomes more settled as parties ripen in power, the cadres are habituated to their roles and status, and people become accustomed to the Marxist-Leninist way of life. It is conceivable that the bloc may expand, as in effect it has expanded: not only Mongolia but Cuba and Vietnam are members of CMEA, and North Korea and Yugoslavia are associates; Laos, South Yemen, Ethiopia, and Angola are observers.

On the other hand, it seems certain that there will be future upsurges of independence in Eastern Europe, which may be more difficult than past ones to suppress. The chief weakness lies in the economy. It is difficult to coordinate planned economies. They inherently tend to autarky, because the way to insure a supply of goods is to produce them domestically, and there is no good way to calculate prices without a market. (Marer, 1984c: 161.) Soviet authorities failed for many years to appreciate the difficulty of integrating centralized economies, and such progress as they have made has been mostly in bilateral, not multilateral, arrangements. (Braun, 1983: 103, 117.) The CMEA has dozens of commissions and institutes but no central decision-making body. A convertible ruble was established in 1964, but it has never functioned well. (Hutchings, 1983: 26–27, 234.)

Although dependence on Soviet oil has been a major bond tying Eastern Europe to the USSR, the backbone of Soviet control is, of course, the military; Soviet and East European forces are coordinated through the WTO. In this area, unlike the economic, the Soviets concede very little to the sensitivities of their dependents; it is less effective to argue that military effectiveness requires autonomy. The WTO has many attached bodies for coordination of maneuvers, training, doctrines, and weaponry. (Jones, chap. 5.) WTO is supplemented by a network of bilateral treaties promising friendship, cooperation, and mutual assistance, and (except for those with Romania) referring to the "drawing together" of socialist states, their "internationalist duties," and the defense of the "historic achievements of socialism." (Hutchings, 1983: 160–65.)

But WTO, like CMEA, has no central decision-making body (for organizational chart, see Hutchings [142]) and no standing army. East Europeans have caused problems regarding extra-European cooperation, national control of forces, defense expenditures, and decision-making procedures. The Romanians have refused WTO maneuvers on their territory and have insisted that their armed forces can be subject only to Romanian command. (Braun, 1983: 91.) East European forces may be of doubtful utility for repression at home or for combat against the West. (Johnson, 1985: 263–80.)

The Soviets are no longer able to pressure Poland and other states by the specter of West German revanchism, as they could until the German-Polish treaty of December 1970. They can no longer name high officials of satellite governments. Apparently the Soviets can require either conformity in foreign policy, as in the case of Hungary, or domestic repressiveness as in Romania, but not necessarily both together. They are in something of a dilemma, as they hope to get better support from voluntary allies, nominally independent states supported by their peoples, but cannot permit real independence and fear any political liberalization. They want close relations, but they are apprehensive that East European deviationism will be contagious and therefore they keep the brother countries at a distance. (Terry, 1984: 24 and Kux, 1980: 23.)

In any event, the Soviet sphere is recognized de facto although not de jure. West Europeans are ambivalent. They regret the unnatural division of the continent, but they fear that any serious meddling with it would be excessively dangerous. The United States similarly decries the "captive nations" but proposes no provocative steps to release them and hesitates between regarding the East European governments as servants of Soviet policy, whose citizens should be encouraged to resist tyrannical rule, and as sovereign powers whose potential independence is to be promoted.

In 1948 the United States was prepared to help Tito's Yugoslavia (which had been the most virulently anti-American of the communist states) after it made good its independence from Moscow. U.S. support saved Yugoslavia from probable defeat, although Tito kept up communist rhetoric and policies (including collectivization) for many months after the break. (Zimmerman, 1984: 130.) A secret National Security

Council paper in 1949 urged working for the separation of Eastern Europe from the Soviet Union by encouraging more independence, Yugoslav-style, and the United States made small-scale efforts to infiltrate some communist countries. (Garthoff, 1985: 318–19.) But, generally speaking, the United States has taken for granted the Soviet domination of Eastern Europe. In the presidential campaign of 1952 the Republicans made noises about "rolling back" Soviet control of that area, but they forgot about it as soon as Eisenhower was elected. In 1956 the United States made it clear that it would oppose Soviet intervention in Hungary only by peaceful means and refused to recognize a rebel government. (Keal, 1983b: 121.)

Following the Hungarian precedent, in 1968 the United States somewhat naively disclaimed interest in Czechoslovakia as the Soviet invasion was obviously brewing, hoping to persuade the Politburo that the United States was not behind the Czech movement and thus that the movement did not represent a threat to the Soviet Union. The Vietnam War also immobilized the United States, somewhat like the Suez conflict twelve years earlier. When the invasion came, the United States limited its reaction to moral indignation and a rather brief chill in relations. Cost to the Soviet Union was minimized, and there followed the warmest spell of U.S.-Soviet détente of the postwar period.

The United States viewed the 1979 invasion of Afghanistan more seriously, although it was a much less important country. The Soviet transgression of the accepted borders was punished, however, only by minor slaps, including a boycott of the Moscow Olympics and an embargo on additional shipments of American grain, which forced the Soviets to buy elsewhere at slightly higher prices. In reprisal against the imposition of military rule in Poland in 1981, the United States undertook a number of retaliatory measures of small importance, which may have increased Polish dependence on the Soviet Union while giving the Polish government an excuse for economic troubles.

Détente between the United States and the Soviet Union seems to have had the effect of sealing the status quo in Eastern Europe. The Helsinki accords of 1975 likewise served to legitimate the existing situation as the price of some international recognition for human rights. On the other hand, American presidents have several times traveled to the more independent countries of Eastern Europe, Poland, Yugoslavia, and Romania, as have secretaries of state and other high dignitaries. The Soviets see these gestures as efforts to divide. (Garthoff, 1985: 336.)

Despite the policy of rewarding deviant East European nations with political attention and commercial concessions, including trade benefits and credits, it would appear that the Western powers would be loath to see any threat to Soviet overlordship because of the uncertainties this would raise. The continuation of the Soviet sphere is less menacing than any probable cause of its breakup. Nevertheless, the West has no wish to accept the bloc as a "well-knit family of nations" and "the foundation of the future worldwide brotherhood of nations," as Brezhnev has characterized Eastern Europe. (Kux, 1980: 23.)

The Two Spheres

The U.S. and Soviet spheres are both reflections of superior power, and both involve economic, political, ideological, and military-strategic considerations. Each superpower is economically dominant in its sphere but does not necessarily find it very profitable; each promotes its own political institutions and beliefs, and each resists intrusions of the other into its reserved space. Relations in both spheres are mostly bilateral, and multilateral bodies lack decision-making authority. Both have been varyingly imperious and overbearing toward weaker states under their aegis, and each has appeared to the peoples of their spheres as an impediment to change. Yet the relations of the superpowers to their spheres have been as dissimilar as the histories and institutions of the United States and Russia/Soviet Union.

The United States and Russia expanded across a continental expanse; for both, expansion came to seem in the nature of the vigorous state. However, the enlargement of American territories was more the work of unorganized migration than deliberate action. Even substantial acquisitions of territory—Texas in 1845 and Hawaii in 1898—were largely accomplished by settlers from the United States who formed themselves into a political power and requested to join the Union. Washington had only to accept the fait accompli. In contrast, there was consistent national purpose in Russian expansionism, and it was carried on much more by the state and by military means, much less by self-governing migrants, such as Cossack bands. Moreover, territorial growth was essential for the Russian autocracy, part of the meaning of its existence. Tsarist and Soviet expansionism, then, have been largely carried out by the state for the state.

In both cases, expansion, both of the national territory and of the hegemonic sphere, was into areas of relative weakness. Much of the Eurasian steppes and Siberia, like the American West, was thinly populated and lacking well-organized powers to seriously resist the intrusion. Here, too, however, the difference is marked. The United States has never swallowed a widely recognized state, and its empire-building has always been at the expense of very poor and weak peoples. After engulfment of the continental expanse gave way to the extension of American power overseas at the end of the nineteenth century, the United States intervened mostly in the very feeblest of states, such as Haiti, the Dominican Republic, and Nicaragua, with minimal bloodshed; and such intervention was usually a result of those states' incapacity and disorder.

If the United States had applied power to empire in the Russian fashion, it could easily have incorporated the entire Western Hemisphere. From the latter part of the nineteenth century there was no force capable of resisting the vast potential strength of what was rapidly becoming the world's premiere industrial power. The Russian empire grew where and whenever it met opportunities, at the expense of more advanced as well as less advanced peoples, taking in large and well-organized historic states as well as tribal peoples. The United States was never prepared for any major sacrifice for the sake of imperial gain, such as would have been implied by the assertion of control over South America. And if the president was prone to push forward, he was commonly checked by the Congress and public opinion; the Senate many times refused acquisitions proposed by the executive.

A corollary is that military force has been and is less central to the American imperial way than to Russian/Soviet expansionism. Force was essential in continental expansion, of course, but the United States after its Civil War and up to the late nineteenth century was a remarkably demilitarized power, in marked contrast to the Russia of that period. The war with Spain marked the leap to American overseas dominion. The growth of American influence abroad, however, was the work primarily of private interests, investors, and entrepreneurs. After 1898 it would not appear that the United States really gained imperial stature by military interventions. To the contrary, the incursions in the Caribbean and Central America in the first decade of this century were clearly irritants in relations with Latin America in general, and the republics were protesting by the 1920s.

The renunciation of intervention in the Good Neighbor Policy of the 1930s brought an increase in U.S. influence, or at least of hemispheric solidarity. Military or paramilitary operations since World War II have been generally counterproductive (Blasier, 1976 passim), as in Guatemala (1954), Cuba (1961), and the Dominican Republic (1965). The exception may be the militarily trivial Grenadan occupation of 1983; judgment of U.S. actions against Nicaragua must await their outcome.

The Russian empire, after the occupation of Siberia, was strictly the result of military power, as has been the Soviet sphere since 1939. For this reason the Soviet sphere is much less natural, in a geopolitical sense, than the American. Turkey, Iran, and perhaps Yugoslavia would fit better in it, while Hungary and especially East Germany do not belong.

Even outlying Soviet dependencies, such as Cuba and Ethiopia, have come about by virtue of the Soviet ability to offer military assistance. And the use of force by the Soviet Union within its sphere, as in Berlin (1953), Hungary (1956), and Czechoslovakia (1968), has been clearly effective. Regarding Afghanistan (1979 and after), judgment is not yet clear. The dimensions of conflict in Afghanistan were certainly not expected; the Soviet Union has rather obvious reluctance to risk major bloodshed. It held back from the use of Soviet armies in Poland in 1981–82. The Soviets apparently hesitated in 1956 and certainly did so in 1968, and they have refrained from using or openly threatening force against Romanian insubordination. The fact that Finland resisted fiercely probably accounted for Stalin's willingness to accept its autonomy, and the strength of Hungarian opposition in 1956 seems to have been a precondition for gentler treatment under Kádár. (Valenta, 1984b.) A display of willingness to use force from time to time may be necessary to restore a sense of order in the bloc.

The basic fact is that there are Soviet forces on the ground in all countries within the Soviet sphere except Romania, which is surrounded; and everyone knows that they would go into action rather than permit departure from the bloc or any deviation threatening to "socialism" as defined by the Soviet Union. Soviet domination is stronger in its military aspect than in other ways. (Kux, 1980: 26.) Soviet dominion is also strategically more important than American. Eastern Europe is essential to the Soviets both for defensive and offensive purposes, and the Eastern European armed forces are closely linked to those of the Soviet Union. (Johnson, 1985: 256–57.)

By contrast, military force is only a dim possibility in the relations between the United States and most Latin American countries, especially the larger and more distant ones. The lesson of Cuba is that a Latin American country, if it refrains from gross provocation and is prepared for economic sanctions, can defy the United States with impunity and more or less ally itself with the Soviet Union. Anti-U.S. movements thrive, even in Central America, and guerrillas dare the United States to intervene.

The military is no longer an important agency of inter-American integration, as the United States has allowed the relations built up in the 1960s largely to lapse. The defense of the United States is concentrated in Europe and Japan; Latin American armies and navies do not count significantly in U.S. strategic calculations. The Panama Canal is no longer crucial, and nuclear weapons make Latin America irrelevant except for the possibility of Soviet bases in the Caribbean area.

As a result of the difference in the way the two spheres were created, economic relations of dependents to the respective hegemonic powers are opposite. The vassal or client states of the United States all have income levels under one-fifth that of the United States. To the contrary, the most important part of the Soviet sphere, Eastern Europe, has income levels in most places substantially higher than that of the Russians (and they are growing more rapidly, for the most part). Only with some impoverished client states, such as Vietnam and Ethiopia, does the Soviet Union have a relation parallel to that of the United States with Central America. The GNP of Caribbean–Central American countries is less than 2 percent of that of the United States, while all Latin America represents about one-quarter. The GNP of Soviet Eastern Europe seems to be slightly over half that of the Soviet Union.

This dissimilarity makes for quite different problems of control. The impoverished peoples of the Caribbean region tend to blame the United States for their poverty; yet at the same time they look to this country for economic aid to pull them out of the morass, they migrate to the United States, and many want their countries to be more like the United States. Peoples of Eastern Europe, on the other hand, generally regard themselves as culturally superior to the Russians, resent Russian hegemony primarily on nationalistic grounds, and see themselves as subsidizing the Soviet economy.

By corollary, the Soviet sphere contributes much more to the standing of the Soviet Union in the world than the American sphere does to the United States. This country could substantially lose control of its "backyard" with only minor economic costs. Only about 12 percent of U.S. foreign trade is with Latin America, only about 1 percent with the Caribbean–Central American region (not including Mexico). In any event, the United States has never tried to exclude other nations from trade in Latin America and has seldom sought special privileges. U.S.–Latin American economic relations do not rest on political arrangements and are unlikely to be destroyed by political developments (unless the United States imposes sanctions against regimes regarded as hostile, as in the cases of Cuba and Nicaragua.) It would be unpleasant for the United States to see much of Latin America under leftist or radical rule, caught up in economic nationalism and fervent anti-Americanism, but it would hardly be threatening to the American system.

On the other hand, Soviet trade is concentrated on its dependents of Eastern Europe (in 1983, 46 percent of Soviet foreign trade was within the bloc) (*Narodnoe Khozaistvo 1983*, 1984: 562), and this trade is politically directed. One might argue over to what extent the economic relations between satellites and hegemon are more profitable to one side or the other, but the Soviets have become highly geared to them. For the Soviet Union, Eastern Europe is very important as a market for large quantities of materials that would be difficult to place in the West and as a source of goods of relatively high quality and technology, the acquisition of which in the West would be costly in hard currency. To shift Soviet trade away from Eastern Europe might well necessitate a major opening and liberalization of the Soviet economy, that is, a change of the Soviet political economy.

Conceivably the Soviet economy might be more productive if it were more oriented to the West. But from the Soviet point of view, the cost is secondary to the military-political benefits, just as is the cost of maintenance of the Soviet armed forces. The East European domain adds to military strength, lends support for Soviet policies, assists Soviet purposes in the Third World, and supports the international communist movement. (Campbell, 1984: 23–24.)

Both superpowers have asserted their rights of intervention in terms of their political ideals—democracy or Marxist-Leninist socialism. In both cases this has been partly a rationalization for the defense of strategic positions. The effect has been rather different, however. It has proved rather easy for the Russians to impose an autocratic order, or, in recent times, a Marxist-Leninist one, and the political systems of the Soviet sphere have always been fairly similar. Only in Poland have the Russians had much trouble in translating power on the ground into political structure. National regimes have correspondingly tended to rely on Soviet support to maintain them.

On the other side, U.S. efforts to make democracies of dependent states have been only moderately successful. Military occupation in particular failed to bring democracy to Haiti and Nicaragua, although the Dominican Republic has moved to fairly effective democracy since the late 1970s, over forty years after the withdrawal of the Marines and a decade after their short return visit in 1965. Democracy is obviously something that cannot be erected simply by decreeing a constitution and holding elections, unlike the mechanisms of party absolutism, which have been effectively copied from Vietnam to Czechoslovakia to Cuba.

The difficulty of reproducing American political institutions derives not only from their greater complexity but from the fact that the American domination has been less systematic than the Soviet. The United States has never set about seriously to change Latin American societies as it did those of Germany and, to a greater degree, Japan after World War II. It has reacted to what were seen as threats without trying to remodel the prevalent order. In the Caribbean countries occupied early in this century it was considered sufficient to make some material improvements and establish an efficient constabulary, which became the instrument of corrupt dictatorship. In 1954 the United States contributed to the overthrow of a leftist Guatemalan government and then walked away, as though what government the country had was of no concern as long as it was anticommunist.

In both spheres, susceptibility to intervention is related to the strength of the governing authority. Civil war or disintegration of government has most invited U.S. attention, from Nicaragua early in this century to the civil struggle in the Dominican Republic in 1965. The removal of the Marxist-Leninist government of Grenada could not have been undertaken if that government had not destroyed itself by factionalism. Likewise, the Soviets moved in the absence of firm party control in Hungary and Czechoslovakia. They have always claimed to have been invited, and even when the invitation was not impressively official, as in Czechoslovakia in 1968, they were welcomed by a group of hardliners. (Valenta, 1984c: 103.) One must suppose the stern power of the Ceaușescu government in Romania enables it to carry on policies of considerable independence in both foreign and economic affairs without too much fear of Soviet coercion.

In sum, the spheres of influence of the superpowers express global bipolarity, both as a simple adversary relationship of the militarily dominant powers and as a contrariety of political tendencies. Not only are the dependent powers allies and supporters of the respective champions, but in the conduct of their internal affairs and external relations they express the politics and outlook of the extremes of the fundamental political spectrum from pluralism to monism, or polyarchy to authoritarianism. In their sphere the Soviets try to manage and coordinate everything: production, cultural affairs, the military, politics, and philosophy. The U.S. sphere is haphazard, often chaotic, relying on the vagaries of private enterprise. The American approach, contrary to what one might expect, seems perhaps the more successful, as economic interaction prospers better unplanned, and the spontaneous cultural integration of the U.S. sphere is far more effective than all the Soviet–East European cultural programs.

Although they express the basic political structure of world politics, the spheres are subject to the erosive effects of integration in the technological world. It seems obvious that the ability of both hegemonic powers to give directions in their spheres has decidedly diminished, although it is difficult to judge, short of a challenging and probably dangerous crisis, how much has actually eroded. The U.S. overlordship of the 1920s clearly is no more, and the prestige of its leadership has receded fairly steadily since the establishment of the OAS in 1948; efforts of the Reagan administration to reassert it have not been notably successful. The Soviet sphere was given organizational form after the death of Stalin removed the personal-dictatorial bond, but in the opacity of bloc affairs it is difficult to judge how much reality there is in the many integrating bodies or how they would react in a crisis; for example, it is not clear how far the Soviet Union can count on East European armies. Both spheres have declined in economic importance for the respective superpower. U.S. trade has grown more rapidly with other areas, especially Asia, than with Latin America, while Soviet trade has increased more rapidly with "capitalist countries" and especially the Third World than with the satellites. (*Narodnoe Khoziastvo 1983*, 1984: 563.)

The idea of regional spheres of influence of superpowers, in which nations are not fully free to direct their economic and political affairs and order their foreign relations to suit themselves, is repugnant to liberal ideals, to international law, and to the concept of an open international system. In the ideal scheme of things the "world village" should have no restricted neighborhoods, but all should be able to join in community affairs as they please. Yet the spheres are not to be undone. Eastern Europe is of secondary concern to the United States, but it is politically, ideologically, and militarily vital to the Soviet Union. Without it the Kremlin would no longer be a superpower. The Latin American sphere, while not so crucial to the United States, is nonetheless important to it while having little significance for the Soviet Union beyond the possibility of causing trouble and embarrassment in it for the global rival.

It may well be that spheres of influence contribute to international stability and to making the nuclear world a little less dangerous. (Keal, 1983b: 3.) The spheres are, of course, areas of danger, but perhaps less dangerous than they would be if there were no looming and unchallengeable power in the vicinity. There may be conflict within a sphere of influence, but it is not likely to lead to a global confrontation because it is understood that the other superpower keeps out. In any case, it seems too dangerous to try seriously to change them.

3

Economic Change and State Development

James R. Kurth

I. Hegemonic Systems in Comparative Perspective

The international system since 1945 has been largely defined by the two superpowers, the United States and the Soviet Union. One of the prominent features of this international system and of the two superpowers that shape it is that each superpower dominates a regional subsystem of subordinate states—the United States in Latin America and the Soviet Union in Eastern Europe. This chapter will examine the relationships between economic change and political change within these two subsystems.

Traditional historians and political analysts have often described such regional subsystems as areas of "hegemony" or "spheres of influence," and they have referred to the subordinate states within them as "client states" or "protectorates." (Kaufman, 1976; Handel, 1981.) Although the United States in Latin America and the Soviet Union in Eastern Europe are the two most obvious hegemonic systems of today, other examples of hegemonic systems since World War II have been

Britain in the Middle East until the 1950s and in the Persian Gulf sheikhdoms until the 1970s and France in sub-Saharan Africa from the 1960s until the present. The hegemonic systems of the two superpowers have had a good deal in common with these two other systems involving states of unequal power and societies of unequal development.

There were also several comparable hegemonic systems in the more distant past. (Kurth, 1973.) Since the Peace of Westphalia of 1648, which ended the Thirty Years War and established the legal grounds for a multitude of small but formally independent states within Mitteleuropa, there have been a number of hegemonic systems or close approximations to them. In addition to the contemporary systems already mentioned, there were also earlier cases such as (1) France in the Rhineland (1648–1713), (2) Austria in the German states (1815–66), (3) Austria in the Italian states (1815–59), (4) Germany in southeastern Europe (1934–45), and (5) Britain in the Indian princely states (1858–1947). (This last system was a limiting case between a hegemonic system and a colonial one, an extreme form of the indirect rule that Britain often employed elsewhere in its empire.) There have also been abortive hegemonic systems, such as Japan in East Asia (1931–45) and Italy in southeastern Europe (1924–43).

Thus almost every great power has undertaken at some time some sort of hegemonic system, be it actual, approximate, or abortive. This suggests that hegemonic systems are one predictable result of great power status.

Several of these pre-1945 hegemonic systems were prototypes, in regard to the strategies and methods of the dominant powers, of the United States in Latin America and the Soviet Union in Eastern Europe. There were, for example, the Austrians in Germany, with their use of an international organization (the German Confederation) for collective legitimation of political intervention; the Austrians in Italy, with their use of military intervention against revolutionary movements and in support of client regimes (Kissinger, 1964); and the Germans in southeastern Europe with their use of their large market for foreign goods as a powerful bargaining tool with underdeveloped countries (Hirschman, 1980.) The hegemonic systems of the two superpowers have had some similarities in their methods with these three hegemonic systems in the Mitteleuropa of an earlier day.

II. Hegemonic Systems and Colonial Systems

Hegemonic systems or spheres of influence, which are composed by a dominant power exercising influence or at most indirect and informal rule over several subordinate states, are to be distinguished from colonial systems, which were composed by a dominant power exercising direct and formal rule over several territories or countries that had no state structure other than that imposed by the colonial administration itself. (Fieldhouse, 1967; Smith, 1981.) Colonial systems were a prominent feature of the international system from the sixteenth to the eighteenth century and again from the 1870s to the 1950s, but of course they are virtually extinct today. (The only major remaining colonial system is the rule by the Russians over other nationalities within the borders of the Soviet Union itself.) It is the hegemonic system that is a prominent feature of the international system in the contemporary era.

Why did dominant powers establish colonial systems in some cases and in some times and hegemonic systems in others? The answer lies largely in the levels of economic development and social modernization of the dominant power and the subordinate region. (Kurth, 1973.)

When the subordinate territories were undeveloped in their economy, traditional in their society, and tribal in their politics—in short, when there was yet no organized state—a colonial system was the normal result. The dominant power itself had to create and organize the state, and it did so in the form of full, direct, colonial rule.

The dominant power was even more likely to take the colonial path if it was itself undergoing the transition between an agrarian and an industrial economy and between a traditional and a modern society. In an industrializing economy and a modernizing society, there still remained a large rural aristocracy or gentry, imbued with traditional values, and this class provided the ideal source for the governors and administrators of traditional, rural subjects in the colonies. As James Mill remarked in the 1830s, the British empire was "a vast system of outdoor relief for the upper classes." (Strachey, 1960: 72.)

With the beginning of the modern state in subordinate regions, however, a different pattern becomes the norm. This frequently occurs when the subordinate region itself is characterized by an industrializing economy and a modernizing society. Here, the dominant power finds it easier, indeed eventually essential, to engage in indirect rather than direct rule. Given the increasing economic development, the elements for a local state become available; and given the increasing social mobilization, the costs of direct administration—and repression —become too costly. A hegemonic system or sphere of influence is the logical result. And it has been even more likely for the dominant power to take the hegemonic path if its own economy is largely industrialized and its own society is largely modernized. Under such conditions, there is no longer a numerous aristocracy or gentry to provide a substantial cadre of effective colonial administrators, or a numerous peasantry to provide a large number of compliant soldiers.

From this perspective, then, the colonial system can itself be seen as a transitional stage in the development of the international system. And the hegemonic system can be seen as a rather normal stage or feature of the international system of our own time, the period since 1945.

In this chapter we will examine three hegemonic systems of the period since 1945 with a focus upon the political consequences of economic changes within the subordinate states: (1) Britain in the Middle East (which survived into the 1950s in the Middle East generally and into the 1970s in the sheikhdoms of the Persian Gulf); (2) the Soviet Union in Eastern Europe; and (3) the United States in Latin America.

III. Britain in the Middle East

When the British created their great empire in the nineteenth century, they organized most of it into a vast system of colonies or direct rule. Other parts were governed as protectorates or with indirect rule. And still other countries, most notably in the Middle East, retained various degrees of formal independence while experiencing pervasive British influence. The way in which the British conducted their relations with the countries of the Middle East from the end of the nineteenth century until the middle of the twentieth tells us something about the dynamics of a hegemonic system and about three interrelated hegemonic logics—strategic, political, and economic.

The British were originally propelled into the Middle East by a strategic logic. They sought to achieve a string of secure territories and bases along their "lifeline" to India. But India itself was primarily of enormous economic value to the British. (Hobsbawm, 1968.)

The British accordingly sought friendly governments, "most loyal allies" in the phrase of the day, in the countries of the Middle East, first in Egypt and in the Persian Gulf, then in Persia, and then in particular successor states of the Ottoman Empire, such as Iraq. At first this was not very difficult to achieve. These were traditional societies, and the kind of government most natural to them was traditional monarchy. This comported well with the form although not the reality, with the "decorative" although not the "efficient," elements of the British political system itself. The form of the British monarchy and the life-style of the British aristocracy provided a natural model for emulation by Arab kings, Persian shahs, and Gulf sheikhs. (Kelly, 1980; Monroe, 1963.)

The strategic logic and the political logic of the British hegemony in the Middle East led, however, to an economic logic too. British hegemony and local monarchies, Pax Britannica and Trucial States, provided both international and internal stability. This stable environment, in turn, became an attractive area for British investors. And so the wealth of Britain flowed out from the home country to foreign countries, "from industry to empire," including the countries of the Middle East. And the discovery and development of oil in Iran, Iraq, and the Persian Gulf sheikhdoms greatly accelerated and accentuated the process of investment and the consequent process of economic growth and social modernization. There was created a large middle class grounded in commercial activities and in local bureaucracies. But this class was a natural source for nationalism and anti-imperialism. Thus a gap opened up between the political system supported by the hegemon and the social system energized by the hegemon, between the "official country" and the "real country."

The strength of nationalist, anti-British (and pro-German) movements was great enough in Iran and Egypt by World War II that the British feared that they might successfully convert their monarchs from most loyal allies into German agents. The British intervened militarily in Iran in 1941, when they deposed the shah and placed on the throne his young son who would become the shah that we would come to know all too well in later years. They also intervened militarily in Egypt in 1942, when they occupied the grounds of King Farouk's palace.

After the war the British no longer had the resources and then no longer had the will to sustain a vigorous hegemony in the Middle East. (Monroe, 1963.) In some countries, those without economic value, they chose to turn their hegemonic enterprises and responsibilities almost immediately over to the Americans, who seemed to have interests similar enough to the British so that one could be confident that they would do the job. The years 1947–48 were the time of the first phase of the Great Recessional of British hegemony in the Middle East and adjacent areas, as they turned over the responsibility for Greece to the United States (which assumed the obligation under the Truman Doctrine) and for Palestine to the American-supported state of Israel. (Polk, 1975.) By 1954 the Americans had assumed dominant responsibility for even oil-rich Iran, after the CIA helped the young shah overturn the populist and nationalist government that had come to power.

By the early 1950s it would have been reasonable to calculate that the authoritarian monarchies of the Middle East were out of equilibrium. The recent history (1910s–1940s) of monarchy in the modernizing societies of Eastern and Southern Europe suggested that the institution was really only a transitional phenomenon, doomed to disappear in political upheaval after a few generations of economic growth and social modernization had brought into being new groups, classes, and conflicts. Given their position on the near periphery of industrial Europe and given the income from their growing oil production, the Middle Eastern states would undergo economic growth and social modernization and, therefore, political stress and strain comparable to that which had occurred on that earlier periphery on the eastern and southern fringes of Europe, including countries such as Greece and Turkey, which obviously had much in common with the states of the Middle East. (Kurth, 1982a.) Indeed, the oil wealth and the new means of mass communications would accelerate and accentuate the process in the Middle East compared to Europe. A warning had been given by the populist and nationalist government of Mohammad Mosaddeq in Iran. But the real prototype of the new political formula was the military-nationalist revolution that overthrew the Egyptian monarchy in 1952.

When Middle Eastern countries were allowed to follow their natural tendency, to line up their political systems with their new social structures, the result seemed to be a nationalist and often populist military regime. The political telos of the Middle East seemed to be Nasserism.

The Middle Eastern countries were at an economic level similar to the "import-substituting industrialization" stage of the major Latin American countries at that time. (O'Donnell, 1973; Collier, 1979; Kurth, 1979a.) And it is not surprising that something like "national-populism," under such leaders as Juan Perón and Getúlio Vargas, would be the political result. The military-nationalist revolution in Egypt was followed by similar ones in later years in other most loyal allies of British power in the Middle East—in Iraq in 1958 and in Libya in 1969.

Finally, in the early 1970s the British cooperated with the Americans in turning over the last remnants of their hegemonic system, in the sheikhdoms of the Persian Gulf, to what they hoped would be a sufficiently powerful and responsible local hegemon, the shah of Iran. However, this hegemon soon turned out to be incapable of protecting his own rule, much less that of the assorted sheikhs of the Gulf. It was in the ancient mosques and bazaars of Tehran amid the revival of Islam that the sun finally set upon the British hegemony. (Kelly, 1980; Sick, 1985; Kurth, 1982a.)

IV. The Soviet Union in Eastern Europe

At the end of World War II and as a consequence of it, the Soviet Union occupied or at least overshadowed each of the nations on its western frontiers. The way in which it organized its relations with these nations of Eastern Europe also tells us something about the dynamics of a hegemonic system and about the three interrelated hegemonic logics —strategic, political, and economic.

Stalin himself observed at the time, "This war is not as in the past. Whoever occupies a territory also imposes on it his own social system [as far] as his army can reach." (Djilas, 1962: 114.) Here, as in so much else, Stalin understood the logic of a great power in international politics in the contemporary era.

Like all great powers, the Soviet Union sought to achieve a ring of buffer states, a protective *glacis*, as soon as it had the military strength to do so. The compulsion, and indeed the justification, seemed especially strong in the case of the Soviet Union. After all, historically the greatest powers of the West had periodically invaded Russia through Eastern Europe and especially through Poland, as in 1812, in 1914, in 1919, and in 1941. The true "Polish Corridor" lay between Germany and Russia and was Poland itself. But the smaller nations to the north and to the south of Poland had also on occasion been springboards for invasions of Russia, as each of them had been once again in 1941. It was thus wholly natural, indeed inevitable, that Stalin would insist that these East European nations become buffer states, with "governments friendly to the Soviet Union."

From early industrialization to communist party-state.   The logic of international politics soon led to a logic of internal politics, however, and the Soviet Union's strategic imperative became the East European nations' political imperative. The social structure and the national traditions in most of the East European nations made it most unlikely that a government friendly to the Soviet Union would issue from a wholly indigenous or independent political process, be it a democratic or an authoritarian one. Most of these countries were still in the initial stage of industrialization, that of the production of light consumer goods (such as textiles, shoes, and processed foods). Their working class was small, their middle class was weak and divided, and their landlord class was powerful. This was the case in Poland, Hungary, Romania, and Bulgaria. In these countries it was likely that, in a few years after World War II, the old conservative elites would regain their political power, just as they had a few years after World War I. (Rothschild, 1974; Seton-Watson, 1967a; Wolff, 1957.) Being anticommunist by class interest and anti-Russian by national tradition (except in Bulgaria), these elites would then readily ally themselves with the newest great power to the West, the United States, and would once again become a threat to the Soviet Union.

This meant that the Soviets had to replace the natural social structure with an artificial one, they would have to manufacture their friendly governments by a revolution from above and from without, and they would have to impose communist party rule and maintain it by authoritarian, even totalitarian, means. This was the pattern and the process in Poland, Hungary, Romania, Bulgaria, and also the Soviet zone of Germany in the years immediately after World War II. (Seton-Watson, 1964; Brzezinski, 1967.)

Missing from this list were Czechoslovakia and Finland, the exceptions that prove the rule. For these nations were considerably more industrialized in 1945, had maintained democratic rather than authoritarian systems in the interwar years, and had large mass-based communist parties. These differences in social structure preserved Czechoslovakian democracy from a Soviet-imposed revolution for three years, until 1948, when the division of Europe and the polarization of the Cold War caused the Soviets to end this particular state of exception. But the similar differences in social structure have preserved Finnish democracy to the present day.

From communist party-state to forced-draft industrialization. The internal political logic in Eastern Europe soon turned into an internal economic one. The communist parties of the Soviet Union and the new satellites were committed to a particular economic program, that of rapid, forced-draft industrialization, particularly in the production of capital goods (such as the steel, chemical, and electrical industries). (Brzezinski, 1967.) This process in turn resulted in rapid urbanization and in rapid growth in the number of industrial workers, bureaucratic employees, and intellectuals. These social changes had something in common with those that occurred in Latin America in the 1970s, with the rapid economic growth encouraged by the United States, by American multinational corporations, and by "bureaucratic-authoritarian regimes" imposed by the local military forces. (Collier, 1979.)

The capital-goods stage of industrialization is a peculiar one. It requires the generation and mobilization of vaster amounts of capital than in the preceding stage of light-consumer-goods production. (Kurth, 1979b.) The construction of heavy industry is a heavy burden for a society and normally requires a rather heavy-handed politics. A communist party, Marxist in its social ideology and Leninist in its political organization, is in many respects the most effective agent for driving a society through the capital-goods stage of industrialization. In other countries such as in Brazil and Argentina a similar function has been performed by the bureaucratic-authoritarian regime. But the purest form of a bureaucratic-authoritarian system is probably not a military regime but a communist party-state.

From forced-draft industrialization to economic obsolescence. The very fact that the Marxist-Leninist party is such a perfect agent for bringing about the capital-goods stage of industrialization means, by a dialectical logic, that it is an imperfect agent for what is normally the next stage of industrialization, the production of consumer durables (such as automobiles, appliances, and consumer electric products). (Kurth, 1979b.) It is no accident that countries ruled by communist parties normally experience growth rates in capital-goods industries that are greater than those in capitalist countries, and growth rates in consumer-durable industries that are lower than those in capitalist countries. The communist pattern of industrialization is a period of dramatic and dizzying growth followed by a period of pronounced and prolonged stagnation.

The paradigmatic example of this pattern is of course the Soviet Union itself. The consumer-durable stage or "auto-industrial age" (Rothschild, 1973) of the Soviet Union has remained on an ever-receding horizon, and the Soviet economic vision remains what it has been since the October Revolution of 1917, a great monument to the leading industries of the Europe of seventy years ago — steel, chemicals, electricity, and armaments.

The communist party and the society that it rules apparently can escape this grim dialectical logic only by devolving substantial economic decision-making down to the level of the industrial enterprise once they seek to move beyond the stage of capital-goods industrialization (as Hungary and recently China have done). But this does not mean that the end result will be a full free enterprise system.

It is probably the case that the most effective agent for bringing a society through the consumer-durable stage of industrialization is neither a full communist party-state nor a full free enterprise system. Rather, it is probably a system of "organized competition," in which the state and perhaps a hegemonic party define the framework in which a half-dozen or so enterprises operate and compete. This has been the case with Japan, a democratic political system under the leadership of the Liberal Democratic party since 1955; and with South Korea, a bureaucratic-authoritarian system under the rule of the military since 1962.

From economic obsolescence to political obsolescence.   The economic obsolescence of the communist party-state has been compounded by its political obsolescence. It is difficult to govern an industrialized and urbanized society with a small authoritarian party, even a highly organized communist one. The Soviet army and the communist party brought into being in East European countries a new society that then pressed upon the bounds of the party and on occasion broke into open rebellion, as in uprisings of workers in East Berlin in 1953, of workers and intellectuals in Hungary in 1956, of intellectuals in Czechoslovakia in 1968, and of workers or intellectuals in Poland in 1956, 1970, 1976, and 1980–81.

Had the East European nations been allowed to follow their natural tendency, to line up their political systems with their new social structures, they probably would have become social democracies. When allowed to vote their preferences, industrial workers tend over the long run to vote for socialist parties, and bureaucratic employees tend to vote for liberal or progressive ones. In a situation where there is a large industrial working class and a large bureaucratic employee class, where there is no longer a powerful landlord class, and where there is a large state sector in the economy as in both Northern Europe and Eastern Europe, there is a natural, solid base for a governing coalition of socialist, progressive, and liberal parties and for social-democratic policies. The political telos of Eastern Europe is probably Finlandization, so to speak. But the Soviets have not dared to permit this.

First, in the historical crucible of Eastern Europe with its traditions of opposition to Russian domination, the Soviets have assumed that there is too great a risk that a newly democratic and newly neutral nation might go all the way and become an ally of the West. Second, the liberalization of an East European communist state carries implications for the liberalization of the Soviet Union itself. Thus, for the

Soviets the monopoly of the communist party (i.e., the Soviet system) in its East European satellites had to be maintained. (Jones, 1977; Ulam, 1965, 1974.)

In East Germany, Hungary, and Czechoslovakia this could be done only by Soviet military intervention and then by continuing military occupation. (Valenta, 1984b.) The general timing of the Soviet military interventions corresponded to the disintegration of local communist party control.

The particular timing of the Soviet military interventions, however, also seems to reflect conditions in the West. In each case the Soviet problem with its ally had been growing for some time, yet the moment that the Soviets invaded was one when the West's attention was diverted and engaged elsewhere (with concluding the armistice negotiations in the Korean War in 1953; the Suez crisis in 1956; and the turmoil surrounding the antiwar protests and the Democratic National Convention in 1968). Similarly, the Soviets invaded Afghanistan in December 1979 when the relationships between the United States and Iran and Pakistan, the two countries most immediately threatened by the Afghan intervention, had never been worse (the occupation of the U.S. Embassy in Tehran and the burning of the U.S. Embassy in Islamabad had both occurred in November, the previous month).

More recently, in Poland in 1981, the Soviet-style system was maintained by a new form of military intervention in a communist state, i.e., by the local military itself. With this political innovation, Poland entered into the era of a military-based bureaucratic-authoritarian regime at just about the same time that Brazil, Argentina, and Uruguay were leaving it. In any case, the Polish military regime has a particular quality absent from its Latin American counterparts; it is supported (and surrounded) by two Soviet divisions in Poland, twenty Soviet divisions in East Germany, and ninety Soviet divisions in European Russia.

The dynamics of the Soviet hegemonic system in its client states, then, seem to have condemned the Soviets to continuing military occupation, to being a "brooding omnipresence," in East Germany, Poland, Czechoslovakia, Hungary, and now also Afghanistan.

There have, however, also been cases where an East European nation was able to gain a very large degree of independence from the Soviet Union without provoking Soviet military intervention, i.e., Yugoslavia in 1948, Albania in 1961, and Romania in 1964. (Zimmerman, 1984.) These exceptions illuminate the rules of the Soviet hegemonic system. In each case, at the time of its move toward independence, the local communist regime was at least as authoritarian, as insistent upon its political monopoly, as the communist regime in the Soviet Union itself. (Later, Tito in Yugoslavia would allow very substantial liberalization.) The move toward independence did not immediately challenge the domestic political formula within the Soviet Union. For the nations of Eastern Europe, it seems, there is a rather sharp contradiction between political liberalization and national independence, between internal freedom and external freedom.

Reverse uneven development and counterfactual history. The Soviet Union in Eastern Europe represents an anomaly among hegemonic systems. As we have seen, most hegemonic systems are characterized by "uneven development," with the dominant power being more advanced than the subordinate states. The classic cases are Britain in the Middle East and the United States in Latin America. However, the Soviet Union in Eastern Europe is a case where the dominant power is less developed economically than most of the subordinate states. (Marer, 1974a; 1984b.) In this respect it is similar to Austria in the German states or even the Italian states during the first half of the nineteenth century. Hegemonic systems characterized by such "even development" or indeed by reverse uneven development are structurally more unstable than a classic hegemonic system, with its more conventional kind of uneven development.

Indeed, there are good reasons to think that the East European nations could even be effective competitors in West European markets if they were not encumbered by command economies. Their economic models and potentials are perhaps best represented by Finland and Austria. And, continuing in counterfactualism, if the United States, rather than the Soviet Union, were the dominant power in Eastern Europe, the subordinate states would likely evolve into something like the small states of Northern Europe (with social-democratic political systems) or like the small states of Southern Europe (with perhaps occasional relapses into bureaucratic-authoritarian regimes, like that in Greece from 1967–1974).

V. The United States in Latin America

Like the British in the Middle East and the Soviets in Eastern Europe, the Americans in Latin America have been propelled by a strategic logic, although like them not by that logic alone. The threat of the Germans in the 1910s and the 1930s and the threat of the Soviets since the 1950s have periodically energized and justified American hegemony in the region, especially in Central America and the Caribbean. (LaFeber, 1983; Newfarmer, 1984; Kurth, 1986a, 1986b.)

The proximity of Central America and the Caribbean to the United States and the smallness of the countries there would have made the region a natural sphere of influence, no matter what the particular political, economic, or ideological character of the "colossus of the North." If somehow either the British, the French, the Germans, or the Russians had established a unified nation on the southern portion of the North American continent by the end of the nineteenth century, they too would have composed a hegemonic system over the states of Central America and the Caribbean. Indeed, given the style of imperial rule of the time and given the actual practice of the British and the French in the region, the system would probably have been a full colonial one rather than a hegemonic one.

In contrast with these other great powers, however, the United States was "born equal," "born modern" (Huntington, 1968: 135), and born anticolonial, and thus it was born to become hegemonic, rather than colonial, once it became a great power. Its colonial possessions (Puerto Rico, the Virgin Islands, the Philippines) were relatively few. The United States had, not uniquely but especially, a propensity for hegemony. (Kurth, 1973.) And Central America and the Caribbean were the arenas in which this propensity was carried to its fullest expression.

Agrarian economies and personalist dictatorships.   With the United States in Latin America, as with Britain in the Middle East and the Soviet Union in Eastern Europe, the strategic logic of hegemony soon worked its way into a political and then an economic logic. In the first half of the twentieth century the social structures of Latin America had much in common with those of Eastern Europe and the Middle East at the time. The countries of Latin America were of course exporters of primary commodities with only the beginnings of industrialization; on the basis of this economic pattern alone, their natural political system would probably have been traditional monarchy, as in Eastern Europe and the Middle East. But, of course, this political form had been made wholly impossible by the revolutions of the nineteenth century, first the Latin American Wars of Independence, then the revolution against the Brazilian monarchy in 1889, and finally the Cuban War of Independence culminating in 1898. Given the role model of the United States in the region, the political form for those countries after their revolutions normally had to be a presidential republic rather than a traditional monarchy. But, given the social structure of the region, a presidential republic could only be a political form that covered a different political reality, that of personalist dictatorship, i.e., rule by traditional caudillos.

Personalist dictatorship lacked, however, an important feature of traditional monarchies, that of dynastic legitimacy. Thus the dictators or caudillos of Latin America often compensated for the absence of this element of political power by resorting to enhanced brutality. Thus it was that the most liberal and democratic of the hegemonic powers, the United States, ended up supporting some of the most brutal and repressive of client regimes.

Still, personalist dictatorship had a certain congruence with the social structure of Latin America in the early decades of the twentieth century; and when that congruence on occasion broke down, American intervention reestablished it, particularly in Central America and the Caribbean. Once again, as with the British hegemony in the Middle East, conditions of international and internal stability largely prevailed. And American investors also found an attractive area for their capital. Once again, economic development, new social classes, and new political strains ensued.

From import-substituting industrialization to national-populist regime.   The United States was thus confronted with the overthrow of several of its client dictatorships in Central America and the Caribbean, and at roughly the same time and the same rate as the British in the Middle East and the Soviets in Eastern Europe (Jorge Ubico in Guatemala in 1944 culminating in the crisis of 1954, Fulgencio Batista in Cuba in 1959, Rafael Trujillo in the Dominican Republic culminating in the crisis of 1965, and Anastasio Somoza in Nicaragua in 1979). (Blasier, 1976; LaFeber, 1983.)

For some of these countries the most natural political formula, given their particular level of economic development and social structure, would have been some form of national-populist military regime, like that of Perón in Argentina or Vargas in Brazil; such regimes had currently come to power in the Middle East and indeed with Jacobo Arbenz in Guatemala. These countries were entering their stage of import-substituting industrialization, the production of light consumer goods. (Villagran Kramer, 1982.) They contained a rapidly growing local business class, an industrial working class, and a class of white-collar employees and intellectuals, with the workers, white-collar employees, and intellectuals adding up to a substantial urban popular sector. The political telos of Latin American countries at this stage of industrialization was perhaps something like Perónism.

The program of national populism included the nationalization of prominent sectors or "commanding heights" of the economy that were controlled by foreign corporations. In those few Latin American countries with little U.S. direct foreign investment, the U.S. government could accept or even support a new national-populist regime (as in Bolivia in 1952). In an economy dominated by U.S. direct foreign investment, however, the political logic of national populism meant that national-populist movements would attack and call for the nationalization of these investments. And this meant a direct political conflict with the government of the United States.

Unlike the British when they confronted nationalist and populist regimes in the Middle East, the United States was at times powerful enough, proximate enough, and determined enough to do something about them—thus the CIA intervention in Guatemala in 1954, the military intervention in the Dominican Republic in 1965, and the support given to the military coups in Brazil in 1964 and in Chile in 1973. (Blasier, 1976.)

More interesting, perhaps, than the successful interventions are the unsuccessful ones—the Bay of Pigs invasion of Cuba in 1961 and the not-so-covert Contra intervention in Nicaragua since 1981 (a sort of prolonged Bay of Pigs). The cases of Cuba and Nicaragua may give a glimpse into possible paths out of the apparently deterministic logic of a hegemonic system.

In both Cuba by 1958 and Nicaragua by 1978 the major portion of the local business class had withdrawn its support from the dictator. This made it reasonable for American businessmen and American officials to withdraw their support too. And relatedly, in both Cuba and Nicaragua, the revolutionary leadership seemed at the time more populist than communist. In each case this conjunction of populist movement with business support temporarily gave rise to hopes among U.S. policymakers for a viable third way between a personalist dictatorship that no longer fit a new social structure and a revolutionary communist regime that might fit it so well that it could do without American investments and U.S. influence. But in Cuba, in the end, the political conflict over direct American investment followed its logic and destroyed the option of a merely populist regime.

The very fate of the Cuban Revolution, moreover, tended to inoculate the business class in other Latin American countries against such national-populist adventures in later years. Cuba became not so much the first domino in Latin America as was feared by U.S. policymakers in the early 1960s, but rather became a barrier to other populist-business alliances in the region for almost a generation. And the fate of the Nicaraguan Revolution may perform a similar inoculation in our own time. It seems to have helped to do so in El Salvador and Guatemala.

From obsolescent personalist dictatorship to premature bureaucratic-authoritarian regime. In several Latin American countries, then, the political telos of national populism appears to be on an ever-receding horizon, resulting in a widening gap between the reality of the social structure and the formula of current politics. This is particularly the case in Central America. The deep structure of political instability is acute in El Salvador and Guatemala and potentially so in Honduras and Panama. The economic development and the consequent social structure of these countries seem to have reached the point that a stable personalist dictatorship (e.g., the Somozas before the 1970s) is no longer possible; the number, the size, and the degree of mobilization of different social groups probably require some degree of "institutionalization" of political and governmental actors. (Huntington, 1968.) On the other hand, the economic development and social structure of these countries seem to have not yet reached the point where a stable bureaucratic-authoritarian regime (such as Brazil or Chile in the 1970s) becomes possible; such regimes probably require the economic resources and social allies found only at a later stage of industrialization than import-substitution, that is, the capital-goods or "deepening" stage of industrialization. (Collier, 1979.) In any event, the small size of these countries alone makes it almost impossible for them to engage in the production of capital goods.

If this is the case, the local political ally of American hegemony may have to be either an unstable obsolescent personalist dictatorship, which is becoming less and less effective, or an unstable premature bureaucratic-authoritarian regime, which has a distinct tendency to resort to the use of death squads. Accordingly, any stability will have to be imposed from without, i.e., by American military advisers, military aid, and perhaps military intervention. Both natural political instability and its alternative, imported political stability, create their own economic logic. Such political conditions result in a flight of local capital, a reduction in private American investments and loans, and a declining economy less and less able to meet political demands; this in turn makes the military solutions even more essential.

Marxist-Leninist reality and counterfactual history. The dynamics of the U.S. hegemonic system in several of its client states, then, seem to have condemned the United States to continuing military support to local military regimes, to being a "brooding omnipresence" in the region for some time to come.

How would the political formula of the other superpower and hegemon fit Central America? Returning again to counterfactualism, if the Soviet Union, rather than the United States, were the dominant power in Central America, the subordinate states would likely be transformed into something like Cuba and Nicaragua. Several Central American countries are at a stage of economic development in which a single-party system, especially one shaped by a Marxist-Leninist party, would be quite congruent with their social structure, that is, with the politically mobilized social groups. Further, since the people of a small state normally see the neighboring great power (in this case, the United States) as the most threatening one, a Marxist-Leninist party and a Soviet presence would be seen as reinforcing, not contradicting, the nationalist principle of national populism. And a socialist economy could be seen as the fulfillment of the populist one.

Thus, it appears that the Soviet system of hegemony would be most compatible with the national-populist telos of the subordinate states of Central America, and the American system of hegemony would be most compatible with the social-democratic telos of the subordinate states of Eastern Europe. Both the United States and the Soviet Union are thus driven to pursue a double containment policy. As superpowers, they are condemned to a policy of containing each other at distant points around the globe. And as hegemonic powers, they are condemned to a policy of containing the political consequences of economic change, the central tendency and the political telos, within their own most immediate neighbors.

II   Concepts and Theories

4

Dominant-Subordinate Relationships: How Shall We Define Them? How Do We Compare Them?

David B. Abernethy

How do dominant and subordinate states interact with one another, and with what consequences for each? A persuasive answer to this question requires reference to empirical evidence from a record of human history that is only too replete with examples. But the presentation of factual material, while a necessary condition for answering the question, can hardly qualify as a sufficient condition. In order to determine which facts are relevant as illustrations of any phenomenon, one must determine independently of these facts the characteristics ascribed to the phenomenon. X cannot be said to be an example of Y until one has some sense of the meaning of Y: how, that is, Y's defining features are conceived and—more or less precisely, more or less objectively—measured. The task of defining and operationalizing key concepts, at the very outset of a discussion employing these concepts, seems rather prosaic and not particularly challenging intellectually. Yet failure to engage in this task, failure to translate from the implicit to the explicit level the meaning of the words we need to communicate our major message, can undermine the intellectual enterprise itself.

The dangers in this regard are particularly acute when the key terms employed are (a) frequently used in common speech, hence subject to widely varying interpretations; (b) broad in application; (c) vague; (d) normatively and emotionally loaded; and (e) often used as verbal weapons in real-world political struggles. Concepts like "dominance" and "subordination" surely qualify on all these counts for the high-danger list. It is therefore especially important to devote attention to conceptual and semantic issues when considering dominant-subordinate state relationships. That one's definition will inevitably be arbitrary, and that one's fellow scholars are not likely to employ it, should not serve as a deterrent. The mere act of stating clearly what one's key terms mean may encourage others to do likewise. When relevant definitions and relevant facts and values are made explicit, the prospects are increased that participants in a debate will actually talk to each other rather than past each other, as is so often and so unfortunately the case.

My first task, then, is to suggest how "dominance" and "subordination" in the international system might be defined. A second task is to suggest how particular instances of dominance and subordination might be compared with one another. The theme of this volume is theoretically interesting because it is clearly within the realm of international politics—we are studying the interactions of unequally powerful states; yet the relevant approaches and methods are those of comparative politics—we are comparing two sets of international asymmetries. In order to compare anything with any other thing, we must identify the similarities and the differences between the two. On the one hand, there must be some minimal level of similarity, below which comparison becomes meaningless: how, for example, can one compare shyness with a shoe? On the other hand, there must be some minimal level of dissimilarity, below which comparison also becomes meaningless: how, for example, could one compare a shoe with another shoe identical to it?

A useful starting point in comparative analysis is the identification of similarities, in order to determine whether two or more phenomena have enough in common to be meaningfully or usefully compared. In this essay I employ two complementary methods to search for similarities. One method, already noted, is to proceed deductively by defining a dominant/subordinate relationship and then determining whether our two cases are covered by such a definition. The other method is to proceed more inductively by identifying additional cases covered by the definition, and in the course of comparing the first two cases with the latter ones to identify characteristics the first two have in common. This I will do by discussing relations between the empire-builders of Western Europe and the people throughout the globe who over a period of five centuries were incorporated into Europe's colonial empires. Employing the history of "The West and the Rest" (Chinweizu, 1975)—with the West as the colonizer, much of the Rest as the colonized—as a standard for comparison with the two contemporary cases of the United States in Latin America and the USSR in Eastern Europe will shed light on several distinctive features shared by our two cases. Identifying the causes, extent, and consequences of the important differences between the two contemporary cases—the aspect of comparative analysis that complements the identification of similarities—is a task undertaken by other essays in this volume.

I

First, an effort at definition. One state may be considered dominant and another subordinate if the following conditions obtain.

(1) The two states interact with each other, usually across a broad range of issue areas. These issue areas include matters of military, diplomatic, economic, and cultural concern to one or both parties.

(2) The interaction has historical depth as well as functional breadth, with certain recurring broad patterns of action and reaction, of the exercise and the receipt of influence, discernible over a period of time—say, at least a decade. It is these recurrent patterns in the past that enable us to generalize with a reasonable degree of confidence and that permit us to make projections and speculations, however tentative they may be, about the future.

(3) The consequences of interaction between the dominant and the subordinate state are significant for the subordinate state.

Two things should be noted about this formulation. First, interaction normally has a greater effect on the domestic and foreign policy of the subordinate state than of the dominant state. The consequences of interaction may also be significant for the dominant state, but this need not be the case. Second, the significant consequence for the subordinate state can be, and often is, harmful to the interests of that state, but this also need not be the case. In theory, at least, the results might actually be positive. (Much depends, of course, on how one chooses to define "harmful" and "positive" effects on a state's interests.) The assertion that a subordinate state loses, along some absolute scale or relative to the dominant state, as a consequence of links with the latter, should be just that: an assertion open to verification, not an assumption that is built into one's very definition of the relationship. If a claim is assumed to be true, then it cannot also be asserted as the empirically demonstrated conclusion of one's study. For this reason, I prefer to employ a narrow definition that looks only at characteristics of a relationship without also prejudging, by semantic fiat, the outcome of that relationship.

(4) One state, the dominant one, has considerably more of an objectively measured, mutually acknowledged, and mutually valued attribute of power than the other. Phrased in another way, the two states differ in their capacities to enforce compliance upon the other if the other prefers not to comply. The difference in "compliance capacity" could if necessary be affirmed by an outside, neutral analyst able to base assessments of power differences upon empirical observations — say, of the size, combat experience, training, and mobility of a country's military forces, the quality of its weapons systems, the level of its per capita gross national product, or the degree to which its industrial sector produces what its citizens consume. (For such indicators see, for example, chapters 3 and 4 in Knorr, 1975; or Sivard, 1985.) The difference in compliance capacity, moreover, is recognized by leaders in both states. And it is defined by these leaders not simply as a difference but also as an inequality, because both sets of leaders value possessing more of the same attribute. Ironically, when interstate disagreements arise as a result of the inequalities or asymmetries of power among states, the problem is precisely that all parties to the conflict are in agreement that a particular objective indicator of power is appropriate, and that having more of that indicator is preferable to having less. Conflict, in such cases, is actually premised on an underlying value consensus.

(5) The dominant state not only possesses the capacity to gain compliance from the subordinate state, but it has also on at least some occasions demonstrated the will to gain compliance. Power is the combined and interactive effect of one's capacity to act effectively and one's will to do so. Just as we would not consider a state powerful if it possessed the will but not the capacity to exert influence over others, so too the state would not be deemed powerful if it possessed the capacity to exert influence but lacked the will to employ that capacity. The objective, readily measurable, and relatively fixed component of

power (capacity) must, in some crude sense, be multiplied by the subjective, far less readily measurable, and often highly fluctuating component (will) in order to assess the actual power of the dominant state and the extent of power asymmetry between it and a subordinate state. If there is indeed a power asymmetry, analysts should be able to identify more than one important instance in which the dominant state has clearly demonstrated the will to act in its own interests vis-à-vis a subordinate state.

(6) The subordinate state's capacity for autonomous action is seriously constrained by the sheer fact of the dominant state's existence. Leaders in the subordinate state must regularly take into serious account the dominant state's possible responses to a proposed change in the subordinate state's domestic or foreign policies. In contrast, dominant state leaders can normally alter their domestic or foreign policies without taking into account the subordinate state's possible responses to such a change as a factor seriously altering the wisdom or feasibility of the change.

(7) Representatives of institutions based in the dominant state penetrate the territory of the subordinate state, playing a direct and relatively visible role as domestic actors in the latter's political life. The range and extent of penetrative action from dominant to subordinate state is much greater than the range and extent of what might be termed counter-penetration from subordinate to dominant state.

I am somewhat hesitant to propose this characteristic as a defining feature of a dominant state-subordinate state relationship. In theory, state A could be subordinate to dominant state B solely by virtue of B's control of resources based outside the boundaries of A, this control enabling B to coerce or induce A's leaders to act in certain ways. In the modern world, however, dependence on external influence is normally accompanied by external penetration of the subordinate polity, so that the subordinate must deal with the dominant state as both a foreign and a domestic actor. Presumably the key penetrative institutions of a dominant capitalist state are based in its private sector (for example, multinational corporations engaged in extractive, manufacturing, trading, and financial operations), while the key penetrative institutions of a dominant communist state are based in its public sector (for example, the political party, economic planning apparatus, and armed forces). Whichever the sector in which these institutions are based within the dominant state, the fact that they penetrate the political space of the subordinate state is the critical common feature as far as the latter state is concerned.

Do the two cases of U.S.–Latin American and Soviet–East European relations possess these general features in common? It is quite clear, to me at least, that they do. Supporting evidence—including instances of the demonstrated will and capacity of each dominant state significantly to affect the domestic and foreign policies of the smaller states in its sphere of influence—is amply provided in other essays in this volume. It is quite likely, moreover, that analysts stressing the differences between the two asymmetrical relationships would nonetheless agree that, given the narrow definition proposed here, both cases should be classified under a common "dominant-subordinate" heading.

II

The next step in identifying similarities between the two cases is to move from semantics to empirics, from reflections on the meaning of key terms to investigation of the numerous historical instances of dominant state-subordinate state relationships. It might be particularly valuable to study cases other than the two we are analyzing, and then to compare our two cases with one or more of these others. Perhaps the most significant such cases in modern world history—taking into account geographic area affected, time span of dominance, and degree of societal transformation wrought by dominance—are the overseas colonial empires established by several Western European states from the fifteenth century onward in conjunction with European exploratory, mercantile, extractive, and proselytizing activities in the rest of the world. These empires, initially concentrated in what Western Europeans termed the "New World," expanded dramatically during the nineteenth and twentieth centuries in the "Old World" of Asia, Africa, the Near East, and Oceania. (For overviews of European imperial expansion and colonial rule, see Betts, 1985; Davis, 1973; Fieldhouse, 1966 and 1981; Kiernan, 1982; Parry, 1966 and 1974; Stavrianos, 1981; Wolf, 1982; and Wright, 1976.) The remainder of this essay is an attempt to take the next step called for by comparing the formal empires established by Western European powers with the two cases analyzed in this volume. I grant at the outset that this attempt is quite preliminary and that it errs on the side of overgeneralizing, across time and space, about a vast and complex and controversial topic.

To be sure, European overseas empires differed among themselves in many significant respects. For example, there are differences in the timing of imperial expansion, in the characteristics of the European states engaged in empire building, in the extent to which Europeans exported themselves as well as their civilization to a given colony, in colonial economic policies, and in the demographic, political, and cultural characteristics of the indigenous peoples who became the colonial subjects of European rulers. Nonetheless, certain broad similarities may be identified in the relationships between dominant European colonial empire-building states and the dependent territories they claimed, whether in the preindustrial "New World" phase or the subsequent industrial-capitalist "Old World" phase of imperial expansion. In the course of identifying these similarities, I will argue that these very features do not obtain in either of the two more contemporary cases we are examining. Thus, U.S. relations with Latin America and Soviet relations with Eastern Europe have in common the fact that they lack key features of Europe's relationship with its colonies.

Consider the following characteristics of Western Europe's colonial empires:

(1) The dominant-subordinate relationship was formalized, the power inequalities between a given colonial ruler and its colony being reflected in the different and quite unequal legal statuses of the two territories. The former was a sovereign state, whereas the latter lacked sovereignty and was defined by various terms (colony, protectorate, mandate, overseas territory, etc.) to indicate that the dominant state considered it in some sense a possession, an extension of the dominant state's own existence. (In extreme cases the colony was defined not as a separate territory but as an integral part of the metropole: witness the official French view that Algeria was three *départements* of France, and the 1951 redefinition of Portugal's territories as Overseas Provinces.) Formal legal control meant that, in practice as well as in theory, Europeans exercised extraordinary powers over people who as a result of imperial expansion had lost their political autonomy. For example, Europeans drew the boundaries of colonial territories, named those territories, determined their legal systems and official languages, created their central administrative structures, and appointed from the metropole the top officials charged with the maintenance of order and the stimulation of colonial economic development. Colonialism was a means by which a metropole located outside a colony could become manifestly the dominant power in the colony's domestic life. Institutions, technologies, patterns of production and consumption, ideas, and values were exported from the metropole, to become in time among the most important features defining the colony's internal identity and character. In this respect, colonialism was the ultimate instance of external penetration.

Because European control was formalized, colonial rulers were normally quite explicit in justifying the exercise of their power in the colonies as a means of advancing the metropole's national interests. After all, the metropole felt it had a legal and moral right to rule, and acting upon this right entailed using force if necessary to put down protests and rebellions in the colonies. Moreover, apologists for colonial empire often argued that the metropole was acting in the best interests of colonized peoples. The inherently paternalistic assumptions of this position were usually quite explicit. (On occasion colonialism was justified as advancing both the metropole's national interests and the interests of the colonized; see, for example, the classic apologia by Lugard for the British (1923) and by Sarraut for the French (1923).)

In sharp contrast, the U.S.–Latin America and Soviet–East Europe relationships are instances of informal influence. The subordinate states in these two cases are legally sovereign just as are the dominant states, and in this respect equal to them in the international political arena. The legal-formal relationship of equality thus masks — instead of reflecting, as in the colonial case — the highly unequal degrees of compliance capacity between dominant and subordinate states. The legal sovereignty of Latin American and Eastern European states serves as a protective device that limits the kind of blatant penetration, and heavy reliance on foreign coercive power and administrative personnel to reshape domestic institutions, that generally characterized European colonial rule. Both the United States and the Soviet Union, moreover, have an anticolonial tradition to uphold — the United States as the first (or the first thirteen!) of Europe's overseas colonial territories to extricate itself from colonialism, the Soviet Union as the exponent of Lenin's doctrine that capitalist imperialism can be successfully attacked by encouraging colonized peoples to break free from the control of the leading capitalist countries. However different in motivation, these two anticolonial traditions probably serve to constrain interventionist behavior by the superpowers that would otherwise be more brutal and unabashedly self-serving than it is.

The combined effect of subordinate state sovereignty and dominant state anticolonialism is a high level of informal, indirect influence — rather than formal, direct control — by the penetrative institutions of the United States and the USSR. (Scott, 1982a.) The United States exerts considerable influence on subordinate state elites through its private profit sector (corporations and banks) and private nonprofit sector (foundations, universities, secular and religious private voluntary organizations), as well as through publicly financed official development assistance. The Soviet Union exerts considerable influence on subordinate state elites through the links between "fraternal" ruling parties and the trade and cultural activities of its public sector institutions. And the rulers of the subordinate states are nationals of those states, with greater autonomy of action than the rulers of colonies who were themselves citizens and employees of the dominant state. In general, the blatant exercise of dominant-state compliance capacity is less evident in the two contemporary cases than in the era of European empire building.

This is not to say that the United States and the Soviet Union have not felt it necessary on occasion to use force to intervene in their respective spheres of influence. When they have done so, however, the fact that the people against whom force is used are citizens of sovereign states has meant that the rationales for intervention have been more convoluted and hypocritical than the rationales for most colonial interventions. On the one hand, the contemporary superpowers are reluctant to state explicitly the national-interest reasons for direct intervention in the affairs of other independent states. On the other hand, Europe's historic rationales for conquering other people and reshaping their societies are no longer acceptable in a world most of whose states were once colonies of European powers and have decisively rejected the paternalistic premises of European imperialism. As if by default, superpower rationales for direct intervention tend to be negative—"we act in order to prevent the opposing superpower and its proxies from entering our sphere of influence or threatening our ideology"—rather than positive statements based quite openly on the alleged right of a dominant party (whether a state or a race or a culture) to rule other people. (On the Soviet justification for invading Czechoslovakia in 1968, and the similarly tortured American justification for invading the Dominican Republic in 1965, see Franck and Weisband, 1971.)

(2) Given the formal character of European colonial rule, and the European penchant for drawing fixed boundaries separating different colonial territories from one another, the geographic limits of a European power's control of foreign territory were often quite explicit. (Important exceptions to this generalization were expansionist pressures of European settlers along an ever-moving frontier, and multiple European spheres of influence in the nineteenth and early twentieth century within a single polity, Ch'ing and later Republican China.) Disputes among European metropoles concerning the boundaries of their respective empires were settled by warfare (the normal pattern

prior to the Congress of Vienna in 1815) or by diplomacy (the normal pattern in the century following the Congress of Vienna). The rules of the game governing global relations among competing imperial powers were thus reasonably clear and widely accepted. It was even possible for the imperial powers to cooperate in drawing up procedures for competitively carving up an entire continent—as they actually did, at Africa's expense, at Berlin in 1884–85. The fact that imperial boundaries existed and had a status in international (i.e., European) law gave a certain clarity and precision to the power struggles among the great states of Western Europe.

By contrast, the boundaries of today's American and Soviet informal empires are not nearly so clear and precise. This imprecision in turn encourages each superpower to engage in a certain amount of testing behavior to determine whether a particular country is or is not within the sphere of influence of the rival superpower. At various times over the past four decades Yugoslavia, Hungary, Czechoslovakia, Poland, Guatemala, Cuba, Grenada, and Nicaragua have each been perceived by one or the other superpower as moving outside the boundary of its own rightful sphere of influence. This perception has led to a series of crises over the international alliance status, as well as domestic policy orientation, of these countries. Arguably, the potential of such crises to threaten international peace has been increased because sphere-of-influence boundaries have not been as clearly drawn as were colonial boundaries, and because the rules for resolving disputes across "informal" boundary lines are less likely to be agreed upon than in a context of formal colonial rule.

(3) The dominant states of Western Europe were geographically separated from their colonial possessions by large bodies of water. This pattern of what has been termed "saltwater colonialism" was a consequence of the exploration of the world's oceans by Western Europeans from the fifteenth century onward, and of the effective military and commercial control of the high seas that followed closely upon exploration. (Parry, 1974.) Because of the substantial physical distance between European metropoles and their colonies, the relationship between dominant states and subordinate territories had several distinctive characteristics:

(a) Colonies were not particularly useful for direct defense of the metropole in time of war with rival great powers. Rather, colonies were valued on other grounds—as contributing, for example, to the metropole's economic development, or as helping to defend other parts of the metropole's farflung empire.

(b) The dominant state's capacity to enlarge its colonial holdings and to retain them depended heavily on the size, speed, and versatility of its naval fleet.

(c) There were enormous racial, cultural, and linguistic differences between European colonizers and those among the colonized population who were indigenous to a particular area.

(d) These highly visible differences in turn encouraged explanations for and justifications of European dominance that were based on the alleged biological or cultural superiority of Europeans (or, more broadly, the "white race").

In the nineteenth century the United States and Russia were also expansionist powers, but for the most part their expansion took place over land, along a moving frontier well away from the oceans. In both instances, people of European background conquered and often displaced peoples racially and culturally distinct from themselves, incorporating these peoples into an ever-larger dominant polity. But neither the Americans, busy "winning the West," nor the Russians, busy "winning the East," considered these expansionist activities instances of colonialism or imperialism. Such terms were to be reserved for the creators of saltwater empires. (The United States, of course, eventually did enter the ranks of saltwater powers when, in spite of its own anticolonial ideology, it took over the island remnants of the Spanish empire that were pressing for national independence at the end of the nineteenth century.)

Likewise, the territorial spheres of influence of these two currently dominant states are connected to them by land. This is most obvious in the case of the Soviet Union, which is contiguous to Poland, Czechoslovakia, Hungary, and Romania—as well as to Estonia, Latvia, and Lithuania, once independent countries that were unceremoniously absorbed into the Soviet Union during World War II. Though the overland link between the United States and the countries of Central and South America is clearly more attenuated, the symbolic significance of common occupancy of a hemispheric landmass should not be underestimated.

This elemental geographic factor has several implications for relations between the superpowers and their respective spheres of influence.

(a) The ultimate value of subordinate states is defined less in economic than in military terms, and the principal military issue is defense of the dominant power itself. Each superpower's sphere of influence is too close to home, too useful as a spatial shield, to permit the rival superpower to become a significant actor within that sphere. For their part the Soviets fear another overland invasion from Western Europe, with Eastern Europe serving as their only available shield. The Americans fear a combination of hostile missiles or planes facing them along a relatively unprotected southern flank, a cutoff of access to the Panama Canal, and the political destabilization (eventually affecting their immediate neighbor, Mexico) that widespread conflict over the extremely unequal distribution of wealth within Latin American countries is likely to produce.

(b) The projection of naval power is less important than in the colonial case. Soviet naval capacity is essentially irrelevant for retaining Eastern Europe as a sphere of influence. Naval power has mattered more for the Americans than for the Soviets; witness the role of the Marines as occupying forces on numerous occasions in Central America and the Caribbean, and the strategic value of the Panama Canal as a transit point for American military and commercial vessels. Nonetheless, the very insulation by sea of the New World from the Old has rendered the continued reliance on naval capacity less necessary for the Americans in their sphere of influence than for the Western Europeans in their far-flung overseas colonies.

(c) The politically dominant groups in the Soviet Union and the United States are not dramatically different in racial, ethnolinguistic, and cultural terms from the dominant groups in their respective spheres of influence. With some exceptions, political elites in all these areas are Europeans (Caucasians) or descendants of Europeans. The Slavic branch of the Indo-European languages encompasses not only Great Russians (as well as Belorussians and Ukrainians) but also Poles, Czechs, Slovaks, Bulgarians, Serbs, Croats, and Slovenes. This broad linguistic connection was the basis for Slavophile movements in the nineteenth and early twentieth centuries, which implied increased political influence by Russia across its western borders among culturally kindred peoples whose misfortune was to be ruled by non-Slavic Ottoman and Habsburg regimes. In the U.S.–Latin American case, although dominant groups are separated linguistically by the different legacies of English and Iberian colonialism, these groups are nonetheless similar in tracing direct descent to earlier immigrants from Western Europe. And Christianity in its varied forms—Eastern orthodox, Roman Catholic, Protestant—has been the predominant religion in Russia, in Eastern Europe, and in the Americas since the arrival of European conquerors and settlers.

(d) Given the commonalities just noted, dominant state rationales for establishing and maintaining regional spheres of influence have not been based on the alleged biological or cultural superiority of the dominant state's population. The overt white racism that was such a powerful element in the psychology of European imperialism—particularly in its nineteenth-century Afro-Asian phase—does not play a role in justifying the regional hegemony of today's two superpowers.

(4) Several Western European states participated actively and often quite competitively in overseas empire-building. Because these states were geographically close (and in many cases actually contiguous) to one another and shared many common elements of history and culture (Tilly, 1975: chap. 1), it was only natural that they interacted with each other continuously and intensely. This was the case regardless of whether interaction was cooperative, competitive, or overtly hostile, or whether it occurred at the diplomatic, military, economic, or cultural and intellectual levels.

Precisely because the European states constructing their parallel empires were in such physical proximity to one another, the analyst can readily imagine the actions of these states, taken collectively, as instances of a more general phenomenon: Western European imperialism. From this perspective the restless energies of Europeans whose countries fronted the North Atlantic seaboard radiated outward in many directions from a single core area to transform the social and physical environment of vast areas of the globe. (Davis, 1973; Wallerstein, 1980.) Europe's colonies may be seen as peripheries of this core in power terms, and as peripheries around this core in geographic terms. European imperialism created, reinforced, and in turn reflected a unipolar global power system.

Not only were dominant imperial states in close proximity to one another, but the colonies of different European states were also, in many cases, close to one another. Notable instances of areas whose now-independent states possess diverse colonial backgrounds are the islands of the Caribbean, the northern littoral of South America, the West African coast, and the islands of Micronesia. Economic and cultural interaction between the colonies of one metropole and those of another was generally minimized. However, if the metropoles should fall to fighting with each other, it was only too easy for their military confrontation to be exported to the periphery. The War of the Spanish Succession (1701–14), the Seven Years War (1756–63), the Napoleonic Wars (1790s to 1815), and of course World War I amply illustrate the tendency of intra-European warfare to replicate itself at the global level among the colonies of the contestants. Predictably, the results of these wars produced changes in formal control of the colonial peripheries; to the victor in the European military contest belonged—or so it seemed to the victor—the spoils of the loser's empire elsewhere in the rest of the world.

By way of contrast, the United States and the Soviet Union are physically very distant from one another. Each is highly aware of the geostrategic challenge posed by its rival in an era when missile warfare can in a sense obliterate the distance factor. Nonetheless, the regularity and the intensity of interaction across a broad range of issue areas are necessarily limited by the basic geographic fact of life that the United States and the Soviet Union occupy different continents, their capital cities separated by over 4,500 air miles. Physical distance, moreover, produces a global system that can no longer be perceived as unipolar. Rather, the world after 1945 is bipolarized—or perhaps multipolarized, if one considers Western Europe, China, and Japan as additional centers of world power. Likewise, the spheres of influence of each superpower are geographically quite distant from one another. This factor alone renders it difficult for the two subordinate regions to develop lateral relations of any significance, whether cooperative or hostile.

What are the political implications of these geographic differences between the European colonial case, on the one hand, and the U.S.–Latin American and USSR–Eastern European cases, on the other? One implication is that the physical distance between the United States and the Soviet Union, coupled with the physical distance between their respective regional spheres of influence, reduces the risks of war between the superpowers and increases the likelihood that a crisis in one dominant state's sphere of influence can be resolved without spreading to the other dominant state's sphere. Another less sanguine implication relates to the effects of a real or perceived loss of global power by a dominant state. When the Western European countries lost formal control of the last of their overseas empires following World War II, they were able in part to handle the psychological burdens of power loss by creatively redefining the nature of their relations with each other. The European Economic Community and associated institutions served as devices to enlarge identities and interests within a single geographic region, even as the scope of European power outside the region was being reduced. In contrast, the perceived loss of a superpower's adjacent sphere of influence would probably lead not to more cooperative but to considerably more hostile relations with the rival superpower, which would be accused of improper intervention far from its own borders. Unfortunately, there does not seem to be an economic or symbolic equivalent to the EEC as a means through which the United States and the USSR could work together to cope creatively with declining hegemony in their respective spheres of influence.

(5) Western European colonial rule was accompanied by prolonged and intensive efforts to change the cultural practices, norms, and beliefs of indigenous colonized populations. The colonial rulers generally assumed that they had little to gain from serious inquiry into the cultures of the people they ruled, aside from the knowledge of how to rule more effectively and efficiently. On the other hand, the rulers assumed that some or even all of the colonized population would become more civilized by substituting the ways of Europeans for those of their own "backward" society. The keys to cultural penetration in the colonial era were Christian missionary bodies, which set as their explicit task the conversion of non-Christians to their particular version of the "true faith," and which often went about this task by establishing schools to teach basic skills of literacy and numbers to young people, usually in a European language.

The introduction of Western European forms of Christianity—and of Western European languages and ideas through the schools that the missionaries or the colonial government itself sponsored—had a substantial impact on the cultures of indigenous colonized peoples. To be sure, this impact varied considerably from one society to another, resistance to the religious and secular ideas of Europeans being particularly effective where the already accepted indigenous religion employed its own sacred texts to convey its fundamental tenets to the populace. Even where indigenous cultural resistance was strong, however, the institutions of European cultural penetration had a significant corrosive effect on the precolonial worldviews and norms of colonized peoples. Not least destructive was the more-or-less explicit message from pulpit and classroom alike that the indigenous cultural tradition was inherently inferior to that of the Europeans. At the same time the institutions of cultural penetration conveyed ideas that could be (and eventually were) employed by emerging leaders of the colonized population to attack the moral foundations of colonialism. (For an overview, see Emerson, 1960; for a country case study, see McCully, 1940.) In Asia and Africa the movement to terminate European rule and create independent states was led by indigenous intellectuals educated in Western-oriented school systems. (Emerson, 1960; Baum and Gagliano, 1976.) These intellectuals occupied an ambiguous position between their own people, whose culture they wished to rescue from the European colonizers' charge of inferiority, and the economically developed societies of the West, many of whose values they had come to accept in the course of their education. (Shils, 1961; Matossian, 1962; for an example, see Nehru, 1960.)

Cultural penetration generally plays a less significant role in Soviet Union–Eastern European and U.S.–Latin American relations than it did in relations between the European metropoles and their overseas colonies. In part this is because the superpowers consider the export of many aspects of their culture to be of secondary importance; in part it is because there is fairly widespread resistance within subordinate regions to the wholesale importation of dominant-state culture. Superpower elites do not have a self-conceived "civilizing mission" in their respective spheres of influence, or a sense that the societies they dominate politically and militarily are distinctly inferior culturally to them. If anything, they confront within their spheres of influence a widely shared sentiment that the religious, linguistic, intellectual, and aesthetic heritage of the politically dominated populations is superior to that of the dominant state.

Penetration through religious institutions is of course irrelevant in the case of the Soviet Union, which is officially wary of organized religion when not actively hostile to it. Interestingly, popular support for the Roman Catholic Church in Poland is an expression of Polish nationalism that simultaneously rejects the atheistic premises of the official Marxist doctrine promulgated by the Soviet Union. In the U.S. case, American Catholics provide funds and personnel for Roman Catholic activities in Latin America. But the church structures that Americans support have long been under local control, and increasingly significant elements within Latin America's Catholic hierarchy find themselves opposing U.S. policy in the region as well as the acquisitive, individualistic values widely associated with the American way of life. Far from serving as mechanisms of external dominance, religious institutions in both subordinate regions tend in fact to express popular sentiments of national counterdependency.

In the language arena, although knowledge of English and of Russian is clearly helpful for upwardly mobile Latin Americans and Eastern Europeans, respectively, the command of these languages is not nearly as necessary a tool for forging successful professional, business, or public service careers as the command of European colonial languages was for indigenous people in Europe's colonial empires.

To be sure, both superpowers desire a certain set of ideas and values to be accepted within their spheres of influence. But these ideas and values are not as closely connected to the notion of dominant-state cultural and intellectual superiority as in the European colonial case. Marxism-Leninism, as interpreted by the Soviet leadership, is taught in Eastern European schools, and its vocabulary is constantly employed by the official media. Of more than passing symbolic significance, however, is the fact that Marx was himself a Western European and that his ideas, developed out of his experiences and research in Germany and England, were initially imported into Russia. Marxism-Leninism, moreover, is supranational in character: its moving historical force is an industrial working class that can develop in any part of the world in the course of capitalist development. Acceptance of the dominant-state ideology by Eastern Europeans does not therefore need to imply acceptance of the superiority of the Russian or Soviet intellectual tradition over the traditions of their own societies.

The United States exports a more diffuse ideology through a more diffuse set of institutions. The essential idea is that large and minimally regulated private profit and private nonprofit sectors are desirable means of ensuring the political liberties of citizens and the satisfaction of ever-rising popular demands for consumer goods. This is not a particularly American idea, however; the search for its intellectual antecedents takes one back to Western Europe and such thinkers as Locke, Say, Smith, Ricardo, and Mill. It is also a supranational idea, the argument being that private sector actors in any society can and should organize to protect their political and economic interests against the self-aggrandizing tendencies of public sector institutions. Acceptance of a capitalist ideology by Latin Americans does not therefore need to imply acceptance of the superiority of the United States' intellectual tradition over the traditions of their own societies. Moreover, Latin American culture retains precapitalist values from its own Iberian colonial heritage, while many of its prominent intellectuals express anticapitalist values precisely because the American imperialism Latin Americans fear is causally linked with American capitalism. In these respects American ideas and norms have a limited impact on Latin American culture, even though the consumptionist life-style that Americans celebrate has undeniable appeal south of the U.S. border.

Because of these constraints on superpower cultural penetration, the attitude of Eastern European and Latin American elites to the superpowers is perhaps less complex and conflicted than the attitude of nationalist leaders in Europe's colonies toward the imperial metropole. Whether successful anticolonial nationalist movements were led by the descendants of Europeans (as in the New World in the late eighteenth and early nineteenth centuries) or by indigenous non-

Europeans (as in the Old World in the twentieth century), what Marshall Singer terms "perceptual/identity ties" between the nationalists and the metropole were quite powerful. (Singer, 1972: chap. 4.) The nationalists, while rejecting the political authority claims of the European metropole, were in a sense the direct products of the colonizer's culture, and their historical mission was to communicate to their own populace many of the externally generated ideas and norms that they themselves had come to accept. Attacking colonialism by identifying its internal contradictions entailed accepting the very values and institutions Europeans wanted for themselves but denied in their colonies —for example, national sovereignty, a free press, a universal franchise, and control of administrative structures by elected politicians. In the Eastern European and Latin American cases, in contrast, political and intellectual elites are less clearly oriented to the dominant state as a normative reference point. Even if political elites owe their power over their own people to military and economic support from the dominant state, they do not necessarily consider their external patrons as the source of ideas to be mediated to their own people. In general, the behavior of these subordinate-state elites is less psychologically burdened than in the colonial case by the complications of ambivalence toward the foreign power dominating their country.

(6) The ability of Western European states to create and maintain overseas empires depended ultimately on their capacity and will to use the most advanced means of coercion at their disposal—means not available in nearly the same quantity or of the same quality to the people they conquered. As the Europeans developed new technologies of warfare—and of transportation and communication relevant to warfare—they readily employed these technologies against the people who eventually were incorporated as subjects into their empires. When Hilaire Belloc wrote in the late nineteenth century:

> "Whatever happens, we have got
> The Maxim gun, and they have not,"

he and his readers knew that the Europeans used this latest military invention with devastating effectiveness when battling, for example, the spear-throwing forces of the Mahdi in the Sudan. It was precisely the demonstrated capacity to coerce non-European peoples and polities into submission that helped to define the leading Western European countries as the modern world's "great powers."

In contrast, the coercive capacities defining the United States and the Soviet Union as the "superpowers" of the post-1945 era are not simply conventional forces but also these countries' large and growing arsenal of nuclear weapons. Virtually the entire period of Soviet dominance in Eastern Europe, and the last four decades of U.S. dominance in Latin America, have occurred in the context of a bipolar world faced with the small but distinct possibility of atomic warfare. But the capacity of the superpowers to employ nuclear weapons against each other is vastly out of proportion to their will to use them, both because the destructive potential of the latest technology is so awesome and because the likelihood of self-destruction is high if one side actually employs these weapons against the other. The very arsenal of weapons that intimidates the enemy renders each superpower vulnerable to annihilation by its enemy. The superpowers must therefore resort to psychological rather than real warfare with respect to the most advanced destructive technology they possess, relying on the threat to use nuclear weapons under certain conditions as a deterrent they hope is sufficiently credible to avoid ever having to carry out the threat. (George and Smoke, 1974; Russett, 1983.)

The uneasy forbearance the United States and the Soviet Union show toward one another in the nuclear arena is demonstrated even more clearly in the relations each superpower has with countries in its own sphere of influence. There is an enormous inequality between the military capacities of each nuclear superpower and the capacities of the states within its sphere: no country in Latin America or in Eastern Europe is a member of the nuclear club, or (with the possible exception of Brazil) is it ever likely to become one. Yet the superpowers do not threaten to employ the advanced military technology that defines them as superpowers on subordinate states in order to maintain dominance. It would be unthinkable for a contemporary superpower to try to effect compliance within its sphere of influence by arguing that

Whatever happens, we have got
The doomsday bomb, and you have not.

If coercion is threatened and on occasion employed, it is "conventional" or prenuclear in character. (For Soviet coercive diplomacy, see Kaplan, 1981; for U.S. coercive diplomacy, see Blechman and Kaplan, 1978.) Thus the imbalance in military capacity between dominant and dependent states—which if anything is even greater in the Soviet and American cases than in the European colonial case—does not translate into a comparable imbalance in coercive power, because each superpower's will to use its full capacity against subordinate states is far more restrained. This restraint, exercised *within* each set of dominant-subordinate relationships, is dictated in large measure by a logic of strategic limitation *between* the superpowers that did not operate in the prenuclear era of the European colonial empires.

One implication of this analysis is that states within the contemporary American and Soviet spheres of influence have greater bargaining leverage with their respective dominant powers than might be imagined from an examination of the dominant power's military capabilities. Another implication is that each superpower is tempted to assert itself indirectly on the world scene through nonnuclear client states whose aggressive actions are deemed less likely to trigger a nuclear holocaust than comparable behavior by the superpower itself. In the colonial era European states were under no constraint to work through proxies or surrogates elsewhere in the world; when they acted out of imperial self-interest they usually acted directly and on their own. (Kiernan, 1982.) The post-1945 international system, in contrast, is a system in which many states are or are perceived to be proxies for superpower interests. Thus at various times the United States has defined North Korea, North Vietnam, China (in both the Korean and Indochinese conflicts), Cuba, Libya, and Nicaragua as surrogates for Soviet expansion. (Ra'anan, 1979; Porter, 1984.) For its part, the Soviet Union has at various times doubtless perceived the states linked to the United States by mutual defense treaties (NATO, CENTO, SEATO), as well as South Korea and Israel, as surrogates for American imperialism. Whether the foreign policy of these allegedly surrogate states is in fact the result of superpower prompting, or is rather the result of relatively autonomous action by decisionmakers in these states, has become itself a critical issue bitterly dividing analysts of contemporary world events.

In summary, a comparison of the two dominant-subordinate cases so extensively analyzed in this volume with the European overseas colonial empires highlights several features the U.S.–Latin American and Soviet–Eastern European cases have in common. The subordinate states are legally sovereign; the dominant states articulate an anticolonial ideology; sphere-of-influence boundaries are not clearly defined; dominant and subordinate states are connected by land; each sphere of influence is physically distant from the principal rival of its dominant state; cultural penetration by the dominant state is relatively limited; and the dominant states lack the will to use the most destructive component of their compliance capacity on their subordinate states. These common features, which stand in rather marked contrast to the features of European colonialism, clearly meet the "minimum similarity" requirement of comparative analysis. Identification of the important differences between the two cases—which other essays undertake as their central task—complements this analysis and provides the basis for theory construction utilizing both the similarities and the differences noted in this volume.

5

On Influence and Spheres of Influence

Paul Keal

In this chapter I will explore the concept of spheres of influence and its contributions to an understanding of superpower dominance over subordinate states. By a sphere of influence I mean a definite region within which a single external power exerts a predominant influence, which limits the independence or freedom of action of states within it.

In contemporary international politics such a region can be either a group of adjacent states or an ocean and the island states in it together with the littoral states around it. Examples of both these kinds of regions are, respectively, Eastern Europe and the Caribbean. The perimeter of such a region lies where the predominance of one power ends, though this may not always be clearly defined as is illustrated by the doubts that long persisted about the status of Yugoslavia. States not in a sphere of influence may either be free of the influence associated with spheres or in gray areas where there is competition between rival powers for influence but in which none has a clear predominance.

In terms of spheres of influence, states are one of two obvious kinds: powers that do the influencing, and the states that are influenced.

Defining the influencing power as outside the region recognizes that influenced states are separate from the influencing power. Some influencing powers have been far removed from their spheres of influence, as Britain, France, and Germany were from Africa and China during the nineteenth century. In the contemporary world, however, definite spheres of influence are generally adjacent to the influencing power.

Describing an influencing power as one that exerts "predominant influence" means that it prevails both over the entities in the region and against the influence of other comparable powers over the region. Contrary to this definition, it is sometimes assumed that a sphere of influence is exclusive to the influencing power and all other powers are completely excluded. There is some degree of exclusion in a sphere of influence, but it is not absolute; it does not extend to all activities of states and their nationals and varies from case to case. American finance penetrates Eastern Europe, while Soviet aid and ideology penetrate Latin America, and so on.

Finally, the limitation of independence or freedom of action of political entities in a sphere of influence covers the range from direct action, such as armed intervention by the influencing power, to much less direct and more diffuse forms of influence, such as, for instance, the mechanisms described by interdependence and dependency theorists. In defining spheres of influence, we must allow for the fact that in the limits placed on influenced states there is a spectrum of qualitative differences. Finland's trade, defense, and foreign policies must have regard for the Soviet Union, but its actions are not restricted to the same degree as, for instance, Poland's.

The concept of spheres of influence as distinct from the actual term is very much the older of the two. As a concept, spheres of influence may be traced back to antiquity. Polybius referred to an agreement between Rome and Carthage that had as its subject what was essentially a sphere of influence. (1912: 55.) Centuries later the concept was central to the Treaty of Tordesillas of 1494 and the papal bulls preceding it, which divided the actual and future discoveries and conquests of Spain and Portugal between the two countries. (*New Cambridge*, 1957: 79.) It was not until the last quarter of the nineteenth century, however, that the concept had the term "spheres of influence" attached to it. During that period the establishment of spheres of influence and the conclusion of agreements about them was an accepted practice of the European great powers.

When the term "spheres of influence" was first used in diplomacy is uncertain. Lord Curzon traced it back to a dispatch, from Count Gortchakoff to Lord Clarendon in 1869, that assured Britain that Afghanistan lay "completely outside the sphere within which Russia might be called upon to exercise her influence." (Curzon, 1907: 42.) Whatever the first use of the actual term was, it became widespread in connection with "the scramble for Africa." This can be said to have started with the Conference of Berlin of 1884–85, after which "the modern era of . . . spheres of influence began." (Lindley, 1969: 209.)

The purpose of this conference, called by Germany and France, was to reach an understanding on the Congo Basin. In its general act, the conference agreed to freedom of trade for all nations within the region watered by the Congo and its affluents and laid down rules about occupation. In essence, during the initial stages of the scramble for Africa the term "spheres of influence" referred to the territorial intentions of European powers with respect to the interior of Africa. To speak of the sphere of influence of France, for instance, was to speak of territory France wished to acquire but had not yet effectively occupied. (Lugard, 1923: 11–12.) Proclaiming a sphere of influence amounted to staking a claim that could be ignored only at the risk of conflict with the claimant.

Why the European powers wanted to acquire these territories is of course a matter of interpretation and conjecture. There is probably no single explanation sufficient to account for the motives of all the European powers engaged in imperialist expansion. It was certainly not a simple matter of acquiring vast territories for the sake of territory per se.

Hobson, and Lenin after him, saw spheres of influence as part of the struggle between monopolists for the division of the world into economic territories. In their view the purpose of spheres of influence was to secure markets regardless of whether this led to the establishment of colonies. Lenin's distinctive contribution was to argue that imperialist powers form alliances against one another in order to protect and extend their possessions and spheres of influence, but that these alliances are nothing but truces in periods between wars. He reasoned that spheres of influence ultimately do not satisfy the needs of rival economic powers, and so they are led to challenge one another. (1977: 119.)

Other interpretations emphasize instead that spheres of influence and the colonies they often became were perceived to play a role in creating national prestige. The statesmen of some powers believed that the acquisition of territory in Asia and Africa was in some way required of a great power or at least that it would bring with it a beneficial increase in status. Thus, whereas the empires of Britain, France, and Russia brought economic benefits, the imperialist aspirations of Germany and Italy were more a matter of national prestige than of national interest or economic advantage.

Regardless of why the European powers wanted to acquire territories, the device of spheres of influence served a common purpose. Whatever their individual motives or intentions, the European powers, in effect, contrived to avoid conflict over territory by agreeing beforehand about which areas each was to have as its own preserve. The term "spheres of influence" referred to such areas, and mutual recognition of them meant relinquishing claims to the sphere designated as another's. In this way there would, in theory, be no conflict over the territory. The function of spheres of influence, in this respect, has not changed in contemporary international politics.

During the last quarter of the nineteenth century the bulk of spheres of influence resulted from mutual agreements or treaties that had status in international law. However, not all spheres of influence have resulted from agreements. In important cases spheres-of-influence agreements have devolved from the existence of spheres of influence. In any case, the sphere of influence of one power or the respective spheres of two or more powers are quite distinct from an agreement or agreements about such spheres. Spheres of influence and agreements about them must not be confused. Yet, as I shall argue later, the place of spheres of influence in contemporary international politics cannot be understood without reference to agreements about them.

To further clarify the concept of spheres of influence, it is useful, especially with regard to Eastern Europe and Latin America, to contrast it with the related but distinct concepts of buffer zone, spheres of restraint, and frontiers.

The first of these was defined by Martin Wight (1949) as "an area occupied by a weaker Power or Powers between two or more stronger Powers," as to which it is in "the vital interest of each stronger Power to prevent the other from controlling." Each of the stronger powers, Wight continued, "will preserve this interest in one of two ways, according to its strength: either by seeking to establish its own control over the buffer zone ... or by maintaining its neutrality and independence." (50–51.) In cases where powers have established control over what they regard as a buffer zone, such zones have coincided with spheres of influence. But precisely because buffer zones may be comprised of states, such as Sweden, which are neutral and independent, not all buffer zones are spheres of influence, and hence the two concepts must be distinguished.

Concerning the two spheres that are the subject of this book, the states of Eastern Europe are both a Soviet sphere of influence and a buffer zone. By contrast, Latin America is a U.S. sphere of influence, but it is not a buffer zone in the sense identified by Wight. Indeed, it is in relation to buffer zones that the contrast between Eastern Europe and Latin America is sharpest. Eastern Europe stands between the Soviet Union and a Western Europe allied to the United States. Latin America is a buffer only between the United States and the unpopulated wastes of Antarctica.

Unlike a buffer zone, a sphere of restraint cannot coincide with a sphere of influence. The term "spheres of restraint" implies a political relationship between powerful and weak states different from what is implied by the term "spheres of influence." Whereas spheres of influence are regions over which one power exerts predominant influence, a sphere of restraint is an area in which no one power is predominant.

In contrast to spheres of influence, there are so-called gray areas, in which much of Africa used to be included, where the nature and extent of each superpower's involvement is unclear. Neither superpower is in any way sure of the extent to which it can act without coming into conflict with or meeting opposition from the other. There may thus be the danger of the two superpowers clashing through being involved on opposite sides of a conflict between their respective clients, as in the Middle East. Consequently, each superpower must exercise restraint in its actions. Rather than intervene unilaterally or become involved in other ways that might risk confronting the other, each should "restrain" itself sufficiently to avoid conflict.

Contrary to this situation, the nature of a sphere of influence is such that the influencing power is reasonably sure about what it can do in its sphere without coming into conflict with its adversary. And the adversary power has a clear understanding of what the influencing power in question will tolerate. This applies to relations between the Soviet Union and United States with regard to their respective spheres in Eastern Europe and Latin America.

Finally, "international frontiers" are also related to but distinct from spheres of influence. The term "frontier" in this context does not mean a boundary between sovereignties; it does not refer to the boundary of any one state or necessarily to anything tangible. Equally as much as a line it denotes an idea in the sense Frederick Jackson Turner meant when he fixed the term to the furthermost and expanding fringe of a civilization. (1961: 39.) It was similarly defined by H. Duncan Hall as "the zone in which the great powers, expanding along their main lines of communication to the limits of their potential and economic influence and defence needs impinge on each other in conflict or compromise." (1948: 3.) Thus the conception of frontier required here is that of a stable line of demarcation separating the influence of one power from that of another. Nations sometimes establish spheres in order to secure a frontier in this sense, as the Soviets did in Eastern Europe, but it would be wrong to conclude that such spheres are established only with regard to frontiers. The U.S. sphere in Latin America does not demarcate a frontier between the Soviet Union and the United States in the way that the western perimeter of Eastern Europe does between the USSR and Western Europe.

The crucial difference between frontiers and spheres of influence is that whereas the idea of a "frontier" can be understood with reference only to relations between two great powers, or between the powers of two civilizations, spheres of influence cannot be understood without reference to relations between influencing powers and the states they influence. Although they are conceptually distinct from spheres of influence, what buffer zones, spheres of restraint, and frontiers have in common with them is reference to the rivalry of great powers. In the practice of states one of the functions fulfilled by spheres of influence has been the establishment of frontiers between the areas of great power interests, and to that extent each concept holds a similar place in the language of diplomacy.

The contemporary relevance of the distinction between these two concepts may be seen in the Helsinki agreements of 1975. These agreements represented settlement of the dispute about the postwar "frontiers" of Europe. For the Western powers, "frontiers" meant, in this case, the boundaries of states. It can be argued, however, that for the Soviet Union it meant acceptance of the Soviet sphere and the demarcation of a frontier in the sense outlined above.

If spheres of influence sometimes establish frontiers, how are spheres of influence themselves established? We have already stated that some but not all spheres of influence have resulted from mutual agreements; others have been established through unilateral declaration. A region may eventually be regarded as the sphere of a particular power after a unilateral declaration by that power that the region in question is in its sphere of influence.

The most important example of a unilateral declaration—moreover one with continuing relevance—is the Monroe Doctrine. Though President James Monroe's message of December 1823 did not contain the term "sphere of influence," what he said about the relationship between the United States and the Western Hemisphere is suitably described by it. In practice, the doctrine has meant that the United States has interfered in the affairs of American states when it has perceived those states as either being, or in danger of falling, under the influence of extracontinental powers. Such outside influence has been perceived as a threat to the peace and safety of the United States. Thus, interference has been explained as necessary for the peace and safety of the United States.

It should be noted that implicit in this process is an interplay between the two distinct aspects of spheres of influence in international politics: on the one hand, the relationship between the influencing power—in this case the United States—and the states it influences, and, on the other hand, the relationship between the influencing power and whichever extracontinental power causes it to perceive a threat. This point is taken up again below.

Of the Monroe Doctrine and other cases it must be observed that a mere unilateral declaration about how a particular region should be regarded by other powers does not mean that those other powers will necessarily so regard the region in question. The British government, for instance, did not recognize the Monroe Doctrine.

Nevertheless, even though an adversary power declares that it does not accept a unilateral declaration, the power that made the declaration may, in time, come to believe its claims have been accepted. It is more the nonverbal acts of the adversary than its verbal acts that count. The longer the declaring power goes unchallenged, the more likely it is to believe that its claims have been accepted. If they are accepted, it may or may not be for reasons of reciprocity. This means that other powers may accept the implications of a unilateral declaration in the expectation that the power that issued the declaration will similarly accept their own claims. Once a unilateral declaration seems accepted, the region to which it refers may become the subject either of explicit agreement or tacit understanding between the power from which it emanated and one or more powers of comparable status. In this way the region to which the Monroe Doctrine refers may be seen as the subject of a tacit understanding between the United States and the Soviet Union about spheres of influence.

Unilateral declarations, such as the Monroe Doctrine, and mutual agreements are directed to the same end. The formal agreements of the late nineteenth and early twentieth century that established spheres of influence in Africa, China, and Persia recognized the predominant interest or influence of one power in a particular region. The recognition of such interest or influence had as its purpose the regulation of relations between the powers concerned insofar as such relations might be affected by that region. Such agreements bound the powers that were party to them but did no more than warn off unfriendly third parties. In these respects the formal agreements of the past about spheres of influence had ends in common with contemporary understandings. But there the similarity ends.

Although there are traces of agreement about spheres of influence in Article 21 of the Covenant of the League of Nations, in the Kellogg-Briand Pact (Zimmern, 1939: 401–2), and the provision for regional arrangements in the Charter of the United Nations, the importance of spheres of influence in contemporary politics does not lie in any degree of recognition they have found in such instruments. Further, the way in which a region comes to be regarded as a sphere of influence is, in contemporary international politics, considerably more complex than was the case in the formal agreements of the past.

In contemporary international politics whatever agreement or understanding exists over spheres of influence is unspoken or tacit. The practices associated with spheres of influence are not compatible with either the rhetoric and imperatives of the principle of state sovereignty or attempts to prohibit the use of force through instruments such as the Kellogg-Briand Pact. For this reason the superpowers formally deny that they have any agreement or understanding, tacit or otherwise, about spheres of influence. (Department of State, 1968: 350; Sovetov, 1968: 9.) As a consequence of these denials the superpowers cannot communicate directly or specifically about any such understanding.

Agreement or understanding is formally denied in the language of the superpowers because they cannot, or do not wish to, be seen in the opinion of international society as openly claiming for themselves or granting each other any rights, which they do not have, to spheres of influence. For the United States to claim or grant such rights would amount to condoning intervention and the violation of state autonomy, thereby undermining the foundations of international society. For the Soviet Union acknowledgment of an understanding about spheres of influence would be to suggest that it acts in its own interests rather than in keeping with those of socialist solidarity.

It is worth emphasizing that what the United States and the Soviet Union each deny is the existence of agreement or understanding as

distinct from the actual spheres of influence. In their official pronouncements they neither deny nor admit that there are spheres of
influence. Of the great powers only China has spoken openly about
spheres of influence, and it has repeatedly denied that it either has or
seeks to have a sphere of its own. (*Peking Review*, 1973a: 14; 1973b: 9;
1973c: 9–11.)

Despite this stance by the Soviet Union and the United States, both
spheres of influence and tacit understanding about them are part of
the reality of contemporary international politics. Both superpowers
have behaved as though they do recognize each other's sphere. Indeed,
it is because of the way they have behaved that it may be inferred they
do have a tacit and reciprocal understanding about the range of behavior each will tolerate of the other with regard to their respective spheres
of influence. Further, it is because of such understanding that spheres
of influence have the importance and role that they do in contemporary international politics.

Before I examine this proposition, three further points concerning
spheres of influence as a concept are apposite. First, important spheres
of influence are intimately connected with the perceived vital interests
of influencing powers. By vital interests I mean those that a state
perceives as worth going to war to defend. Contemporary understanding about spheres of influence stems from the mutual recognition by
the United States and the Soviet Union that each perceives the preservation of its respective sphere to be in its vital interest. Thus, for one to
challenge the sphere of the other would be to risk war.

Further, from time to time commentators have argued that clarity of
thought about vital interests accompanied by acceptance of spheres of
influence should guide the foreign policy of the superpowers. In the
late 1960s and 1970s Ronald Steel (1967: 328; 1971–72: 11), for example,
drew on the writings of Walter Lippmann to argue against the globalist
policies being practiced by the United States. As an alternative to
globalism, he proposed that the United States be more selective about
the areas it identified as crucial to its vital security interests. At the
same time the United States should recognize that the Soviet Union
also has vital security interests and therefore a justified claim to a
sphere of influence insofar as it serves those interests. This, however,
was and remains a brand of realism unacceptable to international
norms.

Second, the spheres of influence of the Soviet Union and the United
States are associated with alliances and security communities. Although
they are definitely not agreements about spheres of influence, treaties

such as the North Atlantic Treaty, the Warsaw Treaty of Friendship, Cooperation and Mutual Assistance, and the provision for regional arrangements in the Charter of the United Nations all have some bearing upon them. The Warsaw Treaty allowed the Soviet Union to coerce East Germany, Poland, Hungary, and Bulgaria into joining in the invasion of Czechoslovakia in 1968. It is one of the means by which the Soviet Union is able to both dominate Eastern Europe and argue for the legitimacy of its actions. Similarly, Article 52 of the UN Charter has enabled the United States to argue that its policing actions in Latin America are consistent with both the aims of the Organization of American States concerning the peace and security of the region and the charter itself.

In essence, the membership of an alliance or security arrangement can comprise an influencing power and the states it influences. Such is the situation in Eastern Europe and between the United States and the states of Latin America with which it has collective security arrangements. In these situations the alliance or arrangement is a vehicle for the influencing power to exert and maintain its dominance over the states in its sphere.

Third, the Soviet and U.S. spheres that are the subject of this book are clear cases from which it may be misleading to generalize about spheres in general. For a time after World War II Western Europe could have been called a U.S. sphere of influence. If so, when did it cease to be and what is it now? Whatever the answer to these questions, a crucial difference between Western and Eastern Europe is that prior to World War II the states that comprise the former were great powers. They were also the source of the institutions upon which international society is founded. This distinction alone could result in propositions that did not fit the states of Eastern Europe and Latin America.

Similarly, it would be instructive to study Australia as a sphere of influence. It is tied to the United States through the ANZUS treaty, which refers to the "peace and security" of a community in much the same words as the Monroe Doctrine; through U.S. command, control, communications, and intelligence (C3I) facilities, which are claimed to be crucial to deterrence; and through shared intelligence arrangements. (Richelson and Ball, 1985.) Further, its economy is permeated with U.S. capital and transnational actors. And its cultural life is increasingly saturated by American culture and values. Australia has not, however, ever been subject to the overt forms of influence, such as armed intervention, that have been applied to Eastern Europe and Latin America. To whatever extent it is within a U.S. sphere of influence, it is in a different, less clear-cut category than the states of Eastern Europe and Latin America.

Bearing these points in mind, what is the role of spheres of influence in contemporary international politics?

The Role of Spheres of Influence
in Contemporary International Politics

Crucial to the argument of this section is the obvious and elementary distinction already drawn between influencing powers and the states that are influenced by them. Discussion of spheres of influence frequently centers on the relationship between influenced states and the power that influences them. Indeed, one of the declared aims of this book is to compare the relationships of the two influencing powers with states in their respective spheres of influence. The significance of spheres of influence in international politics is, however, not confined to the relationship between influenced states and the influencing powers. More significant are those aspects of the relationship between influencing powers that devolve from each of them having a sphere of influence. This relationship is in turn intimately connected with the relationship each of them has with the states in their respective spheres of influence. Without an understanding of the relationship between influencing powers, the conditions that prevail within a sphere of influence cannot be fully understood.

The importance of the Soviet and U.S. spheres of influence in contemporary international politics resides mainly in the tacit understanding each of the superpowers has about the sphere of the other. More explicitly, it can be argued that tacit understandings about spheres of influence contribute to international order.

The way in which such understandings contribute to international order is through providing guidelines by which powers may conduct their relations so as to advance perceived common interests. A basis for the perception of common interests in international order is provided by the fear of war, particularly nuclear war, and by economic dependence among other factors. But to achieve any degree of international order, states need to find guidelines that show them how they must behave if they are to advance their common interests. They must articulate norms or rules and agree upon them.

Such rules need not be formal or explicit but rather may simply be operating procedures or unwritten "rules of the game." The tacit understandings that have devolved from spheres of influence provide just such guidelines or rules. If the general principles of conduct embodied in them are followed, orderly relations between powers that have spheres of influence may be achieved to some degree.

The Soviet Union and the United States both understand that the other expects to be able to limit the freedom and independence of states in their respective spheres without coming into conflict with each other. What is understood as appropriate behavior provides a stability in relations between the two influencing powers that is lacking with respect to areas not in the sphere of either one (unless there is a tacit understanding between them that certain areas are to be the domain of neither). If either one were to upset the expectations of the other concerning spheres of influence, the basis of understanding between them would be upset if not destroyed and relations between them would be destabilized. Thus, to aid rebellious states in another power's sphere of influence would be to go against what is expected, and by challenging the hegemony of the influencing power would be inimical to international order.

A further way in which spheres of influence may be said to contribute to order is with respect to relations between influenced states in the same sphere of influence. States within both the Soviet and U.S. spheres have, by and large, not resorted to force against one another during the last forty years. Disputes between them have been muted and have not become international problems with implications beyond the immediate region in which they occur. For instance, disputes between the states of Eastern Europe, of the sort that were very much in evidence before World War II, no longer reach "the surface of conscious political activity." (Bull, 1977: 219.) It is not that there are no longer any internal conflicts in these states or any rivalries between them, but that the presence of the influencing power keeps them in check. To a certain extent the order that obtains in relations between influenced states in the same sphere of influence is the result of each one of them acting in accord with what they perceive the influencing power to require. By so doing, they maintain order between themselves and the influencing power.

The regard shown by influenced states for what they perceive to be the requirements of the influencing power amounts to the recognition of hierarchy. But the recognition of this hierarchy is the result of its being demonstrated from time to time. The attempt at the Bay of Pigs and the interventions in Guatemala, Hungary, the Dominican Republic, Czechoslovakia, and Afghanistan, together with U.S. support for the Contras against the Sandinistas in Nicaragua, all represent action taken to maintain hegemony. Actions such as these, by which an influencing power polices its sphere of influence, induce recognition of the hierarchy within the sphere. Thus order within a sphere of influence is a condition produced partly by the influencing power actively policing its sphere and partly by passive recognition on the part of the influenced states of the hierarchical relationship.

Intervention, however, is merely the most obvious assertion of hierarchy. Hegemony may also be expressed through an economic arrangement, and, indeed, neo-Marxist literature would cast spheres of influence entirely in this form. For neo-Marxists the relationship between influencer and influenced is one properly explained only in terms of economic dependence, and it is important to recognize that this may be a form of control. I do not propose here to inquire into the empirical plausibility of the truth or falsity of the theory of economic dependence. But if it is true and if spheres of influence can be described in these terms, military intervention to maintain the relationship of hierarchy between an influencing power and the states it influences is generally unnecessary. Through aid, trade, and investment, and through the harmony of interest between the elites both in influenced states and in the influencing power, control has been established and can be maintained.

Finally, whether it is maintained by police actions or through economic structure, order within spheres of influence can be said to contribute to international order by limiting the possibility of conflicts breaking out that might affect the entire international system. When this benefit is added to the contribution provided by tacit understanding between influencing powers, it can be argued that although the practices associated with spheres of influence violate the norms of interstate behavior and are unjust, they have, nevertheless, contributed to international order. (Keal, 1983a: 194–209.)

Having depicted the role of spheres of influence as contributing to order, where does the argument lead? Does it suggest that existing spheres of influence should be maintained, that the establishment of new ones would be a good thing, or perhaps even that they should be openly accepted? Given the prevailing norms of international society, the last of these can be disregarded for the reasons already spelled out as to why there is tacit understanding rather than open agreement. The other two points are more complex. Any answer to whether the maintenance of existing spheres is a good thing or whether an increase in their number is desirable depends on the value that informs it.

Order is only one among other competing values in international politics. Arguably, it takes precedence over other values insofar as it may be a necessary condition for their achievement. In any case, with regard to spheres of influence the requirements for order stand in stark contrast to those for justice. Further, the tension between these two values is closely related to the question of change within spheres of influence. Justice is integral to the relationship between an influencing power and the states it influences. Order, on the other hand, is more closely related to the quality and the relationship between influencing powers.

When order is taken as the principal value, the maintenance and extension of spheres of influence are desirable from two points of view: that of people who do not want war between influencing powers, and that of the influencing powers themselves. From the vantage point of the citizens of influenced states, however, such a valuation is not desirable. To prefer order in relation to spheres of influence is to relegate to secondary importance the injustices inherent in them, such as inequalities in the distribution of wealth, violations of the doctrine of sovereign equality of states, the suppression of human rights, and the denial of equality of individuals. In relation to these it has to be recognized that the requirements of order achieved through the device of spheres of influence conflict with those of justice. It must also be recognized that injustice might lead to disorder or, alternatively, that justice can often be purchased only at the price of disorder.

There are situations in which influencing powers attempt to curb change and to maintain the status quo. Very often this means maintaining an unjust regime, a policy that might ultimately seriously undermine the interests of order. For influencing powers, unchecked changes in their spheres of influence could destabilize their relationship with adversaries. An adversary might try to take advantage of particular situations in ways that could lead to conflict with its rival. Fear of this possibility reinforces the tendency of influencing powers to maintain the status quo by supporting repressive regimes in influenced states. Nevertheless, influencing states do not necessarily seek to maintain the status quo.

A primary reason for resisting change is the stable expectations on which tacit understanding about spheres of influence are founded. Change is perceived as having the potential to destabilize these expectations. It follows from the earlier argument concerning guidelines and rules of the game that changes that involve breaking stable expectations carry with them danger and uncertainty. For this reason, regard for stable expectations reinforces a preference for not upsetting the status quo. Yet suppression of change might merely delay and increase demands for it; the injustices inherent in spheres of influence might simply lead to disorder.

Quite apart from the fact that injustice gives rise to disorder, it is in itself a reason for seeking either to dismantle spheres of influence or at least attempt to infuse the relationship between influencing powers and the states they influence with a higher degree of justice. This, however, comes back to the central argument of this chapter that spheres of influence cannot be seen in terms only of the relationship between influencing powers and the states they influence.

To reiterate, when justice is given highest priority, attention is focused on the relationship between the influencing power and the states it dominates. From the standpoint of justice, the nature of this relationship is such that spheres of influence have to be judged on the whole as undesirable. What can be done to change it?

Change within a sphere of influence may be achieved in three ways. None of them is mutually exclusive, and conceivably some circumstances could arise in which all three coincided. First, the influencing power might modify its behavior. It might do so either because of a conscious choice, independent of outside influences, or because it becomes so preoccupied with other matters that it ceases to maintain its position of hegemony. The latter situation may be associated with the decline of the influencing power as a great power in international politics. Second, influenced states could purposely set out to secure greater autonomy for themselves. Third, another power of comparable status might either seek to force or find means of inducing an influencing power to change the nature of its relationship with the states it influences.

In a sphere of influence, as in international politics in general and in all forms of social organization, there is continual change in some degree. Influencing powers do modify their behavior, and influenced states do sometimes secure more autonomy for themselves. (Jones, 1977.) Nevertheless, with regard to the Soviet and U.S. spheres, whatever changes have taken place have not altered the fundamental nature of the relationships involved. Implicit in much thinking about the subject is the idea that radical change could be achieved only by the third of the ways identified.

But my argument has been that the logic of spheres of influence is such that influencing powers do not challenge each other's authority over their respective spheres. And because spheres of influence are identified with vital interests — those for which powers are prepared to go to war—to offer such a challenge would be to take substantial risk. Since World War II the Soviet Union and the United States have not effectively challenged each other's spheres in the sense of seeking to radically alter the other's behavior. This fact merely reinforces the proposition that the situation within a sphere of influence is, in important cases, connected with relations between influencing powers.

That the superpowers do not effectively challenge each other's sphere allows the inference that they have a mutual understanding about them. Why do they have this understanding? Why does the one acquiesce in the other's actions and dominance?

In answer to this, Franck and Weisband (1971: 135–36) argued that, as a matter of reciprocity, the one power acquiesces in what the other does because it must allow the other what it has claimed for itself. They argue that the superpowers perpetuate spheres of influence through the justifications they give when they intervene within their respective spheres. These justifications have two effects: (1) they "authorize" the other power to also do what is being justified, and (2) when the other power does the same, the first power is tied by its own justifications from impeding the other. Thus the "cumulative effect" of the justifications the United States gave for its actions with regard to Guatemala, Cuba, and the Dominican Republic was that they appeared "to authorize the Soviet Union to do exactly what it did to Czechoslovakia in 1968." (Franck and Weisband, 1971: 8.) To which the invasion of Afghanistan in 1979 can probably be added. (Keal, 1983b.)

For Franck and Weisband the justifications used by the superpowers created a "reciprocal obligation" to acquiesce in each other's actions. But this idea is questionable. Neither superpower is "obliged" to acquiesce in the sphere of the other. Either could choose to upset all existing expectations. In any case, the justifications each superpower employs are not intended primarily or perhaps even at all for the other superpower. They are intended for a wider, mixed audience that includes the allies of the power giving the justification and, in the case of a democracy, the power's own electorate as well. Further, their argument presupposes that if the United States had acted differently with regard to Latin America, then the Soviet Union would have been obliged to act differently with regard to Eastern Europe. This cannot be assumed, and it is also quite doubtful. Consequently, to explain acquiescence in terms of a principle of reciprocity, whereby each must allow the other what it claims for itself, is not satisfactory.

It is far more likely that the reason for acquiescence and the need for tacit understanding lie not in a need for reciprocity in itself but rather in the common interest each superpower has in avoiding nuclear war. Common interest in avoiding nuclear war is the more compelling reason for acquiescence, and it is the primary reason why there is a tacit understanding between the superpowers about spheres of influence.

To summarize, my argument has been that spheres of influence in contemporary international politics are a device for regulating relations between the Soviet Union and the United States; what is most important is how the possession of spheres of influence affects relations between the two nations as influencing powers. Further, primarily because of the unspoken understanding between the superpowers, spheres of influence contribute to international order. But it is an order that inhibits change within spheres and denies the states within them the full enjoyment of international norms such as sovereign equality and autonomy.

The only way the practices associated with spheres of influence can be ended is by fundamentally upsetting the expectations that the superpowers have of each other with respect to spheres of influence. But if spheres of influence really are inseparable from perceived vital interests, the implications of upsetting expectations cannot be taken lightly and might be very dangerous.

We have still to consider more specifically what the concept of spheres of influence contributes to understanding the dominance of the Soviet Union over Eastern Europe and of the United States over Latin America.

Soviet and U.S. Dominance

At the outset, the term *dominance* requires some attention. The late Hedley Bull distinguished dominance as being "characterized by the habitual use of force by a great power, against the lesser states comprising its hinterland, and by the habitual disregard of the universal norms of interstate behaviour that confer rights of sovereignty, equality and independence upon these states." (1977: 214.) As an example he cited "the position of the United States in relation to the states of Central America and the Caribbean from late in the last century until the introduction of Franklin Roosevelt's Good Neighbour Policy in 1933." (Bull, 1977: 214.)

In contrast to dominance, Bull described *hegemony* as a relationship in which "there is resort to force, but this is not habitual and uninhibited but occasional and reluctant." A power that exercises hegemony prefers not to use force and the threat of it. If it does, it is "with a sense that in doing so it is incurring a political cost." While it is prepared "to violate the rights of sovereignty, equality and independence enjoyed by the lesser states, . . . it does not disregard them: it recognizes that these might exist, and justifies violation of them by appeal to some specific overriding principles." (1977: 215–16.)

In the terms of this distinction the relationship between the Soviet Union and the states of Eastern Europe and that between the United States and Latin America are of a kind that are characterized by hegemony rather than dominance. Both the United States and the Soviet Union are scrupulous in declaring their adherence to the norms of interstate behavior. Whenever they have resorted to some policing action or overtly interfered in the affairs of one or more of the states they influence, they have sought to justify their actions in terms of these norms even though they have violated them. This notion of hegemony, in which there is respect for norms but occasional resort to force when other means fail, helps to distinguish the nature of influence in the relationship between an influencing power and the states it influences from influence in a general sense. But how should *influence* as such be defined?

Influence refers to a relationship between two actors in which the actions or inactions of each have reference to the actions or inactions of the other. In other words, what the one does or does not do is said to be "influenced" by what the other has not done or might or might not do. This definition has the virtue of encompassing both the relationship between influencing powers and between them and the states they influence.

Concerning the relationship between influencing powers, the tacit understanding each has is a matter of reference to each other. A refrains from doing x if A expects B will also refrain from doing y, and each understands this to be the case, and so on. Each understands that the other will refrain from interfering with relations between it and the states it influences and that the one will not attempt to extend political influence in the sphere of the other. It is understood by each that the other will allow it to limit the freedom and independence of states in its sphere of influence, principally by maintaining governments of which it approves and that serve its perceived interests. There is nothing immutable in this interaction. One power could choose to break the rules and thereby cease, for a time, to be influenced in its actions by reference to the other. The implications of such a choice have already been discussed in relation to the question of change. The important point here is again that the nature of the influence exercised in a sphere of influence is intimately connected with the relationship between influencing powers.

The relationship between an influencing power and the states it influences also involves the same reference to each other's actions, with the causal factor inherent in it. Influenced states are neither completely controlled nor without all autonomy. They operate instead with a combination of control and autonomy. The relationship is such that the range of options from which A, as an influenced state, can choose is limited by B, the influencing power. Thus A has autonomy in certain actions beyond which B takes control. The range of options and the point at which B does take control may not be explicit and may only be discovered in the course of action. Further, A's perceptions of what B will tolerate may be as important as any explicit limits set by B. Thus A may simply do x because of what A perceives B might do if A instead does y. In this way A's actions are influenced by and have regard for B in what is a mixture of constraint and autonomy. There is a causal relationship between the actions and inactions of both A and B; autonomy is limited, and while B does not always exercise power over A the possibility of doing so at any time is there and is a determinant of A's actions.

The concept of a sphere of influence tells us no more than this. It is not one that specifies any precise degree of influence or even exactly what form the influence takes except in clear-cut examples such as armed intervention. Within a sphere of influence, economic, political, and military factors all interact as causes for action or inaction, and in determining the amount of autonomy an actor may have and the degree of power one actor can exercise over another.

Influencing powers are able to use armed force against the states they influence. But they need not use or even threaten to use force. The mere existence of the influencing powers' preponderant forces may be enough to produce a controlling effect. In the economic realm the penetration of the influencing power may be so great as to be able to achieve the desired degree of control without any resort or reference to force. And military and economic factors combine to give the influencing power political leverage. They are not, however, the only sources of political leverage. Ideological leadership, whether of the Communist party of the Soviet Union over the ruling parties in Eastern Europe or the more subtle means at the disposal of the United States, is another source.

The concept of a sphere of influence simply does not get beyond this level of generality with regard to the "dominance" of the Soviet Union over Eastern Europe and that of the United States over Latin America. This is partly because the mix of factors in each sphere is different and, moreover, different between specific cases within each of these spheres. Another reason is that the importance of the concept in the practice of contemporary international politics has been as a device that defines specific aspects of relations between powers of comparable status. Spheres of influence are primarily a device for regulating relations between the powers that have them. As a function of these relations the sovereignty and autonomy of influenced states, particularly with regard to foreign policy, are limited. The concept is not more specific.

To explain the relationships that obtain within a sphere of influence, a variety of analytical frameworks could be applied. These include theories of dependency, interdependence, and imperialism. Underpinning some of these theories is often a rejection of the idea that great powers should be accorded any special status or role. Indeed, the role taken by dominant powers is explicitly criticized.

When, on the other hand, the analysis is cast in terms of the relationship between influencing powers, it is one that sits squarely in the traditionalist camp of theorizing about the states system and its institutions in the mold of Martin Wight (1977, 1979) and Hedley Bull (1977). In this scheme great powers, whether acting as influencing powers or otherwise, are accepted as having a special status and role in international society. This role may involve the control and suppression of lesser states. Neither approach stands by itself; both are necessary to comprehension of the reality of international politics.

The problem of comparing spheres of influence is a dual one of comparing conditions within two or more spheres and of comparing influencing powers as such. Within any sphere there is a spectrum of qualitative differences in the influence exercised. Between different spheres there are asymmetries. Common to all spheres of influence is the violation of specific norms of international society. The same norms are violated, with respect to the states they influence, by the Soviet Union and the United States alike. As influencing powers per se, the Soviet Union and the United States both behave alike as great powers. For the Soviet Union, Eastern Europe is a buffer zone standing at an international frontier. The aspirations guiding its dominance over Eastern Europe may be seen as essentially those that guided tsarist Russia. In its actions toward Latin America the United States similarly behaves as a great power. The concept of spheres of influence cannot be said to assist in distinguishing between the dominance of democratic and communist powers. To think that it could would be to ignore its history and role in the theory and practice of international politics.

In conclusion, comparison of the United States and the Soviet Union from the perspective of spheres of influence views the behavior of the two in the same light. Their actions are seen as guided primarily by the imperatives of their position as great powers in an international hierarchy rather than by the ideology each espouses. As great powers, they have common aims that are independent of their form of government. Spheres of influence serve to regulate particular aspects of relations between them. Concerning these spheres, they mutually influence each other's behavior, and what they allow each other molds the relationship each has with the states it influences. The relationship between the Soviet Union and the United States, as influencing powers, is thus a key to change within their respective spheres. Without reference to the relationship between influencing powers, the concept of spheres of influence as a framework for analysis is incomplete.

6

Sphere-of-Influence Behavior:
A Literature Search and
Methodological Reflections

Gabriel A. Almond

The chapters in this volume seek to explain the similarities and differences in the sphere-of-influence behavior of the superpowers. Broadly speaking, these behaviors may be influenced by (1) the domestic characteristics of the superpowers, (2) the characteristics of the dominated countries, and (3) the larger conditions in the international environment. This chapter is primarily concerned with the first of these explanatory variables, the characteristics of the hegemonic powers as they appear to affect their sphere-of-influence policies. The first part of the chapter is a search of the literature on (1) the relationship between type of regime and foreign and defense policy, in the classical tradition of political theory, (2) a search of the literature on domestic constraints on U.S. and USSR foreign and defense policy, and (3) a discussion of the literature dealing directly with U.S. and USSR sphere-of-influence policies. In the second part of the chapter I turn to a discussion of the methodological issues that arise in comparing Soviet and American sphere-of-influence behavior.

Politics and Foreign Policy in the History of Political Theory

This brief and selective search of the literature dealing with regime type and foreign policy begins with the consequences of political and governmental characteristics for foreign policy in general and then focuses more sharply on sphere-of-influence comparisons. The earliest known comment on the relationship between regime type and foreign policy, by the Greek historian Thucydides, writing in the fifth century B.C., strikes an extraordinarily modern note. In his report of Pericles' funeral oration after the Chalcidean defeat he imputes these words to the Greek statesman: "We throw open our city to the world, and never by alien acts exclude foreigners from any opportunity of learning or observing, although the eyes of an enemy may occasionally profit by our liberality." (1982, 109.) Thus Pericles represents as a virtue what later writers such as Tocqueville and Bryce cite as weaknesses in the foreign policy-making of democracies.

In a later oration there occurs the greatest celebration of democratic imperialism to be found in the literature, and this after a series of Athenian defeats.

> Remember, too, that if your country has the greatest name in all the world, it is because she never bent before disaster, and because she has expended more life and effort in war than any other city, and has won for herself a power greater than any hitherto known . . . should we ever be forced to yield, still it will be remembered that we held rule over more Hellenes than any other Hellenic state, that we sustained the greatest wars against their united or separate powers, and inhabited a city unrivalled by any other in resources or magnitude. (1982, 124.)

Aristotle, lecturing in the fourth century B.C., makes a number of subtle discriminations among regime types and their influences on foreign policy. He points out that a tyranny cannot afford to relax. It must maintain a high rate of activity, such as pyramid or temple building, to keep its population busy. This same need for keeping people busy and out of mischief "makes tyrants war mongers, with the object of keeping their subjects constantly occupied and continually in need of a leader." (1975, 245.) In certain monarchic polities such as Sparta and Crete "the system of education and most of the laws are framed with a general view to war." (285.) Aristotle makes the case for culture or ideology as determining foreign policy propensities regardless of regime, with the possible exception of tyrannies where there is a built-in need for action and expansion. Thus, he points out, "There are some who dislike the exercise of authority over neighboring states. They regard it as the height of injustice when the authority is despotic; they still regard it as a hindrance to one's own well-being . . . when the authority is constitutional." On the other hand, there are those who "argue that the despotic and tyrannical form of constitution is the only one that gives felicity, and indeed there are states where the exercise of despotic authority over neighboring states is made the standard to which both constitution and laws must conform." (284.)

Machiavelli might be advising the Soviet Politburo on how to maintain control of conquered countries when he points out that there are three ways of governing defeated countries: (1) laying them waste, (2) colonizing them and occupying them militarily, and (3) setting up a friendly dependent government. For conquered republics with some experience of liberty "there is greater life, greater hatred, and more desire for vengeance; they do not and cannot cast aside the memory of their ancient liberty, so that the surest way is either to lay them waste, or reside in them. (1940.) And as Machiavelli suggests, the most extreme measures have been required in those countries with an experience of national independence and/or political liberty.

Machiavelli's *Prince, Discourses on Livy*, and *The Histories of Florence* are full of aphorisms and prescriptions drawn from historical experience — classical and European. He distinguishes between popular republics, monarchies, and tyrannies in their international behavior. Thus he argues that republics are more reliable observers of treaties than principalities, if only because their deliberative processes are slower. But in addition, questions of creditworthiness are likely to be raised in these deliberative processes. Machiavelli counsels against intervening in the internal conflicts of other countries, on the grounds that it might unite the internal antagonists. He points out that republics may expand in three ways: (1) by confederating, as in Tuscany and Switzerland; (2) by subjugating neighboring states, as in the case of Sparta and Athens; and (3) by associating with neighboring states but retaining sovereignty and central power, as Rome did. He recommends the Roman strategy for outwardly mobile republics.

In Books IX and X of Montesquieu's *The Spirit of Laws* (1977) the

French philosopher writes about the international defensive and offensive tendencies of different types of regimes. The most successful defensive strategy for republics is confederation, as manifested in the Greek and Italian city-states. For monarchies the building of fortresses is the best stratagem. "Fortresses are proper for monarchies; despotic governments are afraid of them. They dare not intrust them to anybody for there is no one that has a love for the prince and his government." (186.) With regard to offensive strategies Montesquieu cautions against expansion by conquest for both republics and monarchies. They may attain a size that they are unable to defend effectively. Conquest is more suitable to tyrannies; the tyrant secures control by maintaining a central military force to be deployed against any peripheral mutiny.

Montesquieu also advises conquerors to avoid unnecessary interference in the affairs of dominated countries: "It is not sufficient in those conquests to let the conquered nation enjoy their own laws; it is perhaps more necessary to leave them also their own manners, because people generally know, love, and defend their manners better than their laws." He cites the counterexample of the French, "who have been driven nine times out of Italy, because, as historians say, of their insolent familiarities with the fair sex. It is too much for a nation to be obliged to bear not only with the pride of conquerors, but with their incontinence and indiscretion; these are without doubt, most grievous and intolerable, as they are the source of infinite outrages." (194.)

Thus the theme of comparative foreign policy has something of a history. Indeed, it is as old as the discipline itself. Whenever scholars have speculated about varieties of governments they have tended to pose the question of how different types of regimes carry on war and diplomacy. In more recent times Tocqueville (1945), reflecting on American popular disorders at the time of the French Revolution, took a categorical position on the incompetence of democracies in the conduct of foreign affairs.

> I have no hesitation in avowing my convictions, that it is most especially in the conduct of foreign relations, that democratic governments appear to me to be decidedly inferior to governments carried on upon different principles. . . . Good sense may suffice to direct the ordinary course of society; and among people whose education has been provided for, the advantages of democratic liberty in the internal affairs of the country may more than compensate for the evils inherent in a democratic government. But such is not always the case in the mutual relations of foreign

nations ... a democracy is unable to regulate the details of an important undertaking, to persevere in a design, and to work out its execution in the presence of serious obstacles. It cannot combine its measures with secrecy, and will not await their consequences with patience. These are qualities which more especially belong to an individual or to an aristocracy; and they are precisely the means by which an individual people attains a predominant position. (234.)

But Tocqueville supports this sweeping judgment on the basis of the American case alone. The traditional view of comparative theory has been much more circumspect about the relation between regime type and foreign policy. James Bryce, writing in the immediate aftermath of World War I, took a qualified view of the foreign policy competence of democracy. Writing his chapter on "Democracy and Foreign Policy" on the eve of the 1918 armistice, Bryce pays special attention to the issue of secrecy—the classic weakness attributed to democratic foreign policy-making. He acknowledges that oligarchies do better at engaging in secret diplomacy; but in the depths of the Great War, he asks, to what effect? The issue, as he puts it, is not that oligarchies are better-organized for foreign policy-making than democracies. The breakdown of diplomacy in 1914, and the sordid set of secret agreements among the two alliances then coming to light, had discredited this central argument of Tocqueville and others. The question for Bryce was whether democracies could do better than oligarchies. The solution he reaches is a compromise between oligarchic and democratic arrangements. The specialists and the professionals of the executive branch ought to have the primary responsibility for implementing foreign policy, while the legislative branch, more representative of popular will, ought to have a major responsibility in setting the goals of foreign policy. And here the excitability of the public and its legislative representatives may be mitigated by the formation of foreign policy committees in parliaments that would ensure a modicum of professionalism in the popular branch. (1921, chap. 5.)

Domestic Constraints on Foreign Policy: The United States and Western Europe

The period since World War II has seen major research efforts on the foreign policy behavior of the two superpowers. Recollection of American isolationism after World War I raised speculation about the stability of U.S. commitments in the post-World War II era. Thus a substantial literature treating various aspects of the American political process as they affected foreign policy began to appear in the 1950s and has continued as a major research topic ever since. These writings in the earlier postwar decades included a study of Congress and foreign policy by Dahl (1950); a study of public opinion and foreign policy by Almond (1950); studies of the foreign policy-making process, the press and foreign policy, and the bureaucracy and foreign policy by Bernard Cohen (1957, 1963); and studies of the attentive public and leadership and foreign policy by Rosenau (1968, 1963).

In the late 1960s and 1970s a more sophisticated literature began to appear dealing with the American political process and foreign policy. One of the most distinguished products of this research was the Bauer, Pool, and Dexter study of interest groups, public opinion, and the process of foreign economic policy-making in the United States. (1964.) Even more significant in its methodological impact was Graham Allison's study of the Cuban missile crisis. The innovation in this study, employment of a deliberate policy-process model-fitting procedure in the analysis of a specific case, has been widely adopted in other foreign policy studies and in political studies more generally. (1971.)

There have been two major comparative foreign policy studies in recent decades. The pioneering study, made by Kenneth Waltz, compared British and American foreign policy-making processes and their effectiveness in the period from 1945 to 1965. (1967.) After examining British and American governmental structure, party organization, foreign policy ideology, executive-legislative relations, and public opinion, he reached the conclusion that the American foreign policy process was superior to the British in facilitating the early identification of problems, since it provided for "the pragmatic quest for solutions, the ready confrontation of dangers, the willing expenditure of energies, and the open criticism of policies." (307–8.) This observation was made at the high point of American foreign policy effectiveness — the mid-1960s. The substantial literature that has appeared in the period since 1965 has reported a steady attrition in American foreign policy effectiveness — a decentralization and fragmentation of foreign policy power and a breakdown of foreign policy consensus. (Mueller, 1973; Spanier, 1981.)

More recently the theme of the domestic constraints on foreign economic policy was treated comparatively in a symposium edited by Peter Katzenstein with a number of collaborators who contributed papers describing foreign economic policy-making in the United States,

Britain, Japan, West Germany, Italy, and France during the declining phase of American international hegemony. (1977.) Using a more specific and limited dependent variable, foreign economic policy, and a common international stimulus, the oil crisis, the authors more sharply delineate the differences in the political processes of the major industrial powers and clearly relate politics to policy. The project identified three distinct patterns of foreign economic policy and policy-making processes. "Policy makers in America and Britain, subscribing to the principles of a liberal international economic order, have at their disposal policy instruments which only indirectly affect particular sectors and firms. Japanese policy makers aim for a high rate of growth; they can command selective policy instruments which have a direct impact on particular sectors and firms. The three states on the European continent, finally, mix elements of Anglo-Saxon liberalism and Japanese neo-mercantilism in a third, hybrid pattern." (298.) The principle concern of the six country studies included in this book is the impact of these institutional and cultural characteristics on international economic growth and stability.

But by far the most illuminating and balanced theoretical contribution to the literature on the interaction of domestic and international affairs is the essay of Peter Gourevitch, "The Second Image Reversed: The International Sources of Domestic Politics." (1978.) In the section of that essay in which he deals with the relationship between domestic structures and the international system, he quickly reviews the variety of structures emphasized by the contributions to the literature—the character of the bureaucracy, the characteristics of public opinion, the operational codes and perceptual sets of the leaders, the structure of the economy, the character of domestic coalitions, and the like. Running through all this literature is a tendency, he argues, to "focus on process and institutional arrangement divorced from politics; on structure in the sense of procedures, separate from the groups and interests which work through politics; on the formal properties of relationships among groups, rather than the content of the relations among them; on the character of decisions (consistency, coherence, etc.) rather than the content of decisions. Somehow politics disappears." Gourevitch then proceeds to make the case that the substance of issues must be taken into account as a separate explanatory variable, that the substance of issues may override structural differences of the most striking sort, that, in other words, the explanatory power of structure ought not be exaggerated. (901ff.) As proof, he shows that the prominent structural differences in the political systems of Germany, Britain,

France, and the United States cannot explain the similarities and differences in their policy responses to the world depressions of the 1870s and 1880s. Similarly, structural differences cannot explain the policy responses of these same powers to the world depression of the 1930s. Thus he criticizes the emphasis in the Katzenstein symposium on the "strong-state weak-state" explanation of differences in foreign economic policy. Indeed, it would seem that Gourevitch is following the lead set by Dahl and Lowi in the 1960s when they argued that political structure is a universe of policy decisions stratified by the nature of the issues. (Dahl, 1961; Lowi, 1964.)

Domestic Constraints: The USSR

Though Gourevitch's work on the interaction of international and domestic affairs is rich in historical case material, he draws essentially from Western European and American political-economic historical experience. He does not include the Soviet case in his comparisons. The literature dealing with the domestic constraints on Soviet foreign policy is quite substantial, though not as large as that which deals with American foreign policy. It has become increasingly self-conscious methodologically. Most of the models generated in the political science of the last decades, and particularly in American studies, were applied in the analysis of Soviet political and foreign policy behavior. Thus in the middle 1960s Frederick Barghoorn (1966) applied structural functional theory to the analysis of Soviet politics and policy. Skilling (1971, 1983), Rigby (1972), Hough (1983), Groth (1979), White (1978), and many others applied and tested interest group theory as it related to Soviet politics in a creative polemic in the 1970s and 1980s.

The bureaucratic politics model of Graham Allison was applied with great effect to communist political studies, including an exchange between Karen Dawisha, Graham Allison, Fred Eidlin, and Jiri Valenta (1980), and works by Paul Cocks (1979) and Jerry Hough (1973). Political development models were applied notably in the work of Jan Triska and Paul Cocks (1977). The patron-client and corporatism models were applied in the work of John P. Willerton (1978), T. H. Rigby (1983), and others.

While most of these studies have dealt with Soviet and communist policy-making processes in general terms, some of them have focused specifically on foreign and defense policy, notably studies by Triska and Finley (1968) and Erik Hoffman and Frederic J. Fleron (1971). Triska and Finley's pioneer study of Soviet foreign policy was the first full elaboration of the structure, process, and substance of the foreign and security policy of the USSR. Seweryn Bialer has published a symposium dealing specifically with domestic constraints on Soviet foreign and defense policy (1981). This collection of papers reflects the increased rigor and conceptual sophistication in communism studies resulting from this two-decade creative interaction of social science theories and models and Soviet and East European area studies. Alexander Dallin (1985), in an excellent essay, summarizes the evidence and speculation produced by this research program and provides us with a listing and weighting of domestic factors influencing Soviet foreign policy.

Dallin tells us that (1) Over time specifically Russian cultural patterns have diminished in weight as such explanatory variables as modernization have affected Russian attitudes and behavior. (2) He argues that Soviet ideology has been of decreasing operational weight.

> What remains, it appears, is part ritual and part composite mindsets, which must be plumbed individually to determine what role ideology plays. (3) In the societal sphere, public opinion, mood, and values have typically been a passive constraint on policymakers. Even if they are increasing (as they appear to be) their role remains secondary at best. (4) The political dimensions have all gained in weight over time. In the post-Stalin era this has been true of elite politics, bureaucratic politics, group politics, and coalition politics. The role of experts as advisers and consultants has likewise been on the increase, as has the role of the military. (5) The weight of the geographic, territorial environment has tended to decline in the age of television, jet flights, and space exploration. Economic considerations constitute increasingly important constraints on foreign and defense policy. (6) As for the role of personalities, the relative weight of the individual . . . (as against group or institutional variables) tends to be less in our era of "collective leadership." (380–81.)

Dallin describes most of these trends as aspects of the larger modernizing processes of "secularization, bureaucratization, the growing role of specialists, and an increasing awareness of resource problems," trends shared by other modern countries including the United States. (381.) In his concluding paragraphs Dallin stresses the importance of introducing an explicit comparative perspective. Such comparative work, he argues, should focus on the interplay between external and internal bargaining and postures. He particularly emphasizes the importance of investigating the possibilities and realities of "tacit" or "latent coalitions between adversaries." (382.)

Comparative Research on U.S.-USSR Foreign Policy Behavior

The literature so far reviewed includes the treatment of the domestic sources of foreign policy in classical political theory, and the "inner-outer" relationship in U.S. and Soviet foreign policy examined individually. There are at least three works that make explicit, systematic comparisons of American and Soviet foreign policy, and one of them focuses specifically on comparative sphere-of-influence behavior. These are Zbigniew Brzezinski and Samuel Huntington's trailbreaking study, *Political Power USA/USSR* (1964); Christer Jonsson's *Superpower* (1984); and Edy Kaufman's *The Superpowers* (1976).

A chapter in the Brzezinski and Huntington book contrasts the intervention behavior of the United States and the Soviet Union, respectively, in Cuba and Hungary and their efforts at alliance management with France and China. Thus we have a sphere-of-influence contrast and a diplomacy contrast. Brzezinski and Huntington attribute equal importance to ideological and political structural factors in explaining the differences in intervention behavior of the superpowers in Cuba and Hungary. They point out that the Soviet Union had no problems with the use of force in Hungary since their ideology justifies the use of force in the attainment and maintenance of "Socialist power." On the other hand, the use of force in foreign affairs by the United States is inhibited by moral and legal considerations. In the Bay of Pigs situation the use of American air power to avoid failure encountered a legal-moral boundary that John F. Kennedy was unwilling to cross.

From the structural perspective two factors contributed to the American failure, while their absence on the Soviet side explains the Hungarian success. Given the turnover in American foreign policy leadership deriving from a system of democratic elections, the United States confronted the plans for the Cuban invasion with a new and inexperienced team. The Russian team in the Hungarian case had had decades of experience in foreign policy decision-making. The third factor explaining the U.S. failure and the Soviet success was the contrast between the open and closed character of the American and Soviet political processes.

> Soviet society did not inhibit action on the part of the leaders, while the fear that a Hungarian type of revisionism might spread

to the USSR acted as a spur on the communist regime to destroy the danger quickly. Furthermore, the closed character of that society made it possible for the leaders to weigh alternative policies in the secrecy of the inner sanctum. By the same token, the openness of the American society forced a public discussion of the issue at almost every stage, led to press reports concerning preparations for the invasion, and thus made calm assessment of the situation all the more difficult. The American policy-makers were exposed to the conflicting pulls of the American society—its sense of impatience with international problems, its belief in American supremacy, its willingness to acknowledge that many Latin Americans may genuinely dislike the United States, its desire to remove the "Cuban cancer" in one clean sweep, and at the same time its fear of war, its unwillingness to let "American boys" be involved (especially in a protracted counter-guerrilla activity which might have followed Castro's fall), its underlying conservatism, which would have impeded the necessary reforms in Cuba. All this complicated the response: on the one hand it made impossible the abandonment of the Cuban venture and on the other it encouraged strong reservations and imposed such limits that it prejudiced the outcome. Thus in both cases the respective natures of the political systems in large measure shaped the destiny of the two interventions. (383ff.)

In the case of contrasting alliance behavior between the United States vis-à-vis France within the framework of NATO and the USSR vis-à-vis China in the communist orbit, ideological and political cultural differences again produced contrasting results. It was possible to contain the disagreements between the United States and France within the context of a pragmatic adaptive alliance culture, while the USSR-China disagreement occurred in an ideological context that was principled and dichotomous. From the structural perspective, both the United States and France had leaderships with a long pattern of past cooperation. There were voices on both sides to ease the tensions and explore common ground. In the case of the USSR and China "there was simply no 'Sino-Soviet Establishment' to plead the cause of unity and to moderate the increasingly immoderate language of the debate. Any effort to compensate for this handicap through approaches to individual leaders was inescapably construed as an intrigue, and, in fact, neither leadership had any alternative except intrigue. But this, in turn, further intensified the hostility. . . ." (405.)

The character of the debate in the two cases also affected the outcome. In the case of the United States and France the open pluralistic political process spelled out a greater variety of options and their costs and benefits, while in the USSR-China case the covert character of the interaction contributed to the polarization of the two sides. Brzezinski and Huntington conclude from this comparison of American and Soviet foreign policy behavior that

> factors peculiar to the American and the Soviet political systems were of decisive importance in shaping the character of the two disputes, in delaying adequate responses, and in aggravating the misunderstandings with allies. The same factors, however, allowed a gradual containment of the dispute in the Franco-American case, while they pushed the Sino-Soviet relationship into a spiraling hostility. Analysis of the two interventions and of the two alliances suggests that the Soviet system is better suited for dealing with enemies and that the American system is more effective in coping with friends. (407.)

In their emphasis on ideological as well as structural factors, Brzezinski and Huntington seem to agree with Gourevitch in stressing the importance of ideology and issues, as well as characteristics of political structure, in determining public policy. They seem to be at issue with Dallin on the importance of ideology. But almost two decades separate the Brzezinski and Huntington and the Dallin contributions, and the Dallin view might correspond more closely to reality.

In a more recent study Christer Jonsson (1984) compares the foreign policies of the United States and the Soviet Union and concludes

> More specifically, the Soviet Union has tended to emulate American behavior in its ambition to enact the "superpower role" and acquire equal status with the United States. Soviet-American congruence in role conceptions has, in turn, tended to reinforce and amplify those background factors which portend parallel behavior. In particular, historical, ideological, and bureaucratic factors interact to produce similar foreign policy outlooks and groupings. These similarities notwithstanding, significant dissimilarities can be discerned in American and Soviet foreign policy which are associated with power asymmetries. Differences in capabilities and socioeconomic systems, in combination with differential impacts of changes in the international system, make for Soviet inferiority in comparison with the United States, with respect to potential lever-

age around the world. These power differentials have, in turn, contributed to the failure to establish any effective superpower condominium. (222.)

Jonsson supports these observations on the superpowers' similarities and differences with an analysis of American and Soviet behavior in three issue areas—foreign aid, crisis management in the Middle East, and nuclear nonproliferation—which seems to confirm his downplaying of ideological and political differences and his emphasis on economic capabilities. Had he included sphere-of-influence behavior, his argument would have been more difficult to sustain, as is suggested by the essays in this volume and other works dealing with the politics and ideology of American and Soviet foreign policy. (Bialer, 1976.)

The Israeli political scientist Edy Kaufman presents us with the most comprehensive treatment of the United States–USSR sphere-of-influence comparison. He brings the expertise of an international relations scholar to the analysis of the interaction of the hegemons and spheres of influence in the larger world setting. Along with Huntington and Brzezinski he stresses the importance of political structure and ideology in determining hegemon behavior, although he does not refer to this earlier work. He points out that "A major explanation accounting for the differences is to be found in the distinctive internal political structure and ideology of each of the superpowers. State control of the economy and totalitarianism, private transnational enterprise in an oligopolistic market, respect for civil rights and opposition are important aspects for determining the type of dominance relationship." (Kaufman, 1976.) The differences among the conclusions of Brzezinski and Huntington, Jonsson, and Kaufman show how crucial is the substance of issues in explaining differences and similarities in Soviet and American behavior. Only a careful case study procedure, as is followed in the present book, can bring to light the importance of situation, issue area, and other variables in the explanation of Soviet and American foreign policy.

Methodological Issues in the Comparison of Soviet and U.S. Sphere-of-Influence Behavior

While much has been written about the domestic sources of Soviet and American foreign policy behavior, with increasingly similar methodologies and frameworks, there has been very little systematic empirical comparison of the two. Neither the Soviet and communism specialists, on the one hand, nor the Latin Americanists, on the other, have considered it sufficiently important to invest substantial resources in comparing the sphere-of-influence behavior of the two superpowers. Contributions to this volume represent the first major systematic effort to make such comparisons.

Why should this be so? How may we explain what appears to be an intellectual lag? The phenomenon of two dominant and conflicting powers relating themselves differently to their spheres of influence seems to be an obvious topic of interest for scholars—of interest for the general theory of types of political regimes as well as essential in the evaluation of the performance of regimes. Surely, Soviet behavior in Eastern Europe and American behavior in Latin America are among the most salient foreign policy issues confronting the American public, and in the present ideological division of the world every informed layman is constantly making comparisons.

There are two major reasons for the scholarly neglect of this subject: (1) the limitations of area-related skills and (2) ideology. For obvious reasons scholars specialize by areas. It is the rare scholar who is trained in both Slavic and Latin American languages, cultures, and histories. Empirical comparative work is normally intra-area—among European communist countries, European-American democratic capitalist countries, Latin American countries, African countries, and the like. At this regional-cultural level the skill problem is more manageable, and the methodological problems are more readily controlled. It takes a major investment of resources to mobilize an undertaking such as the present one—to bring together the appropriate talents and skills and to confront the methodological problems in such a cross-area, cross-ideological comparison.

But the problem calls for more than simply identifying and mobilizing intellectual resources. Cross-ideological comparison involves methodological and even metamethodological issues of some complexity. And there is a serious asymmetry here. What little empirical comparison has been done has come almost entirely from the Eastern European side, or from students of international relations. Thus, for example, the Soviet and IR specialist William Zimmerman made a preliminary comparison of Eastern Europe and Latin America in terms of the principal doctrines of dependency theory, which associates the capitalist-dependent relationship with inequality, penetration, exploitation, and trade dependence. (1978.) Zimmerman argues that dependency theory's emphasis on the causal role of capitalism does not hold up in a comparison with socialist "dependency." He concludes "To the extent that conditions which dependency theorists have ascribed to relationships between developed and less developed capitalist states are actually observed, this preliminary inquiry suggests that they are to be found as often, and to an even greater degree, in the Soviet–East European regional system." (621.) Cal Clark and Donna Bahry, both Eastern European specialists, more recently have made a similar comparison of capitalist and socialist dependency, arguing that repression and exploitation are more political on the socialist side and more economic on the capitalist side. (1983a.) It seems that the only Latin Americanist to bridge the ideological-comparative gap is James Lee Ray, who sought to operationalize quantitative indicators of "dependency pathologies" in Latin America and Eastern Europe. His findings on economic performance and political compliance in the two areas suggest that dependency theory cannot explain the important differences "between the foreign policies of capitalist and socialist states." (1981, 133.)

While the communism specialists have engaged in explicit empirical comparisons of the two dominance systems in only a very limited way, they have no methodological rule advising against making such comparisons. The Latin Americanists of the dependency school not only avoid such comparisons, but they explicitly rule against them. The leading dependency authority, Fernando Henriques Cardoso, disposes of the problem in the following language: "Although there are forms of dependent relationships between socialist countries, the structural context that permits an understanding of these is quite different from that within capitalist countries and requires specific analyses." (1979, xxiv.)

This statement seems to be the sole specific reference to this question in the dependency literature, and it appears only in the preface to the English language edition. But it has been accepted virtually without exception by dependency writers. What can we make of such an unelaborated advice of avoidance? What metamethodological logic lies behind it? At the risk of putting words into the mouths of Cardoso and the dependency writers, let me suggest the following. The dependency approach is an application of a number of Marxist-Leninist propositions primarily to the North American–Latin American relationship. If one follows this theoretical framework, then, indeed, the comparison of similar-looking dominance phenomena might be misleading. Thus, for example, capital or trade flows that might on the surface seem to be biased in favor of the Soviet Union cannot be compared with the flows of capital, profits, commodities, and services between a dominant capitalist power and a dependent Third World country. In the first case the bias contributes to the strengthening and growth of socialism at the center, which ultimately redounds to the benefit of the socialist community as a whole. One ought not compare the Soviet, Eastern bloc, or Cuban military dispositions in Eastern European or Third World countries with American military dispositions in foreign countries. Soviet, Eastern bloc, and Cuban troops in foreign countries are there to support the revolutionary socialist aspirations and accomplishments of the peasants and workers. American troops are in Asia and Europe, on the other hand, to prevent the inevitable transformation of these societies into socialist commonwealths. Or finally, one cannot compare the political institutions of the dependent countries of Eastern Europe and Latin America since these political institutions have fundamentally different functions. In the Eastern Europe case, socialist parties, representing the real interests of the working and peasant classes, preside over a process of progressive development, while in the Latin American area bureaucratic authoritarian regimes, or capitalist-democratic ones, maintain order through repression in the interest of a steady flow of profits to the capitalist center.

Lurking behind this argument of noncomparability is Marxist historicism. To compare capitalist with socialist phenomena is to compare systems at different stages of dialectical time. Facts, numbers, and institutions, superficially similar, mean different things when they occur in the backward rather than the progressive parts of the world historical process. This may be the logic behind the Cardoso warning and behind the neglect of the Soviet example in the dependency literature.

But surely we cannot let the matter rest with Cardoso's caveat. If the dependent relationships between socialist countries have a significantly different structural context than that which obtains in capitalist dependency, then Cardoso and his colleagues owe us some elaboration of this methodological point. Mainstream social science scholarship has been wrestling with problems of comparability for a long time. The problem of functional equivalence is almost an obsession with Giovanni Sartori when he criticizes conceptual stretching, straining, and "travelling" in our comparative studies. (1971.) Przeworski and Teune's *Logic of Comparative Social Inquiry* deals with the equivalence fallacy problem in the most detailed and rigorous way. (1970.) Dogan and Pelassy's recent contribution to the methodology of comparison is full of warning to avoid confusing superficially similar but basically unlike phenomena with one another. (1984.)

It is clear that the dependency writers have not made a case for noncomparability, and they have left to the rest of us the problem of elaborating just what the methodological issues are and how they may best be confronted. It may be useful to spell out, even at the risk of being obvious, what the purposes of comparison are. At the most elementary level comparison is the essence of knowledge. None of us could put one foot in front of another without making descriptive comparisons. Knowledge in a fundamental sense rests on discrimination, descrying differences and similarities. The clichéd prohibition against comparing apples and oranges does not apply to comparison in this descriptive sense. We constantly compare apples, oranges, and other fruits. The apples-and-oranges caveat applies to explanatory comparison, which we shall discuss below.

No one would challenge the possibility of descriptively comparing hegemons and their interaction with their spheres of influence. Surely the hegemons may be compared descriptively one with the other in terms of population and natural resources, ethnic composition and distribution, religious composition and distribution, aspects of the economy such as per capita GNP over time, the composition of GNP, the composition of the labor force, the distribution of wealth and income, and aspects of the political system such as centralization of power, separation of power, independence of the judiciary, freedom of party organization and voluntary association, and communications and press freedom. Surely, descriptive data are available on all these items and on the histories of the hegemons in these and other respects.

Similarly, it is possible to get descriptive data on the characteristics of the dominated countries in Eastern Europe and Latin America. For each one of these countries one could acquire the same kinds of data as for the hegemons—size, population, resources, economic and political characteristics, historical background, and their relations with one another.

It is also possible to describe the larger international settings that constrain the hegemon—sphere-of-interest relationships—the state of the world economy, military deployments and actions, the state of world opinion, and the like.

Finally, it is possible to descriptively compare the flows of interaction between the hegemons and their spheres of influence: the extent of penetration into the political and economic structure of the subordinate countries, the extent and character of military penetration, diplomatic bullying or cajoling, media penetration, and so on. An enormous amount of descriptive information is available, making possible a great many descriptive comparisons—so much of this on the Soviet–Eastern European side versus so much of that on the U.S.–Latin American side. Some of these descriptive data are reported in the works cited above.

These descriptive comparisons make possible first-level evaluative comparisons depending on how the various phenomena are weighted —in other words, the weight one places on economic freedom, security, and equality; freedom of organization, movement, and publication; occupational choice and physical mobility; physical safety; human dignity; and the like. The descriptive data may be combined and used as indicators of these values. We should have no problems spelling out how the two systems compare with each other according to these indicators, insofar as data are available, as long as we avoid attributing any objective validity to our own value weightings or to those of particular political and ideological movements.

The comparative analysis runs into trouble when it moves into the explanatory mode, where the apples-and-oranges dictum applies. If we concern ourselves not only with the problem of describing differences and similarities and judging them according to weighted values, but also with the problem of explaining these differences and similarities, then we run into difficulties. When we speak of the "comparative method" it is this explanatory kind of comparison that we mean. We compare things in order to derive some general proposition about a relationship, and this proposition "explains" the relationship. In its simplest form as formulated by John Stuart Mill, if two similar events (let us say revolutions) are preceded by two similar sets of conditions (let us say the breakdown of state authority), everything else remaining equal, then we can defend the hypothesis that revolutions are preceded by breakdowns of state authority. If in addition we find that there are no cases in which revolutions are not preceded by the breakdown of state authority, then our explanation has gained in power. Skocpol describes this Millsian methodological doctrine neatly in her *State and Revolutions*. (1979.)

In other words, when we move beyond descriptive comparison —the what and the how—to explanatory comparison—the why —then we have to proceed with care, matching independent variable(s) in case 1 with independent variable(s) in case 2 and dependent ones with the dependent ones in both cases, holding everything else constant to the extent that this is possible. This is the comparative method in the sense of scientific explanation.

Before turning to the logic of such a comparative explanatory effort, it may be relevant to review the dependency theorists' effort to explain the American half of this hegemon–sphere-of-influence relationship. The dependency writers have generated three predictions from the application of Marxist-Leninist propositions to the North America–Latin America relationship.

(1) The first prediction is that, given the inherently exploitative nature of advanced capitalism, the net effect of economic interaction would be to stunt the economic growth of the dependent countries and to accentuate the inequalities among social classes.

(2) With the disconfirmation of the growth prediction, if not the prediction on inequality, a second economic prediction was that what growth occurred in the dependent countries would be distorted growth (i.e., not an optimal growth pattern from the point of view of *dependencia* needs); and that any growth would redound to the benefit of the capitalist classes in the core and peripheral countries.

(3) A third prediction was that the development of dependent capitalism would inevitably require bureaucratic-authoritarian regimes in order to repress popular resistance to these exploitative patterns.

The record of these predictions is not good. The first one was soon overtaken by the reality of substantial growth in many Latin American and other Third World countries. The second prediction has been neither confirmed nor disconfirmed. In Latin America the record of unequal distribution seems to confirm it. In Asia it has been rather dramatically disconfirmed in successful export-oriented countries such as South Korea, Taiwan, Singapore, and Thailand, where substantial growth has been accompanied by increasing equality. Thus if it is presented as a law, the second prediction has not been confirmed. Development policies in market economies may build in distributive features. The third prediction as to the necessity of bureaucratic authoritarian regimes in Third World development processes has been disconfirmed. Again, the relationship of political and economic development is much too complex to be captured by this dependency formulation.

Observing the rules of mainstream political science and resting all proof on the weight of evidence and the logic of inference, how would we structure the logic of explanation of the hegemon–sphere-of-influence relationship? We are dealing with four interacting sets of variables, as shown in figure 1. In the center box are the sphere-of-influence behaviors of the hegemon — military deployments and actions, diplomatic actions, political actions, economic exchanges, sociocultural penetrations. These are the dependent variables. The independent variables that explain these behaviors are listed in the three boxes surrounding the sphere-of-influence behavior box. At the left are the hegemon characteristics—its political structure, ideology and political culture, economic structure, social structure, and culture. At the right are the sphere-of-influence characteristics—the political structure, ideology and political culture, economic structure, as well as the interactions among the sphere-of-influence countries. Below are the international context characteristics—the diplomatic alliance structure, the military deployment and action structure, the state of the world economy, the state of world opinion.

The independent variables are not of equal weight, and there is a causal directionality in the system. Thus the hegemon characteristics tend to be the dynamic initiators in the system. These characteristics constrain goals pursued by the hegemon. The behaviors in the sphere of influence are the intended means to these goals. Sphere-of-influence characteristics affect the choice of hegemon goals, and the selection of, and emphasis on, the various means. The international environment —diplomatic, military, economic, and ideological—stimulates or constrains the behavior of the hegemon and the sphere-of-influence countries.

The logic of this relationship generates four sets of explanatory hypotheses of hegemon–sphere-of-influence behavior: (1) the international system or strategic hypotheses, (2) political hypotheses, (3) ideological hypotheses, and (4) economic hypotheses.

(1) The strategic hypothesis argues that given very large asymmetries in the power of nation-states in an anarchic world political environment, there is a tendency for the larger powers to dominate and penetrate the smaller contiguous powers. This is a simple power-security model and has some explanatory value, but it surely will not yield our Eastern European and Latin American pattern of penetration and subordination. It explains the direction of influence but not its magnitude, structure, or content. A related strategic hypothesis would hold that given two conflictual hegemons with spheres of influence, there would be an inevitable tendency for each hegemon to seek to enhance its own power-security by penetrating into and encouraging defections within the sphere of influence of the opposing hegemon. While this also has some explanatory power, it cannot generate a Cuban or Nicaraguan defection, on the one hand, or a Czech Spring or Polish Solidarity, on the other.

(2) There are several political structure hypotheses. One that goes back to classic political theory attributes to tyrannies an inherent pro-

Figure I   Logical Structure of Hegemon–Sphere-of-Influence Relationships

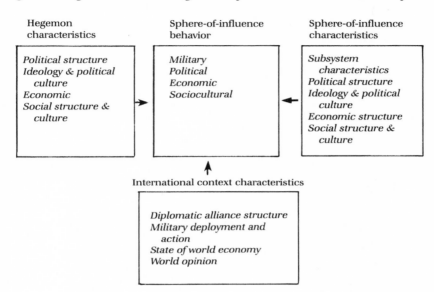

Hegemon characteristics	Sphere-of-influence behavior	Sphere-of-influence characteristics

Political structure
 Ideology & political
   culture
 Economic
 Social structure &
   culture
	Military
	 Political
	 Economic
	 Sociocultural
		Subsystem
		   characteristics
		 Political structure
		 Ideology & political
		   culture
		 Economic structure
		 Social structure &
		   culture

International context characteristics

Diplomatic alliance structure
Military deployment and
   action
State of world economy
World opinion

pensity for mobilization and expansion because of their lack of internal legitimacy. Legitimate monarchies and republics are presumed to be less aggressive. In the form presented by Montesquieu this hypothesis does not seem to hold—there are too many contrary cases. For example, the Athenian, Roman, and British empires were notably aggressive, on the one hand, and authoritarian Turkey and Spain were notably unaggressive, on the other. It is also doubtful that one can sustain Tocqueville's argument of democratic inefficiency and ineffectiveness in foreign and defense policy. Evaluation of the importance of political structure must proceed from the kinds of case studies presented by Brzezinski and Huntington, Christer Jonssen, Edy Kaufman, and notably the present volume in order to generate a more discriminating set of hypotheses regarding the effects of political structure on sphere-of-influence behavior. A centralized and autocratic decision-making process can produce decisions more quickly than a decentralized and democratic one; but a decentralized and pluralistic decision-making process can accommodate more points of view and arrive at compromises more effectively than an autocratic one. The consequences, therefore, would depend on the situation.

It must also be understood that explanations of hegemon–sphere-of-influence interaction based on political structure are two-sided. One has to consider the consequences of different combinations of political structure—heterogeneous combinations in the case of the United States and homogeneous ones in the Soviet case. Here again there do not appear to be simple regularities, and it will be difficult to tease out the political-structure aspects of particular relationships. Finally, the state-society balance has to be considered in formulating political-structure hypotheses. A socialist hegemon in which the economy is dominated by the polity is more likely to follow a political-military-led form of sphere-of-influence penetration than a capitalist hegemon, where the penetration is more likely to be either economy-driven, with political and military penetration dependent on trade and investment, or reactive to threats from the other hegemon.

(3) An ideology-driven theory of hegemon–sphere-of-interest behavior would argue that the assumptions, perceptions, goals, and tactical beliefs of the politically relevant strata of the hegemons would explain their sphere-of-influence behavior. Ideological explanations overlap with political structural ones in that ideologies legitimate political structure; but ideologies may or may not require that sphere-of-influence political structure be identical with or similar to that of the hegemon. One can, of course, argue that there is a propensity for all hegemons to prefer sphere-of-influence political structure to be isomorphic, but this will hardly explain the structural policies followed by the Soviet Union and the United States. The Soviet Union is less inhibited in the use of any and all means necessary to maintain party-dominated political-economic regimes in its sphere of influence, while the United States is ideologically (as well as structurally) more inhibited in the use of force to maintain market economy regimes. One would also have to factor in political cultural explanations of sphere-of-influence resistance to hegemon penetration—the intensity of nationalism, the continued coherence of religious beliefs and organizations, the resistance of social groupings such as workers and peasants.

(4) Finally, there are economy-driven theories of hegemon–sphere-of-influence behavior. We have already presented the early and late version of dependency theory that would apply only to the capitalist part of the comparison. Mainstream economic theories purporting to explain sphere-of-interest behavior include the Kuznets curve hypothesis and its Chenery-Ahluwalia elaborations. Here data on nineteenth-century European economic growth showed a curvilinear pattern, with inequality increasing in the earlier stages of economic development and then

declining once a certain level has been reached. The World Bank study group associated with Hollis Chenery has tested the Kuznets hypothesis on more recent Third World data, spelling out a policy mix (and providing country cases to illustrate it) that might mitigate the trend toward inequality and its political consequences. (1974.) Economy-driven hypotheses also stress the contrasts between the development strategies followed in Latin America and the growth strategies followed in Asia, approaches that have had significant political implications.

This fourfold logic of explanation is unlikely to produce simple, parsimonious theories of hegemon–sphere-of-influence interaction. It is evident that we need strategic, political, ideological-cultural, and economic variables to make sense of Soviet–East European and U.S.–Latin American relationships. But a careful, sequential, model-fitting approach employing an issue-based case study sampling strategy can bring this complex causal structure into relief and lead us to a higher level of understanding and interpretation, as well as to more effective policies dealing with these relationships.

7

On Bargaining

Jeffrey L. Hughes

Great power motivations and mechanisms of influence differ somewhat in their respective spheres of influence, but the dynamics and
resulting dilemmas of strong state–weak state interaction are similar
in important respects. This chapter will explore these dynamics; more
specifically, it will compare U.S. and Soviet bargaining relations with
states in their spheres of influence in Latin America and in Eastern
Europe. The perspective offered here allows a systematic accounting
of the similarities and differences between the spheres. First, I place
the contemporary comparison in perspective by addressing the costs
and benefits inherent in historical variants of predominance-dependency relationships. Second, I develop a generalizable bargaining model
that helps explain the dynamics and variations of strategies in relations between the weak and the strong. It helps make sense of the
varieties of costs and benefits of the historical relations and aids comparisons across the Soviet and U.S. spheres. The framework sets out
conditions for great power control, on the one hand, and weaker
power autonomy, on the other. Illustrative examples will concentrate

on U.S.–Latin American and Soviet–East European relations in the post-World War II period. Third, I then address how great power predominance has changed over time and construct a typology of how different profiles of weaker states affect patterns of diplomacy. The profiles of states that remain complacent dependencies and those that attempt defection can be shown to vary in systematic ways. Finally, I use the implications of the analysis to reflect on the evolving nature of superpower influence in the two regions.

1. Historical Manifestations of Dominance and Dependence Relations

To argue that the superpower spheres are comparable historically and theoretically in a variety of important ways is not to say the spheres must function identically. There may well be different mechanisms for the deliberate exertion of influence in the respective spheres. Kaufman (1976), for example, argues that in general terms, the Soviets' sphere in Eastern Europe has primarily been sustained by political means, while the United States mainly uses economic means to assert its position in Latin America. This difference is implicit in the arguments of critics of each of the superpowers in respect to their particular spheres. Nonetheless, whether one accepts this distinction or not, and irrespective of the intent of either superpower, it is still arguable that each superpower exerts a comparable, major conditioning influence on outcomes in its sphere; each creates a comparable bargaining situation with its neighbors, the dynamics and dilemmas of which are very similar.

Indeed, if one compares each contemporary sphere to historical antecedents of great power systems, it is striking how much the dynamics and consequences of great power–weaker power interactions have in common, despite important changes in the international context. To the extent that the dynamics of each contemporary regional system are also similar to those of their historical precursors, the stronger the case for their own similarity rather than uniqueness. As early as 1948 Soviet expert George Kennan "saw Soviet expansionism as a new form of colonialism, subject to all the frailties, vulnerabilities, and self-destructive tendencies of that earlier phenomenon." (Gaddis, 1978: 194.) It is also intriguing to have an expert on Poland and Eastern Europe argue that "The way the Soviet Union has imposed its domination over Eastern Europe is, in fact, not altogether different from the way Britain ruled colonial India. The direct annexation of the eastern periphery of the region into the USSR makes it resemble those parts of the Indian subcontinent which were run directly from London; while the maintenance of the facade of sovereignty and a degree of actual autonomy in the remaining countries of Eastern Europe comes close to the British doctrine of paramountcy in the various semi-independent Indian states." (Bromke, 1985: 9.) This comparison is particularly significant in that it is usually the U.S. experience as a world power that is compared to the British imperial experience. Thus, some similarities apply over time and across social systems.

The nuclear revolution has not vitiated these comparisons; it has been a technical, not a political, revolution. Niebuhr, in a chapter on "The Two Imperial Nations of Today" in his *The Structure of Nations and Empires* (1959), notes that while "The contest of power between the two alliances and their respective hegemonic powers is involved in an unprecedented situation: the nuclear stalemate. . . . If mankind should have the good fortune to avoid the ultimate and suicidal holocaust, *it will be necessary to turn from the unprecedented factors of our situation, which have naturally preoccupied us, to the perennial and constant factors, which have emerged in all imperial and national rivalries through the ages."* He also suggests that liberalism and Marxism alike are predisposed against analysis of such perennial factors. It is in the spirit of comparison that he later notes, for example, that "it is not wrong to reflect on historical analogies between the monarchical absolutism which gripped Europe only a few centuries ago and the present Russian system," attending to the forces of change and decay in the former to reflect on the latter. (1959: 11–12, 282, emphasis added.)

In the quest for perennial and constant factors, British statesman and scholar George Cornwall Lewis's lucid (1841) *Essay on the Government of Dependencies* is exemplary to develop historical parallels with contemporary relations between great and weaker powers. He was one of the managers of the British empire, but as an analyst he too looked to historical predecessors as far back as Greece and Rome. He examined "the nature of the political relation of supremacy and dependence . . . to develop some of the principal consequences which that relation involves." He conceptualized a dependency as a subordinate government—not to be confounded with a colony—that preserves some of its own laws and institutions, though being exposed to the power of the dominant country either through treaty or conquest (1841: xvi, 156.) Though he wrote in a different epoch, Lewis examined such relationships over a wide range of international history; but besides sections of historical analysis of lasting value, many other portions of his argument have a decidedly contemporary ring. With minor word changes many passages could apply to either contemporary sphere. Of particular value are his chapters separately treating the advantages and the disadvantages repeatedly observed over history in dependency relationships for dominant and dependent powers alike. He states the strongest case for each advantage and disadvantage, while his discussion gives historical examples of why one gets a mixed picture in different time horizons and circumstances.

(a) Ideal-Typical Advantages

In regard to the advantages the dominant country in its relation with a dependency (1841: 120–42) may obtain: the benefit of new fighting forces or a secure position, a source of revenue as a sort of imperial tribute, an advantageously structured trading relationship or place of capital employment, or, failing these, at least a source of prestige. Yet even this enumeration of advantages is developed with countertendencies: the counterpart to security is that dependencies "have furnished incentives to war, and, from their distance and extent have been both difficult and expensive to defend." (130.) In respect to finances: "Even if it be admitted that the dominant country may occasionally derive some temporary benefit from a monopoly of the commerce of the dependency, it may be safely affirmed that a monopoly will, in the long run, be detrimental to those for whose supposed benefit it exists." (132.) A determined effort to monopolize such control ignores the opinion of many dependent people, "wounding them in their feelings, as well as in their economical interests," and "disposes them to throw off their dependent condition on any favorable opportunity for successful revolt." (133.) In regard to prestige Lewis concludes that "if . . . the dependency suffers the evils which . . . are almost inevitable consequences of its political condition, such a possession cannot justly be called glorious." (142.) Such are the "advantages," though Lewis recognizes that states are moved by more than ready-made calculations of interest.*

The advantages that may accrue to the dependent state (1841: 143–46) include the provision of protection and military security at low cost, the protection of its trade, and opportunities for pecuniary assistance or selective favorable trade conditions from the dominant state. It is

*"Thus slow and painful are the advances of human reason, made as it were, by groping in the dark, and retarded at every step by the opposition of short-sighted interest, the listlessness of routine, and the want of confidence of theoretical truths!" (Lewis, 1841: 35–36.)

also possible that the dominant state may bring about an equalizing change in the dependent state's social structure that might not have occurred had the dependent state's elite been more independent. Lewis's assessment of these advantages is no less analytically biting. Protection has to be considered in some sense as an "advantage" because of the weaker state's exposure to aggressions from other states if it had no patron; as a dependency it is "comparatively secure . . . though subject to the evils inherent in its dependent condition." (144.) Having deflated some of the putative advantages of domination, he poses a no less cautionary note to the dependent state's pursuit of autonomy. Any dependent state "too weak to stand by itself, and whose territory possesses advantages rendering it an object of desire to independent states, ought to guard carefully against the natural error of supposing that they will benefit by a change of masters. They ought to remember constantly that they are condemned by natural causes to a state of dependence; that the evils which they suffer under their actual rulers may be inseparable from that condition; and that, though those evils may be partly imputable to the misconduct of their actual rulers, a revolt or defection might transfer them to worse masters, after it exposed them to the evils which are incidental to a political revolution." (144.) This issue and dilemma is no less prominent today than when Lewis expressed it. His analytical consignment of many states to dependency, however, is counterbalanced by his expectation that a dependency will nonetheless continue to rebel, if not revolt, against the dominant state's impositions. He also devotes an entire chapter to more decisive breaks with dependency.

It is not difficult to find examples of the United States or the USSR securing advantages of security positions and leadership prestige in Eastern Europe and Latin America, or favorable relations of trade or investment. There are also instances of dependencies obtaining cheap defense, aid, and subsidization. We will now turn to the many contemporary correspondences to the disadvantages Lewis enumerates in predominance-dependency relations.

(b) Ideal-Typical Disadvantages
Possible disadvantages to the dominant country (1841: 147–50) include increased risks of conflict where efforts to monopolize and defend some dependencies may consolidate rivalries that might otherwise have been moderated; high costs of maintaining control of dependencies, not only in war but during peace; the structured nature of trade

with dependencies that could lead to inefficiencies, and interfere with more fruitful opportunities (for both parties); the possibility of forms of patronage or corruption with respect to relations with the dependency that could lower standards of political morality. Contemporary discussions of whether Eastern Europe is a net liability to the Soviets and the nature of the Latin American debt crisis illustrate the relevance of these points.

The disadvantages to the dependent state (1841: 151–73) include ignorance or indifference on the part of the dominant state about the interests and situation of the dependency; inexpedient interference on the part of the dominant state or failure to involve itself in timely and beneficial ways; and a tendency of the dominant power to try to impose its law, institutions, principles, and language upon the dependency. There is an ineluctable tension between demands on the dependency to apply fundamental principles and laws of the dominant state and their substantive application in the dependency. The dependent state is also subject to the international and domestic vagaries of the dominant power. It necessarily "bears a share, to a greater or less extent, of many of the calamities in which the dominant country may be involved through the errors of its government or from any other cause" in its international policy, while in the event the dependency itself "should happen to excite the attention of the dominant country . . . it is rarely treated . . . with reference to the true interests of the dependency itself, or even of the dominant country as regards the dependency; but it is commonly sacrificed to the temporary interests of the political parties in the dominant country which are contending for the possession of political power." (172, 171.) Lowenthal's analysis (1973) of the United States in the Dominican intervention and Alliance for Progress, and Valenta's analysis (1979a, 1979b) of the Soviet intervention in Czechoslovakia, for example, give Lewis's words a contemporary ring.

Under some circumstances the disadvantages both to the dominant and the dependent state within the relationship may have a reciprocal, cumulative effect. The dominant power may seek security in a world of competing states by forming a sphere of influence; at times, such spheres have moderated great power conflict. (148.) Yet the political or economic disadvantages experienced by dependent states may spur unrest, revolt, or an attempt to throw off their dependence, providing the faultline along which new great power conflict takes place. (149.) In this way, dependencies may be the occasion of insecurity and costs they were intended to forestall. The numerous scholarly scenarios regarding superpower conflict in Europe arising out of disturbances in the GDR or Poland find a counterpart in LaFeber's (1984) "Inevitable Revolutions" taking place in Central America.

(c) Results in Practice

Lewis has a balanced view. Dominant powers may secure advantages in having dependencies, yet they may have to incur increasing costs and risks to sustain them; conversely, there are both disadvantages and advantages to dependencies relative to alternatives that exist in the world as it is rather than as embodied in an ideal of autonomy. It is clear that there is a zero-sum aspect to ideal types: the dominant power's advantages are best expressed through the dependency's disadvantages; and conversely, the dependency's advantages are often registered at the expense of the dominant state. Lewis allows that the interplay between the two countries is critical. He repeatedly notes how results vary significantly on a case-by-case basis. (1841: 123, 143, 151.) The mixture of outcomes reflects compromises. In oversimple terms it reflects a bargaining relationship of punishments and rewards between states, trading advantages on one score for disadvantages on others relative to alternatives. This is particularly true as the world has become more tightly knit than in Lewis's time and the costs of intervention have increased.

The familiarity of Lewis's arguments to those made about contemporary spheres heightens the case for comparability made in chapter 1. His observations about cases other than the superpower spheres examined here provide a backdrop for an analysis that does more than score points for either sphere, but rather roots them both in variants of an historical phenomenon. His arguments indicate the crucial nature of the interplay between dominant and dependent states in producing variations in dependency relations. However, Lewis sets out only the peaks and troughs of these relations without explaining the wide variety of mixtures in the results across dominant-dependent pairs of states.

2. Dynamics and Conditions of Power and Dependence in Spheres of Influence

The very terms "dominant" and "dependent" state imply a marked discrepancy in coercive potential that exists in spheres of influence. There is little doubt that the dominant state could enforce its will by force, though with varying degrees of cost depending on the particular dependent state. Sometimes, of course, dominant states do intervene to sustain their preferred policy line in a dependency. However, this is only a part of the story, and often not the most central part.

The distinction between "fate control" and "behavior control" is important in this regard (Thibaut and Kelley, cited in Singer, 1963). One may be able to decide the fate of another party by exerting force at some cost and risk, without necessarily being able to exert effective day-to-day control over the behavior of that party. There may be a wide range of outcomes that are possible between the dominant state's preferred policy and when it may feel compelled to intervene to control a dependency's fate. Coercion may be an important conditioning factor in the background, but it may be only sporadically important in the politics of dependence. Besides diplomatic persuasion, there are intermediate relations of bargaining through punishments and rewards. The dominant state's threatened punishments to the dependent state raise the potential costs of disagreement, while the rewards it issues lower the costs of agreement on its terms. Nor are such interactions characterized only by material calculations of power. Status and symbols representing other values play an important role, complicating easy deductive calculations of interest alone.*

Peter M. Blau's discussion of "Unilateral Dependence and Obligations" in his *Exchange and Power in Social Life* (1964) suggests a way to conceptualize the complexity of how dominant actors attempt to control behavior of dependents short of outright force, as in fate control. In developing these conditions for dominant control, he also defines the prerequisites for the dependent actor's "autonomy," even if it is only autonomy within the shadow of fate control. Thus, where Lewis's account indicated the repeated consequences of dependency, Blau's arguments show the logic of interaction, and help to explain both the consequences and their variations. While Blau primarily developed his arguments to apply to politics of organizations and individuals within

---

*See Geertz's critique (1980: 121–23, 134–36) of narrow institutional and interest conceptions of state power and argument for the ideational and cultural component in the exertion of power. The empirical case of Bali on which he bases these reflections is also relevant. One set of competing regional lords attempted by virtue of their basin location and resources to control, domesticate, and integrate the upland lords, who in turn sought to retain their independence and to undercut the power of those below them by controlling water runoff. The balance of power dynamics of this case are interesting because they developed in isolation from the rest of the world. (1980: 19–25.) If nineteenth-century Balinese politics manifest some familiar dynamics of power, surely the superpowers manifest even more.

states, he anticipated applying them more widely. (e.g., 1964: chap. 9.) Noted international relations theorists have in fact extended them to great power interactions (Rosecrance, 1981) as well as to great power–Third World relations (Burton, 1972: 79–101).

The general thrust of Blau's arguments deals with the dynamics of power and exchange. Essentially, he presents a conflict theory saying there is a dynamic tendency toward imbalance in social relations. There are tensions between the forces of power competition and exchange integration. On the one hand, competition for power promotes hierarchy and differential control over scarce resources. Hierarchy of power leads to economic exchange. On the other hand, exchange fosters differentiation of success; this may make the services that parties have to offer more unlike and foster exchange, while over time differentiation of success and power may lead to new efforts to compete. Power relations are one-sided and asymmetrical, while more interdependent exchange relations imply a lack of or reduction in power. The benefits of today's power may be the basis for tomorrow's constraint. Granted, the most powerful sometimes can resort to "coercive force, which is the extreme application of negative sanctions" and which may "suppress noxious behavior when all other means for modifying it have failed," but this kind of punishment does not effectively sustain its effect at reasonable cost. Though admittedly it may have a deterrent demonstration effect, "Unless we are in a position to punish the activity every time it appears, it will soon reinstate itself." (1964: 224–26.) "Subjugation by coercive force can hardly be experienced as just, for it offers no compensating advantages for submission. Hence coercion is virtually always resisted and, if possible, actively opposed. But if the power to command services and compliance is derived from the supply of needed benefits, those subject to the power do not necessarily experience their position as disadvantageous, although they may do so." (1964: 228.) Thus reward-based power is more effective, but it may, as noted, undercut its own primacy over time.

The particular facet of Blau's argument relevant here applies to situations where: (1) power is asymmetrical in terms of the net abilities to deliver punishments and rewards; (2) power is recurrently exercised over time; and (3) an element of choice is still retained by the dependent actor despite the severe forms of punishment, either threatened or implicit, for transgressions; voluntarism is reflected in the fact that the punishments are sometimes accepted or brought on. In this context, rewards are not simply gifts, since if the weaker party comes to depend upon them, the threat that they may be revoked carries the weight of punishment. Thus "the threat of punishment, although it exerts the most severe restraints, creates the dependence that is the root of power indirectly, as it were, while recurrent essential rewards that can be withheld do so directly." (1964: 117–18.) These punishments and rewards are not only material in character but involve other social values, e.g., diplomatic recognition and prestige or ostracism and attacks on legitimacy.

Blau's model is particularly useful for comparing the contemporary spheres of influence because it does not allow differences in the nature of economic activity to obscure similarities in the influence process. For example, though it is in some sense significant that the USSR is an exporter of primary products to some of its dependencies and an importer of significant technological goods while the United States is more nearly in the opposite role, when analyzed in terms of the model the resulting influence process in the regions is nonetheless similar in terms of its effects. (See section 4 below on the evolution of types of empire on this point.)

In the form of ideal types Blau (1964: 118–25) states that in a dependency relationship the conditions of power for the dominant actor (A) in respect to dependent actor (B) are (1) indifference to the material benefits B has to offer, (2) monopolization of the "rewards" needed by B, (3) prevention of B's coercive opposition, and (4) representation of the source of relevant values to B. Correspondingly, the conditions of B's independence are (1) possession of strategic resources in respect to A, (2) availability of alternatives to A's rewards, (3) possession of credible coercive ability, and (4) invocation of ideals lessening needs from A. (See table 1.)

In practice, dominant state A's standing varies over time and in respect

Table 1. Summary of Blau conditions of power
and of independence within constraints

Conditions of power (for A):	Conditions enhancing independence (for B):
1. Indifference to benefits from B	1. Possess or represent strategic resources to A
2. Monopoly over what others need	2. Alternatives to A's rewards available elsewhere
3. Prevent coercive opposition	3. Mobilize coercive ability
4. Represent source of relevant values	4. Employ ideals lessening needs

to different dependencies, just as the dependent states present differing profiles on the conditions of relative autonomy or independence. We will address a variety of characteristic interactions below. First, however, the meaning of each of Blau's (a) conditions for power, on the one hand, and (b) the corresponding conditions enhancing independence, on the other, will be developed separately. Brief examples from each sphere will help illustrate the points; however, one cannot infer too much from the relative standing of a great power and a weaker power on any one condition alone. Furthermore, one must distinguish between strategies consistent with the conditions and how they in fact worked out in practice.* The initial discussion here emphasizes strategies; the following section more systematically examines the consequences for particular cases. Also, for simplicity, we will initially treat A and B as fairly unitary actors, though we will modify this assumption later, particularly in respect to the elite of some dependent states who must carefully weigh not only their relations with the dominant power but also with their own publics.

(1) *Indifference to benefits vs. strategic resources.* The basic issue in regard of this pairing is A's ability to extract demands and B's to negotiate counterdemands. (Blau, 1964: 122–23.) Counterdemands are not as threatening or potent if the party is indifferent to them. Among great powers this logic was partly shown by Stalin's "ostentatious unconcern" (Gaddis, 1978: 181) and later Mao's alleged indifference to nuclear weapons at the same time they were both acquiring them (which is to say that feigned indifference is not sufficient to sustain a policy). This logic may also have informed Stalin's rejection of Marshall Plan aid, though other factors were probably more important; but still, Stalin could show that Lend-Lease and Western aid were not the foundations of his military power: he would take what he needed from Eastern Europe on his own. In asymmetrical situations, the extent to which A is not reliant, or dependent, upon resources or services supplied from B is a measure of its indifference.

(a) State A, often simply as a result of size and endowment but also as a result of strategy, secures many needed benefits from outside its proximate subordinates in their sphere of influence, or diversifies to minimize its reliance on them. It may obtain grain, oil, or minerals from a variety of distant suppliers rather than concentrate on available benefits within its own geographic sphere. "The upshot is that this

---

*The conditions are not perfectly exclusive in terms of the empirical referents they consider within their purview; rather, they characterize the capabilities of actors in terms of the feasible modes of response to other actors and the environment.

trade is not crucial for the Soviet economy, but 'all aspects of trade with the USSR—the level, the composition, the terms, and the balance and how it is financed—are critical for the economic development of Eastern Europe.'" (Bornstein in Skurski, 1982: 357–58.) The U.S. position is even stronger in this regard. One might say, however, that simple compliance on the part of the dependency is a benefit that A is not indifferent to. Applying this logic to capitalist powers, one need not expect to find only a paradigm case dependency relation where profit repatriations are high, as some dependency arguments might lead one to expect, but also where they are low but the area is nonetheless deemed important for security reasons. Where state A's benefits (not simply economic) are high, it is not indifferent and is subject to greater reciprocal manipulation, at least over time. Similarly, the Soviet's most loyal dependencies in some cases are the ones from which they receive the least "socialist product" in percentage terms. Ironically, but consistent with the model, the most pliable dependencies in the respective spheres may be the weakest versions of capitalism and socialism and be beneficiaries in economic terms.

(b) Dependent actors, in turn, may attempt to control the use or development of their resources. (Blau, 1964: 119.) The narrower range of their interests may enhance a coherent policy response. (Vital, 1967: 29–31.) Dependent states may try to nationalize control over raw materials and control markets and investments (as in Latin America), or fight against development schemes premised on their endowments (as in Eastern Europe in the 1960s). The requirements of social stability of a dependency can even be a bargaining resource, particularly if it affects the great powers' larger calculations of interests (e.g., Poland or Mexico). Dependent states may also try to manipulate their unique diplomatic role or salient position to A to extract better treatment (such as the GDR in its role in *Ostpolitik*, for example, or Mexico under Luis Echeverría in regard to the developing world, or more recently in its activist policy in Central America). Yugoslavia obtained significant financial support in the 1950s from the West, in spite of earlier disagreements, much as Cuba obtains large amounts of Soviet support today by virtue of its strategic position and the options it offers for the low-risk exercise of influence.

Dependent actors, particularly the stronger ones, may attempt to maintain a policy of indifference on the model of a great power. But unless this stance is combined with an intense counterideology (see condition 4), it cannot be easily upheld. Mexico has repeatedly been reluctant to receive forms of U.S. assistance termed "aid," even in the wake of national disasters, in order to uphold the view that Mexico can handle its own problems. Nonetheless, the dependent cannot usually afford to be indifferent for long on the model of a dominant power.

(2) Monopolization of rewards vs. available alternatives. The basic issue at stake here is the degree of organized restraint on competition: is bargaining fundamentally bilateral, or is it multilateral in important respects? In its strongest ideal-type form, actor A would want to bar alternative suppliers to B, provided it can supply them at reasonable cost to itself. In figurative terms it would want to be "the only firm in town where jobs can be found," "the political society that is the sole source of national security and glory," "the church that is the only avenue to salvation," and "the police that alone can offer protection against violence." (Blau, 1964: 123, 121.)

(a) Variations on the Monroe Doctrine and the Brezhnev doctrine have given expression to these sentiments: in the most general sense they seek to preclude alternatives, with each superpower being the sole interpreter of where to draw the line. The greater the monopolization of trade and finance, of diplomatic support and ideological appeal, and of military protection, the greater A's dominance (though not necessarily economic gain). It is arguable that in many situations in world politics the influence wielded by a great power stems less from coercion and more from its "powers of attraction" in terms of providing markets, capital, technology, skills, etc., to weaker states. (Singer, 1972.) In recent years, for example, trade and finance have become especially important forms of reward offered by the Soviets in some of their East European trade, with implicit subsidization occurring in some years; such "preferential trade treatment serves to sustain the allegiance of and to maintain dominance over the ruling communist parties of Eastern Europe." One can view "Soviet trade subsidies . . . as 'payment' for further limits on East European sovereignty." (Vanous, 1982: 7; debate over the precise measurement e.g., Marer, 1984a and chapter 17 here, while important, does not change the principle.) For the United States in Latin America, the monopoly perks have been eased financial conditions on borrowing and development and military aid. The Alliance for Progress, for example, was fundamentally an intraregional program for the bestowing of rewards.

In both dependent regions, even multilateral forums with great power sponsorship often have crucial bilateral dimensions. A carefully structured dispensation of rewards by the dominant power can be particularly important in forging long-run dependence. To an important extent this stems from the sheer comparative size of the dominant power's economy. This factor is very clear where the United States is concerned. Similarly, the size of the Soviet economy, which is so much larger than all the East European economies put together, makes the USSR the big regional supplier and customer. As a result, a radical pattern of bilateral trade emerges, where each East European state "orients its trade toward the Soviet Union." (Skurski, 1982: 357.) A multitude of CMEA projects and technical exchanges also provide "Organizational controls addressed primarily to the membership of the East European subsystem [that] can, in their own subtle ways, emphasize the acceptable limits of national independence and deviation, preferred objectives for collective support, and economic preferment to those who avoid offending Soviet sensitivities." In other words, these trade and technical relationships help institutionalize rules and reduce the role of force. (Jamgotch, 1975: 416–17.) Soviet energy resources, for example, have been particularly important in recent times. They have recurrently sold to East European countries under the world market price, while simultaneously extracting a commitment from the purchasing states to invest resources and expertise in joint energy acquisition and processing projects within the CMEA framework. (See Gustafson, 1981–82.) Since these projects have crucial elements inside the Soviet Union or involve interdependent electricity-receiving grids, they help promote reliance on the Soviets and commitment to a long-term relationship without enhancing the independent wherewithal of the dependencies; indeed, the East European states also become more interdependent with each other. Similarly, in Latin America such forms of reward as financial loans, aid, technical assistance, and market access have been dispensed within a series of multilateral frameworks, while being fundamentally determined on a bilateral case-by-case basis.

(b) Contrary to actor A's goals, actor B may attempt to develop alternatives to A as sources of supply and make its own services demanded by others. Simply inspiring tacit recognition of these options may enhance B's position. These alternatives need not necessarily be forged with other dominant actors. However, in some instances inspiring "Competition among superiors for the services of subordinates increases the subordinate's independence" (Blau, 1964: 119–20, 123), though it may also call forth more effort to dominate them or more credible threats of fate control.

To the extent state B finds trading alternatives or alternative sources of capital, it has more room for maneuver so long as it can sustain these relationships economically or politically. It may resist economic integration into structures responsive to the dominant actor. The recent opposition of Mexico and even Canada to the benignly intended proposal by the United States of a North American Common Market is but one recent manifestation of this resistance. Thus one can expect "efforts of smaller states within a regional hierarchical system to lessen the barriers which separate the regional system from the global international system . . . to intensify" as circumstances allow. (Zimmerman, 1972: 36.) Latin American states may seek private loans that are not so tied to IMF conditions or form regional trading arrangements that exclude the United States such as the Andean Pact, while East European states may seek Western financing and Third World trade outside of CMEA. Interestingly, the same international market that may be seen as a constraint in Latin America may be (or be seen as) a potential boon to East European independence; conversely, the socialist norms, social structure, and economic links that may be seen as a constraint in the latter region may in turn be (or be perceived as) a vehicle for pursuit of autonomy in the former.

The common element in these cases is the quest for an alternative source of leverage, not necessarily the specific form of social organization itself. (Superpower fears of intrusion by their adversary in their sphere may be right, but because of this quest by the dependencies for alternatives as much as because of concerted adversary policy.) However, development of East European economies in isolation from many pressures of the international market limits their ability to effectively break into it, just as many of the essentials for sustaining Latin American states' economies would not be available to them if they broke out of it and were ostracized in the international financial community, where such economic slack (as opposed to military support) is only rarely ever taken up by the Soviets. (See Varas, 1984: 46.) Under these and other constraints, East European forays into international capitalism may turn out to be less profitable and Latin American into socialism less compelling than the incentives that drive their quest for enhanced autonomy from the superpowers.

Still, alternatives exist to complacent integration. States may, like Romania, extend their diversification, obtaining diplomatic or ideological support from the Chinese (staying "within the same church" as it were) while forging new economic alternatives with the West and the Third World. Similarly, some Latin American states seek to obtain West European (especially French) and Japanese economic involvement, market access, and diplomatic support. The desire to diversify relationships also helps explain why "over the past two decades one of the most striking features of the foreign policy of most South American regimes—regardless of ideology—has been their enduring interest in regularizing their diplomatic and economic ties with Moscow." (Varas, 1984: 35.) The limiting case of low-risk diversification is represented by Argentina under Perón in the 1950s as he sought to optimize his bargaining position by declaring himself nonaligned. More direct challenges by B to A include adopting alternative diplomatic, ideological, or military patrons. Direct transfer of these ties to a rival power entails high risks or can be most readily accomplished by less proximate members of the sphere. Cuba ran high risks in switching economic, political, ideological, and military patrons. Distant and small but strategically important Albania transferred its ties to China for a time, China being just one more in a long line of great power patrons. Albania and to a greater extent Yugoslavia and Cuba have played the high-risk game of exploiting the "competition among superiors for the services of subordinates" to advance what they perceive as their own interests.

(3) Prevention of coercive opposition vs. coercive ability.   The issue at stake is whether or not there is a role for "coercive force in the fight against powers with superior resources." Actor A's aims are to discourage coalitions among subordinates that would enable them to extract demands, to resist political control of exchange processes by supporting, or enforcing, law and order according to sanctioned rules of the game, and, finally, to protect itself or its representatives from the threat of violence and legitimized political opposition. (Blau, 1964: 123, 122.)

(a) Each dominant state wants to control military relations and organizations in its region (including resources, personnel training, material, crisis commands) sufficiently to uphold its objectives and what it perceives as its security requirements, though legitimating them as much as possible through regional participation. The United States wants to keep communism out of its sphere, while the Soviets want to sustain it in theirs. U.S. organization for this purpose has been more informal, the Soviets' much more formal. Both have intervened to rein in governments that have alternative bases of support or ideology. The frequency of U.S. intervention declined from the early years of this century with the advent of the Good Neighbor Policy, which was accompanied by a deliberate strategy of strengthening internal security forces to enable them to keep order on their own, with little concern for democracy, elections having occasioned earlier interventions. But the Cold War revived U.S. efforts to organize military security for the region as it felt compelled to intervene several times to forestall communist threats. Informal links and occasional coordination within OAS was about the limit of organization it could muster in this regard, however, given uneven regional support for an inter-American Regional Military System. The post-1945 Soviet imposition of regimes in Eastern Europe and the later use of the Warsaw Pact as an instrument of integration and control are discussed in chapter 10.

The Soviets exert more formal control than does the United States, but formal control is more subject to direct challenge, as indicated by repeated upheavals and coercive responses since the 1950s. In general terms Soviet–East European relations are politicized in the Soviets' favor, who resist depoliticizing these relations, while the United States has attempted to keep relations with Latin America depoliticized and as economic as possible, resisting politicization except in crises. Both dominant powers try to sustain favorable rules of the game that optimize control and minimize opposition. Thus, in the 1960s the USSR resisted ruble convertibility in Eastern Europe, which would have moved the region more toward a general market under less bilateral control. Similarly, today the United States is opposed to any debt coalition or nationalization, wanting adherence to the free market, GATT, and IMF conditions, rather than politicizing exchange relations. Finally, the United States opposes communist opposition groups in Latin America, even if they have electoral legitimacy, just as in their sphere the Soviets oppose independent labor unions, or sources of dissent outside communist party control.

(b) Dependent actors may try to tap sources of power that help them reduce the dominant actor's interference with its conduct or deter outright intervention. They may also try to maneuver coalitions to best achieve their demands. In some instances leaders use a sense of nationalism to help resist outside constraints on their conduct. A heritage of resistance to invasion (such as in Poland, Mexico, and Yugoslavia) and/or indigenous revolution (Yugoslavia, Cuba, Albania, Nicaragua) may provide a dependent nation with more latitude. Some states (like Romania in the Warsaw Pact, Mexico in GATT) limit their participation in dominant-sponsored coalition arrangements, with refusal to integrate being judged the best possible assertion of autonomy. In other instances states may deftly maneuver within constraints and initiate coalitions that are beneficial to them, while at the same time offering greater benefits than costs to the dominant power in terms of control (e.g., Polish resolution of its postwar border with the GDR reduced its dependence on Moscow for protection, yet aided Soviet-supported *Ostpolitik*). Domestically, some institutions are so inextricably intertwined with national traditions, such as the Church in Poland or universities in some Latin American states, that they may sustain their autonomy and sources of political resistance.

(4) Source of relevant values vs. ideals lessening needs.   The issue at stake is "ideological conflict between social values that intensify the need for the services the powerful have to offer and counter-ideologies that mitigate this need." The dominant actor wants to present itself as a force of progress materially, spiritually, or ideologically in a way "inherently valuable for its members." It has "a stake in helping to perpetuate and spread the relevant social values and in opposing counter-ideologies that depreciate these values." (Blau, 1964: 123, 122.)

(a) It is a basic tendency of great powers to attempt to forward a worldview. This has been repeatedly observed and widely noted in history. The role of Soviet ideology in this respect needs no elaboration; only the degree to which it remains a central motivating force is debated. That the United States has a doctrine or ideology of sorts is less obvious, since there is no explicit set of tenets. But America was founded on a set of tenets that set the parameters of policy debate. Many observers such as Kennan (1951), Hartz (1955), Brzezinski and Huntington (1964), Hoffmann (1968), Schurmann (1974), and Dallek (1983) have noted the key role Lockean liberalism and domestic preoccupations play in America's approach to the world and communism in general, while Packenham (1973) and Krasner (1978) have focused more on Latin America in particular. Indeed, one can cite examples from both great powers where efforts to uphold or forward their ideologies even compromised effective achievement of their interests.

This ideological effervescence, however, is not totally without effect. As Berger notes, words and doctrines not only describe reality, they "also have the power to create and shape realities. The words of the strong carry more weight than the weak. Indeed, very often the weak describe themselves in words coined by the strong. . . . As [Western imperial powers] imposed their military, political and economic power over most of the world, they also imposed the power of their words. It was they who named the others, sort of a negative baptism." Thus he notes a Brazilian song from the 1960s that cheerfully and defiantly asserts "We are the underdeveloped!" accepting both the designation and the developmental path to become like the other—to become developed. (1974: 7.) Similarly, Milosz's evocation of *The Captive Mind* (1953) brilliantly portrays the appeal of Marxist-Leninist doctrine to many intellectuals in Eastern Europe, at least during the time of the communists' consolidation of power.

There has been a decline in the strength of the appeal of both superpowers' ideologies as ordering principles for dependencies. (Resurgence of Islamic fundamentalism, for example, is but one recent manifestation of this.) Capitalist economic development did not always lead to political democracy but sometimes to increasing political violence without effective institution-building, leading to military control of the state. (Huntington, 1966.) Conversely, the Stalinist development model seemed to offer effective institutions for quick development, but in the end the institutions themselves seemed to impede the economic process. The appeal of the Soviet model generally diminished, and the USSR became more of an ally to be used than a model to be emulated (R. Lowenthal, 1977), while in respect to Eastern Europe some argued that the doctrine had come to be a means to inundate the realm of public thought, to fill a vacuum rather than foster appeal (Kolakowski, 1982). Its anticolonial appeal has also lost credibility.

Nonetheless, the ideology of a future transformation from socialism toward communism remains important for the legitimacy of some East European leaders. (Jamgotch, 1975: 414.) The United States has downgraded the axiomatic appropriateness of its social system for others, though in a relative sense it still has great appeal in Latin America. There is the long-standing heritage of the "Western Hemisphere Idea" to draw on. "Much of the behavior of the United States toward Latin America is conditioned by the desire to maintain a positive image and to assure the generally favorable disposition of the Latin Republics." (Wesson, 1982b: 2, 4–5.) While it is difficult to say whether the recent return to democracy in a number of states there reflects more the decline of military governments or an upswell in support for democracy, its basic cultural, ideological, and economic appeal remains in Latin America irrespective of strength or the longevity of the incipient returns to democracy (in Argentina, Brazil, Bolivia, and Panama). Indeed, even the military rulers there justify themselves as temporary expedients resulting from crisis conditions, tacitly recognizing their position is contrary to "the norm," and in some sense presupposing a return to more democratic forms of rule.

(b) Dependent actors may limit their dependence by limiting or reducing their needs in service of an idea and therefore becoming less dependent upon others. "Religious and political ideals [e.g., patriotism, nationalism] derive their driving force in large part from imbuing adherents with values that make the satisfaction of material wants comparatively unimportant and that, consequently, lessen men's dependence on those who can supply material benefits. By reducing material needs, revolutionary ideologies become a source of independent strength and resistance to power." (Blau, 1964: 120–21.)

The role of ideology and political ideals to reduce states' dependence takes several forms. Nationalism is probably the most powerful ideal that can be marshaled in opposition to greater power. Cases involving the Soviet Union illustrate this dramatically; Latvia, Estonia, and Lithuania adhere to their cultural heritage even in the face of a concerted policy to minimize this role, and without a concerted policy of resistance. (Vardys, 1975.) More broadly, one could view the East European experience as a testimony to the persistence of national traditions in the face of efforts to construct a new social order. (Almond, 1983.) Nationalism varies from passive persistence to an active policy of independence. One sees, for example, a deliberate role for nationalism in the policies of Poland and Romania, as well as in Mexico, Cuba, and Nicaragua.

Nationalism may be supplemented by appeals to ideology. The most prevalent usage is to selectively try to hold the dominant power to its own principles and rhetoric, or to use variations on them to one's own advantage. Dependent states reiterate their claims to sovereignty and appeal to the United Nations and international law when their grievance is against the United States; they appeal to principles of socialism when seeking redress from the USSR. Romania, for example, has been particularly adept at invoking Marx and Lenin to fortify its policy preferences, while Mexico long has stressed the relationship between sovereignty and nonintervention in international law and has also tried to use the principles of the OAS and United Nations to strengthen its positions. Socialist polycentrism and Eurocommunism have enhanced the East Europeans' options in this respect, while movements for a New International Economic Order and the Group of 77 have aided the Latin Americans' cause. The advantage of this approach is that it cannot easily be branded as a counter or illegitimate ideology; at the same time it raises the costs of opposing the dependent state on the issue in question.

An alternative use of ideology involves staking out an even more extreme ideological position than the dominant power. Albanian quests for autarky and isolationism have substituted revolutionary ideology for material payoffs; the Cultural Revolution in China, which took a similar approach, showed this to be a less viable strategy for a fledgling great power. In Latin America one finds regime leaderships, particularly military ones, that outstrip the United States in their opposition to communism. In Eastern Europe extreme internal conformity allows external latitude, while in Latin America extreme external conformity can soften U.S. disapproval of various internal policies, such as in Pinochet's Chile. The dependent state may then become, in some respects, a parody of the preferences of the dominant state: extreme revolutionary radicalism in Eastern Europe, and extreme conservative or bureaucratic-authoritarian capitalism in Latin America.

A similar dynamic toward the extremes works in the opposite direction. Internal revolution in a dependent state, accompanied by a quest for autonomy, leads to appeals to the ideology of the opposing sphere. One observes this, for example, in Hungary in 1956, in Cuba since 1960, and in Nicaragua in the 1980s. The result is ideological polarization within a dominant power's sphere. Outside the sphere it is more possible to mix models: to be a capitalist Tanzania and deliberately try to move toward self-reliance, or a Marxist-controlled Angola or Mozambique and sustain a role for international capitalism. Inside, polarization of appeal provides the dependency with an alternative, if high-risk, source of inspiration and leverage. In addition to nationalism and ideology, religion may also provide a resource or haven for autonomy movements. Religion and ideology may separately support nationalism, but they may be in tension with each other as possible bases for supporting autonomy.

How the actor stands in relation to all four conditions helps establish the bargaining potentials of the parties. But as my illustrative examples made clear, these are not simple predictive conditions; to see how they translate into outcomes, one must examine the way dependent states with differing profiles bring these conditions to bear in interaction with the dominant power.

3. Differentiation of Dependent Outcomes for Dependencies in Spheres of Influence

(a) The Superpowers
Without reviewing the historical experience of both spheres since 1945, it is reasonable to argue that both the United States and USSR have experienced a decline in their relative standing on the conditions of power in respect to their spheres. "The great powers now have less freedom of action in their spheres. The small countries in each sphere stand up more to their patron superpower than they used to." (Blasier, 1983: 4.) Both powers have had strong standing on all four conditions of power. The U.S. standing was particularly high after World War II, so

much so that America could focus its attention on Europe and the Far East. Soviet predominance was of a lesser margin, and its attention was more concentrated on East and Central Europe. In recent years the United States has devoted more attention to Latin America, while the USSR has extended its global capabilities as other objectives and commitments came to vie with their earlier concentration on Eastern Europe. While both superpowers retain fate control in respect to their spheres, both have experienced secular declines in their ability to control day-to-day behavior across the board. In Blau's terms, having set up hierarchical relations based on power, they have become more interdependent with their subordinate states through exchange over time and, accordingly, have less power. Thus, on a relative basis, the dependencies as a whole were able to assert more power.

There are differences in specifics; the relationships in each sphere ebbed and flowed differently. However, both superpowers have seen decline in their ideologies as a source of relevant values (condition 4), the Soviets much more so than the United States. Both have seen a decline in their effectiveness in preventing coercive opposition (condition 3); in general, the political costs of intervention have increased. In Eastern Europe the Soviets have seen liberalization movements and worker and consumer dissatisfaction spawn unrest, while the United States has seen rebel movements and revolution reacting against the status quo in Central America. While the Soviets retain greater usable control, facing fewer domestic constraints, they are also less capable of economically sustaining the prolonged disruption some interventions would bring. Neither superpower is indifferent to the benefits of competent performance by its sphere members (condition 1). Both want to sustain stability, yet Eastern Europe has in some cases become an economic burden to the Soviets and a challenge to the legitimacy of their control, while the United States is increasingly concerned about the debt crisis in Latin America where a default could imperil its own banks as well as international financial stability. Finally, the monopolization of key rewards (condition 2) has declined for both superpowers, though this remains a central link in each sphere. Economic links play an essential role in reward and punishment, but now they can be a two-way street; rewards cannot easily be severed as punishment when the results would harm both parties. A monopoly position can mean responsibility, and that too can be costly. Either the superpowers allowed or encouraged dependent states to diversify in some respects, which reduced the costs to them as well as some measure of control, or they were forced to bail out their dependents after these measures foundered, strapping the dependencies in crises. Thus, both the United States and the USSR are hegemonies experiencing leveling in their spheres.

(b) Outcomes to the Dependencies

Generalizations about the dependent states are more complex: rather than the one and the many, we are now talking about the many and the one. Taken individually, one can see a diversification of dependent outcomes on the basis of bargaining profiles. This range includes what I will call (a) consensual, (b) circumventing (successful and unsuccessful), and (c) constrained bargainers. Here we will simplify and classify some states primarily for the contemporary period, though one might have to consider a sequence of profiles over time for more detailed analysis. This typology was basically empirically derived and is adequate for purposes here. It is interesting to note, however, that the outcomes roughly correspond to four responses to "threat systems" that Boulding (1963) derived in a more abstract fashion.* The terms

---

*Boulding notes (1) integrative, (2) counterthreat, (3) submissive, and (4) defiant responses within what he calls "threat systems." His distinctions address, but do not encompass, our more general typology that incorporates uses of "reward power" and dependence. Relating his conceptions to ours: (1) Consensual bargainers pursue an integrative response. In general, it "establishes community between the threatener and the threatened and produces common values and a common interest." He allows that this may take many different forms and may be mixed with the other responses. If combined with submission, for example, the threat system may even disappear. (2) Successful circumventing bargaining is an example of a counterthreat response. This is attempted deterrence. It puts the burden of response on the original threatener: if he does not respond, "the capital value of his threat" may decline, while if he carries it out there is bound to be an escalation of response on a negative-sum situation. (3) Unsuccessful circumventing bargaining results in a "submissive" response: "When the holdup man threatens us we give him our wallet. . . . When the state says, 'Become a soldier or I will put you in prison,' the young man allows himself to be conscripted." This "is likely to be a conflict system; that is, it is likely to move the parties to a state in which the threatener is better off and the threatened is worse off than in the initial condition." Much depends on the perceived legitimacy of the threat. Finally, (4) constrained bargainers may forward a defiant response. "This is somewhat analogous to the nonconsummation of exchange because of a refusal to trade. A says to B, 'You give me X and I will give you Y'; B simply says, 'No, it's not worth it to me,' and the situation returns to the status quo ante." But in threat systems this "defiance puts a burden of response on the threatener and hence is in some sense a challenge to him" and he must decide whether to carry out the negative-sum threat. Except for the integrative response, if the responses become reciprocal it is basically a reciprocation of "bads." Thus Boulding argues that exchange-based systems tend to be more durable over the long haul than threat systems since they are based rather on joint, positive-sum consummations: classical civilizations based on slavery have met their demise while trade has persistently grown. (1963: 426–30.)

used here are preferred, however, since these refer to distinct types of cases, whereas Boulding's threat responses can be variously mixed as components at the same time.

Consensual Bargainers seek rewards or diminished obligations in exchange for compliance. They often rate weakly on the four conditions of independence. They bargain (tacitly or otherwise) to enhance their well-being by staying readily within accepted limits of good behavior. Their domestic systems are consonant with the great powers' objectives. Bulgaria and Costa Rica are examples. Bulgaria is Moscow's most loyal dependency and is a ready extension of Soviet policy. Costa Rica will go so far as to accept arms shipments that it would prefer to reject in order to assuage the United States in pursuit of its Central American policy. One might also place Honduras in this category, and even Brazil, which in the tradition of Rio Branco, has often acted as a stalwart regional agent of the United States, showing that one cannot predict outcomes solely on the basis of coercive potential (condition 3) alone.

Circumventing Bargainers seek enhanced political or economic autonomy. There are two kinds: those who succeed and those who fail. The successful cases rate well on at least three of four conditions (often 2, 3, and 4) of independence. Success requires that the state not be so important as to invoke superpower fate control, or else be strong, distant, or protected enough to deter intervention. Yugoslavia, Albania, and Romania are examples of varying degrees of success, as are Cuba and Nicaragua. The cases are context-dependent, but all are the result of internal revolution and consolidation and have systems directed from the leadership down. The term "circumventing" is preferred to "defection" because unlike a defector a country must retain its geographic locale: it can try to get around the influence of the superpower, but it remains conditioned by it.

The unsuccessful cases are more society-driven than leadership-controlled, and the elite ultimately tends to be polarized between factions. They also have weaker or less advantageous profiles on the conditions of independence (particularly condition 3). Hungary in 1956, Czechoslovakia in 1968, Guatemala in 1954, and the Dominican Republic in 1965 are examples of failed efforts at restructuring relations. Such curtailed cases may, however, result in a revised social contract with the superpower as recompense or insurance against repetition.

Constrained Bargainers may rate fairly high on several conditions of independence (often 1, 3, and 4). It is the high standing on condition 1 that brings forth the special efforts of the dominant power. They may be so strategically important that there is no question of their being allowed to become successful circumventing bargainers. Their often poor standing on condition 2, despite efforts to the contrary, is a reflection of this. But their inherent strength on the other conditions of power rule out a submissive response. On the one hand, they are strong and historically independent enough to command attention, yet this historical distinctiveness may also impede their effective adjustment to the political and economic constraints that they are pressured to abide by. On the other hand, they are so important that their very failures of adjustment can be a source of bargaining strength: they may manipulate constraints or court failure to compel hegemonic assistance or policy change without bringing on intervention. Politics as usual may involve tensions within leadership elites, tensions that stem from differences over the primacy accorded to domestic resistance or external constraints. Crisis politics resolves the split in favor of one side or the other, though in no case does direct dominant intervention result, even when the more society-oriented elites' view predominates for a time.

Poland and Mexico are examples of constrained bargainers. They each possess a certain deterrent capability, as evidenced by Poland in 1956 and 1980–81 and Mexico in 1938. But they also provide dramatic illustrations of when weakness can be turned into a bargaining strength (or make the best of a bad situation not entirely of their own making). As Schelling (1960) notes, this can occur in situations where two bargainers have both conflicting and common interests. It requires that the weaker actor bind itself to a position and do away with or convey its lack of alternatives, and the calculation by the stronger actor that agreement on the weaker party's terms is preferable to no agreement. For example, Mexico's ability to cite "'wounded nationalism' serves today as a useful foreign policy bargaining chip: Mexican policymakers can tell their U.S. counterparts that, restrained by sensitive public opinion, they must negotiate tenaciously." (Levy and Szekely, 1983: 173.) If the United States prefers agreement to no agreement, they may have to accede to the constrained side. Similarly, during crises, Mexico can implicitly threaten default on its massive foreign debt or warn of instability resulting from too stringent financial conditions or restricted emigration in order to pressure the United States for concessions. As a result of Poland's crises, the Poles obtained continued private farming, a role for the Church, and various rescue packages of financial support from the Soviets. In a like manner, the GDR manipulates its domestic public's inevitable comparison with living standards in the FRG to obtain various preferences from the Soviets.

Thus, if a key basis of consensual bargaining is loyalty, and of successful circumventing bargaining the manipulation of internal resistance, the constrained bargainer can manipulate not only its own strength, but also its resulting weakness when things go wrong. This variation of outcomes is systematically comparable in terms of the Blau conditions of power and independence. This differentiation of outcomes also accounts for the diverse applicability of the advantages and disadvantages of dominance and dependency noted by Lewis. However, the classification of a state does not necessarily consign it to that type of relationship forever, and, as Blau argues, the advantages and disadvantages are bound to ebb and flow over time.

4. Evolution of Spheres of Influence

Section 1 focused on the historical *variations* in predominance-dependence relations, which have important contemporary parallels and rooted comparison in the long-standing dilemmas of great power relations. Section 2 offered a general model for the *conditions and dynamics* of varieties of bargaining behavior in the contemporary spheres, while section 3 sorted out the *patterns for particular pairs* in great power–weaker power relations. Thus, while sections 2 and 3 sorted out variations of strategies and results by country, this final section *examines the collective effects* of these patterns on the evolution of spheres of influence.

Reflecting on this evolution in general terms among the states of each sphere one could argue that the following general pattern holds: Each great power has first gone from being just one great power competitor in the region prior to the time shown in table 2 to being the leading manager of it. The timing of the phases were different but converging. The imposed orders of the early period in the table then decayed somewhat as the great powers, becoming superpowers, attended to competing concerns. While continuing to rely on the social orders set in place in the first two periods, each superpower also sought to construct additional institutional arrangements and incentives to sustain its influence at acceptable cost. However, development policies forwarded for this purpose often enriched dependent oligarchs, or *nomenklatura*, while raising popular expectations that were not often fulfilled.

Table 2. Summation of evolutionary trends in spheres of influence

Externally impose order	Rely on internal order	Tacit limits to disorder Reward internal loyalty Punish external threats	Disorder increases Tacit limits challenged Costs of reward and punishment increase
Focus attention on region		Competing strategic foci	Attention reasserted
US–Latin America:	1900–30 Physical dominance	1933–54 Good Neighbor Policy	1954–mid-1970s Cold War: Alliance for Progress; Johnson Doctrine	Late 1970s–present Drift/Crisis "Interdependence"
USSR– East Europe:	1945–56 Physical dominance	1956–68 Khrushchev doctrine: polycen-trism	1968–79 Brezhnev doctrine Material rewards and/or intervention	1979–present Drift/Crisis "Socialist Relations of a New Type"

The flawed development of some dependencies was partly a reflection of the increasing tension between imposed or supported old orders and the level of developing social complexity within states and interdependence between them. In terms of Blauian dynamics, as one shifted from a regional system of hierarchical, pure power arrangements to one based more on exchanged rewards, increasing interdependence began to come in conflict with internal power relations based on the original mandate. Paradoxically, just as old ground rules prove less adequate, increasing social complexity complicates reaching a new negotiated order of obligations and constraints within and among states of the regions.*

The costs of the superpower's policies have therefore been increasing. The broad strategic focus of the superpowers, reflected in increased Soviet involvement in the Third World in the 1970s, and the broad but contracting conception of the U.S. role there over the same period, may refocus with renewed vigor on their neighboring regions out of necessity in the years ahead. Pessimism about opportunities in the Third World combined with increased instability and interdepend-

*See Young's (1982) abstract but interesting arguments explaining why there is an inverse relation between the level of social complexity and interdependence, and the effectiveness of imposed social orders.

ence in adjacent spheres will drive this redirection of attention. As a result, there may be greater constraints on the weaker states in these regions, but as superpower fortunes are increasingly tied to the success of these regimes, their responses will also be more constrained and/or more costly.

The potential costs of superpower intervention are high. Economic relations are therefore increasingly important in sustaining acceptable "behavior control" and allegiance. Emphasis on the critical nature of these relations may help reshape conceptions of the prerequisites of power in the spheres. Jacobs (1984) argues that though the state is a key political unit of analysis, it is *not* the key analytical economic unit in analyzing the fortunes of great or small powers; rather, cities and regions are central in explaining differences in economic success and the consequences of trade and subsidies. Cities are key engines of development to the extent that they can innovate and produce substantial numbers of goods they previously imported, creating new incentives in subsequent trade with other cities. Cities have regional effects that work backward through this process. Industrial development cannot be grafted onto regions in the absence of cities able to engage in import substitution. This argument has implications for the interdependence of the sphere actors. The Blau model itself is not linked to a state-centric formulation; the superpower's conceptions may be antiquated to the extent that they remain rooted in this conception.

There are differences in the constraints and forms of predominance shaping change in the Soviet and American spheres. There are differences in Imperial democracy and authoritarianism, as well as important similarities in consequences. Jacobs (1984; 182–220) maintains that "From an economic point of view there are two types of empires, which we can think of as the English and Roman models." The English model [which could also be called the Greek model] focuses on control over economies more backward than its own, while the Roman model also involves economies as advanced or more advanced than its own. The English model applies more to the United States in Central and Latin America, while the Roman model more aptly characterizes the Soviet role in Eastern Europe.

Jacobs avers that, in general, imperial systems "become too poor to sustain the very costs of empire. The longer an empire holds together, the poorer and more backward it tends to become. . . . Yet if imperialism wins wealth for imperial powers, as it undoubtedly does, how can this be? It is partly a matter of timing. Jacobs maintains that "the very policies and transactions that are necessary to win, hold and exploit an empire are destructive to an imperial power's own cities and cannot but help lead to their stagnation and decay." The military expenditures of the imperial power are subsidized by the earnings of cities, which then do not redound to reciprocal productive interchanges among cities but rather require sustained military spending to maintain one area at the expense of city surplus elsewhere. Empires structure trade between economies in ways that work in the short run, but do not sustain the dynamo cities, particularly in the dependencies. (Jacobs, 1984: 182–220.)

Subsidies may then be necessary to sustain not only any trade at all, but also social stability in the dependencies, precisely when the ability of the imperial power to supply them starts to decrease. The alternative to subsidization is repression. We may note in this regard that the consensual bargainers' cities rely heavily on subsidies. The "successful" circumventing bargainers tend to have somewhat sluggish city economies and thus weak links to the metropole (which is partly a cause not simply an effect of their policy). Constrained bargainer's cities are economically important but warp the economies' incentive structure, drawing workers from the countryside but failing to dynamically sustain employment (and thus are potentially very politically significant). The positions of the capital city elites in bargaining with the metropole differ significantly in each case.

"Today the Soviet Union and the United States each predicts and anticipates the economic decline of the other. Neither will be disappointed." When the Soviet Union "took under its economic control Gdansk, Warsaw, Cracow, Prague, Bratislava, Budapest, part of Berlin and other cities in East Germany, it acquired an additional supply of city earnings to drain for transactions of decline. The chief trade-off for these cities has been export work destined for inert economies in the Soviet Union. Far from continuing to develop, the economies of these cities have been arrested." (Jacobs, 1984: 200.) In the Roman model the core stifles the dependencies. And while the level of Soviet subsidies over the past decade is a matter of dispute, the fact that the issue is raised at all is symptomatic of decline. A certain reversal of the earlier flow of revenues has to occur, or an increase in repression, or the redirection and restructuring of the basis of trade—i.e., political change in Eastern Europe. To avert the worst outcomes, the Soviets would have to relax political control in return for less expense.

In the U.S.–Latin America case, the causes of city decline are more complex. Jacobs argues that exchanges are beneficial to metropole cities when the dependencies pay as they go (that is achieve effective city-based import substitution), whereas when this type of trade is maintained primarily on credit, and unless the city in the dependency is unusually innovative, the exchange drains some long-term sources of dynamic intercity trade (while perhaps being remunerative to individuals in the short term). Rolled-over loans continue the drain, and unrepayable ones (a large percentage) will act like subsidies. A situation arises that unless the loans continue, a default by a major debtor could bring down the U.S. banking system; and one does not want to allow lesser debtors to provide precedents for reneging. Yet continued subsidization simply continues to foster the type of development incentives that were not initially sustainable. The implication is that advanced city trade with other advanced cities (in contrast to advanced-backward trade culminating in the Iranian Revolution) and less-advanced cities trading with less-advanced ones (as Venice started out) are collectively economically better for all parties. The implication of the English model seems to be that the great power's political logic initially overrides economic logic and misstructures the incentives that come to be sustained over time in both metropole and dependency. Ebel (1984) lucidly makes this argument about "The Development and Decline of the Central American City-State." Thus while the Soviets have to sacrifice political control to economize, to forestall the worst trends, the United States would seemingly have to trade less economic expense for less political control.

This argument may be overstated, but it puts forward a coherent dynamic of decline connecting the arguments about reward-based power and the interlinked bargaining fates of weak and strong alike in spheres of influence. It goes beyond simply positing the relative decline of power as an independent variable explaining outcomes to investigate the causes of that decline. It addresses some of the key political problems facing great and weak powers alike. Both face the dilemma noted by Pericles, who told the Athenians: "Perhaps it was wrong of us ... to take or get the international position we now hold; but nothing could be more dangerous now than to pretend we don't hold it, or to give it up without consideration of who gets what we resign." (Adams, 1975: 372.) The United States is in a more advantageous position to avoid the dilemmas of decline outlined in this pessimistic account; like the English model, it has greater opportunity for its fortunes to vary directly rather than inversely with its dependencies than does the Soviet-Roman model. Yet an effective restructuring of relations in either sphere requires not only a more differentiated strategy on the part of the superpowers toward the region but also strengthened tacit restraints toward their adversary's region.

Superpower predominance is declining in their spheres in relative terms despite a refocusing of attention on them. In contrast to previous periods of hegemonic leveling or decline in world politics, however, the contemporary period shows no ready challengers rising to face the superpowers. It might be possible for the superpowers to negotiate an arrangement to avoid the historical tendency of seeing their own security being extraordinarily threatened in such periods of decline. The challenge they face is in moving from a position of begrudgingly granted hegemony by the weaker states, to a position of accepted primacy, from a vision of the "hard sphere of influence" to the "soft sphere," since policies consistent with hegemony contradict effective management of social interdependence.

Working against an optimistic solution is the fact, or the perception, that the superpowers challenge each other's spheres, if only on a peripheral basis. Yet one could also imagine the development of an explicit, hands-off reciprocity. As one Soviet analyst recognized in 1983, "most recently in the Latin American strategy of the U.S., the geopolitical factor is being moved more persistently to center stage, the 'vital significance' is being frankly emphasized for the security of the United States." (Antiasov and Vasilliyev, quoted in Rothenberg, 1983: 17.) The Soviets are likely to limit their probes of U.S. tolerance given that "No area in the world is more tightly integrated into the United States political-economic system, and none—as President Ronald Reagan warned a joint session of Congress in April 1983—more vital for North American security, than Central America." (LaFeber, 1984: 5.) The same argument could be made about the Soviet position in Eastern Europe. Indeed, one could interpret statements of Mikhail Gorbachev linking reduction of U.S. support through Pakistan to Afghanistan (which it has considered in its "soft" sphere) with Soviet aid to Nicaragua as less a threat than as a renewed recognition of spheres of influence. Assessment of the balance of the internal and external sources of instability in each sphere will centrally color the superpowers, relations with each other; as well as the future of development in each sphere.

To the extent that such political reciprocity gained currency, weaker states of the region would benefit by decreased superpower perceptions of threat. East-West trade would not be discouraged. Superpower security reactiveness could be tempered. Reneging on such an agreement would pose costs to each superpower. It could be conducive to more domestic autonomy and social stability in the weaker states, particularly in Eastern Europe. While the weaker states would be analytically consigned to spheres of influence, they would have fuller reign for the considerable skill and effectiveness with which they have often pursued their autonomy, even under the more constrained circumstances that were the major focus of this chapter.

III   Dominant Powers

8

The Dominant Powers and Their Strategies

David D. Finley

This chapter begins with the modern paradox of power that confounds great powers today in their relations with small neighbors. As the late Raymond Aron observed, never in the past have great nation-states disposed so much raw power but never has it been so difficult to convert it to achievement of their purposes. It is that paradox I wish to explore by comparing the capabilities and strategies of the United States and the USSR with respect to their smaller regional neighbors.

The chapter begins by developing a suitable framework for comparison, incorporating concepts that will accommodate both regional systems without imposing on them the prejudices of ideology. My aim is to generate comparative hypotheses. In that sense the chapter aspires to be introductory rather than conclusive.*

The editor has abridged the historical material in this chapter to avoid redundance with respect to events already described in Part I.

*A preliminary version of this chapter was presented and discussed at the American Political Science Association meeting in New Orleans in September 1985 and the World Slavic Congress in Washington, D.C., in November 1985. I am particularly grateful for helpful criticism from Cole Blasier, Cal Clark, Devon Pena, and William Zimmerman, none of whom bear responsibility for the results.

I. Concepts

This volume is addressed to the "dominant" powers and their "subordinate" states. With Modelski, let us think of dominant as connoting substantial control of a system and hence the capacity to regulate its processes. (1978: 216.) But dominance need not imply unchallenged authority, and political dominance though closely related to economic dominance may not be synonymous. Thus one may contemplate a relationship in which the politically dominant partner controls the structure of interaction without controlling the costs and constraints that accrue from it. Let us think of subordinate in the sense of dependent, and let us define dependence, with Keohane and Nye, as net reliance, or, in terms we shall examine more closely below, highly asymmetric interdependence in which the costs and constraints, the sensitivity and vulnerability of a system of transactions, fall disproportionately on one side. (1977: 16–19.) Thus we open at the outset the possibility of complex change in the systems we examine here, and we define both dominance and subordination as relative rather than absolute qualities.

One element in determining the direction of change of these systemic qualities is strategy. Strategy is a term that originated in military discourse about generalship. It denotes directly or by implied analogy a science of planning and directing large-scale military operations, maneuvering forces into an advantageous position prior to tactical confrontation of the adversary. It presupposes a clear purpose and rational calculations of how to achieve that purpose. Tactics in turn refer to the microcosmic choices by which elements of a strategic plan are pursued in specific conditions of threat and opportunity that confront those who are charged with the conduct of battle.

Transposed from the military arena to the politics of international relations, the term strategy is both appropriate and potentially misleading. The vision of unambiguous, consistent adherence to a comprehensive plan is of course cultivated by most political leaders and nurtured by debates about national purpose. But whereas military strategy is devised in a highly structured, hierarchical context that can theoretically provide for comprehensive calculation of detail and coordination of effort, that image dissolves in the broad arena of politics, which arches over elements of military, diplomatic, and economic arenas that are often nonhierarchical and poorly coordinated at best, if not in outright conflict. Politics itself implies at its core an unfinished, practical dialectic rather than the efficient implementation of a plan. This is not to claim the irrelevance of persisting goals and ratio-nal calculation, or of strategic elements, in the conduct of states and leaders. It is simply to remind ourselves to resist the temptation to reconstruct the politics of international relations as merely the inter-play of unified national strategies. Strategy offers one starting point, not a sufficient conceptual framework by itself.

The evident pluralism of American politics and policy-making helps us avoid the futile quest of a single overall strategy to attribute to the United States, in this case as a nation-state engaging its hemispheric neighbors. The unified face and fundamentally different premises of Soviet Leninism tempt us the other way. Thus the specter of a Soviet "grand design" has long haunted Western assessments—compounded of the scientific claims of Leninism, the authoritarian tradition of Soviet domestic politics, the relative secrecy of its policy-making processes, and the fears generated by a simultaneously mysterious, ominous, and powerful adversary. A familiar recipe for American anxiety is the worry that while the United States muddles along with the ineffectual com-promises of interest-group pluralism, a determined, singleminded Soviet Union proceeds with implacable parsimony to implement its calcu-lated long-range plans. Neither the revisionism that characterizes U.S. policy as the relentless imperialism of a military-industrial complex, nor that which characterizes Soviet policy as defensive, opportunistic expediency covered by Marxist rhetoric, is likely to provide a less distorted perception of national behavior. The task rather is to reveal the dynamic in both cases of declaratory strategies that are forced continuously to adapt to both the consequences of strategically moti-vated actions and to circumstances that unexpectedly alter the condi-tions of success or failure.

Thus, for an American example, we look at John Kennedy's Alliance for Progress speech in March 1961 for declaratory strategy:

> We propose to complete the revolution of the Americas, to build a hemisphere where all men can hope for a suitable standard of living, and all can live out their lives in dignity and freedom. To achieve this goal political freedom must accompany material progress. Our Alliance for Progress is an alliance of free govern-ments and it must work to eliminate tyranny from a hemisphere in which it has no rightful place. . . . This political freedom must be accompanied by social change. For unless necessary social reforms are freely made . . . our alliance, our revolution, our dream, our freedom will fail. . . . Let us once again transform the American

Continent into a vast crucible of revolutionary ideas and efforts. (*American Foreign Policy*, 1965: 346–47.)

The following month witnessed U.S. management and support of the Bay of Pigs invasion, then withdrawal.

In January 1965 Secretary of State Dean Rusk discerned strategic progress:

> In country after country, the military establishment is committing itself more deeply to the maintenance of a constitutional and democratic system. . . . In the last two or three years it has become clear that Castro as a threat to the Western Hemisphere has been very, very severely reduced. . . . But then it is also true that the Alliance for Progress is now beginning to take hold. . . . The hemisphere can now see that there is a way to bring about the necessary economic and social changes in the hemisphere without resorting either to repression from the extreme right or to dictatorship from the extreme left. (*American Foreign Policy*, 1968: 948, 1015.)

But later that spring Lyndon Johnson explained the need to deploy 22,000 U.S. troops to the Dominican Republic, in part as follows:

> The revolutionary movement took a tragic turn. Communist leaders, many of them trained in Cuba, seeing a chance to increase disorder, to gain a foothold, joined the revolution. They took increasing control. And what began as a popular democratic revolution, committed to democracy and social justice, very shortly moved and was taken over and really seized and placed in the hands of a band of Communist conspirators. . . . The American nations cannot, must not, and will not permit the establishment of another Communist government in the Western Hemisphere. (962–63.)

The emphasis on a strategy of fostering socioeconomic change in the name of human dignity and a vision of social justice became, in collision with circumstances, a strategy of military intervention to rid the hemisphere of communist conspirators.

Turning to Eastern Europe, we find Leonid Brezhnev taking stock of the international situation there at the Twenty-third CPSU Congress in March 1966, as follows:

> The world socialist system is making steady progress. The basic laws of socialist construction are common to all countries, they

are well known and have been tested in practice. Nevertheless, as the socialist countries develop, they are constantly coming up against new problems engendered by the realities of life in all its complexity and variety. . . . The development of the world socialist system, therefore, requires a constant creative approach, on the tried and tested basis of Marxism-Leninism, to the problems that arise, and it requires the pooling of experience and opinions. . . . Business-like contacts and political consultations between the leaders of the fraternal parties of the socialist countries have developed into a system. . . . Such meetings make it possible to summarize and use, in good time and more fully, all that is worth while in the practical activities of each country. . . . The Council for Mutual Economic Assistance is acquiring increasing importance in expanding the economies of the participant countries. . . . The economy of the socialist countries is developing more rapidly than that of the countries of the bourgeois world. . . . In the sphere of military cooperation, there has been a further consolidation of our relations with the socialist countries in the face of growing aggressive acts on the part of the imperialist forces headed by the USA, a strengthening and improvement of the mechanism of the Warsaw Pact. The Warsaw Pact is the reliable protector of the gains of the peoples of the socialist countries. . . . Comrades, cooperation and solidarity are the main sources of the strength of the socialist system. (Rush, 1970: 295–98.)

The vision is progress toward Marxist-Leninist prosperity. The strategic goal is unity, voluntary cooperation through organizational integration. A year later, at the Karlovy Vary Conference of Communist and Workers' Parties, the same strategy of community progress through solidarity and cooperation was reiterated:

All our parties are united by the common Marxist-Leninist ideology, by common ultimate aims. We know that the fraternal parties work under different conditions and therefore take different tactical steps. . . . But all this does not prevent our parties from cooperating closely, from drawing up agreed positions, from striving for unity of action in the struggle for the communist end. And we are convinced that the solidarity of communists will continue to grow. In this respect, our conference is the best reply to those bourgeois politicians who maintain that communism has split along national lines. (Rush, 1970: 37.)

But by the following year events in Czechoslovakia were entirely out of hand. Exhortations to maintain the discipline of socialist internationalism and defer to unified pursuit of the Soviet course toward communism yielded to lightly veiled threats, then to massive military intervention. The subsequent "Brezhnev doctrine" of limited socialist sovereignty was first formulated as follows in a *Pravda* editorial in September 1968:

> The Socialist system exists in concrete form in individual countries that have their own well-defined state boundaries and develop with regard for the specific attributes of each such country. And no one interferes with concrete measures to perfect the socialist system in various socialist countries. But matters change radically when a danger to socialism itself arises in a country. World socialism as a social system is the common achievement of the working people of all countries; it is indivisible, and its defense is the common cause of all communists and all the progressive people on earth, first and foremost the working people of the socialist countries.... The communists of the fraternal countries naturally could not allow the socialist states to remain idle in the name of abstract sovereignty while the country [Czechoslovakia] was endangered by antisocialist degeneration.... Those who speak of the "illegality" of the allied socialist countries' actions in Czechoslovakia forget that in a class society there is and can be no such thing as nonclass law. Laws and the norms of law are subordinated to the laws of the class struggle and the laws of social development. These laws are clearly formulated in the documents jointly adopted by the Communist and Workers' Parties. (*Current Digest*, 1968: 10–12.)

Under the impact of circumstances, a declaratory strategy of fostering voluntary economic and military cooperation through organizational integration had yielded in practice to a regional strategy of military intervention, or a strategy of dominance made effective by the credible threat of military intervention.

As this chapter will attempt to show, the dialectic between declaratory strategy, on the one hand, and obdurate circumstances and outcomes, on the other, characterizes the recent evolution of relations between each dominant power and its regional neighbors. The repeated eclipse of the declaratory strategies of the dominant powers suggests in both cases a dynamic of international relations strongly at odds with their diagnoses. We can explain the strategies actually adopted as responses to unwanted and largely unanticipated outcomes and circumstances.

But how may we explain the persistent failures of diagnosis on the part of the dominant powers? To answer this question we must prepare conceptual formulations to use in comparing the two sets of regional international relations.

Keohane and Nye elaborate the concept of dependence as "a state of being determined or significantly affected by external forces," and interdependence as mutual dependence, characterized by reciprocal effects among countries or among actors in different countries. (1977: 8.) It is asymmetries of interdependence, in turn, that link interdependence with power. B is sensitive to A when it is significantly affected by transactions in a dimension of their engagement, and it is vulnerable to A when its costs of adjusting or compensating for A's behavior so as to maintain stability of the relationship are high. More concretely, when asymmetries or discrepancies of military or economic resources make B vulnerable to actions by A, to that extent A will have power over B. (11–19.)

While I shall try to follow these definitions in the rest of this chapter, it is necessary to recognize that dependence first gained currency in discourse about international relations as part of the ideologically specific processes of *dependencia*, refined by Marxist theorists who addressed themselves to U.S. exploitation of Latin America. *Dependencia* implies a causal explanation for that particular sort of internal and external dependence, rooted in U.S. imperialism and more generally the world capitalist political economy. (Frank, 1972: 321–97; Caporaso, 1978: 13–43.) To adopt that cluster of propositions by definition, useful as many of its insights have been, would be to define out of our scope the relationship between the USSR and socialist Eastern Europe, just the relationship that we are trying to bring under comparison.

The concept of "dependent development," however, a part of the *dependencia* legacy, is separable from its ideological origins and has already been put to use effectively to analyze the Eastern European political economy. (Clark and Bahry, 1983a: 271–93; Zimmerman, 1978: 604–23.) The internal and external dependence of local elites, reduced control over development priorities, and artificial constraints on economic diversification, in countries peripheral to a dominant regional or global power, will be summed up for our purposes, too, by the term "dependent development."

We shall also adopt from Keohane and Nye their concept of international regimes in general and that of complex interdependence as a particular sort of regime. Keohane and Nye define regimes as "the networks of rules, institutions, norms, and procedures which regularize and control the effects of behavior" within an international system. (24–25.) Complex interdependence is one model of such a regime, characterized by multiple channels of connection among the parties, an absence of hierarchy among issues of importance to the parties, and a general subordination of military force as a legitimate instrument of intrasystem conduct. The model should be thought of as standing at one pole of a continuum of international regimes for which the opposite pole is the traditional regime, defined by the political "realist" as centering on military security concerns of the parties and governed by their competitive pursuit, via the instruments of diplomacy, of maximum political power. (Morgenthau, 1966: chap. 7.)

Finally, we shall invoke the concept of the hegemonic system, in which one party, the dominant state or hegemon, is powerful enough to maintain the essential rules governing interstate relations and willing to do so. The theories of hegemonic stability, associating a hegemonic system with international stability and its decline or absence with instability or chaotic tendencies, have received intense scrutiny over the past decade from the developers of the neorealist school in international political economy. We shall consider their relevance and the long-cycle perspective, pioneered by Modelski, in our comparative analysis. (Kindleberger, 1973, 1981; Gilpin, 1975; Krasner, 1976; Stein, 1984; Modelski, 1978.)

Returning to the point of departure for this section, it is the modern paradox of international power that has pushed these theorists and others beyond the conventions of traditional political realism, not to reject the elements of international politics on which the traditional realists have based their analyses but to add new emphasis to the complicating and sometimes cross-cutting factors of the interdependent international political economy as well.

II. Comparisons

We turn now to comparing the strategies of the two dominant powers: the United States in Latin America and the Soviet Union in Eastern Europe. My aim is to develop a basis for advancing some hypotheses about their similarities and differences, drawing on the common conceptual framework advanced in the first section of this chapter.

First, there is the overriding similarity of common strategic purposes: security first and economic advantage second. Sharp ideological differences between the two dominant powers produce radically different formulations of the prerequisites for security and economic advantage, and different political structures have led to radically different norms, institutions, and procedures for the regional regimes; but these differences should not obscure the underlying similarities of strategic purpose.

A second similarity has been the rising political and economic costs both dominant powers have confronted in their efforts to maintain or restore their hegemonic positions in the presence of frustrating obstacles. Both the United States and the USSR have been thwarted repeatedly in their expectations that regional progress would follow the patterns of liberal and Leninist development, respectively, and that those patterns would unite the dominant powers' strategic purposes with ideological conformity, thus minimizing conflict within the regions. While both regions manifest greater internal diversity than we have described here, it is clear that in neither case has there been widespread subscription to dominant power recipes for domestic organization or regional leadership.

Third, the phenomenon of dependent development has clearly distorted the ways in which some of the smaller countries have attained or pursued socioeconomic modernization. In each region the distortions from a balanced national economy have been induced or directly managed by the dominant power through a combination of political and economic pressures. The distortions are thus a result of being on the periphery of a dominant power and of inability to prevail against the perceived priorities of that dominant power.

Fourth, in both cases the modernization processes themselves, as well as repressed modernization aspirations, have generated domestic pressures and catalyzed indigenous visions of progress. These resist the direction of the dominant powers and place their respective hegemonies under tension, rapidly increasing the political-economic price they must pay for values they seek from the regional system. The externally dependent elites, in both Latin America and Eastern Europe, are caught from behind by these domestic pressures and find themselves in the delicate position of brokers between the hegemon and their own countrymen.

Fifth, in both cases the dominant powers have thus far been unwilling to allow the regional regimes to slip from their control or to contemplate the possibility of leadership without hegemony. The United States and the USSR have responded to regime change, and pressures for more, by establishing rules unilaterally and committing enough political and economic resources to enforce them. Thus, since the defections of Yugoslavia and Cuba, with few exceptions the USSR and the United States have undertaken to restore acceptable regimes wherever the bounds of conformity were threatened. Albania is an exception; apparently the Soviet Union estimated the costs of intervention incommensurate with the anticipated returns. In some ways perhaps Guyana's radical government following independence offers a counterpart for Albania. Both are on the geographical periphery of the respective areas and of minimal geopolitical importance.

As a corollary to this determination displayed by the dominant powers, we may observe that both the United States and the USSR have been more willing to use the threat or reality of military intervention to coerce conformity than to bear the economic costs of cultivating voluntary cooperation among the smaller countries of their regions. The dominant powers' strategic adaptations have been predominantly military-political in character, and they have been employed in the cause of restoring rather than re-creating regimes. Thus, while the rhetoric of mutual assistance for rapid growth in conformity with domestic aspirations characterized the Alliance for Progress (1961) and the Comprehensive Plan of COMECON (1971), both dominant powers turned to military-political coercion when domestic aspirations thereafter took the smaller countries beyond tolerable bounds. Looked at another way, neither the COMECON-based vision of Nikita Khrushchev nor the Good Neighbor Policy of Franklin Roosevelt nor the Alliance for Progress were enduring efforts to establish new relationships within the respective regional regimes.

Sixth, whereas the conservative responses of the dominant powers have stressed their military-political advantages, the forces that have tended to disrupt the regional regimes have usually been economic in origin. While the long cycles invoked by Modelski to describe great power ascendancy and decline gain some substantiation in the U.S. experience, the independent dynamic that has repeatedly confounded both dominant powers is ultimately a function of economic changes. At the risk of oversimplification, one may say that economics has challenged the regimes and politics has tried to beat back those challenges. Thus the political resistance to the USSR in Czechoslovakia and Poland gained its initial impetus from economic breakdowns. The USSR responded politically. The internal revolutions that have discredited dependent elites and the U.S. role in Latin America have been a function of socioeconomic pressure; and the U.S. response has also been primarily political.

Finally, among these similarities in the two regions, social and cultural and attitudinal development has generally been disintegrative rather than integrative. Despite efforts by both dominant powers to promote cultural integration, with measures ranging from intense popular propaganda to educational and cultural exchanges, both dominant powers are less appealing to public opinion in their regional dependencies today than they were forty years ago. Despite the new technological sophistication of cultural penetration, the net regional consequences have been increased rejection of the dominant powers' cultural leadership at all levels.

It is tempting to dwell on the similarities of U.S. and Soviet regional frustrations. They may, however, easily obscure the abiding differences across the two regions. For many people in the global south the differences seem minimal. The symmetries of Soviet and U.S. regional power, though dressed in different rhetorical and visual symbols, seem to present a similar imperialistic threat. But let us try to abstract some of the important differences too.

We have already alluded to the fundamental ideological difference between pluralism and monism. In theory that difference gives an advantage of flexibility to U.S. strategy because the liberal premise defers to aspirations for independence and thus appears to fit historical cases better. As a rationalization of dominant power commitments, however, the Leninist premise serves the USSR better by justifying imposition of a single authority. The more significant consequence of the difference is to limit U.S. capabilities in a way that the USSR need not fear. So far as U.S. pluralist structures of decision-making must be aligned to make government strategy effective, the liberal dilemma about unilateral intervention constrains U.S. action. The effect of deeply divided public opinion was learned in Vietnam. Its Congressional reflection has been evident in ambivalence over aid to the Nicaraguan Contras.

Turning to the theory of hegemonic stability and decline in long cycles of international relations, we must note that the theory has usually been presented as a global characterization, and the argument for decline rests on the assumption of a liberal trading order adopted by the hegemon to maximize its economic advantages. The derivation proceeds from Portuguese, Dutch, British, and American eras of global political-economic ascendance. Thus, while the theory plausibly explains the rising costs of U.S. hegemony and the diffusion of U.S. power globally, and U.S. regional difficulties with Latin America by extension, the same theories do not so easily fit the Soviet Union's case.

The USSR has not, or not yet, come anywhere near inheriting the role of global hegemon from the United States. In contrast to its global military stature, the USSR's hegemony in terms of political economy runs only through its own region, and it has certainly not sought the classical advantage of a liberal trading order there. The United States, even if in decline, remains for the present the only global hegemon. Thus an explanation of Soviet decline within its region depends at best on an analogical application of the general theory. It might be more accurate to conceptualize the USSR as an imperial power, whose empire has been created and maintained by asymmetrical military power, but for which the evolution of multiple political-economic connections has led to more and increasingly burdensome costs. Making this distinction raises the question whether the Soviet regional system is as vulnerable to global economic trends as is that of the United States.

Third, regional economic dependency patterns are quite different between the Soviet and U.S. spheres. Whereas the American role as a manufactured goods exporter accords with the traditional hegemonic theory of advantage against primary materials exporters, single commodity economies, and agricultural economies, the Soviet role is quite different. With respect to most of its region, the USSR is the less-developed country, the primary goods exporter. Several of its dependencies take the part of manufactured goods exporters. (Clark and Bahry, 1983a: 280.) Hegemony predicated upon this reversed state of complementarity not only casts into question the conventional wisdom concerning who inevitably exploits whom, but suggests that external global economic trends may affect Soviet regional hegemony very differently from U.S. hegemony and present each hegemon with different strategic choices.

Our identification of similarities and differences across U.S. and Soviet regional relations must inevitably refer to the external contexts in which these bilateral regional relationships proceed. An understanding of the dominant powers' strategies and their effects clearly requires more explicit attention to external relationships.

The first of these contexts is provided by global East-West conflict. Rigid commitment to maintaining the regional status quo, even at a sacrificial political and economic price, rather than adapting to diffusion pressures and a less insulated, more liberal international regime, is largely a function of the dominant powers' relation *to each other* rather than to their respective regional dependencies.

Both dominant powers historically feared outside great power subversion and thus derived their original strategic purposes from their assessment of global threats. Although the origins of the American strategy in fear of Western Europe are long obsolete, the transposition of that fear toward the USSR's potential role in the hemisphere is reinforced by the traditional wisdom of insulation rooted in the sentiments of the Monroe Doctrine. Just as Dollar Diplomacy was partially driven by the aim to preempt European intervention, the United States feels driven to occupy the political space opened by Latin American socioeconomic convulsions before the USSR can get there. As factors to be considered, the internal dynamics of the Latin American countries have been deeply subordinated throughout.

In Eastern Europe the USSR perceived a vital interest in establishing a buffer to the West in the wake of two near fatal invasions from the West against the Bolshevik government. But control of Eastern Europe quickly became a symbolic issue in the global conflict with the capitalist West and a public barometer for the progress of world socialism. Thus the practical counsel of history as well as the legitimacy of the Soviet elite seem to require maintaining regional dominance.

The similarity between the subordinate regions is limited by differences of degree. Geopolitically, there is a great contrast. For the USSR the East European region is the primary external area on which the Soviet global position seems to depend. For the United States, Latin America has never taken that high a priority. Today Afghanistan is probably a better Soviet equivalent to Nicaragua than is any East European socialist state.

Like Central America, Afghanistan is not on the main geopolitical axis between the dominant power and its principal adversaries. Like Central America, Afghanistan has clearly been within its dominant power's traditional sphere of influence but is not intimately tied to the progress of Marxist-Leninist historical evolution. Neither the United States nor the USSR has a major national interest in seeking to displace the other power's traditional dominance in either small country, and in fact each great power has been notably cautious about such overtures. (Clement, 1984.)

We recognized earlier the tendency of disaffected clients in both regions to seek the external great power as a counterbalancing, alternative champion to the regional hegemon. Set against the Yugoslav and Cuban precedents, that tendency reinforces the dominant powers' inclination to perceive any regional instability as a function of East-West conflict and to respond to it as such regardless of more complex origins. Soviet tolerance of the Albanian defection may in part be explained by the fact that whatever else the turnabout represented it clearly was neither U.S.-inspired nor a product of sympathy toward the United States.

What is notable is not the alacrity with which the external dominant powers have sought to separate regional clients from their hegemons, but their restraint. Ever since the rhetoric of "rolling back the Iron Curtain" was revealed as hollow in the instance of Hungary in 1956, the United States has been deferential to the Soviet sphere of influence. Latin America has clearly occupied the lowest Soviet priority among world geographic areas in the years during which Soviet global capacity has expanded. In each case initiative has come from the disaffected clients, not the dominant powers.

In sum, the East-West global context induces unbending, sacrificial reaction on the part of both the United States and the USSR in their respective regions. It has prevented both countries from evaluating regional pressures on their own merits and from accommodating the diffusion of political-economic power that indigenous regional changes represent.

The second external context we must evaluate is the global North-South tension. The effects of this context are strikingly different in the two regions. For the United States and Latin America the relationship is archetypical of North-South tensions between the highly industrial and less-developed countries. U.S. difficulties of leadership and credibility are in large part attributable to failure to recognize that centrifugal forces result from this dynamic rather than from East-West tensions. But for the USSR in Eastern Europe the regional differences on North-South dimensions do not coincide with the dominant-dependent asymmetries of power. To be sure, Soviet-Yugoslav or Romanian conflicts have strong attributes of North-South exploitation. But dependent development has generally taken a different course in Eastern Europe. Soviet political power has dictated a distorted course of growth, predicated on Soviet needs rather than those of the client itself, and this loss of sovereign control and material advantage is deeply resented. But the balance of primary versus manufactured products has more often favored the East European dependencies than the USSR. In Valerie Bunce's felicitous formulation, the empire has struck back. (1985: 1–46.) North-South disparities complicate the Soviet-East European relationship, for instance, by creating sensitivity to global oil price manipulation and establishing new political-economic tradeoffs of energy dependence. But the disparities cut across the asymmetries of political-military power rather than reinforcing or contradicting them.

Conclusion: Choices of Future Strategy

The comparison drawn so far has not presented an enviable picture of the dominant powers' position. The economic and political costs of maintaining what each envisions as a necessary regional sphere of influence rise rapidly and encroach upon diverse competing claims for their own finite resources. The principal catalyst of each dilemma is the external stimulus of East-West conflict. But there are important differences as well as similarities in these dilemmas. Let us focus the conclusions of the comparison on some of the strategic choices that face each dominant power today.

First, to emphasize the consequences of similarities, it is fair to say that both the USSR and the United States face the basic strategic choice of either maintaining a "restorationist" posture or looking for acceptable ways to pursue vital interests while accommodating the diffusion of regional power. If the principal external context of East-West conflict and competition remains the source of regional policy, then control will take priority. It is no doubt within the resources of both dominant powers to absorb the rising costs of that choice for a long time, but not without increasing sacrifices elsewhere. The costs will include underwriting public debt and artificial support of markets for client exports beyond the real needs of the dominant powers. It will also mean a repressive military-political response to predictable political manifestations of social pressures in each region. That is feasible too, in both regions, but again the prospective price is high. It has been suggested that most of the increased costs to the Soviet Union will be economic in return for political benefits; to the United States the tradeoff will be political costs for economic benefits. That dichotomy is misleading. Both dominant powers must expect to bear heavy political and economic costs if they determine to restore unilateral control at the level of the 1950s because the indigenous regional changes since the 1950s in both Latin America and Eastern Europe have irrevocably changed the respective regimes.

What is far less clear is whether the long-term national interests of either the United States or the USSR really lie in such sacrificial commitments to the past or will continue to be perceived to lie there. The costs are clear and there is no escape from their steady inflation. It is hard to argue for an acceptable economic return that would justify the costs to either of the dominant powers. Although perceptions change slowly, the prospective security return, given the modern global military balance, is certainly less evident than twenty years ago.

From the USSR's perspective the argument for such a continuing priority is more readily made than for the United States. For the former, geography is more compelling; one may argue that a principal global threat to Soviet security lies in the European theater of East-West engagement, that therefore the northern tier of the Warsaw Pact is fundamental and its effective loss into East-West neutrality would isolate Soviet socialism and discredit the ideology on which the Soviet system relies domestically as well as internationally in an essentially hostile world.

In terms of the same East-West engagement, Latin America is peripheral, unless it were to become the locus of Soviet military deployments comparable to that of NATO in Western Europe. Given liberal U.S. values and institutions, the United States, unlike the USSR, does not face an ideological threat; no similar argument attaches to the importance of one or another domestic political or economic order among Latin American states, and no threat attaches to independence per se. Recognizing the distances and diversity of Latin American states, we may conclude that a distinction should be made between the Caribbean Basin and South America, where a security priority for U.S. dominance is less credible and more expensive to maintain. Hegemonic theory suggests greater decline for U.S. influence and greater political-economic diffusion of power among the major nation-states of South America than among the minor states of the Caribbean. (Poitras, 1985.)

We may thus consider the possibilities of the United States and the USSR finding scenarios for their regional regimes that would provide for their global interests without accepting the costs of an indefinite policy of restoration. For the USSR such a choice could imply strategies for maintaining a security veto over foreign policy among East European socialist states that would exclude Western military bases and discourage other concessions to Soviet global adversaries that to the Soviet Union appear threatening to an East-West balance. Such a reduced meaning for a security community might be quite consistent with East European aspirations for a less limited sovereignty than the Brezhnev Doctrine implies. It would mean in effect accepting the Finlandization of Eastern Europe. Just as Yugoslavia today, because of its location, is more tolerable to the USSR than a similar regime would be in Poland, it is reasonable to conceive of such Finlandization in terms that would grant latitude to East European countries according to their relative importance to Soviet security.

Given the difficulties of successful East European participation in the global capitalist economy, the inducements to these countries to maintain a robust COMECON would argue for the continued viability of such regional integration on a voluntary basis. Given the failure of the USSR so far, in terms of Modelski's stages of great power ascent and decline, to achieve broadly recognized legitimacy in Eastern Europe, such a transition could improve its position and thus indirectly contribute positively to Soviet security purposes. No one anticipates an abrupt reordering of Soviet policies in Eastern Europe. Old perceptions change very slowly, and the sharpened East-West conflict of recent years militates against flexibility. But rising costs of hegemony remain persistent and corrosive.

For the United States such a choice could imply greater differentiation among its hemispheric neighbors too, and greater sensitivity to the forces born of North-South tensions as against the East-West conflict. The Monroe Doctrine is fully understandable today in terms of opposition to Soviet penetration into the Caribbean Basin, as understandable as the counterpart Soviet opposition to a U.S. presence in Eastern Europe. The tacit basis for such a symmetrical recognition of adversary interests already exists. Assuming an indefinite prolongation of fundamental Soviet-U.S. conflict, a stable mutual recognition of these regional spheres does not seem farfetched. The Monroe Doctrine did not entail the expanded license for unilateral intervention appropriated by Theodore Roosevelt. In its more modest earlier incarnation it could still be a reasonable guide to real U.S. security interests in Central America and the Caribbean, and also to real Soviet security interests in Eastern Europe. Thus understood, it could also be compatible with neorealist accommodation to the pressures of political-economic diffusion in both regions.

9

The Logics of Hegemony: The United States as a Superpower in Central America

Terry Karl and Richard R. Fagen

Comparative analyses of the United States, the Soviet Union, and their respective peripheries are often pulled toward the identification of nominal similarities and differences at the behavioral level: U.S. troops in Vietnam and Soviet troops in Afghanistan; U.S. use of local client militaries in Central America and Soviet use of a client military in Poland; public protests in Washington against U.S. interventionism in Nicaragua, and deafening silence in Moscow about Soviet interventionism in Afghanistan. Such comparisons, however, tend to obscure as much as they reveal. In fact, they are often little more than thinly veiled devices for suggesting that one hegemon (the Soviet Union from the U.S. point of view) is worse, less reformable, more disastrous for its subordinate states than the other.

What analyses of this sort do not take into account is that these are *not*, at root, equivalent systems of dominant-subordinate relationships and should not be analyzed as such. The United States is formally a political democracy and is overwhelmingly more developed economically than its subordinate states. The Soviet Union is not a political democracy and is less developed economically than most of the states of Eastern Europe. These are qualitatively different regime types embedded in systems of domination and subordination that are also qualitatively different. Moreover, these systems are in flux, not the same today as they were even as little as a decade ago—and not destined to remain in the future as they are today.

What is a more appropriate point of entry? It is our contention that comparison of these two hegemonic systems should begin with a detailed analysis of the "laws of motion" of each system, considered separately. Only after this task has been accomplished does the construction of truly comparative categories become possible. Thus, in this essay, we do not attempt a head-on comparison of the United States in Central America with the Soviet Union in Eastern Europe. Rather, we sketch four separate but interrelated logics that move the United States as a hegemonic power. At certain points we do introduce some illustrative comparisons with the Soviet Union, but this cannot be done systematically because, as will be seen, we believe that at least three of the four logics do not really apply to the Soviet Union at all. Thus the next step is to explore the laws of motion of Soviet hegemony—an ambitious endeavor that is beyond the scope of our current enterprise.

The four logics that we use can be characterized as follows: (1) superpowers in conflict; (2) the United States as the dominant power in the capitalist world system; (3) antirevolutionary politics in a regional context; and (4) regime type (democracy) in the United States. We argue that important symmetries between the United States and the Soviet Union are found only in the first domain where—in reciprocal and mutually reinforcing fashion—each superpower acts to consolidate its global position at the expense of the other within a Cold War context of semi-zero-sum calculations. The other three logics—each in its own way also global in scope—are quite specific to the kind of hegemony exercised by the United States.

From our perspective, logic one, although critically important, actually explains the least of what remains as problematic about the United States in the Third World. In short, we suggest that an understanding of the sources, instrumentalities, and constraints on U.S. attempts to exercise hegemony will not be found primarily in an abstract consideration of superpower behavior in a militarily bipolar world, but rather at the level of the global capitalist system, the contingencies of antirevolutionary politics and regional history, and the specifics of democratic practice (and its violations) in the United States. We use the case of Central America—specifically analyzing a number of U.S. policy dilemmas in the region—to demonstrate this proposition.

The Four Logics of U.S. Hegemony

The strategic logic at work: superpowers in conflict. In an international environment in which the roles of the United States and the USSR are globalized, there is a mutually reinforcing imperative to project power, to sustain credibility, and to punish defectors from the alliance patterns established in the postwar period. Given this imperative, the high-flown notions of moral authority, defense of the free world, and "doing what is right"—common justifications for the exercise of U.S. hegemony—or the rights of the working class, defense of the socialist camp, and "doing what is necessary"—common justifications for the Soviet Union—take on quite specific and different meanings. On the part of the United States the basic message is simply a more elegant formulation of the arguments used by Lyndon Johnson in Vietnam: the United States is a truly global power, and it does not cut and run. From the Soviets the message is that they will maintain and defend the boundaries drawn in the wake of World War II. Neither abstract descriptions of national interests nor specific discussion of threatened sea-lanes, Soviet MIGs, or CIA machinations are at the heart of the matter—at least with respect to subordinate powers and the Third World. Control is at issue, made manifest in specific policy actions. Unhappily for peripheral countries, these actions often have little to do with the real development problems that they face.

From the U.S. point of view, what are the messages that these policy actions are intended to send? First and foremost, U.S. officials believe that vigorous U.S. action in peripheral countries tells the Soviets: "We are tough and we will not condone any change which appears to enhance your influence at the expense of our own." Control of events in the Third World is seen as part of the restoration of an image of U.S. power, so damaged after the debacle of Vietnam. It is, in essence, a preemptive strike for credibility, the proof that a global power can still control global events. The systemic logic is clear: What is important for one hegemonic actor in a two superpower system is to demonstrate a margin of superiority. As Edward Luttwak, adviser to the Reagan administration on military and strategic matters, explains:

Aggression is the one thing the U.S. knows how to deal with easily. The Soviet Union is an empire, in geographical extent and in world power the greatest empire yet seen in history. The military history of empires is not made of aggression. They are not essentially weak powers that suddenly leap on their neighbors. They expand their power by being so powerful that neighbors and neighbors' neighbors deem it prudent to comply with the empire's desires. The threat that we face is not Russian cavalry, but that foreign governments would deem it prudent not to co-operate with the United States anymore. (Epstein, 1985: 16.)

The United States has the capacity to stop a threat of this nature in the Third World. Thus, the maintenance of governments, even in small peripheral countries, that will cooperate with the United States is proof of its ability to project power and to contain the spread of Soviet power. Defeating or defusing radical regimes prevents the tipping of global power toward the Communist bloc, a shift defined *eo ipso* as inimical to U.S. interests. In this vision, involvement in conflict in the Third World is in effect a war by proxy against the USSR.

In addition to warning the Soviets, this mode of behavior is seen as having the advantage of sending crucial signals to U.S. allies—both in Europe and on the peripheries. In essence, the U.S. is demonstrating that it is trustworthy to its alliance partners, big and small. It will stand by its historic friends, if only by raising the costs of defection from its ranks. The "Reagan Doctrine," which actively supports anticommunist insurgencies across the Third World, is an integral part of this strategy. Protracted counterinsurgency wars, even if they are merely "nickel and dime operations" for the United States, are extremely costly in terms of human lives and resources for peripheral nations. In the systemic logic of superpower confrontation they are viewed as projecting power in a manner that inhibits the Soviet Union, reassures allies, and raises the cost of defection from the U.S. sphere of influence.

Somewhat ironically, this logic also accounts for the limited role of each superpower in the regional "backyard" of the other, as well as the conservative or "freezing" effect that each exercises over its neighboring polities. Since World War II both the United States and the Soviet Union have implicitly accepted the notion that each controls regional spheres of influence that are generally out of bounds for military activity by the other power. Just as the United States was unwilling to exploit fully the Polish crisis of 1981–82, the Soviets have been cautious about becoming involved in Central America, which they refer to as the "strategic rear" of the United States. Indeed, they have been quite frank about the limits of their involvement. While they will lend military aid and economic and political support to the Nicaraguan regime, they promise only "solidarity" in the event of a full-scale U.S. invasion. The commitment to Salvadoran rebels, to the extent that it exists at all, is far less. While the Soviets may exploit the Central American crisis in a number of ways, the bottom line is that Managua will have to defend itself.* (Blasier, 1986; Leiken, 1984; Jacobsen, 1984.)

*The political-economic logic at work: the United States and the capitalist world system.*** The twentieth century witnessed the consolidation of a worldwide system of production, exchange, and mass communications. The essential logic of this system is capitalist, and even nominally socialist countries are forced (or choose) to play by the rules of this global game in their trade, financial, and investment relations. In short, for small countries that wish to play on the world stage in our time—even to maintain or introduce a bit of rationality into the domestic economy—many of the key parameters are determined externally: prices, markets, technology, and tastes. And, without question, the most important actor in this international economic system is the United States, not the Soviet Union.

It is increasingly the case that autarchical scenarios of development have become difficult to the point of impossibility. In the aggregate, the much touted interdependence of the world economy means that the "health" of the advanced industrial economies (overwhelmingly capitalist) deeply affects the functioning of smaller economies through trade and finance, not to mention war, immigration, and other mechanisms. The small economies like Cuba that in part escape from the functioning of this system because of some special circumstance (with the USSR and COMECON in the Cuban case) are only the exceptions that prove the rule.

Some argue that the rise of regional and competing powers in today's world calls into question the validity of a "global system" characterization of the environment in which the small economies are attempting

*In this sense, both the Soviet Union and the United States have followed a moderate policy of limited containment, one that is geared to securing existing commitments while recognizing the superpower status of the other. Both recognize that their mutual military buildup has made a dangerous endeavor of tinkering in the backyard of the other. (Tucker, 1980–81.) Recently this stance has brought serious criticism from the ideological right. Formerly strong supporters of the Reagan administration, figures such as *Commentary*'s Norman Podhoretz contend that the United States should be more aggressive in Poland, the rest of Eastern Europe, and Afghanistan. (Podhoretz, 1985.)

**This section is adopted from the introduction in Fagen, Deere, and Corâaggio (1986).

to develop. After all, Japan and other capitalist powers compete successfully with the United States in a variety of ways. And the Soviet Union, and occasionally China, successfully challenge the capitalist world politically and diplomatically. But the world is multipolar in only a limited, albeit important, sense. Certainly there are intracapitalist conflicts and even contradictions. And obviously the Soviet Union is a great power militarily, with impressive capacity to act on the world stage. Furthermore, the actually existing socialist countries (despite all their internal schisms) generally stand as an ideological and political counterweight to the capitalist world—another pole of attraction and an occasional helpmate in difficult times. But the primary, critical features of the world political economy with which nations on the periphery must deal are rooted in the capitalist world system. Multipolarity provides, in some cases, a secondary structure of opportunity or some political, military, and ideological leverage on occasion, but it is not the fundamental architecture within which development on the periphery is played out.

The secondary impact of the socialist world to development on the periphery can be documented at many points: in trade, finance, transfer of technology, and even in foreign aid the world looks much more unipolar (taking the advanced capitalist nations as a bloc) than multipolar. But it is perhaps in the cultural domain, broadly defined, that the dominance of advanced capitalism is most marked. Where are the socialist alternatives to the music, dress, media productions, and consumer goods emanating from the advanced capitalist countries? Coca-Cola in the backlands, "Dallas" on the TV screens of urban shacks, blue jeans on the streets of Canton, and Accra. In the political realm the rule is increasing diversity, but in the realm of consumption the rule is increasing homogenization. There is no multipolarity in the march of contemporary commodity culture from the urban centers of capitalism—and particularly from the United States—into the most distant corners of the globe. In fact, there is no more striking global monopoly in the world today.

The small peripheral economies attempting to develop in the world just described have rather tightly constrained choices. The overwhelming majority have neither the material resources nor the productive skills and capacity to opt out of international trade and finance—even for relatively brief periods of time. In greater or lesser measure, in one way or another, they are subject to the rules of the only game in town. Furthermore, they are, with rare exceptions, passive players. By this we mean that they cannot as individuals affect the rules. They are price-takers in trade, technology buyers or recipients rather than technology generators, and borrowers on terms set elsewhere. Even collectively the record is not encouraging regarding the capacity of consortia of small peripheral economies to change the rules. At the margin, through international organizations—both formal and informal—some rules have been modified and a few changed. But the overall record of the postwar period is hardly studded with successes.

Thus, economic development (defined narrowly as capital accumulation and the augmentation of the forces of production) is extremely complex and difficult in today's world for small economies on the periphery (and for many large ones as well). The system and its rules were not established for their benefit. The rules were set up by the core capitalist players to ensure that their predominant position would be extended into the foreseeable future. These core countries cannot always get what they want, and there are important international and interclass disputes within and among the core countries with respect to what *is* wanted. The debate about debt restructuring and repayment suggests how heated such disputes can be. Nevertheless, the global system remains sharply skewed in favor of the interests of the core capitalist countries, primarily the United States. In this sense, trade, finance, and commodity culture can be considered the gunboats of the 1980s. This is the "international power context" in which the United States relates to its periphery, and it is quite different from the Soviet–Eastern European setting.*

The anti-revolutionary regional logic at work: controlling the neighborhood. The behavior of the United States as a hegemonic power becomes most clear when—through revolution or some sort of electoral (Chile) or negotiated (Zimbabwe) transfer of power—a Third World country begins a fundamental transformation of its own political and economic structures in the direction of "socialism."** Since these countries in transition cannot fully opt out of the global or regional systems in which they are located—at least in the contemporary period—they

---

*In contrast, the situation of reverse uneven development between the Soviet Union and Eastern Europe has produced a distinctive international environment characterized by the highly structured arrangements within COMECON. It can be argued that these arrangements, while they shape the economies of the subordinate countries to suit the Soviet Union, also give greater voice and influence to these subordinate powers vis-à-vis the USSR.

**We are accepting the self-designation of many of these experiments as socialist or "moving toward socialism."

must seek some form of modus vivendi with the United States. They too must trade, borrow, and deal with the material culture of capitalism *while at the same time attempting the transformation of the basic domestic political-economic-social systems that have characterized them in the past.* Thus, while they may well be trying to organize themselves to win more frequently in the global game, they are also dedicated to fundamental transformations at home that necessarily involve the replacement, or at least the dramatic disempowerment, of traditional elites with transnational links. This, in turn, implies a significant erosion of the capacity of the United States to influence the politics and economics of the revolutionary society, either directly or indirectly—not a situation viewed with equanimity in Washington. Put less delicately, Third World experiments in socialism feel the weight of the capitalist system not just in the "impersonal" working out of the harsh rules of the game, but as economic, political, and military pressures designed to turn them back into well-behaved conventional peripheral countries in the U.S. sphere of influence.

Why should this be the case? Conventional explanations usually focus on the tendency of these countries to ally themselves diplomatically with one or another group within the socialist camp. Thus, the conventional argument goes, the enmity of the advanced capitalist countries (usually, but not exclusively the United States) derives from geostrategic concerns and from international relations in the narrow diplomatic-military sense. Throw in a handful of economic interests, and season with liberal developmentalist ideology, and you have the conventional explanatory stew. Samuel P. Huntington exemplifies this view when he explains (and justifies) U.S. opposition to Third World revolutionary movements that are broadly understood as socialist:

> Revolutionary upheavals in Third World countries usually threaten concrete U.S. interests in these countries: investments, trade, military alliances, access to bases. Major revolutions and the regimes they produce generally have a negative impact on human rights, economic development, and regional security. In addition, any revolutionary regime will normally be less sympathetic to and less closely associated with the United States than was its predecessor. It will also normally be more open to Soviet influence, even though the Soviet Union may have played no role in its coming to power. Consequently, preventing revolutionary upheavals in Third World countries has been a recurring concern of U.S. policy. (Huntington, 1982b: 12.)

Erroneous observations about human rights and economic development aside, this kind of explanation is not inaccurate, just superficial
and incomplete. What is missing is an appreciation of the extent to
which serious experiments in revolutionary transitions challenge the
underlying logic of capitalist relations, the traditional alliance patterns
with local elites, and the global system that is the generalized manifestation of those relations. Any individual experiment does not, of course,
by itself threaten the global interests of capitalism—or even, in some
cases, its most concrete local interests, e.g., Angola. But taken together,
the experiments *do* challenge the legitimacy of capitalism and capitalist relations since they represent a rejection of "the system" and the
patterns of development associated with it.

Thus the United States, as the leading capitalist power, has systemic
reasons above and beyond the specifics of the Cold War and simple
calculations of economic interest to oppose the socialist or revolutionary transformation of the Third World. In the post-World War II period
the United States has become the status quo power par excellence, the
global gendarme of a still-unfolding capitalist world that is most at risk
in the Third World.* This is the perspective of a "winner," determined
not to let the immense advantages accumulated in the twentieth century slip from its grasp. It is also the perspective of a missionary,
convinced that its way of doing political and economic business is
generalizable and exportable to most if not all of the world.

Although the reach of the United States as an antirevolutionary power
is now global, the most unremitting application of these policies takes
place in Latin America and particularly the Caribbean Basin. For
example, the Bishop experiment in Grenada would not have received so
much attention, and that tiny island certainly would not have been
invaded, had it been located in the Indian Ocean. Central America and
the Caribbean have always been seen as of special importance in demonstrating continued and even enhanced capacity to control events in
the Third World. In fact, U.S. interventionist policies in the region long
predate both the development of the postwar, bipolar world and the
highly internationalized capitalist economy. From the founding of the
republic, U.S. leaders have believed that they were fated to dominate
Mexico, Central America, and the Caribbean, and, to a lesser extent,
the lands beyond. What subsequently came to be called manifest destiny meant for Jefferson, Hamilton, and others the acquisition of the

---

*The Soviet Union is a status quo power of a different sort. Since its reach is not global in
scope, its anti-change stance is largely confined to the countries on its periphery. Globally,
its stance can be characterized as "cautiously pro-revolutionary."

continent "piece by piece" until "America has a hemisphere to itself."
(LaFeber, 1983: 22.) This foreign policy vision was first institutionalized
in the Monroe Doctrine of 1823. More concretely for Central America,
it subsequently came to be embodied in a series of military, political,
and economic interventions designed to shape the countries of the
region in ways compatible with the expansion of U.S. capitalism. It is
no accident that every twentieth-century intervention by U.S. troops in
the hemisphere has occurred in the Central American–Caribbean
region.

The transformation of the United States from secondary status to the
world's most powerful nation in the twentieth century brought concomitant changes in its relationship with Central America, tightening
the web of political, economic, and security concerns. The notion that
the Caribbean Basin was the "backyard" of the United States was reinforced by the rapid internationalization of U.S. capital. Throughout the
region U.S. entrepreneurs, led by Minor Keith's United Fruit Company,
penetrated local economies and established a network of relationships with local dominant classes. By the 1920s the political and economic elites in each of the five countries had become increasingly
dependent on North America. The United States, in turn, was more
than willing to reinforce this economic dependence with direct military and political intervention. From 1898 with the deployment of U.S.
forces in Cuba to 1920, U.S. marines entered the Caribbean region no
less than twenty times. Their primary goal was to put down local
unrest, often aimed at elites who were U.S. commercial allies. By the
1950s the U.S. had a firm alliance with the dominant economic class,
military and security forces linked to the United States, and the
Church—a coalition that managed to rule most Central American
countries with varying degrees of success and repression until the late
1970s. This created a new rationale for involvement in the region—the
defense of traditional friends.

The current crisis in Central America is a direct challenge to this
ruling coalition, to the historical allies of the United States, and to a
long-standing tradition of regional hegemony. The crisis itself stems in
part from the failure of regional institutions—the Alliance for Progress
and the Central American Common Market—arrangements that had
sustained the traditional form of domination throughout the 1960s.
These setbacks, coupled with poor economic conditions following the
1973 oil price increase and growing violations of human rights, trig-
gered a political chain reaction throughout the isthmus. In every country except Costa Rica the military asserted overwhelming control as

traditional political parties crumbled. In Nicaragua, Guatemala, and El Salvador the new demands of peasants and, to a lesser extent, urban labor were met with state terror, which, in turn, proved unable to curb the growth of revolutionary movements. For the first time since the United States had become dominant in Central America, the area faced the prospect of a widespread regional war that challenged the hegemony of traditional elites and, by definition, the historical role of the "Colossus of the North." A century and a half of U.S. domination was now seen to be at risk.*

The regime logic at work: problems of a democratic hegemon.   There is an additional and crucial way in which the United States differs from the Soviet Union as a hegemonic power. As a relatively open and democratic political regime, the role of global gendarme of a still-unfolding capitalist world order is not entirely congenial to the American political system. Multiple debates and dilemmas of foreign policy are played out in public forums—in the press, the Congress, the judiciary, and the actions of social movements. Thus the American tradition comes into direct conflict at many points with the ideology and practice of an expanding national security state. Yet it is precisely this type of state—with its secrecy, immense budgets, worldwide system of bases, alliances, and covert and overt operations—that is necessary to the enforcement (or attempted enforcement) of the pax Americana. (Wolfe, 1977.)

Until the late 1960s, in the context of a broadly based bipartisan consensus on the formulation and implementation of U.S. foreign policy, the fundamental tensions between the civil-democratic and national security subcultures were not so evident. But the Vietnam war put an end to automatic acquiescence to the basic tenets of Cold War liberalism. For the first time there was significant questioning of the amount and extent of defense expenditures, the necessity for overseas adventures, and the credibility of the U.S. government in these matters. On a deeper level the combined trauma of Vietnam and Watergate produced attempts to make the executive branch more accountable by passing the War Powers Act, strengthening the role of Congress in foreign

---

*Again, there would seem to be sharp contrasts with the Soviet Union and Eastern Europe. Soviet allotments for hegemonic control are more profoundly determined by a mentality of encirclement and a strategy of perimeter defense. Having been invaded through the Polish corridor several times in this century alone, and repeatedly attacked across its borders, Soviet border-centric notions of security have their historic roots in defensive concerns. In this sense, Afghanistan is *not* Vietnam, and it is as yet unimaginable to envision Soviet troops fighting a war in a country 12,000 miles from their borders.

policy-making, providing more open access to information relevant to foreign policy, and protecting the civil liberties essential to democratic dissent. Although the era of easy acquiescence to executive-led decision-making came to an end, no clearly formulated and widely legitimated alternative vision of the new globalism emerged. If the U.S. public and the Congress demanded a more careful allocation of resources (especially American lives) after Vietnam as the quid pro quo for giving minimal public and congressional support for U.S. policy in the Third World, the rules for those allocations were still to be decided. Meanwhile, the actions and words of individual administrations were placed under permanent, if only partial, scrutiny.

The acuteness of the democracy–national security state tension has varied depending on the coalitional makeup and policies of different administrations. The Carter administration, for example, responded to post-Vietnam and post-Watergate pressures in a number of ways. Reinvigorated human rights policies, deeply felt by important public constituencies, some members of Congress, and quite a few officials in the administration, held the promise of becoming a low-cost way of restoring some semblance of consensus in support of U.S. policy. After all, a nation with such a strong civil libertarian tradition should be able to agree on the extension of that tradition to its foreign policy (or so it was hoped). The Carter administration also drew back from certain interventionist practices abroad and made sporadic attempts to limit the reach of the national security apparatus at home. In the Caribbean Basin it accelerated the negotiations for the new Panama Canal treaties and took steps toward a normalization of relations with Cuba. But as numerous critics have pointed out, there was a basic contradiction—or at least a profound tension—between the still-dominant ideology of global management and the particular policies crafted by the Carter administration. (Feinberg, 1983; Blachman et al., 1986.) Human rights, taken seriously, means that an administration cannot continue to be cozy with the shah of Iran. Respect for minimal notions of self-determination and nonintervention implies that one must probably stand by and watch as the Sandinistas assault the increasingly illegitimate dynasty of the Somozas in Nicaragua.* As these tensions surfaced,

---

*The three-way tension between the old hegemony, the reemergent moralism, and the new constraints, both domestic and international, is clearly illustrated in the Nicaraguan case. In June 1979, as the Sandinistas were winning dramatic victories over Somoza's National Guard, the Carter administration went before the Organization of American States to request a "peace-keeping" force to separate the contending forces and, incidentally, prevent a total victory of the Sandinistas. The administration was distancing

the Carter team backed away from its initial innovations.

For the Reagan administration, the lessons of Carterism were clear —supported, of course, by a priori ideological convictions: liberalization, the elevation of human rights concerns to a first order of priority, and a general softening of the traditional stance toward revolution meant the deterioration of the U.S. international position. Credibility would suffer, the hands of enemies would be strengthened as U.S. alliances weakened. Authoritarianism, it was argued, was far preferable to the victory of revolutionary regimes. In fact, to further delegitimize revolutionary regimes, they were simply labeled "totalitarian." (Kirkpatrick, 1979.) In Central America the change of perspective was swiftly felt. Reagan moved aggressively with a new campaign against Cuba, a not-so-secret war against Nicaragua, the introduction of money and military advisers into El Salvador, the construction of eight bases in Honduras, an attempt to renew military assistance to the Guatemalan armed forces, and systematic pressure against Costa Rica's traditional neutrality. At home the president's actions also eroded the domestic commitments made in the wake of Vietnam. The Reagan administration skirted the War Powers Act by initiating a proxy war against Nicaragua; it persistently bypassed congressional controls on military assistance through the use of supplemental appropriations; and it began to limit public access to information through new intelligence classification schemes and travel restrictions.*

But the implementation of this new doctrine has also been deeply constrained by post-Vietnam and post-Watergate realities in the United States—although the correlation of forces at home is different in the

itself from Somoza, yet feared the eventual ramifications of a new regime dominated by the rebels. The OAS, in spite of (or perhaps because of) the 1965 Dominican "peace-keeping" precedent, roundly rejected the U.S. proposal. The administration, committed to multilateral action, was thus unable to intervene to shape events as it would have liked.
*Kenneth Sharpe (1986: 43) points out that Congress did attempt to limit military appropriations to El Salvador from 1981–84, but the president used his authority to reprogram budgetary allocations and to draw down supplemental funds to bypass these restrictions. In 1982, for example, Congress only appropriated $27 million, explicitly turning down an administration supplemental request for $35 million. The White House claimed that an emergency situation existed in El Salvador and used its special draw-down authority to dispatch $55 million—over twice the amount that Congress had authorized. (1986: 43.) Sharpe and various congressmen have documented the administration's refusal to comply with the reporting requirements of the War Powers Act, which states that Congress must be informed within forty-eight hours when U.S. troops are introduced into hostilities. U.S. military personnel have been stationed in zones of conflict and had come under fire on at least eight separate incidents by early 1985, yet Congress has yet to debate or approve this policy. (Leach, 1984: 28–29.)

mid-1980s than it was a decade earlier. Skyrocketing defense expenditures (as well as the national debt), a Senate marginally in the hands of Republicans with a House still dominated by Democrats, an immensely popular president, resurgent nativistic/"patriotic" sentiment, and much more differentiate the context of the Reagan administration from that of its predecessor. Yet neither Democrats nor Republicans have been able to have their way in foreign policy toward the Third World—at least not to the extent that would have been possible during what some still regard as "the good old days."

Finally, it should be noted that the operation of these four logics means that despite differences in administrations, there is substantial continuity in U.S. foreign policy in the Third World—and especially in Central America. U.S. administrations have generally attempted to curtail or destroy the influence of the left, create or sustain an ally who provides an alternative to radical or nationalist regimes, and in general structure the politics and economics of the region in ways that are viewed as compatible with the capitalist world order. All administrations have been faced with the dilemma of carrying out these tasks in the context of a political democracy and a society that demand at least ostensible allegiance to liberal values. Furthermore, since the debacle in Vietnam, each administration has sought to give priority to battles closest to home—where favorable outcomes are most likely and where victories can be won with the least expenditure of resources. The interests and concerns remain global, but no administration wants to be caught fighting a new "test case" halfway around the globe. Thus it is in Central America where the several logics now intersect most explosively.

The United States in Central America:
Policy Dilemmas in the Backyard

There is a puzzle in contemporary U.S.–Central American relations. On the one hand, every U.S. administration (with the possible exception of Carter) since World War II has persistently defined political struggles within Central American nations in terms of the East-West conflict (despite much evidence to the contrary), and subsequently each has called forth a national security vision of the communist menace in the hemisphere to justify intervention. The current administration may have carried this practice to new extremes, yet it is important to remember that U.S. enmity toward the revolutionary government of Nicaragua and commitment to defeat the insurgency in El Salvador are expressions of long-standing traditions in U.S. foreign policy. On the other hand, despite these Cold War definitions and the past history of intervention in the region, the United States has not yet turned its full power on Central America in the 1980s. While the "Colossus of the North" is obviously an overwhelming presence to both policymakers and their opponents in Nicaragua and El Salvador, spending $100 million to arm and aid the Contras, holding endless naval maneuvers, imposing an economic blockade, and supplying fifty-five U.S. military advisers and a billion dollars to El Salvador is hardly full utilization of the U.S. arsenal of hegemony. If Central America is so overwhelmingly important to U.S. national security, why—we might ask—is so *little* being done to destroy our "enemies" in Nicaragua and help our "friends" in El Salvador and elsewhere?* Since it is impossible to trace U.S. involvement in the region in detail here, we shall instead specify the manner in which the collision between the regime logic of a democracy and the other logics developed above creates foreign policy dilemmas that help to explain this seeming paradox. Of course, somewhat similar dilemmas may be found in the Soviet Union or any other power attempting to exercise regional hegemony, but they assume a specific, even unique configuration in a democracy.

Dilemma 1: Defining U.S. interests in Central America.   Most observers agree that beyond the national security rhetoric there is a striking lack of clarity about U.S. interests in Central America—about what is at stake and what should be defended. Take, for example, the Report of the President's National Bipartisan Commission on Central America (the Kissinger Commission Report)—a document whose main purpose was to build a national consensus for the Reagan administration's policy in the region. The report contends that U.S. involvement in Central America is necessary in order "to preserve the moral authority of the United States," as well as to reinforce the perception by others that our nation "does what is right because it is right." Furthermore, the report claims that the United States has an interest in improving the living standards of the people of Central America in order to avoid revolution, to advance the cause of democracy, and to strengthen the hemispheric system. (*Report of the President's National Bipartisan Committee*, 1984: 45.)

---

*Needless to say, this is not the reality as seen from and experienced in Central America. Low-intensity warfare is only "low" from the perspective of the United States; it is experienced as full-scale war in the region. The point here is merely that the United States thus far has not used its full power in Central America, surely a region where a direct confrontation with the Soviet Union is a very remote possibility.

Yet "preserving moral authority," "doing what is right," and "advancing the cause of democracy, broadly defined" are scarcely the operational currencies of foreign involvement. Nor do they translate easily into concrete policies. Additionally, economic concerns do not find a place on most lists of U.S. interests, reflecting the lack of vital raw materials and the peripheral role of Central American markets for the United States (and, incidentally, revealing the limited utility of traditional theories of imperialism for explaining U.S. involvement). Thus it is not surprising that the rhetoric surrounding U.S. national interests and objectives in Central America has changed with remarkable frequency during both the Carter and Reagan administrations. At best, observers can only point to some very general objectives—keeping hostile powers at bay, securing stable governments that are allies of the United States, and promoting change within parameters acceptable to the United States. (Wiarda, 1984; Hayes, 1984; Leiken, 1984.) But objectives such as these leave almost all the tough questions unanswered.

What ultimately seems to knit together these shifting and somewhat vague descriptions of U.S. interests and objectives, however, is a fundamental assumption that equates U.S. security with the absence or suppression of revolutionary regimes. Given the logics that motivate the United States, the rationale for this equation is clear. Nevertheless, it is politically difficult to articulate this antirevolutionary stance as an overriding policy goal in light of the United States' own revolutionary and democratic traditions. Since the goal cannot be articulated publicly, its implementation must always be masked or mystified: Contra mercenaries and killers thus become "freedom fighters." The repressive Salvadoran military must be strengthened to "preserve democracy." Honduras must be turned into a U.S. military base in order to "guarantee peace in the face of a communist threat." Yet at the same time that the entire region is presented as "vital to U.S. national security," no convincing proof of its "vitalness" can be presented. Any attempt to specify and then act appropriately on what is "vital" will destroy the possibility of reaching the foreign policy consensus needed to sustain the "appropriate" actions. Democracy at home and warmaking in Central America do not easily coexist.

Dilemma 2: Defining the enemy. The lack of clarity and candor about national interests, and the absence of any credible security threat from tiny countries to the South, drive the overriding need for U.S. administrations to define the enemy in Central America primarily in terms of international communism—despite the unconvincing nature of this proposition. With the partial exception of Carter, each administration has attributed crises in Central America or the Caribbean to external subversion on the part of the Soviet Union, Cuba, and now Nicaragua. Any attempt to overthrow conservative authoritarian regimes becomes a Russian-Cuban plot—one that is aimed indirectly at the United States. Any change in the Third World that results in a form of international alignment that establishes some relationship with the USSR is perceived as a change in the basic correlation of forces and must be stopped. An East-West definition of the roots of the crisis in the Caribbean Basin means that any significant opposition or insurgency is transmuted into a tool of the Soviets, actual or potential.

Yet this manner of labeling the enemy has domestic credibility costs. There is a general consensus among most informed observers that the crisis in Central America is primarily rooted in internal problems, not external subversion. Scholars may differ on whether the chief cause lies in changes in landholding patterns, the closing of the traditional escape valves of migration, the failure of the Central American Common Market, the rapid growth of population, the repressiveness of local military and security forces, the intransigence of traditional economic and political elites, or some combination of these. Yet virtually every expert (with the exception of those working in the Reagan administration) rejects the notion that external actors, meaning either the USSR, Cuba, or the United States, have been the central source of conflict in the region. (Fagen and Pellicer, 1983; Newfarmer, 1984; Wiarda, 1984.)

Furthermore, links with the Soviet Union, where they do exist, cannot credibly be demonstrated to constitute a security risk in the conventional military sense. In fact, when attempts have been made to document the relationship between the Nicaraguan regime or the Salvadoran rebels and the Soviet Union (such as the State Department's 1981 White Paper on "Communist Interference in El Salvador" [State Department Bulletin, no. 2048] or the 1982 Special Report on "Cuban and Nicaraguan Support for the Salvadoran Insurgency"), they have violated conventional rules of evidence by containing forgeries as well as completely unsubstantiated accusations. (*Wall Street Journal*, June 8, 1981.) Unable to rely on reality, the Reagan administration has resorted to demonology and endless name-calling: "totalitarian dungeon," "Dictator Ortega," and the like. Since nuns, students, peasants, and trade unionists critical of the existing order do not evoke automatic enmity from the U.S. public, a credible enemy—one that is linked to international communism—must be created. In this sense, government disinformation and demonology are inevitable consequences of the conflict between democracy and hegemony.*

Dilemma 3: Creating friends in Central America. The erosion of traditional dominant coalitions in Central America and the concomitant rise of revolutionary urban and peasant-based groups has presented the United States with a seemingly insolvable problem. It can attempt to prop up its friends of the past—a solution that does not seem feasible in light of their human rights abuses, the strength of opposition forces, and powerful demands for change. Or it can embrace these newly emerging forces—an unlikely alternative given their nationalist, populist, and anti-imperialist character as well as their challenge to the capitalist economy as currently organized. This choice, so vexing to decisionmakers, has led to a now familiar formula for policy: create a moderate, viable "center" or third force that can provide a stable government friendly to the United States and an economy still oriented to private ownership. In an echo of what was originally the formula of the Alliance for Progress, both the Carter and Reagan administrations (in different degrees and with somewhat different motivations) have sought to build such a "center" in Central America to undercut the appeals of the radical left. This notion, which draws upon the successful defeat of a guerrilla movement in Venezuela led by the reformist Acción Democrática party, has been put into practice most thoroughly through support for El Salvador's Christian Democratic party. (Karl, 1985.)

The dilemma for U.S. policy, however, is rooted in the effort itself. Where such forces do not exist, e.g., Nicaragua, they must be created, or simply invented. As the tremendous problems in establishing the credibility of the Contra-supported Nicaraguan "democratic" alliance demonstrate, this is no easy task. Ex-Somocistas and mercenaries require more than a sophisticated public relations campaign to make them a palatable alternative to either Nicaraguan or U.S. public opinion,

---

*We should note that the Soviet government's problems in defining the enemy in Eastern Europe are less acute. On the one hand, Germany has invaded the Soviet Union in the not-too-distant past. Thus there is a historically legitimate and potentially powerful enemy on which to focus. Furthermore, since the Soviets are operating in a context of reverse uneven development, they do not face the disbelief inherent in the contention that a small underdeveloped country can be a security threat to one of the world's greatest military powers. On the other hand, the nature of the Soviet political system permits mobilization without the same necessity for prior legitimation and precludes the mechanisms of accountability in foreign policy found in a democracy.

even if they have the help of figures like Arturo Cruz and the backing of the Central Intelligence Agency. Where such middle forces do exist, e.g., the Christian Democratic party in El Salvador, the existence of deeply entrenched elites, the long history of authoritarian rule, and the present virulence of class conflict do not create propitious conditions for their success. In either case, the creation or maintenance of these "centers" requires an unusually high level of foreign involvement in economic, political, and military domains—a reality that mitigates against their legitimacy and eventually reveals them as yet another group dependent on external subsidization. Thus the "center," whether invented or partially indigenous, is always in danger of becoming unfit for what it is intended to accomplish—the creation of a new, change-oriented, yet stable basis for an alternative regime-type friendly to the United States. Even if it manages to survive, prospects for fundamental reforms remain dim since it can almost never move dramatically against its opponents on the right.

These three dilemmas are built into the structure of the U.S. global role, its history of domination in the region, and the nature of its democracy. Thus they are not easy to resolve. It is not surprising, then, that the Reagan administration, like its predecessor, has found it next to impossible to implement its version of U.S. policy in Central America. It has had, however, demonstrably more success in El Salvador than in Nicaragua.

Take, for example, the administration's problems in selling an East-West version of the Central American conflict. From the outset, Reagan's efforts were hindered by the fact that a very substantial portion of the U.S. Congress, the news media, and the public in general would not accept the premise that Central American problems derive essentially from communist subversion. To the contrary, informed opinion saw revolutionary upheaval in Nicaragua, El Salvador, and Guatemala as a response to decades of repression and exploitation as well as the systematic destruction of reformist politics and politicians. When coupled with the public's concerns for human rights and for "no more Vietnams," it has been difficult for the administration to secure the support and financing necessary to carry out its policies. Even after Nicaragua predictably turned more openly to the Soviet Union in the wake of the U.S.-sponsored war and the economic blockade, the Sandinistas still could not be credibly presented as fierce and dangerous enemies of America. And despite massive efforts to drum up enthusiasm for the Contras, including charity balls and society women sending CARE packages to the Nicaraguan-Honduran border, there has been remarkably little enthusiasm generated for these "freedom fighters." Furthermore, public opinion polls have consistently demonstrated at least 60 percent opposition to direct military intervention in the region, even during the high point of support for the Reagan administration after the invasion of Grenada.

Thus, in a series of votes and resolutions on Central America, Congress has almost always refused to give the full dollar amount requested by the administration for its undeclared war on Nicaragua and its propping-up of the Salvadoran military. Skepticism over the administration's descriptions of the enemy in Central America has even penetrated the armed forces. In July 1983 the then-retiring army chief of the Southern Command, General Wallace Nutting, was quoted as saying: "The fundamental causes of dissatisfaction [in Central America] are the existing social, political, economic inequities." Other officers concurred: "Guerrilla uprisings, no matter how anti-American or dependent on Soviet assistance, spring largely from genuine economic and political grievances that can't be swept away by U.S. troops." (*Wall Street Journal*, July 20, 1983.) This skepticism—which, according to one Reagan official, has made the military "the strongest pacifists in the whole place"—is a fundamental reason why Nicaragua has not been the target of even harsher actions on the part of the United States.*

If the administration has been less than successful in defining a credible enemy in Central America in general, or a Contra "friend" in Nicaragua, it has been notably more capable in El Salvador. While it was barely able to glean $27 million from a reluctant Congress for the war against Nicaragua in 1985, it raised a full *half-billion dollars* for El Salvador in that same year, making that small country one of the largest recipients of U.S. aid in the world. The administration moved from a situation in 1982, where all allied NATO governments with the exception of Britain disassociated themselves from the fraud of the Salvadoran elections of that year, to widespread international recognition of the Duarte alternative by 1985. The short-term explanation is not hard to find. The combination of U.S.-sponsored elections and the figure of President José Napoleón Duarte, a leader with a genuine internal base (who has the added advantage of speaking English on U.S. television), have been the stimuli for an uneasy U.S. consensus for current administration policy in El Salvador. For the time being, Duarte

*Interview by author with official responsible for Central America policy in the Department of State, Washington, D.C., September 1983.

permits the United States to avoid the stark dichotomy of either supporting friendly but military-authoritarian regimes or living with (or directly attacking) radical nationalists. Whether he can survive as a political force, keep the right in check, undercut a powerful revolutionary movement, and put El Salvador on a new development path—even with hundreds of millions of U.S. dollars—is, however, dubious at best.

We have come to the end of our brief analysis of the hegemonic logics of the United States. Our fundamental methodological assumption has been that comparability between the United States and the Soviet Union is possible only after the laws of motion of both systems are in full view. Thus we suggest that the parallel development of logics to explain the actions of the Soviet Union in Eastern Europe as well as the dilemmas it faces in the exercise of hegemony would be the next step in an ambitious comparative endeavor of this sort.

We have limited our empirical discussion to U.S. policy in Central America—from the most global considerations of superpower rivalry to more micro aspects of the tactics by which the Reagan administration, using high-intensity symbolism and low-intensity warfare, is attempting to turn back the clock in Nicaragua and shape the politics of El Salvador. Time will tell if these efforts are ultimately successful, and—if so—at what cost to Central America and the United States. But even now, at least one critical feature of this effort is clearly in focus. Despite the fact that both superpowers attempt to export their own political and economic formulas through military intimidation, the creation of client political groupings, and the violation of national sovereignty and human rights in subordinate states, only the United States carries the "burden of capitalism and democracy" abroad. As we have seen, this is a two-edged sword. In the very process of attempting to maintain the global system that it heads, the United States must proclaim that it is doing so in the name of certain values. And in allegedly championing the spread of these values, it violates them at every turn. Furthermore, since many Americans have the temerity to believe and the freedom to argue that those values should be practiced by their government both at home and abroad, imposing hegemony on the Third World will continue to meet constraints, opposition, and—at least in many areas—defeat. Coca-Cola and rock music travel on their own wings from one corner of the globe to the other. But more fundamental political and economic arrangements are usually exported only at gunpoint, and even then, only under very special circumstances.

10

The Military as an Instrument of Influence and Control

Condoleezza Rice

The United States and the Soviet Union enjoy overwhelming military superiority within their regional spheres of influence, Latin America and Eastern Europe. In any military confrontation between these two giant states and the smaller states there would simply be no contest. Several times in the twentieth century the Soviet Union and the United States have resorted successfully to military intervention to forestall unwanted change. But police actions can be politically costly, and both the United States and the Soviet Union have been cautious in the use of overt power. Military intervention is a policy of last resort.

Military power does not have to be used in its rawest form, however. Threateningly visible military maneuvers and gunboat diplomacy have long been standard fare when the United States and the Soviet Union wish to remind smaller states of their military vulnerability. The course of domestic development within subordinate states can be influenced, even altered, by a range of actions that draw on military assets. In strong state–weak state relations there are important links that tie the interests of indigenous political elites to those of elites in the dominant state.

Military assistance is but one good that dominant powers are able to provide for political elites in smaller states, and since security is critical, the promise to give or the threat to withhold that assistance can be a powerful lever. Moreover, it is important to note that dominant powers maintain links directly with military elites. The military is only one of the political institutions through which influence and control over the course of domestic development can be maintained. But for the USSR and the United States, status quo powers within their own regions of influence, it is a particularly important institution. Control of those who control the guns is an obvious advantage in any attempt to ward off unwelcome change. Denial of the military instrument to recalcitrant political leaders or the ability to turn to the military to support one's own interests are essentials in times of crisis.

The successful exercise of these options rests heavily on the existence of effective levers long before they are needed. But in structuring military relations within its sphere, the dominant power is pursuing a number of competing, even conflicting, objectives. There are the control objectives, mentioned above, through which the dominant powers maintain coercive means to assert final authority in domestic development. On the other hand, the dominant states also wish to build influence based on persuasion that is broad and deep enough to avoid situations in which military power needs to be used overtly. These normative objectives include socialization of the population through military service, legitimation of the indigenous regime, creation of an identity of interests with indigenous elites, and the inculcation of the dominant power's values and principles within the military elites and the society as a whole. If one adds a functional objective, the need to create military institutions that are capable and cohesive fighting forces, it can be seen that it is not easy to meet all objectives simultaneously.

This chapter examines the way in which the United States and the Soviet Union pursue these objectives in structuring relations with the indigenous military. It examines and compares the mechanisms employed and compares them on three dimensions; penetration, integration, and sustainability. But before turning to these issues, it is important to examine more closely the contexts in which American and Soviet power is exercised.

Regional Power Asymmetries and Domestic Development

Power has been defined in numerous ways by social scientists. It has been called the ability to "force adaptation through control of the environment," "the ability of strong states to impose costs on others in ways that weaker states cannot," and "the ability to produce a discernible effect on the actions of another." (Baldwin, 1979: 177.) Power is observable when one actor sets out to determine the actions of another and succeeds. Power is presumed to flow from certain attributes: economic wealth, military strength, and political, ideological, and cultural influence. The ability to translate power attributes into manifest power is the essence of international relations.

The interactions between the dominant states and subordinate states in Eastern Europe and the Americas are power relationships. By all objective measures the United States and the Soviet Union have significantly greater power than their allies in each region. Moreover, the smaller states rely on the United States and the Soviet Union for a variety of "goods." The list ranges from political support and military guarantees to trade relations. At times some leaders in subordinate states have been dependent on Moscow and Washington for their political lives. The power that accrues to the dominant states under these circumstances is obviously great. Because these relationships include some perception of mutual benefit and the threat of coercion, the alternatives are few and the costs for the small state in finding a substitute sponsor are very high. The highly asymmetric dependence is self-reinforcing. The term dependence should not be taken as pejorative here. It is simply recognition of the fact that states do not bring equal assets to relationships. Every state (in the modern system) is dependent on someone for something. It is a simple fact that weaker states (those with fewer attributes of power) are likely to be more dependent on stronger states than the other way around.

But power does not float freely. It is necessary to exercise it upon some object. An assumption of this study is that dominant powers like the United States and the Soviet Union are able to exercise their power at many levels. They are able to forge personal relationships with political and military leaders because they can promise (even if they cannot deliver) to keep elites in office. Institutional relationships are forged because identification with the institutions of the dominant state can lend legitimacy to governing elites and, perhaps more important, stability and immunity from challengers. At the state-to-state level the stronger power is likely to dominate trade and economic relations. These regional hegemons lead multilateral organizations that reinforce their domination at other levels. The dominant regional power is thus able to reach down below the level of state-to-state relations and influence domestic events directly. The ability of the small states to act autonomously, without regard for the preferences of the dominant power, is severely constrained. The costs of testing the more powerful actor may be so great that the small state does not test the limits of autonomy. Moreover, domestic institutions and elites may see their interests as tied simultaneously to the external power and the internal political system. When there is conflict between the two sets of interests, the Januslike elites, looking in opposite directions, are in a most difficult position indeed.

Comparing the Context and Exercise of American and Soviet Power

The differences between the United States and the Soviet Union are obvious. The democratic political system of the United States fashions foreign policies that are openly debated and determined by a multitude of important governmental and nongovernmental actors. The Soviet foreign policy process is hidden from view and, like Soviet politics generally, conducted by a chosen handful of very powerful men. The American economy is the "locomotive" of the capitalist world economy, which includes all of the great industrial powers (except the Soviet Union) and most of the smaller, dependent economies of the Third World. The Soviet economy is hardly a locomotive even for itself any longer, and though it still dominates socialist economic relations, both the Soviet Union and its allies have found it increasingly necessary to draw upon the resources of the industrialized capitalist world.

One common attribute is the ideological content of American and Soviet power, especially within their spheres of influence. The fear of contagion—the spread of unwanted change—is very strong in both cases. It has become fashionable to dismiss ideology as an important force in the conduct of foreign policy. But ideology, while it is clearly not the sole determinant of foreign policy preferences, continues to play an important role in coloring political leaders' perceptions of their environment. It is not that ideology is a blueprint. Rather, it is a constraint upon the imagination of political leaders. It limits alternatives because some are judged to be out of the realm of the possible. Unlike capabilities, which can be acquired through effort and the devotion of resources, ideology can be quite difficult to alter. It is true that both powers have shaped and stretched ideology to justify many actions. But the argument here is that ideology has itself shaped and stretched the actions of the superpowers and is, in part, an explanation for the rigidity they exhibit in relations with the subordinate powers in their regional spheres of influence.

For the United States the ideological content of policy is a marriage of the Monroe Doctrine and containment. The security concerns that spawned the Monroe Doctrine are no longer relevant. While some continue to worry about Soviet bases in the Caribbean, the overwhelming military power of the United States in the region makes this argument less than forceful. But the exclusionary ideology remains. It is virulently anticommunist, and as a consequence the United States is able to tolerate any form of government, whether military dictatorship or constitutional democracy, that is not communist. It is unlikely that a communist state could ever be an ally of the United States, at least in this region. Ideology plays an essentially proscriptive role, defining that which the United States wishes to forbid. For the United States, democracy can never emerge from a communist environment, while a dictatorship at least preserves the future possibility. Even in the face of evidence that dictatorships beget new dictators at least as often as they do democracies, this distinction between authoritarianism and communism governs American policy in the region.

The ideological component of Soviet policy in Eastern Europe is more complex. Clearly, Eastern Europe is important to the Soviet Union for many reasons; it is a security buffer, and the states are economic and political allies. But for the Soviet Union the socialist world community has significant value in being socialist. The Soviets exercise a kind of prescriptive control. They know precisely what form of government they prefer and exclude other alternatives. One-party systems, state control of the media, and even some economic sacred cows (central planning for heavy industry, for instance) are essentials of acceptable government. Commitment to these institutions and to other deeply held tenets helps to explain why the Soviet Union cannot tolerate deviation even though there may be no objective threat to economic or security ties. For the Soviet Union, ideology is a constraint because loyalty and reliable economic and security relations are defined as relations between communist states. For the Soviet ideologue a deviant Romania with a tightly controlled political system is less threatening than a compliant Czechoslovakia well on its way to political liberalism. Perhaps Joseph Stalin put it best in explaining that socialism in one country was a temporary condition, and that a ring of brother states would be needed to secure the Soviet revolution itself. (Stalin, 1974.)

There are also important differences in the nature of the regional spheres themselves that help to explain how American and Soviet power differ in their impact. Latin America is a region of great diversity, with several states that could be considered regional powers in their own right. Brazil, Argentina, Venezuela, and others have many levers of influence of their own within the region, and their domestic institutions are probably more resistant to American influence. No state in Eastern Europe enjoys the regional status of these Latin American powers. The richest of them, East Germany, has so many political liabilities that its room for independent maneuver in foreign policy is very small. In viewing the American sphere of influence, it is perhaps useful to draw a distinction between Latin America as a whole and the weaker states of the region, particularly those of Central America. No such distinction needs to be made within Eastern Europe, although the Soviets were, at an earlier time, completely incapable of penetrating and manipulating the institutions of Yugoslavia, where the revolution had been led by the nationalist Josip Broz Tito.

Another important asymmetry is in the relative importance of the regions to the security of the dominant power. Latin America does not share a border with powerful American enemies, and though an argument can be made that sea-lanes and open access to the ocean are important, the great power of the American fleet and protective oceanic boundaries are the final guarantors of American security. The importance of Eastern Europe as a security buffer is generally acknowledged. The historical memory of invasions through the Polish corridor and the creation of NATO on the Soviet Union's western border are surely assuaged by Soviet control of Central Europe. But the security buffer zone argument can be drawn too simply. Perhaps the Soviet Union, even with overwhelming conventional strength in Europe, does still fear a repeat of the German invasion of June 1941. It is more likely, however, that the real value of East European territory is not as a *cordon sanitaire* but as a forward base for Soviet and Warsaw Pact military forces, which, if Soviet leaders decide that war is inevitable, could be dispatched rapidly across NATO borders. The Soviets claim that their political doctrine is defensive, that the West would have to start or at least provoke a war. But seemingly without concern for the inherent contradiction, the Soviets also proclaim that their military strategy is offensive. They would not wait to be attacked and would seek to press their forces onto the territory of Western Europe in a rapid offensive. If this preemptive strategy of Soviet military policy is to be carried out,

East European territory is critical. Thus, Eastern Europe is both a *cordon sanitaire* and an absolutely vital staging ground for the successful prosecution of Soviet military strategy should war in Europe begin. (Gareev, 1985.) Eastern Europe plays a far more central role in the military strategy of the Soviet Union than Latin America does for the United States.

The differences in the regions and in the nature of the two states themselves can be easily stated. In examining the structure of military relations between the dominant powers and the smaller states, it is clear that a great deal can be explained by the factors cited above. Before exploring this thesis further, we will examine the types of levers that flow from the military power of the United States and the Soviet Union.

Levers of Military Influence

The levers of military influence fall into two broad categories: the use of military assistance and arms sales to forge security dependence, and contacts between military officers that give the dominant power influence with indigenous military elites. The components of the first category are obvious, but it is probably worth noting that security dependence is an effective lever only if there are no viable alternatives for substitution. In a multiseller market this can be difficult to achieve. Nevertheless, the United States and the Soviet Union control almost 70 percent of the arms trade, and the figure is somewhat higher if small arms and less sophisticated weaponry are excluded. (Arms Control and Disarmament Agency, 1985.) Other states are gaining, but this is still a two-player game. Moreover, the costs of substituting one supplier for another are very high. Inoperability of parts for weapons made by different suppliers, sunk costs in terms of training, and the inability to buy spare parts for weapons already in the arsenal are three problems that come to mind.

The second set of levers can be described rather easily, but it is difficult to assess their potential for successful influence-building. Military assistance agreements often include arrangements for personnel training and officer education in the sponsoring country, and the stationing of the dominant power's troops on long-term training missions in the recipient country. There is also the practice of bringing military officers to the military academies of the dominant powers. These opportunities for contact between officers and soldiers of the dominant and subordinate states are sometimes believed to be important in forging unity and identity of interests between the militaries. Some even believe that the values and traditions of the parent military can be transmitted through such contact. The problem is that familiarity can also breed contempt, and the values and traditions of the indigenous military are shaped by a host of factors, not least important among them the values and traditions of ancestral institutions. Try as they might, the parent states often fail miserably at value transmission.

Both the United States and the Soviet Union have established military relationships based on military assistance and contact with the indigenous military. Figures for arms sales to any region are always subject to some doubt, especially in the Soviet case where problems associated with costing Soviet hardware abound. But broad trends are readily observable. The United States and the Soviet Union are the primary suppliers of arms within their respective regions. Between 1979 and 1983 the Soviet Union transferred arms to Bulgaria, Czechoslovakia, East Germany, and Poland whose worth exceeded $1.1 billion for each country. Sales to Hungary during the same period totalled $650 million and to Romania $420 million. These transfers accounted for about 75 percent of the intra-Warsaw Pact arms sales. (Arms Control and Disarmament Agency, 1985: 133.) It is generally believed that all weapons within the Warsaw Pact are purchased, albeit at special alliance prices. There are no known grants of equipment.

Clearly, grants make substitution more difficult than sales, but even in their absence there is little supplier substitution within the Warsaw Pact. Czechoslovakia is the other major Warsaw Pact supplier and is, itself, self-sufficient in small and light arms. But since arms sales are coordinated through the alliance machinery, these arrangements supplement rather than supplant Soviet assistance. There are constant struggles within the Pact, however, as the smaller suppliers, Czechoslovakia and Poland in particular, fight to maintain indigenous production. The East Europeans want to maintain flexibility in this relationship, while the Soviets have made it clear that they prefer a fully integrated arms production and transfer package. The Soviets defend their position in the name of efficiency. One Soviet commentator stated that it would be inefficient for national industries to build everything: "Only the USSR can achieve this. It is better for the socialist countries to specialize." (Iakubovskii, 1975.) The policy of division of labor and specialization has not been a complete success. Redundancy continues, and there are few signs that the East Europeans are convinced of the wisdom of this policy. Czechoslovakia, in fact, has so ignored the policy that it is now self-sufficient in small arms and produces (under license from the Soviet Union) a good deal of its own heavy weaponry. Only Romania has dared venture outside of the pact for significant assistance, however. Romanian suppliers include France, the United Kingdom, and West Germany. About 15 percent of Romania's arms trade was with Western countries in the period from 1979 to 1983. Romania has also increased its own arms production capacity.

The United States is also the dominant supplier of arms to Latin America, accounting for a little over 65 percent of sales in the region. Mexico and Venezuela were America's biggest customers, receiving about $1.1 billion worth of equipment in the period from 1979 to 1983. In Latin America, however, there is a greater diversity of suppliers. Argentina, Colombia, and Brazil have numerous West European suppliers. Brazil has become a net exporter of arms and has an active trade with her Latin American neighbors — a trade that, unlike Czechoslovakia's, is not coordinated through regional alliance machinery. The possibilities for substitution are numerous for most of these states. Peru has even signed a military assistance agreement with the Soviet Union and obtained $440 million in aid from the Soviet bloc. (Arms Control and Disarmament Agency, 1985: 133.)

On the other hand, the security dependence of the Central American states is considerably greater. Though Central American states do buy arms from other suppliers, security assistance from the United States is by far the most significant component. American military assistance is channeled to Central America through three different programs: the Military Assistance Program, which provides direct grants for the purchase of military equipment, facilities, and maintenance; the International Military Education and Training Program, which underwrites the training of officers; and the Foreign Military Sales Financing Program, which provides longer-term loans and credits for the purchase of equipment. Military assistance is also provided through the Foreign Military and Constructions Sales Agreements Program and in the transfer of nonlethal equipment (bridge laying equipment, for example) through the Arms Control Export Licensing Act.

From 1950 to 1979 U.S. support for Central America (Costa Rica, El Salvador, Guatemala, Honduras, Nicaragua, and Panama) totaled $127 million, almost evenly divided among the three major programs. (U.S. Department of Defense Security Assistance Agency.) But between 1980 and 1982 alone U.S. aid exceeded that almost thirty-year total (1980–82 aid amounted to $176 million). For 1984, the last year for which data are available, the Reagan administration proposed aid packages of $135 million for Central America, with 90 percent of that aid designated for

El Salvador and Honduras. These figures clearly show the refocusing of American effort in this area. Moreover, for these small countries the possibilities for substitution are somewhat constrained. The assistance programs take the form of credits and loans rather than cash purchases and should theoretically provide the sponsoring power with a better lever of influence than cash payment (or even short-term credit) deals.

We find fewer parallels when we examine the ways in which the two dominant powers provide contact between their own militaries and the indigenous elites. One way to compare these policies more effectively is to examine them on the common dimensions of penetration, integration, and sustainability. Penetration refers to activities within subordinate states of military officers from the dominant states—in management of military affairs, development of doctrine, and training. Integration refers to the subsumption of national command functions in a larger, regional military organization. The ability to sustain these ties over time is also important.

The Soviets have made very good use of their military institution in achieving and maintaining dominance in Eastern Europe. Soviet troop maneuvers and exercises have been used a number of times to remind recalcitrant political elites of Soviet power. In the Hungarian crisis of 1956 and during the Prague Spring of 1968, unscheduled and very visible troop maneuvers took place on the borders and on the territory of Hungary and Czechoslovakia. Many believe that they were, in fact, a prelude to invasion, but it is equally plausible that they were undertaken for their coercive value. (Valenta, 1979b; Jones, 1981.) For instance, in June 1968, troop maneuvers conducted in Czechoslovakia were extended well beyond their announced date of cessation. It is probably no accident that sensitive negotiations with the Dubček regime were being carried out during this time; the military exercises were certainly timed to coincide with a vitriolic press campaign against the Czechoslovak reform movement. The same tactic was employed in the fall of 1981 just prior to the imposition of martial law in Poland and the crackdown on Solidarity. It is not clear whether the audience was the Polish leadership or the Polish people, but this time the Soviets did not invade. They were able to turn instead to General Wojciech Jaruzelski and segments of the Polish military.

The Soviets have also achieved thorough penetration of subordinate militaries, perhaps making possible the Jaruzelski solution. The structure of the relationships is such that at the level of the high command, there is a Soviet counterpart for each East European officer. (Rice,

1984.) There are Soviet advisers with each staff, with the political administration, and within the ministry of defense. These contacts are made somewhat easier by the stationing of Soviet troops on the territory of four of their six allies. Cultural and sporting events and, of course, military training allow frequent contact between the Groups of Soviet Forces in Europe (nineteen to twenty divisions in East Germany, five in Czechoslovakia, four in Hungary, and two in Poland). If one adds the Soviet military missions at embassies and the Soviet representatives to the Warsaw Pact missions in East European countries, the depth of Soviet involvement in the day-to-day management of East European militaries is clear. Bulgaria has many Soviet advisers but no Soviet troops, and Romania has neither Soviet troops nor Soviet advisers.

The Soviet–East European military structure also scores high on integration. This is due, for the most part, to the tautly integrated Warsaw Pact structure. Soviet coalition doctrine envisions Soviet and East European forces as one. The commander in chief of the Warsaw Pact is a Soviet marshal, but many believe that even his role would be subsumed by the commander in chief of the Western Theater of Military Operations. The Groups of Soviet Forces and their corresponding East European armies would become military front-sized formations against the West in the event of war, without distinction by national command.

Because the Soviets expect the Warsaw Pact armies to fight as one, they have increased pressure on the East Europeans to specialize in certain military tasks (the Hungarians in bridge-building and engineering, for example) and to train as one multinational entity. Whole functional units of the East European militaries train with Soviet units, and no attempt is made to maintain the integrity of national command. In the Warsaw Pact there is a common doctrine and strategy; tactics, weapons, and training are similar, if not identical. This is an extremely effective military strategy, but there are political payoffs as well. It is clear from one Czechoslovak statement that military efficiency is not the only goal of tighter integration. "The closest cooperation ... has been expanded ... a new form was added to the existing ones: the mutual exchange of whole units between motorized riflemen and other formations of our fraternal armies...." The account goes on to proclaim that the new form gives Soviet commanders and soldiers a chance to get to know their Czechoslovak counterparts personally. "This is far more effective than brief conversations or short meetings." (*Rúde Právo*, October 5, 1978.) The ability of forces that are so thoroughly penetrated to resist Soviet invasion is very limited. Here the motives for control and for efficiency are completely consonant.

Finally, this military structure has endured over time. If anything, it has been strengthened by the 1968 invasion of Czechoslovakia, which placed Soviet troops on Czechoslovak soil for the first time since 1945. The Soviets were startled by the rapid deterioration of their networks of influence and control within the Czechoslovak army and emerged from the crisis dedicated to tighter integration. New efforts to coordinate the formation of military doctrine were launched after 1975. There has been a remarkable proliferation of joint works on military history, the history of the Warsaw Pact, and coalition doctrine. New institutions like the Joint Technical Committee, which coordinates weapons production and procurement, and a rejuvenated Defense Ministers Council also foster integration. The East Europeans point to positive features of this system, primarily enhancement of "consultation and operational direction of the Joint Armed Forces." (Holloway and Sharp, 1984.) In fact, the Soviets have been careful to give the Warsaw Pact a new aura of equality. At the same time they have worked within the new institutions to tie the East European armies more closely to their Soviet counterparts and to transfer many decision-making functions from the national context to the multilateral context of the Warsaw Pact, thus moving toward tighter integration.

All has not been rosy for the Soviets in this regard, however. Romania has been a constant gadfly and a source of some embarrassment. But even though Nicolae Ceauşescu has attempted to completely de-Sovietize his own military elite, the Soviets have lived up to the bargains Khrushchev made with him almost thirty years ago. Perhaps Soviet patience with Romania will be rewarded some day. There are reportedly rumblings within the Romanian military elite as they see sophisticated weapons pass them by, and some have suggested that great instability in Romania could lead to the reestablishment of Soviet influence with the Romanian military. Some would say that this is possibly the underlying cause of Ceauşescu's recent concessions to his own military that have substantially enlarged their role in economic policy. It should also be noted that Romania walks a very thin line in Warsaw Pact affairs and has, in spite of protestations of independence from the alliance, participated in staff exercises. Finally, Romania's geographic position, far from the central front, has undoubtedly helped Ceauşescu to maintain his relative independence.

The levers of the United States appear to be both less penetrative and less integrative. Joint maneuvers have been carried out on occasion with Brazil, Argentina, and Colombia. The responsibilities of the

Southern Command do not require the deployment of large contingents of American ground forces. There are small contingents in Antigua and Cuba (420 marines at Guantánamo Bay). The American military presence is represented largely by naval forces steaming in nearby waters. The total number of American forces in the Caribbean and Latin America is 15,500. This number pales in comparison with the 355,600 Americans in Europe or the 147,500 in the Pacific. (International Institute for Strategic Studies, 1984.)

There is far greater U.S. penetration of the small militaries in the Central American countries of El Salvador, Honduras, and, to a lesser extent, Guatemala. According to most reports, this activity has increased significantly in the last four years. (White, 1984; Arnson, 1984.) American attention was refocused on the region after the Nicaraguan Revolution. Since that time the United States has actively participated in training and arming these militaries. The primary goal has been to train them in the rigors of counterinsurgency doctrine to prevent yet another communist victory.

The most immediate concern has been the Salvadoran army. In 1977 the United States cut off military assistance to El Salvador and Guatemala because of persistent human rights violations. A coup d'état by more moderate elements in the army laid the groundwork for the resumption of American aid in 1980. Many in the Carter administration had been concerned that El Salvador's army was on the verge of collapse and urged the immediate resumption of aid. When aid was resumed, the package was accompanied by considerable pressure from the United States for the restructuring of El Salvador's army and the professionalization of its officer corps. The centerpiece of this effort was the adoption of counterinsurgency doctrine and training. This doctrine, which relies on unconventional warfare methods to fight guerrilla movements, first surfaced in the United States during the Kennedy administration. President John F. Kennedy was concerned that the Soviet Union and its communist allies would engage in what the administration termed "salami tactics," slicing off pieces of the "free world" through defeat of weak American allies from within. Kennedy ordered the study of methods of guerrilla warfare and the development of American Army Special Forces prepared to fight it. The first test came in Vietnam, but persistent battles between the proponents of conventional warfare and the officers trained in counterinsurgency slowed the full-scale development and use of these methods in the American military. (White, 1984; Summers, 1984.) Nevertheless, counterinsurgency strategies were used in Vietnam.

After Vietnam, in a time of budgetary stringency, counterinsurgency lost much of its support within the American military. Small units, trained not to fight conventional battles but guerrilla warfare, virtually disappeared. Then, with the victory of the Sandinista insurgency, the hostage crisis in Iran, and the growth of terrorism, they were resurrected, first in the late days of the Carter administration and then more fully by the Reagan administration. Counterinsurgency training enjoyed a renaissance at the American Special Forces Center at Fort Benning, Georgia, and at the U.S. Army School of the Americas in Panama, which was revitalized to train Latin American officers. In 1982 five hundred officers from El Salvador alone were training in Georgia.

To assist in the training of the Salvadoran military, whose numbers had increased fourfold in five years, the United States initially sent nineteen advisers. In 1983 that number was increased to the congressionally imposed ceiling of fifty-five. The advisers participate in the training of Salvadoran forces and also help in the maintenance of equipment. Five officers act as liaisons between the regional and national command. Of the fifty-five advisers, fifteen are reportedly counterinsurgency experts training newly organized "rapid reaction battalions."

This effort has not been entirely successful. In spite of their almost total dependence on the United States for military assistance, Salvadoran military officers have been extraordinarily resistant to American suggestions for reorganization of forces and to calls for the adoption of counterinsurgency doctrine. These officers, trained in more conventional American methods as cadets, reportedly do not like the prospect of becoming essentially "guerrilla armies." (White, 1984; Arnson, 1984.) Moreover, the American-trained counterinsurgency battalions are in short supply, and because they are the most active in battle, their survival rate is extremely low. Nevertheless, the American effort has helped the Salvadoran army stem the tide of what seemed a few years ago to be an inevitable rebel victory.

American penetration of the Honduran and Guatemalan armies has been somewhat less thorough than in El Salvador. U.S. military assistance to these countries has risen significantly and they have American advisers, but their commands have not been reshaped to any significant degree. Some observers of the region point to the relationship between the American ambassadors and the defense ministers of these countries as promoting a strong American role in their defense and foreign policy-making, especially in Honduras. (White, 1984.) Until the late 1970s there had been occasional multilateral exercises between

Honduran and American forces. In 1982 the largest maneuvers ever took place: the "Big Pine I" maneuvers were strategically placed not far from the Nicaraguan border, with 4,000 Honduran troops and 1,600 American soldiers participating. At the same time the USS *William V. Pratt* cruised the Caribbean coast to show the flag. Even larger-scale "Big Pine II" maneuvers took place in July 1982, this time involving 5,600 American soldiers with two full naval battle groups deployed in the Caribbean.

Honduran territory also plays a major role as a U.S. base for training military personnel, and there have been repeated calls for a Regional Military Training Center to be permanently established there. Between 1970 and 1980 over two thousand Honduran officers were trained by American army instructors. Argentina has also sent advisers to Honduras to train officers from that country, El Salvador, and Guatemala. The rift between the United States and Argentina over the Falkland Islands/Malvinas War caused Argentina to temporarily cease participation in this activity, but it has reportedly resumed.

Growing criticism, however, is making it increasingly difficult for the United States to use Honduran territory for military purposes. Mild protests were heard at the end of 1984 from the Honduran president, and the Contradora group has expressed concern about the "regionalization" of the conflict with Nicaragua. Much of the discomfort with the U.S. presence in Honduras stems from concern over the purpose of its military activities, which are said to be too closely linked with support for the Contra insurgency against the Sandinista regime in Nicaragua. American support for the Contras is carried out primarily through the CIA, not the American armed forces. But whatever the depth of American involvement, Honduran territory has been the primary haven for Contra training and the staging ground for their raids against Sandinista territory and assets. The problem for the Reagan administration has been to sustain support domestically for any American activity in support of the Contras.

Even with the increased training and equipping of the armies of these states, American activities are considerably less penetrative than those of the Soviet Union. The Soviets have developed essentially isomorphic structures in the East European armies that provide for Soviet counterparts to East European officers throughout those militaries. Sometimes these advisers are found all the way down to the unit level. The military organizations of the Central American states are not symmetrical with their American counterparts. Interestingly, one would have to go back to the end of World War II and look at

American-sponsored military reforms in Japan to see any evidence that the United States once attached importance to isomorphic structures in its relations with allies. Not surprisingly, those structures were created precisely for the purpose of transmitting democratic values and the means for civilian control of the military to Japan and, to a lesser extent, West Germany.

While American military activities have become more penetrative in recent years, efforts to integrate the forces of Latin America have been largely absent. This is mainly because the Organization of American States, which was formed in 1948 with the express purpose of repelling communist aggression, has failed to produce a collective military force. Joint task forces have been formed at times, as in 1965–66 for the invasion and occupation of the Dominican Republic, but no permanent structure exists. There is an Inter-American Defense Board to coordinate planning. The other attempt to form a permanent military bloc against communism, the July 1965 agreement between El Salvador, Guatemala, Honduras, and Nicaragua, became dormant with the Sandinista revolution in 1979. A less formal alliance was later forged between El Salvador, Guatemala, and Honduras against Cuba, Nicaragua, and domestic guerrilla movements; and a similar grouping, the Communidad Democratica Centroamericana, composed of Costa Rica, Honduras, and El Salvador, agreed in January 1982 to a mutual assistance pact. (International Institute for Strategic Studies, 1984.) The structure of military relations in the Americas is far looser than that of Eastern Europe, and in all cases the integrity of national commands has been maintained.

Nevertheless, the United States, sometimes with allies in tow, has been able to use military force to forestall change in the region. The joint effort by Grenada's small neighbors and the United States in the 1983 invasion of Grenada is the latest case in point. But the lack of attention to penetration and integration of the militaries probably reflects, first and foremost, Latin America's relative lack of importance in the overall security equation of the United States. Moreover, American forces are far more mobile and easily deployable, given the navy's power projection capability, than those of the Soviet Union, which, as they did in the invasions of Hungary and Czechoslovakia, must move across great expanses of land. The militaries of Latin America vary a great deal in their level of professionalism and in the degree to which they play an external security role. Many of the militaries of the smaller states resembled palace guards rather than professional militaries for a very long time. (Wesson, 1982a.) Even now, few of them are really devoted to protection of the regimes from external threat. With some exceptions, the opportunities for and interest in joint tactics, doctrine, and training are relatively few in this region.

Arguably, the real difference between the two blocs in the structuring of military relations lies not in the degree of penetration or integration, but in the sustainability of dominant state–subordinate state ties. The Soviet Union's system of military ties in Eastern Europe dates back to the end of World War II, when it built isomorphic military institutions in the region. Those ties have been developing and maturing, albeit with important breaks with Romania and temporary troubles in Czechoslovakia, since 1945. The inconsistent nature of American foreign policy has bedeviled any attempt to build long-term, consistently strengthening ties with the Central American states. The relative importance attached to the region has shifted over time, and a period of intense interest, like the present one, may well be followed by benign neglect in a few years. Moreover, persistent concerns about the human rights violations of military friends in the region and differing opinions in Congress and the Executive make consistent military assistance programs in the region difficult to maintain.

In spite of these differences, both the United States and the Soviet Union do have military levers within their regions; the problem is how to manipulate them in order to meet political objectives. This is especially difficult because each superpower must often deal with conflicting objectives within its sphere of influence. While the United States often seems to value control above transformation of the societies of Latin and Central America, social change remains an objective. Pressure upon elites, especially military elites, to allow this process to take place can have an unsteadying effect on already vulnerable governments. The United States has often failed in trying to employ these levers to promote human rights in the region. Both Guatemala and El Salvador refused American aid rather than comply with human rights standards. Some have argued that the United States encouraged and helped to make possible the coup d'état by moderate officers in El Salvador in 1979. Nevertheless, the massive military aid given to this region by the United States has not carried commensurate leverage in shaping internal events.

The Soviet Union does not face the same kind of conflict because social change in Eastern Europe is low on the Soviet agenda. Sometimes, however, the Soviet desire to inculcate the military with values held dear by the Soviet Union itself must be put aside. The most obvious example is Poland. The Soviets have strong fears of Bonapartism and military rule and have spent endless time and effort preaching the virtues of party control of the military. In the crisis of December 1981 the control objective took precedence, and General Jaruzelski was at least tolerated if not encouraged. Now the Soviets face the unhappy task of trying to get the Polish army back into the barracks.

In 1968 the Soviets faced a conflict between control and normative objectives in Czechoslovakia as well. The Soviet Union spends endless effort and money to promote the image of "friendship in arms." Privileged East European officers have been trained at Soviet military technical schools and academies since 1946, and the political education curriculum is heavy on promoting goodwill. Soviet cultural and sports clubs from the armed forces travel among the East European armies for the same reason. But the need to invade Czechoslovakia and purge the army clearly unravelled the entire investment in military friendship between the two countries.

Sometimes the conflict between objectives comes about quite unintentionally and is not foreseen by the dominant power. In the 1960s there was great hope that the professionalization of the militaries of Brazil, Argentina, and other countries of the region and their contact with their apolitical American counterparts would foster the same values of political neutrality in the Latin American militaries. But professionalization fostered precisely the opposite values as technocrats within the military took it upon themselves to lead their countries to modernization. The Soviets are not without experience in the disappointments of professionalization of the armed forces either. After Nikita Khrushchev decided that the East European militaries should modernize, the call went out for the professionalization of the armed forces. But it was assumed that professionalization would result in undying loyalty to the Soviet Union and identity of interests between the militaries. In fact, it fostered just the opposite response. The better-educated officers questioned their second-class status in the development of strategy and doctrine and demanded a greater role. Eventually, at least in the case of Czechoslovakia, the Soviets had to oversee the intentional dismantling of the professional officer corps it had built, in order to construct one that was politically loyal, if professionally weak. (Rice, 1984.)

In spite of the difficulty of balancing these conflicting concerns, the Americans and Soviets have had their successes in wielding the levers at their disposal. As a rule the control objective has been easier to meet than the normative one. The Soviets had to swallow their own fears of Bonapartism in bringing Jaruzelski to power, but he has certainly ruled more effectively than most would have expected. In any case, his assent was far better than a politically costly Soviet invasion of Poland. The number of juntas in Latin America, ruling in the name of anticommunism and enjoying American assistance as a result, is testimony to the value of having friends among those who have guns. In Chile, after the United States initially failed to convince the military to intervene against Salvador Allende, a coup did take place. (Sigmund, 1982.) The degree of American complicity is a matter of some debate, but in this case, as in others, the military, allied with other forces, was considered preferable to Allende, who threatened American interests. The ability to reestablish and then maintain stability in places like Panama and Guatemala, East Germany, Czechoslovakia, and Poland are certainly in the interest of the dominant power, even if the nature of the regimes has often been embarrassing.

Given their great power, however, it is startling how often the United States and the Soviet Union have failed in their use of military influence and control. Twice the Soviets have had to openly intervene. In Hungary in 1956 they actually met resistance from renegade military units, from a minister of defense who was an anti-Soviet freedom fighter, and from armed members of the population. The Czechoslovak armed forces did not resist, but they proved to be completely unreliable as an internal instrument against the Dubček reforms. In fact, the military leadership was so caught up in the reform that they refused to denounce it. For their part in the Prague Spring, the armed forces of Czechoslovakia lost 11,000 officers in a postinvasion purge.

The United States has been even less successful in employing its military influence effectively. The American bloc has had outright defections to the other side after the defeat of indigenous military forces allied with the United States. Perhaps the most striking example is Cuba, where, in 1959, Fulgencio Batista's armies went down to defeat in spite of American assistance. Cuba is now an important Soviet military ally, and Nicaragua is moving in that direction. It should be noted that both Cuba and Nicaragua are obliged to follow certain rules. The prohibition against the basing of offensive weaponry capable of striking the American homeland is a case in point. When the Soviets challenged this principle in 1962, the United States demonstrated that it was willing to go to war to uphold it. The Soviets, of course, relented and have for the most part respected this sometimes rather blurry line of demarcation. Less dramatic evidence of the weakness of American levers in this region can be seen in the political independence of more powerful states like Peru and Argentina during periods of military rule.

One could argue that the lack of penetration and integration of the military forces of the region is a handicap for the United States. In the case of Peru and Argentina the militaries remained wholly national and independent forces and could thus, albeit at some costs, be free to act against American interests. On the other hand, in Cuba and Nicaragua the United States enjoyed influence with the professional militaries, but not with the rebels. Whereas victorious armed rebellion in the Soviet bloc, given the depth of Soviet military and police control, is unthinkable, such a development is entirely possible in the more loosely controlled U.S. sphere of influence.

As a substitute for sophisticated levers of military influence, the United States is blessed with economic supremacy in the region, a fact that makes life difficult for those states that do challenge American power. The economic pressure that contributed to the rise of General Augusto Pinochet is a case in point. American governmental and private ties to economic elites are extremely important as well. Often alliances between these interests and the military are born without the assistance of American levers of influence. But as Western Europe has regained its own economic strength and has shown a willingness to violate American economic sanctions, the efficacy of this economic lever may be weakening.

One final key to understanding America's failures to use military levers more effectively lies in the fact that implied American threats lack credibility in the post-Vietnam era. First, there is always the question of whether America can mobilize domestic opinion to support the use of force. Second, the building and maintenance of military ties is best done covertly, and it is very difficult to do anything covertly in the United States. Third, the American political system has so many actors that insurgents can certainly plead their cases to different segments of the population. Dubček had to deal with a united Soviet government. Pictures such as those of Roberto D'Aubuisson meeting with Senator Jesse Helms or of American volunteers helping the Sandinistas would never appear in the Soviet bloc. Finally, a lack of consistency in American foreign policy as a whole makes it difficult to sustain levers of influence and control. American ideology, except possibly during the Carter administration, has been remarkably consistent toward the region. But the short attention span of American foreign policy and shifting budget priorities have led to frequent neglect. As a result, when crises refocus American attention, the levers of influence are in disrepair.

The Soviets, on the other hand, know exactly where their power lies, and consistent attention to the all-important military instrument should not be surprising. It should be reiterated that the security situation is much more pressing and immediate in Eastern Europe and that integration has real value in military terms. But the Soviets have paid careful attention to the political side of this instrument, valuing politicization and socialization of the militaries of Eastern Europe very highly. They do make mistakes, as in the 1960s when Khrushchev's encouragement of renationalization of the region's armed forces led to instability in Czechoslovakia and set Romania on her independent course. But the Soviets understand that the military lever is their most consistent and sustainable one. It is dangerous for the Soviets to contemplate economic sanctions against their allies because this would undermine the stability of the regimes and unleash forces of popular resentment that are just beneath the surface. One student of the situation has noted that there is marginal correlation between Soviet economic assistance and the political loyalty of the recipient. (Reisinger, 1983.) The Soviets have also displayed a willingness to force integration in the military sphere while allowing diversity in others. The Czechs once accused the Soviets of substituting military integration for failed economic, social, and political integration. (*Lidová Armáda*, 1968.) The depth of attention that the Soviets give to the military dimension would tend to support that judgment.

It is easy to fall into the sin of parallelism when comparing these two great powers. This analysis was intended to show that the United States and the Soviet Union use these seemingly similar instruments differently and that the impact of these differences upon the freedom of maneuver of subordinate states is significant. It is possible to draw a few conclusions about the usefulness of this instrument in general. In the final analysis the ability of the superpowers to use their military assets for influence and control depends fundamentally on the character of the task at hand. The use of these assets for influence-building seems to work best in small, politically vulnerable states, a category into which most East European states and the states of Central America and the Caribbean fit. In states that have few assets of their own, leaders who are dependent on a regional hegemon are likely to choose policy options carefully. They are less likely to test the limits of autonomy and to tailor their policy preferences in accordance with the expectations of the dominant power. The states of Central America, like El Salvador, that are unable to look to other patrons for political and military support are prime examples. Not surprisingly, little deviation from the American line is observable in the policies of José

Napoleón Duarte. Deviation in Eastern Europe does occur, but when it comes to important decisions in the Warsaw Pact, the Soviets are very good at forcing monolithic unity.

On balance, military levers would appear to be better suited for control and functional objectives than normative ones. A recent army officer's critique of American policy in Vietnam criticizes the Kennedy and Johnson administrations for trying to use the American military as a vehicle to democratize Vietnamese political institutions and to build popular legitimacy of the Saigon regime. (Summers, 1984.) The Soviet Union has also tried to use its military in this way and to create indigenous militaries that would give to the states of Eastern Europe the trappings of sovereignty and legitimacy and provide a vehicle for the socialization of the population. But in insisting that there is no tension between their roles as national protectors and their roles as protectors of international socialism, the Soviets have often deceived themselves. In a conflict between the two, the control objective and the normative one have come into violent opposition.

Still, it is better to have these levers than not. At times it is possible to ask "Who is serving whom?" as military elites learn to manipulate the system to strengthen their own power within their societies. But used in conjunction with other levers, for example economic ones or effective coordination with police forces, the military instrument can be quite potent. At least when a superpower intervenes with its own forces in the region, it can hope for neutrality at the worst and cooperation at best. When crisis comes, therefore, there is probably no better lever within the region than the military instrument. As a means to long-term influence, however, this lever is much less promising. But it is always important to ask what the prospect for influence would be without the military ties. Put in that light, it is easy to understand why the military instrument receives so much attention in the policies of dominant powers within their spheres of influence.

11

Military Interventions: Doctrines, Motivations, Goals, and Outcomes

Jiri Valenta

Cuba [is] the most interesting addition which could ever be made to our system of States. The control which with Florida Point this island would give us over the Gulf of Mexico, and the countries and isthmus bordering on it, as well as all those whose water flow into it, would fill up the measure of our political well being.—Thomas Jefferson, 1823

Poland is a capitalist monstrosity and the last bulwark of imperialism [which] continues to . . . isolate Germany from Soviet communism.—Vladimir Lenin, 1920

Military interventions are a ubiquitous political phenomenon, infinitely varied by virtue of their motivational causes, modes of implementation, and outcomes. Of specific interest here is that restricted concept of intervention developed by Stanley Hoffmann, whereby a state, through direct or indirect application of its military might, seeks primarily to

*I am indebted to my colleagues at the University of Miami for their insightful comments: Dean Ambler Moss, former Ambassador to Panama; Prof. Enrique Baloyra; and Prof. Jaime Suchlicki. I also benefited from the comments of Virginia Valenta, Prof. Alex Pravda and Prof. Robert Wesson.

affect another state's domestic affairs and, by extension, its external affairs, with the understanding that the capability to substantially control the internal politics of a country is the most effective way of shaping its politics abroad. (1984: 6–28.) Such interventions occur when a target state's authority apparatus is in question because of internal revolution, civil war, military takeover, or other sources of serious instability.

This conceptual framework allows considerable latitude for interpretation and multiple focuses. My analysis here is restricted to a broad and, I hope, dispassionate comparison of interventions by the great powers in countries along their peripheries or within perceived spheres of influence, i.e., East-Central Europe (hereinafter Eastern Europe) in the case of the USSR, and the Caribbean Basin (Mexico, Central America, and the Caribbean islands)** in the case of the United States. Both superpowers have far-reaching interventionist capabilities that in times of perceived necessity have been used to directly or indirectly influence the domestic affairs of neighboring states. Usually such transgressions have not conformed to what many observers envisage as clear-cut interventionist doctrines. The motives more often have been multifaceted and changing, reflecting, as they do, evolving images of national security. Superpower interventions, like the motives that incite them and the decision-making processes that sanction them, do not readily conform to neat categories. In spite of similarities, the interventionist activities of the Soviet Union and the United States have been highly dissimilar since World War II, primarily because the underlying motives and conditions and the coherent political-ideological approach that facilitate the USSR's structural interventionist continuity in Eastern Europe have been lacking in the last several decades on the part of the United States vis-à-vis neighboring Caribbean countries.

The following discussion will revolve around four basic points: (1) the explanations and justifications for superpower military interventions can be strikingly similar; (2) the Monroe Doctrine and the so-called Brezhnev doctrine, which have been used by analysts to help explain interventions by the great powers at their peripheries, have had an uneven and sometimes limited effect on the actual development of U.S. and Soviet national security and interventionist policies; (3) instead of resulting from static doctrines, such interventions, particularly in the post-World War II era, reflect ever-evolving images of national security and often-changing motivations; (4) because of different political sys-

**These regional concepts are employed for lack of better ones, although both present some problems.

tems and differing concepts of national security, asymmetry in the implementations and long-term effects of superpower interventionism is pronounced.

I. Similarities

Post-World War II superpower interventions have involved international Goliaths, on the one hand, and, on the other, small and, in the case of Grenada, even minuscule Davids. Consider the Soviet interventions in Hungary in 1956, Czechoslovakia in 1968, and the indirect intervention in Poland in 1980–81; and the U.S. interventions in Guatemala in 1954 (indirect), the Dominican Republic in 1965, and Grenada in 1983. The unequal nature of these struggles was commented on by UN Secretary General U Thant in the introduction to his annual report in 1968: "It is, certainly, a frightening commentary on the ominous state of world affairs that one super-state or the other can become exercised to the point of resorting to military action because of a liberalization of a regime in a small country like Czechoslovakia or because of an internal upheaval in another small State such as the Dominican Republic." (Hoyt, 1985: 145–48.)

A second common feature of Soviet and U.S. interventionist policy in peripheral states is both superpowers' attempts to legitimize their interventions by securing the assent and token participation of other friendly states in the region, as well as the support of recognized regional organizations. Thus the United States, following intervention in the Dominican Republic, persuaded the Organization of American States (OAS) to take nominal command of token OAS forces under the leadership of a Brazilian general. In Grenada in 1983 the United States also secured the token military participation of a majority of the members of the smaller and regionally more confined Organization of East Caribbean States (OECS). The Soviets, in turn, justified their invasion of Hungary on the need to conserve Warsaw Pact Organization (WTO) cohesion, which Hungary's activities supposedly threatened. The Soviet invasion of Czechoslovakia also derived legitimacy from WTO associations; the invasion was conducted under WTO cover and with active, although token, military participation by most WTO members.

A third feature characteristic of most superpower interventions has been the intervenors' compulsion to justify and explain their behavior; and in spite of actual differences in the conduct and outcome of their interventions, superpower alibis are often very similar. Related to this is the Soviet and American tendency to try to prevent the United Nations from debating these issues. Thus Alexander Dubček's government was coerced into withdrawing the matter of the Soviet invasion of Czechoslovakia from the UN Security Council agenda, and the United States lobbied to block a similar UN debate concerning U.S. intervention in Guatemala and the subsequent collapse of the Jacobo Arbenz government. Both superpowers, furthermore, take advantage of inflated rhetoric about "humanity" and "morality" ("communist brotherhood in arms," "duty to Western civilization," or "duty to socialism") to justify their use of force. The exaggeration of external threats often obscures the real motives behind their actions. Though the Soviets have become more and more innovative in providing such justifications, these sometimes reach ridiculous proportions, such as their stated need to invade Czechoslovakia in 1968 because of an "international Jewish conspiracy." (Valenta, 1979b: 106.)

Often superpower explanations of interventionist behavior appear to echo one another. Thus President Lyndon Johnson's justification for intervening in the Dominican Republic in 1965, based on the need to preempt the rise of "another communist country" in the Caribbean, i.e., a "second Cuba," appeared to be echoed three years later by General Secretary Leonid Brezhnev, who spoke of the necessity of preventing Czechoslovakia from becoming "another Yugoslavia." It might also be ventured that the so-called Brezhnev doctrine, which provided the Soviet justification for the Czechoslovak invasion, in some sense replicated U.S. pronouncements following the indirect intervention in Guatemala and the invasion of the Dominican Republic.

The superpowers (and especially the USSR) have supported the argument that a military intervention undertaken in response to an invitation from a lawfully established government is free of any illegality. This line of reasoning has been used repeatedly by the Soviets, who euphemistically refer to their interventions as "fraternal assistance." This rationale governed the invasions of Hungary and Czechoslovakia as well as the invasion of Afghanistan in 1979. A comparable U.S. example in the Caribbean Basin was the intervention in Grenada in 1983.

Given these and other similarities, many analysts conclude that superpower interventions and the motivational impulses behind them are symmetrical. As this *myth* goes, the Monroe Doctrine and the Brezhnev doctrine advance equally the hegemonic ambitions of their author states while protecting their respective national interests. Accordingly, differing ideologies are immaterial in the face of similar outcomes, that is, the subordination of small states to the will and benefit of greater powers.

II. Doctrine Versus Reality

The Monroe Doctrine was of serious policy relevance primarily during the first three decades of the twentieth century, at which time it was closely limited to the Caribbean Basin region. After being weakened by substantial revisions in the 1930s, its importance declined further, except for resurrections during the Cold War and following the emergence of communist Cuba in the 1960s and Leninist-oriented Nicaragua in the 1980s.

In contrast, the Brezhnev doctrine of limited sovereignty of communist states—gradually distilled from Soviet justifications of repeated, structural interventions inside the East European regional framework—is of more considerable viability. (Windsor, 1984: 62–64.) Whereas the Monroe Doctrine seems to have diminished in applicable range and importance, contemporary Soviet behavior and pronouncements point to the strengthening and broadening applicability of the doctrine of limited sovereignty, especially as it may now be applied beyond the confines of Eastern Europe, for which it was first intended.

What is known as the Monroe Doctrine originated in 1823 in President James Monroe's proclamation against reimposition or extension of European colonial rule. While repeating some of the basic propositions advanced in earlier correspondence of Thomas Jefferson, Monroe's statement unequivocally declares that "We owe it to candor and to amicable relations existing between the United States and [the European powers] to declare that we should consider any attempt on their part to extend their system to any portion of this hemisphere as dangerous to our peace and safety." (Mecham, 1965: 48–49.)

Unlike Soviet declarations of limited sovereignty, Monroe's statement was wishful and visionary, and, as Ernest May concludes, to a certain extent the by-product of the U.S. election campaign at that time. (May, 1975: x.) In fact, it had almost no effect on actual U.S. national security policy until the middle of the nineteenth century. Before that time, for example, the United States did nothing to impede the activities of Great Britain, which annexed the Falkland Islands in 1833, consolidated its power in British Honduras (today Belize) and along the east coast of Nicaragua between 1823 and 1860, and sought otherwise to stake claims in Nicaragua for purposes of building a future transoceanic canal. (This would conform with the interpretation that there was a tacit understanding between the United States and Great Britain whereby the British would remain dominant in the area until circumstances dictated otherwise.) During this period the United States clearly lacked the necessary means to block interventions in America by major European powers. At the same time, however, there existed no serious possibility of any European power establishing a proxy state that would challenge the United States.

Throughout the nineteenth century, influence of the Monroe Doctrine was restricted almost entirely to the North American continent. This is not to say that the doctrine was totally without effect farther south. At the least it seems to have provided an inspiration to the likes of American filibusters such as soldier of fortune William Walker, who intervened in Nicaragua on behalf of Nicaragua's Liberal party and declared himself president for a short period in 1856 and 1857, after which he was defeated and executed.

Though President James Polk revived the spirit of the Monroe Doctrine in 1845 (the term itself did not come into use until 1853), the doctrine was not a policy-making consideration during the U.S.-Mexican War of the 1840s. This war was undertaken with no major concern for the influence of European powers in the Americas.

Keeping pace with growing U.S. geopolitical interests in the Caribbean Basin and with Anglo-German naval competition and perceived ambitions in the Caribbean Sea, the Monroe Doctrine acquired new policy-making relevance only at the turn of the twentieth century. The Anglo-German blockade of Venezuela in 1902–3 and European moves to collect bad debts in the Caribbean showed the necessity of denying potential enemies access to the Caribbean and provided the background, though not necessarily the primary reasons, for President Theodore Roosevelt's corollary to the Monroe Doctrine, which constituted a specific interventionist clause. As Roosevelt put it: "Chronic wrongdoing, or an impotence . . . may in America, as elsewhere, ultimately require intervention by some civilized nation, and in the Western Hemisphere the adherence of the United States to the Monroe Doctrine may force the United States, however reluctantly, in flagrant cases of such wrong-doing or impotence, to exercise an international police power." (Mecham, 1965: 68.) Subsequently Roosevelt and some of his successors embarked on a practical policy of sporadic interventionism that was to last almost three decades. The first of these interventions, the war with Spain over Cuba in 1898, preceded the actual enunciation of the Roosevelt corollary.

In practice, the Monroe Doctrine and its interventionist amendment formed the basis for a regional strategy limited almost exclusively to the Caribbean region. The only direct U.S. military interventions in the Americas have taken place in the Caribbean islands (Cuba, Haiti, the

Dominican Republic) or in countries with connections to this region such as Mexico and Central America (Nicaragua, Panama), but not in remote regions of South America.

The Monroe Doctrine was further strengthened in 1902 following the withdrawal of U.S. forces from Cuba. At this time the United States went so far as to extort from Cuba a treaty ceding the United States the right to intervene at its discretion in Cuba's internal affairs. The Platt Amendment, introduced to the new Cuban constitution, was in effect a U.S. version of limited sovereignty, if only pertaining to Cuba. It gave the United States the right to intervene "for . . . the maintenance of a government adequate for the protection of life and property, and individual liberty," and for discharging U.S. "obligations with respect to Cuba." (Perkins, 1981: 7–12.) The only other country that agreed to give the United States a very qualified right of intervention in its own affairs was Panama in 1903. The idea of limited sovereignty would later be revived and restated, though in a much different mold, by the Soviets in their treaties with several WTO allies.

As Dexter Perkins points out (1961: 24), the U.S. State Department's Clark Memorandum of 1928 expressly repudiated Roosevelt's principle. The Kellogg-Briand Pact of the same year limited the Monroe Doctrine itself. Later, in 1933, the U.S. government signed the Montevideo Declaration that termed illegal any intervention by one state in another, and in 1934 it abrogated the Platt Amendment.

The spirit of the Monroe Doctrine was revived somewhat with the rise of fascism during World War II, and also thereafter during the Cold War. Thus the Inter-American Treaty of Reciprocal Assistance (the Rio Treaty), adopted by the United States and the Latin American nations in 1947, called for joint commitment against external aggression, as did the Charter of the Organization of American States (OAS). (Both the OAS and Rio Treaty were prototypes of Cold War pacts, later refined and perfected in the NATO Pact of 1949 and the Warsaw Treaty Organization Pact of 1955.) Much later, President Lyndon Johnson's intervention in the Dominican Republic (1965) and a number of statements by other officials (e.g., "the principle of nonintervention has become obsolete") also appeared to reinvoke the Monroe Doctrine, or at least echo its rhetoric.

But actions speak louder than doctrines: following failure of a U.S.-backed Cuban exile brigade to liberate Cuba in 1961, President John Kennedy chose not to reinforce the Cuban exiles with all-out U.S. intervention. Kennedy also chose to employ a naval blockade, but did not follow the blockade with a military invasion. In short, U.S. tolerance of a communist regime having close military ties with a hostile, extrahemispheric power in the most strategically located country in the Caribbean rendered the Monroe Doctrine obsolete, in spite of previous acts and statements to the contrary. Soviet leader Nikita Khrushchev certainly saw it this way in the 1960s and so boasted. Finally, the Panama Canal Treaty (concluded in 1977) and President Jimmy Carter's decision not to intervene against the victorious FSLN in Nicaragua in 1979 further reinforced growing perceptions of an outdated, inoperative Monroe Doctrine.

What was first called the Brezhnev doctrine was derived from Brezhnev and his colleagues' ex post facto justification of the invasion of Czechoslovakia in 1968. As I have argued elsewhere, it was also a by-product and crystallization of the Politburo's long debate on the resolution of the Czechoslovak issue. As Brezhnev explained in 1968:

> When external and internal forces hostile to socialism try to turn the development of a given socialist country in the direction of restoration of the capitalist system, when a threat arises to the cause of socialism in that country—a threat to the security of the socialist commonwealth as a whole—this is no longer merely a problem for that country's people, but a common problem, the concern of all socialist countries. It is quite clear that an action such as military assistance to a fraternal country to end a threat to the socialist system is an extraordinary measure, dictated by necessity. (1–2.)

To call the Soviet doctrine of limited sovereignty the Brezhnev doctrine is ahistorical if not inaccurate. The idea of limited sovereignty for strategically located neighboring states was first conceived by the Russian tsars in the centuries-long struggle with Poland, a country that was and still is to the USSR what Cuba and Mexico are to the United States. The limiting of Poland's sovereignty was an explicit policy of the Russian tsars and, later, Soviet commissars. The Bolsheviks were responsible for adding a Leninist ideological context to the doctrine and for perfecting and extending it to the whole of Eastern Europe. Thus Brezhnev did not inaugurate an interventionist policy doctrine but only perfected an old Leninist strategy that commenced with the Soviet intervention in Poland in 1920. This strategy was perpetuated by Stalin's interventionist policy vis-à-vis the Baltic republics (excepting Finland, which successfully resisted a Soviet invasion in 1940), and by Stalin's and later Khrushchev's interventionist policies toward Eastern Europe after 1944–45. (Only geographically remote Yugoslavia and Albania were

excepted.) Specifically, Brezhnev could be described as having implemented the Khrushchev Doctrine inasmuch as his justification for the
Czechoslovak invasion, though more elaborate, comprehensive, and
theoretical, was similar to Khrushchev's justification for crushing the
East German workers' revolt in 1953 and for invading Hungary in 1956.

While the Roosevelt corollary was repudiated by the United States,
and the Monroe Doctrine, although not officially repudiated, has
become obsolete by virtue of continuous U.S. tolerance of Cuba and
inability to reverse the pro-Soviet orientation of Nicaragua, the doctrine of limited sovereignty has become not only a political principle,
but, in the Soviet mind, a principle of international law. Though primarily directed toward East European communist countries, the
Brezhnev doctrine articulates the Soviet right to intervene militarily in
the internal affairs of all communist states.

The Soviet doctrine of limited sovereignty is not, like the Monroe
Doctrine, a statement on national security policy, mainly concerned
with the intrusion of external powers at the U.S. periphery. It is, rather, a
Leninist version of the repudiated Roosevelt corollary and Platt
Amendment, which seeks to rationalize military intervention against
both external and internal (though more often internal) challenges to
the prescribed Soviet-modeled, European Leninist system. Whereas
the Monroe Doctrine was conceived to prevent great powers from
intervening in smaller, less powerful (American) states, the reverse is
true of the Brezhnev doctrine of limited sovereignty, which is designed
primarily to control, manipulate, and finally coerce the domestic policies of less powerful (communist) nations by continuous, structural
interventionism.

The Soviet doctrine of limited sovereignty implies that even internal
challenges, such as pluralistic communism, are not acceptable in the
regional Leninist system constructed by the Kremlin in Eastern Europe.
Accordingly, the Soviet Union and other communist nations presume
the right to intervene militarily to crush such challenges.

The Soviet doctrine of limited sovereignty was not applied in the
case of Yugoslavia. Thus Yugoslavia's "defection" to the West in 1948–49
is often compared with Cuba's defection to the East in 1960. However,
both cases are actually dissimilar insofar as Yugoslavia has not evolved
into a de facto capitalist country allied with an extrahemispheric power.
Also, in contrast to communist, Soviet-allied Cuba, Yugoslavia has managed to preserve its status as a nonaligned communist regime. This is
also true, but to a lesser extent, of Albania.

The interventionist clauses of the doctrine of limited sovereignty were not repudiated as were the Roosevelt corollary and the Platt Amendment. Nor have Soviet treaties with important East European countries been modified to Soviet disadvantage, as was the 1978 Panama Canal Treaty with the United States. Whereas U.S. intervention in the Caribbean Basin was limited and made much more difficult because of these policy changes, Soviet interventionism vis-à-vis the East European countries was perfected and further facilitated by new Soviet treaties with these countries in the 1970s. The original Soviet treaties with East European communist countries of the late 1940s were primarily aimed against external threats from the West. By virtue of new amendments, the treaties with Czechoslovakia and East Germany now provide for dealing with internal threats by explicitly authorizing intervention at the discretion of the USSR, a major element of the doctrine of limited sovereignty. Portions of the language of the doctrine of limited sovereignty—"mutual assistance" among communist countries on the basis of "socialist internationalism"—were even incorporated into the new Soviet Constitution of 1977. (*Constitution of the USSR*: 32–33.)

Finally, unlike the Monroe Doctrine, the Soviet doctrine of limited sovereignty is not necessarily regionally limited. It can be interpreted as pertaining to all communist countries, and, some argue, Leninist-oriented countries, regardless of where they are located. Though the doctrine, at its inception, apparently was not intended as a means to justify global Soviet interventionism, the Soviets have not tried to dispel this convenient ambiguity. Some Soviet officials even justified the invasion of Afghanistan on the basis of this self-proclaimed right to support Leninist-oriented regimes on a global scale. (Valenta, 1980: 140–41.) Thus the option for future global applications of the doctrine of limited sovereignty cannot be ruled out.

III. Intervention in Light of National Security Motivations and Goals

The Soviet and American political systems differ fundamentally, as do their perceived national security requirements. The bulk of the disparity stems from the Soviets' differently defined concept of security. The physical security component, requiring that the needs of physical security and logistics be met at the nation's peripheries, is central to both the Soviet and U.S. concepts. However, while ideological concerns are not absent from U.S. national security considerations, the American concept of national security includes large economic stakes in neighboring countries. The Soviet concept is dominated by overriding political-ideological interests at the Soviet periphery, which are best served by establishing and maintaining Leninist systems modeled on the Soviet system.

It is difficult to generalize about the motives and goals behind U.S. and Soviet interventions, given the variety of circumstances surrounding each case. The U.S. role would need to be assessed on the basis of interventions in seven countries of the Caribbean Basin region (Mexico, Cuba, Nicaragua, the Dominican Republic, Haiti, Panama, Puerto Rico [which was incorporated as a commonwealth], and Grenada.) The Soviet case would be judged on the basis of interventions, sometimes followed by annexations (in the case of the Baltic states), in Latvia, Lithuania, Estonia, Poland, Czechoslovakia, Hungary, East Germany, and Finland. A careful study of each intervention suggests a degree of parallelism along motivational lines. In each instance, although in widely varying degrees, perceived or potential threats to physical security requirements figured into the policy-making equation. All the above nations are located in areas adjacent to the superpowers and have traditionally been considered vital to each nation's ability to safeguard its security interests. However, in none of the mentioned cases was a threat to the physical security of a superpower unambiguously and imminently present. At best such threats were only perceived or potential. (The one instance of real and immediate danger occurred during the Cuban missile crisis of October 1962 when the United States threatened to use force, but only to ensure removal of Soviet missiles from Cuba.) Outside of these broadly traced similarities, there is little real symmetry.

As noted, a systemic ideological impetus to interventionism has been comparatively weaker in American motives, which have been decidedly more oriented toward security concerns and economic interests. The heyday of U.S. interventionism at its periphery was the period between 1898 and the late 1920s. The only direct U.S. military interventions in the Western Hemisphere during the post-World War II era involved the Dominican Republic and Grenada. (The Soviet trajectory has been different, with repeated Soviet interventions in Eastern Europe both during and after World War II.) U.S. interventionism in the Caribbean Basin from 1898 to 1928 coincided with an evolving reappraisal of the physical requirements of U.S. national security in the region. This reassessment was carried out under the influence of Captain Mahan's writings (1889) and the growing possibility of a transfer of sea dominance from Great Britain to Germany. The progression of the Caribbean region from an area of potential strategic importance to one of immediate and vital national security priority occurred during construction of the Panama Canal, which was completed in 1914.

Ideological stakes were also a contributory factor in U.S. interventionism during this period. Such ideological concerns, though more practical than profound or proselytizing, were already foreshadowed by Monroe's message of 1823: "The political system of the allied powers," he said, "is essentially different . . . from that of America." Ideological undertones were also present, though not crucial, in the subsequent Caribbean Basin interventions of 1898–1929. Thus the decision of 1898 to enter into war with Spain and "liberate" Cuba was not prompted so much by the desire to liberate Cuba's oppressed as by long-range security calculations, coupled with strong economic interests ($50 million in U.S. investments by 1898) and heightened by pressure from the U.S. sugar industry. (Pressure by factions within the U.S. sugar industry, though not coordinated, is shown to have exerted a significant influence on the decision of the hesitant and reluctant William McKinley administration.) The jingoism of an irresponsible press also helped to whip up a frenzy in the U.S. Congress and among the American people.

With the Cuban venture and growing U.S. sensitivity about security matters, the Pandora's box of U.S. interventionism was flung wide. Subsequently the United States embarked on the acquisition of Panama in 1903, a new intervention in Cuba in 1906, and interventions in Haiti in 1915, the Dominican Republic in 1916, Panama in 1918, and Nicaragua in 1912 and again in 1927. During this period, the United States also intervened twice in Mexico: once after a military coup, when ensuing violence resulted in a brief U.S. naval occupation of Vera Cruz in 1914; and again in 1916 when the U.S. Army pursued the rebel Pancho Villa into Mexican territory following the latter's attack on a New Mexico settlement.

The acquisition of Panama as a U.S. dependency was motivated by clear strategic considerations, i.e., the need to control "a strategic bridge" for the militarily and commercially important Panama Canal. Other U.S. interventions in the region were essentially cautionary measures aimed at preventing potential security problems, stabilizing anarchic conditions or civil war, and protecting U.S. business interests in determined areas. In some cases there was also a perceived threat of involvement by European powers. In Haiti in 1914 pressure by officials of the City Bank of New York was influential in the decision to send in the marines to take custody of gold claimed by U.S. and European bankers. The marines returned to occupy Haiti in 1915 because of anarchy following the assassination of the Haitian president. The U.S. intervention in the Dominican Republic in 1916 was designed to put an end to instability there. In each of these cases U.S. policymakers appeared sincere in believing the threats were real. However, there is no conclusive evidence of an alleged German threat of intervention in the Dominican affair, or of an alleged economic threat from German and French economic activities in Haiti.

Although the major U.S. motivation for intervention in Nicaragua during this period was to safeguard U.S. business investments, a prior and probably still viable concern was that Nicaragua might negotiate to provide a competing Pacific-Atlantic canal site to some foreign power. This suspicion was aroused when, in 1909, Nicaraguan President José Santos Zelaya hinted at the possibility of opening such negotiations with the Japanese.

The brief and limited U.S. intervention in Mexico in 1914 was in response to a military coup and civil war in that country. A more direct and decisive U.S. intervention occurred after the Mexican rebel Pancho Villa attacked Columbus, New Mexico. However, unlike Lenin during the Soviets' comparable involvement in Poland in 1920, which escalated into a full-blown case of "fraternal assistance" in the name of "proletarian internationalism," President Wilson exhibited great restraint in resisting the temptation (spurred by U.S. oil interests) to engage in all-out war against Mexico.

U.S. interventionism declined considerably in the three decades beginning in 1930, only to reemerge as a more sporadic phenomenon in the post–World War II era when potential threats from an imperial Germany were replaced by the tentative probings of an acquisitive Soviet Union. At that time the perceptions of U.S. national security requirements showed the influence of the World War II experience when German submarine activities made it difficult for Washington to keep logistics lines open to Europe and Africa. However, the indirect U.S. intervention in Guatemala in 1954 (via proxies led by Colonel Carlos Castillo Armas and operating out of Honduras and Nicaragua) was not motivated by perceived challenges to U.S. physical security in the Caribbean but by conditions within Guatemala, particularly the growing influence of communist elements in Jacobo Arbenz's government, the threat to the United Fruit Company's interests from Arbenz's agrarian reform, and the fact that Czech arms had been sent to Guatemala. While the intervention was a significant determinant in Guatemalan affairs at that time, the Arbenz government did not collapse under the pressure of the invasion, but rather from a variety of internal and external pressures that came into play after the USSR failed to heed Arbenz's appeal through the UN Security Council.

The motivation for U.S. intervention in the Dominican Republic in 1965, like previous interventions in Caribbean nations (Cuba in 1906, the Dominican Republic in 1916, Haiti in 1915), was to halt widespread instability, anarchy, and ensuing civil war. The 1965 action was occasioned by a poorly executed pro-Juan Bosch coup. Evidence does not support President Lyndon Johnson's claims of a creeping communist takeover or communist infiltration of the government, though there may have been a threat to American lives. As critics of the intervention persuasively argued, the Johnson administration failed to demonstrate the imminent emergence of a Castro-type regime, although this was ostensibly the main U.S. concern. The U.S. overreacted to a perceived threat that at worst had only potentially harmful ramifications.

In Grenada in 1983 there was also no conclusive evidence of an immediate, direct threat to U.S. security interests. However, the potential security threat to Grenada's East Caribbean neighbors and, ultimately, to U.S. security and regional interests was much more serious than in the case of the Dominican Republic. The captured Grenada documents demonstrate that a Soviet- and Cuban-backed military buildup was occurring at a mounting pace, and this was the prevailing consensus among OECS members. While in the Dominican Republic an impending duplication of the Cuban scenario was exaggerated, in Grenada, as captured documents illustrate, a Leninist, pro-Soviet regime was clearly in place. (Valenta and Ellison, 1986: 334–41.) The bloody coup and murder of a popular Marxist prime minister by more orthodox Leninist forces was only the beginning of the bloodshed in what was to be the consolidation of a much more brutal, pro-Soviet regime. The intervention interrupted and prevented this chain of events. The ongoing, indirect U.S. intervention in Nicaragua is motivated by a similar rationale, i.e., the need to obstruct the consolidation of a Leninist-oriented regime having military ties with a hostile, extrahemispheric power.

This is not the place to examine the motives behind traditional Russian interventions in Eastern Europe, except insofar as these serve as a prelude to present-day Soviet interventionist policy. In contrast to the young, comparatively weak United States at the close of the eighteenth century and several decades into the nineteenth century, Russia by those years had achieved the status of a great power, an empire imbued with its own manifest destiny. Various foreign conquests and numerous episodes of tsarist "fraternal assistance" to neighboring states in Eastern Europe (especially Poland and Hungary, but also states south and east of Russia) regularly punctuated Russian history during this period.

Subsequent Bolshevik rule, commencing in 1917, proves that old habits die hard. Take the Polish war of 1920. It started with a Polish attack on Soviet territory. At this stage the main Soviet motive for entering into combat was to repulse the Poles and counter a real threat to the physical security of the Soviet state. Yet, unlike Wilson in Mexico, Lenin gave in to the temptation to follow up a retaliatory intervention into enemy territory with an all-out offensive war motivated not only by security concerns but also by ideology.

This dual motivation was again demonstrated in 1939–40, following Hitler's and Stalin's partition of Poland. The Soviets, dissatisfied with mere security guarantees, annexed, incorporated, and Leninized the western part of Poland. This pattern, by now well established, was repeated in the Baltic republics of Lithuania, Latvia, and Estonia. The Soviets had similar objectives in Finland, whose Finnish commissars, exiled in the USSR, had already formed a new Leninist government of "the Democratic Republic of Finland" that they were planning to impose on Finland following an all-out Soviet invasion of that country. Fierce Finnish resistance prevented the Soviets' planned "Balkanization" of Finland.

One perdurable motive in all Soviet interventions has been the perceived necessity of bolstering the country's physical security in anticipation of an eventual conflict with Germany. (U.S. policymakers felt this same necessity in 1914–17 and again in 1939–41.) The USSR's anxiety was graphically demonstrated in the case of Finland, where, before the invasion, the Soviets had proposed to the Finns a territorial quid pro quo by which the Finns would cede certain strategic areas to the Soviets in return for Soviet territorial concessions elsewhere at the Soviet-Finnish frontier. The deal made security sense (to the Soviets), given Leningrad's location only twenty miles from Finnish territory. However, after the Finns refused the deal, Soviet motives again appeared to fracture and multiply. The subsequent all-out Soviet invasion, with the intention of establishing a Leninist, puppet regime in Finland (as the Soviets later succeeded doing in the countries of Eastern Europe and in Afghanistan), suggested a coupling of the ever-powerful Soviet ideological motive with the security motive requiring permanent control.

The ideological component of Soviet national security perceptions has played an important role in Soviet interventionism following World

War II. Extensive Soviet suffering in World War II makes understandable the Soviet preoccupation with physical security in sensitive areas of Eastern Europe. The bilateral treaties with the East European nations and the Soviets' permanent and massive occupation of Eastern Germany are manifestations of this concern. The Warsaw Treaty Organization system, which was formed to guarantee Soviet physical security requirements, is the culmination of this drive as it allows the Soviets to keep logistics lines open to forward bases in Eastern Europe.

However, to accomplish this objective it would have been sufficient for the Soviets to establish only a physical security system—a *cordon sanitaire* of buffer states linked with the USSR by the kind of treaties the Soviets concluded with Finland in 1948 and with the East European nations themselves in the late 1940s. For purposes of security alone, the Soviets did not need to Leninize six East European nations in what has become a process of perpetual intervention necessary to enforce the Leninist model. The fact is that the Soviets have two main goals at their periphery: one is political-ideological, the other, military-security.

The crushing of the workers' revolt in East Germany in 1953, the invasions of Hungary (1956) and Czechoslovakia (1968), and the indirect interventions in Poland (1956 and 1980–81) clearly demonstrate the motor power of Soviet political-ideological concerns. In Hungary, contrary to Soviet rhetoric, there was no threat of a U.S. or West German intervention, but the Hungarian revolution, with its anti-Soviet undertones, did bring immediate political and ideological consequences for Hungary, as well as for the rest of Eastern Europe and the USSR. Unlike Władysław Gomułka during the almost simultaneous crisis in Poland, Imre Nagy, communist prime minister of Hungary, did not entirely succeed in restoring order, even though he was assisted by Soviet military intervention. Nagy committed a second grave mistake by proclaiming the establishment of a multiparty government, organized around a coalition of several parties, much like the government that had existed in 1945. Though neither anti-Soviet nor anticommunist, this government violated the first commandment of Soviet rule, which predicates political control by the local communist party. The Soviet decision to intervene for a second time, on a massive scale, was taken because of these two conditions, not because of Nagy's desperate move to withdraw from the Warsaw Treaty Organization, which came later. Thus the Soviet argument that the threat of WTO dismemberment prompted the invasion is highly inflated. (Valenta, 1984a: 127–51.)

In Czechoslovakia (1968) Soviet political-ideological stakes were much greater than any actual or potential security concerns. (The same was true of Poland in 1980–81.) Alexander Dubček's continuous implementation of radical reforms was the factor that tipped the balance in favor of the ultimate Soviet solution. The Soviets did not fear a dramatic change in Czech foreign policy, such as withdrawal from the WTO, for it was clear that the Dubček government would not deviate from the basic Soviet foreign policy line. Moreover, Soviet intelligence discounted any threat to Czechoslovakia from NATO or West Germany, in spite of Soviet postinvasion propaganda to the contrary. What Kremlin leaders did fear was the threat that "creeping counterrevolution" in Prague posed for the Soviet Union itself.

Soviet leaders' shared images of the stakes in Eastern Europe, such as preservation of the political and ideological status quo, were important issues during the August 1968 Politburo debate. Soviet fears were not that Czechoslovakia would withdraw, like Hungary, from the Warsaw Treaty Organization or from the Council for Mutual Economic Assistance, but rather that, like Poland in 1980–81, it would continue to belong to these organizations and influence other members. If democratization of the Czechoslovak Communist party had been validated at the subsequent Czechoslovak party congress in September, the repercussions and spillovers would have been felt by other WTO members and perhaps ultimately by the Soviet Union.

Like the Prague Spring, the popular revolt in Poland in 1980–81 was not violent; nor was it a direct challenge to Soviet security interests. On only a few occasions were the Soviets moved to express concern about those interests. However, from the Soviets' perspective, developments in Poland were unpredictable. The fundamental Soviet concern was that the East European political-ideological *cordon sanitaire* would be eroded by unrestricted changes. Moreover, a truly successful Polish workers' revolution, originating "from below," was even more threatening to the USSR than the revolutionary program of reform instigated "from above" by Czech party intellectuals in 1968. Soviet acceptance of Poland's free trade unions would have amounted to nothing less than recognition of a mass, non-Leninist, working-class organization rivaling the communist party's self-proclaimed monopoly of political power. East German and Czechoslovak leaders shared the Soviets' fear that Solidarity's legalized right to strike would undermine the party's authority and lead to the establishment of a dual power base in Poland, with detrimental spillover effects in their own and other East European countries. Thus they conducted vitriolic campaigns against "counterrevolutionary" forces in Solidarity and "revisionists" in the party and pressed for military intervention, using continuous military exercises inside and around Poland to finally prompt an inside intervention by Soviet proxies (in this case the Polish security and military forces).

IV. Interventionist Behavior and Outcomes

The most significant differences between U.S. and Soviet interventionism in their respective spheres of influence have occurred during the actual interventions and in their aftermaths. By and large the U.S. mode of intervention has been much more limited in scope and intensity. Some U.S. interventions were conducted on behalf of legitimate, although minor, parties during civil or political strife, and a few were even welcomed by substantial segments of the populations affected. The Soviet interventions were conducted on behalf of small groups, fictional government cliques, and even Quislings. Although both U.S. and Soviet interventions have been questionable on legal grounds, if not in flagrant violation of international law, some U.S. interventions have had beneficial socioeconomic and political results. Unlike the Soviet cases, most U.S. interventions have been the subject of domestic controversy, or at least ambivalence, and U.S. forces were eventually withdrawn and sovereignty restored, even to those nations that had been occupied. Most U.S. interventions were not conceived or used as a means of establishing permanent control.

Most Soviet interventions (the most recent one in Poland in 1980–81 being an exception) could be described as invasions. They have, furthermore, been massive and brutal, especially when compared with most U.S. interventions, in the Caribbean Basin at least, which were carried out by small forces and directed at selected targets. Soviet invasions, without exception, have been aimed at territorial acquisition or the establishment or maintenance of permanent Soviet control. This has necessitated a type of perpetual interventionism whereby Soviet troops stationed within or around a country are always poised to reestablish Soviet norms when a country steps out of line. Although some of the parties supported by U.S. government interventions were not necessarily the best alternatives available to U.S. policymakers and/or did not enjoy majority support at home, at no time have U.S. interventions brutally imposed Quisling-type governments. This, however, has been a commonplace tactic of Soviet interventionist policy in Eastern Europe, and in Afghanistan in 1979. In Grenada, as I can testify, after having made three visits to that country, U.S. forces were welcomed as liberators by a majority of the Grenadan people.

Undeniably, some U.S. interventions (Nicaragua, Haiti), have been resisted by prolonged guerrilla warfare on the part of various groups. (In at least one of these countries, Haiti, there were reports of marine cruelty.) Yet the pre-World War II interventions, followed by brief occupations (Cuba, Haiti, and the Dominican Republic), had at least some beneficial socioeconomic results, admitted to even by leftist writers: the establishment of orderly financing, the strengthening of administrative control, and some improvements in public health. To be sure, not all U.S. postinterventionist activities in occupied countries have been successful. This was true of U.S. agricultural operations in Haiti, for example. The impact of post-World War II U.S. interventions is much more difficult to judge, as they were either indirect or short-lived. The judgment on the impact of the Grenada intervention is not yet in.

The crux of the matter is that U.S. interventions have been conducted in underdeveloped Third World countries. Recent Soviet interventions have been conducted in more developed European countries, all having Western cultural traditions, and some even political systems akin to those of the United States. This was surely the case in Czechoslovakia and Finland, but also to some extent in East Germany, Hungary, Poland, and the Baltic republics. Unlike upheavals in the Caribbean, the incipient revolutionary transformations witnessed in Poland and Hungary in 1956, in Czechoslovakia in 1968, and in Poland in 1980–81 were brief attempts to adapt communism to the social and cultural fabric of what, until recently, was known as Central or East-Central Europe.

In spite of the complex interaction of a number of different internal and external factors, the revolutionary ferment in these countries was similar. In each case broad segments of the population had become dissatisfied with political and economic conditions, especially the suppression of individual liberties, the Sovietization of the way of life, and the inefficiency of the centralized, Byzantine economic system. Revolution and subsequent intervention followed. Given their Western heritage, it is no wonder that overwhelming majorities in those countries resented the Soviet interventions. The Soviets brought few short- or long-term benefits to the countries affected, in comparison with what their development might have been had they remained integrated in the Western cultural and economic community.

In neither the Dominican Republic nor Grenada did U.S. invading forces attempt to set up Soviet-style puppet regimes like those established after the interventions in Hungary, the Baltic republics, Finland,

and Czechoslovakia. Even earlier, in Cuba, Nicaragua, Haiti, and Guatemala, U.S. interventions did not represent gains for the U.S. brand of democracy equivalent to what the Soviets garnered for Leninism by intervening in Eastern Europe. (In Hungary, years after the invasion, such ideological gains would be modified somewhat.) In Cuba and Nicaragua, despite U.S. efforts to establish democratic rules of the game, the interventions actually helped to set the stage for long and abusive authoritarian dictatorships. Yet in the Dominican Republic (1965) intervention opened the way for twenty years of democratic rule and some socioeconomic progress.

Unlike interventionist policy in the USSR, U.S. interventionism at times has been highly resented by powerful domestic sectors—the U.S. press and members of Congress—who, in turn, have influenced the U.S. decision-making process. In the case of some of these interventions U.S. public opinion, at first deeply ambivalent, has become entangled in heated controversy. Exaggerated interventionist rationales have often been ridiculed by domestic critics. For example, Secretary of State Frank Kellogg's defense of the U.S. intervention in Nicaragua, which made exaggerated claims about "Bolshevik aims and policies in Mexico and Latin America," was thought by a leading newspaper to be "utterly indecent intellectual exposure" and was severely criticized in the Congress in 1926. (Perkins, 1981: 115.) Similarly, critics in the Congress and in the press assaulted the Johnson administration's exaggeration of the communist threat in the Dominican Republic. In Moscow there was sporadic criticism of the Soviet invasion of Czechoslovakia, not openly in the Soviet press or among members of the Supreme Soviet, but by a few dissidents who subsequently found themselves jailed or in mental hospitals.

Most U.S. interventions were not undertaken to impose irreversible mechanisms of control or to effect a permanent systemic transition. Unlike the old colonial powers (the British, the French, the Russians), the United States rarely planned to remain indefinitely in possession of an occupied country, notable exceptions being the northern territory of Mexico in 1848–49, Puerto Rico in 1898, and the Panama Canal Zone in 1903. On occasion, political realities and unrelenting domestic criticism have prompted the U.S. government to apologize for or repudiate certain interventionist policies. Thus, according to the treaty of 1922, the United States made amends with Colombia and, as Robert Wesson reminds us, apologized for having partitioned the country to form the independent state of Panama. Only the fury of Teddy Roosevelt barred the United States from offering a more explicit apology. (1982b: 12.)

Also, in contrast to Moscow, Washington has resisted the temptation to include the interventionist Platt Amendment in later postinterventionist treaties with other nations in the region. (A notable exception was Senator Dennis DeConcini's reservation to the first of the two Panama Canal treaties. The Platt Amendment was not invoked during the subsequent Cuban crisis of 1933–34, after which it was abrogated. In the 1970s, when the Soviets negotiated a number of treaties that formalized their system of limited sovereignty in some of the East European countries, the United States negotiated a new canal treaty with Panama, elevating that country from a subordinate position to one of greater equality and more fully realized sovereignty. The only comparable episode in Soviet history was the Soviet military withdrawal from Austria and support for Austrian neutrality in 1955. This feat, however, was tempered by the fact that Austria was not communist and that the USSR was only one of four occupying powers, with a minor territorial holding at that. In contrast, most countries having experienced intervention by U.S. forces have subsequently seen their jurisdiction and sovereignty fully restored. Even in Panama, the United States is obliged by treaty to complete this process by 1999. (The United States will retain control over only one vital defense and operational facility.) Whereas some nations in the Caribbean Basin are still clearly dependent on the United States in economic and political affairs, and may remain so indefinitely, not a single one, including Grenada, has had its national sovereignty limited in perpetuity by a treaty.

V. Conclusions

A modicum of parallelism and symmetry between U.S. and Soviet interventionist strategies in neighboring countries is undeniable. The justifications and defenses put forward in support of interventionist acts and the attempts to legitimize them are notable for their similarities. A degree of parallelism is also present in the supporting doctrines.

But differences override the similarities. The finely honed Soviet doctrine of limited sovereignty of communist countries proclaims the Kremlin's right to preserve the achievements of Leninism in the countries of Eastern Europe. In spite of the U.S.-OECS military intervention in Grenada and the ongoing indirect U.S. intervention in Nicaragua (via the so-called Contras), continuous U.S. tolerance of a Cuban regime allied de facto with an extrahemispheric, hostile power attests to the obsolescence of the Monroe Doctrine and, even more certainly, the already repudiated Roosevelt interventionist corollary.

But superpower policies are shaped by differing concepts of national security, and stated doctrines are not necessarily the crystallization of these images. (Often unwritten "doctrines" are just as viable as official ones.) Here again there are similarities, particularly each country's sensitivity to potential security threats posed by developments in adjacent regions. Beyond the aforementioned similarities, however, one is struck by a more fundamental asymmetry in U.S. and Soviet interventionist modes and their outcomes. U.S. national security interests in the Caribbean have rested on powerful economic investments, especially before World War II when the United States was willing to protect them with military muscle. The Soviet concept of national security differs from the U.S. concept, primarily because of the existence of overwhelming political-ideological stakes perceived by the Soviets in Eastern Europe. The Soviet need to maintain a Leninist regional system necessitates ongoing structural interventionism. On balance, the United States is more prone to tolerate political-ideological defiance from its closest neighbors. Though all interventions are shaky on legal grounds, most U.S. interventions were not conceived as a means for establishing permanent control over another nation.

Unlike the United States, the USSR has well-established rules about what is permissible at its own periphery. Soviet leaders have political-ideological stakes in Eastern Europe that are conditioned by history and Leninist doctrine; the region is vital not only to the physical security but also to the political and ideological well-being of the Soviet Union. To maintain maximum influence in the region, the Soviet Union must prevent the spread of what it views as anti-Soviet tendencies, be these "bourgeois," "revisionist," or "Eurocommunist." Accordingly, (a) the withdrawal of an East European country from the Warsaw Treaty Organization (the Hungarian scenario of 1956) is not permissible; (b) the revolutionary restoration of a genuine multiparty system in any of the WTO countries (again, the Hungarian scenario of 1956) or the existence of genuinely pluralistic forces such as independent trade unions (the Polish scenario of 1980–81) would jeopardize the control of the communist party and therefore cannot be tolerated; (c) the weakening of a regime's loyalty (Czechoslovakia in 1968) or the inability of a regime to contain pressures for revolutionary change within acceptable limits (Poland in 1956 and 1980–81, Czechoslovakia in 1968) cannot be tolerated.

True, the Soviet rules of the game in Eastern Europe provide considerable leeway for implementing the Leninist model. This was demonstrated most persuasively in Hungary in the 1970s. One thing that can be ascertained from the events in Hungary, Czechoslovakia, and Poland is that the Soviets are determined not to permit pluralistic socialism. Another is that postinterventionist policies are not predetermined. The postinvasion periods in Hungary and Czechoslovakia have been markedly different, with greater importance attached to the preservation of political orthodoxy in Czechoslovakia than in Hungary.

In contrast to the USSR, the U.S. threshold for tolerating political-ideological deviations among its Caribbean neighbors is quite high. The subject of what and how much to tolerate has actually not been thought through consistently and over a long period of time by U.S. policymakers. But who could imagine the Soviet Union even considering Contadora-type negotiations (mediation of the Nicaraguan conflict by Panama, Mexico, Venezuela, and Colombia) for Hungary in 1956 and Czechoslovakia in 1968 (with some of the other Warsaw Pact allies constituting the Contadora group); tolerating in Poland the type of defiance the United States has faced over oil supplies and prices from Mexico and from Venezuela in OPEC; or tolerating a Haitian-type revolution (1986) in any of the WTO states?

Though the USSR showed some restraint in handling the most recent Polish crisis, Eastern Europe has not begun to forget or dismiss the Soviets' real and looming interventionist capabilities. Soviet power and the threat of invasion were sufficient to reverse the revolutionary situation in Poland. Previous invasions had demonstrated the limits of autonomy set by the Soviet leadership and served as warnings to other ruling communist parties. The invasions of Hungary in 1956 and Czechoslovakia in 1968 made a Soviet invasion of Poland unnecessary in 1981. Instead, fear fostered by Soviet military exercises prompted an "inside job" by the Polish military and security forces.

Overwhelming U.S. power, on the other hand, did not achieve the same effect in Nicaragua as late as 1985. This is because the United States has made some strides toward abandonment of the Platt Amendment psychology, which sanctioned permanent semicolonial solutions to revolutionary problems. The repudiation of the Roosevelt corollary and Platt Amendment and the new Panama Canal Treaty are good testimony to that, as are the resolutions of the crises in Haiti and in the Philippines in 1986. The United States is no longer the hegemonic entity it was in the early twentieth century; it no longer can or will coerce subordinate states in its environs without the substantial support of other regional actors, as occurred in Grenada. Meanwhile, the

Soviets as yet fail to see that their own continuous policies of intervention and of granting only limited sovereignty heighten the very insecurity and instability in Eastern Europe that such policies were designed to forestall.

IV   Subordinate States

12

The Subordinate States and
Their Strategies

Paul M. Johnson

The main function of this chapter in our collective research enterprise
is to analyze the strategies of the subordinate states in the regional
systems of Latin America and Eastern Europe. But as David D. Finley
has already had occasion to point out in his chapter, attributing the
qualities and characteristics of "strategists" to states acting in the international arena already presupposes a lot. In our ordinary understanding of the term, strategists are persons bent upon achieving a limited
number of well-defined goals by means of carefully coordinated measures that are sustained over considerable periods of time and ration-
ally calculated to overcome or circumvent expected resistance or
obstruction from other actors. The ideal strategist analyzes the
resources at his (and at his opponents') disposal and exercises his
creativity in devising ways to minimize his opponents' relative advantages and to maximize his own, given the structural constraints imposed
on each by the surrounding environment to which they both must
adapt.

The leaders of a small number of historical states evidently have been in a position to conduct foreign affairs in the manner of a chess grand master, but more typically national leaders face a situation in which potentially important resources for exerting international influence remain under the control of relatively autonomous organizations or individuals unwilling to subordinate themselves unquestioningly to centralized direction. A state's effectiveness in subsuming all its international interactions under the control of a single guiding rationality varies enormously with the character of the particular country's political, economic, social, and cultural institutions. The task of maintaining coherence and consistency of purpose in foreign policy-making is particularly difficult in highly penetrated countries (including a significant proportion of the Latin American and East European countries that are the focus of this volume), where both state and nonstate actors from outside the country (including actors we would like to conceptualize as at least potential "opponents" against whose machinations foreign policy strategies are to be devised) routinely play important roles in "internal" decision-making processes. Unless we can sensibly postulate that the small-state decisionmaker cum national strategist has as one of his goals the establishment, or at least the maintenance, of meaningful limitations on the interference of external actors in the domestic decision-making process, it would make little sense to analyze the interactions of a small *state* with its hegemon in terms of alternate strategies (though of course at a more micro level of analysis one might still wish to apply some such approach to explicating the decisionmaker's efforts to pursue his special personal, group, or class interests against the opposition of *domestic* opponents). The institutionally determined *capacity* to deal with the hegemon at arm's length needs to be accompanied by the *will* of the decisionmaker to do so before the question of devising strategies for the purpose can logically arise.

Subordinate States' Goals in Regional Relations

Casting our discussion of regional relations in the emotion-laden terms of *dominance* and *subordination* perhaps sets us up for the premature conclusion that the primary foreign policy goal of the subordinate state is (or ought to be) the achievement of "genuine sovereignty" by eliminating or at least dramatically reducing outside influences on the country's political and economic affairs. Nationalist political and philosophical norms very widely prevalent in the twentieth century both affirm the intrinsic value of national self-determination and tend to make the domestic legitimacy as well as the international prestige of any regime critically dependent upon its ability at least occasionally to demonstrate that its policymakers place some concept of the core national interests above the interests of all other actors in the international community. Prevailing state-centered theories of economic and social development imply as their logical corollary that minimizing both internal and external impediments to discretionary state control over the national population and their economic assets is a necessary (albeit hardly sufficient) instrumentality for bestowing both national prosperity and distributive justice, which are in their own right widely embraced national goals. Even on a cynical view of elite political motivations as primarily the promotion of narrow personal self-interest, we may expect that small-power political leaders striving to maximize their personal power will often find attractive the prospect of reducing the constraints imposed upon their sovereign will by the country's subordinate position in the international system. We thus have good reason to expect the preservation of an essential core of national sovereignty to figure among the objectives guiding foreign policymakers in even rather highly penetrated polities, yet nevertheless it remains far from clear that active measures to substantially reduce the country's accustomed level of dependence on the regional hegemon typically have a high priority in the concerns of national decisionmakers in the smaller states.

Sometimes countries acquire national leaders who have adopted normative systems that deny or deprecate the value of national sovereignty and instead define higher loyalties that demand the polity's subordination to more encompassing political communities. Such situations are historically rather rare, but at least some of the founding fathers of the East European peoples' democracies in the immediate postwar period seem to have fallen into this category, as evidenced by their long previous service to, and extensive personal sacrifices on behalf of, the Comintern, as well as by the frequency of their public statements in the early 1950s justifying contemporary economic austerity by ascribing to the popular masses a sacred obligation to shoulder burdens imposed by "internationalist duty." Where a substantial portion of the population remained unconvinced of the value of many of the revolutionary leadership's new institutions and policies, the availability of the Soviet Army as the ultimate guarantor of the socialist order permitted these committed revolutionaries to proceed more rapidly and ruthlessly with their revolution than would otherwise have been possible or prudent. (Once the basic institutions of the new order had finally been successfully established, however, some of the erst-while revolutionaries began to see basic drawbacks to their by now well-earned reputation as stooges for a foreign power seemingly bent upon a permanent policy of repression and austerity—among them that their resulting problems of legitimacy tended to make it more and more difficult to secure the voluntary cooperation from the citizenry needed to make the new socialist institutions function efficiently.)

Most commonly, national political leaders do indeed desire greater national independence. But they also wish to achieve other, more pressing objectives that they see as potentially ill-served by a too single-minded preoccupation with its pursuit—carrying out (or, for conserva-tive regimes, avoiding) particular kinds of socioeconomic reforms; main-taining great power protection against third powers thought to be entertaining aggressive intentions toward the country or against domes-tic insurgents committed to unacceptable changes in the distribution of power, status, and wealth; safeguarding access to international trade, aid, and investment as necessary to foster economic development, and the like. Ideological preconceptions, preferences about economic devel-opment strategies, and national security considerations may all stand in the way of a more assertive pursuit of national independence. Finally, a leader's narrow personal desire to remain in office, coupled with a perception of helplessness to change the existing distribution of power, may seem to him to dictate that he undertake only those policies that are acceptable to foreign patrons and/or to powerful domestic constitu-encies with vested interests in the international status quo.

U.S. and Soviet Goals in Regional Relations

As a practical matter, smaller powers' opportunities for asserting inde-pendence in policy matters from the dictation of the regional hege-mon are very substantially shaped by the character and intensity of the most important demands made by the hegemon upon the coun-tries in the particular region. Independent pursuit of policies diametri-cally opposed to the hegemon's definition of its more important inter-ests in the region are likely to evoke powerful sanctions, while small-state initiatives in other spheres of policy more likely will be viewed with indulgence or unconcern and allowed to proceed unhindered. Small-country leaders' sense of their own autonomy (or lack thereof) is less dependent upon the actual means the hegemon has to compel compliance when it chooses than upon the degree to which leaders in fact feel strong domestic pressures to undertake particular concrete policies known to be antagonistic to one or more of the hegemon's more salient interests.

The most prominent of the enduring objectives that seem to animate Soviet and U.S. policies toward the smaller powers in their own regions can be briefly categorized under the common general headings of geopolitical or military security objectives, economic objectives, and ideological-cultural objectives. The intensity and tenacity of Soviet and American efforts to obstruct or overcome the initiatives of the smaller powers in their regions has usually been roughly proportionate to the degree the particular small-power actions were perceived as threatening to these overriding objectives. However, the overall importance of each of the two regions to their respective hegemons' broader foreign policy interests also differs considerably, and this too has had its impact on the degree of constraint each superpower has felt it necessary to enforce in its region.

At a minimum, the two superpowers wish to deny the military accessibility of countries in their vicinity to the forces of other larger powers constituting an actual or potential threat to their homelands. Additionally, both superpowers see advantages in being in the position to mobilize the military and military-economic potential of neighboring states as a supplement to their own military capabilities in the event of large-scale hostilities. Both find it geopolitically advantageous to maintain military bases or support installations on the soil of at least some of their neighboring countries and consider it important that they have long-term assurances for the continued use of such facilities.

In general, it would seem that Eastern Europe has weighed more heavily in the USSR's quest for military security and advantage than Latin America has in that of the United States. The USSR shares the same continent with the advanced industrial powers of Western Europe united in the anti-Soviet NATO alliance, and the Soviet Union's Warsaw Pact allies lie athwart the main lines of advance in any conventional land war between East and West, whether offensive or defensive. U.S. policymakers have faced no strategic threat of comparable magnitude in Latin America during the postwar period, and so long as the USSR and its allies lack major offensive capabilities in the hemisphere, U.S. regional security problems will focus primarily on protection of the approaches to the Panama Canal and the maritime shipping lanes through the Caribbean and across the Atlantic. The location of Eastern European countries in the main likely theater of conflict, as well as the more advanced character of their industrial base, has made the mobilization of Warsaw Pact military forces as a major adjunct to Soviet forces a much more useful endeavor for the USSR than anything the United States can hope to achieve with the relatively smaller, more distant, and more poorly equipped military establishments of Latin America.

Economic considerations have also played a part in shaping the policies of both superpowers in their regions. Both have found significant complementarities between their own economic resources and capabilities and those of their near neighbors and have sought to turn these to advantage. Latin America has traditionally served as a source for U.S. imports of inexpensive raw materials and semifabricates, provided export markets for U.S. manufactures and agricultural products, and afforded an outlet for U.S. direct investment and financial capital. Eastern Europe's role in the Soviet economy has been almost the reverse of Latin America's in the U.S. economy. The USSR is a heavy net importer of East European machinery and industrial consumer goods, which it pays for almost entirely through large exports of fuels, raw materials, and semimanufactures. Since the mid-1970s, the Soviets have also initiated a number of joint projects with their CMEA partners providing for very large direct investments of East European capital for the development of expensive new energy and mineral reserves in the Arctic regions and Siberia.

In economic terms, as in the area of military strategy, Eastern Europe's utility looms larger for the Soviets than Latin America's does for the United States. Whereas its Eastern European CMEA trade partners have accounted for about 40 to 45 percent of total Soviet foreign trade in recent years, Latin America has accounted for about only 15 percent of U.S. foreign trade—and about one-half of that is normally with a single country, Mexico. Latin America is the locus of about 15 percent of U.S. direct investment abroad. (Department of Commerce, 1985; United Nations, 1984.)

There is a further asymmetry between the two regional systems in the area of economic policies. Because of the radically different domestic character of U.S. and Soviet economic systems, economic considerations enter policymakers' deliberations in quite different ways. America's foreign economic transactions are mainly driven by profit-seeking initiatives from the private sector and are only exceptionally prescribed in directive fashion by state policymakers in pursuit of broader foreign policy objectives (most typically justified in the name of national security rather than economic interest). In the USSR the fusion of economic and political authority and its concentration in the hands of a relatively small group of collegial decisionmakers in Moscow mean that the same people in the Politburo who form the country's diplomatic and military policies also directly supervise the machinery of macro-economic planning and microeconomic management, both in regard to domestic production and in regard to international trade. Whereas U.S. government policies in Latin America during noncrisis periods very often seem to be driven by private economic interests (the routine promotion of American trade and episodic initiatives to protect American private investments against threats of destruction, confiscation, or disadvantageous over-regulation at the hands of Latin American governments), the Soviet leadership rather self-consciously politicizes foreign trade decision-making at both the macro and the micro levels. Consequently, Soviet policy-making commonly has displayed both a willingness to subordinate purely economic concerns to political objectives in certain issue areas and a marked propensity for mobilizing political pressures to gain economic advantages in others.

The impact of ideology on the determination of U.S. and Soviet objectives in their foreign relations is an extraordinarily complex topic. Ideology establishes a conceptual framework through which policymakers organize their perceptions of the international environment. It prescribes for them an image of an ideal future state of the world and legitimizes institutions and policies in the eyes of other believers to the extent that these institutions or policies can be persuasively linked to eventual achievement of such an ideal world. It may provide clues as to which social and economic interests in the current world order are most apt to support or oppose efforts to achieve Utopia. If the ideology is sufficiently well developed, some of its doctrines may also provide prescriptions for particular sorts of strategies or policies most likely to be efficacious in bringing about movement toward the ultimate goal—or at least they may serve to rule out (on either moral or predictive grounds) some classes of policies or strategies as essentially unworthy of consideration.

Without going deeply into this much-analyzed but still insufficiently clarified subject here, suffice it to say that both the United States and the Soviet Union count among their self-defined roles in world affairs that of "missionary" (and occasionally "knight-crusader") for a universalistic ideology. The Soviet Union espouses Marxism-Leninism and professes to accept an internationalist duty to provide unwavering support for worldwide proletarian revolution to overturn all capitalist and precaptialist politicoeconomic institutions and replace them with distinctively socialist institutions, of which present Soviet institutions are seen as the prototype. American ideology, while neither so analytically complex nor so formally codified as Marxism-Leninism, has traditionally envisaged an ideal international order as one composed entirely of independent, affluent, liberal democratic states peacefully enjoying the benefits of the free-enterprise system and conducting their mutual relations according to the rules of free trade and respect for international law. The promotion or protection of democratic politics and free-enterprise economic institutions abroad has thus been an enduring ideological objective of U.S. foreign policy.

To recognize the reality of ideologically sanctioned goals in the two superpowers' foreign policies is of course not to assign them absolute priority. Securing the blessings of democracy and free enterprise for the downtrodden of the world is not the only objective of U.S. policy abroad, nor is every Soviet diplomatic initiative part of a carefully formulated plan to bolshevize the globe. Both display stubborn propensities to promote their own ways of life abroad, but where other more immediate interests and objectives (especially those connected with national security considerations) have seemed to be in conflict with this long-range goal, neither has been dogmatically unwilling to accept agonizing tradeoffs. Soviet commitment to the cause of communist revolution has not prevented them from establishing the most cordial relations with anti-imperialist Third World regimes that vigorously repress the local communist party, while American attachment to liberal democracy does not always (or, in my view, often enough) stand in the way of opportunistic alliances with countries ruled by anticommunist military juntas or ostentatiously pro-"free-enterprise" kleptocrats.

Of the two superpowers, the USSR has historically shown the greater concern for seeing to it that its neighboring states emulate its politicoeconomic institutions and policies. In part, this may be because in the Soviet ideology the domestic legitimacy of the Soviet regime is intimately connected with the concept that the revolutionary regime is a harbinger of, and a means to, a new and qualitatively superior world order. American ideology, on the other hand, essentially accepts the permanence of the nation-state and demands only that it be suitably responsive to the current preferences of its citizenry to be legitimate, without having to demonstrate progress toward the accomplishment of a world historical mission. From 1948 to roughly 1956 the Soviets demanded, and nearly always got, detailed conformity by the new people's democracies to Soviet-approved patterns in virtually every sphere of political, economic, and cultural policy; the Soviet road to socialism was to be the sole guide for all of the people's democracies. Since 1956 the Soviets have rather grudgingly conceded the need for some local variation on the basically established Soviet model in the interests of political stability. But they have made clear that they regard the maintenance of a "socialist" politicoeconomic order as an absolute requirement for normal peaceful relations with the states of Eastern Europe, and that the only genuine socialism is one in which a disciplined Leninist political party maintains monopolistic control over policy-making in all important spheres, including not only state administration but also the press, culture, and the economy. To admit the acceptability of radically different institutions or policies in another socialist country is implicitly to call into question the legitimacy of the Soviet Union's own basic institutions, which are justified by reference to universalistic iron laws of socialist development.

While the United States has been broadly on the record as favoring liberal institutions in Latin America (and has even at times withheld recognition from or cut off aid to governments coming to power by "illegal" means), this has seldom been a sine qua non of peaceful relations. Similarly, while the United States has clearly favored the maintenance or extension of free enterprise in the Latin American countries, disputes with neighboring countries engaged in large-scale expropriations or nationalizations of private property have centered on U.S. demands for "prompt, adequate, and effective compensation" of its affected citizens rather than any outright denial of the state's sovereign discretionary right to seize and administer or redistribute the property of its own citizenry within its own borders. Still, the immense expense involved in complying with the demand for adequate, prompt, and effective compensation for the expropriation of foreign-owned property may well as a practical matter preclude a rapid socialist transformation of at least the more penetrated Latin American economies, an outcome certainly congenial to American ideological preferences.

Mechanisms of Subordination

It is often suggested that the root cause of the special dominant positions of the superpowers in their regions is simply the massive disproportionality of their economic and military capabilities in comparison with their smaller, weaker, and/or less affluent neighbors, coupled with the prudent unwillingness of other major powers to accept the risks of challenging the regional hegemon in his own backyard by competing vigorously for influence there. There is much to be said for this view, and surely both a major preponderance of power capabilities and restraint by great power rivals are necessary preconditions for the kind of clout the United States and the Soviet Union have wielded in their respective regions. However, more is involved in the durability of these regional hegemonies than merely the raw power to forcibly overcome armed resistance. In both cases the ability of the hegemon to exert its influence has become regularized and even institutionalized. The subordinate countries of the respective regions over time have become entangled in a diverse multitude of international and transnational influences that reinforce one another and together drastically limit their autonomy. When small countries' leaders find themselves compelled to pursue policies that in some measure are sure to be perceived by the regional hegemon as damaging to its interests, the kinds of strategies that can be effectively pursued are largely determined by the character of the mechanisms for exerting influence that are institutionally available to the regional hegemon inside the country.

A full catalog of the mechanisms predisposing East European and Latin American elites in particular countries to conform to Soviet and U.S. interests would have to summarize two enormous literatures and cannot be attempted here. But among the more prominent categories of the mechanisms of dependency one should list at least the following:

(1) Military-coercive capabilities. Both the United States and the Soviet Union have on occasion used their own military forces to intervene directly in their respective regions. Since World War II the Soviets have deployed their troops for interventions to affect internal politics during crises in East Germany (1953), Hungary (1956), Poland (1956), and Czechoslovakia (1968). Soviet troops in multidivision strength are permanently stationed in East Germany, Poland, Czechoslovakia, and Hungary. In the same period the United States has intervened with its own troops in the Dominican Republic (1965) and Grenada (1983) and has given support to military interventions by exile forces in Guatemala (1954), Cuba (1961), and currently in Nicaragua. Other than the installations protecting the Panama Canal, bases in Puerto Rico, and the embattled Guantánamo naval base in Cuba, the United States does not permanently station large operational military forces in Latin America. However, the U.S. naval presence in the Caribbean and the availability of two marine divisions plus the 82nd Airborne Division in high-readiness status in the continental United States mean that American leaders can carry out small-scale military interventions in less-populous Caribbean Basin countries on relatively short notice. U.S. military intervention in South America or in the larger and better-

armed countries of the Caribbean Basin is not a practical option without a full-scale mobilization, since the bulk of existing U.S. ground forces are committed to Western Europe or the Far East. In contrast, the Soviet Union is able to bring massive force to bear anywhere in Eastern Europe because the main body of its ground forces are already located in the region to oppose NATO.

In addition to their raw capabilities for defeating the armed forces of the subordinate countries once battle is joined, the regional hegemons have the potentiality in many cases of directly influencing the local military leadership in such a way as to greatly reduce the chances of armed resistance or even to organize a coup against an uncooperative chief executive. The Soviets have the advantage of a highly institutionalized military alliance (the Warsaw Pact) that provides for extensive Soviet liaison at all levels of the East European military, the extended training of all higher-ranking East European military officers in Soviet academies, and regular training exercises in which East European divisions operate under the command of Soviet officers. Furthermore, the communist party's "political officer" apparatus in every Warsaw Pact country but Romania carries out extensive direct liaison with their Soviet counterparts in the MPA, and the extensive political education programs directed at military personnel lay great emphasis upon the necessity for the strictest cooperation with the Soviet Union and the Soviet armed forces as the touchstone of internationalist duty. The East European internal security police directorates for insuring the loyalty of the armed forces function under the close supervision of the Soviet KGB's Third Directorate (again, Romania is an exception). (Jones, 1981.)

U.S. penetration of the Latin American militaries is much less institutionalized but nevertheless extensive enough to be of importance. There are relatively few U.S. liaison officers with most Latin American military forces. The presence of U.S. military advisory group personnel in Latin America reached its peak in 1968 and amounted to only about eight hundred men; by 1979 their numbers had diminished to fewer than one hundred. (Stepan, 1981: 20.) Joint maneuvers are primarily naval and do not involve subordination of Latin American forces to American command. (Recent American training exercises in Honduras represent a considerable departure from past practices.) Substantial numbers of higher-ranking Latin American officers have undergone training courses in the United States or at least in U.S. military training facilities abroad, especially during the heyday of counterinsurgency doctrine in the 1960s.

(2) Political intervention capabilities. Both the United States and the Soviet Union attempt to maintain contact (both openly through diplomatic staff, military advisory groups, and trade representatives, and clandestinely through intelligence operatives) with interest groups, factions, and influential individuals inside the political elite but not currently in top posts. Such contacts may be employed to generate or support opposition to the incumbent leadership in the event of severe discord with the hegemonic power. Soviet involvement in factional infighting in the top ranks of Eastern European communist parties is well known. (For unusual firsthand insider accounts dealing with events in Czechoslovakia and Hungary, see Mlynar, 1980, and Nagy, 1958.) Such involvement has been greatly facilitated by the institutionalized practice of extensive party, state, military, security service, and economic liaison and regular exchange of low-, medium-, and high-level visiting delegations. While U.S. political action operatives in Latin America generally have fewer such formally institutionalized opportunities to look over and recruit among the local political elite, the more open and less security-conscious atmosphere prevailing in Latin American regimes offers ample opportunity for less formal contact to be initiated. The U.S. contribution to the destabilization of Allende's regime in Chile demonstrated in extreme form the potentialities of such covert political intervention, at least when used under relatively favorable political conditions in conjunction with other instrumentalities of economic pressure. (Marchetti and Marks, 1974; Meyer, 1980.)

(3) Economic mechanisms of control. The literature on Latin America (and especially the so-called *dependencia* literature) tends to greatly emphasize the role of economic factors in the vulnerability of the countries of that region to external manipulation. The most-dependent countries in the region display high geographical concentration and high commodity concentration in their foreign trade patterns, are host to sizable foreign investments concentrated in key areas of the economy, owe extensive debts to banks and international financial institutions dominated by the United States and thus find it necessary to orient their economic policies almost entirely to passive coping with essentially uncontrollable externally generated economic forces of the world capitalist market. In addition to difficulties arising from the anarchy of the marketplace, these economic structural features render the subordinate states of the region vulnerable to calculated manipulation or blackmail by the U.S. government, which is in a position to impose dire economic sanctions (refusal of credit, trade boycotts) that can virtually shut down the economies of at least the more-dependent countries.

More recently, there has begun to emerge a literature on Eastern Europe suggesting that parallel phenomena of socialist *dependentsia* on the Soviet Union exist and have had similarly deleterious effects in distorting economic development of the countries in that region. (See Zimmerman, 1978; Clark and Bahry, 1983a.) That the Soviet leaders are aware of their economic leverage is made clear by their efforts at organizing economic sanctions against Yugoslavia in 1948, China in 1960, and Albania in 1961, as well as by their skillful employment of economic carrots and sticks in their dealings with Romania since the mid-1960s.

(4) *Ideological, cultural, and other normative mechanisms of manipulation.* Because of their subjective character, these elements of the hegemon's power are the most difficult to characterize precisely or observe in action, yet in the long run they may be extremely potent. Essentially I am referring here to those recurrent social processes whereby decision-making elites in the subordinate states come to share the values, beliefs, and attitudes of the elite in the hegemonic power and hence are spontaneously predisposed to identify their own and their country's interests with those of the hegemon and to devise their own policies accordingly. These elites of subordinate states may be educated abroad, rely on foreign technical experts, read mass media dominated by imported wire service reports, attend movies imported from the hegemonic country, travel extensively there, associate with the foreign diplomatic community, adopt a foreign life-style, and so on. The Soviet Union, with its characteristic mistrust of "spontaneity" in important matters, deploys a sizable bureaucracy to manage cultural exchanges with the people's democracies and services a worldwide net of "friendship societies" with carefully crafted written and spoken propaganda. Every year hundreds of carefully selected and instructed military, state, party, scientific, trade union, and youth delegations are dispatched to Eastern Europe or are received in the USSR for the purpose of meeting with their counterparts. While the U.S. government's consciously planned programs for spreading American values and culture pale by comparison with the USSR's historically unprecedented devotion of resources to the science of Agitprop, the American high-consumption life-style publicized abroad quite unconsciously has proved tremendously attractive (some might say seductive) in the post-1945 world generally and in Latin America as well. Tourism, advertising, exported movies and TV programs, and the like have provided American policymakers with a difficult-to-measure but surely significant advantage through the impact on the leaders and mass publics

with which they must deal. The most satisfactory form of control is almost always voluntary cooperation based on perceptions of shared interests and values, if it can be attained.

Occasions and Strategies for Conflict

Despite the great disparity of power between the regional hegemons and the subordinate states in their systems, the subordinate states almost always enjoy at least some bargaining power in at least some issue areas when there are low-intensity conflicts of interest. Perhaps history's closest approach to a perfect across-the-board "that's-it-and-no-backtalk" relationship between hegemon and subordinate states prevailed in Eastern Europe in the period from roughly 1949 to 1953, the years of the great purges in the region. Stalin's secret police terrorized the East European communist elites, regarding even indirect or inadvertent criticism of anything Soviet as prima facie evidence of treason. During this period the USSR pursued a straightforward policy of economic exploitation of its East European neighbors in order to accelerate the Soviet Union's postwar recovery and to facilitate the military buildup that accompanied the Korean War. The principal methods used by the Soviets included war reparations payments, plant dismantlements, joint-stock enterprises, and trade treaties that imposed large delivery obligations on the East European partners at prices vastly below prevailing world prices. Paul Marer has conservatively estimated the Soviet take during this period at no less than $16 billion, approximately the same size as the total of U.S. Marshall Plan assistance to Western Europe. (Marer, 1974: 238.)

The explosions of popular discontent that rocked the Soviet empire from 1953 to 1956 proved the shortsightedness of such a policy to Khrushchev, and the post-1956 period brought Soviet economic and political concessions—relaxation of the police terror, an end to reparations payments, liquidation of most of the hated joint-stock enterprises, and revisions in the terms of the trade treaties. Since that time the conduct of international trade between the USSR and its East European partners, while by no means unaffected by political power considerations, nevertheless has resembled the familiar patterns of international trade negotiations more than it has resembled the levying of tribute.

Owing to the paucity and poor quality of the available trade data, there has been a lively dispute among Western econometricians as to whether (and to what degree) the USSR continued to exploit its trade partners through discriminatory pricing arrangements from 1956 to 1972. (See, inter alia, Menderhausen, 1959; Menderhausen, 1960; Holzman, 1962; Holzman, 1967.) The upshot of the available evidence is that both sides probably suffered in their terms of trade as compared to the gains prospectively available to them on world markets. More recently Marrese and Vanous (1982) have suggested that, roughly since the Arab oil embargo in 1973, Eastern Europe has been a substantial economic burden on the USSR, extracting substantial economic subsidies by pointing to the credible danger of economic collapse and political turmoil on the Soviet border if the states of the region are left to cope alone with the economic shocks inflicted by the world economy. Rising world market prices for oil (the USSR's largest single export to Eastern Europe) coupled with the more slowly rising prices payable under CMEA rules, combined from 1973 to 1982 to provide the people's democracies with a substantial cushion for their still seriously deteriorating terms of trade. Since the world market price for oil peaked in 1982, world market prices are now for the first time in a long while below the five-year moving average on which CMEA prices are based, meaning that the direction of the subsidy is now in the process of reversing itself. This may touch off yet another round of hard bargaining in the meeting rooms of the CMEA as the East Europeans seek counterbalancing concessions on other controversial but negotiable issues such as the details of CMEA specialization agreements, the volume of Soviet fuel deliveries to be guaranteed to each country, the size of East European contributions to the Soviet foreign aid program in the Third World, and the East European share of Warsaw Pact defense spending.

Another example of how the threat of collapse serves as a bargaining value has of late been visible in negotiations over Latin American debt repayments. A number of the countries of the region borrowed heavily during the 1970s to finance ambitious economic development projects that were to increase production and exports sufficiently to make possible a painless liquidation of the original debt and provide additional profits for the state or local enterprises. Errors in planning and forecasting, cost overruns, diversion of investment resources into consumption for politically favored groups, rising interest rates, shortfalls in export revenues due to falling prices, and other factors have left many of these countries heavily in debt and unable to service these debts on their present export earnings without imposing politically unacceptable degrees of austerity on the population. The U.S. government, the IMF, and private creditor banks have been demanding tough austerity measures from the debtor governments as the prerequisite for rescheduling existing loans over longer payback periods and extending new credit. Major debtor governments have in effect threatened to collapse and unilaterally reduce payments or stop them altogether unless the financial and political terms are dramatically eased. While the bargaining is still very much under way, it appears that the indebtedness of such countries as Mexico, Argentina, and Brazil constitutes such a major proportion of the assets of major American and European banks that forcing them into default could create major bank failures and deflationary economic shocks for the U.S. economy. In effect, the debtors' weakness has now become an asset in bargaining, and major concessions seem likely. The same factors may well in the end prove useful to subordinate states in bargaining over other issues as well, such as tariff reductions by the United States and the West Europeans that would permit substantial increases in Latin American exports.

There is another form of implicit bargaining from a position of weakness that is scarcely bargaining at all. The more loyal subordinate states in the regional systems (such as Bulgaria, Czechoslovakia since 1969, East Germany, Haiti, the Dominican Republic, and Nicaragua under Somoza) often pursue a conscious strategy of seeking to form a "special relationship" with the regional hegemon by striving so hard to please in every respect that the hegemon's leaders will feel moved to reciprocate in the grand manner by showing special favoritism or generosity. These are often the states whose regimes have the greatest problems of legitimacy in their relationships to their citizenry and/or special security problems that lead them to seek great power protection at almost any cost.

These and other kinds of low-key bargaining behind closed doors can often achieve acceptable (if unequally beneficial) compromises of the conflicting interests of hegemon and subordinate state on issues where common elite interests are relatively apparent (for example, the prevention of economic disaster from sparking political unrest that might spread across state boundaries). Unfortunately, there are also occasions when conflicts of interest arise that are seemingly too fundamental to be compromised within the parameters of acceptability set by the hegemon.

A decision by small-country policymakers to actively seek a greater degree of national autonomy vis-à-vis the regional hegemon is apt to depend mainly on whether they (and their principal constituencies) ultimately perceive progress toward one or more of their most vital and pressing objectives as being blocked or seriously inhibited by rigid constraints imposed by the hegemon's own definition of its interests in the region. Most often it is issues closely connected with economic development strategy that have provided at least the initial impetus for the subordinate state's efforts in Latin America, while both economic and political factors seem to have been causative factors in the East European cases. In both regions, however, there is an evident tendency for conflicts to broaden and escalate once the hegemon perceives its position to be threatened.

Situations in which a subordinate state leader pursues a plan of economic development incompatible with the preferences of the regional hegemon, eventually leading to conflict, are most evident in Latin America where populist-nationalist and/or socialist movements come to power (or seem about to come to power) and attempt to implement programs calling for large-scale nationalizations or burdensome regulation of foreign business. Mexico's nationalization of the oil industry, Bolivia's takeover of the tin mines, Guatemala's expropriation of land belonging to the United Fruit Company, and Cuba's various measures in the early 1960s, all precipitated major difficulties with the United States. The first two instances were resolved peacefully; the last two were not. Other economically motivated initiatives leading to serious friction include the assertion of claims by Chile and Peru to 200-mile territorial limits in the Pacific and recent threats by several Latin American countries to declare unilateral moratoria on debt repayments owed to foreign banks.

In Eastern Europe, social discontent directly attributable to the austerity imposed by Soviet development plans resulted in the ascension to power in Hungary and Poland, in 1956, of reformist communist leaders whose readiness to make unorthodox concessions precipitated conflicts with the Soviet Union. Romania's assertion of its independence beginning in the early 1960s was, in contrast, precipitated by an incumbent Stalinist leadership's determination to maintain orthodox development strategies in the face of innovative Soviet proposals. The Soviets had called for a supranational CMEA planning authority that would impose upon Romania a role in the new socialist division of labor emphasizing priority for the agricultural, light industrial, and extractive economic sectors. Yugoslavia's departure from the bloc in 1948 evoked polemics from the Soviets about that country's insufficiently militant approach to the collectivization of agriculture (identified as a critical precondition for genuine socialist economic development). However, there is reason to believe that Tito's refusal to accept the penetration of the Yugoslav military and security services by large numbers of Soviet advisers may have been a more important immediate issue. Albania's exit from the bloc in the early 1960s seems to have been precipitated by the incumbent leadership's resistance to Soviet pressures for rather limited political reforms (de-Stalinization) and to newly reaffirmed Soviet policies seeking to woo Yugoslavia back into the bloc through "unprincipled concessions" to various Yugoslav ideological heresies. There was a likelihood that such reform, if applied to Albania, might well entail the removal from office of General Secretary Enver Hoxha and his close associates. The change in Czechoslovakia's leadership that resulted in the initiation of the Prague Spring of 1968 was substantially due to disgust on the part of one large faction of the party elite at Antonin Novotny's prolonged delays in implementing a controversial reform of the system of economic planning and management. The plan had already been approved by the party central committee but was still viewed with suspicion in certain quarters in Moscow. However, the ground swell of support for more fundamental political reforms that soon followed was probably more critical than the economic reform issue in pushing relations with the Soviet Union to the breaking point. The dispute that led to the sacking of Walter Ulbricht from his leading position in East Germany in 1970 is generally believed to have arisen primarily from Ulbricht's efforts to obstruct and reverse a major Soviet foreign policy decision to move toward normalization of relations with West Germany without securing prior West German agreements to recognize the permanence of the division of Germany and the legitimate sovereign status of the East German government.

The most serious conflicts have occurred in those instances where the leaders of the subordinate state have found themselves strongly committed to important policies radically at variance with the current demands of the regional hegemon. When this is the case, only rather high-risk and unattractive strategies are available. They will have to recant and resign, openly and resolutely defy the hegemon and hope to weather the worst that comes, or find some sort of new leverage for striking an unprecedentedly tough bargain.

Making a bid for complete independence through a strategy of open defiance predictably leads to the hegemon's exploitation of many, if not all, of the levers of control implicit in the structure of regional relations. When such radical breakaways have been attempted, the most important element in a successful strategy has been timely measures to avoid military intervention or heavy-handed measures intended to spark an internal power grab by rival factions willing to be more accommodating. Replacement of the leadership by rival factions cooperating with the regional hegemon is unlikely if the top elite is already substantially united and committed to the policy that precipitated the dispute. It becomes still more unlikely if the incumbent leadership has taken pains to secure in advance the support of the internal security organs and hence is capable of detecting and forestalling such conspiracies. Tito and Hoxha had evidently never been willing to allow the extensive penetration of their security police by Soviet advisers that was characteristic of the other people's democracies in the 1940s and 1950s, and Gheorghe Gheorghiu-Dej carried out an extensive purge of the Romanian security apparatus in the late 1950s in conjunction with the elimination of his principal political rivals. Dubček's reluctance to take decisive action to purge potential Quisling elements in the Czechoslovak security police (and elsewhere among the party elite) was no doubt intended to reassure the Soviets of his lack of counterrevolutionary intentions, but it proved to be a serious mistake (see Mlynar, 1978).

One possible technique for reducing the prospects for a military intervention is to seek support from other states. This may be moral support, consisting of little more than verbal representations to the hegemon that such an event will damage relations with the third party (which may be another subordinate state in the region, an outside major power, representatives of the nonaligned movement, or other factions). Or support may be offered of a more material kind, indicating a willingness to assist in the event of combat breaking out. Cuba has been able to parlay its new relationship with the USSR into a security treaty that has effectively forestalled further armed U.S. intervention, and Albania hoped to receive similar guarantees in its cozying up to China.

Direct military intervention is perhaps most effectively deterred by ostentatious measures of preparation for massive armed resistance by both the professional military and the general population. (Jones, 1981.) This will very often entail the promulgation and exploitation of idiosyncratic nationalist, populist, and perhaps even xenophobic ideologies. The more monolithic communist regimes of Eastern Europe, with their disciplined political parties, ubiquitous security services, sizable military forces, and well-oiled propaganda machines, would seem to have certain built-in advantages in resisting such interventions as compared with the less organized Latin American countries (either democratic or authoritarian). But this organizational advantage is considerably offset by the much larger forces readily available to the Soviets for intervention in their home region. Defiant Latin American leaders in countries of any size are reasonably safe from invasion by the United

States if (and this is a big if) they have found ways to secure the active loyalty of the armed forces. The United States simply does not have available in the region the necessary preponderance of force to overcome large-scale determined resistance, and the matter in dispute would have to be extremely weighty indeed before its resolution could justify a general mobilization of the reserves and the recall of significant forces from Europe or the Far East. Where the military leadership is derived from the same revolutionary struggle that brought the top leadership to power (as in Cuba and present-day Nicaragua), or where the defiant political leadership group is itself drawn from the ranks of the military (as in Peru) the loyalty of the troops may not be seriously in question. But throughout much of Latin America the tradition of military evasion of strict civilian control means that extraordinary measures might be necessary. Extensive efforts by the leadership to mobilize, organize, and equip supporters from the civilian population for armed resistance seems to be a particularly valuable asset both as an additional deterrent to invasion and as a buttress of support to help insure against a military coup or sellout by less committed members of the elite.

The great danger in an all-out confrontational strategy is that to make the threat of resistance credible virtually requires such an unequivocal declaration of hostility toward the regional hegemon that it becomes extremely difficult to keep the conflict from escalating and involving the country in multiple unresolvable disputes with the hegemon. These disputes in turn may call forth the entire array of available sanctions that might otherwise have been avoided through some form of compromise. Władysław Gomułka's success in reassuring the Soviet leaders of his basically moderate reformism and solid commitment to the Warsaw Pact after he openly threatened Khrushchev with armed resistance in 1956 represented a remarkable achievement in intrabloc diplomacy, as did Nicolae Ceauşescu's managing to stay within the bloc despite his massive mobilization of Romania's military forces at the time of maximum Soviet pressure in 1968. In such tense circumstances, if the break becomes obviously irrevocable and total and if the hegemon considers the country involved to be of major national security significance, military intervention may prove impossible to deter.

The attractiveness of economic sanctions to the outraged hegemon is that they are not likely to be either so politically costly at home or so dangerous to the stability of the broader international arena as is military intervention. They have fewer risks of provoking counterintervention by other great powers, and they do not require cooperation from within the insubordinate state as political intervention does. If administered in graduated doses, economic sanctions are also less likely to bring about an irrevocable break, since they can be variable in their harshness and maintain some basic proportionality to the severity of the initial dispute. If the hegemon wishes to avoid bloodshed but is resolved that serious remedies are in order as a deterrent to others and an incentive for the errant leadership to learn the error of their ways, imposing economic sanctions is apt to seem the low-risk option. The vulnerability of the subordinate states to economic pressures, however, is highly variable, and the impact of economic deprivation is rather difficult to calculate in advance. The record of success in obtaining compliance by actually imposing massive economic sanctions (as opposed to merely threatening to do so) is not particularly good in either Eastern Europe or Latin America—as witness the ineffectiveness of the American economic boycott in bringing Castro to heel or of the Soviet Union's spectacular but ultimately fruitless attempts to reunify the socialist commonwealth by savaging the economies of Yugoslavia in 1948 and Albania and China in the early 1960s. (The United States did, however, achieve success in its efforts to destabilize the Allende regime in Chile in the early 1970s.)

Measures to counteract economic sanctions basically involve two kinds of actions—efforts to reduce the severity of the effects of the sanctions on the economy by reducing the vulnerability of the country's position (preferably well in advance), and efforts to moderate the political impact of whatever degree of economic distress unavoidably still ensues once the sanctions are actually in place.

Given a few years of slowly increasing friction to prepare in advance of full-scale confrontation, most states (even initially very dependent ones) are capable of substantially reducing their vulnerability to economic sanctions through such measures as trade diversification, accumulation of stockpiles, arrangement of lines of credit, cultivation of potential aid givers, and enhanced self-sufficiency in the production of highly critical commodities. Once sanctions have actually been imposed, further measures, such as rationing and conservation campaigns, are apt to suggest themselves as the leaders settle in for the long pull. Since complete economic collapse is unlikely to take place immediately (critical shortages take at least a few weeks or a few months to develop), even relatively unprepared leaders will have time to take counsel and seek to arrange substitute markets and sources of supply.

Perhaps just as important as purely economic measures to prevent or alleviate hardship is the task of channeling the frustrations that they are likely to cause into politically safe or advantageous channels. The decision of the hegemon to rely on economic sanctions rather than more swift and violent actions allows the small power's leaders time to mobilize public and elite opinion behind them on the basis of nationalist reactions to foreign aggression. Identification of the cause of the national leadership's continued incumbency and the implementation of their program with maintaining the sovereignty of the nation helps to deter potentially disloyal elements of the elite from undertaking collaboration or attempting to arrange a separate deal. It also facilitates the more willing mobilization of the population for unpleasant sacrifices that might otherwise lead to grumbling or disorder. Tito's, Hoxha's, Ceauşescu's, Castro's, and even Lázaro Cárdenas's elaborately tended personality cults effectively established them as not merely left-wing revolutionary heroes but also as veritable nationalist icons, and effectively discouraged serious public criticism of their policies for many years after the initial crises that spawned them were largely resolved. (Where the policy departure or departures that precipitated the original conflict are themselves internally highly divisive, however, the hardships imposed by the economic sanctions are more likely to polarize further, rather than unite, the population and the political elite, as seems to have happened in Chile under Allende.)

Inspection of table 1 reveals that most of the Latin American countries, especially the larger South American nations, have already markedly reduced their likely vulnerability to U.S. trade sanctions over the last twenty to thirty years through diversification in the structure of their trade. Whereas a number of them conducted around half of their trade with the United States in the 1950s, proportions for many of these countries nowadays run more in the vicinity of one-fourth to considerably less. Around the Caribbean, U.S. trade connections have also declined considerably, but since the levels of the 1950s were so much higher to begin with, enormous vulnerability still remains, as exemplified by worst case Mexico's 1980 figure of 63 percent (compared with a 1955 figure of 77 percent.)

The most noticeable pattern in East European trade with the USSR is that the more loyal people's democracies (Bulgaria, Czechoslovakia, and East Germany) have displayed very little improvement in the high proportion (more than 50 percent in Bulgaria's case) of their trade with their regional hegemon, while the more assertively independent states (Albania, Yugoslavia, and Romania) achieved dramatic success in reduc-

Table 1. Percentage of Foreign Trade with Regional Hegemon

Country	1955			1980		
	exports	imports	total	exports	imports	total
Mexico	75	79	77	63	62	63
Honduras	69	66	67	53	42	48
Venezuela	39	59	49	46	46	46
Panama	95	60	78	46	33	40
Ecuador	61	52	57	34	39	37
Costa Rica	55	60	58	35	35	35
Colombia	74	63	67	27	40	34
Guatemala	74	65	70	29	35	33
Nicaragua	35	65	50	39	27	33
Bolivia	60	40	50	33	28	31
Peru	36	50	43	30	30	30
El Salvador	64	57	61	30	25	28
Chile	42	43	43	12	27	20
Brazil	42	24	33	17	19	18
Argentina	13	13	13	9	23	16
Uruguay	9	19	14	11	10	10
Paraguay	18	14	16	5	10	8
Bulgaria	51	48	50	50	57	53
Czechoslovakia	34	35	35	36	35	36
East Germany	40	36	38	36	34	35
Poland	31	34	33	31	33	32
Hungary	25	18	22	29	28	29
Romania	50	53	52	18	16	17
Yugoslavia	8	7	8	4	4	4

ing their vulnerability in this regard. Poland and Hungary, whose leaders since 1956 have mostly taken conformist positions in foreign policy while pursuing modestly reformist domestic policies, show, respectively, little improvement and modest deterioration in their trade diversification over this period.

Measures to deal with and attenuate the effects of cultural or ideological penetration of the homeland by alien values or ways of thinking seem to be a part of virtually every sharp and sustained confrontation between hegemon and subordinate state in either region. Once the small state's leaders find themselves competing with the hegemon for the loyalty of key subordinates and influential members of the public, they find it useful and probably necessary to debunk past ways of thinking that legitimized their (or their predecessors') former subordination to the hegemon. Drawing clear lines between "us" and "them" based on attitudes toward ultimate values discourages defection and collaborationism. However, the task calls for considerable creativity, since the set of ideas or doctrines that legitimized the state's subordination typically is also closely related to the set of ideas that legitimize the state itself. Consequently, the most common response is to make only selective changes in doctrine while insisting all the while that the hegemon is guilty of having originally perverted the noble ideals formerly affirmed in common. Thus the evolution of a distinctive "Yugoslav road to communism" began with the assertion that Stalin had twisted and distorted the true teachings of Marx and Engels on postrevolutionary socialist development. Hoxha lashed out at the pernicious effects of Soviet "revisionism" on the pure heritage of Stalin's thought and assumed the mantle of successor in the line of world proletarian leaders running from Marx to Engels, Lenin, Stalin—and Hoxha. Ceauşescu attempted to blend Leninist orthodoxy with nationalist and chauvinist sentiments widely latent among the Romanian population as survivals from the precommunist period. In Latin America populist nationalism is typically the ideology of choice, overlaid with calls for self-sacrifice to achieve a breakthrough in the country's economic development by overthrowing American-imposed impediments to the practical attainment of the American-endorsed goals of prosperity, social justice, and democracy. In most cases the grander ideological campaigns also coincide with less theoretically elegant but highly symbolic attempts to displace (or at least stigmatize) such "corrupting" foreign cultural artifacts as imported movies, TV shows, books, magazines, phonograph records, clothing fashions, linguistic borrowings, street names, and holiday customs.

Conclusion

The sovereign equality of all states began as a formalistic legal norm of narrow applicability that eventually became an aspiration. Since the late 1950s it has been brought forward as a moral imperative confronting the brute fact of massive power inequalities in the contemporary international system. Regional hegemonies are no longer looked upon as natural or as artifices to moderate great power competition and conflict but rather as somewhat shameful marks of our failure to progress toward a more just form of international order. Elites in the subordinate states in the Soviet and American regional systems, with few exceptions, are constantly on the lookout for opportunities to expand their elbow room, either incrementally within the familiar structure of their alliance, or on occasion radically by a dramatic break with the regional hegemon. While neither superpower's entourage shows much prospect of melting away entirely, the tendency over the past three decades has clearly been toward a loosening of the bonds that tie the subordinate states to their hegemon. For every state that dramatically stands up and wins another major concession, there are many that benefit by deftly appropriating some part of that concession by using it as a precedent in quiet bargaining behind the scenes.

The process of loosening ties has clearly gone further in Latin America than in Eastern Europe—and Eastern Europe clearly had further to go in the first place. In Eastern Europe it is only the socialist states of the Balkans that have enjoyed the good fortune of successful self-assertion, while the more economically developed and strategically more critical countries of the Northern Tier have thus far had to content themselves with incremental gains in their still remarkably weak bargaining positions. It remains to be seen whether their now seriously dilapidated, increasingly dependent economies and sharpening East-West tensions will be compatible with further progress in the years immediately ahead.

13

Capitalist Dependency and Socialist Dependency: The Case of Cuba

Robert A. Packenham

Introduction

Is socialism a means to eliminate or reduce dependency and its alleged concomitants? According to a number of authors, including some of the most influential in the field of Latin American politics and development, it is. Indeed, for most of these authors socialism is the only desirable or acceptable way to address the problems of dependent capitalism. For them, capitalism is inherently exploitative and repressive; socialism is the only desirable or acceptable path to a more autonomous, egalitarian, free, and just society (e.g., Cardoso and Faletto, 1979: ix–xxiv, 209–16).

As is obvious to anyone familiar with the literature, for many authors

An earlier version of this essay was presented at the panel on "The Dominant Powers and Their Dependencies," Annual Meeting of the American Political Science Association, New Orleans, Louisiana, August 29–September 1, 1985.

the truth or falsity of this view is not a matter amenable to resolution by anything so mundane as reference to historical experience. For such analysts, this view is true by definition. The analyst using this perspective first "assumes" it to be true and then "demonstrates" that it is true by citing data that support it. (x.) In this interpretation the practice of comparing hypotheses against evidence and rejecting or modifying the hypothesis if the evidence fails to be supportive is "formal," undialectical, positivist, ethnocentric, and bourgeois. (Cardoso, 1977: 15.)

Additionally, there is another problem having a slightly different origin but the same consequences. Edy Kaufman (1976: 14–15) has well noted that many policymakers and partisans of both communist and capitalist countries reject a priori the possibility of any analogies, parallels, or comparisons between the influences of the two superpowers on smaller countries. "Extreme partisans of both camps," Kaufman reports, "reach the point of absurdity by denying the possibility of a comparison, on the grounds that the policies of the superpowers are not identical and are therefore incomparable." In this essay it is assumed that comparisons are possible. Indeed, without this assumption the claim that socialism is superior to capitalism is nonsense.

For those who do believe that historical experience can and should be examined as a means to illuminate the truth and value of such claims, however, comparative analyses of capitalist and socialist cases are indispensable. Kaufman reports that on his visits to both Latin America and Eastern Europe he "encountered criticism of the paramount superpower yet very little awareness of the restrictions imposed by the rival superpower in other regions." (15.) The present study hopes to heighten that awareness through the comparative analysis of the rival superpowers in the same region. Broadly speaking, two kinds of comparisons of capitalist and socialist dependency immediately suggest themselves and appear to dominate the literature: cross-sectional comparisons and longitudinal comparisons. In doing cross-sectional comparisons, one typically compares, say, the situation of Eastern European countries vis-à-vis the USSR with the situation of Latin American countries vis-à-vis the United States. In doing longitudinal analysis, one can compare the situation of the same country before and after the advent of socialism: say, Cuba before and after 1959, Chile before and after 1970, Nicaragua before and after 1979, Grenada before and after 1979. In this chapter the longitudinal method is used and the case selected for analysis is Cuba.

The longitudinal method normally enables the analyst to hold variables constant to a greater extent than he can when he studies two different countries. Language, historical tradition and memory, cultural baselines, basic geographic and material circumstances, and population are all factors that are more or less constant whenever one studies a particular case over time. When some profound event, like the Cuban Revolution, occurs in one country, one can more or less hold these other factors constant and make reasonable inferences about the degree and form of changes in the country that may (or may not) have been brought about by that profound event. Of course, in fact other variables do change; it is not true that the profound event is the only alteration. So the method is not airtight (to say the least). No method is airtight. However, longitudinal analysis—comparing different systems within the same country over time—clearly has natural strengths that deserve to be exploited. Comparative politics can be done by comparing different systems over time within the same country as well as by comparing different countries to one another.

Within Latin America Cuba is by far the best case available if one wants to make systematic longitudinal comparisons of capitalism with socialism. Its experience with socialism is now more than a quarter-century old. By contrast, the socialist experiments in Chile and Grenada were short-lived—Salvador Allende's socialist experiment lasted only three years, the New Jewel regime only four. The Nicaraguan experiment has had only six or seven years. Moreover, the emotionalism, politicization, and theatricality that have pervaded analyses of Cuba and that dominate writing about the other cases are now abating in the Cuban case, although they are still common.

Structural Economic Dependency Before and After 1959

Basic to the dependent condition is structural dependency: monoculture, reliance on exports, trade partner concentration, capital dependency, technological dependency, and the like. Not only Cuba's leaders but many intellectuals outside Cuba thought Cuba's structural economic dependency would change significantly under socialism. Some think it has changed significantly. (e.g., LeoGrande, 1979.) Let us see what has happened.

Diversification of Production/Monoculture in Production

The more diversified a nation's economy, the less dependent it is. The less diversified the economy, the more dependent it is. Thus, an economy with a varied production structure—e.g., one that produces industrial goods rather than just primary products, a variety of agricultural products rather than just one, and so on—is less dependent than an economy based overwhelmingly on just one product.

Before the Revolution, Cuba was a classic case of monoculture —reliance on one crop, in Cuba's case sugar, as the main prop of the national economy. In the early stages of the Revolution, diversification "was an idealistic goal ... promoted vigorously but irrationally in 1961–63 with poor results. Since 1964 economic reality pushed diversification down to the bottom of Cuba's priorities. In spite of great expectations, sugar continues to be the dominant sector in the economy, and only modest advances have been made in the diversification of the nonsugar sector." (Mesa-Lago, 1981: 179.) The overall result is that "Sugar monoculture is more pronounced now than before the Revolution." (64.) In the 1950s and early 1960s Fidel Castro and other Cuban leaders insisted that the economic doctrine of comparative advantage used to justify Cuba's sugar monoculture was a mystification of capitalist economic ideology, designed to keep Cuba in economic servitude. By the mid-1970s, however, Castro was attacking what he called "antisugar" attitudes and he pledged that Cuba would "stick to sugar" precisely because of the comparative advantages of that product. (65.)

Overall Dependency on Trade
The larger the trade sector in relation to total economic activity, the more dependent the country's economy. From 1946 to 1958 the average ratio of Cuba's exports to GNP was 30.6 percent and declining, while that of imports was 25.7 percent and increasing. Total trade as a percentage of GNP was 56.3 percent and stagnant. What happened after the Revolution?

A rigorous comparison is difficult if not impossible to make because after the Revolution the Cubans stopped computing GNP and instead began to make other computations—global social product (GSP), total material product (TMP), and gross material product (GMP). These concepts were developed in the Soviet Union and are not directly comparable to the Western concept of GNP. (199–202.) If one ignores this problem and makes a direct comparison between trade/GNP before 1959 and trade/GMP after 1959, there appears to be a reduction in overall trade dependency. From 1962 to 1978 the average proportion of exports in relation to GMP was only 21 percent, and the average ratio of total trade to GMP was only 48.5 percent. (Mesa-Lago: 79; LeoGrande: 5–8.) However, GNP and GMP are not the same, and therefore this comparison is misleading. Moreover, as we shall see below, the export figures are massively distorted by the world sugar price, whereas import ratios are much more stable and reliable indicators of trade dependence.

Some of these problems are avoided if one looks at trends in trade dependency after the Revolution, using consistent definitions and indicators from 1962 to 1978. These data show a deepening of Cuba's trade dependency in the 1970s compared to the 1960s. This pattern holds on all three indicators of trade as a percentage of GMP: exports went from an average of 16 percent of GMP in the 1960s to an average of 26 percent in the 1970s; imports from 24 to 31 percent; and total trade from 40 to 56 percent. In 1978 total trade was 69 percent of GMP, which was twice the figure (34.6) for 1962. (Mesa-Lago: 80.)

The world price of sugar affects the export and total trade indicators. High prices in the early 1970s increased them, and low prices in the 1960s decreased them. However, there is no parallel distortion with respect to imports, which are consistently and significantly higher than export/GMP ratios. Thus Castro complained in 1978 that "we have an importer's mentality . . . exports must be increased with (capitalist countries) and with the socialist region as well." (82.) In this respect dependence under socialism is at least as great as it was under capitalism.

Monoculture in Exports
The more diversified the export structure, the less dependent the country, and vice versa. The early attempt by the revolutionary government to diversify the export structure was no more successful than the early drive to industrialize and diversify the overall economy. Thus, from the 1920s to the 1950s, the share of sugar exports ranged from 70 to 92 percent of total exports, with an overall average of 81 percent. From 1959 to 1976 the share of sugar exports over total exports ranged from 74 to 90 percent, with an average of 82 percent. In short, Cuba's export structure has been as dependent during the revolutionary period as before. (Mesa-Lago: 82–83; LeoGrande: 8–11.)

Trade-Partner Concentration
A country that relies heavily on one or a few trading partners is more dependent than a country that has a larger number of trade partners. Before the Revolution—from 1946 to 1958—an annual average of 69 percent of Cuba's trade was with the United States. A higher proportion of this total was imports from the United States (77 percent) than exports to the United States (63 percent). (LeoGrande: 14.) After the

Revolution—from 1961 to 1976—the average annual share of Cuba's trade with the USSR was 48.5 percent. Again, a higher proportion of the total was imports from the Soviet Union (52 percent) than exports to the Soviet Union (43 percent). (15.) Thus, if one compares the average of the years before and after 1959 in Cuba's trade with the two principal countries only, there has been a significant reduction of trade-partner concentration.

One additional point should be noted, however. The trade-partner concentration is much higher after 1959 if the indicator is not only the Soviet Union but also the countries of the CMEA (Council for Mutual Economic Assistance) whose trade policies the Soviet Union influences much more strongly than the United States influences the trade policies of its allies. Using this more inclusive indicator, which is a more appropriate one than the USSR alone, the difference between the pre-1959 and post-1959 periods vanishes. From 1961 through 1978 the socialist countries absorbed an annual average of 73 percent of Cuba's trade (Mesa-Lago: 92) as compared with the average 69 percent figure for the United States before 1959. Also, by 1978—the last year for which I have figures—Cuban trade with the USSR alone reached 69 percent. (92.) Bearing in mind this trend, plus the close political and economic relationship between the USSR and the CMEA countries, "it can reasonably be maintained that in terms of trade-partner concentration, Cuba today is as vulnerable to external economic and political influence as it was before the Revolution." (Mesa-Lago: 94; LeoGrande: 13, 17.)

Finally, even if one uses the lowest possible indicator, the absolute level of trade-partner concentration is still very high.

Capital Dependency
Although direct private foreign investment was virtually eliminated in Cuba after the Revolution, this does not mean dependency on foreign capital has disappeared. To the contrary, it is massive. The largest source by far of this foreign capital dependency is the Soviet Union. Soviet capital comes mainly in the form of repayable loans; nonrepayable credits to finance Soviet-Cuban trade deficits; direct aid for economic development; subsidies to Cuban exports (especially sugar and nickel) and Cuban imports (especially oil); and grants for military assistance. Total Soviet capital inflow to Cuba as of 1976 was estimated to be at least $10 billion, of which about half ($4.9 billion) had to be repaid. (Mesa-Lago: 103.) Total economic aid from the Soviet Union to Cuba through 1979 has been estimated at $16.7 billion. Military aid for the same period is estimated at $3.7 billion. (Blasier, 1983: 100, 125.)

It is very difficult to make precise comparisons of levels of Cuban capital dependency before and after 1959 because of problems of data comparability. However, everyone who has studied the problem agrees that the USSR "has clearly replaced the U.S. as the major source of Cuban investment capital." (LeoGrande: 18.)

Of course, by their very nature Soviet investments do not involve either Soviet ownership of Cuban properties or repatriation of profits in the normal senses of those terms. Whether there are other ways in which the Soviets do "own" Cuban properties and/or extract "profits" from their investments are topics to be discussed below.

Debt Dependency

In 1959 Cuba's foreign debt was $45.5 million. This was less than in 1951 when it had been $68.2 million. (19.) In 1976, before the economic crisis hit Latin America, a conservative estimate of Cuba's debt was $6.2 billion. This was 136 times the 1959 figure. In 1975 Cuba's debt was the third largest in Latin America in absolute terms, after Brazil and Mexico, and the largest by far in per capita terms—four times that of Brazil, three times that of Mexico. (Mesa-Lago: 106.) By the end of 1977 Cuba owed $5.2 billion to socialist countries and $4.2 billion to capitalist countries. The interest rates to the socialist countries ranged from zero to 2.5 percent. For capitalist countries the interest rates varied but in general were much higher. In 1972 Cuba signed an agreement with the USSR suspending its debt payments until 1986. It appears that Cuba is even less likely to be able to pay in 1986 than it was in 1972. (Mesa-Lago: 104, 105.)

In short, twenty-five years after the Revolution Cuba's debt dependency was hundreds of times greater than it had been under capitalism. Cuba's situation with regard to the debt crisis was certainly no better than that of capitalist countries in the region. A strong argument could be made that it is worse.

Energy Dependency

Cuba's dependency on foreign energy is immense. Its natural endowments in energy resources—oil, gas, coal, hydropower—are very poor. Dependency on oil is particularly acute. The level of Cuban oil imports is on a par with countries that are much larger and more industrialized. Astonishingly, virtually all of Cuba's oil comes from one country. "In 1967–76 the USSR supplied an average of 98 percent of Cuban oil

imports. This oil comes from Black Sea ports 6,400 miles away." (99.)
The freight costs are enormous, amounting to 7.3 percent of total costs
in the 1970s. The implications of this particular kind of oil dependency
for Cuba's political and diplomatic dependency are profound, as we
shall see below. (Mesa-Lago: 101; LeoGrande: 26; Thomas, 1971: 701,
719–20; Dominquez, 1978: 162–63.)

Clearly, with respect to these statistical indicators, which are surely
fundamental and essential, Cuba's energy dependency has not declined.

Technological Dependency
In analyzing capitalist countries, dependency theorists have put great
weight on technology. Their argument is that no matter what may
happen on other indicators, Latin American countries tied to international capitalism are constrained and exploited by their lack of an
autonomous capacity in basic technology. Technology dependency is
thus seen as an almost absolute barrier to autonomous development
within the context of world capitalism. Socialism is supposed to be the
way to break this barrier.

Although data are scarce, it is possible to make inferences about
Cuba's technological dependency based on whether or not Cuban
technological innovations are observable in the economic or other
spheres. On this basis there is no evidence of a reduction in the degree
of Cuba's technological dependency compared to its level under
capitalism. By contrast, the technological dependency of capitalist countries in Latin America and other parts of the Third World, though very
great, declined in some areas. (Grieco, 1982; Street and James, 1979.)
Although there is no evidence that Cubans have reduced their technology dependency since 1959, there is consistent and firm evidence
showing that they have a more balanced appreciation of the benefits of
Western, capitalist technology now than they did in earlier years. Thus
the Cuban economist (later vice president) Carlos Rafael Rodriguez
stated publicly in 1975 that the socialist camp lacks a whole range of
technology that is only available from the West. Fidel Castro himself
stated in 1977 that "the United States is the most advanced country in
the world in technology and science; Cuba could benefit from everything that America has." (Mesa-Lago: 9.)

Summary
Summing up this survey of Cuban structural economic dependency
since 1959, we see the following:

Aspect of Economic Dependency	*Change/No Change Since 1959*
Monoculture of National Production	No Change
Overall Trade Dependency	No Change
Monoculture of Exports	No Change
Trade-Partner Concentration: U.S./CMEA Countries	No Change
Trade-Partner Concentration: U.S./USSR	Less Dependency
Capital Dependency	No Change
Debt Dependency	More Dependency
Energy Dependency	More Dependency
Technological Dependency	No Change

This analysis makes it clear that Cuba's structural economic dependency since 1959 has neither been eliminated nor significantly reduced in terms of basic economic indicators. Given the centrality of economic factors — modes of production and exchange — in Marxist theories and in neo-Marxist "perspectives" and "heuristic orientations" toward analyses of dependency, and given the optimistic predictions in these theories, perspectives, and orientations about the transformative effects that socialism would supposedly bring to economic relationships, these facts are manifestly of great significance.

Socialist Dependency: A Nonexploitative, "Benevolent" Form?

Despite the foregoing facts, many analysts continue to reject or minimize the degree and significance of Cuba's post-1959 dependence. There are several ways to do this. One way is simply to ignore the subject. Thus Cardoso affirms that the Cuban Revolution proved that "dependency can be broken." He does this by referring in detail to Cuba's relationship with the United States, while remaining silent on the subject of Cuba's relationship with the Soviet Union. (Cardoso, 1973a: 2.)

A second way is to dispute the analysis that has just been presented and to argue that in terms of those indicators Cuba's dependency has declined. The most important analysis of this sort is by LeoGrande (1979). He compared Cuban structural economic dependency before and after 1959 and found that out of twenty-eight indicators six showed no significant change in dependency, while sixteen showed improvement. LeoGrande's work is serious and useful in many respects. However, it has serious methodological flaws. As Mesa-Lago (1981: 229) points out, "of those sixteen indicators, ten were used to measure one variable (trade partner concentration in which a significant reduction in dependency was registered) while in another variable (that is, the foreign debt that showed a significant increase in dependency) only one indicator was used." LeoGrande also defines dependency in terms of capitalist characteristics such as profit remittances and income inequalities, and then points to the absence or reduction of those characteristics under socialism as proof that dependency is eliminated or reduced *because of* socialism. This is tautological. Also, when an indicator shows a decline in dependency, he attributes it to socialism; when dependency does not decline, it is a legacy of capitalism. In other words: heads, socialism wins; tails, capitalism loses. Even so, LeoGrande concludes that structural economic dependency has not been eliminated, only (in his view) reduced. While LeoGrande's work is interesting, it does not effectively challenge the idea that structural economic dependency under socialism remains very high.

A third approach has perhaps been the most subtle and influential way of dealing with the evidence of continued structural economic dependence under socialism. In this approach it is conceded that the transition to socialism has not eliminated or massively reduced dependency measured in the foregoing structural economic terms. The proposition some analysts now put forward, however, is that although dependency in those terms—"conventional" dependence—has continued since 1959, the exploitation that characterized capitalist dependency has been eliminated or at least massively reduced under socialism. The USSR is seen as a socialist country whose relationship to Cuba is nonexploitative. As Fidel Castro himself has put it: "How can the Soviet Union be labeled imperialist? Where are its monopoly corporations? Where is its participation in the multinational companies? What factories, what mines, what oil fields does it own in the undeveloped world? What worker is exploited in any country of Asia, Africa, or Latin America by Soviet capital?" (Fagen, 1978a: 74.) According to this view, the Cuban regime and its foreign and domestic policies are fundamentally "Cuban, un-Soviet and independent" of Soviet influence except in ways that have helped Cuba. (69–78.) Richard Fagen, for instance, argues that "even though structurally Cuba's international ties and situation still imply a significant level of vulnerability, these ties and situation have not in the main conditioned the Cuban economy in negative ways as far as achieving the primary goal of directing development toward human well-being and more equitable distribution." (1978b: 300.) Thus, in his view Cuban foreign policies have been nationalistic, autonomous, and "authentically Cuban" rather than influenced by the USSR. Some theorists lay great stress on an alleged "convergence of interests" between Cuba and the USSR. (Erisman, 1985; Duncan, 1985.) In the domestic sphere, according to this interpretation, the transformation to socialism has met the "real needs" of the "vast majority" of the Cuban people. Whereas dependency on capitalism is said to have been malign in its consequences for the Cuban population, ties of "conventional" dependency to the Soviet Union, which is seen as a socialist country, are said to be benign or "benevolent" in their consequences for the Cuban people. (Fagen, 1978a and 1978b; Brundenius, 1984; Halebsky and Kirk, 1985.)

Proponents of this third approach have advanced their claims at two levels, which are empirically interrelated and intertwined but analytically separable. First, they argue in abstract terms that the mechanisms of capitalist exploitation are eliminated under socialism and replaced by nonexploitative socialist mechanisms. Second, they argue that specific, concrete features — both internal and external — of Cuba's dependency under socialism have been much more benign and less exploitative than those of capitalist dependency. Let us consider these arguments and see to what extent the evidence supports them.

Socialist Dependency: Mechanisms of Influence and Exploitation

According to the *dependencia* approach to Latin American development, exploitation in peripheral capitalist countries does not occur through simple domination by foreign powers but through an alliance of foreign capitalists, domestic capitalists, and the dependent capitalist state. According to this model, these actors together dominate and exploit the popular classes. There may be disputes within the camp of the dominant actors, but such disputes do not alter the fundamental character of the relationship in which the "triple alliance" (or "tri-pe" alliance) of foreign, national, and state elites dominates and exploits the popular classes. (Cardoso, 1973b; Evans, 1979; Cardoso and Faletto, 1979.) Socialism is supposed to help remedy all this. Indeed, in most of these formulations the only way to bring about "the achievement of a more egalitarian or more just society" is to destroy capitalist institutions and to "construct paths toward socialism" defined in Marxist terms. (Cardoso and Faletto, 1979: xxiii–xxiv.)

The evidence from the Cuban case since 1959 does not support these arguments. Although the mechanisms and specific features of Cuban dependency under socialism are somewhat different from those under capitalism, in the Cuban case after 1959 various mechanisms and processes of domination and exploitation have been at work. These mechanisms and processes have not been discussed or even noted in the *dependencia* literature. Although in some ways they may be more benign than their capitalist counterparts, in most ways they are much more malign, repressive, and exploitative. In the remainder of this section I will sketch the main mechanisms of influence and exploitation in analytical terms. The next section will provide a more detailed discussion of the way they have operated in concrete terms in Cuba since 1959.

One of the main mechanisms by which the Soviet Union influences Cuban domestic and foreign policies and institutions is through the leverage established by Cuba's structural economic dependency on the Soviet Union. In other words, the structural economic characteristics described in the first part of this chapter are "fungible," or translatable, into influences on specific policies and institutions within Cuba of the sort that will be described in detail in the next section. A Russian embassy official, Rudolf Shliapnikov, told the Cuban Communist party official Anibal Escalante in 1967 that "We have only to say that repairs are being held up at Baku for three weeks and that's that." (Thomas, 1977: 701.) (Baku is the Soviet Union's port for shipping oil to Cuba.) If one multiplies that chilling comment across the broad spectrum of the USSR's points of economic leverage, then one begins to appreciate the magnitude of Soviet influence on Cuban affairs. Mesa-Lago (1981: 187) sketches some of these points of leverage as follows:

> The USSR has the capacity to cut the supply to the island of virtually all oil, most capital, foodstuffs, and raw materials, about one-third of basic capital and intermediate goods, and probably all weaponry. Additionally, loss of Soviet markets would mean an end to their buying about half of Cuban sugar at three times the price of the market as well as purchase of substantial amounts of nickel also at a subsidized price. The USSR could also exert powerful influence over such COMECON countries as the GDR, Czechoslovakia, and Bulgaria, which are particularly the key ones in trade with Cuba, to stop economic relations with Cuba. Finally the USSR could stick to the 1972 agreements and ask Cuba to start repaying in 1986 the debt owed the Soviets. These are not hypothetical scenarios because in 1968 the USSR used the oil stick and in the 1970s the economic-aid carrot to influence crucial shifts in Cuban foreign and domestic policies.

LeoGrande (1979: 26), who in general sees Cuba as less constrained by the USSR than Mesa-Lago does, writes in a similar vein as follows:

> Cuba is highly vulnerable to a conscious policy of politicoeconomic coercion on the part of the Soviet Union. Most analysts of Cuban-Soviet relations are convinced that the USSR took advantage of this vulnerability in late 1967 and early 1968 by delaying petroleum shipments to Cuba and by moving very slowly in the 1968 annual trade agreement negotiations. Shortly thereafter Cuban foreign policy moved more into line with Soviet policy; e.g., Cuba toned down its denunciations of pro-Soviet communist parties in Latin America, retreated from its active support of guerrilla forces in the continent, and in August 1968 gave qualified support to the Soviet intervention in Czechoslovakia.

This first mechanism is much more potent in the case of dependency on the Soviet Union than it ever was under capitalist dependency. The reason is that the Soviet state controls and coordinates the instruments of economic leverage to a far greater degree than the U.S. government ever controlled U.S. economic activities in Cuba. Indeed, the failure of the U.S. government to guide U.S. private investment and trade policies in directions conducive to U.S. public interests in the 1950s has been identified (Johnson, 1965) as a major flaw in U.S. policy that contributed to difficulties with Cuba and eventually to the collapse of the U.S.-Cuba relationship.

A second mechanism—really a large, complex set of mechanisms—is organizational. Many organizations provide institutionalized linkages between the Soviet Union and Cuba. It has been suggested (Blasier: 68) that "studying Soviet relations with Latin America without studying the relations between the Communist party of the Soviet Union (CPSU) and the Latin American Parties would be as unrealistic as ignoring multinational corporations in examining U.S. policies toward the area." This point certainly holds for Cuba. Yet many *dependencia* analyses of Cuba that are greatly concerned about multinational corporations before 1959 are silent on the subject of the CPSU after 1959.

On the basis of a detailed study by Andres Suarez, Jorge Dominguez has concluded that in the first half of the 1960s

> Prime Minister Fidel Castro acquiesced in the formation and development of a revolutionary party, and eventually a Communist party, first as an effort to obtain further support from the Soviet Union, then as a condition of continued Soviet support.

Subsequent events further validated Suarez's analysis, when he extended it into the 1970s. As the disastrous year of 1970 came to an end, the Soviet Union once again rescued Cuba, but this time on condition that a major reorganization of the Cuban government, under Soviet guidance, be undertaken. (Dominguez, 1978: 159.)

Thus not only the Cuban Communist party but the entire Cuban bureaucratic apparatus was reshaped in significant measure by the Soviet Union. The main instrument for this reshaping was the Cuban-Soviet Commission for Economic, Scientific, and Technical Collaboration, established in 1970. According to Dominguez, the details of this agreement "made evident how vast and decisive Soviet influence would become within the Cuban government." The commission henceforth coordinated the efforts of the Cuban ministries of foreign trade, merchant marine and ports, basic industries, and mining and metallurgy. It also coordinated the activities of the Agency for Agricultural Development, the Agricultural Mechanization Agency, the Institute of Fishing, the Institute of Civil Aeronautics, and the Electric Power Enterprise. The Cuban-Soviet commission itself became a new agency that pushed the Cuban government toward further bureaucratization and centralization of power. The commission met "frequently and regularly." All the agencies it coordinated were required to have "systematic, formal bureaucratic procedures under the guidance of Soviet technicians (whose numbers in Cuba consequently increased vastly in the early 1970s) in order to make effective use of Soviet assistance." (159–60.)

In 1972 Cuba joined the Council for Mutual Economic Assistance (CMEA, or COMECON). From the mid-1970s on, the Cuban five-year plans (themselves a conceptual device borrowed from the USSR) have been fully coordinated with the Soviet five-year plans. Even the Cuban system of national accounting has been reshaped along Soviet lines. (Dominguez, 1978: 159–60; Mesa-Lago, 1981: 199–202.) In short, the Soviets are deeply involved in every sector of Cuba's economy and in most government ministries. In addition to the ones mentioned above, they are also involved in the Ministry of Interior and its espionage branch, the DGI (General Directorate of Intelligence), which works closely with the Soviet KGB. (Talbott, 1978b: 39; Dominguez: 160.)

A third mechanism is the commonality of interests between Fidel Castro and the Cuban leadership on the one hand, and the Soviet leaders on the other. This commonality of interests is not total by any means, but it is great by any standard and very great indeed compared to the area of common interests between either of them, on the one hand, and the interests of the Cuban people, on the other.

What are the major interests of Fidel Castro and the Cuban ruling elite? As Hugh Thomas and his colleagues have pointed out (1984: 5), these interests or priorities have remained unchanged over the life of the regime since 1959. They are, in order of importance: (1) maintaining undiluted power for Castro; (2) making Cuba a "world class" actor with major international influence; and (3) transforming Cuban society. Castro has had considerable success in achieving these goals, and the degree of success has been directly related to the order of priority. This success owes a very great deal to the Soviet Union. Soviet support has been indispensable economically and militarily for the survival of the Castro regime. It has enabled Castro to play an international role he otherwise could never have played, and it has helped him greatly in his efforts to reshape Cuban society.

What are the main interests of the USSR in Cuba? Cuba has been, in Blasier's terminology, an "economic liability" for the USSR but a "political asset."

> Cuba may be the Soviet Union's most important political windfall since World War II. . . . Cuba has played a unique role in bolstering the authority and appeal of Soviet doctrine, the universal claims of which require intermittent validation. Communist Cuba has helped make the Soviet contention that communism is the wave of the future more believable. Thus the Marxist-Leninist regime in Cuba has strengthened Soviet influence, most particularly in the Third World. But Cuba has had more than a demonstration effect; Castro has sought to mobilize revolutionary forces around the world and supported, where it suited him, Soviet political objectives. Soviet leaders have been particularly pleased that Cuba introduced the first Communist state in the Western Hemisphere, and it has been a useful ally in political competition with the United States. (Blasier: 99.)

In addition, Cuba has been able to do in Africa, the Middle East, the Caribbean, and Central America things that the Russians cannot do as well or at all. It represents Soviet positions in the nonaligned movement. It supports unpopular Soviet actions in Czechoslovakia, Afghanistan, and Poland.

Thus, although the interests of Fidel Castro and the Soviets are not identical by any means, they are relatively congenial. Each is useful to the other and both sides know it. With respect to these two sets of actors, therefore, the widely held thesis of "convergence of interests" has a great deal of validity.

However, it is critically important to make a distinction between the Cuban ruling elite and the Cuban population as a whole. What Cuban interests are served by supporting the Soviet invasions of Czechoslovakia and Afghanistan and Soviet sponsorship of military suppression in Poland? These policies make no sense in terms of the interests of the Cuban people. They make great sense, however, in terms of the interests of Fidel Castro. Thus:

> Castro has his own reasons for approving Soviet military support for faltering socialist governments in Czechoslovakia, Afghanistan and Poland. He would hope to have such support if the Cuban government were similarly threatened.... The main justification for Soviet military suppression is that socialist regimes are being threatened with "foreign intervention" by "imperialist" nations ... if Castro is counting on the USSR to protect him from "imperialism" (or local forces linked to "imperialism"), he must necessarily approve the Soviet defense of "socialism" elsewhere. (Blasier, 1983: 109.)

What this example suggests, and the next section documents in a more systematic and comprehensive fashion, is that most policies in Cuba do not serve the interests of the Cuban population as a whole nearly so much as they serve the interests of the Cuban ruling elite and its Soviet sponsors. If, as Evans, Cardoso, and other *dependencia* writers claim, there is a *tri-pe* alliance of multinational, state, and local capital in countries on the periphery of capitalism that exploits the population of these countries, then there is also a *bi-pe* alliance of Soviet and Cuban elites that exploits the Cuban population in ways and to degrees never realized in pre-1959 Cuba or most other peripheral capitalist countries.

Unfortunately, this sort of analysis is never made by partisans of the Castro regime or by proponents of the *dependencia* perspective on Latin American development. They reject or ignore even the possibility of conflicting interests between the Cuban elite and the Cuban population. They claim or assume that what has been good for the Cuban and Soviet elites has also been good for the Cuban people. Yet, if the standards they use to critically analyze such peripheral capitalist countries as, say, Brazil or Cuba before 1959 are applied to Cuba after 1959, then it becomes clear that the Castro elite, whose interests are dialectically and intimately intertwined with those of the Soviet government, is systematically dominating and exploiting the Cuban people. The concrete manifestations of those common interests, and of the other mechanisms just described, are the topic to which we now turn.

Socialist Dependency: Specific Features

Dependencia authors, defenders of Cuban socialism, and other analysts have offered a number of hypotheses about the concrete processes, institutions, and policies they believe have characterized socialist dependency in Cuba. First, they say, under socialism there is no capitalist investment and therefore no profit repatriation from Cuba to the USSR. In this view, whereas capitalist economic dependency involved investments and profits and therefore was exploitative, socialist economic dependency does not involve investments and profits and therefore is not exploitative. Second, socialism has made possible changes in Cuba's internal social structure that were impossible under capitalism and that are more just and equitable than the pre-1959 capitalist social system. Third, socialism has broken the pattern of dependency on imported U.S. culture and replaced it with authentically national cultural expressions. Fourth, socialism has made possible true, "substantive" democracy rather than authoritarianism or the merely "formal," procedural political democracy that obtained before 1959. Finally, since 1959 Cuba's foreign diplomatic and military activities have been autonomous, independent, authentically national policies in the Cuban national interest, whereas before 1959 these activities and policies were subordinated to and exploited by the interests of the United States.

Notice that these hypotheses stress the internal aspects of post-1959 Cuban development as much as—if not more than—the external ones. This is consistent with the analysis these authors make of peripheral capitalist countries, where the main emphasis is also on the internal manifestations or "expressions" of dependency. (See Cardoso and Faletto, 1979: passim.) Their idea is that internal development patterns are inextricably intertwined with the external context, whether capitalist or socialist, and that the transformation from capitalist to socialist dependency will be associated with the benign patterns of development just hypothesized.

Let us examine specific features of Cuba's domestic and foreign policies and institutions in the context of socialist dependency in order to see how these hypotheses stand up. It will be shown that, far from confirming these five hypotheses, the evidence strongly rejects them and supports instead the hypotheses about the mechanisms and processes of socialist dependency and exploitation that were presented in the preceding section.

Social and Economic Aspects

Most discussions of this topic say that the Revolution's accomplishments in the social sphere have been magnificent. Economic problems are noted but blamed on the U.S. economic embargo. They are not taken very seriously or given much weight as a commentary on the Revolution. While this picture has its elements of truth, it makes two kinds of errors. It is one-sided and incomplete in its assessment of the social gains. It also misperceives and underestimates the economic failings.

We begin with the Revolution's proudest achievements—the social sphere. Post-1959 accomplishments—many real, some imagined—in the areas of literacy, educational opportunity, rural development, land reform, housing, health care, nutritional standards, employment, class relations, "moral reforms" (against prostitution, gambling, corruption, and homosexuality), and racial and sexual equality are widely noted and have been described in detail by many authors. There is no need to repeat those accounts here. However, even in this sphere of greatest accomplishment, the record is by no means universally positive or nonexploitative. Nor is all this social progress related to the Revolution, socialism, and Soviet support; much of it has roots in the capitalist period.

In the first place, in comparison with other Latin American countries Cuba before 1959 was not only relatively well off in per capita income but also quite progressive in terms of such social indicators as literacy, educational opportunity, per capita levels of energy consumption, daily newspaper circulation, radios, television sets, and physicians. Indeed, on these indicators Cuba was on a par with many European countries. If it is true that these patterns refer to aggregate statistics of resources concentrated in the cities, it is also true that in 1959 Cuba's population was two-thirds urban. This point is not sufficiently noted. In addition it was 75 percent literate and 99 percent Spanish-speaking. How many radios did the rich listen to compared to the poor? Nutritional levels were higher and infant mortality rates were substantially lower than in most of Latin America. And there was never the phenomenon of boat people, even under Fulgencio Batista.

Second, some of these accomplishments in the social sphere are more apparent than real. Much "employment" is still disguised unemployment. Rural-urban disparities persist. The political elite, which is ipso facto also the economic and social elite, is still over-whelmingly male and white. In these respects and others the unequal and/or exploitative features attributed to capitalism continue under socialism—sometimes in lesser degree, sometimes in the same or even greater degree. The political power of Cuban women is no greater today than it was in 1959. Homophobia is far greater under Cuban socialism than it ever was under capitalism, in part because it now has not only cultural predilections but also the weight of Fidel Castro's personality and the capacity of the Cuban state apparatus to back it up. Access to the political elite was as great for blacks and mulattoes before 1959 (Batista himself was mulatto) as after 1959.

Third, during the course of the Revolution there have been dramatic worsening trends in many areas of early apparent achievement. The first impulses toward social equality have been replaced by powerful trends toward social elitism—not the old capitalist forms but the new socialist forms. Thus the initial opposition to "sociolismo"—buddyism or cronyism—has given way to a new class of party functionaries and state bureaucrats with privileged housing, department stores, vacation villas, access to hard currencies and luxury goods. As in the Soviet Union, rates of divorce have increased dramatically since 1959 and now stand at very high levels on a world scale. Corruption and illegal economic profiteering have increased.

Fourth, given the nature of the Cuban state and of state-society relations since the Revolution, most of these social benefits have very high political costs directly and necessarily associated with them. The government apparatus that provides food, housing, health care, and educational opportunity simultaneously, and for that very reason, also has enormous power over individuals and groups in Cuban society. Every Cuban knows this, and such knowledge, together with the other political mechanisms of the Cuban state, makes significant dissent by Cuban citizens virtually unthinkable except by those few—very few —who are willing to accept the most severe risks and costs. A state that has the power to deny food to political nonconformists, and that is willing to use that power, has unique instruments for maintaining "popular support."

Finally, the argument that a socialist transformation, a profoundly undemocratic political system, and massive economic decline were necessary in order to make social changes is dubious. For example, Costa Rica has had a comparably progressive socioeconomic profile

—low unemployment, high health standards, low illiteracy—at the same time that it has retained a pluralistic, democratic political system. And it also enjoys a higher standard of living and much greater economic dynamism than Cuba.

Viewed in light of these considerations, the social achievements are less compelling than many analyses would suggest. Undoubtedly some of the achievements were easier to bring about under socialist dependency, but it was not the only way to achieve them, and it obviously has a dark exploitative side as well, which we have just begun to describe.

There is also, of course, the enormous economic price that has been paid and is still being paid. Before 1959 Cuba had one of the most impressive socioeconomic profiles of any country in Latin America. In 1952 it ranked third among all Latin American countries in per capita GNP. Since 1959 Cuba has been transformed into one of the least productive countries in the region. In 1981 it ranked fifteenth in a list of twenty countries in per capita GNP. No other country dropped in ranking from 1952 to 1981 by more than three places; Cuba dropped twelve places. (Thomas et al., 1984: 29.) The Cuban Revolution, in short, has performed extremely poorly in terms of productivity and creating new wealth (as distinguished from dividing up wealth that had already been created).

It is of course true that there have been no capitalist investments by the Soviet Union, and thus no profit remittances. By definition, socialist systems do not make capitalist investments or remit capitalist profits. Moreover, since in Marxist economic terms profit is by definition exploitative, it follows that a system without profits is in that respect nonexploitative. These points are true not because of any facts but, in this view, by definition. However, to anyone not dogmatically loyal to Marxist definitions, it is manifest that capitalist investment and the profit system can be positive features of a generative, productive, positive-sum process. Such a notion is unacceptable to Marxists —including sophisticated Marxists—but outside the Marxist view it is nothing more than elementary economics. Critics of capitalist investment often cite examples where profits exceeded total investment to illustrate the exploitative effects of capitalism. Such arguments are fallacious for several reasons. They ignore the multiplier effects of the capital invested. They also ignore cases where investments were unproductive and the investor lost his investment. The risk of such losses is one of the factors that entitles an investor to profits. Finally, they ignore the fact that the Cubans themselves at the practical level now frequently reject their theoretical premises about the exploitative effects of capital when they appeal for direct private investment, commercial loans, and hard capitalist currencies. The intellectual and policy fallacies of Marxist theory are also shown in relation to protests against the economic embargo on Cuba at the same time that free trade and investment are said to be exploitative. If trade is exploitative, as they claim, the embargo—pejoratively but inaccurately called a blockade—logically has to be a plus for Cuba. Yet, illogically, they claim it hurts them. If it does in fact hurt them, then obviously trade—and its inevitable concomitant economic dependency—must also be positive in its effects.

Increasingly it looks as if the social gains of the Revolution largely have come from simply dismantling the productive mechanisms of capitalist dependency without replacing them in effective ways. A once productive island has thus been transformed into a massive economic liability. Its problems have a variety of sources, including the frequent arbitrary and ill-informed interventions of Fidel Castro himself. The U.S. economic embargo is also cited as a reason. The most fundamental problems, however, are not random, or personal, or inspired by capitalism; they are inherent in the character of Cuba's associated-dependent socialist situation. The economy's weaknesses, in other words, are fundamentally structural. They are, as Leontiev pointed out more than a decade ago, "fundamentally the same as those that plagued the Soviet Union and other socialist countries," namely, "the characteristically low productivity of labor, rooted in the basic differences between a socialistic and an individualistic society." Leontiev went on to argue that the productivity of labor

> seems to be lower now than it was before the revolution. With the same equipment and under otherwise identical physical conditions the same worker, or the same group of workers, seems to produce in all branches of industry and agriculture smaller amounts of goods, or goods of lower quality, or both, than would have been produced before the revolution.
>
> The so-called moral incentives ... seem ineffective as a means of inducing laborers, white-collar workers, managerial and supervisory personnel to perform their respective jobs as well as they did before the revolution. ... (1971: 19, 21.)

Subsequent events have confirmed this analysis. While the Cubans have made some adjustments, given their ideological and political commitments they cannot really correct these structural defects, which are inherent in the Cuban model.

Thus, once socialist Cuba divided up—fairly rapidly—the fruits of earlier capitalist development, the economic and other costs have become more evident.

To be sure, there are those who say these economic and social costs exist only for the Cuban upper and middle classes—i.e., for *gusanos*, literally, worms, nonhumans, the epithet used by the Castro regime (and many U.S. intellectuals) to refer to Cuban exiles. However, most of the approximately 125,000 Cuban boat people in 1980 were working and poor people. (Moreover, it may be permissible to note that even middle-class persons are human beings.) To date, a full tenth of the Cuban population has fled the island. Many more—up to two million more according to some responsible estimates—would leave if they could. Nothing remotely resembling these phenomena existed before 1959, not even during the worst days of Batista.

Political Aspects
But if there are problems and costs in the social and economic areas, even more profound modes of exploitation under socialist dependency occur in the political, cultural, and military-diplomatic areas. Again, they affect not only the affluent but also the middle-class, working-class, and poor people of Cuba directly and intensely.

In Cuba there is not even a pretense of democratic rule in the sense of citizens controlling governmental officials. To the contrary, the logic of the Revolution both publicly and within the ruling circles is the reverse: leaders guide, direct, and control citizens in the ways of revolutionary truth and virtue. The idea of citizens controlling leaders is characterized by the leaders as bourgeois, reactionary, and counterrevolutionary. In Cuba "the Revolution and its leaders legitimate the constitution, the courts, the administration, the party, the mass organizations, and the elections—and not vice versa." (Dominguez, 1978: 261.)

Accordingly, within Cuba itself power centers first and foremost on Fidel Castro, and second on the people closest to him. Fidel Castro has been the undisputed "socialist caudillo" of Cuba for more than a quarter century—that is, for most of his adult life and the entire life of the post-1959 system. It is a remarkable achievement with few parallels on a world scale. Castro has well met his first priority of maintaining undiluted power for himself during this period.

Especially in the 1970s and 1980s the Cuban Communist party, the civilian bureaucracy, and the military have grown in numbers, organizational capacity and complexity, and influence—although all of them remain systematically subordinate to Fidel Castro and the CPP. At the next level down in the hierarchy of power are the mass organizations: the Committees for the Defense of the Revolution (CDRs), the Federation of Cuban Women (FMC), labor unions, and youth organizations. Finally there are elected legislative bodies (assemblies) and judicial structures at national, provincial, and local levels. However, except in strictly limited and sharply controlled ways, these bodies do not have the functions associated with them in political democracies.

These political mechanisms are used for various domestic and foreign policy objectives set by the political elite. One of the main stated objectives is to create new socialist citizens who will be free of the values and characteristics that are glorified and practiced in politically liberal, capitalist societies. The regime is explicitly and resolutely antiliberal. Liberal societies place a high value on individualism, competition, pluralism, the basic freedoms, and group autonomy. From the point of view of the Cuban system, these values and practices are egotistical, alienating, atomizing, divisive, and undisciplined. The aim of the Revolution is, and must be, to get rid of them. Cuba's leaders have argued that since capitalism was in place for hundreds of years in Cuba, these values and practices are deeply ingrained. To get rid of them, therefore, a vanguard is needed of enlightened teachers and leaders who will transform the unenlightened masses into realizing their true needs and interests.

Thus, the Cuban political system is explicitly and comprehensively elitist and hierarchical both in the principles that undergird and legitimize it and in its political institutions and processes. These principles and institutions are enormously powerful devices for controlling and exploiting Cuban citizens. Under these principles there is literally no sphere of human activity that is immune from state supervision and control. In other words, there are no moral or ethical constraints on state action vis-à-vis the individual except the "needs of the Revolution" as determined by the top leadership. Any degree of state penetration of any area of individual and group life is legitimate. The elaborate and powerful organizational structures of the Cuban state, the legitimating myths of the Revolution, Fidel Castro's charisma, and other factors all assure that in practical terms the actual degree of that penetration is enormous.

In these circumstances, civil liberties have no meaning either conceptually or practically. Neither does the idea of the autonomy of individuals and groups from state power. In Cuba the idea of a "legitimate opposition" is totally foreign and subversive. The operative principle is, "Within the Revolution, anything; outside the Revolution, nothing." This standard is very elastic. It can mean whatever the state chooses it to mean.

In Cuba the communications media are totally controlled by the political elite. Criticisms of the regime and its leaders—even (especially?) jokes about them—are rigorously prohibited. According to Hugh Thomas (1971: 1463), "Compared with the Cuban press, that of Spain (under Franco) might be considered sparkling." Lee Lockwood (1970: 18) notes that the media in Cuba are not only dull, dogmatic, repetitious, and sycophantic but also uninformative. "In fact," he writes, "the Cuban press is so mediocre that even Fidel can't stand it; I had personally witnessed how every morning at breakfast, he read the AP and UPI wire service reports first (and carefully) before skimming idly through *Granma*." Castro has railed at the U.S. media because of their alleged elitism, monopoly power, and subservience to government policies, yet these charges fit his own system infinitely more accurately than the U.S. system. Clearly such control of the media—both print and electronic—affords Castro a powerful instrument for controlling and exploiting the Cuban population. Just to give one concrete example, the Cuban government controls entirely information about the human and material costs of Cuba's military activities in Africa. It is inconceivable that the government would (or could) tolerate investigative reporting or a pluralistic, free press.

The political elite have several mass organizations to enforce loyalty to the regime and its objectives and to supervise and punish possible counterrevolutionaries. Of these the most important are the CDRs. They were founded in 1960 with a membership of about 800,000 persons; by 1983 there were more than 5 million members, or more than half the entire population (and about 80 percent of the adult population). The specific goals have been many and somewhat varied over time: e.g., vigilance, local government, public health, civil defense. However, the major continuing theme has been vigilance. CDRs exist primarily to ensure that Cubans are "integrated" into the Revolution. Being "integrated" is in effect "a requirement for normal life in Cuba, whatever one's feelings toward revolutionary rule and policies." Thus, "even former members of the prerevolutionary upper class, still living in Cuba in mansions with domestic servants, have been reported belonging to a committee, because being a member makes life easier." (Dominguez,

1978: 264.) By contrast, "nonintegration" is more than inconvenient; it is dangerous. "Nonintegrated" persons are publicly vilified. CDR militants hold "repudiation meetings" to "chastise, browbeat, and humiliate" those who want to leave Cuba. Merely not belonging to the CDRs is a political act. In a society that insists on revolutionary militancy, those who stand on the sidelines are vulnerable. (Dominguez, 1978: 260–67; del Aguila, 1984: 154–56.)

Under such circumstances the regime does not need to use a large amount of physical violence or imprison large numbers of people in order to operate a totalitarian system. Of course, politically motivated violence, imprisonment, and torture have been used by the regime on thousands of Cubans. However, the circumstances just described, plus the U.S. escape hatch through which a full tenth of the population has passed, have kept at relatively low levels the amount of overt physical violence and imprisonment in Cuba compared to such cases as the USSR, the People's Republic of China, or Cambodia. But the system is no less totalitarian for all that. Moreover, there are other effective forms of violence besides political murder and physical torture and imprisonment. This is a point that is made frequently against capitalist culture but seldom against Cuba, where it applies with even greater force.

Culture and Education

Nowhere are the influences of the Soviet model of development in Cuba more evident, and more contrary to human well-being, than in the cultural and educational spheres. Intellectual work at all levels is intensely politicized. All cultural, artistic, and educational activity is evaluated and rewarded exclusively in terms of its contribution to the Revolution, as judged by the political elite. Intellectual independence and criticism of the regime are met with official contempt, mass humiliation, and various forms of psychological and physical repression. The most notorious examples are those of the poets Heberto Padilla and Armando Valladares and the dramatist Anton Arrufat, but they are only the tip of the iceberg. (Ripoll, 1982.)

Today the vast majority—one estimate is 95 percent—of Cuban writers and creative artists are in exile. Most of them are not ex-Batistianos. Most opposed Batista. Many were actively involved in the fight against his regime, and some even had positions in the Castro government in the early years. But the cultural regimentation and dogmatism were intolerable to them and they left. Many of these exiles have made and are now making distinguished contributions in the cultural sphere. One has only to mention, for example, the works of Carlos Franqui, Cabrera Infante, or a dozen distinguished social scientists. On the island itself, however, the picture is very different. As Thomas et al. (1984: 42–43) report:

> In 1964, in a famous interview in Paris, novelist Alejo Carpentier was asked why he had not written a novel about the Cuban Revolution. He answered that unfortunately he had been raised and educated long before the Revolution and the burden of creating new revolutionary novels would have to fall on the shoulders of a younger generation. "Twenty years from now," he affirmed, "we will be able to read the literary production of the new Cuba." Those 20 years have elapsed. Tragically, the Cuban revolution cannot offer a single notable novelist, a famous poet, a penetrating essayist, not even a fresh contribution to Marxist analysis. . . . Censorship and fear have smothered creativity in Cuba. What is left on the island is merely the incessant voice of official propaganda.

The situation would seem to be better at the level of mass education. However, as is often the case, impressive figures regarding aggregate gains in educational opportunity are misleading. For one thing, "despite claims to the contrary, higher education remains elitist in Cuba." (Thomas et al., 1984: 41.) Tests of political loyalty and political achievement are applied at all levels of the educational system to determine who has access to the best facilities and training.

Second, the quality of education has not kept pace with the increases in the overall quantity of educational opportunity—which, as noted earlier, were already relatively great before 1959. To the contrary, the dogmatic and politicized character of education has impoverished its quality. The quality is now much inferior to what it was before 1959 and is today in democratic countries such as Costa Rica. For example, when liberal U.S. Congressman Stephen Solarz of New York visited Cuba in 1978, he met with a group of sixteen students at the University of Havana. According to journalist Strobe Talbott, the students were impressive in delivering set pieces consistent with current government policy, but "on subjects where the government's line was not yet clearly defined, students and teachers alike were intellectually incapacitated. At the end . . . Solarz thanked (his hosts) for a revealing demonstration of 'democratic centralism' at work. The students seemed unaware of his irony." (1978a: 31.)

Scholarly analyses of Cuban education confirm this journalistic impression. According to a very sympathetic study of "the Enterprise of History in Socialist Cuba":

> As long as problems persist in Cuba (and they do persist), as long as the security of the Revolution is challenged from without, the emphasis will continue to fall on the exhortation to revolutionary duty and patriotic sacrifice. Appreciation of the present, together with a recognition of the achievements of the Revolution, require awareness of a certain version of the past. It is this central task that Cuban historiography is given. It is with the old past that the new present is compared, a comparison that seeks to underscore the vices of capitalism and the virtues of socialism. The recent literature has examined the nature of capitalism in prerevolutionary Cuba, an inquiry that begins with the Spanish conquest and emphasizes exploitation, corruption, and oppression in the old regime—in short, a chronicle of how truly bad the old days were. The achievements of the Revolution, by implication, are thereby set off in relief—accomplishments never to be taken for granted. (Perez, 1985: 4.)

At the level of secondary education Cuban officials themselves have conceded publicly various shortcomings in quality: shoddy construction and low durability of school buildings and facilities, rising drop-out rates, increases in cheating on the part of students and teachers. (Thomas et al., 1984: 42.)

The Militarization of Cuban Society
The regimentation and politicization of education and culture have parallels in the militarization of society, which in turn has both internal and external aspects. The militarization of Cuban society is partly rooted in the guerrilla experience that defeated Batista. The concepts and habits forged during those years continue to affect Cuba, and they are now reinforced and supplemented by the penetration into Cuban political organizations and processes of numerous aspects of the Soviet model. In 1980, for example, thirteen out of sixteen members of the Political Bureau of the PCC had been early guerrilla followers of Fidel and Raul Castro. (Thomas et al., 1984: 15.) The regular armed forces of Cuba are the largest in all of Latin America with the possible exception of Brazil, a country with thirteen times as many inhabitants and seventy-four times as much territory. Even if Cuba's defense needs are greater, this huge disparity is still notable. There are now between

200,000 and 375,000 members of Cuba's regular armed forces. In addition, there are another 100,000 to 500,000 men and women in the militia, several thousand border guards, 10–15,000 state security police, a "Youth Labor Army" of 100,000, and several hundred thousand members of the military reserves. (Aguilar, 1985: 160–61; Thomas et al., 1984: 57; Dominguez, 1978: 346–50; Fagen, 1978a: 77.) If one adds the paramilitary aspects of the CDRs and other mass organizations, one sees that virtually the entire population is militarized in one way or another. Indeed, Castro has stated that instead of a vote for every citizen, he would offer them a gun, and he has said many times that he had created an armed camp in his nation. (Thomas et al., 1984: 57.) All this is a far cry indeed from the 47,812 (Dominguez, 1978: 346–47) poorly trained, ineffective troops of Batista's army, navy, and reserve forces at their greatest strength. It is these facts that have led Thomas (1984: 784) to say that in Cuba "the emphasis on war and weapons, on the importance of fighting, borders on the psychopathic."

Foreign and Military Policies
The subject of Cuban foreign policy before 1959 is complex. U.S. government influence was enormous at times, as the history of the Platt Amendment and many aspects of U.S. relations with the governments of Ramón Grau San Martín and Fulgencio Batista attest. U.S. private interests also were very influential in Cuba. In these respects, among others, Cuban politics was heavily influenced by the United States. On the other hand, the pluralistic character of U.S. government institutions, and of its public-private relations, diluted and complicated U.S. influences and provided some political and economic space for Cuba's domestic affairs and foreign policy. The character of Soviet institutions, and therefore of their influences on Cuba, are very different. Today Cuba is much more tightly tied in its foreign and domestic policies to the Soviet government than it ever was to the United States. In fact, the major constraint on Soviet influence is its physical distance from Cuba. This leaves both the USSR and Cuba somewhat vulnerable. Ironically, physical distance is one of the factors *dependencia* thinkers reject as relevant to dependency because it is not per se an aspect of their touchstone distinction between capitalism and socialism.

Soviet influence was not significant at the beginning of the Revolution. It became important only about eighteen months after Castro came to power in January 1959. (Blasier, 1983: 100–103.) Through most of the 1960s the relationship grew, but there were also major differences between the Soviet and Cuban governments on domestic and foreign policies. The Cubans veered from one extreme to another in their economic policies and favored insurrectionary violence against established governments in Latin American countries. The Soviets opposed both these tendencies. In the 1970s, however, conflicts over both domestic and foreign policy decreased. In the domestic sphere after 1970 the Cuban polity, economy, and society have increasingly been reorganized along Soviet lines. In the international sphere, particularly after 1968, the Cuban government has accepted the Soviet government as its senior partner in foreign policy. Thus Cuba has supported Soviet policy in Czechoslovakia (1968), Afghanistan (1979), Poland (1981), Angola (1979), Ethiopia (1979), Nicaragua (1979), and El Salvador (1979). The Cubans have been an ideal and effective sponsor for Soviet policies in Africa and Central America and in regard to the so-called nonaligned movement of Third World countries. They have sided with the USSR against the People's Republic of China.

Since the late 1960s there has been no important foreign policy question on which the Cubans have publicly challenged the Soviet Union. On the contrary, the Cubans have followed the Soviet lead as loyally as any Eastern European country (perhaps more loyally than most) even on such distasteful issues as Czechoslovakia, Afghanistan, and Poland. If private disagreements or qualifications exist, they are not expressed publicly.

The scale and scope of Cuban involvement with Soviet foreign and military policies are astonishing for a country of ten million people that never imagined, let alone implemented, such levels of military activity in the context of capitalist dependency. Cuban military operations in Africa and the Middle East exploded in magnitude during the collaborative phase of Cuban-Soviet relations that began in the late 1960s and is still going on. The highest total number of Cuban troops and military advisers in those regions at any time in the 1960s was an estimated 750–1,000 in 1966. In 1976 it had increased to an estimated 16–19,000 and by 1978 to an estimated 38–39,000. (Blasier: 112.)

> Cuban forces abroad in the late 1970s accounted for two-thirds of the military and technical personnel stationed by all Communist states in the Third World — exceeding Soviet troops in Afghanistan and Vietnamese forces in Southeast Asia. In addition to troops, Cuba dispatched technicians, advisers, and construction workers to Algeria, Iraq, Jamaica, Libya, Mozambique, Nicaragua, Vietnam, and Grenada in the late 1970s and early 1980s. (Thomas et al., 1984: 12; Mesa-Lago: 50–53; del Aguila: 125.)

In 1978 Cuba had not only about 35,000 military troops and advisers in Angola and Ethiopia but two hundred in Libya, a thousand in Mozambique, three to four hundred in South Yemen, one hundred to a hundred and fifty in Guinea-Bissau, fifty in Tanzania, twenty in Iraq, and fifteen to sixty in Zambia. (Blasier: 112.) By 1981–83 Cuba's overseas military presence had remained at the same levels in most of the foregoing countries (except for Guinea-Bissau, where it had dropped to fifty) but increased to 3,000 in Libya, 2,200 in Iraq, and 800 in South Yemen. In addition, there were 170 Cuban military personnel in Algeria and 2–4,000 in Nicaragua. Another 22–25,000 economic technicians were operating in these countries. (del Aguila, 1984: 125.) According to Fidel Castro, more than 100,000 members of the Cuban armed forces had served in Africa by the end of 1980. In 1982 Cuba had about 70,000 military troops, military advisers, and civilian advisers in twenty-three countries around the world. (Thomas et al., 1984: 12.)

Not only military personnel but weapons capabilities increased very rapidly during this period. In 1981 there were about 2,400 Soviet military advisers in Cuba to provide training and support for the military equipment that had flowed into Cuba since 1975. (There were also several thousand Soviet civilian advisers.) Cuba's ground and air forces, nearly all provided by the Soviets, included two hundred MIG fighters and fifty combat aircraft of other kinds; thirty-eight combat helicopters; 650 tanks; 1,500 anti-aircraft guns; and dozens of military transport aircraft, including at least seven long-range jets each capable of carrying 150 to 200 combat-equipped troops. (Cirincione and Hunter, 1984: 175.)

In short, the military has been by far the most dynamic sector of the Cuban economy for at least a decade. The Soviets have paid most of the economic costs in this sector. One of the main arguments of *dependencia* writers is that foreign capital is concentrated in the most dynamic sectors of the associated-dependent countries, and that therefore foreign capital is more influential than mere aggregate investments would suggest. By this logic of "dynamic-sector analysis" the Soviet role in Cuba is greater than U.S. capital ever was in Cuba.

Many commentators maintain that Cuba's foreign policy reflects Cuba's own interests. However, it is not plausible that a country of Cuba's size, location, and precarious economy would, in its own interests, have 70,000 troops and military advisers in twenty-three countries around the world—most of them in Africa and the Middle East, where the troops are Cuban but the officers and the uniforms are Russian. It is also argued that this foreign military involvement is popular in Cuba. But what does "popular" mean in Cuba, where dissent is "counterrevolutionary" and "antinational," where the media and the means of production are state-controlled, and where a massive, powerful apparatus of political mobilization and vigilance is in place? If it is "popular," and in Cuba's interests, why are data on casualties unreported in Cuba, the dead buried outside Cuba, and the wounded kept out of public exposure? (Leiken, 1981: 100; Pastor, 1983: 191.) Why, despite intense political pressures and safeguards against release of information on the subject, is there still evidence of resistance to the African wars among the managerial elite; of "insubordination among some troops"; and of "widespread unhappiness among the Cuban people concerning compulsory military service"? (Dominguez, 1978: 355.)

Conclusion

This essay has not established — nor has it sought to establish — that Cuban revolutionary institutions and policies are a total, mechanical replication of Soviet models and preferences. Even less was pre-1959 Cuba a mechanical response to influences from the United States. The chapter does reject, however, the proposition that Cuba's domestic development and foreign relations under socialism have been autonomous and nonexploitative. It makes an analytical and empirical case for a very different hypothesis, namely, that a *bi-pe* alliance of Cuban and Soviet elites is systematically dominating and exploiting the Cuban people for its own ends.

These conclusions are sharply at odds with the claims of *dependencia* authors about the character and consequences of socialist dependency. These authors have frequently called for studies of "concrete situations" of capitalist dependency, and occasionally they have done such studies. But they have never done studies of concrete situations of socialist dependency. It is hoped that this examination of the specific features and mechanisms of socialist dependency will contribute to the comparative analysis of capitalist and socialist dependency.

The barriers to such comparative analysis are many. They include not only the intellectual strictures of Marxism but also numerous and complex sociological, historical, and political obstacles. Because of these barriers, it is difficult for most scholars writing about Latin America even to think of analyzing socialist cases in anything like the same critical spirit one routinely uses to analyze capitalist cases. Critical analyses of capitalist cases are not necessarily perceived as inherently critical of capitalism; even if they are, that is regarded as permissible. Studies that are critical of socialist cases, by contrast, are perceived as inherently anti-socialist, which is not permissible, even if they are merely trying to find out what is going on.

These kinds of sociological, historical, and political barriers go back to the Vietnam War and to taboos generated during the era of Joseph McCarthy in the United States. But the roots extend even deeper and more broadly. In the 1930s George Orwell discovered to his immense sorrow that the intelligentsia "could not conceive of directing upon Russia anything like the same stringency of criticism they used on their own nation." In Catalonia Orwell learned that while the communist-controlled government was filling up the jails with "the most devoted fighters for Spanish freedom, men who had given up everything for the cause," the intelligentsia that controlled the Western press did not know and refused to know, because "they were committed not to the fact but to the abstraction." (Trilling, 1952: xvii, xxii.)

In considering socialist dependency it is time to examine not the abstraction but the fact. If real-world cases of capitalism are compared to ideal-world cases of socialism, the socialist cases look better, and always will. Real-world cases always have flaws, and ideal-world cases never do. That comparison is bogus. A genuine comparison will not, and should not, necessarily lead to any particular set of conclusions and opinions about the relative merits of the two kinds of dependent situations. But it does allow the debate to become realistic and serious and thus more conducive to human well-being in dependent countries.

14

The Politics of Dependence
in Poland and Mexico

Jeffrey L. Hughes

In international history great power spheres of influence arise in a
variety of ways and may be sustained by different mechanisms. But
they all share a key purpose: to forestall external threats at acceptable
cost. Yet over time the effort to achieve this purpose may foster a
greater challenge to a great power's security, economic stability, and
the legitimacy of its strategies and ideals: indigenous unrest and costs
incurred to contain it. Here I compare U.S.-Mexican and Soviet-Polish
bargaining relations, with emphasis on the recent past. Comparison of
Mexico and Poland is justified by parallels of history, culture, location,
size, and the unfolding of severe contemporary internal crises. These
countries' strategic importance and propinquity to a superpower mean
they are too important to be allowed to significantly diverge from or
threaten the dominant power's preferences; yet their distinct national
traditions and inherent strength as middle powers preclude complacent political or economic dependence. Their development is shaped

by their position, yet the very difficulties attending this process enmeshes each dominant power in complicated and costly efforts to sustain a viable continuing basis for the relationship. The dependent state can neither escape nor enjoy its condition, while the dominant state cannot simply control it.

In chapter 7 I presented a bargaining model and a typology of outcomes that were standardized and illuminated by it. Poland and Mexico were classified as examples of constrained bargainers. This chapter pursues the comparison further. It addresses the paradox of the contemporary constrained bargainer: Why is there an association of increasing dependent state internal *weakness*, crisis, and dependency, with (1) its *increased challenge* to superpower preferences in important respects, and (2) simultaneously a *diminished* superpower capacity to effectively resist changes or effectively cope with the sources of challenge in these weakened dependencies at low cost? When is a weakened dependency not more but less pliable? What are the implications of this question for the evolution and sustenance of spheres of influence?

First, I will give a preliminary overview of why this comparison is valid and interesting in the context of weak state–strong state bargaining. Second, I briefly compare the two countries' characteristics and capabilities and offer parallels of cultural and historical experience, bringing the account up to the 1970s. Third, I sketch the common internal crisis symptoms manifest in Poland and Mexico that burgeoned in the 1970s and after. Fourth, I summarize the joint bargaining profiles of U.S.-Mexican and Soviet-Polish relations for each Blau condition, allowing the similarities and differences to be noted. Then the similar dynamics of constraint and rescue for the parallel cases are explored from 1968 to the present. My argument is that we have analogous dependent cases; constraints differ between the spheres, but similar bargaining dynamics help explain the paradox noted above. This illustrates the utility of the model. Finally, the analysis raises larger implications about the exercise of power and the achievement of stability in spheres of influence.

1. Justification and Overview:
Why Compare the Mexican and Polish Cases?

There are several sets of reasons for comparing Mexico and Poland, with a focus on the last decade and a half. A body of literature exists anticipating or making this a logical comparison. The situations of

Poland and Mexico are analogous in important respects, as are the problems they pose to the superpowers. These similarities make them useful cases for examining within the context of our bargaining framework.

Author and former diplomat Carlos Fuentes, after being introduced by Jerzy Kosinski to a PEN gathering, remarked: "The wily old dictator, Porfirio Díaz, who ruled my country for over three decades ... once remarked: 'Poor Mexico, so far from God and so near to the United States.' I believe, my dear Jerzy Kosinski, that with one toponymical change, this singular remark could equally well be applied to Poland. ... A case could be made for the view that Mexico is the Poland of Latin America, and Poland the Mexico of Eastern Europe—when things go badly for us. When they go well—well, then we are both Finlands of the mind and can start counting our blessings." (Fuentes, 1974: 131.) Czeslaw Milosz had anticipated this comparison from the opposite direction: he compared the Spanish conquest of the Aztecs and the imposition of a foreign belief system in the Caribbean and Mexico to the Soviet conquest of the Baltic region and parts of Poland. Engaging in a sort of comparative commiseration, he suggests that the "incorporation of the Baltic states into the Soviet Union may seem an unimportant incident to a Mexican ... but not to the millions of people living in the people's democracies. For years they have been pondering over this rather extraordinary action on the part of a great power, an act analogous only to some of the misdeeds of colonial politics," only more foreboding. (1953: 223, 227, 245–46.)

By virtue of their historical positions and development, Mexico and Poland present almost metaphorical parallels: "North Americans consider the world something that can be perfected," subscribing to an ideology of progress, "while [Mexicans] consider it something that can be redeemed." (Paz 1961: 24.) Similarly, the Soviet state is officially committed to a doctrine oriented toward future perfection, while Poland has looked to its past for inspiration, where "past and future are bound together for the Poles in a dialectic of liberation," much as its literature has implied that a "Poland, enslaved and innocently suffering, was eventually to redeem the world." (Gross, 1983: 4.)

In an earlier period the relative stability and legitimacy of the essentially single-party Mexican government was used as a standard of comparison with the Soviet Union and East European countries. (Croan, 1970.) The article, "Is Mexico the Future of Eastern Europe?," sensibly noted the differences standing between Mexican stability and East European instability; but a decade and a half later, one is more inclined to answer the question raised in the title: "yes," in terms of comparative instability, bureaucratization, corruption, indebtedness, failed development plans, and opposition to liberalization movements. Indeed, at about the same time Paz was comparing the instability in Mexico and bureaucratization of its autonomous party with the "so-called Socialist countries of Eastern Europe," arguing that: "The experiences of Russia and Mexico are conclusive: without democracy, economic development has no meaning. . . . Moscow and Mexico City are full of gagged people and monuments to the Revolution." ([1969] 1972: 130, 40–41, 10–11.)

Besides such suggestive parallels, the comparison between Poland and Mexico also follows logically from analytical literature comparing middle powers. There have been comparisons of Canada and Poland (Matejko, 1980); Finland and Poland (Allardt and Wesokowski, 1978, 1980); Mexico and Canada (Baker Fox, 1977; Wyman, 1978; Spykman, 1942: 47, 59–60); and Mexico and Finland (Orton, 1983). Both Poland and Mexico have been compared to Canada and Finland, but not to each other, though Holbraad (1984: 85, 87, 90) treats them as analytically comparable middle powers. Thus it is a sensible comparison on its own terms, but it also follows logically from specialized literature accepting it as worthy.

The propinquity of Mexico and Poland to their dominant neighbors destined them to face pressures to make and keep them dependent and secure, but their size and sense of national resistance prevent a complacent response. In each case, dominant power influence has an impact that is almost irresistible; it argues for the priority of international obligations (to socialism, the IMF, and foreign investors) over national preferences. The Soviets are committed to political development in Poland primarily on their own terms, while the United States is committed to upholding economic development on its terms. Yet such pressure sets dynamics in motion in each dependent state that impede the ready success of the favored policies: a case of the irresistible international force versus the immovable domestic object. The Blau bargaining model helps account for these dynamics, while the outcomes over time make many of the disadvantages of both dominance and dependency outlined by Lewis (cited in chapter 7) ring true. This is not to say, however, that there were (or are) any easy or ready historical alternatives to such a predicament.

Soviet political constraints are fundamental to Polish political and economic performance and social adjustment. U.S. economic preponderance is central to Mexico's economic and social policy and political performance. Polish unrest and dissatisfaction challenge the Soviet Union politically and its basis of legitimacy, while Mexican fiscal problems challenge the stability of the U.S.-backed international economic order. The Soviets are concerned that the forms of resistance in Poland could prove contagious in other states of some of its own regions, while the United States remains concerned over debt failure and renegotiation precedents, as well as harboring subtle fears about massive emigration northward in the train of any economic collapse. Both Mexico and Poland have set down developmental paths from which there is no going back, but the dynamics of their politics and economics have painted them into a corner. In both countries sustained economic growth is central to maintaining social stability and co-opting the opposition, while government and party institutions seem increasingly ill-adapted to either sustain the growth or allow meaningful political reform.*

The dramatic internal crisis in Poland, particularly since 1980, involving political alienation of the regime and society and economic debacle is well known. Sober observers of the Mexican scene have pointed out comparable difficulties. Since the late 1970s they have argued "that the trend most important to note ... is a *weakening* in the capacity of the Mexican political system to escape the constraints placed on it by the highly conservative private sector. The greater this constraint, the less able will be the political regime to respond to ... many of the socioeconomic problems that presently produce so much potential for growing political instability." (Hansen, 1981: 43–44.) Indeed, "unless major changes in the organization and functioning of the political system occur, a structural crisis remains a strong possibility." (Scott, 1978: 472; also see Fagen, 1977: 698–700; Johnson, 1984.) The August 1982 economic crisis and the subsequent austerity measures, which "represent the most sustained attempt at austerity in postrevolutionary Mexican history" as well as "its worst ... economic and political crisis ... in fifty years" (Cornelius, 1985: 117, 83), make Mexico a compara-

---

*There are important interrelationships between the spheres that this chapter does not investigate. For example, the United States has important common interests with Poland in keeping it solvent after Western banks recycled many petrodollars through Poland in the 1970s. The stability of Poland is linked in some way to the stability of Western banking. These risks were taken, however, because it was perceived that the USSR would always be a lender of last resort. Similarly, the USSR and Mexico have a common interest in higher oil prices, important to both of them for crucial foreign exchange. These commonalities of interest, while important, are derivative of the bilateral relations examined here.

ble case to Poland. Many observers feel that the financial crisis unfolding in 1986 will be even more serious.

The path to improved performance in Poland "is rent by two conflicting and perhaps irreconcilable requirements: to placate the powerful protector, and to keep the continuing specter of domestic dissatisfaction to manageable proportions." (Dziewanowski, 1977: 228.) In Mexico "the basic dilemma for the . . . government is how to plan for the expansive development necessary to relieve unemployment, hunger and shortages of goods, while practicing the austerity dictated by conventional monetary and fiscal policy" required by its international financers. (Street, 1983: 434.) The superpowers now join Poland and Mexico in being painted into a corner. To recover economically, Poland needs renewed political reform, yet the Soviets discourage this as it may presage loss of control again; for Mexico to repay its debts, it needs to increase trade and perhaps emigration, yet international economic pressures and U.S. domestic politics and protectionism may discourage the necessary levels of trade. Still, both superpowers have to try to rescue or salvage the situations in these important states: the Soviets in spite of what they see as the domestic heresies of the Poles, and the United States in spite of Mexico's foreign policy divergence over Central America. The Soviet political model and the U.S. economic model are on the firing line. In neither case is there much hope of an effective early remedy.

Mexico and Poland, therefore, present cases of dependent states in a similar type of bargaining predicament across spheres. The dilemmas that Poland and Mexico face, and in turn pose to the superpowers, are those of constrained bargainers. While one may agree that "Mexico's relations with the United States . . . have been much healthier and mutually beneficial than Poland's relations with the USSR" (Blasier, 1983: 152), the comparison is still warranted in important respects. The Polish position of constraint and resistance comes readily to mind. While the United States has not directly intervened in Mexico for over half a century "there is a relatively high degree of consensus among Mexican elites . . . [today that in] terms of national security . . . the principal threat to Mexico is not Soviet-Cuban subversion . . . but rather the United States itself. This perception is clearly rooted in Mexico's historic vulnerability to its dominant northern neighbor." (Bagley, 1981: 355.) In U.S.-Mexican relations, "whenever peace prevailed, United States economic penetration occurred, and on the two occasions when this has taken place—1880 to 1910 and 1945 to the present—Mexico's

internal peace and stability have been threatened partly by the consequences of that process." (Schmitt, 1974: xii.) Thus "if Yankee imperialism has any dominant meaning in Mexico today, it clearly refers to the
U.S. economic presence, not the dusty troops and steaming gunboats
of times past"; this is "imperialism in the more modern sense of the
extension of financial and corporate control across frontiers in ways
that distort the development of the host country, denationalizing and
stripping power from ostensibly sovereign elites and peoples." (Fagen,
1977: 686.) Therefore, while Mexico's predicament is for the time being
more benign and less dramatic, it may still be compared to Poland as a
constrained bargainer.

2. Background to Comparison of Mexico and Poland*

General Similarities Today: Comparative Fact Profiles
Mexico and Poland both share a long common border with a dominant power that, because of its strategic location, tries to deny influence
in its subordinate neighbor to possible adversaries. This external presence has conditioned political and economic development of both
countries. Furthermore, in each case the relationship with the dominant power was not always so unequal. Poland once had an empire of
its own that rivaled Russia, while in the early nineteenth century the
power discrepancy between Mexico and the United States was not
very great: "The two countries began their independent lives relatively
equal in resources and expectations." (Schmitt, 1974: xi.) A conscious-
ness of this historical relationship works against being a complacent
junior partner.

Both Mexico and Poland are basically single-party states. While both
have certain traditions of authoritarian or centralized politics, in each

*Besides the specific attribution of sources by direct quotations or points of fact, I would
also like to acknowledge my general reliance on the following sources for the cases,
though none might agree with the use I have put them to: *Mexico*: Bagley, 1981, 1983;
Cornelius, 1985; Deagle, 1983; Fagen, 1977, 1983; Ferris, 1984; Hansen, 1981; Johnson,
1984; Levy and Szekely, 1983; McShane, 1981; Meyer, 1981; Middlebrook, 1981, 1985;
Needler, 1982; Ojeda, 1983; Pellicier de Brody, 1983; Poitras, 1981; Purcell, 1980, 1981;
Ronfeldt and Sereseres, 1977; Sanderson, 1983a, 1983b; Scott, 1978; Smith, 1985; Street,
1983; Wyman, 1978. *Poland*: Bialer, 1980; Bielasiak, 1981, 1983, 1984; Bromke, 1985; Brus,
1983; Davies, 1983; Dziewanowski, 1977; Fallenbuchl, 1982; Garnysz, 1982; Hough, 1982;
Jamgotch, 1975; Kanet, 1981, 1983; Kemme, 1984; Korbonski, 1983, 1984a, 1984b; Larrabee,
1981–82; Marer, 1984a, 1984b; Mason, 1984; Miller, 1984; Misztal, 1985; Rachwald, 1982,
1983; Sar, 1984; Schoplin, 1983; Simon, 1981; Skurski, 1982; Touraine, 1983; Vanous, 1982.

case there is an underlying diversity. Their domestic political structures are not only related to the external constraints they faced, but also to their comparable patterns and timing of industrialization as late developers; to some extent one can find Diaz's counterpart in Pilsudski's "colonels regime," with the subsequent unrest and vacuum being consolidated under one-party systems. Development was most dramatic for both in the post-World War II period. The resulting balance between industry and agriculture is proportionally similar in both cases. Concentration on raw material exports has given way to an increasing role for manufactures (though selling them is a different matter). Both also have exported fossil fuel—-coal from Poland, oil from Mexico, though the recent oil finds in Mexico make this a more central factor to the country's economy.

Today both are classified as middle powers using GNP as the prime criterion. (Holbraad, 1984: 85–90.) While it is possible to argue that even though both Mexico's and Poland's GNPs qualify them as middle powers, Poland is too openly dependent in domestic and foreign policy on the USSR to be considered one. But even this position, in attempting to go beyond the GNP criterion, is forced to note that Mexico behaves in a similarly dependent way, suggesting that it is "frustrated and overwhelmed by their giant neighbor, next to whom they feel dwarfed." The explanation that "Their political, economic, and military dependence on the United States makes them perceive themselves as much much weaker than they really are" (Handel, 1981: 23–27, 51) is thus distinguished by how the analyst evaluates the potentials of behavior rather than by how it does behave. Poland's GNP is slightly higher, while Mexico is larger and more populous. Both have young populations. "Poland has one of the youngest populations in the world" (Dziewanowski, 1977: 241), while Mexico's is even younger. This could affect future patterns of political socialization and mass politics in both countries.

Neither state, of course, has developed in isolation. Mexico has developed under U.S. economic tutelage to an important extent, while Poland under Soviet influence has followed an extensive model of development —though moments of confrontation have occurred in each case. The result, however, has been a comparable trade concentration and dependence. There is great trade asymmetry in these relationships, with the Soviets accounting for about one-third of the market for Polish goods (and with influence over other outlets), while the United States accounts for about two-thirds of Mexico's imports and exports.

Furthermore, aspects of the salience of this trade are comparable: the Soviets supply oil that is crucial for Poland, while the United States provides vital grain to Mexico.

Mexico and Poland even face comparable economic difficulties. Their international debt, for example, is indicative of their problems: Mexican debt approaches $100 billion, while Poland's is about $30 billion, with the debt service ratio being very high in both instances. They even have parallel problems of underemployment and migration. Both countries are experiencing politically significant migration from rural areas to cities, fostering further underemployment or unemployment there. International migration is an obvious symptom in the Mexican case. In Poland too "the problem of what to do with surplus labor is serious. Mass labor migration . . . has recently become more common in the Soviet orbit. The two most industrially advanced countries, East Germany and Czechoslovakia, import the most foreign labor, and Poland, with its considerable surplus of manpower, has been their principal supplier." (Dziewanowski, 1977: 218.) In Mexico the problem is an order of magnitude larger, but the sources of the problem in each country bear comparison. Furthermore, if one includes the Polish diaspora, "approximately fifteen million Poles, or one third of the entire nation, resides outside the country" (Rachwald, 1983: 133), a figure not so different from Mexico. And while Mexican emigration is perceived as a U.S. domestic issue, the Soviets must be wary of having Polish workers migrating around Eastern Europe.

Historical and Cultural Similarities: Comparable Profiles
These contemporary parallels are not simply accidental but are rooted in the past. Mexico and Poland have both been the contesting ground of empires and have experienced periods of colonial control as well as independence. Mexico has faced Spanish control, European imperial contestation, and American encroachment. Poland has faced invasion and periods of control by the Habsburg, French, and Russian empires, as well as by the Germans and Soviets. These colonial legacies have left their marks on both countries. Both share a common religious background. Spain brought Catholicism to Mexico, where it merged in unique fashion with Aztec and Indian tradition. In Poland, Catholicism, a partial outgrowth of the Habsburg empire, became the bulwark against the East and a perpetual link with Western culture, merging with the concept of nation itself. With this common Catholic background, the subsequent developmental and revolutionary experience in both countries has led to analogous paradoxes. In Mexico, just as the nineteenth-

century positivism of the *cientificos* and the ideology of the Revolution spawned an anticlerical Catholic country, so too has Marxism-Leninism been grafted onto Polish development to make a Catholic communist country!

Perhaps paradox is reflective of the territorial divisions and partitions each country has undergone. Poland and Mexico have had their countries divided and have been at war and in revolt against their dominant neighbors several times. Russia was a party to the divisions of Poland in the eighteenth century, while as a bastion of order it squelched uprisings in Poland in the 1830s and 1860s. During this time the United States supported the independence of Texas from Mexico in the 1830s, went to war with Mexico in 1846–48, and purchased more territory in 1854, which Mexico sold to relieve the war's resulting financial duress. The net result of the war "that the most careful scholars of the conflict . . . have labeled . . . a U.S. war of aggression" was that "the United States appropriated almost half of Mexico's national territory." (Meyer, 1981: 30.) The United States was more successful, sooner, than Russia in its territorial conquests, primarily because there were fewer other competing predators for Mexico. There were, however, real security concerns in each case. The United States was concerned over: British and French efforts in 1842–44 to try to foster accommodation between Mexico and Texas as prelude to supporting the latter's independence as a bulwark against U.S. power (Bourne, 1970: 52–54); France's role in Mexico in the 1860s; and German efforts prior to World War I and World War II to bring Mexico and Latin America into balance-of-power politics. Similarly, Russia had faced Napoleon's invasion, feared Napoleon III's threats to stimulate unrest in Poland at the tail end of the Crimean War, and later anticipated invasion from Germany through Poland. Even today one sees divided loyalties on both sides of Soviet-Polish (Andelman, 1981–82: 90, 101) and U.S.-Mexican (Levy, 1983: 14–16) borders as a result of this reshuffling.

Despite territorial division, Mexico and Poland retained a basic strength. This was evident by 1920. The Mexican Revolution was indigenous, a rebellion against legacies of the Spanish colonial past and the humiliation of being "a virtual economic satellite of the United States." (Schmitt, 1974: xi.) The revolutionaries consolidated power asserting the primacy of national interests and proceeded to appropriate foreigners' property. This was a complex process. The United States was important in the ascensions of Francisco Madero and then Victoriano Huerta to power, and in their subsequent removals when neither seemed appealing or forthcoming on issues like expropriation or implementing democratic constitutional provisions. Woodrow Wilson's occupation of Vera Cruz was instrumental in bringing Venustiano Carranza to power, but he ultimately proved no more pliable. Emiliano Zapata and Pancho Villa also contested for power, with Villa attacking New Mexico in 1916 in reprisal for U.S. support of Carranza. U.S. troops pursued him into Mexico, which even helped unify the competing Mexican factions that feared further intervention. Diversion of U.S. attention by World War I and the coup by Álvaro Obregón mark the consolidation of the Revolution. "For the first time in the modern industrial age a weak, underdeveloped, and economically penetrated state insisted on modifying if not abolishing its dependence on a highly industrialized, militarily powerful overlord" (Schmitt, 1974: 158), though economic dependency soon returned. U.S. policy in Mexico was motivated partly by security considerations and partly by liberal ideology and sense of mission, though they were sometimes counterproductive in both respects.

The consolidation of the Mexican state was coterminous with revival of Poland as a state after World War I. With as much prospect of success as Villa, Poland attacked the Soviet Union in 1920, making initial inroads, but then was pushed back to its own capital, which symbolically, like Villa, was never captured. The attack demonstrated the basic strength of the reconstituted state, a point that would be made again in late 1939. For a time Poland exerted independent discretion in foreign policy, playing one great power off against another as best it could. Stalin exerted some influence on Polish domestic politics in the 1930s, decimating the indigenous Polish Communist party, while after World War II he was able to implant a Stalinist form of communist party in Poland using loyal trainees. But it essentially lasted in this form only from 1949 to the mid-1950s. Even in the wake of a devastating war the Soviets had difficulty in grafting their preferences onto Poland, despite its having recently been partitioned, overrun, and recombined in a new form. Indeed, the Soviets retained their influence more by engineering the territorial settlement to place Poland under the threat of future German revanchism, setting themselves up as protector, rather than by their ability to force internal compliance. The Soviets justified their position in Poland as a spoil of war by their security concerns and by ideology. Thus, while after World War II Poland was enmeshed in a sphere more based on coercion, and Mexico in one more based on rewards, Mexico's earlier historical conflicts pose telling if less well-remembered parallels.

In both cases distinct historical and national identities emerged out of the caldrons of their developmental experiences. Some have even noted cultural parallels common to Polish and Spanish traditions, not the least significant being a willingness to fight in the name of honor. Salvador de Madariaga developed the parallel of Spanish and Polish culture in the last century, while more recently Arthur Rubenstein notes: "Poland is a very touching, proud little country. They have something in common with the Spaniards, a certain noble pride. A bit stupid, some practical people might say. They will go a thousand strong against an army of a million, fighting with forks and spoons and I don't know what." (Dziewanowski, 1977: 251, 232.) Both states have developed a keen sense of nationalism vis-à-vis its great power neighbor. In Poland the Church merges with nationalism, while in Mexico a commitment to the ideals of its Revolution merges with nationalism.

Mexican-U.S. relations from 1846 to 1910 are analogous to 1946 to 1956 in Polish-Soviet relations. Years of social upheaval, such as Mexico endured during its Revolution, were imposed on Poland as a consequence of World War II. The Polish reassertion of independence in 1956 is the analog of Mexico's standing firm during the Revolution in the face of U.S. threats, and sustaining the nationalization of its oil fields in 1938 in the face of possible U.S. intervention. In both cases internal opposition to the great power led to economic or political change while deterring significant intervention. In Poland, as in Mexico, the regime was able to resist external pressure "because of the strength of national feeling" that "represented more than nationalism: it was primarily a desire to free society, politically but also economically and culturally, from foreign control brutally and incompetently managed by the country's leaders." (Touraine, 1983: 25.)

In 1956 Władysław Gomułka started off in the manner of Mexico's Lázaro Cárdenas, who had resisted outside pressure and forwarded land reform. Just as Cárdenas's (1934–1940) position benefited from the U.S. Good Neighbor Policy, Gomułka benefited from the Khrushchev doctrine of "many paths to socialism." Hopes ran high. But just as Manuel Ávila Camacho (1940–46) had effected a reconciliation with the United States regarding development policy, so too did Gomułka with the Soviet Union. While Gomułka sustained efforts to modify his foreign policy position vis-à-vis Germany in order to reduce dependence on his Soviet protector (much as Adolfo Lopez Mateos [1958–64] and even more Luis Echeverría [1970–76] sought to sustain an independent diplomatic position without really threatening the basis of U.S. relations), domestically he ended up like Gustavo Díaz Ordaz (1964–70): pulling to the right, with intellectuals revolting against both regimes in 1968. Subsequently neither Edward Gierek in Poland nor José López Portillo (1976–82) in Mexico could rely on the strength of party ideals or the support of revisionist intellectuals; effective management of a troubled economy became their central concern, and as their technocratic strategies foundered, so did their political fortunes. Both regimes came to face severe crises.

Hence there are parallels in their internal developments, which have increasingly converged as they both have industrialized. There has also been a convergence of parallels in terms of the incorporation of Mexico and Poland into spheres of influence, though here Poland has lagged behind Mexico. Similarities have increased as the superpowers have risen to superpower primacy.

General Political and Economic Characteristics of the Developing Crises
Mexico and Poland's domestic structures achieved their modern single-party form in both Mexico and Poland in the post-World War II period. The Partido Revolucionario Institucional (PRI) in Mexico superseded its progenitors in the 1940s after Cardenas, while the Polish United Workers' party (PUWP) took its modern form under Gomułka. Elite recruitment was carefully controlled in both cases. Industrialization and reasonably high growth rates in the 1960s to the mid-1970s transformed both countries into middle-income powers of increased complexity. This affected the structure of both parties. In Mexico co-optation has been the essence of politics. This has applied to specialized bureaucrats who are necessary to maintain a more complex economy as well as to opposition groups that arose as a result of modernization. Co-optation was equally important to Poland over this period. (Bielasiak, 1981: 96, 102, 112, 122.) Both countries have also adopted forms of inclusionary politics as a means to bridge opposition between state and society. Yet, in the main, co-optation and inclusion did not affect the real levers of policy. The Mexican Revolution became institutionalized, while a "new class" arose in Poland protecting its communist prerogatives; dominant factions in both countries had vested interests in co-opting opposition (Huntington [1970: 37] explicitly draws this parallel between the two countries). Elite élan and upward mobility declined, while inequality increased. The overriding result in both states was increasing institutional rigidity and maladaptation to change. Bureaucracy and corruption grew; investments were misapplied or excessive; and effective agriculture was not encouraged.

3. The Unfolding of Crises in the 1970s and 1980s

These developments take us to the brink of the 1970s. The internal tendencies of the impending crises that snowballed in Poland and Mexico throughout the decade include: (1) the reliance of each system on economic growth for political stability and the co-optation of opposition and thus the severe challenge presented by economic crisis; (2) the attempt to defend the status quo and party rule through technological innovation rather than by implementing promises of effective reform and political liberalization; and (3) an incipient loss of state control over mass politics that increased into the 1980s; and finally (4) ultimately a severe crisis as earlier economic strategies failed and indicated a need for reform, while fears of further government loss of control were too great to allow its implementation.

Reliance on growth for stability. A symptom of the excessive reliance on economic growth for political stability was the increasing debt contracted in the beginning of the 1970s on the premise that sufficient consumer consumption could accompany the buildup of an effective export capability to repay it. But the new industries were not well managed or sufficiently effective, while international market conditions became less favorable. At the same time older or more traditional industries languished. It became more difficult to produce or consume as payment obligations mounted and inflation increased. Belt-tightening often hit those who could least afford it, challenging the fragile tacit bargain that linked society and state. Even successful programs tended to increase inequality or raise expectations faster than they dispersed rewards.

Furthermore, the economic downturns led to socially paradoxical results. For example, while both nations had significant agricultural sectors, each ended up producing and exporting agricultural products oriented toward earning foreign exchange, while at the same time they had to import basic foodstuffs central to social stability. This either structured produce away from basic staples toward cash crops (Mexico), subjecting them to the vagaries of the world market and protectionism of others while not fulfilling needs at home; or it exacerbated internal shortages (Poland), driving up domestic prices and discontent. Economic crisis increased external reliance on others to sustain social stability.

The failure of technocratic fixes. During the 1970s Poland tried to reconcile an authoritarian-ideological regime with the need for reform and the existence of democratic pressures. Mexico faced the task of trying to reconcile the maintenance of an economic environment attractive to foreign investment with stability and a sense of independence. Each party faced opposition to its coping strategies, and each tried to preempt and control political reform without changing fundamentals. Gierek sought a technocratic solution to Poland's difficulties through his "New Economic Mechanism." He hoped to more effectively use bureaucratic specialists and rational criteria to achieve growth, while retaining control over the political consequences. Economic change was to be accompanied by a reassertion of communist principles. Resistance to changing the Polish constitution along these lines was evident in 1976, while the economic strategy foundered over the decade. In Mexico López Portillo sought to preempt and co-opt opposition by electoral reforms in 1977. This measure has been more symbolic than real, declining in importance as new oil finds temporarily bolstered the finances of the regime in the latter part of the decade, and only reemerging as a principle to allow certain opposition movements to be elected in certain regions as a sop, as even the regime's oil-backed fortunes foundered. Furthermore, the role of the PRI itself was decreasing somewhat in prominence relative to the state bureaucracy, a trend exemplified by Miguel de la Madrid's selection as president. Essentially this choice implied an effort to move Mexico forward industrially with less direct reliance on classic populism and PRI patronage, while relying more on technological solutions. In both cases, however, the economies failed to sustain exchange-earning exports. In defense of the status quo and in response to continuing perceptions of bureaucratic inefficiency and corruption and failures of technocratic strategies, minions of order in Mexico attribute these problems to insufficient use of capitalist markets, while Polish communist ideologues attribute them to insufficient socialism and imperialist interference.

Such defenses have not prevented the emergence of corruption as a political issue. In Poland the economic "dissatisfaction was compounded by the widespread perception that the elite was increasingly looking after its own interests only and that benefits and privileges were accruing only to those in power." (Mason, 1984: 30; Milewski, 1986: 341.) In Mexico López Portillo essentially had to flee the country at the end of his term, facing questions about where the oil revenues went. This was reflective of the loss of control over mass politics.

Loss of control of mass politics.   In 1968 the Tlatelolco massacre of students alienated Mexican intellectuals from the regime and raised more general questions about its legitimacy. In Poland, also in 1968, a crisis occurred between the party bureaucracy and more independent Marxist humanist intellectuals, resulting in their alienation from the party and reducing the range of viable party-directed alternatives. In 1970 Polish workers angered by food price increases engaged in strikes, erupting in riots and fatalities that brought down Gomułka's rule and resulted in the reinstatement of subsidies. Similarly, the rural and urban terrorism in Mexico in the early 1970s was more a sign of reduced peasant and worker support for the PRI than a concerted political movement, though it did spur land reform to a certain extent. Consequently, for a variety of reasons there were rumored threats about an increasing role for the military to reclaim Mexico's image of stability by the end of Echeverría's term, "as the precariously balanced system nearly tottered during 1976." (Scott, 1978: 471.) In Poland in 1976 a more fundamental revolt occurred, again spurred by food price increases. It was notable for the alliance formed between workers and intellectuals, whose previous opposition had unfolded independently. This alliance proved instrumental in forwarding Solidarity, which epitomized the party's loss of control of mass politics. Eventually, even the party was thoroughly permeated by Solidarity sympathizers, basically bringing the struggle down not to a party-nonparty conflict but to a more unlegitimated relation of force (Mason, 1984: 34), with the military supporting the state as an alternative to Soviet intervention.

In Mexico the fortuitous oil finds of the late 1970s delayed the government's political reckoning with its diminished ability to guide mass politics. But since the boom went bust, there have been important new developments in labor politics. The Confederation of Mexican Workers (CTM), the PRI's former mainstay in controlling the bulk of industrial workers, became more assertive because of discontent within the union. "In a first ever break with party tradition" in 1981 the CTM leader publicly stated that the PRI no longer could count on its unqualified support, but that support would be accorded only to the extent that the union's demands were addressed by the president. This resulted from the defection of some workers for rival unions, including one union of more elite service sector workers (CROM) with which de la Madrid has fostered accommodation, in contrast to confrontation with the CTM. (Sanderson, 1983b: 402–3.) Thus the CTM becomes more assertive precisely when it is less able to channel dissent and support, while independent unions with differing interests grow outside of PRI control. As Scott presciently noted a number of years ago: "After repeated rebuffs, many Mexicans simply stop trying to work through the political system, and instead operate as best they can outside it. The real danger to the party is that pressure on government by these proliferating interests may eventually be coordinated by some other political movement, one that can satisfy their aspirations." (1978: 473–74.) For example, "A highly organized and sophisticated trade union movement can undermine austerity programs and . . . IMF . . . agreements that threaten labor's class and organizational interests." (Sanderson, 1983b: 403.) While this has not yet occurred, the process bears comparison to the Polish case. Furthermore, Mexico City is so central to Mexican politics that the initial impact of such a movement would not have to extend far beyond it to have a major impact. This may explain de la Madrid's sensitivity to unrest in the border state of Coahuila in 1984 stemming from protests against electoral fraud, where his calling in the army "was possibly more provocative than the problem itself." But "the government will increasingly run up against the choice it faced [there]: either give in to the opposition, or call in the army. This is a no-win situation." (Castenada, 1985–1986: 290–93.)

Crises highlight both the need and risks of reform. Both Poland and Mexico have reached a point where the need for reform is greater than ever, but the political consequences of such reform are less controllable and politically suspect. This is why in Poland "The economic reforms of General Jaruzelski's government are, to put it mildly, inconsistent. They are intended to introduce some market elements into the economy without diminishing the decision-making power of the political leadership." (Milewski, 1985–1986: 345.) The need for reform is in tension with its consequences. As Solidarity leader Jacek Kuron notes: "Everybody knows that the tempo of production will not improve unless people are allowed to have a say about their work and lives. But the Government knows that if it liberalizes the old Solidarity demons of 1980 will rise through the cracks. So it refuses to enter into any real dialogue, the economy worsens, conditions of life decline and any idiot can see what can happen." (*New York Times*, February 16, 1986: 7.) The tension is between overcentralized and inefficient bureaucratic central planning and the consequences of introducing needed market elements. (Milewski, 1985–1986: 344.) For the present the Polish dilemma will be measured in terms of overcentralization.

The situation in Mexico today reflects similar dilemmas. Like Poland, the political system "can no longer deliver the economic growth and prosperity that [particularly the middle] classes now expect as a matter of course. At the same time, the political system does not feel it can grant them the additional measure of democracy which might be an acceptable alternative. Political wisdom dictates that one does not open up a political system in the midst of a severe economic crisis." Thus while the Mexican system faces a decline in credibility and effectiveness that may even challenge the viability of its one-party system, the obstacles to reform are also political. (Castenada, 1985–1986: 289, 287, 291, 297.) The prospects for transcending this impasse, however, are better for Mexico than Poland (though one cannot be too optimistic). Under recent U.S. pressure Mexico has taken a series of steps reducing government control of the economy and allowing less mediated integration with the U.S. and world economy. These reforms taken "as a whole . . . reflect a significant policy shift as important as any since the Mexican revolution began in 1910. What remains to be seen, of course, is whether the plan will work. Numerous obstacles stand in the way, the most potentially troublesome of which is Mexican politics," since this economic "liberalization flies in the face of long held and cherished tenets of Mexican political philosophy." (*New York Times*, February 16, 1986: 4.) The prospect of a nationalist reaction cannot be discounted.

While Poland has been forced to turn more inward in response to superpower pressure, Mexico has in some sense been forced to turn more outward. Whether it will transcend its similar internal dilemmas in a different way, or be forced to backslide, like Poland, into more repressive and stagnating policies in the face of forces of social protest unleashed by U.S. preferences, remains to be seen. It is clear, however, that there is more than one path to a similar outcome, irrespective of intentions.

4. U.S.-Mexican and USSR-Polish Bargaining Relations Compared, 1968–85

Having now examined the comparability, development, and internal crises of Mexico and Poland, it is important to explore their contemporary bargaining relations with their hegemonic neighbors in terms of the Blau model. There are similarities and differences in their bargaining profiles, but the dynamics of interaction are similar. Mexico and Poland are reasonably strong states in weak positions, undergoing internal crises, yet superpower responses to them are constrained as well, and they are often called to the economic rescue despite their reluctance to bear the costs.

Table 1 summarizes the bargaining profiles. The conditions and varieties of concomitant strategies are defined in some detail in chapter 7.

Table 1. Summation of Blau bargaining profiles and their trends
for paired actors in the contemporary period

Conditions	Actors	
	United States	Mexico
1. Indifference versus strategic resources	Not indifferent to position, social stability, debt repayment, migration.	Status of social stability. Oil supply.
Prognosis:	International security and domestic economics potentially affected.	
2. Monopoly versus alternatives	High trade monopolization. Supplies defense. Market access, private capital, tourism, grain.	Foreign policy diversification. Attempt some trade and investment diversity. Promote own oil industry.
Prognosis:	Economic monopoly, low direct political control but domestic condition central.	Foreign policy diversification substitute for domestic ideals.
3. Coercive ability versus resistance	Economic leverage central. Market access, lender conditions. Military potential high; only resurfaces as perceived threat with Mexican oil finds of 1970s.	Nationalism: anti-Yankee. Political resistance: limit role in U.S.-sponsored organizations that reduce independence or bargaining position. Threat to fail.
Prognosis:	High but lowering economic leverage. Military intervention in Central America would indirectly hurt Mexican stability.	Politically high, economically increasing.
4. Value attraction versus opposition	Stable material, cultural emanation and appeal. Anti-communist.	Rhetorically revolutionist, pro-socialist, in Latin America; raises U.S. fear of domino theory.
Prognosis:	High.	High (issue-oriented).

Actors	
USSR	Poland
Not indifferent to position, social stability, legitimacy of role in Eastern Europe.	Status of social stability. Role of railroads and communications for Warsaw Pact.
International security and domestic legitimacy potentially affected.	
High political control. Supplies "defense." Some trade subsidies, especially energy.	Economic trade diversification; also sources of capital.
Political-military prime, but economic increasingly important.	Quest for economic alternatives as standard operating procedure for domestic political malaise.
Military threat conditions, political leverage delivers. Economic leverage increasing.	Nationalism: anti-Russian. Reputation to fight. Threat to fail and unravel if too constrained.
Politically high but decreasing. Intervention in Poland would be very destabilizing.	Economic: high in short run, lower in long run. Political leverage could grow.
Communist ideology of Soviet brand having diminished appeal.	Catholicism. Workers accept central role doctrine gave them to challenge state.
Low/split (high to certain elite).	High.

Analysis of *condition 1* focuses on the dynamics between the degree of saliency or indifference of an issue to the superpower and the strategic resources by which the weaker state affects that calculus. Many issues in Mexico and Poland potentially affect the international *and* domestic interests and stability of the superpowers' positions. This motivates the superpowers to monitor and ultimately exert control over these states to a degree not applicable to, for example, Albania or Argentina. Still, Mexico and Poland are no pushovers; the resources they possess (e.g., Mexican oil) or the capabilities of the superpower that their positions allow them to affect (e.g., transit in the Warsaw Pact) may aid them in bringing implicit counterpressure to bear in some instances. (Middlebrook, 1981; Nau, 1981; and Ronfeldt and Sereseres, 1977: 49–51, 85–96—on Mexican oil; Andelman 1981–1982: 90—on Poland's strategic place in the Warsaw Pact.)

Examining the relationships from the perspective of *condition 2*, the interaction between the superpowers' monopoly over what others need and the weaker states' quests for alternatives lessening their dependence, shows a real lever of superpower advantage. While Mexico's and Poland's diversification efforts are noted, there are real economic and political limits to them in practice. Even at the height of Poland's expansion of international economic ties, one could still note that its "economic dependence on its eastern neighbor is still staggering." (Dziewanowski, 1977: 217.) Similarly, despite Mexico's more salient foreign policy role in Central America, widely analyzed over the past five years (e.g., Poitras, 1981; Ferris, 1984), the fact is that many of these initiatives have been nonstarters. Some observers now caution against U.S. actions that would exacerbate perceptions of the impotence of Mexican policy for fear that Mexico's stability would be compromised. (Castenada, 1985.) Even in pursuit of an independent foreign policy, Mexico did not oppose vital U.S. interests outside of Latin America or rally an actively opposed coalition within it. Mexican economic diversification has also been of limited effectiveness in practice. (Ronfeldt and Sereseres, 1977: 72; Wyman, 1978: 127.) Some argue that in fact Mexico tends to do better in bilateral as opposed to multilateral forums. (Levy, 1983: 171; Story, 1982: 790.) Mexico's reluctance to become a GATT member in 1980 and her lack of enthusiasm for proposals of a North American Common Market seem to support the latter argument. As a constrained bargainer, Mexico will deal directly with the hegemon if it cannot obtain alternatives from less politically interested parties. Of course, superpower monopolization has its own costs, which we will note momentarily.

Condition 3 focuses on the relation between the superpower's ability to prevent coercive opposition and the weaker state's ability to marshal it in credible ways. The balance is heavily weighted toward the dominant powers, but internal characteristics of Poland and Mexico deter and pose limits on its use. Militarily, both Mexico and Poland have perceived increasing coercive threats in the 1980s (Mexico feared for its oil fields in the 1970s, and the United States was increasingly prone to use force in Central America; while Poland faced threats of Soviet intervention in 1981). Economic threats, as opposed to monopolizing the source of rewards, have also been used with effect. For example, in a matter of central importance, such as Mexico's possible membership in OPEC, the United States deliberately linked Mexico's continued favorable market and financial access to remaining separate from the cartel. (Wyman, 1978: 78, 104, 130.) Conversely, Mexico has retaliated on occasion, such as in 1972 when it nationalized U.S. shares in a firm, linking it to a U.S. trade-dumping ruling; but this had no effect on U.S. policy, and the action might have been taken in the future for other reasons anyway. (Odell, 1980: 222.) Information regarding Polish cases is scarcer. In recent years this type of direct confrontation of wills has tended to be replaced by the great powers' recognition of the threatened costs of disruptive failure within Poland and Mexico and of the need to prevent it.

Finally, *condition 4* examines the ways the superpowers' values attract or influence others and the responses of the weaker parties. Interactions on this dimension show important contrasts as well as similarities. Mexico, like Poland, shows a certain sense of cultural autonomy and resistance to foreign mandates, especially in regard to ideology and foreign policy. But it also endorses many values both as put forth and as represented by the United States. There is far more fundamental opposition between Poland and the USSR. Some view Poland's rejection of the Soviet model as a harbinger of attempts by other East European states to slough off a moribund ideology. (Kolakowski, 1983.) Mexico operates largely within a system of U.S. values, while many Poles would prefer to see a reconstitution of the rules. Mexico can attempt even to use U.S. laws, interest groups, and specialized information to argue its cases on a technical and juridical basis. (See Odell, 1980.) This is less true of Poland, though there are important divisions of loyalty among Poles, and some of the more technical elites and intelligentsia may even embrace martial law on Soviet terms as a way to end disorder (Garnysz, 1982: 77), a situation reminiscent of bureaucratic-authoritarian regimes in Latin America. (Touraine, 1983: 3, 191.)

Poland and Mexico garner special attention by virtue of their strategic and political importance (condition 1). But despite their attempts to foster alternatives, the superpowers' monopoly of rewards ensures continued superpower influence in these states, but at the price of deep involvement and economic or political investment (condition 2). As internal problems arise in the dependencies, even the dominant state's coercive power is not very effective (condition 3), while its ideology and value systems become either less relevant or antagonistic (condition 4). Consequently, the dependencies are constrained but not complacent; they are influenced but establish an important degree of reciprocal interdependence. There are few retaliatory actions that the superpower can take without simultaneously hurting itself more than by shelling out the resources to try to salvage a crisis situation partly brought about by its own prior position of predominance. This summary gives a sense of the recent dynamics of interaction. We will now focus briefly on the constrained bargaining power of the dependent state, as well as on its limits.

Constrained bargaining in the developing crisis period appeared earlier and more clearly in the Polish case. In the aftermath of the 1970 crisis, for example, one sees Gierek bargaining with Moscow and obtaining not only a $100 million loan, but also an adjustment in the terms of trade with the USSR, and Soviet trade credits that for all appearances were to compensate for the previous incorrect rate. As the communiqué put it, Poland had obtained "new, fairer prices," surprisingly seeming to admit the previous rate was unfair. (Dziewanowski, 1977: 216.) Not long afterward the Soviets also had to supply oil to Poland during the energy crunch. A similar type of relief had to be supplied after the 1976 crisis when "the Soviet leadership came to the assistance of their colleagues in Warsaw with a substantial loan to help mitigate the domestic economic problems in Poland." (Kanet, 1981: 390.) The bailouts increased as Polish growth rates slowed to a crawl in 1976–80 and thereafter actually moved into a decline. Consequently, Poland has the highest present value of ruble credits and high overall combination of debt and Soviet aid in Eastern Europe, second only to the GDR (which can pay them back). Similarly, it owes the largest debt to the West by a factor of two over any East European state (Vanous, 1982: 3, 7), a debt that is in effect underwritten by the Soviets.

Solidarity was more a consequence of Poland's declining economic trend than a cause. Despite Soviet dismay at internal Polish developments, they continued to come to her financial rescue. "By far the most important source of financial assistance to Poland after summer

1980 was the Soviet Union," which provided $4.2 billion in new credits, almost one-quarter of it in convertible currency, between August 1980 and mid-June 1981. Furthermore, almost $90 billion worth of food and consumer goods was channeled in from other East European states, with payments deferred to the 1983–89 period. (Kanet, 1984: 332–33; Marer, 1984b: 324.) Before and during the time of martial law Poland was faced by a repayment crisis with the West "that threw Poland into the arms of its fellow members of COMECON. Russia has been pumping billions of rubles and hard currency into Poland this year. There is no other way that Poland could have met its obligations." Indeed, immediately after martial law the Soviets themselves sought out a Eurocurrency loan for the precise amount of Poland's obligations. (*Economist*, December 19, 1981: 73–74.) Though the outcome has not been pleasant, intervention was deterred and rescue support was compelled. The drama is far from over, however.

Mexico's predicament also built slowly in the 1970s before peaking in the 1980s. A financial crisis in 1976, partly caused by capital flight resulting from laws and policies supported by Echeverría, "confirmed that the United States had enormous financial as well as capital stakes in Mexico," which is why it then "provided greater support to Mexico's monetary system than to any other developing country." An elaborate set of IMF drawing rights, consortium bank loans, and U.S. treasury and Federal Reserve aid helped stabilize the Mexican economy. Mexico then bargained for an exemption of its oil sector from further constraints on borrowing, while López Portillo "meanwhile warned about a potential 'South Americanization' of Mexico's politics if the United States should prove unresponsive to Mexico's economic needs." (Ronfeldt and Sereseres, 1977: 48–49; see Fagen, 1977: 695.)

Mexican oil wealth temporarily disguised underlying development problems; indeed, to some extent it exacerbated them. It was thought that oil wealth would provide the basis for a "Global Development Policy," the Mexican equivalent of Poland's "New Economic Maneuver." Like the latter policy, the former faced both internal and international market constraints on its effectiveness. As Mexican debt went from the $30 billion range around 1978 toward its present $100 billion figure, however, it also increased Mexican leverage. It was not only the attraction of profit that had led bankers to continue making large loans to Mexico, but that the "United States, bankers reasoned, could not afford to let Mexico go bust." However, the bankers as a group did not realize how high a percentage of short-term loans from private banks Mexico had in its portfolio. (By using private short-term loans Mexico sought to reduce the political constraints tied to loans, even at added economic cost.) At some point in 1982 Mexican policymakers knew they were in dire financial straits. But rather than heading off the crisis through preliminary consultations, they tried some measures on their own (e.g., devaluation), and only at the last minute, in August, did they approach the IMF. "By then holding out a begging bowl, [they] wanted the quickest service on the best terms." (*Economist*, December 11, 1982: 69–76.)

The severity of the Mexican crisis compelled favorable terms. "The world's financiers have put together a rescue package for dollar-dry Mexico with the speed of a conjuror's hand. But Mexico's financial crisis has not disappeared. It threatens to haunt the international credit market for years" (much as Poland's will haunt the Soviets). The IMF knew of impending problems, but there are limits to information and crisis management without a joint approach. "The Americans have overseen the rescue package. They have the most to lose from economic troubles south of the border," particularly as 90 percent of the debt is denominated in dollars. The United States granted about $1 billion in immediate credit; $1 billion in advance purchases of Mexican oil; $1 billion in crop export guarantees; and backed a three-month debt moratorium. (*Economist*, August 28, 1982: 59.) At the same time Mexico had to make some headway in implementing IMF austerity measures.

The wider implications of the Mexican crisis were readily apparent. This was to be "an intricate poker game being played between Latin American finance ministers and western financial institutions," with the "cards everyone wants to see [being] Mexico and the IMF." (*Economist*, October 23, 1982.) Such bargaining continues in the present period. In a later "hand" the banks wanted to reach agreement with Mexico prior to a meeting of Latin American debtors, thereby showing that it paid to deal with the IMF and the United States rather than form a debt cartel. Consequently, observers speculated that "the banks must make some big concessions" to Mexico. (*Economist*, September 1, 1984.) Subsequently, Mexico "wrung from the 13-bank advisory panel . . . most of the concessions which Mexico had sought." Without going into specifics, "the $48.7 billion package [was] the largest sovereign debt ever rescheduled," which "offers at least a sporting chance that default will be avoided in the future." (*Economist*, September 15, 1984: 85.) In fact, the "terms are highly favorable by prevailing international banking standards—indeed, the best achieved to date by any

Latin American country which has experienced a debt crisis in recent years." (Cornelius, 1985: 120.)

Mexico, therefore, provides a dramatic, well-documented case of effectively bargaining from weakness. (Sar [1984: 69–70] notes the problems of getting such good data for the Polish case.) One Mexican scholar and adviser argues that by the time of the 1976 crisis, Mexico had a *weakened* standing on many of the factors that had traditionally bolstered its more capable negotiating posture when compared to many Latin American states. Some of these factors were solid political stability; high growth rate; low inflation; food and energy processing self-sufficiency; more reliable sources of sufficient foreign exchange than tourism and migrant remittances; and ample international financial solvency. (Ojeda, 1983: 120.) While in an absolute sense Mexico might be more dependent on the United States, in a relative sense it is not. The effectiveness with which it achieved favorable outcomes in negotiations despite bargaining from an absolutely weakened condition is a reflection of growing U.S. interdependence. Obviously, everyone would have been better off if Mexico had been better off, but the point is that Mexico's bargaining position did not weaken as its economic and political stability did. A slightly more slowly unfolding Solidarity movement in Poland (see Hough, 1982: 30) might have brought Poland into an even closer parallel with Mexico's position.

It is difficult to be overly optimistic about the temporary resolution of these crises. Certainly the Mexican case has thus far had a more beneficent outcome than the imposition of martial law in Poland, though the human toll of several years of IMF austerity measures should not be underestimated. It is not clear, however, that the short-term superpower responses in either country forwarded more than they impeded effective, long-term structural adjustments. Economically, Mexico has been temporarily bailed out, but social tensions and inequalities remain and may be more salient in a period of economic hardship; necessary social reforms for long-term stability are constrained by the more immediate requirements of economic logic. (Sanderson, 1983a: 332–33.) The Baker plan of the fall of 1985 holds out the prospect of some relief, but the effects of declining oil prices on Mexico's revenues cancel any forward progress; even debt payments on interest seem problematic. Martial law with Soviet blessing temporarily bailed out the communist party in Poland, but it is not clear how the government will garner legitimacy for effective economic management without domestic reforms. (Rachwald, 1982: 392.) However, given the domestic constraints and commitments of both superpowers, it is not easy to propose alternatives. Present solutions channeled by these constraints take precedence over more costly preventative measures to forestall future, more severe problems that may not develop.

5. Security, Autonomy, and Interdependence

Still, one should not overlook the fundamental difference of this crisis period from the earlier periods outlined above. The well-being of superpower and dependent is coming to vary directly rather than inversely. Problems are also more symmetrical than asymmetrical in their distribution of consequences, particularly negative ones. The direct territorial contest for power of earlier periods has given way to exchanges of tribute and dispute over the relative balance of exchanges of rewards. Both parties are more differentiated and dependent upon the other for services. The relations are still very unequal. There is joint dispute over how best to economically achieve or politically define national well-being. But it is hard to deny, for example, that "the United States actually lacks instruments to hurt Mexico deliberately without also harming its own interests—a true mark of interdependence. Mexico may not be able to escape from dependency, but neither can the United States escape from interdependence." (Ronfeldt and Sereseres, 1977: 88.)

The same could easily be said about the Soviets' relations with Poland. The Soviets could cut back on aid or credits to Poland, but this could cause contagious instability that would threaten their own interests; on the other hand, continued Soviet aid simply tightens the direct link between aid and political stability, thereby committing the Soviets to continued costly future bequests. (See Bunce, 1985: 44.) Hence neither can Poland escape its dependency, nor the USSR its interdependence.

The constrained bargainers highlight dilemmas for the superpowers. It is uncertain how these pairs of states will attempt to reconcile their conflicting imperatives between security and autonomy in the future. But it is hard to see how present circumstances can be sustained in Mexico or Poland indefinitely.* General Wojciech Jaruzelski compared Soviet fears about Poland in 1980 and 1981 to a volcano (and interest-

---

*The fact that one could say the same thing about Egypt cautions against overemphasizing the positional location in a sphere, while the same foreboding analysis that applied to Ferdinand Marcos's Philippines before his departure shows that unexpectedly favorable outcomes can occur. Both countries provide interesting comparisons with Poland and Mexico.

ingly compared Soviet security concerns to a magnified version of U.S. concerns in Nicaragua). (*New York Times*, March 9, 1986: E21.) Volcanoes percolate and erupt again. Perhaps the proper metaphor for Mexico's problems is an earthquake; what and where the problem will be is not an issue, only the question of when. Both are physical metaphors and stress the contiguity of their effects on the superpowers.

A distinction noted by Fox (1944) between the quest for security (the power not to be coerced) and the quest for domination (the power to coerce) is as relevant today as when he was speculating on the shape of the post-World War II world. In the past both superpowers have, in varying degrees, pursued domination strategies. In the period since 1945 the United States has been more concerned with security strategies in its sphere of influence in Latin America. Only now may the incentives for *both* powers be simultaneously turning to security strategies in their spheres. One superpower does not challenge another superpower so much by seeking to control his backyard as by disrupting it. Since the threat is now reciprocal, and domination is not politically or economically feasible, there are incentives for seeking security —freedom from coercion—by a mutual observance of spheres of influence that simultaneously allows greater autonomy for the development of the weaker states. In any event, the way this transition period is managed will determine whether the spheres of influence forestall external instability or are the source of it.

V Evolution of Spheres of Influence

15

Costs of Domination, Benefits of Subordination

Paul Marer and Kazimierz Z. Poznanski

This three-part chapter presents a sweeping overview of postwar economic developments in Eastern Europe, a general discussion of the evolution of Soviet–Eastern European economic relations during the last four decades, and a detailed analysis of "who subsidizes whom and by how much?" in those relations. Throughout this chapter we compare Soviet–Eastern European relations with U.S.–Latin American relations, focusing particularly on the economies of the Southern Cone and Mexico in Central America.

The intersystem comparisons deal primarily with three forms of superpower influence on subordinate states: the promotion or imposition of an "appropriate" economic system; the structural dependence arising from the superpower's dominant role as supplier or market; and the net transfer of wealth between the superpower and its dependent states.

We conclude that because the East European countries have by and large exhausted the resources that could be mobilized from domestic, Soviet, or Western sources under their Soviet-imposed economic and political system, they face not temporary but fundamental economic difficulties. No obvious or likely solutions are in prospect, a fact of fundamental, long-term importance for the USSR also. This contrasts with the situation of the developing Latin American countries within the U.S. sphere of influence, where constraints on development are less severe and can be traced more to domestic than to external factors.

We document the changing nature of Soviet economic relations with Eastern Europe. While it has been well established that in the first postwar years Eastern Europe was exploited by the Soviet Union through unfair trade, some recent studies have alleged that since the early 1970s the Soviet Union has been providing huge subsidies to its dependent states by means of distorted prices in energy, materials, and machinery, as well as in other ways.

These findings have made the Soviet Union appear to be a generous superpower compared to the United States, which is not involved in any large-scale and continuous transfer of wealth to the Southern Cone states or Mexico. Even now, when most Latin American countries suffer from heavy indebtedness—costing them increased unemployment because of forced economic austerity—no substantial nonrepayable aid is granted to them by the United States. But neither is there evidence of any significant uncompensated transfer of wealth from the region to the United States, although critics of U.S. involvement in Latin America have made unsubstantiated claims of U.S. exploitation.

After pointing out the many pitfalls of trying to quantify the dollar tag on subsidies in Soviet–East European economic relations, we provide evidence that the cumulative Soviet subsidy to Eastern Europe appears to be considerably below the most recent and best-known Western estimates. Moreover, it seems that while the Soviet Union has been a net subsidizer, it has also been subsidized by Eastern Europe in various ways and forms. We conclude that the whole question of "what price tag on subsidy?" must be placed in a broader economic context. We also speculate briefly on how the Soviets may view the economic "costs" of their hegemony and the East Europeans the "benefits" of their economic dependence.

I. Economic Systems and Overall Performance

Soviet Dogma of Central Planning
Since the late 1940s the economic systems and industrialization strate-

gies of the six East European countries—East Germany, Czechoslovakia, Poland, Hungary, Bulgaria, and Romania—have closely followed the Soviet pattern. This has largely determined their overall economic and trade performance. Although during the past several decades important differences among the East European countries—rooted in eacñ nation's unique historical, cultural, and political experience—have reemerged, the similarities that stem from their Soviet-type economic and political systems remain important.

During the whole postwar period the Soviet Union exerted pressure to preserve systemic uniformity in Eastern Europe, though it was not always successful. Yugoslavia slipped away from Soviet domination in the late 1940s, while in Hungary several elements of Soviet-type planning were dismantled after the 1968 reform. But everywhere in Eastern Europe the means of production are predominantly collectively owned, key positions are controlled by a monolithic party (the *nomenklatura* system), and flexibility of decision-making at the enterprise level remains limited, particularly on investments.

One fundamental feature of this system is that producers face no domestic or import competition. Domestic competition is weak because the production of most goods is concentrated in a single, large organization. In addition, continuous excess demand for goods—under the permanent state of soft budget constraint faced by producers —provides firms with a high degree of safety. Import competition is weak, in turn, because all trade transactions are centralized; there is no link between world and domestic prices; and nothing is imported if a domestic supplier can produce the item, irrespective of cost comparisons. As a result, producers need to pay little attention to product quality, modernity, variety, or service, with negative consequences for economic welfare and competitive abilities.

The commonalities of Soviet and East European industrial strategies also have important implications. Beginning in the early 1950s the share of investment in national income was raised to very high levels, at the expense of consumption. Investment was concentrated in mining, metallurgy, machine-building, and (since the 1960s) in petrochemicals. Greatly neglected was investment in agriculture (Hungary and Bulgaria were partial exceptions), the light industries, services, and infrastructure.

This pattern of investment priorities, together with the basic features of the economic system, were responsible for certain other fundamental shortcomings of economic performance: exceedingly high costs of production and a rapidly growing structural imbalance. Much of these countries' industrial and agricultural output is produced at very high cost, that is, typically using much more material, labor, and (often) capital than is used in market economies at comparable development levels. A further problem is that much of the output of their manufacturers is not competitive, or becomes rapidly obsolete, when judged by world market standards.

The fundamental economic problems of the Soviet Union and the countries of Eastern Europe have, to a certain extent, been obscured by the rapid growth rates of their total output. For approximately three decades—during the 1950s, the 1960s, and the 1970s—these countries achieved an impressive rate of economic expansion. Their own leaders—and the rest of the world—interpreted this as evidence of economic success, even though in most countries the officially reported growth rates were greatly exaggerated, as is documented in Marer. (1985b.) Moreover, little attention has been focused on whether the production of the right or the wrong kinds of goods and services was growing.

Until the end of the 1970s East Europe was able to rely on three consecutive but temporary growth-supporting mechanisms. During the 1950s the East European regimes used military-like methods to mobilize the labor force and squeeze agriculture and the consumer to finance a rapid growth in investment and output. During the 1960s, as it became increasingly difficult (more in some countries than in others) to mobilize new labor and material resources for a rapid growth of investment, economic integration of a special kind with the USSR helped to prop up their growth rates. That is, East European countries (Romania was partly an exception) imported growing quantities of energy and raw materials from the Soviet Union at reasonable prices in exchange for machinery and other manufactures whose quality and modernity were typically not on a par with those of Western and newly industrialized country (NIC) producers.

During the 1970s East Europe turned to the West for large credits. The large import surpluses made possible by Western credits, together with significant Soviet subsidies (which took the form of charging less than world market prices for energy and raw materials and providing low-interest credits), made possible a new industrialization spurt. Its essence was the parallel creation throughout Eastern Europe of large new capacities in crude oil refining, chemicals, metallurgy, and certain other branches of heavy industry, with increased reliance on Soviet energy and raw materials as well as on Western technology and inputs. The intention was to market the output both in the CMEA and the West.

By the late 1970s the indebtedness of the East European countries reached dangerously high levels. Exports to the West lagged behind imports, owing to the shortcomings of East Europe's centrally planned economic system, mistakes in economic policy (especially regarding the allocation of investment), and unfavorable economic conditions in the West. Since 1979 the East European countries have been forced to cut their imports from the West sharply to reestablish their credit-worthiness. In every country this adjustment involved deep cuts in investment and stagnating or declining living standards.

Although East Europe's creditworthiness has now by and large been reestablished, except in the case of Poland, these countries cannot count on large new credits from the West; in fact, they must generate export surpluses to service their substantial debts to the West. In the absence of large new credits a net outflow of resources from East Europe to the West will have to continue, even if existing debts are refinanced by the lenders. Soviet ability and willingness to provide additional quantities of energy and raw materials—and subsidies on them—appear to have ended too, as we discuss below.

The economic systems and policies pursued by the East European countries (and the USSR) thus have led them into a crisis of economic structure. That is, much of their production is excessively energy- and material-intensive and is exceedingly wasteful of inputs; a large share of output is obsolete and thus unsalable on the world market (Poznanski, 1984); and significant production capacities now stand idle. The energy elasticity of production increased throughout the 1970s (each 1 percent increase in industrial output requiring, depending on the country, a 1.4 to 1.8 percent growth of energy); while in the West, industrial restructuring and energy conservation lowered the energy intensity of production into the 0.4 to 0.7 percent range.

Thus, in terms of industrial restructuring, East Europe is about a decade behind the industrial West. There is much talk about the need to undertake industrial restructuring but little evidence of its implementation. The main focus of the planners seems to be, still, on how to obtain, from domestic and CMEA sources, the energy and raw materials needed to increase output based on the prevailing structure rather than how to change the structure and thus free expensive resources for more productive uses.

The broad trends we describe suggest that the East European countries face not temporary but fundamental economic difficulties. They have, by and large, exhausted the resources that could be mobilized from domestic, Soviet, and Western sources under the prevailing industrial structure and Soviet-type economic system. Looking ahead, say, to the year 2000, East Europe's fundamental economic problems will be manifested in slow or stagnating rates of economic growth (but even those will overstate true performance, for the reasons mentioned); continuous and occasionally severe problems in their convertible currency balance of payments; a growing technological gap not only vis-à-vis the industrial West but vis-à-vis the NICs also; and increased tensions in Soviet–East European and intra-East European economic relations.

U.S. Policy of Free Trade

Turning to U.S.–Latin American relations, one has to note that the United States has also continuously promoted the institutional setup of its choice—the market system. To be sure, in Latin America the market mechanism plays a predominant role in resource allocation, although in many countries distortions due to "crony capitalism" and corrupt government do not allow the system to operate efficiently.

Pressure by the United States is, however, generally of an indirect character, exerted mostly through economic incentives offered in exchange for access to U.S. credits (e.g., through IMF requirements in recent years that Latin American debtors cut down on public spending and encourage private activities) or direct investment by U.S. multinationals (which condition their investment on the operation of market mechanisms in the Latin American economies).

In addition, the United States does not insist on systematic uniformity as the Soviets do. It would not like the Latin Americans to turn to centralized planning because that system is viewed as an integral part of a communist political structure. But deviations from a pure version of the market system do not incur the wrath of the United States as significant moves toward "capitalism" in Eastern Europe do on the part of Soviet leaders. This higher tolerance results not only from limited U.S. ability to control domestic elites in Latin America, but also from the fact that the United States puts much less value on the ideological aspect of the economic system than do the Soviets regarding central planning.

The other important difference is that the United States pays less attention to internal systemic changes; its main focus is on the regulation by Latin America of its foreign trade and foreign investment. The U.S. interest is to keep the regional economy relatively open; this, of course, has certain implications for the internal workings of those economies. The Soviets are concerned with the domestic aspects of the East European economies and also prefer to keep those countries less than fully open to world trade and investment.

The implications of external forces working to promote relatively free trade for the Latin American economies have been long debated by social scientists (Poznanski, 1984). Scholars identified with the so-called dependency school claim that this policy is fundamentally detrimental to the region, stressing such negative effects as increased income inequality, technological backwardness, and the undermining of domestic accumulation. This view has been contradicted by those who point out the generally advantageous impact of relatively open economies. (See evidence on the higher rate of growth in export-oriented economies in Krueger, 1982.)

Assessments of the costs and benefits of market orientation and free-trade policies depend in part on the choice of economic indicators. Here we are concerned mostly with the long-run prospects for economic growth and comparative growth performance of Latin America and Eastern Europe. Is Latin America performing better with more market-oriented systemic institutions than Eastern Europe with an economic mechanism imposed or promoted by the Soviets?

Based on research by Poznanski (1985), a key finding is that most Latin American countries, with more open economies than those in Eastern Europe, have built considerably greater economic potential than have the countries in Eastern Europe. This is reflected in comparative production, export, and technological performance. While in the 1950s and 1960s the major Latin American economies, such as Argentina, Brazil, and Mexico, lagged behind Eastern Europe, by the 1970s and 1980s the lags have turned into leads, not only in the production and export of goods in the consumer industries—sectors of lower priority in Eastern Europe—but also in the capital goods industries (e.g., steel, automobile, shipbuilding), and in such high-technology fields as computers, semiconductors, and aircraft.

The key variable as far as economic potential is concerned is export competitiveness. Given the small or medium size of the economies being compared and the high levels of external debt of nearly all the countries in the two regions, ability to earn foreign exchange is a key predictor of future economic performance. The major Latin American nations—exposed to foreign competition—have proved able to gradually expand their market shares in the OECD during the last two decades. In contrast, the East European share in that market has been shrinking. During 1970–81 the newly industrializing countries of Latin America (Argentina, Brazil, Mexico) increased their share of OECD imports from 2.4 to 3.0 percent, while East Europe's share declined from 1.5 to 1.2 percent. In machinery trade the contrast is even more striking; Latin American countries increased their share from 0.3 to 1.4 percent, while Eastern Europe experienced a drop from 0.6 to 0.5 percent. (Poznanski, 1985.)

Because enterprises in Latin America are more exposed to world market pressures, they were forced to undertake a basically more sound adjustment to the debt problem than were the countries of Eastern Europe. As some recent studies show (Tyson, 1986; Poznanski, 1986b), the Latin Americans have aggressively reallocated their resources to the most competitive sectors and squeezed their public spending; the East Europeans, by contrast, refocused their efforts on sectors where they do not have a comparative advantage (e.g., energy production generally, and agriculture in Czechoslovakia and Poland). Thus, while lately most Latin American countries have been able to accelerate their exports, East Europe allowed its trade with the non-CMEA countries to decline sharply.

An assessment of comparative economic performance should also include income distribution. Income distribution is more uneven in the market-type economies of Latin America than in the centrally planned economies of Eastern Europe. On the one hand, the degree of income uniformity and lack of good incentives among workers and white-collar employees causes widespread apathy in Eastern Europe; on the other hand, income distribution between the majority of employees and the elite is much greater than is revealed by earnings data because of the many perquisites, not quantifiable, that the elites in East Europe enjoy. To be sure, the extreme income inequalities throughout Latin America do hinder economic development.

The East European countries have a clear advantage in terms of having little apparent unemployment, although excessive job security regardless of performance limits productivity improvements. In many Latin American countries unemployment is very high, for many reasons. Foremost among them is the high rate of population growth in the region. In contrast, the population of Eastern Europe, except in Poland, has been stagnating or growing very slowly.

As far as poverty is concerned, several major Latin American economies, after years of rapid growth, have made some progress in reducing mass poverty, though vast areas of misery still prevail in many countries. Less well known is the fact that in some countries in Eastern Europe a significant segment of the population has been allowed to fall below the poverty line. In Poland and in Hungary, where unofficial sources and the state-controlled media provide more honest assessments than can be found elsewhere in Eastern Europe, recent estimates show that 20 to 30 percent of the families are close to or below the poverty line. Eyewitness reports from Romania suggest that the economic situation of the population in that country has deteriorated as rapidly, if not more so, than in Poland.

II. Structural Dependence on the Superpowers

The Soviets have been instrumental not only in forcing Eastern Europe to adopt central planning, but also in getting these countries to create and maintain structural dependence on the Soviet economy. It has been a persistent goal of the Soviet leadership to integrate the Eastern European economies into the Soviet economy. The expansion of East-West trade does not interfere with this goal because it helps make East Europe a supplier of badly needed Western goods, technology, and know-how.

After World War II the East European countries developed certain industrial branches and created much capacity specifically to supply the USSR—in some cases initially under reparation requirements, in other cases, or subsequently, under commercial arrangements. There were several reasons for this. The Soviets probably believed—certainly during the 1950s—that their pattern of industrialization was the only correct one for all socialist states. During the 1950s and 1960s the USSR preferred, whenever possible, to obtain its supplemental requirements for machinery and other strategic and nonstrategic goods from its allies rather than from the West, since the latter could not be counted on to be a dependable supplier. Furthermore, the Soviets have always valued economic integration with Eastern Europe in order to keep the region economically dependent, thus providing itself with political leverage and limiting the influence of the West.

As a consequence of the industrialization and trade policies of the 1950s and 1960s, each East European country became locked to a greater or lesser extent into trade with the Soviet Union. In particular, the USSR became an increasingly large net supplier of fuels and raw materials to Eastern Europe. As table 1 shows, for five of the six East European countries, the USSR supplies about one-third of energy consumption and nine-tenths of energy imports. Romania's dependence is much smaller. Soviet energy exports to all destinations account for about 15 percent of domestic production. Approximately half goes to the West, where in 1984 the Soviets earned $25 billion (83 percent of the USSR's total convertible currency revenue of $30 billion); much of the rest goes to Eastern Europe and Cuba. In recent years Soviet energy exports to East Europe accounted for 40 to 50 percent of the USSR's total exports to the region, much of it sold for clearing rubles, some for convertible currency.

The Soviet Union has become a major net importer of Eastern European manufactures. On average, more than 50 percent of East European exports of machinery, for instance, now goes to the Soviet market, while almost 30 percent of East European imports of machinery are supplied by the Soviets. Some East European exports are almost totally dependent on the Soviet market (e.g., Hungarian buses, Polish helicopters, Bulgarian computer equipment), and the Soviets are monopoly suppliers to the East Europeans of many products (e.g., aircraft and nuclear energy equipment).

This double-edged dependence of the East Europeans seems, at first glance, to be advantageous to the region rather than to the Soviet Union. In fact, some statements to that effect are occasionally made by the Soviet leadership. They point out that Eastern Europe enjoys uninterrupted supplies of fuels and raw materials from Soviet sources that require huge, capital-intensive investment projects in order to be productive. At the same time the East Europeans are in a position to sell their less capital-intensive machinery, transport equipment, and other manufactures on the immense and stable Soviet market.

However, this trade pattern is not without certain costs for the East European economies. One of the most significant is that it has helped to freeze the region into an excessively energy- and raw material-

Table 1. Share of the USSR in East Europe's consumption and import of energy, 1982 (in percentages)

Country	Energy consumption	Energy imports
Bulgaria	75	92
Hungary	41	75
Czechoslovakia	37	92
GDR	32	81
Poland	16	90
East Europe Five	32	87
Romania	3	13
East Europe Six	28	78

Source: Bethkenhagen (1984).

intensive production structure. The Soviets provide Eastern Europe with machinery that requires uneconomically high inputs of energy to manufacture and operate. Such a structure may be more readily affordable by the resource-rich Soviet economy than by the poorly endowed East European countries. Good examples are the Soviet steelmaking industry, the primary source of equipment for East European steel producers, or Soviet-designed prefabricated urban housing systems.

The Soviet market for machinery is by and large characterized by a demand for mass volumes of relatively simple types of products that will not require much servicing. In addition, on the Soviet market the East Europeans do not face much competition from domestic suppliers, whose products are often inferior. As a result, the external pressure for product modernization and differentiation—so critical for success in promoting exports to the world market—is low. And although a great deal of lip service has been paid in recent years to the need to improve the quality of manufactures traded within the CMEA, neither the prices paid nor the bilateral barter that best characterizes the payment mechanism promotes modernization or the customer orientation of suppliers.

An additional factor that reinforces East Europe's isolation from the world market is the incompatibility of many Soviet technical standards with those in the rest of the world. In recent years almost all East European manufacturers have been forced to join the Soviet Union's program of computer production in the so-called RIAD system. The family of computers now made in these countries is therefore not fully compatible with major Western systems, so that their sales outside the CMEA are impeded. For the same reason color television sets manufactured by several East European countries are hardly salable on the world market.

The most important aspect of Eastern European dependence on the Soviet Union is that it undermines the region's ability to choose trading partners, a situation with important political implications. Under the circumstances, any substantial shift away from the Soviet Union would require a fundamental change in production patterns that would be extremely difficult, costly, and time-consuming to implement. The current economic crisis in Poland can be interpreted in some sense as the failure of such an attempt. (Poznanski, 1986b.)

A brief look at simple statistical indicators—market shares—suggests that the major Latin American countries are as dependent on the U.S. economy as the East Europeans are on the Soviet Union. As much as one-third of Latin American exports go to the United States (close to the share of East European exports to the USSR). Both regions sell around half of their machinery exports and one-third of their total exports of chemicals to the respective superpowers (table 2). With almost 70 percent of its trade with the United States, Mexico appears to be even more tied to this superpower than are Bulgaria and East Germany—the most dependent East European states—with the Soviet Union.

If one looks more closely, however, it becomes apparent that such general statistical comparisons are misleading. This is because the nature of U.S.–Latin American structural interdependence is fundamentally different from the Soviet-East European relationship. The most critical difference is that while the U.S. economy serves as a growth locomotive for its Latin American partners, dependence on the Soviet Union in many ways undercuts the long-term prospects for economic growth in Eastern Europe, particularly in the relatively more advanced countries.

The more positive U.S. impact on the major Latin American countries is particularly evident in the technical sphere. Unlike the Soviet

Table 2. Indicators of Soviet–East European
and U.S.–Latin American trade,[a] 1983

	USSR Share in East European exports	U.S. Share in Latin American exports	Ratio of East European exports to imports from USSR	Ratio of Latin American exports to imports from United States
Total	37.9	33.1	—	—
Food	56.7	25.7	1595	146
Fuels	7.0	37.6	−1332	2266
Chemicals	26.9	27.8	198	−277
Machinery	51.2	52.9	352	−172
Nonferrous metals	1.8	—	−401	—
Iron and steel	19.3	—	−5700	266[b]
Clothing	53.1	—	—	133[c]

Note: [a] Includes Argentina, Brazil, Columbia, Peru, Venezuela, Mexico, Chile.
[b] Manufactured goods by material, including iron and steel.
[c] Miscellaneous goods, including clothing.
Source: Calculated from the *Monthly Bulletin of Statistics*, United Nations, New York, 1985; data for the last column from *U.S. Foreign Trade Highlights, 1984*, U.S. Department of Commerce, March 1985.

Union, the United States is more technically advanced than its partners. The main exceptions to this generalization are in some military areas, but given Soviet secrecy, the Eastern Europeans do not have much direct access to Soviet technology in this field. At the same time the United States—in contrast to the Soviets in Eastern Europe—is a net supplier of machinery and transport equipment to Latin America.

The United States also plays a more positive role because it provides large direct investment to Latin America, while the Soviet Union drains investment capital from Eastern Europe. Whatever the overall assessment of the impact on host countries of investment by multinational corporations, such flows do provide expertise in marketing, manufacturing, and management. By contrast, East European investments in Soviet-based projects do not offer many benefits of that kind.

The critical role of the United States as trading partner and financier for Latin America surely provides it with considerable economic leverage. But the Soviets appear to have even greater leverage, stemming both from differences in institutional arrangements and from the nature of East Europe's structural dependence itself. For example, goods that Latin America supplies to the United States are by and large competitive products, which are therefore not as difficult to reorient to other markets as is the flow of East European exports to the USSR.

A further consideration is that due to its democratic political regime, the United States finds it more difficult to impose economic sanctions than do the nonelected Soviet leaders. The historical experience shows that strong and lasting sanctions have been imposed by the United States mostly on countries that moved from the U.S. to the Soviet political orbit (e.g., Cuba and Nicaragua), in which case it was not too difficult to reach domestic consensus. Otherwise, sanctions are seldom used or are weak and short-lived because it is difficult to mobilize the political support necessary to make them effective. The Soviet Union has employed sanctions in Eastern Europe (against Yugoslavia and Albania), and has exerted economic pressure on its allies, although such acts are less publicized than is economic pressure exerted by the United States in Latin America.

III. The Wealth Transfer Issue

One of the most critical issues in any assessment of superpower–subordinate state relations is that of uncompensated transfers of wealth between them. This issue tends to be perhaps the most strongly debated, even though other forms of economic impact might be of greater significance. The reason is that unrequited wealth transfers are easier to identify, trace, and interpret than the effects of superpower influence discussed in the previous sections.

We use the phrase "unrequited wealth transfers"—viewed as grants or subsidies by one party and as exploitation by the others—to mean all flows of resources that are not caused by the unimpeded workings of competitive market forces. Thus a remittance of profits by a superpower's multinational corporations to their home country is not seen as exploitative as long as profits seem to fairly compensate for capital services rendered. To give another example, if freely determined world market prices leave a subordinate state with a smaller fraction, or none, of gains from trade because of existing demand-and-supply conditions, we will not consider the case an example of a grant-type transfer.

Soviet Opportunity Costs

While Soviet policies toward Eastern Europe have always been guided, fundamentally, by the political imperative of keeping these countries within the USSR's ideological-political-military orbit, economic relations since World War II have evolved through stages. Thus, until after Stalin's death, East Europe was economically exploited through reparations transfers (mainly from East Germany but also from Bulgaria, Hungary, Romania, and, indirectly, Poland), by means of so-called joint-stock companies, and through discriminatory foreign trade prices, particularly well documented in the case of Poland. One computation estimated that during the first postwar decade, the uncompensated resource flow from East Europe to the Soviet Union was of the same order of magnitude as what the United States transferred under the Marshall Plan to Western Europe. (Marer, 1974b.)

However, by the second half of the 1950s and in the late 1960s and 1970s, just about the time that East Europe became heavily dependent on Soviet energy and certain raw materials, the opportunity cost to the Soviets of supplying these goods to East Europe began to rise. One reason was the slowing rate of growth and rapidly increasing cost of extracting and transporting these resources; production had to be shifted to the more remote and inhospitable western regions, requiring large increases in capital investment, imported technology, and high-priced and difficult-to-attract labor. These problems were compounded by the rapidly declining mineral content of key ferrous and nonferrous metal ores and by the growing technical and transportation problems in the extractive sectors. (Dobozi, 1985.)

The opportunity cost of supplying growing quantities of energy and raw materials to East Europe also increased because the Soviets needed more convertible currency to take advantage of the trading opportunities opened up by détente with the West. However, between 1973 and 1982 (the year world energy prices began to decline) the Soviets earned large windfall gains in convertible currency from the rising world prices of energy, raw materials, and gold, and from the export of military equipment to the Middle East (through which the USSR tapped into the OPEC surplus). These windfall gains, estimated on the order of $50 billion,* helped mitigate the opportunity cost of being a growing net supplier of hard goods to Eastern Europe.

Nevertheless, during the 1970s the Soviet Union took several steps to reduce the opportunity cost of supplying energy and raw materials to East Europe. First, it reduced the exports' rate of growth. Second, after world market prices quadrupled in 1974, the Soviets changed the CMEA pricing formula from a fixed five-year average to a moving average of world market prices in order to adjust CMEA prices more rapidly to those prevailing on the world market. The increased world market prices of its exports, together with the new CMEA pricing formula, improved the USSR's 1975–82 terms of trade with East Europe overall by about 30 percent and its energy terms of trade by more than 50 percent; from 1983 to 1985 the improvement continued. Although the Soviet Union did not cash in fully because it also extended significant credits, the East European countries had to ship large additional quantities of exports to pay for a given volume of fuel imports.

Third, the USSR successfully pressed the East European countries to provide during 1976–80 about $6 billion in long-term credits to help finance joint projects in the USSR to extract and transport energy and raw materials. These credits accounted for 3 to 4 percent of the total domestic investment of five of the six East European countries (less in the case of Romania); a significant portion of the contributions was made in convertible currency. Fourth, it expanded the share of intra-CMEA transactions in hard goods priced at current world market prices and settled in convertible currency.

These actions notwithstanding, since 1974 the USSR has provided East Europe with large implicit subsidies through various channels. Most important has been the underpricing, mainly as a result of the CMEA pricing formula, of its net energy and raw materials exports relative to the world market prices of these goods. The underpricing

---

*The method of estimation can be found in Hewett (1983); the estimates are ours.

was temporary in the case of nonfuel minerals and lasted for about a decade (until 1984) in the case of fuels. Additional subsidies have taken the form of extending substantial trade credits, in the form of trade surpluses, at low (2 to 3 percent) interest, with some risk of non-repayment.

The Soviets may have provided further subsidies by paying, on balance, attractive prices to the net exporters of machinery, equipment, and consumer goods, but the facts regarding this matter are not known fully and the interpretations are controversial. There is no debate over the fact that the Eastern Europeans obtain attractive prices from the USSR and from each other. It is also well documented that during the 1950s and 1960s the prices of intra-CMEA manufactures were relatively high even if judged not on the basis of low East-to-West but of higher West-to-West (i.e., true world market) price standards. To put it differently, importers within the CMEA have not insisted on receiving large discounts for relatively poor-quality packaging and service that Western buyers obtain when they import similar goods from Eastern Europe.

Very little is known, however, about what happened to the intra-CMEA prices of manufactures during the 1970s and early 1980s relative to price trends on the world market. Moreover, the true worth to the importers of manufactures obtained from CMEA partners is a matter of speculation, perhaps not only in the West, but perhaps in the importing countries as well. Some of the goods that would be considered insufficiently modern in the West may be often perfectly suitable for Soviet needs. For instance, much of Soviet industry is not equipped, in terms of infrastructure and skills, to use numerically controlled machine tools, and thus the Soviets prefer the older models—many built according to Soviet specifications—for which there would be little demand in the West. Thus the estimate of how much subsidy one CMEA country grants to another will be influenced greatly by the assumptions made about the true worth of intra-bloc trade in manufactures.

A Western Interpretation of the Soviet Perspective

A well-publicized attempt to quantify the sum total of these subsidies was made by M. Marrese and J. Vanous. They calculated that from 1974 to 1984 the Soviet Union provided to the six East European countries more than $100 billion in subsidies as under-the-table payments for the military, political, and ideological support they received from East Europe's leaders. (Marrese and Vanous, 1982; Vanous and Marrese, 1983; Marrese, 1986.) These findings have received wide publicity.

Because the computations appear to be precise and scientific, the subsidy estimates have been given a great deal of currency by many observers, often without understanding fully the method of estimation that undergirds them.

The wide publicity given to the huge Soviet subsidy estimates has made many observers of Soviet–East European relations alter their views of the Soviet Union. Stalin's USSR was an exploitative superpower. Stalin's successors evidently manipulate dependent states through the granting and withholding of subsidies, i.e., exercising economic leverage. This interpretation also suggests that the Soviet Union is converging with the United States, in that both superpowers now rely on economic instruments and positive incentives to exert their influence.

We are in some disagreement with the Marrese-Vanous subsidy estimates and also with their interpretation of how and why they have originated. Their estimates are based on a complex set of computations that, in our view, embody a significant upward bias. One of us has elaborated elsewhere a criticism of their estimates (Marer, 1984); other experts have also registered disagreements with their computations or interpretations. (Dietz, 1985; Brada, 1985; van Brabant, 1984.) Here, let us just state briefly, without the technical details, our views about the sources of their bias.

First, there are enormous gaps in the data that one would need in order to quantify, with any degree of accuracy, the actual Soviet losses in trade with Eastern Europe. Little detail is known, for example, about the quantities and prices of the manufactures traded within the CMEA, or how suitable they are to the importing country for the uses intended, given that requirements and standards are not identical to those in the West.

Second, one must conceptualize and then try to apply empirically the price standard against which the true worth of intra-CMEA trade will be evaluated. Using the world market standard turns out to be a slippery process as soon as quantification is attempted. For example, in the case of manufactures, it makes a great deal of difference whether East-to-West, West-to-East, or West-to-West prices are used as reference points, and within each standard there is a range of estimates, depending on which Western country (or countries) is used as a reference point.

Third, the computations neglect to take into account a series of items that represent explicit or implicit subsidies from Eastern Europe to the USSR, such as investment contributions, especially those made in convertible currency; East Europe's surplus in invisible trade, such as transport and tourism, and a settlement mechanism that favors the net importer; and East Europe's economic contributions to promote the Soviet Union's global political interests, e.g., subsidies to countries such as Cuba, Vietnam, Mongolia, and Nicaragua.

It is not possible to devise a purely scientific method or approach to quantify intra-CMEA subsidies with precision. But since our criticism of the Marrese-Vanous estimates typically evokes the response, "what would, in your view, be a more realistic estimate of the subsidy flow?," in the next section we will present an alternative methodology and a set of preliminary estimates based on it.

Turning to the Marrese-Vanous interpretation of the reasons for Soviet subsidies to East Europe, we must also register disagreement with their views. In our interpretation the subsidies exist largely because it is not in the Soviet Union's long-term economic or political interest to tear up economic agreements or commercial contracts they have signed. One such key agreement is the CMEA pricing formula. Now that world oil prices have dropped, the Soviets are benefiting, whereas in some earlier years they incurred a disadvantage.

Maintaining the sanctity of signed commercial contracts is also important. For example, in 1966 and 1967 Czechoslovakia and East Germany entered into commercial contracts with the USSR to provide the Soviet Union long-term credits in exchange for each country receiving during 1973–84 5 million tons of oil each year at the fixed price of fifteen transferable rubles ($16.70) per ton. (Von Brabant, 1984.) At the time the agreed price was somewhat above the then prevailing world market price, world oil prices were stable, and there was no expectation of a rapid oil price escalation. That those contracts turned out to be such good deals for Czechoslovakia and East Germany is due to the actions of OPEC rather than to veiled payments by the Soviets for services rendered.

Moreover, in trying to understand Soviet motives it is important to note that during the first half of the 1980s the Soviet Union took new steps to limit the opportunity cost of being a net supplier of hard goods to Eastern Europe. In 1980 it informed the East European countries that the level of energy exports would be frozen for five years. In 1982 it cut oil exports to East Europe by 10 percent (increasing natural gas exports to some countries in partial compensation). Between 1982 and 1985 it cut trade credits to East Europe substantially and is now insisting that during 1986–90 a significant portion of East Europe's outstanding debts should be repaid. In fact, debts owed to the USSR are in some respects harder to repay than those East Europe owes to the West. Although the USSR charges a lower rate of interest, apparently it will not be possible to roll over those credits, whereas much of the debt to the West almost certainly will be refinanced.

In addition, the Soviet Union has insisted—and the East European countries have apparently agreed—to a new round of East European investment participation in the USSR, to help build a giant new natural gas pipeline from western Siberia to East Europe. The cost of the Yamburg project is estimated at 12 billion transferable rubles (about $16 billion); based on past experience with such projects, the actual cost will be substantially higher.

Furthermore, Soviet spokesmen have stated that future supplies of hard goods will depend on their availability, and that the Soviet Union is more interested in delivering industrial products than supplying more fuels and raw materials to Eastern Europe. The USSR has also been pressing the East European countries to improve the quality of their manufactured exports (which has declined in recent years as East Europe has been forced to cut imports from the West) and to restructure the composition of exports to meet new Soviet priorities.

However, given the well-known shortcomings of the CMEA mechanism (Pecsi, 1981, Marer and Montias, 1980, and van Brabant, 1980), it is difficult to see how the East European countries will be able to comply with this Soviet demand—or more generally, how the growth of economic tensions within the CMEA can be avoided. The main shortcomings of the CMEA mechanism include the inability of planners to calculate reliably comparative advantage in manufactures; the existence of parallel capacity throughout the region in certain products while specialization in parts, components, and subassemblies is neglected; the isolation of the producers of exports from foreign users; the unavailability of reliable information about the future needs and import intentions of CMEA partners; a CMEA price mechanism that does not reward modernity, quality, or Western import content; and the inconvertibility of the currencies of the CMEA countries or of the transferable ruble.

A Proposed New Approach to Quantification
For several years after the explosion of world energy and raw material prices, the Soviet Union charged Eastern Europe prices below those prevailing on the world market. However, not only have fuel prices lagged behind the world level (given the intra-CMEA pricing formula) but possibly also those of nonfuel products. Thus, one cannot rule out the possibility that the Soviet Union has been able to obtain compensa-

tion through its imports of underpriced machinery and other nonfuel products, of which it is a net importer.

To evaluate the impact of intra-CMEA prices of both fuel and nonfuel products on subsidy flows, we propose a different method (Poznanski, 1985) from that applied in the Marrese-Vanous studies. The essence of this two-step method is (1) to base the calculation of wealth transfers on a comparison of the export-purchasing power of Soviet fuel in Eastern Europe with that of fuel supplied by the main world exporters of this product to Western countries; and (2) to adjust the results so obtained for the presumed quality differences between East European and Western manufactures.

Step one.   The basic question we are posing is this: Since 1972, has the Soviet Union gained more in terms of the additional volume of nonfuel products it obtained for one unit of its fuel exports to Eastern Europe than fuel-exporters gained in intra-Western trade?

If we found, for example, on the basis of actual intra-CMEA prices, that in a given year the Soviet Union doubled the tonnage of, say, machine tool imports from Eastern Europe per one ton of its fuel exports, while at the same time fuel exporters in the West tripled the tonnage of machines they obtained per ton of fuel, then, in relative terms, the Soviet Union would have been losing, i.e., subsidizing Eastern Europe. Summing up the results of a large and representative sample of such "oil-for-product commodity terms of trade" comparisons is the first step toward arriving at a subsidy estimate.

The basic source of statistics for this calculation is annual country data for (a) Soviet trade with Eastern Europe and (b) intra-Western trade. The trade data have to be in terms of both values and quantities (kilograms or units). Unit values (i.e., prices per kilogram or unit) of imported fuels and of nonfuel products traded in the CMEA and the West, respectively, are determined each year, followed by the calculation of changes in those unit values over time, taking, for instance, 1972 (pre-OPEC price rise) as the base year.

These individual product indices are then used to determine changes in the individual "oil for product commodity terms of trade." Next we aggregate these results (using the export shares of individual nonfuel products as weights) to obtain an overall estimate of changing commodity terms of trade in Soviet–East European and in West-West trade. Then, dividing the aggregate for the West by the aggregate for Eastern Europe in the same year, we establish whether the USSR as fuel supplier lost or gained in relative terms in comparison with fuel exporters in the West.

The absolute size of wealth transfers in a given year—neglecting for the moment quality differences—can be readily calculated. One first finds the dollar value of Eastern European imports of Soviet fuels (multiplying the quantity of those imports by the actual dollar unit values of fuels traded in the West in that year). Then, multiplying the dollar value of Eastern European fuel imports by the aggregate ratio of West/East European purchasing power for fuels, one obtains an estimate of the absolute size of the annual wealth transfers. The annual transfers add up to a cumulative transfer over a specific period.

Step two. The method described in step one helps us to estimate transfers of wealth related only to price differences between Soviet fuels sold to Eastern Europe and fuels sold on the world market. However, there is another potential source of wealth transfer related to the fact that the Soviet Union, as a net importer of Eastern European machinery, gets products of lower quality than it would be able to obtain if it reoriented its net fuel export surplus to the West and imported Western products instead. In step two, we try to estimate the price at which a CMEA country would be able to buy in the West manufactured goods of East European quality, and we combine the estimates with the results obtained in step one.

It has been well documented that when either the East Europeans or the Soviets sell their machinery or other manufactures on the world market, they have to sell at a substantial discount compared with West-to-West prices of similar (but not, of course, identical) products. Marrese and Vanous estimate that discount, on average, as 30 percent. Although the discount factors they use in the case of individual Eastern European countries are arbitrary (+ or – of the 30 percent, on the assumption that the quality of Czech and East German products is above average and those of Romania and Bulgaria below average), we do not consider them unrealistic and thus do not challenge them. Marrese and Vanous also assume that the intra-CMEA prices of manufactures exceed the West-West prices of comparable goods by 10 to 20 percent. While this was apparently the case during the early 1960s, there is little reason to assume that it remained so during the 1970s or early 1980s. In any event, our step one obviates the need to make a more or less arbitrary assumption about this.

While both of the assumptions Marrese and Vanous make—about the East-to-West and East-to-East prices of East European manufactures—are within the plausible range, it is the implications they draw from them for estimating Soviet subsidies that is the Achilles' heel of their estimate. How their reasoning differs from ours is best illustrated by showing the following relationship between price concepts, with some illustrative numbers.

120   Intra-CMEA price
100   West-to-West price
 60   East-to-West price

Marrese and Vanous assume that if the Soviets reoriented their hard good surplus in intra-CMEA trade to the West, they would be able to import the manufactures they now buy from Eastern Europe (at, say, 120) for the same price at which the West buys East Europe's manufactures (at, say, 60). Thus, since the Soviets now pay approximately twice what the goods are really worth, they are continuously providing large subsidies to Eastern Europe, regardless of the export price of fuels and raw materials.

In our view this assumption is incorrect. The Soviet Union could not buy the same or similar goods from a Western country at anywhere near the same price at which a centrally planned economy sells its goods in the West. This is because only a portion of the East-to-West price discount (40 percent in the above illustration) can be attributed to the low quality of Eastern European manufactures; the rest of the discount results from Western discrimination and poor marketing by Eastern Europe.

Table 3. Weighted average oil-nonfuel products purchasing power ratio for Hungary and West Germany

	Absolute ratio		Relative ratio
	West Germany (1972 = 100)	Hungary (1972 = 100)	West Germany/Hungary
Year	(1)	(2)	(1)/(2)
1973	111.7	99.9	111.8
1974	267.3	111.7	239.3
1975	244.4	184.2	132.7
1976	252.2	212.2	118.8
1977	188.9	233.2	81.0
1978	213.0	252.9	84.2
1979	281.7	305.8	92.1
1980	538.4	304.6	176.7
1981	546.1	301.7	181.0
1982	502.4	312.7	160.6
1983	420.8	369.8	113.8

Source: Poznanski (1986b).

Thus an important problem with the Marrese-Vanous method is that they have not provided plausible estimates of the prices the Soviet Union would have to pay to the West if it tried either to purchase Eastern European goods through the Western market or to buy Western analogs — in quality terms — of those goods. The fact that Eastern Europe has to sell its goods to the West at a large discount does not mean that the Soviet Union could obtain them, or their Western analogs, with an identical discount from the West.

A further important point is that while conventional wisdom says that centrally planned economies (CPEs) are shrewd buyers, so that they can import from the West at approximately the same price as Western buyers import from each other, we should not take this for granted without first testing it empirically. That is, are the prices CPEs pay, on the average, less than, equal to, or higher than West-to-West prices? Finding this missing evidence is the essence of the second step in our alternative methodology of estimating wealth transfers in intra-CMEA trade.

Preliminary Results of the Proposed New Approach
We carried out some preliminary illustrative calculations of step one, or estimating fuel-type transfers of wealth, based on the methodology presented above, in comparing Hungary's trade with the USSR with that of West German trade with the world.* The following review of the quantitative results should be considered a research progress report, not a final product. It is intended to elicit comments and to stimulate a search for alternative approaches to estimating wealth transfers within the Soviet bloc.

The results of our calculation of the ratio of each country's commodity terms of trade show that from 1973 to 1986 world oil was buying more in West Germany than Soviet oil bought in Eastern Europe, with the most dramatic difference in 1974 (table 3). However, during 1977–79, Soviet oil was being exchanged for larger quantities of Hungarian nonfuel goods than was the case for world oil sold to West Germany. After 1980 world suppliers of oil again received a better deal in West Germany; the differential was substantial until 1982, declining rapidly thereafter.

The absolute value of wealth transfers between Hungary and the Soviet Union is presented in table 4. During 1973–76 the Soviet Union

---

*The data for Soviet–Eastern European trade are based on a Hungarian source: *Foreign Trade Yearbook* (annual, in Hungarian). Trends in the West are estimated using West German statistics: *Aussenhandel der Bundesrepublik Deutschlands* (annual, in German).

provided Hungary with an oil subsidy of around $600 million, with almost $300 million transferred in 1974 alone. During 1977–79 the situation was reversed, with Hungary losing $450 million to the Soviet Union. During 1980–83 the Soviet Union was subsidizing Hungary again, by approximately $2.75 billion. Thus during 1973–83 the net Soviet subsidy to Hungary through oil was close to $2.9 billion, and about $4 billion if gas subsidies—estimated in the same way as oil subsidies—are added.

This cyclical movement in relative purchasing power is explained by the time lag between Soviet oil prices in the CMEA and those prevailing on the world market. The other contributing factor has to be the difference in price pattern for nonfuel exports from Hungary and West Germany. This is obvious since during 1972–83 the prices the Soviets charged to East Europe were continuously below world market levels. Thus, if at any point the commodity terms of trade for Soviet oil were more favorable than those in the West, as they were during 1977–79, it was because the prices obtained by Hungary for its nonfuel exports (based on our limited sample of products) were relatively lower than those for West German exports of similar (but of course not identical) products.

If we make the rather strong assumption that Soviet trade with Hungary is representative of Soviet trade with the rest of Eastern Europe,

Table 4. Alternative estimate of fuel subsidies for Hungary
and the estimate by Marrese-Vanous, 1973–83 (in millions of dollars)

	1973	1974	1975	1976
1. Alternative	19.6	323.6	165.6	121.3
2. Marrese-Vanous	54.0	397.0	277.0	348.0
3. Difference (1 − 2)	− 34.4	− 73.4	− 111.4	− 266.7

	1977	1978	1979	1980
1. Alternative	− 205.3	− 180.3	− 112.4	1,499.9
2. Marrese-Vanous	292.0	303.0	709.0	1,501.0
3. Difference (1 − 2)	− 497.3	− 483.3	− 821.4	− 51.1

	1981	1982	1983	1970/83
1. Alternative	1,246.1	953.7	254.7	4,018.5
2. Marrese-Vanous	1,597.0	1,400.0	907.0	7,825.0
3. Difference (1 − 2)	− 350.1	− 446.3	− 652.3	− 3,806.5

Source   Poznanski (1986) These two estimates are not fully comparable given methodological differences.

then we can estimate the wealth transfers involved in its total trade with Eastern Europe. This is done by multiplying the Hungarian figures for each year by the factor of 10, since Hungary accounts for about a 10 percent share of Soviet fuel exports to East Europe (excluding Romania).

Our subsidy estimate for Eastern Europe (excluding Romania, for which such estimates were not computed) differs considerably from that of Marrese and Vanous, with respect both to order of magnitude and duration. While Marrese and Vanous conclude that the Soviet Union continuously subsidizes Eastern Europe through fuel supplies, our alternative estimate indicates that Soviet subsidies occurred only during 1973–76 and 1980–83, while in 1977–79 it was the Soviet Union that was being subsidized by Eastern Europe. In addition, we estimate the net fuel-type subsidy by the Soviet Union to Eastern Europe during 1973–83 as about $40 billion, about half of the figure produced by Marrese and Vanous for the same period.*

During 1977–79 Eastern Europe subsidized the Soviet Union with $5 billion, a sum close to the subsidy of Eastern Europe by the Soviet Union during 1973–76 ($6.1 billion). This means that by 1979 the Soviet Union was almost even with Eastern Europe as far as implicit transfer of wealth through the fuel trade is concerned. Simple extrapolation suggests that in 1984 the Eastern Europeans again began to subsidize the Soviet Union, and that it is very likely that the Soviet Union will recover its subsidies from 1980–83 during 1984–86, as it did earlier, i.e., during 1977–79.

The second line of our preliminary research was to determine whether there is any price discrimination when a centrally planned economy purchases machinery in the West. We selected thirty-six types of machine tools exported by West Germany in 1978 and 1982. We found that in 1978 out of thirty-three types of machine tools that were imported by Eastern Europe from West Germany, in only one case did the region pay less than did the Western Europeans. The weighted average East European prices were 68 percent above the intra-West European level. For 1982, five instances of lower prices were found in Eastern Europe, while the average price for all imported machine tools was 45 percent above the level reported in the intra-West European trade. Interestingly, the respective average prices paid by the newly

---

*We disagree with the formula used by Marrese and Vanous to decompose the total subsidy into the part due to Soviet underpricing of primary product exports (including oil) and Soviet overpayment for imported manufactures. If a correct formula were used, a much larger share of the subsidy would be attributable to the overpricing of the manufactures.

industrializing countries exceeded the intra-West European prices by much less, both in 1978 and 1982.

The above results have to be treated with great caution. To obtain more solid evidence one would have to base conclusions on more than one product group, however significant it may be. It will also be necessary to look at more than one Western supplier of goods to Eastern Europe, and to repeat this kind of price comparison for the Soviet Union itself, since the Soviets are probably in a stronger bargaining position in dealing with Western exporters of manufactures than are the East Europeans.

In any event, one must offer a viable explanation for the price differentials found above. One possible reason could be that the East Europeans tend to buy more sophisticated types of machines in particular categories of machine tools. However, this is not a likely explanation given Western controls on the export of certain kinds of technology under COCOM arrangements (whether machine tool exports are controlled would have to be checked) and the questionable capacity of the CMEA countries to absorb the most advanced types of Western manufactures.

A more plausible explanation seems to be that this surcharge reflects various hidden costs Western exporters incur only when operating in Eastern Europe. Western sellers might try to include in their selling price a compensation for the low (i.e., below market) level of interest on credits the planners insist upon, the costs of buy-back deals they may be pressured into as a precondition of sales, and the cost of certain inconveniences accompanying their marketing effort in the CMEA countries (e.g., longer than usual negotiations, expensive local facilities).

If we assume that our results for machine tools are representative, then we can address the following question: what would such a surcharge imply in terms of real Soviet opportunity costs in the imports of manufactures? The following example illustrates the implications of such a price surcharge, assuming it to be in the middle range of our findings for 1978 and 1982, namely 55 percent. We will analyze these implications within the hypothetical scheme of intra-CMEA, West-to-West, and East-to-West price levels introduced earlier.

Let us assume, admittedly arbitrarily, that 50 percent of the price discount on products sold in the West by centrally planned economies can be attributed to quality differences, the remaining 50 percent to discrimination and poor marketing. Since the only realizable opportunity cost for the Soviets when they import East European manufactures would be the quality-related 50 percent of the discount, this means that the true worth of those products would in this case be not 60 but 80. This we call the "corrected East-to-West" price.

124	West-to-East
120	Intra-CMEA
100	West-to-West
80	Corrected East-to-West
60	East-to-West

Further, when the Soviet Union buys manufactures from the West, it apparently has to pay a 55 percent surplus on the top of the 80. The total price, called here West-to-East, would be 124, meaning that to purchase products of Eastern European quality in the West, the Soviets would have to pay a slightly higher price (4 points, or 5 percent) than what they apparently pay in intra-CMEA trade.

If the assumed quality-related discount were not 50 but 25 percent of the total discount, then the adjusted East-to-West price would be 90. With the 55 percent surcharge the Western price to the Soviets would be around 140, or 20 points above the intra-CMEA prices. If, on the other hand, we assumed that the quality-related discount is 75 percent of the total, then the corrected East-to-West price level would be 70 and the West-to-East price 110, i.e., 10 points below the intra-CMEA price.

Our analysis casts serious doubts on the accuracy of the Marrese-Vanous estimates of machine-type subsidies. It might just be possible that, considering prices alone, the Soviets are actually benefiting by not going to the West for the products they now buy from their East European dependencies. However, much more work has to be done to refine estimates of the actual quality discount in East-to-West sales and to document the surcharge on West-to-East transactions.

The results of our analysis suggest that our figure presented earlier for fuel-type subsidies is likely to be the maximum total subsidy on all (fuel- and nonfuel-type) transfers to Eastern Europe from the Soviet Union attributable to price-tag considerations only. Our estimate of $40 billion represents less than half of the $106 billion in implicit Soviet subsidies calculated by Marrese and Vanous for both fuel-type and machinery-type transfers. To be sure, our estimates do not include Soviet subsidies generated by its trade surplus on which below-market rates of interest are charged. This might increase the subsidy estimate by only a few billion dollars.

IV. Conclusions

Our analysis of relative purchasing powers is offered as an alternative to the Marrese-Vanous method of measuring wealth transfers. The preliminary results of our analysis, based on comparison of West Germany and Hungary, reveal that the estimates produced by Marrese and Vanous appear to be strongly inflated. In addition, our analysis shows a substantially different time pattern of wealth transfers within the Soviet bloc during the post-1972 period. While Marrese and Vanous show a more or less persistent increase in one-way subsidies by the Soviet Union to Eastern Europe, our approach suggests a cyclical pattern, with both the Soviet Union and Eastern Europe periodically subsidizing one another.

Also, we find that the temporary subsidies by the Soviet Union resulted more from the inflexibilities of the trade system (particularly rigid price formulas) than from a deliberate Soviet policy of paying Eastern Europe for services rendered. This interpretation is supported by the fact the Soviet Union did not make any additional price adjustments (i.e., downward corrections) in 1979 when the second fuel price shock took place. Finally, unfairness in Soviet–Eastern European trade —involving wealth transfers in both directions—seems to be a permanent feature of commercial relations in the CMEA, where prices are arbitrary and noneconomic considerations affect trade flows.

The huge estimates of Soviet subsidies produced by Marrese and Vanous have stimulated many scholars and policy analysts to speculate on their possible implications. The argument is made that since Eastern Europe has become such a large and persistent economic burden for the Soviet Union, which it is not likely to be willing to bear indefinitely, the Soviets will have to find ways to reduce East Europe's dependence. They may do so by allowing or promoting fundamental economic restructuring, basic economic reforms, or increased trade dependence on the West. Each alternative, of course, has significant political implications.

Our findings suggest that Eastern Europe is less of an economic burden for the USSR than conventional wisdom in the West asserts, and that, in fact, by the mid-1980s Soviet subsidization has ended. To be sure, it is not possible to make precise estimates because we lack sufficient information and a good understanding of how Soviet decisionmakers view these matters. We admit that both the Marrese-Vanous approach and our own approach to estimating subsidies are rather static, focusing on finding the right price tag on the goods actually traded. Our purpose in undertaking such an exercise has been primarily to call attention to the immense difficulties of doing this scientifically.

Soviet and East European views on the costs of hegemony or benefits of dependence are more complicated. For the USSR the real burden of inter-CMEA trade may indeed be growing, not so much on account of price-tag considerations but because of increasingly severe supply constraints on oil and many raw materials, a growing shortage of convertible currency earnings (owing to the supply constraint and the sharp decline in world market prices of energy and raw materials in 1985–86), and the realization that CMEA integration is not a stimulus but a drag on the economic development of most of its members. For East Europe the price-tag benefits of its economic dependence on the USSR, whether temporary or permanent, are most certainly outweighed by the cost of being locked into economic, political, and systemic dependence on the USSR, with its adverse effect on technological progress and therefore on economic growth.

This detrimental impact of the Soviet economy on Eastern Europe contrasts with the generally positive impact of the United States on the economies of Latin America. By exerting pressure to keep the region open to world trade and investment, the United States reinforces competitive pressures on the Latin Americans to react to market shifts and to upgrade their technology. It also provides them with capital equipment far more advanced than what the Soviets can offer the Eastern Europeans. Moreover, U.S. importers provide a convertible currency that exporters can spend freely, whereas the USSR pays primarily in inconvertible rubles—a chief obstacle for East Europeans who wish to attract investment by Western multinational corporations.

16

Dominant Powers and Subordinate Regions: 1914 and Today

Richard Ned Lebow

As other chapters in this volume make apparent, the relationship between dominant powers and subordinate regions can profitably be studied from either vantage point. It is also important to examine the phenomenon in historical perspective. Comparisons of this kind shed light on the full range of possible interactions between dominant states and subordinate regions. They are also useful in identifying the structural characteristics of such relationships and the full range of national strategies and responses associated with them. This chapter will take a step in that direction by attempting to compare the contemporary pattern of relations between superpowers and subordinate regions with that which prevailed among the great powers in the years before 1914. This comparison is not only theoretically interesting but may hold important policy lessons for the superpowers because great power competition for influence in subordinate regions was one of the principal causes of World War I.

1900—1914

One of the more important similarities between prewar Europe and contemporary Europe is the intense great power competition for influence among lesser developed and weaker states. In both periods, this competition was particularly acute in former colonies that only recently had gained their independence.

In prewar Europe most of these countries were located in the Balkans and were former provinces of the Ottoman Empire. Ottoman rule had once encompassed all of the Middle East from Persia to Morocco and extended into Europe up to the gates of Vienna. But by the middle of the nineteenth century the empire had shrunk considerably. The "sick man of Europe," as it was now known, suffered from multiple ailments, including a corrupt and unusually inefficient administration and a political leadership that until the Young Turk revolution of 1908 was unresponsive to change. In addition, ethnic and religious diversity in its population was a certain cause of political discontent in an age of nationalism.

Ottoman weakness encouraged a series of national uprisings whose success only hastened the pace of imperial decline. The Greek War of Independence in the 1820s, the 1875 revolt in Bosnia and Herzegovina, and the 1912 Balkan War succeeded in all but expelling Turkey from Europe. The new Balkan allies also fought among themselves. In 1885 war broke out between Serbia and Bulgaria. In 1913 Bulgaria, unhappy with its share of the spoils of the First Balkan War, attacked Greece and Serbia, which were supported by Romania and Montenegro. Independence, it was apparent, had created more conflicts than it had resolved. (Jelavich, 1973.)

Balkan rivalries were primarily attributable to geographic intermixing of nationalities. Hungarians and Romanians both laid claim to Transylvania on national grounds. For the same reason Bulgaria and Greece contested Thrace; Romania and Bulgaria, the Dobrudja; and Romania and Serbia, the Banat of Temesvar. Almost everyone asserted a right to all or part of Macedonia. Joachim Remak (1967) observes: "Claims and rights were so contradictory and so entangled that the wisest and most disinterested of judges imaginable could never establish one side's justice except at the cost of another's injustice. No matter what the solution, resentment would flourish." The problem of competing national claims was compounded by the fact that most of these new or relatively new states were economically unstable, had no recent history of self-government, and were led by faction-ridden and politically insecure leaderships. These internal problems made the several Balkan governments more prone to adventurous foreign policies than they might have been otherwise.

The combination of internal weakness and external ambition encouraged individual Balkan states to look for great power support. Several of the great powers were more than willing to oblige, and all of them, wittingly or not, were soon drawn into the complex web of Balkan politics. Russia, Austria-Hungary, and Italy harbored territorial ambitions at Turkey's expense and encouraged national uprisings against her empire as both a means of weakening it and a pretext for their own intervention. In 1877 Russia, under the guise of "Pan-Slavism," came to the aid of Bulgaria and expelled the Turks from Eastern Rumelia. St. Petersburg sought to use the "autonomy" of a greater Bulgaria as a means of extending her own influence in the southeast Balkans with the ultimate aim of controlling the Dardanelles. She was stopped from doing so by the other powers, who at the Congress of Berlin the next year compelled her client, Bulgaria, to settle for much more limited gains. (Jelavich, 1973.)

Russian greed ran afoul of both Britain and Germany. British leaders were anxious to shore up the Ottoman Empire as a counterweight to Russian and Austrian influence in the region. They were prepared to go to war to keep the Straits out of Russian hands. Bismarck's Germany, allied with both Austria and Russia, was concerned that their rivalry in the Balkans would lead to a major falling-out, something that would seriously impair German security. Although this outcome was averted by the Congress of Berlin, Austro-Russian competition in the Balkans later became too intense for successful regulation by the other powers. With Bismarck's departure from the scene, Germany, the one state that might have succeeded in restraining this competition, lost its influence in St. Petersburg.

Austria and Russia began to pursue a more aggressive policy in the Balkans in the decade prior to 1914. Austria sought first to limit the size and influence of Serbia, and then to destroy her independence and annex her. In October 1908 the Austrian foreign minister, Count Alois Aehrenthal, proclaimed the annexation of the Turkish provinces of Bosnia and Herzegovina, formerly only administered by Vienna. The Serbians, who viewed the provinces as an essential component of a greater South Slav state, were furious; crowds gathered in Belgrade and called for war. The government, seemingly anxious to oblige, mobilized its army and looked toward St. Petersburg for support. (See Albertini, 1952, vol. 1: 190–300; Taylor, 1971; Schmidt, 1937.)

Russian leaders were also outraged. Izvolski, the foreign minister, was convinced that Aehrenthal had violated a prior understanding between them, while Pan-Slav opinion regarded it as a serious setback to what they envisaged as Russia's "historic mission" in the Balkans: the protection and eventually liberation of all Slavs under foreign rule. Some influential Pan-Slavs dreamed of a Federation of the East that would include Orthodox Greece and Constantinople—to be renamed Tsarigrad—and give substance to Russia's oft-repeated claim that she was the Third Rome.

Such fantasies could not be too openly ridiculed by a regime that depended upon Pan-Slavic opinion as one of the most important remaining props of its support. The Russian government accordingly condemned Austria's fait accompli and demanded territorial compensation for itself and Serbia. In the end, however, Russia was forced to acquiesce to the Austrian initiative and to put pressure on Serbia to do likewise. Russia's capitulation was prompted by her military weakness and diplomatic isolation. Still recovering from her disastrous war with Japan five years earlier, deserted by France, and faced with the combined might of Germany and Austria, Russian leaders reluctantly chose diplomatic humiliation in preference to certain military defeat.

Austria's victory was a Pyrrhic one. It heightened separatist feelings, especially among South Slavs who felt particularly aggrieved. It also led to renewed Austro-Russian rivalry in the Balkans, which had been held in abeyance since the 1890s, and now assumed increasingly acute proportions. The crisis altered the balance of power within the Russian policy-making elite; it undercut the influence of the pro-Germans and correspondingly strengthened the hand of those who favored the French connection. It also promoted a friendlier attitude toward Britain as well. Finally, the crisis provided the incentive for Russia to embark upon an ambitious rearmament program, one that caused deep concern in Germany as it threatened to render the Schlieffen Plan obsolete.

The power vacuum in the Balkans was a necessary but insufficient condition of Austro-Russian hostility. For most of the first decade of the century, leaders of the two empires actually pursued their respective interests in the Balkans with a fair degree of harmony. Conflict between them escalated, however, when domestic political problems pushed leaders in both countries into pursuing expansionist and confrontational foreign policies.

Austria-Hungary's ills were attributable to its multiethnic population, the narrowness and rigidity of its political elite, and a cumbersome administrative structure that squelched innovation and forestalled reform. (Jasczi, 1929; Macartney, 1969: 721–39; Zeman, 1961; Konirsh, 1955: 231–62.) The Empire was dominated by Germans and Magyars who ruled over a larger, increasingly resentful population of Czechs, Slovaks, Poles, Romanians, Croats, Slovenes, Serbs, and Italians. Economic development and the social transformation it helped to promote had given rise to an articulate intelligentsia and middle class among the subject peoples. Some minority spokesmen, the vanguard of the growing nationalist movements, called for dissolution of the Empire, but most aspired only to a greater voice in its affairs. They demanded a more liberal electoral franchise, greater representation in the various regional assemblies, and legislation to put their languages on an equal footing with German and Magyar in the army, assemblies, and civil service. Zealous German and Hungarian defense of the status quo only provoked further agitation.

The Austrian leadership saw no way of reconciling the divergent strands of domestic opinion. Reforms could only be carried out at the expense of the Germans and, even more so, the Hungarians, the peoples upon whose support the system ultimately depended. Reform might also have paralyzed government. This had happened in Bohemia where German obstructionism in the *Landtage*, a tactic designed to forestall electoral reform, followed by Czech disruption of the *Reichsrat*, had made any legislation impossible. The alternative of repression was also unsatisfactory, because it only encouraged the various nationalities to seek cultural expression and political rights outside the Empire. The separatist tide was particularly strong among the South Slav nationalists, many of whom looked toward Serbia as the nucleus of a greater South Slav state. The Serbian government played up to this sentiment and waged an extensive propaganda campaign among Slav subjects with the aim of hastening the Empire's demise.

Incapable of resolving their national problem by constitutional compromise, Austro-Hungarian leaders sought to overcome it through external action. In the Bosnian crisis of 1908–9, Foreign Minister Aehrenthal tried to combat South Slav nationalism by annexing Bosnia-Herzegovina, rendering impossible the unification of Serbia and Montenegro, and with it the growth of a greater Slav state. When this action failed to quell the rising tide of nationalism, Austrian leaders began to plan for the destruction of Serbia and her incorporation into the Empire. This they hoped would deliver a deathblow to South Slav political aspirations. Vienna was also convinced that such a dramatic coup would strengthen the Empire's international position, deemed equally crucial in the struggle to suppress the centrifugal forces of nationalism.

The Russian Empire faced an equally severe but somewhat different problem: a revolutionary challenge from disaffected bourgeois and intelligentsia. Her leaders envisaged a nationalist foreign policy as a means of mobilizing the politically relevant population in support of the political system and its rulers. At the height of the Russo-Japanese crisis, Viascheslav Plehve, the reactionary minister of the interior, is said to have stated this quite bluntly. He is alleged to have confided to the minister of war: "What this country needs is a short victorious war to stem the tide of revolution." (Witte, 1921: 124.)

On the eve of the July crisis Russia's leaders were even more favorably disposed toward war as a means of keeping the bogey of revolution at bay. Russia's domestic crisis had intensified following the assassination of Stolypin in 1911, and tensions were particularly acute in the spring and early summer of 1914. The Duma was incensed by rumors of a possible coup against it by the government, and protests against the limitation of legislative rights were voiced all over the country, even by some otherwise conservative bodies. Industrial strife also reached a new peak in the wave of strikes that swept the country in July. In the resulting disorders the army was called out to seal off the industrial quarters of St. Petersburg. Workers spoke of a new spirit of *buntarstvo*, a violent but diffuse opposition to all authority, and fought back with a sense of desperation that surprised observers. (Haimson, 1964: 619–42; 1965: 1–22; Rogger, 1966: 229–53.)

Some Western historians support the official Soviet contention that the economic and social disintegration of Russia had progressed far enough to have led to revolution even in the absence of the shattering military experience of 1914–17, but there is disagreement on this point. (Black, 1960: 60; Schapiro, 1959: 1–23; Mendel, 1965: 23–33; and Von Laue, 1965: 34–46.) Whether or not the Soviet interpretation is correct, the magnitude of the domestic crisis must have been very much on the minds of Russian leaders during the fateful month of July 1914. They knew that their acquiescence in Serbia's destruction would have been a far greater humiliation than their inability in 1909 to prevent Austria's annexation of Bosnia-Herzogovina. Such a political setback was certain to have had profound domestic repercussions; in the opinion of most contemporary observers it would have alienated conservatives from the government and have given considerable encouragement to revolutionary elements. There was also something of a consensus that war was bound to arouse patriotic sentiments and rally support behind the government, as in fact it did, at least initially. Opposition to Austrian expansion in the Balkans was thus a given for Russian leaders and a policy from which they never deviated during the course of the crisis, even though Sazonov and those around him realized from the very beginning that it would probably lead to war.

Let us return to Austria-Hungary's nationality problem. It is unclear what the other powers could have done to alleviate the insecurity her leaders felt by virtue of this problem. If asked, they would almost certainly have requested support in squelching South Slav aspirations to statehood. Even if such a policy had been politically feasible for the other powers—and for Russia certainly it was not—it would have succeeded only in postponing the day of reckoning. If a solution to the Empire's nationality problem was to be found, it had to be an internal one. However, this was precluded by German and Hungarian opposition to any reforms that threatened their political and economic privileges. Imperial Russia, the other empire in difficulty, faced a similar dilemma. Plehve's apparent belief in the political utility of "a short victorious war" was a dangerous fantasy. Like its Habsburg rival, Russia's internal problems could only have been dealt with in the long run by meaningful structural reforms, a course of action that was anathema to those in power.

If there was little the other powers could do to dampen Austria-Hungary's perceived need to act aggressively, there was much they could do to make it more pronounced. This was so because Vienna's effort to alleviate her nationality problem through territorial expansion ultimately assumed a significance out of proportion to its original intent. The Empire's success, or lack of it, in imposing her political will on the southern Balkans became the template others used to judge her capability and even her will. Once Vienna had defined the destruction of Serbia as an essential condition of her security, her apparent hesitation to act decisively toward this end led the Germans in particular to question her political spine. Austrian fears that Germany would dismiss her as *bundnisunfähig* (unworthy of alliance) and that Russia would as a result pursue a more aggressive policy in the Balkans led the Empire's frightened leaders to seize on the assassination of Archduke Franz Ferdinand as a pretext for war with Serbia. In the words of the chief of the general staff, Conrad von Hötzendorf:

It was . . . the highly practical importance of the prestige of a Great Power, and indeed of a Great Power which, by its continual yielding and patience (herein lay its fault), had given an impression of impotence and made its internal and external enemies continually more aggressive, so that these enemies were working with increasingly aggressive means for the destruction of the old Empire.

A new yielding, especially now after Serbia's act of violence, would have unloosed all those tendencies within the Empire which were already gnawing at the old structure anyway, in the shape of South Slav, Czech, Russophil and Rumanian propaganda, and Italian irredentism. (von Hötzendorf, 1921–25, vol. 4: 31; Feldner, 1953–54, vol. 1; Ritter, 1970, vol. 2, 227–63; Albertini, 1952, vol. 2: 120–80, 254–57, 284–89, 372–85, 651–86.)

As our discussion indicates, serious domestic problems can create two kinds of incentives to pursue aggressive foreign policies. The first incentive is a function of the problems themselves. If these initiatives are frustrated, they can generate, or be perceived to generate, doubts about that state's capability or resolve in the minds of third parties. Concern for a state's international reputation in the context of unresolved domestic problems intensifies its perceived need to act "tough." The most dangerous situation of all is when, for these reasons, two powers or blocs feel the need to display resolve in the same arena. This is what happened to Austria-Hungary and Russia on the eve of World War I.

Contemporary Superpower Relations

Between 1870 and 1914 colonial disputes periodically strained great power relations but never led to war. In the decade prior to 1914 the most serious of these crises could not properly be called colonial disputes. The First Moroccan Crisis of 1904–5, which pitted Germany against France and Britain, was superficially about competing French and German claims in Morocco. Berlin really pushed its claim for compensation in order to provoke a war scare with France, the real purpose of which was to disrupt the nascent Anglo-French rapprochement signalled by the recent colonial agreement between them. (Anderson, 1930; Albertini, 1952: 151–68; Sweet, 1977: 216–35; Steiner, 1977: 22–69.) The Agadir Crisis of 1911–12 was similar. It too concerned colonial claims, but once again these were an expression, not a cause, of differences between Germany on the one hand and France and Britain on the other. (Albertini, 1952, vol. 1: 318–34; Barlow, 1940; Taylor, 1971: 467–74; Fischer, 1975: 71–94; Dockrill, 1977: 271–87.) The Fashoda crisis, which brought Britain and France to the brink of war in 1898, also conformed to this pattern. (Brown, 1970; Langer, 1960: 550–69; Grenville, 1964; Hargreaves, 1963; Lowe, 1967; Renouvin, 1948: 180–97; Sanderson, 1965; Taylor, 1950: 52–80.)

The Balkans were the arena for the most serious prewar crises. The 1909 Bosnian Annexation crisis and the July crisis of 1914 concerned the relative influence of Austria-Hungary and Russia in territories that had formerly been part of the Ottoman Empire. These Balkan disputes also had more fundamental causes than the competitive expansion of the two powers into this region. Austro-Russian antagonism was largely the result of internal structural problems and the domestic political pressures they produced, which leaders in both countries sought to cope with by means of expansionist foreign policies. In periods when neither power felt these pressures, their leaders were often able to pursue their respective interests in the Balkans quite harmoniously. The power vacuum in the Balkans was thus a necessary but inadequate proviso for Austro-Russian hostility.

Soviet-American rivalry in the Third World seems to conform to a similar dynamic. It is an important source of tension between the superpowers, but is unlikely in and of itself to cause a war between them. Almost from the beginning of the Cold War, Washington and Moscow have sought to extend or consolidate their influence among the nonaligned countries of the world, many of which have only recently gained their independence. Superpower penetration into the Middle East, Africa, and Southeast Asia, just like earlier Austro-Russian involvement in the Balkans, has been facilitated by internal local rivalries that encouraged one or more regional antagonists to look for outside support.

Superpower competition in the Third World also resembles the scramble for colonies in Africa and Asia during the late nineteenth century. The colonization was at first limited to territories that had obvious strategic and economic value to the powers involved. Later, expansion became a goal in its own right, even if it was always justified in the name of some strategic imperative. Today's superpower search for influence is similar. At first, it was concentrated along the peripheries of the Soviet Union where for obvious strategic reasons Americans and Russians both sought to establish their political primacy. Competition in countries farther afield has also been motivated by compelling reasons of state. In the Middle East, for example, important economic and strategic prizes have been at stake. However, this is not true for much of Africa or for the peripheral backwaters of the Middle East where the competition for influence has been no less intense.

Soviet-American competition in the Third World seems increasingly unrelated to any tangible interest of either superpower. As often as not, influence appears to be sought as an end in itself, and a costly end at that. Both Moscow and Washington have spent vast sums in pursuit of primacy in Third World countries, even though the political and strategic payoffs of this quest have often proved marginal or transitory. The Soviet experience in Guinea, Angola, and Egypt, and the American involvement in Iran, are all cases in point. Each superpower nevertheless remains on the lookout for an opportunity to supplant its rival's influence in some Third World capital. When the opportunity to do so arises, as it did for the Soviet Union in Ethiopia, or for the United States in Egypt, leaders are willing to expend considerable resources toward this end. The superpowers have made the importance of these struggles self-justifying. Like the great game of colonial competition in the nineteenth century, these struggles have become one means of determining the relative status of the superpowers. Successive American administrations have also given every evidence of believing that important third parties will draw inferences about American power and resolve on the basis of their success or failure in Third World encounters.

So far, the superpowers have avoided any really acute showdowns over their respective levels of influence in Third World countries. The most serious confrontation to date took place at the height of the October 1973 War between Israel and Egypt when Moscow threatened military intervention to save its sorely pressed client, Sadat's Egypt. (Kissinger, 1982: 575–90; Heikal, 1975; Nixon, 1978; Sadat, 1978; Quandt, 1977; George, 1983; Stein, forthcoming; Blechman, 1982; Hart, 1982: 132–56; Garthoff, 1984; Golan, 1984: 185–217.) President Nixon, in his strongly worded response to this threat, actually drew a parallel between the pre-1914 Balkans and the contemporary Middle East. (Rabin, 1979: 178.)

Moscow raised the prospect of intervention in the Middle East not only because its position in Egypt was at stake but also because of the way in which it was being challenged. The Soviets were certainly displeased about Egypt becoming a client of the United States, but, as later events demonstrated, they were prepared to live with this setback. However, they were unwilling to accept Egypt's total military humiliation, and, by extension, their own, as they had equipped and trained her army and air force. This would have diminished their standing as a great power. It would also have lessened their value as an ally throughout the Third World, as the arms and military training they were prepared to offer constituted their principal appeal to so many of these countries.

The United States was sensitive to Soviet concerns; anticipating a strong Soviet response, Nixon and Kissinger forced a cease-fire on a reluctant Israel at the point when it was about to achieve a decisive victory over its Egyptian adversary. The Soviet threat to intervene actually came after the cease-fire had broken down. There is some evidence that Soviet leaders believed that they had been tricked by Kissinger; they apparently concluded that he had proposed a cease-fire to lull them into inaction while all the time secretly encouraging Israel to continue its advance. Subsequent American insistence that Israel respect the cease-fire overcame Soviet suspicions and quickly brought the crisis to an end.

The October War demonstrates the extent to which the superpowers are sensitive to each other's important interests. So does the fact that for over twenty years they have avoided a confrontation as serious as the Cuban missile crisis, despite their sometimes intense competition for influence. Third World rivalry is nevertheless dangerous because there is always some risk that the superpowers will be dragged into a military conflict by virtue of the actions of their clients. This "tail wagging the dog" phenomenon has brought about superpower confrontations on more than one occasion in the Middle East and may also have been responsible for the Korean War.

In this competition it is well to remember the immediate origins of World War I. Tails wagged dogs in 1914 because of three structural attributes of the international political system: (1) minor powers with major grievances; (2) well-publicized great power commitments to these allies that made it impossible to abandon them without suffering intolerable loss of prestige at home and abroad; and (3) a fragile alliance structure that made the leading powers of the two opposing alliance systems more willing to risk war than the breakup of their alliances. Two of these conditions exist today. The world is full of minor powers that harbor territorial ambitions at the expense of their neighbors or would like to do away with them altogether. Some of these states are clients of the superpowers. Moscow and Washington back regional antagonists in the Korean peninsula, south Asia, the Middle East, Africa, and Latin America. The two Koreas, Vietnam, India, Pakistan, Israel, and Syria have sufficiently close and important enough relationships with their respective superpower backers to be confident of the support they require to maintain themselves as powerful regional entities.

The Paranoia of the Powerful

Until now, the superpowers have been anxious to avoid any head-on confrontation provoked by their respective clients or allies. They have not only studiously avoided issuing blank checks but rather have sought to restrain their clients in situations that threatened to provoke a wider superpower confrontation. Unlike their 1914 counterparts, they do not perceive their respective alliances as threatened by imminent dissolution. They give every evidence of fearing the prospect of a super-power war much more than the loss of a client.

The fear of war and the caution it engenders constitute one of the major differences between today and 1914. Fear and caution act as an important barrier to war but one that may not exist indefinitely. In 1914 several of the great powers became more disposed to risk-taking because of the serious problems they faced at home and abroad. Their leaders were willing to assume the risks associated with adventurous foreign policies because they were convinced there was no other way to cope with or overcome their countries' problems. Should the superpowers come to confront domestic and foreign problems of the same magnitude, their leaders might be tempted to act in similar ways.

We can hope that such a situation never arises. There are even reasons for being cautiously optimistic in this regard. Neither super-power confronts the kind of escalating domestic problems that threatened the very survival of several of the great powers in 1914. Nor, given the basis of superpower military strength, is it likely that the balance of power will swing decisively against one or the other of them, or be perceived by either to do so. Nevertheless, the possibility of either development cannot be entirely discounted. Let us therefore speculate about the circumstances for both superpowers, starting with the Soviet Union, by which such threatening circumstances could come to pass.

The view from the spires of the Kremlin cannot be very encouraging. Soviet domestic and foreign problems can only be expected to become more acute in the years ahead because of the continuing hostility of China, a frustrating war in Afghanistan, intensified strategic competition with the United States, and the declining reliability of the Warsaw Pact. A stagnant economy will impose serious constraints on efforts to cope with all of these problems.

In Eastern Europe the combination of nationalism and economic stagnation has already touched off a revolution in Poland. For the time being the threat of radical change has been contained by the imposition of a military dictatorship. But Poland's new leaders appear as incapable as their predecessors in coping with the root causes of unrest. The conditions that led to the emergence of Solidarity in Poland exist in varying degrees elsewhere in Eastern Europe and must constitute a cause for serious concern in Moscow. (Lebow, 1982: 185–236.)

Soviet military intervention in East Germany, Hungary, Czechoslovakia, and by proxy in Poland makes it apparent that Moscow views its primacy in Eastern Europe as an essential precondition of its security. One reason for this is the permeability of the Soviet Union to events in Eastern Europe, an ironic outcome of almost four decades of Soviet efforts to orient the political, economic, and cultural lives of these countries toward the East. At the time of the Czechoslovak invasion, Brezhnev is reported to have told Władysław Gomułka that all Warsaw Pact nations must contribute forces for the operation because in the absence of East bloc solidarity the unrest might spill over into the Ukraine. (*New York Times*, August 28, 1980: 8.)

The Soviets thus appear to subscribe to their own domino theory, one that makes more sense than the American fear in the 1960s of falling dominoes in Southeast Asia. Soviet leaders, like the tsars before them, fear that political liberalization anywhere in Eastern Europe will lead to demands for similar freedoms within the Soviet Union itself. The actual defection of a satellite from Soviet-style socialism or the Warsaw Pact would have even more profound repercussions. If all or even part of Eastern Europe ever succeeded in breaking away, Soviet control of the Baltic republics and the Ukraine would be threatened. Both these areas, as well as most of the other border regions of the Soviet Union, are populated by nationalities that are antagonistic to Russian domination but quiescent because of their respect and fear of Soviet power. This is one important reason why the Soviets had to crush the workers' uprising in East Germany in 1953 and invade Hungary in 1956 and Czechoslovakia in 1968.

The communist governments of Eastern Europe will have an increasingly difficult time in maintaining themselves. They must satisfy two masters: the Kremlin and their own people. Most have attempted to do this by following Soviet guidance with respect to their internal political and economic structure and foreign policy while at the same time trying to win popular support by raising the living standards of their people. Hungary, Poland, and East Germany have all followed this strategy, one that Khrushchev derisively dubbed "goulash communism." Since the end of the Prague Spring, the Czech government has attempted to pursue this approach as well. Romania has developed a variant: ideological rigidity at home and a semi-independent policy abroad, the latter designed to appeal to the national feelings of the Romanian people. Bulgaria, with a history of close relations with Russia, is a special case. (*East European Assessment*, 1981.)

In the years ahead it will become increasingly difficult for Eastern European governments to satisfy both their constituencies. Most of these governments have never really succeeded in making affluence a substitute for political freedom and meaningful national indepen-dence. As the events in Poland demonstrated, Eastern Europeans are far from satisfied with their standard of living and attribute much of the problem to mismanagement. For many reasons, of course, Poland is a special case. But even in East Germany, certainly the most prosper-ous of the satellites, people are disgruntled over the differences between their standard of living and that of the West. They are also well aware of the differences, as 60 to 65 percent of East Germans watch West German television every night. Dissatisfaction is almost certain to increase as the economic prospects for Eastern Europe decline.

Economic problems in Eastern Europe are likely to have political consequences, as the troubles in Poland have made apparent. Wide-spread unrest in any of these countries will compel its government to make economic or conceivably even political concessions in order to keep the lid on protest. However, Eastern European governments can go only so far in this direction without running afoul of Moscow. And to the extent that Soviet leaders feel threatened by international developments, the latitude they allow the Eastern Europeans is likely to diminish. The point may be reached where these governments can no longer satisfy their two disparate constituencies. The Soviets will then face the choice of intervening directly or of allowing their satel-lites to become more responsive to popular demands. Either alterna-tive could have dire consequences for Soviet security and would be certain to make the Soviets feel more insecure and accordingly more committed to demonstrating their resolve.

Abroad, the picture is equally bleak. Sino-Soviet relations, poisoned for more than a decade, show no signs of improving. Mao Tse-tung's successors continue to insist on the same terms for rapprochement: demilitarization of Mongolia and the Sino-Soviet border. The Soviet-Chinese Friendship Treaty expired in April 1980 and was not renewed. Bilateral contacts have continued to decline, and contacts in interna-tional forums remain cool and formal. Chinese propaganda efforts against the Soviet Union have increased in scope and intensity as have Chinese attempts to foster subversion within the USSR. The Chinese also seem on the road to putting their own house in order and are intent on pursuing more pragmatic policies aimed at rapid economic development. At the same time they have continued with their strategic weapons program, although they have made no major effort to modernize their largely obsolescent conventional forces. (Tajima, 1981.)

On China's southern flank the Soviet Union has provided billions of dollars of military assistance to Vietnam. Since the Soviet-Vietnamese Friendship Treaty of March 1978, the Russians have become ever more deeply involved in the training, resupply, and logistics of their Vietnamese ally. Soviet aid, estimated to represent some 25 percent of the Vietnamese GNP, has enabled that country to pursue the conquest of Indochina. Soviet support of Vietnam constitutes another source of Sino-Soviet tension as Chinese-Vietnamese hostility remains acute in the aftermath of their 1979 war. For the duration of the 1980s, relations between the two giants of the Eurasian landmass will be severely strained although they probably will not lead to hostilities. (Pike, 1984: 67–90.)

If the Soviets have become more concerned for their security in the East, they must also be more anxious about their position in the West. The failure of détente touched off a new Cold War with the United States. Following the Soviet invasion of Afghanistan, American defense spending increased dramatically under both the Carter and Reagan administrations. Moscow now faces an intensified and more diverse strategic threat. The Pershing IIs currently being deployed in Europe put many Soviet ICBM command and control centers at risk. Trident II missiles, scheduled to be deployed later in the decade aboard Ohio Class submarines, constitute an even greater threat. Trident II is the first sea-based intercontinental ballistic missile with sufficient accuracy to destroy hardened point targets. These missiles could be launched from submarines in the Indian Ocean and reach the missile fields of southern Russia in less than half the time of a missile launched from the continental United States. (Wit, 1982: 163–74; Arkin, 1984: 5–6.) Pershings and Tridents will be augmented by air- and ground-launched cruise missiles, new bombers making use of "stealth" technology, a burgeoning antisatellite capability, and perhaps even a limited defensive capability against ICBMs. Collectively, these weapons will make Soviet strategic systems and their command and control much more vulnerable. The Soviets must also contend with the strategic force modernization being carried out by France and Britain, the latter committed to replacing its obsolescent Polaris missiles with the new Trident system.

Whatever the actual extent of the strategic shift in favor of the West, it is almost certain to be perceived by the Russians as greater and more threatening than reality warrants. Strategic calculations are almost always based on worst-case analysis. Force comparisons of this kind result in exaggerated perceptions of threat. They also tend to make analysts blind to an adversary's fears for his own security, fears derived in part from his own worst-case estimates of the strategic balance. Insensitivity to an adversary's insecurities encourages analysts and policymakers alike to infer aggressive intentions from his force structure. If, by their calculations, that country possesses more than enough military capability for what they consider its legitimate defensive needs, any further buildup can only be motivated by aggressive designs. The alarm in the United States in the 1970s in response to the Soviet strategic buildup was to a great extent the result of such a perceptual process. The same kind of response can be expected from the Soviets in the late 1980s when the new American forces are deployed.

Our analysis has treated threats to Soviet security sequentially. Moscow, however, must consider them collectively. The ultimate Soviet nightmare is encirclement: a United States–Japan–China–NATO coalition directed against the USSR and capable of being exploited by Beijing in support of its "revanchist" goals. Georgy Arbatov, director of the Institute on the United States and Canada, has acknowledged this concern. According to Arbatov:

> the most important geo-political reality is the fact that the Soviet Union under present circumstances has to regard as its potential adversaries not only the United States but also the NATO allies of the United States, China and Japan. As soon as one includes this factor in the equation the picture becomes radically different. . . . The ratio of the Warsaw Treaty Organization and the NATO budgets is 1:1.5 in favor of NATO. If one brings Japan and China into the picture the correlation will be at least 1:2. (1982: 179–80.)

The Soviets themselves must recognize that encirclement is nowhere close to becoming a reality. NATO countries are reluctant to enter into any commitment outside of Europe, and they become positively nervous when the United States does; Japan, although it recently decided to spend more on defense, is not on the verge of rearming and has been very cautious about being drawn into the Sino-Soviet dispute; and the United States, while anxious to use China as a means of offsetting Soviet power, has carefully avoided entering into any kind of formal alliance with Beijing and, until recently, has refrained from selling her anything that could be put to direct military use. If anything, Sino-

American cooperation has stalled since Reagan came to power because of his administration's solicitous attitude toward Taiwan. Encirclement will therefore remain only a fear in the Soviet mind unless *they* themselves act in ways to bring such an alliance into being. Here, the experience of pre-1914 Germany offers a disturbing precedent.

Ever since the creation of the German Reich in 1871, the nightmare of German leaders was their encirclement by hostile neighbors. In the West, French antagonism was taken for granted. In the East, Bismarck maintained friendly relations with both Russia and Austria-Hungary, a task that required all of his considerable skill. His successors possessed neither his finesse nor wisdom and allowed Russo-German relations to deteriorate to the point where Russia moved closer to France. The Franco-Russian alliance of 1893 appeared to lend credence to German fears of encirclement. These fears intensified in the succeeding years. Italy loosened her ties with Germany and moved closer to France. Anglo-German relations, carefully nurtured by Bismarck, also deteriorated as a result of German naval pretensions. Worst of all, the Anglo-French Entente of 1904 raised the specter of Britain joining the Franco-Russian alliance against Germany. The Entente prompted desperate German leaders to provoke a confrontation with France, the Moroccan crisis of 1905–6, in the hope of separating France from Britain. But the crisis had the opposite effect; it brought Britain and France closer together and encouraged them to initiate staff talks with the purpose of coordinating their military planning in case of war with Germany. Subsequent crises provoked by Germany in 1909 and 1911 to break the ring of encirclement were similarly self-defeating and brought into being the very combination of alliances that she had feared.

The Soviets undeniably have a similar fear of encirclement and, alas, a similar propensity for diplomatic clumsiness. The Russo-Finnish War and the Stalin-Hitler Pact, it must be remembered, were part and parcel of the Soviets' last response to the threat of encirclement. If the Soviet Union's relations with her neighbors continue to deteriorate, it is conceivable that some future Sino-American or Sino-Japanese security initiative will provoke sufficient anxiety in Moscow for Soviet leaders to contemplate a drastic response in the hope of preserving their strategic position. However, heavy-handed efforts at brinkmanship are just as likely to strengthen their adversaries' resolve. This would only exacerbate Moscow's insecurity. The danger here is that such a threatening environment would encourage the Soviets, as it did the Germans in 1914, to contemplate even more desperate measures in the hope that they could keep matters from getting too far out of hand.

I have described a less than encouraging future for the Soviet Union; admittedly, this is something of a worst-case analysis. In practice, we must hope that neither the domestic nor the international situation deteriorates to the point where Soviet leaders feel so threatened that they are attracted to risky foreign policies. But even less dramatic setbacks at home or abroad would still leave Moscow in a less favorable strategic position and facing intensified Chinese hostility and greater Sino-American collaboration. Within the Soviet empire, Eastern Europeans will become more restive and difficult to control, as may some of her own national minorities. Finally, a lower growth rate, and possibly even economic stagnation, will make it impossible for Soviet leaders to continue their current level of military spending and still hope to satisfy growing domestic demands for more consumer goods. A cutback in either area—a reduction in domestic spending seems the more likely of the two—will have detrimental implications for Soviet security.

At the very least, therefore, Soviet leaders are likely to see themselves as vulnerable and on the defensive. Historically, policymakers in such circumstances have tended to exaggerate, not to minimize, the extent of their own weaknesses. They have also exhibited an exaggerated concern for their credibility, convinced that any sign of weakness on their part will encourage more aggressive behavior by their adversaries. Austria-Hungary and Russia behaved this way on the eve of World War I. American policymakers displayed a similar response in the aftermath of their foreign policy failures. The Soviet dilemma, which objectively is likely to be greater in magnitude and more enduring in its consequences, can be expected to engender an even more irrational and pessimistic outlook among Soviet leaders. Their fear of the future does not bode well for the security of either superpower.

Moscow will not be alone in its pessimism about the future. From the vantage point of Washington the world will also look increasingly bleak and threatening. America's position of leadership in the West will almost certainly continue to decline, for both economic and political reasons. NATO's cohesion will erode as will that of other American alliances around the world. In addition, one or more of Washington's clients in the Third World may be replaced by regimes hostile to the United States and everything it stands for.

Widespread opposition in Europe to the deployment of Pershing IIs and cruise missiles made the nuclear question an important and divisive political issue in the United Kingdom, Belgium, and the Federal

Republic of Germany. The peace movements in these countries, even though they failed to prevent deployment of the new weapons, have become formidable political forces by virtue of their opposition to them. They compelled important Northern European socialist parties to disassociate themselves from Alliance policy with regard to nuclear weapons. While it is true that socialist parties generally adopt more extreme positions when they are in opposition, their commitments to antinuclear policies mean that when either the British Labour party or the German Social Democrats next return to power, the political-military strains between one or both of the two most important European members of NATO and the United States will become more pronounced. Heightened tensions between the superpowers, brought about perhaps by the likely failure of the Reagan administration to reach any arms control agreement with the Soviets, will strengthen the European peace movements and facilitate the electoral prospects of the socialist parties. U.S. military intervention in Latin America, Libya, or anywhere else in the Third World would make such developments even more likely.

Even in the absence of left-wing electoral victories, growing political-military tensions between Washington and most NATO capitals will place serious strains on the Alliance. Among the most important issues that divide Washington from the Europeans are NATO's possible role beyond the confines of Europe, the nature of NATO's military strategy on the Central European front, and the appropriate political approach to pursue toward the Soviet Union. To the extent that the Reagan administration or its successor pushes its European allies toward adopting controversial American positions on any of these issues, tensions will arise regardless of the political coloring of the governments in London, Bonn, or The Hague. The American commitment to an increasingly offensive strategy on the Central European front, if seriously pursued within the NATO context, could become one of the most divisive political-military issues of the next decade, for it runs directly counter to the current German tendency to place more emphasis on defense. If political relations with the Soviet Union remain frozen, such a strategy will also be seen by many Europeans as unduly provocative.

The Strategic Defense Initiative (SDI) also has the potential to be extremely divisive. As of March 1986 the Germans, British, and Italians have agreed to participate in the American-sponsored research program. However, all these governments have expressed the hope that the real effect of a Western commitment to SDI will be to facilitate an arms control agreement with the Russians. If this fails to come about because of an overriding American commitment to forge ahead with space weaponry, the political backlash in Western Europe will be enormous. If Washington renounces the ABM Treaty in order to test components of SDI, as the Reagan administration appears committed to doing, it will provoke an even more serious division between European conservatives and socialists and a greater rift within the Alliance itself. Beyond these specific policy disagreements, the Alliance confronts a more general crisis brought about by the growing assertiveness of Western European governments and peoples. Europeans across the political spectrum are increasingly reluctant to accept unquestioningly American leadership on political-military issues. European assertiveness has many causes: a growing sense of political confidence on the part of European elites, greater recognition of the ways in which American and European interests diverge, and, perhaps above all, the inept way in which the last two American administrations have dealt with their allies.

Changing European attitudes put a premium on political skill, more than ever essential to both sides of the Atlantic in order to steer the Alliance safely through the shoals of discord that lie ahead. Political skill requires sensitivity to the worldviews and political forces that shape allied policy preferences. This kind of understanding has been noticeably absent in the Reagan administration. Instead, it has lectured to the Europeans, publicly at times, about the evils of the Russians and the rightness of the American strategy for coping with them. To some degree this behavior is a result of the remarkably parochial worldview of an administration staffed by officials with limited foreign policy experience and with uncompromising ideological convictions that are at odds with the outlook of most of their Western European counterparts. However, it is also a reflection of the fact that American and European elites share less in common with each other than they did ten or twenty years ago. They also know less about each other, given increasingly divergent educational, professional, and political experiences. In the long term, this divergence may constitute the greatest threat to the survival of the Alliance.

The political challenge to the American alliance structure is not limited to Europe. Important allies in other parts of the world have become increasingly alienated and assertive. New Zealand's Labour government declared that country a nuclear-free zone and categorically rejects visits by American warships that are nuclear-powered or carry nuclear weapons. Australians are debating their country's role in

ANZUS, and there is growing opposition to installations in that country that help to provide intelligence for U.S. strategic forces. Japan, America's most politically important ally in the Far East, is for the moment quiescent. In response to Washington's prodding, the Nakasone government broke with tradition and raised the defense budget beyond 1 percent of GNP. However, the currents affecting other allies are likely, sooner or later, to influence Japan, touched off perhaps by other developments in the Far East. (Morrison, 1985: 22–24; Tsurutani, 1982: 175–87; Mochizuki, 1983: 152–79.)

American influence in the Third World is also on the wane. (Feinberg, 1983; LaFeber, 1983; Leiken, 1984; *Washington Times*, June 6, 1985: 3D.) This is most obvious in Latin America where Washington may confront even more serious challenges than the ones it currently faces in El Salvador, Guatemala, Honduras, and Nicaragua. Failure to topple the Sandinistas or at least to moderate their alleged support for revolutionary movements in Central America will make the American government feel acutely threatened in its own political backyard. The collapse of one or more of the conservative regimes it now supports in Central America and their replacement by leftist juntas with close ties to Cuba or Moscow would make the situation all the worse. Nor can one foreclose the possibility of a revolution in South Korea or the Philippines with strong anti-American overtones. Another possibility is some kind of shock in the Middle East, perhaps the overthrow of the Saudi monarchy and the subsequent demise of the Western position in the Gulf. Any development of this kind, coupled with a continuing political-military challenge in Latin America and the further questioning of U.S. policy by important European allies, would seriously aggravate the already existing American sense of isolation and vulnerability.

By the end of the decade the world may witness the bizarre and frightening phenomenon of two awesomely powerful but painfully insecure superpowers, each acutely sensitive to its own vulnerabilities and deeply concerned about the other's efforts to exploit them. The paranoia of the powerful can and has constituted a profound source of international instability. History teaches that policymakers in such circumstances tend to exhibit an exaggerated concern for their credibility, convinced that any sign of weakness will only encourage further challenges from their adversaries. In the case of Germany, this concern found expression in a series of aggressive foreign policy ventures that brought about the very encirclement German leaders feared and ultimately drove them to war.

If anything is more disturbing than a great power acting in this manner, it is the prospect of two superpower adversaries doing so.

Both already display tendencies in this direction. The United States has a remarkable, some call it pathological, concern for its credibility. Democratic and Republican policymakers alike also exaggerate the extent to which Soviet or Soviet-Cuban machinations lie behind every threatening Third World upheaval. The Shaba invasion, Nicaragua, and El Salvador are all cases in point. A series of foreign policy setbacks in Indochina, Angola, and Iran have prompted American leaders to case about for cheap and dramatic ways of displaying resolve. They have succumbed to what could be called "the Mayaguez mentality," as this was the first effort to use force to signal resolve in the immediate aftermath of the American failure in Indochina. In this episode President Ford launched an air, sea, and land attack against Cambodia, which had intercepted the freighter Mayaguez and briefly held its crew. The seamen were already in the process of being released at the time of the U.S. attack. Thirty-eight U.S. Marines and unknown numbers of Cambodians were killed in the attack.

American willingness to consider intervention in the Middle East in 1970 during the Jordanian crisis was also a self-conscious attempt to demonstrate resolve as a response to Watergate. (Garfinkle, 1985: 117–38.) So was the 1973 alert during the Yom Kippur War. According to Henry Kissinger, there was a deep fear, shared by many of the members of the Washington Special Action Group (Kissinger, Schlesinger, Colby, Moorer, Haig, and Scowcroft) that the Soviet leadership might be tempted to intervene unilaterally in the belief that the United States was paralyzed into inaction by Watergate. (Kissinger, 1982: 587.) When Reagan administration officials write their memoirs, it would not be surprising to learn that the invasion of Grenada, that came hard on the heels of the ineffectual U.S. intervention in Lebanon and the suicide bombing of Marine headquarters in Beirut, was motivated at least in part by the perceived need to demonstrate resolve and foreign policy competence.

American policymakers are not alone in their paranoia. Soviet policymakers also appear to exaggerate the malevolent influence of their adversary. Soviet spokesmen have repeatedly charged the United States with responsibility for the turmoil it confronts in Afghanistan and Poland. Some of these charges are obviously propaganda, but to some extent they may also reflect the real views of Soviet officials, as sincerely held if equally farfetched as some of the anti-Soviet charges made by their American counterparts. (Griffith, 1984: 3–51.) Distortion of reality may be particularly pronounced with respect to the Polish situation, which must pose a serious cognitive dilemma for Soviet leaders. To recognize the events of 1980 for what they were, a workers' revolution against a bureaucratic dictatorship imposed and maintained by Moscow, would entail calling into question the most fundamental myths of Soviet-style Marxism. The men of the Kremlin accordingly have every psychological and political incentive to explain away Polish developments by any means they can. The long arm of American imperialism can play a useful role in this regard just as the Soviet-communist conspiracy was invoked by Americans a generation ago to explain their "loss" of China. Unfortunately, such illusions, while comforting, also tend to have damaging long-term foreign policy consequences.

The dynamic we have just described has led to a situation in which the political or strategic advantage either superpower can gain by one-upping its rival in any arena of competition is more than likely to be offset by the cost of the heightened threat it conveys. "Victories" of this kind only encourage the other superpower to look for some way of recouping its loss, setting in motion an escalating spiral of competition and risk-taking. We are currently witnessing such a process with respect to Euromissiles.

A deteriorating situation of this kind calls for mutual restraint. Unfortunately, the Reagan administration, at least, is committed instead to a policy of confrontation. Many of its leading officials are convinced that American security will be enhanced by pushing the Soviets up against the wall, politically, economically, and strategically. Their unspoken but frequently hinted-at assumption is that a strategically outclassed and economically strapped Soviet Union would respond by moderating its foreign policy and perhaps even loosening the reins of repression at home. With this end in mind they are pursuing a major strategic and conventional arms buildup, a major part of which is an expensive quest for a ballistic missile defense, and are on the verge of renouncing arms control agreements that stand in the way of this quest.

The history of this Cold War, and of other great power rivalries before it, reveal that the side that perceives itself at a strategic or political disadvantage rarely responds by offering concessions. It is much more likely to act tough in the hope of covering up its perceived weakness. This is what happened on the eve of World War I. The Reagan administration, in its historical and political ignorance, seems intent on replicating the same kind of international environment. We must hope that the American people and their elected representatives, many of whom are already disturbed by the course of this administration's policy, compel it to moderate its strategic and foreign policy before it succeeds in provoking the very behavior it is striving so hard to prevent.

17

The Future of Dominant-Subordinate Systems

Michael I. Handel

Although many of the traditional descriptions of relations between the strong and the weak in the period since 1945 seem to conform to the realist model, a new trend in this relationship has been evolving. (Handel, 1981.) Initially, changes in the international system during the late 1940s and early 1950s were so subtle that they could still be interpreted in light of the old paradigm of power politics; since the late 1960s many anomalies have surfaced that now raise serious questions about the continued validity of that paradigm. Despite having under-gone numerous changes, the relationship between strong and weak nations can still be explained by the traditional analysis of power politics, but applying the same model today produces very different results. Relations between the strong and the weak are no longer determined by considerations of pure power. Military and even eco-nomic strength cannot, as in the past, simply be translated into or correlated with political influence, spheres of influence, or hegemonic control. While the decline in the direct utility of power is unmistakable today, its origins go back to the period following World War II, and its full implications will become evident only in the years ahead.

The concepts of *dominant* and *subordinate* have become relics of the past, as irrelevant as "gunboat diplomacy," "open door policies," and "capitulations." The evidence is in every daily newspaper. The dominant powers do not seem to dominate, and the subordinate refuse to obey. In fighting against France and the United States, the Vietnamese refused to behave according to the conventional wisdom, which would have had them bow to the logic of the superior power or the great powers. Just as the Soviets have not been able to impose their will in Afghanistan despite their superior military power, the Iranians occupied the U.S. embassy in Tehran with impunity (something a subordinate would not be expected to do, considering the power differential involved). The United States did not send its gunboats to the Persian Gulf, nor did it threaten major military action. The Greeks do not try to please the United States, nor do the Israelis, who depend upon the United States, exhibit the subordinate type of behavior expected of a client state. The Soviet Union could not control Yugoslav or Chinese behavior to accommodate its interests nor can it dictate Romanian or Albanian foreign policy. The United States could not prevent Cuba from becoming a communist client of the USSR or today modify the behavior of the Nicaraguan leftist government. Following the bombing of the U.S. Marine position at the Beirut airport, the United States quickly withdrew from Lebanon. Such experiences not only reflect the changing attitudes and behavior patterns of the great powers but also those of middle powers and smaller states. Israel had to leave most of the territory it occupied in Lebanon, still unable to impose its will on a much weaker state. These and many other examples seem to indicate that our frequent resort to the terms dominant and subordinate is unrealistic. If current trends in the relations between the powerful and weaker states continue, these terms will become even less relevant in the future. Perhaps we are reaching a stage in international politics in which the use of raw power is becoming more and more difficult, as it has within modern societies.

Why are the strong reluctant to use their power? Why has the use of raw military power become increasingly less effective in recent years? Why have direct intervention and dominance become so much more costly than indirect intervention or no intervention at all? In this chapter I will identify and briefly discuss five interrelated major trends that are helpful in answering these questions:

(1) Democratic values.

(2) The slow but steady decline in the importance assigned to foreign policy since 1945 and the gradual increase in the relative importance of domestic politics.

(3) The nuclear revolution.

(4) The increasing cost of direct dominance and use of power.

(5) The realization that almost all raw materials can be obtained without the necessity of having direct control over other states.

Hegemony and the Rise of Democratic Values

Since the beginning of the nineteenth century democratic values have become the accepted norm for a modern state, regardless of the degree to which they have actually been implemented. Democracy is considered the ideal form of government for constitutional monarchies, republics, socialist states, and communist states. It is interesting to note that from the nineteenth century onward, democracy flourished in the countries that were often also the most important hegemonic powers. In the long run this generated a considerable amount of tension between the values of the domestic political systems and the use of force and power in relations with other states. Inasmuch as democracy became the accepted ideal political system domestically, the contradiction between the patterns of domestic and foreign policy could only be modified in the long run by adjusting the pattern of foreign policy behavior to conform to the values of domestic politics. The right to self-determination, to freedom of choice and expression, had to be extended to the outside world. Before World War II the British, French, Belgians, and Dutch could maintain thriving democratic political systems at home and still control vast colonial possessions. The inherent tension in this situation was not evident. But after World War II the contradiction between these two worlds became too obvious to be continued for long. The Wilsonian diplomacy of self-determination was one of the earliest manifestations of this trend (although it did not prevent Woodrow Wilson or subsequent presidents from pursuing a form of gunboat diplomacy in the Caribbean and Central America). After World War II the great European powers found it impossible to continue their direct control of vast overseas colonial empires; having been weakened by the war, they needed to focus most of their energies on the reconstruction of their own economies. Aside from this decline in power, the principal explanation for the demise of the colonial era had to do with the mood of public opinion in Paris and London.

France lost its wars with Vietnam and Algeria as much in Paris as it did on the battlefield. British public opinion was not prepared to support the Suez expedition and pay the price of maintaining British colonial possessions. Likewise, the United States lost the war in Vietnam not so much on the battlefield as in the prolonged fight involving American opinion, the mass media, and congressional support. As the war dragged on, the American public asked more and more questions. Finally, the choice was between breaking the fiber of American society and its national consensus, or continuation of the war. Since the United States preferred democracy to success in war, the choice became inevitable.

Israel had a similar experience in its war in Lebanon. Israeli democracy could accept a military operation on a limited scale—but not a prolonged war and the occupation of another country against the will of its people. Again the choice was between the survival of Israeli democracy and continuation of the war. Israel decided to withdraw from Lebanon. (Israel's control of the West Bank will ultimately create a clash between Israeli democracy on the one hand and continued control of the West Bank population against its will. Since many Israelis view the West Bank as important to Israel's national security, it is not clear that democracy will triumph in this case.)

The weaker states have learned that the key to victory is not on the battlefield but in the enemy's capital. In fact, the campaign on the battlefield is conducted and directed with an eye to its influence on the adversary's domestic public opinion. This was very clearly understood by the Vietnamese and Algerians and is increasingly understood by Israel's Arab neighbors.

Both the black opposition in South Africa and the anti-Marcos forces in the Philippines have come to understand that the best way to achieve their goals is by an appeal to American public opinion, to American democratic values. Indeed, the Philippine opposition to President Marcos achieved a great and bloodless victory by winning the battle for U.S. public opinion, by obtaining congressional support, and as a result also the support of the U.S. president. The blacks in South Africa have begun to make progress since they captured the attention of the American mass media and hence U.S. public opinion. Similar policies are being pursued by Central and Latin American states as well as by other weaker states. The weaker states will increasingly rely on manipulating and convincing public opinion within the great powers in order to achieve their goals. In this respect, of course, the USSR cannot be manipulated as easily (if at all) as the United States. This does not mean that in the long run, as changes occur in the Soviet domestic system, that the weaker states will not also develop access to Soviet "public opinion." (See Handel, 1981: 265–77.)

From the Primacy of Foreign Policy to the Primacy of Domestic Politics

The instability of the European system throughout history and until the end of World War II gave rise to the Rankeian axiom that the foreign interests of a state must take precedence over its domestic affairs. Domestic affairs cannot be addressed as long as the survival of the state has been placed in jeopardy by external threats. The Rankeian insistence on *Der Primat der Aussenpolitik* can be traced back to Machiavelli and Thucydides and to the beginnings of recorded European history.

All of this changed by the end of World War II for reasons that will be discussed below, but the recognition of such changes in the European system has come about very slowly because of the long tradition of the primacy of foreign affairs and the centuries of continued instability. As is always the case, human perception and the theories reflecting these perceptions always lag behind the changes that take place in the environment.

It is not surprising that the major powers were forced to give foreign policy precedence over domestic politics in view of the instability of the European system and as a result also the global system before and after World War I. During this period both balance of power and the traditional alliance systems of the League of Nations failed as Europe went through a transition from a homogeneous system to a tense antagonistic ideological-revolutionary system. The tensions over state borders in the 1930s, the revisionist and aggressive policies of the fascist countries, the inability to solve problems through compromise and negotiation, the frequent resort to naked force, and the rise of communism in Russia all indicated the need to view the external environment as being of paramount concern. States could and did disappear from the map of Europe (e.g., Austria, Latvia, Lithuania, Estonia, Czechoslovakia). If anything, events leading up to World War II, the war itself, and no less its aftermath and the subsequent Cold War only further buttressed belief in the primacy of foreign policy and the implications flowing from this axiomatic assumption.

Although the seeds for the emphasis on domestic politics were already present by 1945, the great powers continued to implement policies based on the primacy of foreign affairs. The fascist powers had disappeared, but the communist regime in the Soviet Union not only remained in power, it exported the communist revolution to Eastern Europe and later attempted to export it on a global scale.

The imperatives of the emphasis on foreign policy are clear: create spheres of influence as broadly as possible in order to directly control the immediate environment and secure your own borders. Direct control is preferable, but where not feasible, supportive alliance systems must be created. These policies were premised on the prolonged traumatic events preceding the two world wars. After World War II significant changes in the international system were completely ignored for two or three decades. The result was the continued reliance on military power, heavy investment in military strength, the acquisition and control of territory (in particular by the USSR), and the development of the zero-sum game mentality. Past experience and fear led to a self-fulfilling prophecy—a tight bipolar system and the tensions of the Cold War.

The realization that the international system had undergone a radical transformation came about only very gradually and in many ways has not been fully recognized even today. The invisible grip of history and past experience is too tenacious to be dissolved through logical and rational analysis alone. Thus, as long as new generations of Soviet citizens are indoctrinated with accounts of the traumatic events of World War II, they will continue to believe that the international environment has not changed since that time.

Objectively speaking, the great powers' need to directly control adjacent spheres of influence has diminished if not disappeared. Neither Germany nor Japan threaten the great powers, and there is no need for directly controlled spheres of influence or buffer zones. Poland or Finland certainly pose no threat to the Soviet Union. If any threat exists, it emanates from the other superpower, and it is primarily based on the existence of intercontinental ballistic missiles, not the danger of conventional war. Territorial acquisitions, spheres of influence, and buffer zones are all irrelevant to the mutual nuclear threat and do nothing to diminish it. Whether or not the USSR controls Cuba is immaterial to the direct security of the United States. The security of the superpowers rests increasingly in their relations with each other but not in the direct control of outside territories. Security as an excuse for pursuing hegemonic policies is irrelevant for the great powers. Other factors reduce the importance of direct or even indirect control over other states in enhancing the national interest. The British, French,

Dutch, Belgians, and Portuguese suffered no harm whatsoever to their political, military, or economic interests when they lost control of their colonial empires. If anything, such disengagement strengthened rather than weakened those states. The same can be said for U.S. involvement in Vietnam and potentially for the USSR in Afghanistan and Eastern Europe. Indirect control is much cheaper and by far more effective. The great powers have discovered the hard way that their interests are best served by indirect involvement and, wherever possible, by no intervention at all.

In the final analysis, control of the external environment is intended to enhance a state's security and thereby add to its quality of life, economic development, material welfare, and political stability. Security is a means to an end, not an end in itself. The rationale for direct intervention in or control of the affairs of other states can only be justified if the cost of control and involvement is smaller than the benefits to be reaped. Since the end of World War II direct intervention has rarely paid off. The French wars in Vietnam and Algeria weakened rather than strengthened France. The U.S. war in Vietnam was not only a negative investment economically and militarily, but almost disrupted the whole fiber of American domestic politics. There is little sense in assigning priority to foreign affairs in the absence of a threat to the survival of the nation—if in the process the state destroys itself from within. In a democratic age when all economic and commercial benefits can be secured without direct control and in which the costs of war have become unbearable, the focus of attention must be on the domestic affairs of the state. Of what value is control by the USSR over Eastern Europe or Afghanistan if its price is retardation of the Soviet Union's economic development (and hence ultimately also its security).

This new order of priority (i.e., the primacy of domestic over foreign politics) already dominates the policies of the European powers, is becoming more and more visible in the post-Vietnam policies of the United States, and is certain to influence the policies of the USSR in the post-Afghanistan era as we approach the end of this century.

The Nuclear Revolution and the Primacy of Avoiding a Nuclear Confrontation Between the Superpowers

Following the development of nuclear weapons by the USSR in 1949, and the subsequent development of fission bombs and intercontinental missiles, the superpowers gradually recognized that a nuclear war between them could only mean the end of civilization as we know it and that there can be no winners in any type of nuclear conflict. They have therefore reluctantly and independently come to the realization that the most important interest they have is the avoidance of nuclear war.

The emergence of this post-World War II interest caused a shift in the paradigm of great-power relationships and to a lesser extent the relationships between the superpowers and the weaker states as well as among the weaker states themselves. Unlike the squaring off of Germany and France in 1914 and 1939, Germany and Russia in 1914, Germany and the USSR in 1941, and Austria and Russia in 1914, a direct confrontation and certainly war between the superpowers has become highly unlikely. The very possibility of a direct confrontation between the United States and the Soviet Union that could lead to war and hence to nuclear escalation is now unthinkable and could serve no rational end. In today's world we can in fact speak about the "primacy of avoiding a nuclear confrontation," hence about "the primacy of avoiding a direct confrontation between the superpowers," rather than about "the primacy of foreign policy."

Although it is clearly understood by most politicians and experts in the 1980s, awareness of the full danger of superpower confrontation was not in evidence during the 1950s and early 1960s, as indicated by the two Berlin crises, by the Quemoy and Matsu crisis, and by the Cuban missile crisis. The outcome in each of these cases indicates that the logic of "the primacy of avoiding a nuclear war" was already pervasive, but at the same time that this understanding was tacit, subconscious, and not as yet clearly formulated.

The Cuban missile crisis was the turning point: it forced the logic of the situation to emerge from the background into the forefront of the relationship between the superpowers. They had finally, albeit reluctantly, arrived at the realization that they could not afford any direct confrontations and that therefore they must also avoid those direct interventions in other parts of the world that could lead to such a confrontation. The ramifications were clear: each could employ direct force only in areas that were not critical to the other side. In other words, the superpowers realized that they could not intervene (as they did in earlier historical periods) in each other's hegemonial spheres of influence (i.e., the United States could not directly or even indirectly intervene in Poland, East Germany, or Czechoslovakia, while the Soviet Union could not risk a large-scale direct intervention in the Western Hemisphere, Western Europe, or the Middle East).

The development of this interest in avoiding a direct confrontation clearly explains why each of the Middle Eastern wars has ended in politically indecisive results. Each superpower had to intervene with its own clients and allies to stop the fighting short of a politically and militarily decisive outcome in order to prevent a superpower confrontation and the possibility of a nuclear war. This is one reason why the United States failed to support and in fact came out against the British, French, and Israeli attempt to take the Suez Canal in 1956. This is also why Israel was twice (in 1967 and 1973) forced to halt its military operations before reaching the culminating point of victory. Although slow to recognize this situation, the regional powers have gradually realized that there is a very definite limit to the utility of military power, and that even if they win on the battlefield, they will find it hard to translate military victories into political gains. The recognition of these constraints on their freedom of action may become more clear to them in the future and may be taken more into account in the formulation of their foreign policies as well as in the design of their military doctrines.

The superpowers could not intervene in each others' spheres of influence or in a region in which their interests are shared (e.g., the Middle East), but each could fight or intervene (outside its own sphere of influence) in Korea, Vietnam, Angola, Ethiopia/Somalia, and Afghanistan. In other words, the only wars they could afford to wage were precisely those that were not worth fighting and where the costs would exceed any benefits. In the modern world of the superpowers what it is possible to fight for without risking a nuclear war is almost by definition not worth the effort.

Intervention in areas of secondary or tertiary importance was in many cases a knee-jerk response to the dictates of the zero-sum game of the bipolar world, in which a missed opportunity was automatically perceived as the other side's gain. In addition, each war was viewed almost exclusively as part of a global contest, rather than in the context of its immediate causes. Intervention was therefore seen as part of a signaling process, that is, part of a global deterrence policy. In the process of fighting these wars of secondary and tertiary importance, the superpowers lost more often than they won. The costs of each war weakened them in relation to the rival superpower instead of augmenting their strength. From its perspective, the Soviet Union could not devise any better policy than that of allowing the United States to waste its power in Vietnam, an involvement that curtailed U.S. ability to pay attention to the rest of the world and simultaneously weakened the popular consensus at home. In the end the Vietnam conflict reduced

U.S. willingness to intervene in other areas. (The Soviet Union did indeed hope to cash in on the American intervention in Vietnam through a redistribution of power in the Middle East. This explains the Soviet policy of encouraging if not pushing the Arabs to go to war against Israel in 1967.)

Although the United States vehemently opposed the Soviet Union's intervention in Afghanistan, from a Machiavellian point of view nothing better could have happened. The Soviet Union has thereby alienated many countries in the Muslim world and has become mired down in a quagmire reminiscent of Vietnam.

The Increased Costs of the Use of Direct Power

The cost of conventional and irregular warfare has increased to such an extent that the readiness and incentive of the great powers to use force and intervene directly have been considerably reduced. The myriad reasons for this can be discussed only briefly in this context.

To begin with, the weaker states have learned that they need not fight to win, but rather not to lose; they must simply try to hold out long enough to win—not on the battlefield—but in their adversary's capital. They have learned that a political victory is more important than a military victory. This type of victory requires patience and time, ingredients that are not always the strongest suit of the great powers. The weaker states have learned that this goal can best be accomplished by penetrating the domestic system of their adversary. To do this they need time; in the process they are, paradoxically, helped by their adversary.

Given the secondary or tertiary importance of their country to the superpower, the military and political leadership of the superpower will find it very difficult initially to send a large number of troops to fight their weaker adversary. As a result, the number of troops first sent to fight in Vietnam or Afghanistan is never large enough to be decisive at the outset; in the meantime, the weaker state or guerrilla force can continue to hold out while the superpower decides whether or not to invest still more resources in an area of relatively little importance. In this sense, time is on the side of the weak.

One reason that the real or absolute power of the superpowers is irrelevant is that they can never apply all the power at their disposal at any given point in time against the weaker state. Concepts such as "compliance capacity" are not applicable here because the superpowers can only commit their troops and employ their superior force in a piecemeal fashion. (See Clausewitz, 1976: book I, chap. 1, section 3; pp. 75–80; and section 8.) This is true not only because the weaker states are not of central importance to the superpowers' survival but also because they must constantly look over their shoulders and maintain power sufficient to support their interests in other regions as well.

A corollary is that this issue of lesser importance for the superpower is the single most vital interest of the weaker state. Thus the stronger power will always have less of an incentive to fight than the weaker state. What is a matter of survival for the weaker state is a matter of choice for the superpower.

Other explanations for the increased cost of direct military intervention are these:

(1) The superpowers' conventional forces are designed for war against each other, not against weaker and less-developed armies. The tanks, aircraft, electronic equipment, etc., procured by the great powers are meant for high technology warfare in Central Europe, not for jungle or desert warfare in difficult terrain. All of this sophisticated equipment is of little relevance in the jungles of Vietnam or the mountains of Afghanistan.

(2) As a result of their potential—though, as argued, not actual —superiority, quantitatively as well as qualitatively, the superpowers tend to dangerously overestimate their own strength and underestimate that of their opponents. This often unintended arrogance can produce tactical defeats and unpleasant surprises on the battlefield. To its detriment, the stronger side may indulge its predilection for straightforward quantitative calculations while ignoring the balance in morale and motivation. It is the very vulnerability of the weaker states that gives them the impetus to develop more creative military doctrines and employ innovative tactics; the more complacent powerful states are, in the meantime, usually content to fight according to existing military doctrines tailored for another type of warfare. Furthermore, the forces of the superpower are often controlled from a distant capital and limited by the political leadership in their choice of tactics and strategy.

(3) The great powers fight, on the whole, according to the accepted rules of the game (particularly the Western democracies, less so the Soviet Union and other authoritarian states), whereas the hard-pressed weaker state will frequently resort to any possible means: terrorism, attacks on civilian population centers, avoidance of combat, and other

advantages provided by guerrilla and other types of irregular warfare.

In many cases the superpower (again, more so the Western democracies) will be much more sensitive to casualties and losses than their weaker opponents who are fighting for mere survival.

(4) The weaker states or indigenous forces are more familiar with the local terrain and climate as well as with the culture and languages of the region. By the time the soldiers and officers of the superpower have become acquainted with the local conditions, they are "rotated" —that is, sent home for recuperation and other duties. More determined from the beginning, the local forces will stay and fight on a continuous basis.

(5) Another important factor that has increased the costs of military intervention is the support provided to the weaker state by the rival superpower, either directly as by the USSR in Vietnam, or indirectly by proxy, as by the United States in Afghanistan through Egypt, Pakistan, and other states. In this "game" the superpower backing the weaker state can never lose. It is not directly involved, and the material support it provides comes with a low price tag relative to the benefits it produces. Normally, the rival superpower provides the weaker state with large quantities of obsolete weapons for which it has no more use. This type of support has an impressive multiplier effect. For every dollar's worth of weapons furnished to the weaker state by one superpower, the opposing superpower will have to invest ten to twenty times as many resources in weapons and manpower. Indirect intervention has made the costs of direct intervention unbearable, for it is not only much cheaper—it is the only cost-effective form of military intervention.

The post-World War II era demonstrates that direct military intervention on a large scale is not a viable proposition and does not promote the interests of the intervening power. In the majority of cases the great powers lived up to their reputations—they did not lose the war militarily. They lost politically when the price being paid was considered too high, and public opinion turned against the war.

The French did not lose militarily in Vietnam or Algeria, the British, French, and Israelis did not lose militarily in the Suez campaign, nor did the United States in Vietnam or Israel in Lebanon. The Soviet Union cannot and will not lose the war in Afghanistan in a military sense, but it cannot win either. In the end Soviet intervention and imperialist hegemonic policy will suffer the same fate as that of the Western democracies. If there is a lesson to be learned from the British victory (to be sure, only by the smallest of margins) in the Falklands/Malvinas

War, it is that the cost of success was much too high. Israel's victory over the PLO in Lebanon was a psychological victory. The only lesson that the Israelis can draw is that the direct application of force should be used only as a last resort.

Perhaps the best indication of the increased cost of direct military intervention can be found in the evolution of U.S. national security policy toward military intervention and the support of other nations. The United States has come a long way since John F. Kennedy's enthusiastic "blank check" type of support for direct U.S. involvement in world affairs. Kennedy declared that the United States was willing to "pay any price, bear any burden, meet any hardship, support any friend, oppose any foe to assure the survival of liberty." (Kennedy, 1961.)

By 1969, at the height of the Vietnam trauma, President Nixon had formulated a radically different and more sober doctrine. According to the Nixon doctrine, the United States would avoid direct intervention whenever possible and instead provide military and economic support to those who were ready to help themselves. "We shall furnish military and economic assistance when requested and as appropriate, but we shall look to the nation directly threatened to assume primary responsibility of providing the manpower for its own defense." (Nixon, 1978.)

The dangers and increased costs of direct military intervention abroad were also recognized by the U.S. Congress in November 1973 in its War Powers Resolution. Under this resolution, the president must consult with Congress "in every possible instance" before introducing armed forces "into hostilities or into situations where imminent involvement in hostilities is clearly indicated by the circumstances." He must report to Congress on the status of American troops in such situations and is required to withdraw such troops within sixty to ninety days unless Congress authorizes their continued presence. The president must in any case immediately withdraw the troops if directed to do so by a concurrent congressional resolution, which is not subject to a presidential veto. (Javits, 1985; Ford, 1977; Holt, 1978; Turner, 1983; Glennon, 1984; Franck, 1977.) The War Powers Resolution certainly makes it more difficult to get U.S. troops directly involved in military action abroad and clearly reduces the president's incentive to do so.

Oddly enough, this trend has been reinforced by none other than the secretary of defense, as representative of the interests and views of the U.S. military. The Weinberger doctrine, "On the Use of Military Power," first enunciated on October 28, 1984, requires the fulfillment of six conditions before the United States should be ready to commit its forces to military action abroad:

(1) The vital interests of the United States or its allies must be at stake.

(2) Sufficient force should be applied to unequivocally reflect the intention of winning (i.e., no half-measures).

(3) Political and military objectives must be clearly defined.

(4) The U.S. involvement must be continuously reassessed to keep cause and response in synchronization.

(5) Before troops are committed, there must be a reasonable assurance of support from American public opinion.

(6) A combat role should be undertaken only as a last resort.

Strict adherence to the Weinberger doctrine would place insurmountable barriers in the way of any large-scale American military use of force abroad. (Weinberger, 1984; Foster, 1983; Cohen, 1984.) Who would decide what a vital interest is? Who can calculate in advance the necessary size of a force required to win a war? Can political and military objectives be clearly defined and by whom? How can public support, even if initially favorable, be guaranteed to last as long as the war effort requires it? These and a multitude of other questions raised by the Weinberger doctrine indicate the obstacles in the way of using forces abroad in accordance with this doctrine. It is not surprising that such a doctrine originated in the Defense Department, for no one is more aware of the prohibitive costs of war and intervention than the U.S. armed forces. The pressures to resort to military force, as Richard K. Betts (1977) has shown, are stronger in the civilian than in the military community.

The trend against the direct use of force as reflected in U.S. law and policy doctrines is clear. The use of force is too expensive, too ineffective. Indeed, force has finally become the *ultima ratio*. Although no such declarations have been made by the Soviet Union, its cost of using force abroad is not very different from that incurred by the United States. Whether made public or not, a doctrine similar to the Weinberger doctrine will have to be developed in the Soviet Union after the war in Afghanistan has ended.

Free Trade: Benefits Without Responsibility

Another relic of the mercantilistic age is the idea that a country will fare better if it has direct control over other states. Today the old mercantilist theories have been replaced by strategic theories declaring the need to secure direct access to raw materials in the name of national security. From an economic point of view as much as from the political and military points of view described in the preceding text, the costs of direct control of resources have become too high.

In the age of high technology there is no need to be in direct control of the silicon mines overseas. All raw material, as recent history has shown, can be obtained more easily and cheaply through free international trade. In the first place the greatest volume of trade by far is between the industrial, developed states. The volume of trade between the highly developed and less-developed countries is much smaller and much less vital. The United States, or for that matter any other great power or state, does not need to be in control of any other states in order to acquire all the raw materials or industrial goods it needs. All commodities, from oil to coffee, bananas, titanium, rubber, or gold, can be obtained most cheaply in the free market. The underdeveloped countries are in fact competing to sell their raw materials and goods to the great powers. This competition tends to push the prices of all raw materials downward. If oil cannot be purchased in Libya or Saudi Arabia, it can be bought in the USSR or produced in Alaska and Mexico.

The strategic argument for the need to directly secure access to raw materials is patently fallacious for the following reason: we have seen that the supreme interest of both superpowers is avoidance of a nuclear confrontation. Any attempt by one superpower to deny the other access to vital raw materials such as oil will inevitably lead to a direct confrontation and hence to a risk of nuclear war. For this reason, the possibility that either of the superpowers would be denied access to vital raw materials is unacceptable and virtually nonexistent.

For years it has been argued that South African raw materials are crucial for the United States. Since the system of apartheid has become a U.S. domestic political issue, very little has been heard of the importance of that country's raw materials. Even if South Africa were to become a Soviet republic, it would, in any event, still have to trade and sell its raw materials in the West. Furthermore, an increasing number of raw materials can be replaced by synthetic substitutes readily available to any industrialized country. Direct control of lesser-developed states forces the more developed and stronger state to take into account their needs and may even force it to subsidize their weaker economies by paying higher than market prices for their products. Responsibility comes with control, and such responsibility is not good for the maximization of profit.

The USSR can be said to control lesser states, yet it is not better off economically for doing so. Countries in Eastern Europe such as Poland

and Romania might collapse economically, and the resulting political instability would force the USSR to bail them out in order to avert political disaster. Direct influence or control over Cuba or Poland may be politically advantageous for the USSR but is a net loss in economic terms.

In contrast, the USSR does not directly control Finland, with which it has developed excellent and profitable relations. Should the Finnish economy collapse tomorrow morning, the USSR owes it nothing. The USSR can have its cake (political influence) and eat it too (economic benefits). Indirect control or Finlandization are politically and economically more effective than direct control because under this arrangement both countries have a common interest. Poland and the USSR, on the other hand, have antagonistic interests. In Schelling's words, Poland can play the game of "coercive deficiency"; it can threaten, having no positive incentive, to commit economic suicide, and the USSR will have to come to its rescue. (1960.)

A similar type of logic can be applied to U.S. policies. U.S. responsibility for the economic well-being of Latin American countries will increase in proportion to the degree of direct control it assumes.

Given the wealth of the USSR in raw materials, there is little doubt that in principle the Soviet Union could do much better without the economic burden of Eastern Europe. Such benefits, however, could only materialize if the Soviet Union were able to concentrate all of its energy inward and develop an economic incentive for its population to work harder. The key to the strength and survival of the USSR lies in its domestic, not its external, environment.

According to the analysis presented in this chapter, future considerations of power politics will rely less and less on direct intervention and the direct application of power. If, in the past, the best way to augment power was through its actual use, in the modern world, the safest, least costly, and most rational way to maximize power is by conserving it. Such a policy was adopted by the European great powers in the 1960s, and was adopted de facto by the United States (with minor exceptions) following the war in Vietnam. The Soviet Union's difficult economic situation and experience in Afghanistan will most likely lead to the adoption of a similar policy in the 1990s. Those states that might continue to resort to the use of raw power against one another are the weaker states, not the great powers. Wars between nations such as Iran and Iraq, Israel and her Arab neighbors, Somalia and Ethiopia,

Egypt and Libya, and perhaps Greece and Turkey will probably continue to flare up.

Paradoxically, a rational cost-benefit type of analysis leads one to conclude that the days of direct use of power by the superpowers have almost come to an end. Unfortunately, the actions of states in the international system, like those of individual political leaders, are not always governed by standards of rationality; therefore, the trends I have identified could conceivably be impeded by illogical or fanatical behavior.

Summary and Conclusion

Jan F. Triska

Domination of the strong and powerful over the weak and powerless is as old as the world. Its history is intimately bound with the spread of civilization. Whether called empires and colonies, sovereigns and suzerains, patrons and clients, hegemons and dependencies, dominant powers and subordinate states, or spheres of influence, hierarchical orders, mandates, or trusteeships—and whatever the differences among them over time and space—relationships between the strong and the weak share two basic features: (1) the strong keep the weak inside, and (2) they keep the rivals out. Keeping the weak inside relates to a power asymmetry between the dominant power and the subordinate state—a relationship of inequality between those who have more power and are in that sense superior and those who have less power and are in that sense inferior. Keeping the rivals out relates to the protection of the domination from external danger. Its principal function is preventive—to shield the area from rival powers, to endow the domination with a prophylactic security screen and thus, ultimately, to protect the protector. The domination results in (1) a net power increase for the dominant state at the expense of the subordinate state as well as (2) a protective shield for the dominant power against international power rivalry.

Inequalities of power have always tempted the strong to dominate the weak. But when geographical areas adjacent to the strong possess substantially inferior capabilities, the opportunities for the strong to fill the relative power vacuum become even more enticing. In fact, the greater the power asymmetries between the strong states and the weak ancillary areas or regions, the more irresistible the temptation for the strong to make demands on their neighbors.

Power is influence. It has the capacity of causing the weak to follow the choices of the strong. It can coerce as well as attract. It is contextual and may be manifested in various forms—strategic, economic, or ideological. (Singer, 1972.) Historically, "almost every great power has undertaken at some time some sort of hegemonic system, be it actual, approximate, or abortive. This suggests that hegemonic systems are one predictable result of great power status." (Kurth.)*

The relationship between the dominant powers and subordinate states is the prominent feature of contemporary international relations. Colonies are virtually extinct in the world today; but dominant powers and subordinate states, such as the United States in Latin America and the Soviet Union in Eastern Europe, are very much in evidence. The issue here, and the major theme of this concluding essay, is that while dominant powers seek to acquire and maintain domination over others, subordinate states try to minimize their subordination and maximize their autonomy. The dominant powers and the subordinate states are on a collision course.

It is my conclusion, supported by collective evidence presented in this volume, (1) that domination, as practiced in the past, is no longer in the national interest of dominant powers, and (2) that the dominant powers will eventually have to yield, however grudgingly, to the subordinate states.

Similarities and Differences: The United States and the Soviet Union

The two dominant powers, the United States and the Soviet Union, and their spheres of influence, Latin America and Eastern Europe, display many significant similarities and differences. The similarities stem from power distribution in international relations (Waltz, 1959); the differences stem from the unique attributes of the two dominant powers

*Citations of authors without a year of publication refer to contributors to this volume.

—the nature of their respective political institutions, ideologies, and historical experiences—as well as from their spheres of influence, their geopolitical and geostrategic locations, their levels of development relative to the dominant power, their cultural backgrounds and sense of community, the relative value of the area to the dominant power, and other factors.*

The United States and the Soviet Union play many important roles in

*On the subject of the two spheres of interest, Latin America and Eastern Europe, a definitional clarification is in order. In his "Historical Comparability" chapter Jeffrey L. Hughes cites Milan Kundera's preference for the cultural-historical term "Central Europe" over the post-World War II political designation "Eastern Europe" and explains why in this book we stick with the conventional political designation. In the following passage James Kurth explains our use of "Latin America," "Central Europe," and "the Caribbean Basin": "Analysts of international affairs often use the term sphere of influence and hegemony interchangeably. Here we felt the need for a term that would describe a relationship of unequal influence (i.e., sphere of influence), which, however, did not reach the point of being a relationship of dominance (i.e., a hegemonic system). We wanted to distinguish between the role of the United States in South America (influence) and its role in Central America and the Caribbean (hegemony). One way to sharpen these distinctions and definitions would be to begin with the central dimensions of unequal influence between states. These could be conceived as (1) economic dependency; (2) military integration; and (3) political intervention, i.e., the general expectation within a small state that under certain conditions a great power will intervene within it in order to protect or to replace the local regime. Various regional systems composed of a great power and several lesser states can be interpreted in the light of the above three dimensions: The United States in South America is characterized by economic dependency, but not by military intervention or even by political intervention (with occasional, and disputed, exceptions such as Chile, 1970–1973). The United States in Western Europe is characterized by military integration (NATO), but not by economic dependency or by political intervention. (The last such case was Greece, 1947–1949.) The United States in Central America and the Caribbean is characterized by economic dependency and political intervention, but not by military integration (although Terry Karl and Richard Fagen argue that there is substantial military integration of the United States with El Salvador and Honduras.) The Soviet Union in Eastern Europe is characterized by military integration and political intervention, but not, for the most part, by economic dependency. *The quantitative definition.* One approach is to define (1) a sphere of influence as a regional system characterized by *one* of these dimensions of influence (i.e., the United States in South America and the United States in Western Europe; and (2) a hegemonic system as a regional system characterized by *two* (or more) of these dimensions (i.e., the United States in Central America and the Caribbean and the Soviet Union in Eastern Europe). A hegemonic system would be a double-barreled (or triple-threat) sphere of influence. *The qualitative definition.* An alternative approach is to define political intervention as the necessary and sufficient condition for a hegemonic system, with a sphere of influence being a region characterized by economic dependency and/or military integration but lacking political intervention. As it happens, this qualitative approach arrives at the same designation of the four regional systems as does the quantitative approach." (James Kurth, letter to the volume editor, February 10, 1986.)

the world. (Jönssen, 1984: 15ff.) Some of these roles are similar, and others are different. The similarity in their roles arises from the fact that the two nations are the major power competitors on the world scene. The dissimilarities stem from the radical differences in their respective political, economic, and social systems: one is a democracy, the other an authoritarian state.

Both the United States and the USSR are superpowers, global powers, adversary alliance leaders, economic powers, status quo proponents, and superordinate regional powers. In these major roles they pursue many objectives, engage in major strategies, employ many means, display many preferences, indulge in many excesses, and exercise many restraints that are similar. This similarity derives from a well-established proposition, originally formulated by Eugene Dupréel, which states that in an extended, sustained competition and conflict, opponents must emulate each other and match their means in order to meet and neutralize each other. If they do not, they risk loss and defeat. (1948.) The issue of democracy versus dictatorship is irrelevant to the outcome of the conflict, which is determined by the balance of the means and forces: "Engaged in mortal combat with a monster, one must become a monster." (Waltz, citing Nietzsche: "Whoever battles with monsters had better see that it does not turn him into a monster"; 1967: 13.) The more intense the conflict, the greater the emphasis on the similarity of roles, objectives, strategies, means, preferences, restraints, and excesses. As Jeffrey L. Hughes points out, "The frequency of U.S. interventions declined with the Good Neighbor policy. But the Cold War revived U.S. efforts to organize military security for the region as it felt compelled to intervene several times to forestall communist threats." When the pendulum swings back to tension reduction, détente, emphasis on arms control, and cooperation between the two powers, the differences between them tend to be more pronounced. In the more hostile periods the two opponents do their best to surpass—and as a consequence continually meet, balance, and neutralize—the capabilities of the other. To many outsiders they look pretty much the same: dangerous, reckless, and aggressive.

"When Brezhnev sends tanks to massacre the Afghans, it is terrible but it is, so to say, normal—it is to be expected," maintains the Czechoslovak novelist Milan Kundera. (1985.) But the United States—the oldest liberal democracy in the world—sending tanks to Central America: is this not a contradiction in terms?

It is not. Democracies have often been belligerent. Classical Athens, republican Rome, revolutionary France, nineteenth-century Britain, the nineteenth- and twentieth-century United States and Israel have all been at times aggressive and expansive dominant powers. As Gabriel Almond reminds us, we should avoid falling into a "trap of monocausal explanations." (1971: 284.)

The United States plays many important roles in international politics because it is a powerful polity, not because it is a democracy. A weak democratic state such as Czechoslovakia between the two world wars did not matter much either way in the power play among nations. The 1938 Munich appeasement is as good an example of that fact as any.

Some of the roles the United States plays abroad are more important than others. Its role as a global power, an alliance leader, a dominant regional power, a status quo nation, and an economic power are often subordinate to its role as a superpower—a strategic behemoth attempting to defend itself from destruction by the other superpower, the USSR. This is not to say that the other roles are not important; they are critical both in their own right and because they directly and significantly support the U.S. role as a superpower. Given the present world balance of forces, U.S. leaders argue, the United States cannot slacken its efforts in any of them.

This role subordination, however, helps to explain the stress and strain on the democratic values of the United States. Some authors in this volume argue that the United States is a hegemon because its overriding foreign policy concern is its competition with the USSR; herein lies "the cosmic anxiety of United States' demise," as Jean-Paul Sartre put it. The Soviet Union serves as a constant reminder to the United States of its mortality (and vice versa).

Other authors argue that even without Soviet competition for world primacy, the United States would still be a hegemon in its own right. (Waltz, 1967: 306.) If all the countries of the world were liberal democracies and the United States were the sole hegemon, the scope, severity, and intensity of conflicting interests would be considerably reduced, but some conflicts would still remain. Conversely, U.S.-Soviet competition and conflicting interests would still exist, even if the USSR were a democracy: superpowers, like all states whether or not they are democratic, attempt to maximize their power at acceptable cost and risk in the international system. Unlike other states, however, superpowers possess superior capabilities that they use as leverage to enforce their demands. To increase their own power, the superpowers reduce the autonomy of states in adjacent regions. To that end, whether autocracies or democracies, they create and maintain conditions consistent with their domination over the region.

The United States, James Kurth points out, was born equal, born modern (Huntington, 1968), and born anticolonial. This is why it was destined to become hegemonic, once it became a great power. It has a "propensity for hegemony. And Latin America was the arena in which this propensity was carried to its fullest expression." The USSR, on the other hand, is a hegemonic anomaly. Because it is less developed economically than most of its subordinate states, its hegemony is structurally unstable. It is condemned by its hegemonic dynamics to continued military occupation of its allies. The Soviet Union is politically unable to move either forward or backward; it is "standing still." While Eastern Europe is a vital Soviet buffer zone, a *cordon sanitaire*, a forward base for Soviet forces, and a critical security area, Latin America is a buffer only between the United States and Antarctica. (Keal.)

At the same time a democracy such as the United States cannot help but be constrained from being a successful hegemon. Its own constitution, with its checks and balances, separation of powers, and protection of civil and human rights, as well as U.S. public opinion, political culture, bureaucratic complexities, and group interests—all militate against an effective U.S. hegemony. Playing the role of a hegemon is often a tense, anguished, and tortuous business. The cognitive and conceptual dissonance between a democracy and a hegemony affects both roles. Domination of some over others is repugnant to a democracy. And there are dangers on both sides. Military interventions seldom result in new democracies, and the new dictatorships they produce are often worse than the old ones. There is always the danger that a democracy could turn into a dictatorship for the sake of self-preservation.

Although it is a democracy, the United States is no slouch as a hegemon. It is sometimes asserted that authoritarian systems have a natural advantage over democracies in foreign policy-making. Kenneth Waltz argues persuasively that this is not always the case: "Coherent policy, executed with a nice combination of caution and verve, is difficult to achieve in any political system, but no more so for democratic states than for others." (1967: 311.) The authors in this volume tend to agree. But they also maintain that the United States is a force for democracy in Latin America not because it is a mighty hegemon but because it serves as an attractive, powerful, distinctive role model. It is considered worthy of emulation because it displays remarkable long-term economic growth and productivity while maintaining social peace, political liberty, and respect for human rights. (Peceny, 1986.)

While approximately equal as military superpowers, the United States and the Soviet Union are unequal as centers of influence. The U.S. economy, its culture, its democracy, its respect for equality and other human rights, and its openness and attractiveness to others ("Yankee go home but take me with you") make the United States a hegemonic success story. As a hegemon, the United States is in the comfortable position of being rich, established, and influential. The Soviet Union, after seventy years of trial and error, cannot match that record. I do not mean to overstate the case. This book is a testimony to the many serious problems the United States faces as a dominant power. Also, the economies of Japan and Korea are more efficient, the culture of Western Europe is richer, British democracy is more representative, Scandinavian democracies are more egalitarian, and Canada is more open to emigrants than the United States. Conversely, we must be careful not to sell the USSR short. In spite of many setbacks, it has accomplished a great deal in the seventy short years of its existence. Since October 1917 the face of Russia has changed fundamentally. Under the hammer and sickle a predominantly agrarian land that had barely entered the industrial age has been transformed into a technotronic giant. The costs were high—enforced hardship, brutal deprivation and sacrifice, and the loss of millions of lives. But the Soviet Union has become a weapons-saturated superpower whose military potential can be matched only by the United States. It has not succeeded in creating a worldwide revolution, subverting social orders, transforming social values, eliminating the exploitation of man, outlawing repression and war, and providing a better life for all. It has not created a "new man," a man free of fear and hunger, of egoism and aggression, a man liberated in the gratification of his needs. But it has improved the lot of its citizens and achieved a power, status, prestige, and external security that tsarist Russia never had. The success of the Soviet Union may well be Stalin's creation, but his successors have tried and will try their utmost to do even better. (North, Ike, and Triska, 1985.)

The fact remains, as Robert Wesson reminds us, that many countries can be counted on to follow U.S. preferences in the world, as compared to only a few states on the Soviet side. The USSR is obsolete both economically and politically (Kurth) and stagnant culturally—a closed society, unattractive even to other communist parties. The Soviet Union lags behind most of its allies; it is no role model for Eastern Europe to emulate. Moreover, communism is in a historical decline globally. The USSR does not wield the influence commensurate with its superpower status. It is not a country that attracts; except for a handful of foreign spies and communists, few seem to wish to emigrate to the USSR.*

The Two Spheres of Influence

Paul Keal argues that spheres of influence are international devices regulating relations between the superpowers. In that sense they contribute to peace, international order, and stability in the world. They protect the dominant powers' vital interests by exempting two large geographical areas from strategic superpower competition. They provide stability that is lacking in other areas of the world: their existence checks rivalries between the two powers within their respective regions by legitimizing a hierarchy of authority and by the use of police power to maintain it. As long as the dominant powers maintain order — through inertia, police actions, interventions, institutions, or structures — the regional stability contributes to international stability.

The two spheres of influence also testify to the mutual dependence of the United States on the Soviet Union and vice versa. The two dominant powers, by entering into the tacit agreement concerning their respective hegemonies, which Paul Keal describes in his chapter "On Influence and Spheres of Influence," provide eloquent testimony of their mutuality of interests. They see each other as "responsible powers." What is more, the outside world also has a vested interest in this

---

*In the recent novel *A Minor Apocalypse* by Tadeusz Konwicki, generally regarded as Poland's finest contemporary novelist, a member of the Polish Communist party argues that Poland's survival depends on the failure of the Soviet Union as a model to be emulated by others: "You should thank your gods," he tells his countrymen, "that the Russians have been rendered inert by their idiotic doctrine, depraved by their ghastly life, and exhausted by their moronic economic system. Every night you should thank heaven that they cannot stop writing those huge books, that those scraps of ideas from the nineteenth-century idealists are still flitting through their brains, that they are standing in lines, that they are hungry for fashionable clothes, that, in a word, they are splashing about in the mud of humanity. Imagine a free, democratic Russia with a capitalist economy. . . . In a few years a Russia like that would produce art of such genius that it would have the world on its knees. A Russia like that would indeed overtake America in industry, and would suck us Poles up like a vacuum cleaner sucks up cobwebs. Without tanks and without deportation to Siberia, it would swallow us up by virtue of its cultural supremacy, by the height of its civilization." (1983: 38.)

U.S.-Soviet collusion and relies on it, viewing it as a positive development for the maintenance of peace.*

The two spheres of influence thus represent double containment: the United States is contained in Eastern Europe just as much as the Soviet Union is contained in Latin America. (Kurth.) While it is true that "American finance penetrates Eastern Europe while Soviet aid and ideology penetrate Latin America" (Keal), U.S. military bases in Eastern Europe are out of the question, just as Soviet military bases are out of the question in Central and Latin America. There is probing, yes, and impassioned speeches are delivered frequently by both sides. But just as the 1956 Hungarian revolution brought no U.S. challenges to Soviet hegemony, so Cuba "became a barrier to other populist-business alliances in the region for almost a generation. And the fate of the Nicaraguan Revolution may perform a similar inoculation in our own time." (Kurth.)

"Obviously," argues Arthur Schlesinger, Jr., "it would be wonderful to have in Central America a set of devoted, tranquil, prosperous, pro-United States countries. Equally, it would be unacceptable to let Central America become a Soviet base. Actually, both extremes are beyond the power of either the United States or the Soviet Union to achieve. . . ." (1984.)

Still, each dominant power keeps pointing to the rival power as the principal danger and challenge to its own sphere of interest. In Eastern Europe the United States and NATO (or "capitalist imperialism") are the major perceived threat. In Latin America it is Cuba and Soviet power (or "communism"). Michael Handel calls this superpower behavior "irrational." Richard Ned Lebow calls it "paranoia of the powerful."

Just as the dominant powers are constrained, despite what they say, in their rival's sphere of influence, they are also constrained in their relations with states within their own spheres. This restraint is dictated in part by their nuclear capabilities. In a nuclear age the superpowers cannot use all the coercive power at their command. David B. Abernethy thinks that this constraint gives the subordinate states "greater bargaining leverage . . . than one might imagine." Condoleezza Rice concurs: "The ability of the superpowers to use their military

---

*U.S. Secretary of State George Shultz, in a curious speech in West Berlin on December 14, 1985, reportedly said that "the United States would not accept the incorporation of any of the East European countries into the Soviet sphere of influence." (*New York Times*, December 15, 1985.) Was he unaware of the tacit U.S.-Soviet agreement on spheres of influence? Or was he challenging that agreement?

assets for influence and control depends fundamentally on the character of the task at hand." Small, weak, vulnerable states, with few assets of their own, are ideal for the purpose. It is startling, Rice points out, how often the dominant powers' effective control has failed. Used alone, the military is not always effective. Its potency is increased when it is used in conjunction with other instruments of influence —economic, political, social, or cultural. By itself, in police actions and interventions, the military tends to do more harm than good.

At the same time the two spheres of influence also represent important assets valued by the two dominant powers. Latin America, while not as important to the United States as Eastern Europe is to the Soviet Union, is nevertheless of value in a variety of ways. Eastern Europe, on the other hand, is perceived by the Soviet Union as crucial. It adds to Soviet military strength, supports Soviet policies at home and abroad, and gives credence to the Soviet claim of the universality of communist absolutes. Eastern Europe scores much higher when it comes to Soviet requirements for security, the economy, politics, and ideology than Latin America does for the United States". But the U.S. requirements, as the authors in this volume show, are much less stringent in Latin America than are the Soviet requirements in Eastern Europe. The Soviet Union's lower threshold of toleration for defiance and deviation reflects both historical Soviet concern for security as well as the geostrategic location of Eastern Europe. (Valenta.) Defection, however, is another story; it is anathema to both powers. They both demand order in their subordinate regions. Depending on the dominant power, the emphasis may vary, but it must be effective to assure stability, which, after all, is the reason for maintaining spheres of influence in the first place—a crude hierarchy of power that permits strong powers to stabilize whole continents.

Capitalism and Socialism

The two economic and social systems, the American and the Soviet, are radically different. The distinction between the market economy and the centrally planned economy is important for understanding the two types of domination. Soviet hegemony in Eastern Europe is overwhelming because it is unified, hierarchic, and carried out by the Soviet party-state apparatus acting in complete unison. The Soviet Politburo, which makes routine decisions on political, social, military, and diplomatic matters affecting Eastern Europe, also decides issues of economic planning and management, production, and trade. Nothing important that concerns Eastern Europe can easily escape the attention of Soviet decisionmakers. They politicize East European economics, at times subordinating economic objectives to political concerns and at other times pulling the other way for the sake of economic gains. (Johnson.) U.S. control in Latin America is much looser because it is neither centralized nor concerted; nor is it primarily governmental. The separate logics that govern the relationship, that of commercial banks and private companies on the one hand and the U.S. government and its agencies on the other, seldom operate in tandem and only when overwhelming political issues are at stake. The two do not harmonize easily. The USSR has ways and means "to keep track of the little things as well as the larger milieu goals." This, the United States cannot do: "Because of the structural separation of political and economic elites in the U.S. capitalist democracy, the majority of America's wealth and resources is simply beyond the direct control of the U.S. government. The commitment of economic elites to a market economy reinforces the U.S. inability to tap these resources." (Peceny, 1986.)

The tight Soviet regional, ideological-organizational, and political bonds are inclusive, exclusive, and complementary. In the short run this gives Soviet domination leverage that the United States does not have in Latin America. In the long run, however, this tight structure ties the more advanced economies of Eastern Europe organically to the less advanced economy of the USSR in an unprofitable, parasitic relationship.

Neo-Marxist *dependencia* literature portrays spheres of influence based on economic dependency as a form of capitalist hegemony. Through aid, trade, and investment, and through the harmony of interest between the elites in both subordinate states and dominant powers, capitalist control can be established and maintained. (Keal; Cardoso, and Faletto, 1979.) The *dependencia* literature focuses on the vulnerability of countries in Latin America to economic manipulation and exploitation by the United States. It stipulates that those Latin American countries that display high commodity concentration in their foreign trade patterns show sizable foreign investments concentrated in the key areas of the economy. Their ability to repay extensive debts to banks and financial institutions controlled by the United States depends on economic forces of the international capitalist market dominated by U.S. companies and, in the last analysis, by the U.S. government. The Soviet Union does not have this kind of economic leverage over Eastern

Europe. But as Paul Johnson points out, the Soviet leaders applied economic sanctions against Yugoslavia in 1948, against China in 1960, and against Albania in 1961, and they have manipulated Soviet-Romanian economic relations since the mid-1960s.

As it is formulated by authors in the *dependencia* tradition, the concept of dependency is not hospitable to comparative analyses of hegemony, autonomy, and exploitation under socialism and capitalism. However useful it may be for understanding and explaining the relationship between the United States and Latin America (as rooted in the world capitalist political economy), the dependency literature as presently constituted is not well suited for orienting comparative study of the United States and the USSR as dominant powers vis-à-vis subordinate states. The reasons are not hard to find. Authors in this tradition not only have focused all their substantive propositions and empirical inquiry on Latin American situations, but they also have embedded their ideas and studies in nonfalsifiable Marxist epistemologies. (Packenham, 1983.) Therefore it is impossible within the framework of *dependencia* premises to conduct the kinds of empirical and theoretical analyses that are central to this volume.

However, it is possible, outside those premises and with a falsificationist epistemology, to examine the substantive propositions of the *dependencia* school in a comparative fashion. Broadly speaking there are two ways to do this: by comparing the same country over time under capitalism and socialism, and by comparing different sets of countries under the two kinds of hegemony. Let us consider each of these in turn.

Cuba provides an unusual opportunity to use the first method. As Robert A. Packenham shows, dependency was neither eliminated nor significantly reduced when Cuba switched its allegiance from the capitalist hegemon, the United States, to the socialist hegemon, the Soviet Union, after 1959. Sugar, trade, capital, debt, energy, and technology dependency are all as high or higher now than they were before. The Soviet Union provides substantial economic subsidies to the Cubans, but it extracts a price for its largesse: Cuba is vulnerable to a policy of economic and political coercion on the part of the Soviet Union. True, some Soviet policies can be seen as helpful and benign, but others can not. In Cuba the mechanisms, forms, and specific features of socialist dependency are not the same as those of capitalist dependency, but the facts of domination and exploitation continue under socialism. Indeed, Packenham concludes that the "*bi-pe* alliance of Soviet and

Cuban elites . . . exploits the Cuban population in ways and to degrees never realized in pre-1959 Cuba or most other peripheral capitalist countries."

The second method is to compare U.S.–Latin American relations with Soviet–Eastern European relations. None of the authors in this volume has used this method to examine the issue of capitalist dependency and socialist dependency. Therefore it may be useful to quote here at length the work of Cal Clark and Donna Bahry. In an article published in 1983 they apply the framework of dependency and dependent development to Soviet–East European relations. Their conclusions about this relationship have much in common with Packenham's about Cuba. They argue that the economic growth in Eastern Europe between the 1950s and the 1970s can be termed "dependent development" because "the process of economic growth and structural transformation made Eastern Europe more dependent economically upon the USSR and created 'class linkages' of common interest between the Soviet and East European elites." (1983a: 271.) The principal difference between capitalist and socialist dependency, the authors maintain, is that

> in contrast to the basically economic nature of dependence under capitalism, the primary thrust of Soviet domination over Eastern Europe [is] political and military with economic control being . . . derivative from political conquest. As a result, the interrelationship of dependence, the nature of class stratification, and external political subservience are significantly stronger in the Socialist model. . . . [Moreover] the centrality of political relationship in Soviet bloc dependency . . . has countervailing implications regarding exploitation and structural distortions. . . . [This] gives rise to an unhappy paradox for these communist regimes: on the one hand their power position depends upon "distorted" economic structures; on the other hand, their failure to change these institutions creates a deteriorating economic situation which also erodes their basis of support and power positions. . . . (1983a: 279, 288.)

Clark and Bahry conclude that socialist-dependent development in Eastern Europe, like capitalist-dependent development in Latin America, has not solved "the problem of classic dependency. Instead, it ultimately created major economic, political, and social 'contradictions' which seemingly can be solved only by some type of radical structural transformation—a possibility all but precluded within the context of the present power structure in the system." (1983a: 288.)

Stability, Choice and Change

Those who make peaceful revolution impossible make violent revolution inevitable.—John F. Kennedy.

The stability of a political system depends on political changes taking place in an orderly manner. As a consequence, institutionalization of political changes is the surest way of guaranteeing stability. At the core of the literature on political change is the notion of rational choice —individual choice made with the aim of maximizing benefits and affecting resource allocation.

Choice, however, must be free, not dictated. As David E. Apter put it, "Choices are illusory if people are victimized by them or afraid to utilize them, and dangerous if they are manifestly incapable of directing them." (1971: 6.) In such situations, choices cease to have meaning; political change, if any, becomes a response to something else.

States in spheres of influence may be viewed as systems within a system—political systems within a regional system. This treatment makes it possible to pinpoint relationships among area components. If one of the member-states is system-dominant, and the other member-states are system-subordinate, and if the system-dominant member has a monopoly over both common purposes and individual choice in member-states, then political change in system-subordinate member-states is but a response to systemic pressure. This line of reasoning suggests the hypothesis that there is a direct relationship between freedom of choice and regional stability: the more limited the choice the more unstable the members and hence the greater the regional instability. Without freedom of choice, political change ceases to have meaning and comes to depend on whimsical choice of the dominant member; its suppression tends to have a cumulative effect, as in the explosive cases of Hungary in 1956, Czechoslovakia in 1968, or the Dominican Republic in 1965.

The most significant variable in explaining political stability and change in the two spheres of influence is the dominant powers' perceptions of their own security interests. These perceptions are the most important causal factor of change, the most persistent system destabilizer, and the most reliable predictor of change. Concern for security lies behind the dominant powers' apprehension of subordinate states' deviation and defection. The Soviet–East European hegemony differs from the U.S.–Latin American hegemony principally in that the USSR insists not only on the fidelity of the elites of the subordinate states but on the fidelity of their respective societies as well.

(Triska and Johnson, 1975.)

If curbing social change and maintaining the status quo in subordinate states have come to mean maintaining oppressive regimes that later destabilized their countries, as did Fulgencio Batista in Cuba, Anastasio Somoza in Nicaragua, Jean-Claude Duvalier in Haiti, Antonín Novotný in Czechoslovakia, Edward Gierek in Poland, and Mátyás Rákosi in Hungary, then why do the dominant powers resist social change in their subordinate states? Because they value the stability of expectations on which a tacit understanding concerning spheres of influence is built, argues Keal. A change that may destabilize those expectations involves uncertainty and danger—an abomination to the orderly world of spheres of influence. And yet, suppression of change bottles up social frustrations and leads to violence.

The United States values control over social change, but with the exception of radical change to the left, Marxism-Leninism, it does not desperately try to prevent such change. The Soviet Union does, and for good reason. It fears contagion. Social change in Eastern Europe threatens the Soviet Union because the Soviet regime lacks political legitimacy among those it presumes to govern. If workers in Warsaw or Prague succeed in changing their governmental structures, workers in Leningrad or Kiev or Tashkent would be likely to try to follow their example. Only by assuring that fundamental questions are never asked on its periphery can the Soviet regime assure its survival within its own homeland. "The threat to Soviet power is thus profound.... A Poland or Czechoslovakia whose population had enjoyed genuine self-determination would threaten Moscow whether or not it were armed.... By contrast, political change in Central America poses no political threat to the United States, because the legitimacy of its governing structure is not in doubt. Revolutionaries who throw off a repressive regime in Nicaragua or Guatemala do not call North American institutions into question." (Ullman, 1983: 51–52.)

Both dominant powers want to maintain the status quo in their regions. The people in these areas, on the other hand, want change. Not all social change is frowned upon by the superpowers, of course. The Hungarian economic experiment in "free enterprise" is allowed to coexist with a socialist planned economy. General Wojciech Jaruzelski's government, embraced by the Soviet leadership, would have been an unthinkable and unacceptable "Bonapartism" twenty years ago. Eduardo Frei's "Chileanization" program in the late 1960s received special dispensation: Chile, loyal and friendly to the United States, acquired a controlling interest in U.S. copper mining companies in

Chile with almost no U.S. opposition.

Dominant power–subordinate state relations do not develop in a uniform fashion. These relations—depending on issues, geopolitical locations, bilateral ties, changes in the domestic system of the dominant (and sometimes rival) power, changes in the international system, and other significant changes sometimes involving the mood of the several involved constituent groups—evolve in staggered modes. Certainly, not all East European countries are alike today, nor are the Latin American states. There has been a great deal of progressive differentiation and stratification in both regions as time passes.

The dominant powers' attitudes to social change in subordinate states depend also on their relations with their rival power. (Keal.) This is part of what Richard Ned Lebow calls the "paranoia of the powerful." The history of great power rivalries, he writes, "reveal[s] that the side that perceives itself at a political or strategic disadvantage rarely responds by offering concessions. It is much more likely to get tough in the hope of covering up its perceived weakness."

But by and large, in dealing with social change both the USSR and the United States are treating symptoms—violent changes—rather than causes of the social problems in their subordinate areas. As Adam Michnik put it in "Letter from Gdansk Prison," in subordinate nations "social changes follow not from violent collisions of various forces but above all from confrontation of different moralities and visions of social order." (1985.) Similarly, Louis Burstin, Costa Rica's former secretary of information, has argued that "Revolutions most commonly occur in countries where political access is closed to newly emerging social classes." In Nicaragua, El Salvador, and Chile, "political reform . . . is the key. Something must be done about the political ignominy that has produced the meadow that ignites with just one spark." (1984.) Economic assistance by itself cannot resolve the outstanding issues, especially since both the United States and the USSR are forcing on their subordinate areas an East-West political dimension that they would not have on their own.

Thus while spheres of influence contribute to peace, stability, and international order, they also contribute to conflict, instability, and disorder within the subordinate states and regions.

Peace vs. Justice

The principal aspirations and hopes of mankind are the achievements of peace and prosperity and the diminution of human inequality. Since no country in our interdependent, finite world can hope to achieve these core values alone, collective efforts are required. Unfortunately, international relations still display very few rules for determining the processes and the substance of national behavior. For this reason, negotiation and bargaining, both explicit and tacit, loom large on the international horizon; countries must cooperate with each other to increase their own well-being, peace, and equality in the world. But because coercive power has not yet been eliminated, states must also protect themselves as well, singly and collectively, against others.

While order, stability, and peace are the major concerns of the dominant powers, justice, equality, and autonomy are the values cherished by the subordinate nations. The two sets of values are in conflict. Whether the maintenance of spheres of influence is a good thing or not depends on the values that inform it. Injustices such as inequalities in the distribution of wealth, violations of the sovereign equality of states, the suppression of human rights, and the denial of equality to individuals lead to instability, disorder, and violence. Moreover, justice can often be purchased only at the price of disorder. But since war between the dominant powers could lead to the end of the world, how do we decide? What do we choose? As Kenneth Waltz put it, there is no real stability without justice, and no enjoyment of justice without order: "In times of relative quiescence the question men put is likely to be: What good is life without justice and freedom? Better to die than live a slave. In times of domestic troubles, of hunger and civil war, of pressing insecurity, however, many will ask: Of what use is freedom without a power sufficient to establish and maintain conditions of [peace and] security? . . . In the absence of order, there can be no enjoyment of [justice and] liberty." (1959: 11–12.) The problem is that injustice and slavery undermine order and lead to chaos, and troubled states could sustain order and peace simply by surrendering.

In his *Politics* Aristotle wrote about justice as it relates to equality. He maintained that justice really meant equality, that inequality led to injustice, and that injustice led to rebellion: "Inequality is always the cause of sedition," he wrote (1947: 143.) If inferiors seek equality, their cause is just; but if equals seek superiority, their cause is unjust. And "without justice . . . no state can be supported." (1947: 90.)

Subordinate nations demand equality. But by equality they do not mean equality of opportunity but equality of condition. Given their subordination, they argue, only equality of condition, i.e., equality that is social and political, as well as economic, assures justice. Therefore, they challenge the order shaped by the spheres of influence.

Inequality and coercion undermine the stability of spheres of influence; external security is threatened by internal instability. The curious thing is that both the U.S. and Soviet role models emphasize equality and voluntary consent. "The U.S. had its own problems with social, political and economic inequities," wrote Richard McCall. "However, the ethos of 'life, liberty, and the pursuit of happiness' and the relative decentralization of economic power eventually enabled the United States to undertake profound social change. These changes did not come easy," but they have prevailed and are here to stay. (1984: 17.) Lenin put it this way: "We want a voluntary union of nations — a union which precludes any coercion of one nation by another — a union founded on complete confidence, on a clear recognition of brotherly unity, on absolutely voluntary consent. Such a union cannot be effected with one stroke." (Dudinsky, 1964: 5.) And Palmiro Togliatti, the late secretary general of the Italian Communist party, later restated the sentiment: "The unity one ought to establish and maintain lies in the diversity and full autonomy of the individual countries." (1964.)

The growing universal challenge to hegemony today proceeds in tandem with the post-World War II process of decolonization, a universal and irresistible march of Third World peoples toward human equality and autonomy. The principles embodied in *The Declaration on the Granting of Independence to Colonial Countries and Peoples*, approved by the General Assembly of the United Nations as Resolution 1514 (XV) on December 14, 1960, are hard to argue with: "The subjection of peoples to alien subjugation, domination and exploitation constitutes a denial of fundamental human rights, is contrary to the Charter of the United Nations and is an impediment to the promotion of world peace and cooperation." (Official Records, 1960: 8.)

In the past forty years these principles have served well the formerly colonial peoples; given the evidence presented in this book, they may serve the subordinate peoples just as well. In fact, today the dominant powers cannot even reveal their tacit understanding regarding their spheres of influence by discussing the agreement publicly because they would be admitting to violation of the sovereign rights and autonomy of others and claiming for themselves superior rights. And this they feel they simply cannot do. (Keal.) As Paul Johnson put it, "The sovereign equality of all states began as a formalistic legal norm of narrow applicability that became an inspiration and that since the late 1950s has been brought forward as a moral imperative confronting the brute fact of massive power inequalities." Respect for others; the realization that all men possess inherently equal personal worth wherever they live; the understanding that subordination implies incomplete self-determination; and the view that a perpetual state of subordination is untenable—are reaching a universal audience. As Robert A. Dahl points out, "Domination has never assured full protection of interests of subordinate people," even under the most benign paternal conditions. (1986.) Comprehensive domination is increasingly on the defensive because it lacks legitimacy. The process of redress has begun; it is more critical in Eastern Europe because it has much further to go there, but the march is on elsewhere as well.

The realization that there is no lasting peace without justice is gaining ground. As Konrad Braun, in his 1950 Swarthmore lecture explained it, "Those who want to establish the realm of peace . . . must work for justice too, indeed for justice first. If we regard peace not as a negative and stagnant posture, the absence of war, but as a constructive and dynamic process, then social justice and international justice . . . are indispensable as compelling forces to carry it forward." (Curle, 1981: 81.)

Dilemmas of Subordinate States

When a small state is forced to pursue its destiny on the periphery of a dominant power its choices are limited. Accommodation with the dominant power may be safe, but it leads to continued subordination as well. Alliance with a rival power may be an effective road toward independence, but it is risky. It is also attractive; for a frustrated dependent state the rival power offers ready-made hope: "A poor nation pitted against a superpower can look in only one direction for help, and that is toward the other superpower." (Dickey, 1985.)

It is not easy for the dominant power to sympathize with this built-in dilemma of the subordinate state. And yet the outcome depends on the dominant power's ability to convince the dependent state that its security and well-being lie neither in the model of Cuba's antagonism to the United States nor of Poland's hostility to the USSR, "but rather in something like Finland's friendly, though wary, independence from the USSR" (Toai and Chanoff, 1984)—symbiotic accommodation rather than parasitic subordination.

Even under the best of circumstances, the cost of subordination for the dependent state is high. It must deal with the dominant power as both an outside force and a domestic one. (Abernethy.) But the cost of deviation is even higher, as is the risk of retaliation. Deviant cases are not easily tolerated because they deny the region's subordination; also, their condition is contagious. One case could lead to other attempts at defection from the subordination, the worst-case scenario of the dominant powers and one to be prevented at all costs.

Defectors and would-be defectors are high risk-takers. They must be popular at home to be able to use that constituency as a base to challenge the dominant power (as did Tito in Yugoslavia and Castro in Cuba). But the benefits and rewards from successful defections are high. Given that trade-off, with time the dominant powers have learned to differentiate between nuisance cases of deviation and defection and cases of strategic loss. At first Cuba and Yugoslavia were perceived as strategic loss cases, but they now tend to be viewed as nuisance cases. (Other nuisance cases are Peru and Romania.)

For both the dominant powers and the subordinate states, for better or worse, the reference point is almost automatically the rival power. Inexorably pushed and pulled by the force that defines the spheres of influence—the East-West conflict—the dominant powers as well as the subordinate states relate prima facie to the rival power. Reacting to problems in their subordinate areas, the dominant powers see rival schemes and plots in every nook and cranny. Similarly, responding to the stresses and strains of domination, subordinate states look to the rival power for relief. The rival gets all the credit and all the blame. Both fears and hopes, however, are exaggerated if not misplaced; for the U.S.-Soviet collusion still works.

There have been substantial changes in both Eastern Europe and Latin America in the last four decades, and there are more to come. But as Keal argues, "Whatever changes have taken place have not altered the fundamental nature of the relationship involved.... The Soviet Union and the United States have not effectively challenged each other's spheres in the sense of seeking to radically alter the other's behavior." Or, as Jeffrey L. Hughes puts it, the dominant powers are loosening their day-to-day "behavior control," but they still retain their "fate control."

In their mutual relations, however, neither dominant powers nor subordinate states always behave prudently. Neither of them always follows appropriate strategies that serves its best interests. Both sides tend at times to exaggerate, to dramatize, and to behave inconsistently. Except during crises, the dominant powers do not view the subordinate states as high on their list of priorities. The subordinate states, on the other hand, often needlessly antagonize the dominant powers. For example, Imre Nagy called for a neutral, national, non-Marxist, independent Hungary in the 1956 Hungarian Revolution—an impossible demand; Alexander Dubček offered the Czechoslovak "socialism with a human face" as an all-socialist model; and President Daniel Ortega Saavedra of Nicaragua took an ostentatious trip to Moscow in 1985, thereby antagonizing many friendly legislators in the United States. Given the odds, wisdom dictates that dependent states employ prudent strategies—strategies that preserve their self-respect while assuaging the dominant power's apprehensions, yet achieve relations that are mutually favorable, benign, and symbiotic.

Let me give some examples.* First, *the stratagem of the wooden horse*. Latin Americans are masters at this strategy. My favorites are the Sandinistas, who compliment U.S. democracy by repeatedly proclaiming that "the battle for Nicaragua is not being waged in Nicaragua but is being fought in the United States" (Tomas Borge, the minister of the interior of Nicaragua; Martz, 1983. Borge said that the only hope for Nicaragua to avoid war was to mobilize American public opinion.) In an op-ed article published in the *New York Times* entitled "Why the U.S. Must End its War," Saavedra appealed to U.S. public opinion. He argued, on March 15, 1985, that "the covert war is illegal, immoral, futile, and unnecessary." Ortega concluded his argument by repeating that the Sandinista government will not cry "uncle": "As for trying to make us cry 'uncle,' this only stiffens our resistance. We know only one cry —the cry for peace with dignity. That is what we seek from the United States. Despite the crimes committed against us, we extend our hand in friendship." The Nicaraguan government has even employed a New York public relations firm, Agendas International, to handle its account in the United States. (In turn, U.S. administration officials have accused Nicaragua of a vast campaign to influence United States public opinion.) (*New York Times*, February 26, 1986: 8.)

Second, *competition for the dominant powers' favor*. This stratagem is practiced successfully in Moscow as well as in Washington on a full-time basis by emissaries from subordinate states, both directly as well as through international institutions such as the Organization of American States, the World Bank, the International Monetary Fund, the Council of Mutual Economic Assistance, and the Warsaw Pact. My favorite example is the manipulation of the U.S. flag by Haitian demonstrators:

*Several of these stratagems were discussed by William Zimmerman of the University of Michigan at our two 1985 panels on dominant powers and subordinate states, at the American Political Science Association meeting in New Orleans, and the American Association for the Advancement of Slavic Studies' Third World Congress meeting in Washington, D.C., respectively.

Protesting against the government of the President-for-Life, Jean-Claude Duvalier, in January, 1986, demonstrators unfurled an American flag. Haitian officials dismissed the gesture as merely a Communist trick. But the United States officials in Washington said they saw no reason to doubt the sincerity of these demonstrators. . . . "I sense that people are saying they've had enough of the poverty, the hunger, the hopelessness," a State Department official said in Washington. "If Duvalier wants to call that communism, let him. But I don't see people in Haiti searching for communism or socialism as a solution." (*New York Times*, January 26, 1986: 3.)

The U.S. flag was improvised out of red and blue cloth: "We have used the American flag so as not to confuse us with Communism and Socialism," said the protestors.

Third, *salami tactics*. A slow but successful stratagem of gaining a little advantage here, a little opportunity there; before long this can amount to a sizable step forward. It is practiced both in Latin America and Eastern Europe with finesse and shrewdness. My favorite examples are the East European "Soviet proxies" in the Third World who turn into independent traders and national agents working for their own countries' (and sometimes their own) interests.

Fourth, *the threat to collapse* stratagem is well described by Paul Johnson. The debts of Latin American countries such as Mexico, Argentina, and Brazil constitute a major proportion of the assets of major American and European banks. Many of these countries are unable to service their debts without introducing politically unacceptable austerity programs. But forcing them into default could create bank failures and deflationary shocks for the U.S. economy. In this way, debtors' weakness—the threat to collapse—becomes a strength and a significant bargaining chip.

Fifth, the *permit-and-encourage pluralization of penetration* stratagem consists of increasing one's own permeability to others, thus watering down the penetration by the dominant power and pluralizing subordination. This stratagem has worked well for Yugoslavia and Nicaragua, but it is tricky. Compatibility of the subordinate state's actions with the dominant power's perceptions of what is permissible is often the issue.

Sixth, the *exploitation of turbulence at the top* stratagem is useful. Usually, subordinate states have more elbow room in periods of leadership tension. But when the attention of the dominant power is absorbed elsewhere, "when East Europeans sense division and drift in Moscow, when they believe they can get away with more," they exploit the situation. (Gati, 1985: 86.)

The subordinate states practice these and similar strategies as they go along. Subordination has been a learning process. And, as we have seen, subordinate people are inventive in their probes of changing relational dynamics. Still, as authors in this volume point out, time is on the side of the subordinate states, not the dominant powers. And to this issue I will now turn.

Dilemmas of the Dominant Powers

Do superpowers' security interests continue to be served well by the maintenance of such costly, rigid, and inequitable control mechanisms as spheres of influence? The international system at large appears to be heading toward a stage of depolarization: nuclear weapons are less persuasive today than they were twenty years ago; China is free from the Soviet hegemony; Japan, South Korea, Taiwan, and other Asian countries are economically more powerful; diversity and heterogeneity increasingly characterize the international system. A loosening of alliances by both members and leaders into more fluid coalitions is taking place: not only organizations such as the Central Treaty Organization (CENTO) and the Southeast Asia Treaty Organization (SEATO) but also major alliances such as NATO and the Warsaw Pact find it increasingly difficult to sustain growth. Small and medium-sized countries seek more independence for greater maneuverability; the fidelity of allies appears to be less reliable; changes in military technology have reduced the value of forward bases for alliance leaders, and leaders are often reluctant to meet the growing cost of maintaining alliances. New opportunities and greater incentives to cultivate a broader range of international friendships have appeared. Changing issues and needs have tended to determine new relationships. The result has been shifting, temporary, cross-cutting, partial alliances and coalitions, to be changed again when new issues emerge, a tendency to say "we will support you on this issue if you support us on that issue." Interdependencies of both small and large states are rising sharply, while dependencies shift around new issues and problems; and many different levels and layers of relations are opening up between two or more countries, where one level or layer seems unaffected by other layers or levels. Good examples of these shifting, cross-cutting alliances can be found among the nations in the Middle East, in U.S.-Chinese relations, in Angola, in Latin American politics, in Israeli-African relations, and among the Common Market countries. (North, Ike, and Triska, 1985: 15–16.)

This broad trend favors the subordinate regions; it points not only toward complete decolonization in the world but also to a new respect for equality, autonomy, and self-determination of subordinate states and peoples. Both the United States and the Soviet Union have suffered a secular slump in their spheres of interest. In particular, their respective ideologies have weakened as have the value bonds in their respective spheres; both powers' effectiveness of control has deteriorated; and the cost of intervention has gone up. The two dominant powers are both experiencing leveling in their spheres of interest, and there are increasing constraints on their behavior in their own regions. (Hughes.) For the two dominant powers to cling to what they had in the past would slow down, but not arrest, the historical devaluation of spheres of influence as relatively limited structures in their power arsenal. The dominant powers would be paying too high a price for their continued resistance to the rising expectations and legitimate aspirations of the subordinate peoples who want to exercise their historic rights. The United States is secure enough in its values to serve as a role model to the campesinos who need assistance but defy domination. The USSR has seemingly more to lose.

This is an irony of history, the paradox of domination. Citing the cases of Poland and Mexico, Jeffrey L. Hughes shows how increasing reluctance to accept subordination leads to an increasing challenge to domination, which in turn leads to diminished superpower capacity to cope with the challenge. Simply sending money to Latin America seems to impoverish recipients further, while it deprives the United States of its financial capability; and Soviet artificial support markets for the shoddy exports from Eastern Europe degrade East European economies while they drain the Soviet economy.

In Latin America and Eastern Europe discipline, obedience, compliance, and conformity have been declining. The rates of change may be differential, but the trend is unmistakable. In Eastern Europe, Hungary, Czechoslovakia, and Poland tried but failed to move toward less repressive government. In Latin America thirteen of the twenty countries were ruled until recently by generals; Haiti was ruled by a family dynasty, and Cuba by a communist dictator. Then in 1984 Uruguay became a democracy and Brazil followed suit, as did Argentina, Guatemala, and now, it would seem, Haiti. Today only Chile and Paraguay are ruled by right-wing dictators. The democracies of Mexico, Costa Rica, Colombia, and Venezuela have proven their resilience. Peru,

Ecuador, Honduras, Panama, and Bolivia are trying to cope as best they can, but they all face the challenge of proving their viability under adverse economic conditions.

The dominant powers want order and tranquility in their regions. Loyalty is important, too, but whether forced or voluntary, it is expensive; neither coercion nor self-interest comes without cost to the dominant power. The subordinate states, on the other hand, want autonomy and prosperity. Because they lack either one, they want change. Given their geostrategic position, their value to the dominant powers—preoccupied with East-West conflict—is growing. Their freedom to maneuver is increasing.

The question comes down to the reliability of subordinate states. This is now the crux of the matter: inferiors coerced into obedience, like conscripts pressed into service, are of dubious value. Instead, the emphasis is on volunteers, on allies, on friends. The nature of a hegemony has changed. Its primary objective is no longer economic exploitation or regional security. Instead, the United States, as well as the USSR, feels pressed to adopt a strategy that values subordinate states as ideological allies, cognates, and supporters. The strength of coalitions tends to be measured more in symbolic than in real terms. Both the United States and the USSR perceive themselves as vulnerable. Because of this perception, they invest scarce resources, moral as well as material, into their hegemonic systems. As Thucydides argues in the Melian Dialogue in the *Peloponnesian War*, symbolic relations and strategies assume importance in direct proportion to the perceived external threat. The symbolic value of a hegemony is out of proportion to its intrinsic value. (Lebow.) The irony is that, in fact, conditions in the world are changing, too. The strategic significance of spheres of influence is decreasing; the utility of power in the nuclear age is going down; the cost of influence is increasing while its utility is decreasing; the universal respect for democratic values—equality, autonomy, and justice—is increasing. The age of colonization is over, and it is now time for superpower domination to release its grip. (Handel.)

This development, however, is difficult for the dominant powers to accept. As Jiri Valenta views it, while "the United States is no longer the hegemon it used to be, [Soviet leaders] fail to see that their own continuous policy of intervention and limited sovereignty heightens the very insecurity and instability in Eastern Europe that such policies were supposed to prevent." Eastern Europe is losing its former strategic significance for the USSR. Fear of Germany is receding in the region.

The Warsaw Pact has become an economic drain on the Soviet Union. Instability in Eastern Europe might advance the widespread feelings of separatism in the Ukraine and the Baltic states. Moscow, too, needs willing respondents, not despondent dependents. "Strategic allegiance of friends and allies is vastly preferable to forced loyalty of uncertain satellites," wrote Valerie Bunce. "The Soviet role in Eastern Europe has evolved from one of coercion to one of captivity. The empire had become a burden, limiting Soviet power; Soviet-installed elites in the client states became vulnerable to economic calamities; the end of economic autarchy in Eastern Europe may lead to the end of political autarchy; and the USSR, now a losing broker rather than a winning hegemon, sees its dominant interests undermined rather than extended.... Indeed, the domestic and the foreign goals of empire [are] at increasing variance." (1985: 45–46.)

Charles Gati disagrees. He argues that "it is quite likely that [Eastern Europe] may succeed in obtaining more 'elbow room' from the Kremlin and move inch by inch toward the West. . . .'" But even if such gradual Europeanization does take place, "it remains wishful thinking to anticipate the 'collapse' of the Soviet empire in Eastern Europe. Diversity is not independence, tolerance is not liberty. While Soviet–East European relations are almost certainly entering a new phase, and one or more mini-coalitions are posing a very serious challenge to Moscow's concept of bloc cohesion, the empire, though rather unwell, is still alive." (1985: 86.)

Eastern Europe came into existence as a new international reality and a political concept in 1945. The formal plan for Allied occupation zones of Nazi Germany agreed upon at Yalta in 1945 became the effective instrument of the East-West division of Europe. The Russian zone of occupation became East Germany, and the three western zones, American, British, and French, became West Germany. Berlin was divided the same way, as was Austria. The Soviet Union added countries to the east that lay on their side of the (agreed-upon) line of occupation—Poland, Hungary, Romania, and Bulgaria. Albania, Yugoslavia, and Czechoslovakia joined Soviet Europe as well. Outside of West Germany and West Berlin, the new "Western Europe" that emerged from World War II was ratified as a friend and ally of the United States through the Truman Doctrine in Greece and Turkey in 1947, and the Marshall Plan for countries west of the new East European boundary line in 1948. Creation of the Warsaw Pact and NATO formalized the two groups as Soviet and American alliances. The division of Europe into

East and West was cast and, over three decades, confirmed; the 1957 Helsinki Agreement legitimized it.*

Zbigniew Brzezinski, the national security adviser to the Carter administration, wrote (1982) that the time had come for the United States "to disassociate" itself from the Yalta order, a symbol of "American-Soviet collusion" to divide Europe. W. W. Rostow, the national security adviser to Presidents Kennedy and Johnson, argued (1982) that what we need is a "farsighted plan to end the confrontation in Central Europe that for 35 years has passed for normality." Joseph C. Harsh questioned the Yalta legacy in a thoughtful analysis. (1982.) Mark Hopkins, reflecting on the fact that Solidarity in Poland upset the old European balance imposed at Yalta, pointed out that "a new arrangement must be worked out, in the Soviet national interest, not to please the Americans." (1982.) Hodding Carter, official spokesman for the State Department during the Carter administration, wrote (1982–83) that "what is desperately needed is a transatlantic 'Great Debate' similar to the one that preceded America's decision to promote and join the Alliance in the late 1940s."

Since World War II the nature of world military and strategic change has been crucial in rate, volume, and direction. NATO and the Warsaw Pact have been left behind by this extraordinary metamorphosis in technological and strategic development. The Russians and the Americans, through these two alliance structures, have frozen the status quo in Europe for over thirty years. On the one hand, NATO today is "the same basic alliance that presupposes a unilateral West European dependence on the United States to survive." On the other hand, in Eastern Europe "the system of dependent, conformist regimes created by Stalin now fulfills inadequately its function as a glacis for the Soviet Union." (Bloemer, 1983: 24–25.) What was once essential to world security interests has shrunk to regional importance—very significant but not vital. "Perhaps the time has come to take Europe out of the superpower game, where it no longer belongs, not only for the sake of world security, but for the sake of Europeans themselves." (Bender, 1981.) After almost four decades of division the 420 million Europeans (250 million in Western Europe and 170 million in Eastern Europe) can look after their own destinies. It would be in their interest to control and direct their own affairs, while freeing the superpowers to worry about each other, about their own global roles, and about their own world interests, without endangering Europeans through their search for

---

*This discussion is based in part on Triska, 1982.

accommodation. The interests of Europe and the interests of the super-powers have seldom been as divergent and heterogeneous as they are now, and they will grow more so with time.

The major argument against this kind of analysis is that the Soviet leaders, traditionally obsessed with security, would never voluntarily agree to a Soviet withdrawal from Eastern Europe, their *cordon sanitaire*. And indeed they may not. But this is an empirical question. With an appropriate set of guarantees making Soviet security in Europe inviolable, with balanced military disengagement, perhaps with neutral and/or nuclear-free zones (as proposed to the United States by Polish Foreign Minister Adam Rapacki in 1958 and approved by Moscow), the Russians may consider a comprehensive peace plan for Europe worthy of consideration. After all, there are precedents. The Soviet leaders did agree to withdraw from Soviet-occupied Austria in 1955 in exchange for Austrian neutrality. Moreover, between 1958 and 1964, following the Rapacki Plan (which they endorsed), they came out with a number of proposals of their own concerning arms limitation in Europe: they offered to enter into negotiations on neutralization and demilitarization of both Germanies; disengagement of armed forces on both sides of the Iron Curtain; a ban on nuclear weapons in Central Europe (in Poland, Czechoslovakia, and in both Germanies); to make Berlin a free city with open and guaranteed routes through East Germany; and even a step-by-step withdrawal of Soviet troops from Eastern Europe in exchange for U.S. withdrawal of its troops from Western Europe. The U.S. rejected all these Soviet proposals on many grounds but principally because they did not provide for German reunification. But the West has not advanced any new ideas of its own. In fact, lack of initiative on the part of the United States has been a continuing problem.

The negotiations would be difficult, long and frustrating. But the possible benefits could make the necessary costs a good investment for all concerned—the Americans, the Russians, and of course the Europeans.

Would West Europeans welcome such a development? With its high technoeconomic and managerial capability, diplomatic skills, cultural assets, large markets, energy supplies, and working connections to former colonies, Western Europe could forge ahead on its own. In fact, West Europeans claim they are ready to assume a share in global responsibility once they gain greater freedom of decision in their own European affairs: "Countless historical, geographic, cultural and strategic interests require that West European countries enter into some kind of security relationship with the Soviet Union," on their own terms, defending their own interests, speaking on their own behalf. (Bloemer, 1983: 26.) The only worry is over the two Germanies.

Admittedly, that is a problem. Many fear that East Germany would gravitate to West Germany. No one wants German reunification any more—neither the West Europeans, the East Europeans, the USSR, the United States, nor the Germans themselves. (Bloemer, 1983.) The memories of prewar Germany are still vivid (Kiep, 1984–85), and a unified Germany would disturb the balance of power in Europe as it did after the reunification of Germany in the nineteenth century. Neutralization of Germany à la Austria is not realistic: the largest country in Europe with eighty million people, a united Germany would hardly be a candidate for neutrality. Germany would have to remain divided. As Klaus Bloemer, a government official in the Federal Republic of Germany, put it, "The great majority of Germans—East and West—would accept the existence of two states in their homeland if a peace treaty between both the four former occupation powers and the two German states insured that the German Democratic Republic emerged with a democratic-pluralistic social order. The GDR—enjoying a status similar to that of Finland—would be obliged to support Soviet foreign policy actively and to cooperate with the Soviet Union economically." (1983: 36–38; Lowenthal, 1984–85.)

"The two German states could then enter into an agreement similar to the 1955 Austrian State Treaty that would prohibit them from developing any political links—be it in the form of a special relationship, a confederation, or the preparation or implementation of a merger. . . . Such an agreement would be in line with the general West German policy of 'freedom before unity' and would not differ from the present status—the existence of two sovereign German states." (Bloemer, 1983: 36–38.)

East Europeans would welcome the new development. It would give them a freedom of maneuver they have not had since World War II. They would still live in the shadow of the USSR, just as Finland does. Soviet troop withdrawal from Eastern Europe would not mean Soviet disappearance from the European continent. The USSR would still be the only superpower in Europe; its capability, influence, and leverage would remain. As David Abernethy pointed out, East European states' capacity for autonomous action would still be seriously constrained by the sheer fact of the Soviet existence. East Europeans would keep a healthy respect for their mighty neighbor; but at home they could experiment in many worthwhile ways.

Undoubtedly, many serious problems would first have to be resolved. But as Zbigniew Brzezinski argues, American-Soviet relations are at a critical turning point: "Both sides are becoming prisoners of a dangerous dynamic." (1984–85.) What is needed is an imaginative, broad strategy rather than the usual tinkering at the margins. "Comfortable coexistence, without danger, is not yet possible; but confrontation can no longer be envisaged," warned Flora Lewis. (1982: 572.) Doing nothing may be more dangerous for maintenance of peace than starting such a dialogue. And a dialogue could lead to a "new global understanding between the United States and the Soviet Union." (Bloemer, 1983: 32.)

For the Soviet Union there is more to be gained by greater flexibility and tolerance of social reality than by grimly standing still. Eastern Europe is important but no longer central to Soviet global strategy. Soviet reliance has been shifting increasingly to its own military power, to its own economy, to domestic political considerations. Perceptive observers maintain that Eastern Europe has on occasion retarded rather than advanced Soviet interests. (Campbell, 1984: 27.) Eastern Europe is "becoming a problem which can not be solved by military means alone." (Brown, 1984: 204.) The pressure there for political and social change is unremitting. The ethos of the times is on the side of the oppressed population, which presses the local communist elites (who are increasingly anxious to please their constituents) to improve the economies, to become more competitive abroad, to offer broader personal scope and more elbow room. But "on occasion, however cautiously, pressure for change will [also] come from the Soviet Union itself, concerned for the success of the Warsaw Treaty system.... Individual aspects of more pluralistic polities will be built into East European political systems ... and the seeds of still more far-reaching change will be gestating." (Dean, 1984: 261.)

The trend is unmistakable. It is moving from more rigid forms of control to more flexible forms of management, and from simple dependence, pure power, and a strict hierarchical arrangement to a more complex social interdependence based on exchanges, promises, and rewards. It is no longer true, as someone said, that when Russia spits, Czechoslovakia swims, and when the United States sneezes, Nicaragua catches cold. Paying greater attention to the interests of their regions, which is almost inevitable, will not bring more satisfaction to the dominant powers either. While their influence will continue to diminish, their sheer presence in the two regions will continue to exercise restraint on the two subordinate areas. In fact, neither side will get what it wants. While the political telos of both regions is equality, justice, and autonomy, the subordinate states will have to settle, given the international realities, for prudent neutrality at home and power-friendly relations abroad.

Great power status requires a doctrine, a worldview, a set of social values; their purpose is to portray the great power as a leader toward a better future, and to malign the rival power and its doctrine and values. The American vision of freedom, human dignity, material progress, and social justice is often coupled with anticommunism; the Soviet aspiration of eliminating the exploitation of man, outlawing repression, and providing a better life for all is coupled with anticapitalism and anti-imperialism. These doctrines and beliefs normally support the powers' national interests. At times, however, they collide with them and are counterproductive.

This book presents collective evidence that domination, as practiced in the past, is no longer in the national interest of either superpower; in fact, it is detrimental to their interests. They cling to it from habit reinforced by old fears. But the practice is now losing the very purpose for which the dominant powers erected their spheres of influence in the first place, namely to preserve the status quo and order.

However, as long as the two superpowers feel threatened, more comprehensive formal changes in their spheres are not very likely; still, informal but effective changes will continue to take place. Forms may stay, but content will surely alter. The old laws may remain on the books, but they will be enforced only selectively. There may not be a dismantling of structures, but much of the substance will take a new direction. Should the two superpowers find a way of breaking through the wall of mistrust, fear, and insecurity—which does not appear likely—then domination of the strong over the weak in Latin America and Eastern Europe may become a welcome casualty in improving the international climate. In any case, as several chapters in this book have made clear, letting go little by little will be easier for the United States than for the USSR.

Sources

(Those entries marked with an asterisk, although not cited in the text, have been added by the volume editor because of their relevance to the book's subject matter.)

Adams, Robert M. (1975). "Machiavelli Now and Here: An Essay for the First World." *American Scholar* 44, 3:365–81.

Aguila, Juan M. del (1984). *Cuba: Dilemmas of a Revolution*. Boulder, Colo., and London: Westview Press.

Akzin, Benjamin (1971). "On Great Powers and Super-Powers," in K. von Beyme (ed.), *Theory and Politics*. The Hague: Martinus Nijhoff: 610–26.

Albertini, Luigi (1952). *The Origins of the War of 1914*. 3 vols. Isabella M. Massey (trans. and ed.). Oxford: Oxford University Press.

Allardt, Erik, and W. Wesokowski, eds. (1980). *Social Structure and Change: Finland and Poland, Comparative Perspectives*. Warsaw: Polish Scientific Publishers.

Allison, Graham (1971). *Essence of Decision: Explaining the Cuban Missile Crisis*. Boston and New York: Little, Brown.

Allison, Roy (1985). *Finland's Relations with the Soviet Union, 1944–84*. London: Macmillan in association with St. Anthony's College, Oxford.

Almond, Gabriel A. (1950). *The American People and Foreign Policy*. New York: Harcourt Brace.

——— (1971). "National Politics and International Politics," in Albert Lepawski, Edward H. Buehrig, and Harold D. Lasswell (eds.), *The Search for World Order*. New York: Appleton Century Crofts: 283–97.

——— (1983). "Communism and Political Culture Theory." *Comparative Politics* 15, 2:127–38.

American Foreign Policy, Current Documents, 1961 (1965). Washington, D.C.: U.S. Government Printing Office.

American Foreign Policy, Current Documents, 1965 (1968). Washington, D.C.: U.S. Government Printing Office.

Amis, Kingsley (1953). *Lucky Jim*. New York: Viking Press.

Andelman, David A. (1981/82). "Contempt and Crisis in Poland." *International Security* 6, 3:90–103.

Anderson, Eugene N. (1930). *The First Moroccan Crisis*. Chicago: University of Chicago Press.

Apter, David E. (1971). *Choice and the Politics of Association: A Developmental Theory*. New Haven: Yale University Press.

Arbatov, Georgy (1982). "A Soviet Commentary," in Arthur M. Cox (ed.), *Russian Roulette: The Superpower Game*. New York: Times Books: 179–80.

Aristotle (1947). *The Politics of Aristotle*. William Ellis (trans.). London: J. M. Dent and Sons.

——— (1975). *The Politics of Aristotle*. Ernest Barker (trans.). London: Oxford University Press.

Arkin, William M. (1984). "Sleight of Hand with Trident II." *Bulletin of the Atomic Scientists* 40:5–6.

Arms Control and Disarmament Agency (1985). *Worldwide Military Expenditures and Arms Transfers*. Washington, D.C.: U.S. Government Printing Office.

Arnson, Cynthia (1984). "The Salvadoran Military and Regime Transformation," in Wolf Grabendorff and Heinrich Krumweide, eds., *Political Change in Central America: Internal and External Dimensions*. Boulder, Colo.: Westview Press.

Aron, Raymond (1963; trans. 1967). *Eighteen Lectures on Industrial Society*. London: Weidenfeld and Nicolson.

——— (1969). *Democracy and Totalitarianism*. New York: Praeger.

——— (1974). *The Imperial Republic: The United States and the World, 1945–1973*. Englewood Cliffs, N.J.: Prentice-Hall.

Ash, Timothy Garton (1984). "Back Yards." *New York Review of Books* 31, 18:3–9.

*Aspaturian, Vernon V. (1974). "The Soviet Impact on Development and Modernization in Eastern Europe," in Charles Gati (ed.), *The Politics of Modernization in Eastern Europe*. New York: Praeger: 205–74.

*——— (1984). "Eastern Europe in World Perspective," in Teresa Rakowska-Harmstone (ed.), *Communism in Eastern Europe*. Bloomington: Indiana University Press: 8–49.

*Bacharach, Samuel B., and Edward J. Lawler (1981). "Bargaining Power," in their *Bargaining: Power, Tactics, Outcomes*. San Francisco: Jossey-Bass: 41–79.

*Backer, B. (1982). "Self-Reliance Under Socialism: The Case of Albania." *Journal of Peace Research* 19, 4:355–67.

Bagley, Bruce M. (1981). "Mexico in the 1980s: A New Regional Power." *Current History* 80, 469:353–56, 386, 393–94.

——— (1983). "Mexican Foreign Policy: The Decline of a Regional Power?" *Current History* 82, 488:406–9, 437.

Bahry, Donna, and Cal Clark (1980). "Political Conformity and Economic Dependence in East Europe," in R. H. Linden (ed.), *The Foreign Policies of East Europe: New Approaches*. New York: Praeger: 135–58.

Bailey, Thomas A. (1950). *America Faces Russia: Russian-American Relations from Early Times to Our Day*. Ithaca, N.Y.: Cornell University Press.

Baker Fox, Annette (1977). *The Politics of Attraction: Four Middle Powers and the United States*. New York: Columbia University Press.

Baldwin, David (1979). "Power Analysis and World Politics." *World Politics* 31, 2:161–94.

*——— (1980). "Interdependence and Power: A Conceptual Analysis." *International Organization* (Autumn): 471–506.

Baloyra, Enrique (1985). "Central America on the Reagan Watch." *Journal of Interamerican Studies and World Affairs* 27, February.

Barghoorn, Frederick (1966). *Politics in the USSR*. Boston: Little, Brown.

Barlow, Ima C. (1940). *The Agadir Crisis*. Chapel Hill: University of North Carolina Press.

Barraclough, Geoffrey (1964). "From the European Balance of Power to the Age of World Politics," in his *An Introduction to Contemporary History*. Baltimore: Penguin Books [1968]: 93–123.

Bauer, Raymond, Ithiel Pool, and Lewis Dexter (1964). *American Business and Public Policy*. New York: Atherton Press.

Baum, Edward, and Felix Gagliano (1976). *Chief Executives in Black Africa and Southeast Asia*. Athens: Ohio University Center International Studies.

Bemis, Samuel F. (1943). *The Latin American Policy of the United States*. New York: Harcourt Brace.

Bender, Peter (1981). *Das Ende des Ideologischen Zeitalters (The End of the Ideological Era)*. Berlin: Severin und Siedler.

Berger, Peter L. (1974). *Pyramids of Sacrifice: Political Ethics and Social Change*. Garden City, N.Y.: Anchor Press.

Bethkenhagen, Jochen (1984). "Oil and Natural Gas in CMEA Intrabloc Trade." *Economic Bulletin* (of the German Institute for Economic Research), West Berlin: 20, 12.

Betts, Raymond F. (1985). *Uncertain Dimensions: Western Overseas Empires in the Twentieth Century*. Minneapolis: University of Minnesota Press.

Betts, Richard K. (1977). *Soldiers, Statesmen and Cold War Crises*. Cambridge, Mass.: Harvard University Press.

Beveridge, Albert J. (1903). *The Russian Advance*. New York: Harper and Bros.

Bialer, Seweryn (1976). "Ideology and Soviet Foreign Policy," in George Schwab (ed.), *Ideology and Foreign Policy*. New York: Cyrco Press: 76–102.

———— (1980). "Poland and the Soviet Imperium." *Foreign Affairs* 59, 3:522–39.

———— (1981). *The Domestic Context of Soviet Foreign Policy*. Boulder, Colo.: Westview Press.

Bielasiak, Jack (1981). "Recruitment Policy, Elite Integration, and Political Stability in People's Poland," in M. D. Simon and R. E. Kanet (eds.), *Background to Crisis: Policy and Politics in Gierek's Poland*. Boulder, Colo.: Westview Press: 95–134.

———— (1983). "The Party: Permanent Crisis," in A. Brumberg (ed.), *Poland: Genesis of a Revolution*. New York: Random House: 10–25.

———— (1984). "The Evolution of Crises in Poland," in J. Bielasiak and M. D. Simon (eds.), *Polish Politics: Edge of the Abyss*. New York: Praeger: 1–28.

Bitar, Sergio (1984). "United States–Latin American Relations: Shifts in Economic Power and Relations for the Future." *Journal of Interamerican Studies and World Affairs* 26, February.

Blachman, Morris, William LeoGrande, and Kenneth Sharpe, eds. (1986). *Confronting Revolution in Central America: Security Through Diplomacy in Central America*. New York: Pantheon Books.

Black, Cyril E. (1960). *The Transformation of Russian Society*. Cambridge, Mass.: Harvard University Press.

Blackmur, R. P. (1980). *Henry Adams*. New York: Harcourt Brace Jovanovich.

Blasier, Cole (1976). *The Hovering Giant: U.S. Responses to Revolutionary Change in Latin America*. Pittsburgh: University of Pittsburgh Press.

———— (1983). *The Giant's Rival: The USSR and Latin America*. Pittsburgh: University of Pittsburgh Press.

Blau, Peter M. (1964). *Exchange and Power in Social Life*. New York: John Wiley & Sons.

Blechman, Barry (1982). "The Political Utility of Nuclear Weapons: The 1973 Middle East Crisis." *International Security* 7, Summer: 132–56.

———, and Stephen S. Kaplan (1978). *Force Without War: U.S. Armed Forces as a Political Instrument*. Washington, D.C.: Brookings Institution.

Bloemer, Klaus (1983). "Freedom for Europe, East and West." *Foreign Policy* 5:23–38.

Boulding, Kenneth E. (1963). "Towards a Pure Theory of Threat Systems." *Economic Review* 53, 2:424–34.

Bourne, Kenneth (1970). *The Foreign Policy of Victorian England, 1830–1902*. Oxford: Clarendon Press.

*Boyd, G., and W. J. Feld, eds. (1980). *Comparative Regional Systems: West and East Europe, North America, the Middle East and Developing Countries*. Elmsford, N.Y.: Pergamon Press.

Brabant, Jozef van (1980). *Socialist Economic Integration*. Cambridge: Cambridge University Press.

——— (1984). "The USSR and Socialist Economic Integration: A Comment." *Soviet Studies* 34, 1.

Brada, Josef (1985). *Soviet Subsidizing of Trade with Eastern Europe: The Primacy of Economics Over Politics*. Munich: Ost-Europa Institute, paper no. 104.

Braun, Aurel (1983). *Small State Security*. New York: Macmillan.

Brezhnev, Leonid (1968). "Address to the Polish United Workers' Party." *Pravda*, November 4.

Broadhurst, A. I. (1982). *The Future of European Alliance Systems: NATO and the Warsaw Pact*. Boulder, Colo.: Westview Press.

Bromke, Adam (1985). *Eastern Europe in the Aftermath of Solidarity*. New York: Columbia University Press.

Brown, Archie (1983). "Pluralism, Power, and the Soviet Political System," in Susan Gross Solomon (ed.), *Pluralism in the Soviet Union*. London: Macmillan.

Brown, J. F. (1984). "The Future of Political Relations within the Warsaw Pact," in David Holloway and Jane M. O. Sharp (eds.), *The Warsaw Pact: Alliance in Transition?* Ithaca, N.Y.: Cornell University Press: 197–214.

*Brown, Kent N. (1977). "Coalition Politics and Soviet Influence in Eastern Europe," in Jan F. Triska and Paul Cocks (eds.), *Political Development in Eastern Europe*. New York: Praeger: 241–55.

Brown, Roger Glenn (1970). *Fashoda Reconsidered: The Impact of Domestic Politics on French Policy in Africa, 1893–1898*. Baltimore: Johns Hopkins University Press.

Brundenius, Claes (1984). *Revolutionary Cuba: The Challenge of Economic Growth with Equity*. Boulder, Colo.: Westview Press.

Brus, Wlodzimierz (1983). "Economics and Politics: The Fatal Link," in A. Brumberg (ed.), *Poland: Genesis of a Revolution*. New York: Random House: 26–41.

Bryce, James (1921). *Modern Democracies*. New York: Macmillan.

Brzezinski, Zbigniew (1967). *The Soviet Bloc: Unity and Conflict*, revised ed. Cambridge, Mass.: Harvard University Press.

——— (1970). *Between Two Ages: America's Role in the Technetronic Era*. New York: Viking Press.

——— (1982). *Wall Street Journal*, February 19.

——— (1984). "To End Yalta's Legacy." *New York Times*, December 27:A21.

——— (1984/85). "The Future of Yalta." *Foreign Affairs* 63, 2:279–302.

———, and Samuel P. Huntington (1964). *Political Power USA/USSR*. New York: Viking

Press.

Bull, Hedley (1971). "World Order and the Superpowers," in Carsten Holbraad (ed.), *Superpowers and World Order*. Canberra: Australian National University Press: 142–54.

————— (1977). *The Anarchical Society: A Study of Order in World Politics*. London and New York: Macmillan.

Bunce, Valerie (1985). "The Empire Strikes Back: The Transformation of the Eastern Bloc from a Soviet Asset to a Soviet Liability." *International Organization* 39, 1:1–46.

Burstin, Luis (1984). "Myths on Latin Upheavals." *New York Times*, February 9.

Burton, John W. (1972). *World Society*. Cambridge: Cambridge. University Press.

*Buzan, Barry (1984). "Security Strategies for Disengagement Policies," in J. G. Ruggie (ed.), *Antimonies of Interdependence: National Welfare and the International Division of Labor*. New York: Columbia University Press.

Campbell, John C. (1984). "Soviet Policy in Eastern Europe: An Overview," in Sarah M. Terry (ed.), *Soviet Policy in Eastern Europe*. New Haven: Yale University Press: 1–31.

Caporaso, James A. (1978). "Dependence, Dependency, and Power in the Global System: A Structural and Behavioral Analysis." *International Organization* 32, 1:13–43.

Cardoso, Fernando Henrique (1973a). "Cuba: Lesson or Symbol?" in David P. Barkin and Nita R. Manitzas (eds.), *Cuba: The Logic of the Revolution*. Andover, Mass.: Warner Modular Publications: 1–9.

————— (1973b). "Associated-Dependent Development," in Alfred Stepan (ed.), *Authoritarian Brazil*. New Haven: Yale University Press: 142–76.

————— (1977). "The Consumption of Dependency Theory in the United States." *Latin American Research Review* 12, 3:7–24.

—————, and Enzo Faletto (1979). *Dependency and Development in Latin America*, revised English ed. Berkeley and Los Angeles: University of California Press.

*Carnoy, Martin (1984). "The Dependent State," in his *The State and Political Theory*. Princeton, N.J.: Princeton University Press: 172–73, 184–207.

Carr, Edward Hallett (1947). *The Soviet Impact on the Western World*. New York: Macmillan.

Carter, Hodding (1982). "A Great Debate on the Atlantic Alliance." *Wall Street Journal*, March 11:27.

————— (1983). "The Generational Fissure in the Atlantic Alliance." *Wall Street Journal*, February 3:31.

Castaneda, Jorge G. (1985). "Don't Corner Mexico!" *Foreign Policy* 60:75–90.

————— (1985/86). "Mexico at the Brink." *Foreign Affairs* 64, 2:287–303.

Central America Crisis Monitoring Team (1985). *In Contempt of Congress: The Reagan Record of Deceit and Illegality on Central America*. Washington, D.C.: Institute for Policy Studies.

Chenery, Hollis, et al. (1974). *Redistribution with Growth*. New York: Oxford University Press.

*Child, John (1980). *Unequal Alliance: The Inter-American Military System, 1938–1978*. Boulder, Colo.: Westview Press.

Chinweizu (1975). *The West and the Rest of Us*. New York: Random House.

Cirincione, Joseph, and Leslie C. Hunter (1984). "Military Threats, Actual and Potential," in R. S. Leiken (ed.), *Central America: Anatomy of Conflict*. Elmsford, N.Y.: Pergamon Press: 173–92.

Clark, Cal, and Donna Bahry (1983a). "Dependent Development: A Socialist Variant." *International Studies Quarterly* 27, 3:271–93.

————— (1983b). "Political Relationships as a Reversal Mechanism in the Soviet Bloc," in

C. F. Doran, G. Modelski, and C. Clark (eds.), *North/South Relations: Studies of Dependency Reversal*. New York: Praeger: 205–21.

Clausewitz, Karl von (1976). *On War*. Princeton, N.J.: Princeton University Press.

Clement, Peter (1984). "Moscow and Nicaragua: Cultivating a New Client?" Paper presented at the annual meeting of the International Studies Association. Atlanta, March 29.

Cocks, Paul, Robert Daniels, and Nancy Heer (1979). *Soviet Politics: Essays in Memory of Merle Fainsod*. Cambridge, Mass.: Harvard University Press.

Cohen, Benjamin J. (1973). *The Question of Imperialism: The Political Economy of Dominance and Dependence*. New York: Basic Books.

Cohen, Bernard C. (1957). *The Political Process and Foreign Policy: The Making of the Japanese Peace Settlement*. Princeton, N.J.: Princeton University Press.

———— (1963). *The Press and Foreign Policy*. Princeton, N.J.: Princeton University Press.

Cohen, Eliot A. (1984). "Constraints on America's Conduct of Small Wars." *International Security* 9, 2:151–81.

*Coleman, Kenneth (1980). "The Political Mythology of the Monroe Doctrine," in John Martz and Louis Schoultz (eds.), *Latin America, The United States, and the Inter-American System*. Boulder, Colo.: Westview Press: 95–114.

Coles, Robert, and John Mack (1985). "If We Ended the Arms Race." *New York Times*, November 19:23.

Collier, David, ed. (1979). *The New Authoritarianism in Latin America*. Princeton, N.J.: Princeton University Press.

"Communist Interference in El Salvador" (1981). *State Department Bulletin* no. 2048.

Connell-Smith, Gordon (1974). *The United States and Latin America*. London: Halsted Press.

Constitution (Fundamental Law) of the Union of Socialist Republics (1978). Moscow: Novosti.

Corêaggio, José Luis, Carmen Diana Deere, and Richard Fagen, eds. (1986). *Transition and Development: Problems of Third World Socialism*. New York: Monthly Review Press.

Cornelius, Wayne A. (1985). "The Political Economy of Mexico Under De la Madrid: Austerity, Routinized Crisis, and Nascent Recovery." *Mexican Studies* 1, 1:83–124.

Cox, Aurthur M. (1982). *Russian Roulette: The Superpower Game*. New York: Times Books.

*Crabb, Cecil V., Jr. (1982). "The Monroe Doctrine: Palladium of American Foreign Policy," and "Conclusion: Doctrines in the American Diplomatic Tradition," in his *The Doctrines of American Foreign Policy*. Baton Rouge: Louisiana State University Press: 9–55, 371–437.

Croan, Melvin (1970). "Is Mexico the Future of Eastern Europe?: Institutional Adaptability and Political Change in Comparative Perspective," in Samuel P. Huntington and C. H. Moore (eds.), *Authoritarian Politics in Modern Society*. New York: Basic Books: 451–83.

Cuevas Cancino, Francisco (1977). "Bolivar's Commonwealth of Nations," in R. Meyers and K. Thompson (eds.), *Truth and Tragedy: A Tribute to Hans Morgenthau*. Washington, D.C.: New Republic Books: 322–32.

Curle, Adam (1981). *True Justice*. London: Quaker House Service.

Current Digest of the Soviet Press (1968). New York: Joint Committee on Slavic Studies, 20, 39: 10–12.

Curzon, G. N. (1907). *Frontiers: The Romanes Lecture, 1907*. London: Clarendon Press.

Dahl, Robert A. (1950). *Congress and Foreign Policy*. New York: Harcourt Brace.

———— (1961). *Who Governs?* New Haven: Yale University Press.

———— (1986). "On Practicality of Democracy." Cited in a Robert Wesson lecture. Stanford, Calif. February 6.

Dallek, Robert (1983). *The American Style of Foreign Policy*. New York: Mentor Books.

*Dallin, Alexander (1985). "Some Lessons of the Past," in Mark Garrison and A. Gleason (eds.), *Shared Destiny: Fifty Years of Soviet-American Relations*. Boston: Beacon Press: 59–81.

*————, and Gail W. Lapidus (1983). "Reagan and the Russians: United States Policy Toward the Soviet Union and Eastern Europe," in Robert J. Leiber, Kenneth A. Oye, and Donald S. Rothchild (eds.), *Eagle Defiant: United States Foreign Policy*. Boston: Little, Brown.

Dallin, David J. (1945). *The Big Three: The United States, Britain, Russia*. New Haven: Yale University Press.

Davies, Norman (1982). *God's Playground: A History of Poland*, vol. 2. New York: Columbia University Press.

Davis, Ralph (1973). *The Rise of the Atlantic Economies*. Ithaca, N.Y.: Cornell University Press.

Dawisha, Karen, Graham Allison, Fred Eidlin, and Jiri Valenta (1980). *Studies in Comparative Communism* Winter.

*Dawisha, Karen, and Peter Hanson, eds. *Soviet–East European Dilemmas*. London: Heineman for the Royal Institute of International Affairs: 41–60.

Deagle, Edwin A. (1983). "United States National Security Policy and Mexico," in C. W. Reynolds and C. Tello (eds.), *U.S.-Mexico Relations: Economic and Social Aspects*. Stanford, Calif.: Stanford University Press: 193–203.

*Dealy, Glen C. (1984/85). "The Pluralistic Latins." *Foreign Policy* 57, Winter: 108–27.

Dean, Jonathan (1984). "The Warsaw Pact in the International System," in David Holloway and Jane M. O. Sharp (eds.), *The Warsaw Pact: Alliance in Transition?* Ithaca, N.Y.: Cornell University Press: 238–62.

Department of Commerce (1985). *Statistical Abstract of the United States*. Washington, D.C.: U.S. Government Printing Office.

Department of Defense (Assistant Secretary for International Affairs). *Foreign Military Sales and Assistance Facts*. Washington, D.C.: U.S. Government Printing Office.

Department of State (1968). "Address by Secretary Rusk." *Department of State Bulletin* 59:1528.

Dickey, Christopher (1985). *With the Contras: A Reporter in the Wilds of Nicaragua*. New York: Simon & Schuster.

Dietz, Raimund (1986). "Advantages/Disadvantages in the USSR's Trade with Eastern Europe: The Aspect of Prices," in *Eastern Europe: Slow Growth in the 1980s* (a compendium of papers submitted to the Joint Economic Committee, U.S. Congress). Washington, D.C.: U.S. Government Printing Office.

Diskin, Martin, ed. (1983). *Trouble in Our Backyard*. New York: Pantheon Books.

Djilas, Milovan (1962). *Conversations with Stalin*. New York: Harcourt Brace and World.

Dobozi, Istvan (1985). "Intra-CMEA Mineral Cooperation." Paper presented at the ninth U.S.-Hungarian Economic Roundtable, Berkeley, June 10–12.

Dockrill, M. L. (1977). "British Policy During the Agadir Crisis of 1911," in F. H. Hinsley (ed.), *British Foreign Policy Under Sir Edward Grey*. London: Cambridge University Press: 271–87.

Dogan, Mattei, and Dominique Pelassy (1984). *How to Compare Nations*. Chatham, N.J.: Chatham House.

Dominguez, Jorge I. (1978). *Cuba: Order and Revolution*. Cambridge, Mass.: Harvard

University Press.

Dore, Isaak I. (1984). *International Law and the Superpowers: Normative Order in a Divided World.* New Brunswick, N.J.: Rutgers University Press.

Dudinsky, J. (1964) "A Community of Equal and Sovereign Nations." *International Affairs* (Moscow) 11:4.

Dukes, Paul (1970). *The Emergence of the Superpowers: A Short Comparative History of the U.S.A. and the U.S.S.R.* London: Macmillan.

Dulles, Foster Rhea (1962). *The United States Since 1865*, revised ed. Ann Arbor: University of Michigan Press.

Duncan, W. Raymond (1985). *The Soviet Union and Cuba: Interests and Influence.* New York: Praeger.

Dupréel, Eugene (1984). *Sociologie Général.* Paris: Presses Universitaires de France.

Dziewanowski, M. K. (1977). *Poland in the Twentieth Century.* New York: Columbia University Press.

Ebel, Roland H. (1984). "The Development and Decline of the Central American City-State," in H. J. Wiarda (ed.), *Rift and Revolution: The Central American Imbroglio.* Washington, D.C.: American Enterprise Institute: 70–104.

Emerson, Rupert (1960). *From Empire to Nation.* Cambridge, Mass.: Harvard University Press.

Epstein, Barbara (1985). "The Ideologies, the Pragmatists, and the Reagan Cold War Consensus." Unpublished paper, University of California, Santa Cruz.

Erisman, H. Michael (1985). *Cuba's International Relations: The Anatomy of a Nationalistic Foreign Policy.* Boulder, Colo.: Westview Press.

Evans, Peter (1979). *Dependent Development: The Alliance of Multinational, State, and Local Capital in Brazil.* Princeton, N.J.: Princeton University Press.

Fagen, Richard R. (1977). "The Realities of U.S.-Mexican Relations." *Foreign Affairs* 55, 4:685–700.

——— (1978a). "Cuba and the Soviet Union." *Wilson Quarterly* 2, 1:69–78.

——— (1978b). "A Funny Thing Happened on the Way to the Market: Thoughts on Extending Dependency Ideas." *International Organization* 32, 1:287–300.

——— (1983). "The Politics of the United States–Mexico Relationship," in C. W. Reynolds and C. Tello (eds.), *U.S.-Mexico Relations: Economic and Social Aspects.* Stanford, Calif.: Stanford University Press: 331–47.

———, and Olga Pellicer, eds. (1983). *The Future of Central America: Policy Choices for the U.S. and Mexico.* Stanford, Calif.: Stanford University Press.

Fagen, Richard, Carmen Diana Deere, and José Luis Corâaggio, eds. (1986). *Transition and Development: Problems of Third World Socialism.* New York: Monthly Review Press.

Falk, Richard A. (1972). "Zone II as a World Order Construct," in J. N. Rosenau, V. Davis, and M. A. East (eds.), *The Analysis of International Politics.* New York: Free Press: 189–206.

*——— (1974). "Counter-Revolution in the Modern World: Soviet-American Consensus and Continuities Between Counterinsurgency Abroad and at Home," in L. H. Miller and R. W. Pruessen (eds.), *Reflections on the Cold War.* Philadelphia: Temple University Press: 183–201.

Fallenbuchl, Zbigniew M. (1982). "Poland's Economic Crisis." *Problems of Communism* 31, 2:1–21.

Feinberg, Richard (1982). *Central America: International Dimensions of the Crisis.* New York: Holmes & Meier.

———— (1983). *The Intemperate Zone: The Third World Challenge to U.S. Foreign Policy.* New York: W. W. Norton.

Feldner, Fritz (1953/54). *Schicksaljahre Osterreichs 1908–1919: Das Politische Tagebuch Josef Redlich.* Graz: Bohlaus.

Ferreira, Olivieros S. (1985). "Política externa e liberdade de maniobra." *Política e Estrategia* 3, January–March.

Ferris, Elizabeth G. (1984). "Mexico's Foreign Policies: A Study in Contradictions," in J. K. Lincoln and E. G. Ferris (eds.), *The Dynamics of Latin American Foreign Policies: Challenges for the 1980s.* Boulder, Colo.: Westview Press: 213–27.

Fieldhouse, D. K. (1966, 2nd ed., 1981). *The Colonial Empires: A Comparative Survey from the Eighteenth Century.* New York: Dell.

———— (1967). *The Colonial Empires.* New York: Grosset & Dunlap.

———— (1981). *Colonialism 1870–1945: An Introduction.* New York: St. Martin's Press.

Fischer, Fritz (1975). *War of Illusions: German Policies from 1911–1914.* New York: W. W. Norton.

Ford, Gerald R. (1977). *The War Powers Resolution.* Washington, D.C.: American Enterprise Institute.

Foster, Gregory D. (1983). "On Selective Intervention." *Strategic Review* 11, 4:48–63.

Fox, William T. R. (1944). *The Super-Powers.* New York: Harcourt Brace.

Franck, Thomas M. (1977). "After the Fall: The New Procedural Framework for Congressional Control Over the War Power." *American Journal of International Law* 71, 4:605–41.

————, and Edward Weisband (1971). *Word Politics: Verbal Strategy Among the Superpowers.* New York: Oxford University Press.

Frank, Andre Gunter (1972). "Sociology of Development and Underdevelopment of Sociology," in J. D. Cockcroft et al., *Dependence and Underdevelopment.* Garden City, N.Y.: Anchor Press.

Fuentes, Carlos (1974). "Central and Eccentric Writing," in A. Fremantle (ed.), *Latin-American Literature Today.* New York: Mentor Books [1977]: 130–45.

Gaddis, John Lewis (1978). *Russia, the Soviet Union, and the United States: An Interpretive History.* New York: Alfred A. Knopf.

Galtung, Johan (1971). "A Structural Theory of Imperialism." *Journal of Peace Research* 8, 2:81–118.

———— (1980/81). "A Structural Theory of Imperialism—Ten Years Later." *Millennium: Journal of International Studies* 9, 3:181–96.

Gareev, M. A. (1985). *Frunze: Voennyi teoretik.* Moscow: Voenno-izdatel'stvo.

Garfinkle, Adam M. (1985). "U.S. Decisionmaking in the Jordan Crisis: Correcting the Record." *Political Science Quarterly* 100, Spring: 117–38.

Garnysz, Casimir [pseud.] (1982). "Holding a Bear by the Tail: The Polish Crisis." *Encounter* 59, 3–4:73–86.

Garthoff, Raymond L. (1984). *Détente and Confrontation.* Washington, D.C.: Brookings Institution.

———— (1985). "Eastern Europe in the Context of U.S.–Soviet Relations," in Sarah M. Terry (ed.), *Soviet Policy in Eastern Europe.* New Haven: Yale University Press.

Gati, Charles (1982). In a letter to Jan F. Triska, March 24.

———— (1985). "Soviet Empire: Alive But Not Well." *Problems of Communism* 34, 2:73–86.

Geertz, Clifford (1980). *Negara: The Theatre State in Nineteenth-Century Bali.* Princeton, N.J.: Princeton University Press.

George, Alexander L. (1969). "The Operational Code: A Neglected Approach to the Study of Political Leaders' Decision-Making." *International Studies Quarterly* 13, 2:190–222.

———— (1983). "The Arab-Israeli War of 1973: Origins and Impact," in his *Managing U.S. Soviet Rivalry.* Boulder, Colo.: Westview Press: 139–54.

————, and Richard Smoke (1974). *Deterrence in American Foreign Policy.* New York: Columbia University Press.

Gerschenkron, Alexander (1960). "Problems and Patterns of Russian Economic Development," in Cyril E. Black (ed.), *The Transformation of Russian Society.* Cambridge, Mass.: Harvard University Press.

Gilbert, Guy (1974). "Socialism and Dependency." *Latin American Perspectives* 1, 1:107–22.

Gilpin, Robert (1975). *U.S. Power and the Multinational Corporation.* New York: Basic Books.

*Gitelman, Zvi (1972). "Beyond Leninism: Political Development in Eastern Europe." *Newsletter on Comparative Studies of Communism* 5, 3:18–43.

Glennon, Michael J. (1984). "The War Powers Resolution Ten Years Later: More Politics Than Law." *American Journal of International Law* 78, 3:571–81.

Golan, Galia (1984). "Soviet Decisionmaking in the Yom Kippur War," in Jiri Valenta and William Potter (eds.), *Soviet Decisionmaking for Security.* London: Allen & Unwin: 185–217.

Goochman, C., and James Lee Ray (1979). "Structural Disparities in Latin America and Eastern Europe, 1950–1970." *Journal of Peace Research* 16: 231–54.

*Gorostiaga, Xabier (1982). "Dilemmas of the Nicaraguan Revolution," in Richard Fagen and Olga Pellicer (eds.), *The Future of Central America: Policy Choices for the U.S. and Mexico.* Stanford, Calif.: Stanford University Press: 47–66.

Gourevitch, Peter (1978). "The Second Image Reversed; The International Sources of Domestic Politics." *International Organization* 32, 4:881ff.

Grenville, J. A. S. (1964). *Lord Salisbury and Foreign Policy.* New York: Oxford University Press.

Grieco, Joseph (1982). "Between Dependency and Autonomy." *International Organization* 36, 3:609–32.

Griffith, Franklyn (1984). "The Sources of American Conduct: Soviet Perspectives and Their Policy Implications." *International Security* 9, Fall: 3–51.

Gross, Jan Tomasz (1983). "In Search of History," in A. Brumberg (ed.), *Poland: Genesis of a Revolution.* New York: Random House: 3–9.

Groth, Alexander (1979). "USSR: Pluralist Monolith." *British Journal of Political Science* 9:445–64.

Gustafson, Thane (1981/82). "Energy and the Soviet Bloc." *International Security* 6, 3:65–89.

*Haas, Ernest B. (1980). "Technological Self-Reliance for Latin America: The OAS Contribution." *International Organization* 34, 4:541–70.

Haimson, Leopold (1964/65). "The Problem of Social Stability in Urban Russia, 1905–1917." *Slavic Review* 23:619–42, and 24:1–22 , 47–56.

Halebsky, Sandor, and John M. Kirk, eds. (1985). *Cuba: Twenty-Five Years of Revolution, 1959–1984.* New York: Praeger.

Hall, Duncan H. (1948). *Mandates, Dependencies and Trusteeship.* London: Stevens.

Handel, Michael (1981). *Weak States in the International System.* London: Frank Cass.

———— (1982). "Does the Dog Wag the Tail or Vice Versa? Patron-Client Relations." *Jerusalem Journal of International Relations* 6, 2:24–35.

Hansen, Roger D. (1981). "The Evolution of U.S.-Mexican Relations: A Sociopolitical Perspective," in R. D. Erb and S. R. Ross (eds.), *United States Relations with Mexico: Context and Content.* Washington, D.C.: American Enterprise Institute: 39–48.

Harcave, Sidney (1968). *Years of the Golden Cockerel*. New York: Macmillan.

Hargreaves, John (1963). *Prelude to the Partition of West Africa*. London: St. Martin's Press.

Harsh, Joseph C. (1982). "Mr. Reagan's Sanctions." *Christian Science Monitor*, January 5:23.

Hart, Douglas M. (1982). "The Political Utility of Nuclear Weapons: The 1973 Middle East Crisis." *International Security* 7, Summer: 132–56.

Hartz, Louis (1955). *The Liberal Tradition in America*. New York: Harcourt Brace Jovanovich.

Hayes, Margaret Daly (1984). "Coping with Problems That Have No Solutions: Political Change in El Salvador and Guatemala," in A. Adelman and R. Reading (eds.), *Confrontations in the Caribbean Basin: International Perspectives on Security, Sovereignty, and Survival*. Pittsburgh: University of Pittsburgh Press.

Heikal, Mohammed (1975). *The Road to Ramadan*. New York: Times Books.

Hewett, E. A. (1983). "Foreign Economic Relations," in Abram Bergson and Herbert Levine (eds.), *The Soviet Economy: Towards the Year 2000*. London: Allen &. Unwin.

Hinsley, F. H. (1977). *British Foreign Policy Under Sir Edward Grey*. London: Cambridge University Press.

Hirschman, Albert O. (1978). "Beyond Asymmetry." *International Organization* 32, 1:45–50.

* ——— (1979). "The Turn to Authoritarianism in Latin America and the Search for Its Economic Determinants," in D. Collier (ed.), *The New Authoritarianism in Latin America*. Princeton, N.J.: Princeton University Press: 61–98.

——— (1980). *National Power and the Structure of Foreign Trade*, revised ed. Berkeley: University of California Press.

Hobsbawm, E. J. (1968). *Industry and Empire*. New York: Pantheon Books.

Hoffmann, Erik, and Frederic Fleron, eds. (1971). *The Conduct of Soviet Foreign Policy*. London: Butterworth.

Hoffmann, Stanley (1968). *Gulliver's Troubles or the Setting of America's Foreign Policy*. New York: McGraw-Hill.

——— (1984). "The Problem of Intervention," in Hedley Bull (ed.), *Intervention in World Policies*. Oxford: Clarendon Press.

Holbraad, Carsten (1984). *Middle Powers in International Politics*. London: Macmillan.

Holloway, David, and Jane M. O. Sharp (1984). *The Warsaw Pact: Alliance in Transition?* Ithaca, N.Y.: Cornell University Press.

*Holsti, K. J. (1982). *Why Nations Realign*. Boston and London: Allen &. Unwin.

Holt, Pat M. (1978). *The War Powers Resolution*. Washington, D.C.: American Enterprise Institute.

Holzman, Franklyn D. (1962). "Soviet Foreign Trade Pricing and the Question of Discrimination." *Review of Economics and Statistics* May: 134–47.

——— (1965). "More on Soviet Bloc Trade Discrimination." *Soviet Studies* July: 44–65.

Hopkins, Mark (1982). "Goodbye Poland, Hello Summit." *New Leader*, January 11: 3–5.

Hötzendorf, Franz Conrad von (1921–25). *Aus Meiner Dienstzeit*, 5 vols. Vienna: Rikola.

Hough, Jerry (1973). "The Bureaucratic Model and the Nature of the Soviet System." *Journal of Comparative Administration* August.

——— (1982). *The Polish Crisis: American Policy Options*. Washington, D.C.: Brookings Institution.

——— (1983). "Pluralism, Corporatism, and the Soviet Union," in Susan Gross Solomon (ed.), *Pluralism in the Soviet Union*. London: Macmillan.

——— (1985). "Russia and the Third World: The Revolutionary Road Runs Out." *Nation* 240, 21:666–68.

Hoyot, Edwin C. (1985). *Law and Force in American Foreign Policy*. Lanham, Md.: University Press of America.

Huntington, Samuel P. (1968). *Political Order in Changing Societies*. New Haven: Yale University Press.

——— (1970). "Social and Institutional Dynamics of One-Party Systems," in Samuel P. Huntington and C. H. Moore (eds.), *Authoritarian Politics in Modern Society*. New York: Basic Books: 3–47.

*——— (1982a). "American Ideals Versus American Institutions." *Political Science Quarterly* Spring: 14–37.

——— (1982b). "United States Foreign Policy and the Third World." Prepared for "Third World and Third Powers," Friedrich Ebert Stiftung, Bonn, West Germany, May 10–11.

*——— (1984). "Will More Countries Become More Democratic?" *Political Science Quarterly* 99, 2:193–218.

Hutchings, Robert L. (1983). *Soviet–East European Relations: Consolidation and Conflict, 1968–1980*. Madison: University of Wisconsin Press.

Iakubovskii, I. I. (1975). *Boevoe sodruzhestvo bratskikh narodov i armii*. Moscow: Voenizdat.

International Institute for Strategic Studies (1984). *The Military Balance*. London: IISS.

Jacobs, Jane (1984). *Cities and the Wealth of Nations: Principles of Economic Life*. New York: Vintage Books.

Jacobsen, C. G. (1984). "Soviet Attitudes Towards Aid to and Contacts with Central American Revolutionaries." Washington, D.C.: Report for the U.S. Department of State.

Jamgotch, Nish, Jr. (1975). "Alliance Management in Eastern Europe." *World Politics* 27, 3:405–29.

Jasczi, Oscar (1929). *The Dissolution of the Habsburg Monarchy*. Chicago: University of Chicago Press.

Javits, Jacob K. (1985). "War Powers Reconsidered." *Foreign Affairs* 64, 1:130–41.

Jelavich, Barbara (1973). *The Ottoman Empire, the Great Powers and the Straits Question, 1870–1887*. Bloomington: Indiana University Press.

Johnson, A. Ross (1985). "Soviet Military Policy in Eastern Europe," in Sarah M. Terry (ed.), *Soviet Policy in Eastern Europe*. New Haven: Yale University Press.

Johnson, Kenneth F. (1984). *Mexican Democracy: A Critical View*. New York: Praeger.

Johnson, Leland (1965). "U.S. Business Investments in Cuba and the Rise of Castro." *World Politics* 17, 3:440–59.

*Johnson, Paul M. (1977). "Modernization as an Agent of Political Change in East European States," in Jan F. Triska and Paul M. Cocks (eds.), *Political Development in Eastern Europe*. New York: Praeger: 30–50.

Joint Economic Committee, 97th Congress (1981). *East European Economic Assessment*, 2 parts. Washington, D.C.: U.S. Government Printing Office.

Jones, Christopher (1977). "Soviet Hegemony in Eastern Europe: The Dynamics of Political Autonomy and Military Intervention." *World Politics* 29, 2:216–41.

——— (1981). *Soviet Influence in Eastern Europe: Political Autonomy and the Warsaw Pact*. New York: Praeger.

Jonsson, Christer (1984). *Superpower: Comparing American and Soviet Foreign Policy*. London: Frances Pinter.

Jowitt, Kenneth (1978). *Social Change in Romania, 1860–1940*. Berkeley: Institute of International Studies, University of California.

——— (1985). "A Political Anthropology of Leninist Regime Relations." Unpublished paper, University of California, Berkeley.

Kanet, Roger E. (1981). "Poland, the Socialist Community, and East-West Relations," in M. D. Simon and R. E. Kanet (eds.), *Background to Crisis: Policy and Politics in Gierek's Poland.* Boulder, Colo.: Westview Press: 371–92.

———— (1983). "The Polish Crisis and Poland's 'Allies': The Soviet and East European Response to Events in Poland," in J. Bielasiak and M. D. Simon (eds.), *Polish Politics: Edge of the Abyss.* New York: Praeger: 317–44.

Kaplan, Stephen S. (1981). *Diplomacy of Power: Soviet Armed Forces As a Political Instrument.* Washington, D.C.: Brookings Institution.

Karl, Terry (1985). "After La Palma: The Prospects for Democratization in El Salvador." *World Policy Journal* Spring.

———— (forthcoming). "Imposing Consent: Electoralism Versus Democratization in El Salvador," in Paul Drake and Eduardo Silva (eds.), *Elections in Latin America.* San Diego: University of California Press.

Katzenstein, Peter J. (1977). "Between Power and Plenty: Foreign Economic Policies of Advanced Industrial States," a symposium. *International Organization* 31, 4, Autumn.

Kaufman, Edy (1976). *The Superpowers and Their Spheres of Influence: The United States and the Soviet Union in Eastern Europe and Latin America.* London: Croom Helm, and New York: St. Martin's Press.

Kaufman, Michael T. (1986). "East Europeans and Party Congress." *New York Times,* February 23.

Keal, Paul E. (1983a). "Contemporary Understanding About Spheres of Influence." *Review of International Studies* 9, 3:153–72.

———— (1983b). *Unspoken Rules and Superpower Dominance.* London: Macmillan.

Kelly, J. B. (1980). *Arabia, the Gulf, and the West.* New York: Basic Books.

Kemme, David M. (1984). "The Polish Crisis: An Economic Overview," in J. Bielasiak and M. D. Simon (eds.), *Polish Politics: Edge of the Abyss.* New York: Praeger: 29–55.

Kennan, George (1951). *American Diplomacy, 1900–1950.* Chicago: University of Chicago Press.

———— (1985). "Morality and Foreign Policy." *Foreign Affairs* 64, 2:205–18.

Kennedy, John F. (1981). "Inaugural Speech, January 20, 1961." *Department of State Bulletin* 44, February 6:175–76.

Keohane, Robert O., and Joseph S. Nye (1977). *Power and Independence.* Boston: Little, Brown.

*Keylor, William R. (1984). "The Confirmation of United States Supremacy," in his *The Twentieth Century World: An International History.* New York: Oxford University Press.

Kiep, Walther Leisler (1984/85). "The New Deutschland-politik." *Foreign Affairs* 63, 2:316–29.

Kiernan, V. G. (1982). *European Empires from Conquest to Collapse, 1815–1960.* London: Fontana.

Kindleberger, Charles P. (1973). *The World in Depression, 1929–1939.* Berkeley: University of California Press.

———— (1981). "Dominance and Leadership in the International Economy." *International Studies Quarterly* 25:2.

Kinzer, Stephen (1986). "Sandinistas Get Tough But Politics Are Lively." *New York Times,* March 20:4.

Kirkpatrick, Jeane (1979). "Dictatorships and Double Standards." *Commentary* 68, 5:34–45.

Kissinger, Henry A. (1964). *A World Restored.* New York: Grosset & Dunlap.

———— (1982). *Years of Upheaval.* Boston: Little, Brown.

*Klare, Michael T., and Cynthia Arnson (1979). "Exporting Repression: U.S. Support for Authoritarianism in Latin America," in Richard Fagen (ed.), *Capitalism and the State in U.S.–Latin American Relations.* Stanford, Calif.: Stanford University Press: 138–68.

Klein, Robert A. (1974). *Sovereign Equality Among States: The History of an Idea.* Toronto: University of Toronto Press.

Knopf, Jeffrey William (1986). Unpublished paper, Stanford University.

Knorr, Klauss (1975). *The Power of Nations: The Political Economy of International Relations.* New York: Basic Books.

Kolakowski, Leszek (1982). "Ideology in Eastern Europe," in M. M. Drachkovitch (ed.), *East Central Europe: Yesterday, Today, Tomorrow.* Stanford, Calif.: Hoover Institution Press: 43–53.

———— (1983). "General Theory of Sovietism: A Word About Dangers and Hopes." *Encounter* 60, 5:19–21.

Konirsh, Suzanne (1955). "Constitutional Aspects of the Struggle Between Germans and Czechs in the Austro-Hungarian Monarchy." *Journal of Modern History* 27:231–62.

Konrad, George (1984). *Antipolitics: An Essay.* New York: Harcourt Brace Jovanovich.

Konwicki, Tadeusz (1983). *A Minor Apocalypse.* Richard Lourie (trans.). New York: Farrar, Straus & Giroux.

Korbel, Josef (1959). *The Communist Subversion of Czechoslovakia.* Princeton, N.J.: Princeton University Press.

Korbonski, Andrzej (1983). "Eastern Europe," in R. F. Byrnes (ed.), *After Brezhnev: Sources of Soviet Conduct in the 1980s.* Bloomington: Indiana University Press: 290–344.

———— (1984a). "Poland," in T. Rakowska-Harmstone (ed.), *Communism in Eastern Europe.* Bloomington: Indiana University Press: 50–85.

———— (1984b). "Soviet Policy Toward Poland," in Sarah M. Terry (ed.), *Soviet Policy in Eastern Europe.* New Haven: Yale University Press: 61–92.

Kovalev, S. (1968). "Sovereignty and the International Obligations of Socialist Countries," *Pravda,* September 26. Translated in *Current Digest of the Soviet Press* 20:39.

Kramer, John M. (1985). "Soviet CMEA Energy Ties." *Problems of Communism* 34, July/August.

Krasner, Stephen D. (1976). "State Power and the Structure of International Trade." *World Politics* 28, 3:317–47.

———— (1978). *Defending the National Interest: Raw Materials Investments and U.S. Foreign Policy.* Princeton, N.J.: Princeton University Press.

Kryzanek, Michael J. (1985). *U.S.–Latin American Relations.* New York: Praeger.

Kundera, Milan (1984). "The Tragedy of Central Europe." *New York Review of Books* 31, 7:33–39.

———— (1985). "A Talk with Milan Kundera." *New York Times Magazine,* May 19:72ff.

Kurth, James R. (1973). "United States Foreign Policy and Latin American Military Rule," in Philippe C. Schmitter (ed.), *Military Rule in Latin America: Functions, Consequences and Perspectives.* Beverly Hills: Sage Publications: 244–322.

———— (1979a). "Industrial Change and Political Change: A European Perspective," in David Collier (ed.), *The New Authoritarianism in Latin America.* Princeton, N.J.: Princeton University Press: 319–82.

———— (1979b). "The Political Consequences of the Product Cycle." *International Organization* 33, 1:1–34.

———— (1982a). "American Leadership, the Western Alliance, and the Old Regime in the Persian Gulf," in Steven L. Spiegel (ed.), *The Middle East and Western Alliances.* London: Allen & Unwin: 117–28.

———— (1982b). "The United States and Central America: Hegemony in Historical and Comparative Perspective," in Richard F. Feinberg (ed.), *Central America: International Dimensions of the Crisis*. New York: Holmes & Meier: 39–57.

———— (1986a). Letter to Jan F. Triska. Swarthmore, Pa. February.

———— (1986b). "The United States, Latin America, and the World: The Changing International Context of U.S.–Latin American Relations," in Kevin J. Middlebrook and Carlos Rico (eds.), *United States–Latin American Relations in the 1980s: Contending Perspectives on a Decade of Crisis*. Pittsburgh: University of Pittsburgh Press.

Kux, Ernst (1980). "Growing Tensions in Eastern Europe." *Problems of Communism* 29.

LaFeber, Walter (1963). *The New Empire: An Interpretation of American Expansionism, 1860–1898*. Ithaca, N.Y.: Cornell University Press.

———— (1983). *Inevitable Revolutions: The United States in Central America*. New York: W. W. Norton.

Langer, William (1960). *The Diplomacy of Imperialism, 1890–1902*. New York: Alfred A. Knopf.

Laquer, Walter, and George L. Mosse, eds. (1966). *1914: The Coming of the First World War*. New York: Harper & Row.

La Rochefoucauld, F. (1959). *Maxims*. New York: Penguin Books.

Larrabee, Stephen F. (1981/82). "Instability and Change in Eastern Europe." *International Security* 6, 3:39–64.

Lasswell, Harold D. (1958). *Politics: Who Gets What, When, How*. New York: Meridian Books.

Laue, Theodore H. von (1965). "The Chances for a Liberal Constitution." *Slavic Review* 24, March: 34–46.

Lavigne, Marie (1985). *Economie Internationale des Pays Socialistes*. Paris: Armand Collin.

Leach, James, et al. (1984). *U.S. Policy in Central America: Against the Law?* Washington, D.C.: Arms Control and Foreign Policy Caucus.

Lebow, Richard Ned (1982). "The Soviet Response to Poland and the Future of the Warsaw Pact," in Arlene I. Broadhurst (ed.), *The Future of European Alliance Systems: NATO and the Warsaw Pact*. Boulder, Colo.: Westview Press: 185–236.

———— (1984). "The Paranoia of the Powerful: Thucydides on World War III." *PS* 17, 1:10–17.

Lee, Rensselaer W., III (1983). *Influence in Soviet Relations With the Third World*. Princeton, N.J.: Everest Associates.

Leiken, Robert S. (1981). "Eastern Winds in Latin America." *Foreign Policy* 42, Spring: 94–113.

———— (1984). *Central America: Anatomy of a Conflict*. Elmsford, N.Y.: Pergamon Press.

———— (1985). "Twin Threats to Democracy in Nicaragua," *New York Times*, October 27:E23.

Lenin, V. I. (1977). *Imperialism, the Highest Stage of Capitalism: A Popular Outline*. New York: International Publishers.

LeoGrande, William M. (1979). "Cuban Dependency: A Comparison of Pre-Revolutionary and Post-Revolutionary International Economic Relations." *Cuban Studies* 9, 2:1–28.

Leontiev, Wassily (1971). "The Trouble With Cuban Socialism." *New York Review of Books*, January 7:19–23.

Levinson, Jerome, and Juan de Onis (1970). *The Alliance That Lost Its Way*. Chicago: Quadrangle Books.

Levy, Daniel, and Gabriel Szekely (1983). *Mexico: Paradoxes of Stability and Change*. Boulder, Colo.: Westview Press.

Lewis, Flora (1982). "Alarm Bells in the West." *Foreign Affairs* 60, 3:551–72.

Lewis, George Cornwall (1841; reprinted 1901). *Government of Dependencies*. London: M. Walter Dunne, Universal Classics Library.

Lidová Armáda (1968). July 2.

Linden, Ronald H. (1986). "Regarding Impact of Interdependence: Yugoslavia and International Change." *Comparative Politics* 18, 2:211–34.

Lindley, M. F. (1969). *The Acquisition and Government of Backward Territory in International Law*. New York: Negro Universities Press.

Liska, George (1967). *Imperial America: The International Politics of Primacy*. Baltimore: Johns Hopkins University Press.

——— (1978). *Career of Empire*. Baltimore: Johns Hopkins University Press.

Lockwood, Lee (1970). "Introduction to 'This Shame Will Be Welcome . . .': A Speech by Fidel Castro." *New York Review of Books*, September 24:18–20.

Lowe, C. J. (1967). *The Reluctant Imperialists: British Foreign Policy, 1878–1902*. London: Routledge & Kegan Paul.

Lowenthal, Abraham (1973). "United States Policy Toward Latin America: 'Liberal,' 'Radical' and 'Bureaucratic' Perspectives." *Latin American Research Review* 8, 3:3–25.

*——— (1974). "'Liberal,' 'Radical' and 'Bureaucratic' Perspectives on U.S.–Latin American Policy," in J. Colter and Richard R. Fagen (eds.), *Latin America and the United States: The Changing Political Realities*. Stanford, Calif.: Stanford University Press: 212–35.

——— (1979). "The United States and Latin America: Ending the Hegemonic Presumption." *Foreign Affairs* 55, 1:199–213.

*——— (1983). "Ronald Reagan and Latin America: Coping with Hegemony in Decline," in Robert J. Leiber, Kenneth A. Oye, and Donald S. Rothchild (eds.), *Eagle Defiant: United States Foreign Policy*. Boston: Little, Brown: 311–35.

*Lowenthal, Richard (1974). "On 'Established' Communist Party Regimes." *Studies in Comparative Communism* 7, 4:335–58.

——— (1977). *Model or Ally? Communist Powers and the Developing Countries*. New York: Oxford University Press.

——— (1984/85). "The German Question Transformed." *Foreign Affairs* 63, 2:303–15.

Lowi, Theodore (1964). "American Business, Public Policy: Case Studies and Political Theory." *World Politics* July.

*——— (1967). "Making Democracy Safe for the World," in J. N. Rosenau (ed.), *Domestic Sources of Foreign Policy*. New York: Free Press: 295–303, 315–31.

Lugard, F. D. (1923). *The Dual Mandate*. London: Blackwood.

Macartney, C. A. (1969). *The Habsburg Empire, 1790–1918*. New York: Macmillan.

*McCall, Richard (1984). "From Monroe to Reagan: An Overview of U.S.–Latin American Relations," in Richard Newfarmer (ed.), *From Gunboats to Diplomacy*. Baltimore: Johns Hopkins University Press: 15–34.

McCully, Bruce (1940). *English Education and the Origins of Indian Nationalism*. New York: Columbia University Press.

Machiavelli (1940). *The Prince*. New York: Random House.

*McNeill, William H. (1984). "International Alliances," in Lisa Taylor (ed.), *The Phenomenon of Change*. New York: Cooper-Hewitt Museum: 56–57.

Mahan, Alfred T. (1889). *The Influence of Sea Power Upon History, 1660–1783*. Boston: Little, Brown.

Marcella, Gabriel (1985). "Defense of the Western Hemisphere: Strategy for the 1990s." *Journal of Interamerican Studies and World Affairs* 27, Fall.

Marchetti, Victor, and John Marks (1974). *The CIA and the Cult of Intelligence*. New York: Dell.

Marer, Paul (1974a). "The Political Economy of Soviet Relations with Eastern Europe," in S. J. Rosen and J. R. Kurth (eds.), *Testing Theories of Economic Imperialism*. Lexington, Mass.: D. C. Heath: 231–60.

———— (1974b). "Soviet Economic Policy in Eastern Europe," in *Reorientation and Commercial Relations of the Countries of Eastern Europe* (a compendium of papers submitted to the Joint Economic Committee, U.S. Congress). Washington, D.C.: U.S. Government Printing Office.

———— (1984a). "East European Economies: Achievements, Problems, Prospects," in T. Rakowska-Harmstone (ed.), *Communism in Eastern Europe*. Bloomington: Indiana University Press: 283–328.

———— (1984b). "Intrabloc Economic Relations and Prospects," in D. Holloway and J. Sharp (eds.), *The Warsaw Pact: Alliance in Transition?* Ithaca, N.Y.: Cornell University Press: 215–37.

———— (1984c). "The Political Economy of Soviet Relations with Eastern Europe," in Sarah M. Terry (ed.), *Soviet Policy in Eastern Europe*. New Haven: Yale University Press: 155–88.

———— (1985a). *Dollar GNPs of the USSR and Eastern Europe*. Baltimore: Johns Hopkins University Press.

———— (1985b). "Prepared Statements Before the Subcommittee on Europe and the Middle East, Committee on Foreign Affairs, U.S. House of Representatives." October 7.

————, and J. M. Montias (1980). "Theory of Measurement of Eastern European Integration," in their *East European Integration and East-West Trade*. Bloomington: Indiana University Press.

Marrese, Michael (1986). "CMEA: Effective but Cumbersome Political Economy." *International Organization* 26, 2.

————, and Jan Vanous (1983). *Soviet Subsidization of Trade with Eastern Europe*. Berkeley: Institute of International Studies, University of California.

Martz, Larry (1983). "Next Target: Nicaragua?" *Newsweek*, November 14:44.

Mason, David S. (1984). "The Polish Party in Crisis, 1980–1982," *Slavic Review* 43, 1:30–45.

Matejko, Alexander J. (1980). "Canada and Poland: Two Countries, Two 'Big Brothers.'" *Jerusalem Journal of International Relations* 4, 4:31–55.

Matossian, Mary (1962). "Ideologies of Delayed Industrialization: Some Tensions and Ambiguities," in John H. Kautsky (ed.), *Political Change in Underdeveloped Countries: Nationalism and Communism*. New York: John Wiley & Sons: 252–64.

May, Ernest R. (1968). *American Imperialism: A Speculative Essay*. New York: Atheneum.

———— (1975). *The Making of the Monroe Doctrine*. Cambridge, Mass.: Harvard University Press.

Mecham, John Lloyd (1965). *A Survey of United States–Latin American Relations*. Boston: Houghton Mifflin.

Mendel, Arthur P. (1965). "Peasant and Worker on the Eve of the First World War." *Slavic Review* 24, March: 23–33.

Menderhausen, Horst (1959). "Terms of Trade Between the Soviet Union and Smaller Communist Countries, 1955–1957." *Review of Economics and Statistics* May: 106–18.

———— (1960). "The Terms of Soviet-Satellite Trade: A Broadened Analysis." *Review of Economics and Statistics* May: 152–63.

Merk, Frederick (1963). *Manifest Destiny and Mission in American History: A Reinterpretation*. New York: Alfred A. Knopf.

——— (1966). *The Monroe Doctrine and American Expansionism, 1843–1849*. New York: Alfred A. Knopf.

Mesa-Lago, Carmelo (1981). *The Economy of Socialist Cuba: A Two-Decade Appraisal*. Albuquerque: University of New Mexico Press.

Meyer, Cord (1980). *Facing Reality: From World Federalism to the CIA*. Lanham, Md.: University Press of America.

Meyer, Michael C. (1981). "Roots and Realities of Mexican Attitudes Toward the United States," in R. D. Erb and S. R. Ross (eds.), *United States Relations with Mexico: Context and Content*. Washington, D.C.: American Enterprise Institute: 29–38.

Michnik, Adam (1985). "Letter from the Gdansk Prison." Jerzy B. Warman (trans.). *New York Review of Books* 32, 12:42–48.

Middlebrook, Kevin J. (1981). "Energy Security in U.S.-Mexican Relations," in D. A. Deese and J. S. Nye (eds.), *Energy and Security*. Cambridge, Mass.: Ballinger Publishing: 152–80.

——— (1985). *Political Liberalization in an Authoritarian Regime: The Case of Mexico*. Research Report Series 41. San Diego: Center for U.S.-Mexican Studies, University of California.

Milewski, Jerzy, Krzysztof Pomian, and Jan Zielonka (1985/86). "Poland Four Years After." *Foreign Affairs* 64, 2:337–59.

Miller, George, Mark Hatfield, and James Leach (1985). *U.S. Aid to El Salvador: An Evaluation of the Past, a Proposal for the Future*. Washington, D.C.: Arms Control and Foreign Policy Caucus.

Miller, Robert F., ed. (1984). *Poland in the Eighties: Social Revolution Against "Real Socialism."* Canberra: Australian National University Press.

Milosz, Czeslaw (1953). *The Captive Mind*. New York: Alfred A. Knopf.

——— (1983). *The Witness of Poetry*. Cambridge, Mass.: Harvard University Press.

——— (1986). "An Interview with Czeslaw Milosz," *New York Review of Books* 33, 3:34–35.

Misztal, Bronislaw, ed. (1985). *Poland After Solidarity: Social Movements Versus the State*. New Brunswick, N.J.: Transaction Books.

Mlynar, Zdenek (1980). *Nightfrost in Prague: The End of Humane Socialism*. New York: Karz-Cohl Publishing.

Mochizuki, Mike M. (1983). "Japan's Search for a Strategy." *International Security* 8, Winter: 152–79.

Modelski, George (1978). "The Long Cycle of Global Politics and the Nation-State." *Comparative Studies in Society and History* 20:2.

*Moneta, Carlos (1973). "The Latin American Economic System as a Mechanism to Control Conflicts," in M. A. Morris and Victor Milan (eds.), *Controlling Latin American Conflicts*. Boulder, Colo.: Westview Press: 99–116.

Monroe, Elizabeth (1963). *Britain's Moment in the Middle East, 1914–1956*. Baltimore: Johns Hopkins University Press.

Montesquieu (1977). *The Spirit of Laws*. Berkeley: University of California Press.

*Moore, Barrington, Jr. (1971). "Of Predatory Democracy: The USA," in his *Reflections on the Causes of Human Misery*. Boston: Beacon Press: 105–50.

Morgenthau, Hans J. (1966). *Politics Among Nations: The Struggle for Power and Peace*. New York: Alfred A. Knopf.

Morrison, David C. (1985). "Japanese Principles, U.S. Policies." *Bulletin of the Atomic Scientists* 41, June/July: 22–24.

Mueller, John E. (1973). *War, Presidents, and Public Opinion*. New York: John Wiley.

Muñoz, Heraldo (1981). "The Strategic Dependency of the Centers and the Economic

Importance of the Latin American Periphery," in his *From Dependency to Development*. Boulder, Colo.: Westview Press: 59–92.

Nagy, Imre (1957). *On Communism: In Defense of the New Course*, New York: Praeger.

Nairn, Ronald C. (1982). "Why NATO Doesn't Work." *Wall Street Journal*, March 26:26.

Narodnoe Khozaistvo SSSR 1983 (1984). Moscow: Finantsy i statistika.

Nau, Henry R. (1981). "U.S.-Mexican Oil and Gas Relations: A Special Relationship?" in R. D. Erb and S. R. Ross (eds.), *United States Relations with Mexico*. Washington, D.C.: American Enterprise Institute: 195–211.

Needler, Martin C. (1982). "Mexico: Wary Neighbor," in R. Wesson (ed.), *U.S. Influence in Latin America in the 1980s*. New York: Praeger: 185–97.

Nehru, Jawaharlal (1946; 1960 ed.). *The Discovery of India*. London: Meridian.

The New Cambridge Modern History, vol. 1 (1957). Cambridge: Cambridge University Press.

Newfarmer, Richard, ed. (1984). *From Gunboats to Diplomacy: New U.S. Policies for Latin America*. Baltimore: Johns Hopkins University Press.

New York Times (1980). August 28:8.

Niebuhr, Reinhold (1959). *The Structure of Nations and Empires*. New York: Charles Scribner's Sons.

Nixon, Richard M. (1978). *The Memoirs of Richard Nixon*. New York: Grosset & Dunlap.

*Nogee, J. L., and J. W. Sloan (1979). "Allende's Chile and the Soviet Union: A Policy Lesson for Latin American Nations Seeking Autonomy." *Journal of Interamerican Studies and World Affairs* 21, 3:339–68.

North, Robert N., Nobutake Ike, and Jan F. Triska (1985). *The World of the Superpowers*, revised ed. Stanford, Calif.: Notrik Press.

Odell, John S. (1980). "Latin American Trade Negotiations with the United States." *International Organization* 34, 2:207–28.

O'Donnell, Guillermo A. (1973). *Modernization and Bureaucratic Authoritarianism: Studies in South American Politics*. Berkeley: Institute of International Studies, University of California.

Ojeda, Mario (1983). "The Future of Relations Between Mexico and the United States," in C. W. Reynolds and C. Tello (eds.), *U.S.-Mexico Relations: Economic and Social Aspects*. Stanford, Calif.: Stanford University Press: 315–30.

*Organski, A. F. K. (1968). "The New Colonialism: Economic Dependencies and Satellites," in his *World Politics*. New York: Alfred A. Knopf: 245–71.

Orton, Keith (1983). "Finland and Mexico: A Comparative Historical Analysis," in C. F. Doran, G. Modelski, and C. Clark (eds.), *North/South Relations: Studies of Dependency Reversal*. New York: Praeger: 187–204.

O'Toole, G. J. A. (1984). *The Spanish War: An American Epic, 1898*. New York: W. W. Norton.

Packenham, Robert A. (1973). *Liberal America and the Third World*. Princeton, N.J.: Princeton University Press.

——— (1983). "The Dependency Perspective and Analytic Dependency," in C. F. Doran, G. Modelski, and C. Clark (eds.), *North/South Relations: Studies of Dependency Reversal*. New York: Praeger: 29–47.

Parker, W. H. (1969). *An Historical Geography of Russia*. Chicago: Aldine.

——— (1972). *The Superpowers: The United States and the Soviet Union Compared*. New York: John Wiley & Sons.

Parry, J. H. (1966). *The Establishment of the European Hegemony, 1415–1715*. New York: Harper & Row.

——— (1974). *The Discovery of the Sea*. New York: Dial.

Pastor, Robert (1982). "Sinking in the Caribbean Basin." *Foreign Affairs* 60, 5:1038–58.

———— (1983). "Cuba and the Soviet Union: Does Cuba Act Alone?" in Barry B. Levine (ed.), *The New Cuban Presence in the Caribbean*. Boulder, Colo.: Westview Press: 191–209.

Paz, Octavio (1961). *The Labyrinth of Solitude: Life and Thought in Mexico*. New York: Grove Press.

———— (1972). *The Other Mexico: Critique of the Pyramid*. New York: Grove Press. (Lectures initially presented in Spanish, 1969.)

———— (1985). *One Earth, Four or Five Worlds: Reflections on Contemporary History*. San Diego: Harcourt Brace Jovanovich.

Peceny, Mark (1986). Unpublished paper, Stanford University.

Pecsi, Kalman (1981). *The Future of Socialist Economic Interpretation*. Armonk, N.Y.: M. E. Sharpe.

Peking Review (1973a). No. 16.

———— (1973b). No. 29.

———— (1973c). No. 43.

Pellicer de Brody, Olga (1983). "National Security in Mexico: Traditional Notions and New Preoccupations," in C. W. Reynolds and C. Tello (eds.), *U.S.-Mexico Relations: Economic and Social Aspects*. Stanford, Calif.: Stanford University Press: 181–92.

*Perez, Louis A., Jr. (1982). "Intervention, Hegemony, and Dependency: The United States in the Circum-Caribbean, 1898–1980," *Pacific Historical Review* May: 165–94.

———— (1985). "Toward a New Future, From a New Past: The Enterprise of History in Socialist Cuba." *Cuban Studies* 15, 1:1–13.

Perkins, Dexter (1955 and 1963). *A History of the Monroe Doctrine*. Boston: Little, Brown.

———— (1961). *The United States and Latin America*. Baton Rouge: Louisiana State University Press.

———— (1966). *The United States and the Caribbean*. Cambridge, Mass.: Harvard University Press.

Perkins, Whitney T. (1981). *Constraint of Empire: The United States and Caribbean Interventions*. Westport, Conn.: Greenwood Press.

Pike, Douglas (1984). "Communist vs. Communist in Southeast Asia." *International Security* 8, Spring: 67–90.

*Pike, Frederick B. (1974). "Corporatism and Latin American–United States Relations," in F. B. Pike and T. Stritch (eds.), *The New Corporatism*. Notre Dame, Ind.: Notre Dame University Press: 132–70.

Plesur, Milton (1971). *America's Outward Thrust: Approaches to Foreign Affairs, 1869–1890*. De Kalb: Northern Illinois University Press.

Podhoretz, Norman (1985). "The Reagan Road to Détente." *Foreign Affairs* 63, 3.

Poitras, Guy (1981). "Mexico's Foreign Policy in an Age of Interdependence," in E. G. Ferris and J. K. Lincoln (eds.), *Latin American Foreign Policies: Global and Regional Dimensions*. Boulder, Colo.: Westview Press: 103–13.

———— (1985). "The State of Hegemony and the Hegemonic State: The U.S. and the Caribbean Basin." Paper presented to the annual meeting of the International Studies Association, Washington, D.C., March 5–9.

Polk, William R. (1975). *The United States and the Arab World*, 3rd ed. Cambridge, Mass.: Harvard University Press.

Polybius (1912). *The Histories*. W. R. Paton (trans.). London: Heineman.

Porter, Bruce (1984). *The USSR in Third World Conflicts: Soviet Arms and Diplomacy in Local Wars, 1945–1980*. Cambridge: Cambridge University Press.

Poznanski, Kazimierz (1984). "Competition Between Eastern Europe and Developing Countries in the Western Market for Manufactured Goods," in *Compendium of Papers, Eastern European Assessment*, vol. 2. Foreign Trade and International Financing, Joint Economic Committee of the U.S. Congress, Washington, D.C.

———— (1985). "Implicit Trade Subsidies: Discussion of New Methodology and New Evidence." Troy, N.Y.: Department of Economics, Rensselaer Polytechnic Institute.

———— (1986a). "Economic Adjustment and Political Forces: Poland Since 1970." *International Organization* 40, 4.

———— (1986b). "The Newly Industrializing Countries in Product Cycle in Manufactures." Troy, N.Y.: Department of Economics, Rensselaer Polytechnic Institute.

Przeworski, Adam, and Henry Teune (1970). *The Logic of Comparative Social Inquiry*. Particularly chaps. 4 and 5. New York: John Wiley & Sons.

Purcell, Susan Kaufman, ed. (1981). "Mexico–United States Relations." *Proceedings of the Academy of Political Science* 34, 1:1–32, 97–157, 189–208.

————, and J. F. H. Purcell (1980). "State and Society in Mexico: Must a Stable Polity Be Institutionalized?" *World Politics* 32, 2:194–227.

Quandt, William B. (1977). *Decade of Decisions*. Berkeley: University of California Press.

Ra'anan, Gavriel D. (1979). *The Evolution of the Soviet Use of Surrogates in Military Relations with the Third World*. Santa Monica: Rand Corporation.

Rabin, Yitzhak (1979). *The Rabin Memoirs*. Boston: Little, Brown.

Rachwald, Arthur R. (1982). "Poland: *Quo Vadis?*" *Current History* 81, 478:371–75, 389–92.

———— (1983). *Poland Between the Superpowers*. Boulder, Colo.: Westview Press.

*Rakowska-Harmstone, Teresa (1984). "Nationalism and Integration in Eastern Europe: The Dynamics of Change," in her *Communism in Eastern Europe*. Bloomington: Indiana University Press: 360–81.

Ray, David (1973). "The Dependency Model of Latin American Underdevelopment: Three Basic Fallacies." *Journal of Interamerican Studies and World Affairs* 15:4–20.

Ray, James Lee (1981). "Dependence, Political Compliance and Economic Performance: Latin America and Eastern Europe," in C. W. Kegley, Jr., and P. McGowan (eds.), *The Political Economy of Foreign Policy Behavior*. Beverly Hills: Sage Publications: 111–36.

Reisinger, William (1983). "East European Military Expenditures in the 1970s: Collective Good or Bargaining Offer?" *International Organization* 37, 1:143–55.

Remak, Joachim (1967). *The Origins of World War I, 1871–1914*. New York: Holt, Rinehart & Winston.

Renouvin, Pierre (1948). "Les Origines de l'expédition de Fachoda." *Revue Historique* 200, December: 180–97.

Report of the President's National Bipartisan Commission on Central America (1984). New York: Macmillan.

Rice, Condoleezza (1984). *Uncertain Allegiance: The Soviet Union and the Czechoslovak Army, 1948–1983*. Princeton, N.J.: Princeton University Press.

Richelson, J. T., and D. Ball (1985). *The Ties That Bind*. Boston: Allen & Unwin.

Rigby, T. H. (1972). "Totalitarianism and Change in Communist Systems." *World Politics* January: 433ff.

———— (1983). *Leadership Selection and Patron-Client Relations in the Soviet Union*. London: Allen & Unwin.

Ripoll, Carlos (1982). "The Cuban Scene: Censors and Dissenters." *Partisan Review* 48, 4:1–16. (Reprinted by Cuban-American National Foundation, Washington, D.C.)

Ritter, Gerhard (1970). *The Sword and the Scepter*, vol. 2: *The European Powers and the Wilhelminian Empire*. Coral Gables, Fla.: University of Miami Press.

Roberts, Henry L. (1962). "America and Russia," in his *Eastern Europe: Politics, Revolution, and Diplomacy*. New York: Alfred A. Knopf [1970].

Rogger, Hans (1966). "Russia in 1914," in Walter Laquer and George L. Mosse (eds.), *1914: The Coming of the First World War*. New York: Harper & Row.

Ronfeltdt, David, and Caesar Sereseres (1977). "The Management of U.S.–Mexico Interdependence: Drift Toward Failure?" in C. Vasquez and M. G. y Griego (eds.), *Mexican-U.S. Relations: Conflict and Convergence*. Los Angeles: University of California Press: 43–107.

Rosecrance, Richard N. (1981). "Reward, Punishment, and Interdependence." *Journal of Conflict Resolution* 25, 1:31–46.

Rosenau, James N. (1963). *National Leadership and Foreign Policy: A Case Study in the Mobilization of Public Support*. Princeton, N.J.: Princeton University Press.

——— (1968). *The Attentive Public and Foreign Policy*. Princeton, N.J.: Princeton Center for International Studies.

——— (1981). *The Study of Political Adaptation*. New Brunswick, N.J.: Transaction Books.

Rostow, W. W. (1982). "New Peace in Europe," *San Francisco Chronicle*, January 28:45.

Rothenberg, Morris (1983). "Latin America in Soviet Eyes." *Problems of Communism* 32, 5:1–18.

Rothschild, Emma (1973). *Paradise Lost: The Decline of the Auto-Industrial Age*. New York: Random House.

Rothschild, Joseph (1974). *East Central Europe Between the Two World Wars*. Seattle: University of Washington Press.

*Rowland, Benjamin M. (1973). "Economic Policy and Development: The Case of Latin America," in Robert E. Osgood et al., *Retreat From Empire? The First Nixon Administration*. Baltimore: Johns Hopkins University Press: 241–77.

Rúde Právo (1978). October 5.

Rush, Myron, ed. (1970). *The International Situation and Soviet Foreign Policy*. Columbus, Ohio: Charles E. Merrill.

Russett, Bruce (1983). *The Prisoners of Insecurity: Nuclear Deterrence, the Arms Race, and Arms Control*. San Francisco: W. H. Freeman.

Sadat, Anwar (1978). *In Search of Identity*. New York: Harper & Row.

Sanderson, G. N. (1965). *England, Europe, and the Upper Nile*. Edinburgh: University of Edinburgh Press.

Sanderson, Steven E. (1983a). "Political Succession and Political Rationality in Mexico." *World Politics* 35, 3:315–34.

——— (1983b). "Political Tensions in the Mexican Party System." *Current History* 82, 488:401–5, 436–37.

Sar, Marcin (1983). "Economic and Political Interdependence in Poland's Foreign Economic Policy," in J. Bielasiak and M. D. Simon (eds.), *Polish Politics: Edge of the Abyss*. New York: Praeger: 56–76.

Sarraut, Albert (1923). *La Mise en Valeur des Colonies Françaises*. Paris: Payot.

Sartori, Giovanni (1971). "Concept of Misinformation in Comparative Politics." *American Political Science Review* 15, 3:682ff.

Schapiro, Leonard (1959). *The Communist Party of the Soviet Union*. New York: Random House.

Schelling, Thomas C. (1960). *The Strategy of Conflict*. Oxford: Oxford University Press.

Schlesinger, Arthur M. (1951). *The Rise of Modern America, 1865–1951*. New York: Macmillan.

Schlesinger, Arthur M., Jr. (1984). "Failings of the Kissinger Report." *New York Times*,

January 17:29.

Schlesinger, Stephen C., and Stephen Kinzer (1983). *Bitter Fruit: The Untold Story of the American Coup in Guatemala*. New York: Anchor Press.

Schmidt, Bernadotte (1937). *The Annexation of Bosnia, 1908–1909*. Cambridge: Cambridge University Press.

Schmitt, Karl M. (1968). "Contradictions and Conflicts in U.S. Foreign Policy: The Case of Latin America," In J. B. Gabbert (ed.), *American Foreign Policy and Revolutionary Change*. Pullman: Washington State University Press: 33–47.

——— (1974). *Mexico and the United States, 1821–1973: Conflict and Coexistence*. New York: John Wiley & Sons.

Schmitter, Philippe C. (1978). "Reflections on Mihail Manoilescu and the Political Consequences of Delayed Dependent Development on the Periphery of Western Europe," in Kenneth Jowitt (ed.), *Social Change in Romania, 1866–1940*. Berkeley: Institute of International Studies, University of California.

Schopflin, George (1983). "Poland and Eastern Europe," in A. Brumberg (ed.), *Poland: Genesis of a Revolution*. New York: Random House: 123–34.

Schou, A., and A. O. Brundtland (1971). *Small States in International Relations*. Uppsala: Almqvist and Wiksells Botryckeri.

Schurmann, Franz (1974). *The Logic of World Power*. New York: Pantheon Books.

Scott, Andrew M. (1965; expanded ed. 1982a). *The Revolution in Statecraft: Intervention in an Age of Interdependence*. Durham, N.C.: Duke University Press.

——— (1982b). *The Dynamics of Interdependence*. Chapel Hill: University of North Carolina Press.

Scott, Robert E. (1978). "Politics in Mexico," in G. A. Almond and G. B. Powell (eds.), *Comparative Politics Today: A World View*. Boston: Little, Brown: 435–78.

Seton-Watson, Hugh (1964). *The East-European Revolution*. New York: Praeger.

——— (1967a). *Eastern Europe Between the Wars, 1918–1941*, 3rd ed. revised. New York: Harper & Row.

——— (1967b). *The Russian Empire, 1801–1917*. Oxford: Clarendon Press.

*Sharp, Paul (1977). "Eastern Europe and the Soviet Union: Convergence and Divergence in Historical Perspective," in H. W. Morton and R. L. Tokes (eds.), *Soviet Politics and Society in the 1970s*. New York: Free Press: 340–67.

Sharpe, Kenneth E. (1986). "U.S. Central American Policy: Abroad at Home." Paper prepared for the Conference on the United States and Central America, a Five-Year Assessment, 1980–1985, University of Southern California, February 20–22.

Shils, Edward (1961). *The Intellectual Between Tradition and Modernity: The Indian Situation*. The Hague: Mouton.

Shipler, David K. (1986). "Is Nicaragua's Revolution Exportable?" *New York Times*, March 16.

Sick, Gary (1985). *All Fall Down: America's Tragic Encounter with Iran*. New York: Random House.

Sigmund, Paul E. (1982). "The Military in Chile," in Robert Wesson (ed.), *New Military Politics in Latin America*. New York: Praeger; and Stanford, Calif.: Hoover Institution Press.

*Silvert, Kalman H. (1977). "Leadership Formation and Modernization in Latin America," in his *Essays in Understanding Latin America*. Philadelphia: Institute for the Study of Human Issues: 17–30.

*Simes, Dimitri K. (1984a). "The New Soviet Challenge." *Foreign Policy* 55, Summer: 113–31.

*——— (1984b). "America's New Edge." *Foreign Policy* 56, Fall: 24–43.

Simon, Maurice D. (1981). "Poland Enters the Eighties," in M. D. Simon and R. E. Kanet (eds.), *Background to Crisis: Policy and Politics in Gierek's Poland*. Boulder, Colo.: Westview Press: 405–18.

Singer, J. David (1963). "Inter-Nation Influence: A Formal Model." *American Political Science Review* 57, 2:420–30.

Singer, Marshall R. (1972). *Weak States in a World of Powers: The Dynamics of International Relationships*. New York: Free Press.

Sivard, Ruth Leger (1985). *World Military and Social Expenditures, 1985*. Washington, D.C.: World Priorities.

*Skidmore, T. E., and P. H. Smith. "Latin America: The United States and the World." *Modern Latin America*: 321–58.

*Skilling, H. Gordon (1983). "Interest Groups and Communist Politics Revisited." *World Politics* 36, 1:1–27.

——— (1984). "The Crisis in Eastern European Communism: National and International." *International Journal* 49, Spring: 429–55.

———, and Franklyn Griffith (1971). *Interest Groups and Soviet Politics*. Princeton, N.J.: Princeton University Press.

Skocpol, Theda (1979). *States and Social Revolutions*. Cambridge: Cambridge University Press.

Skurski, Roger (1982). "Trade and Integration in East Europe." *Current History* 81, 478:357–61, 386–88.

Smith, Gaddis (1984). "The Legacy of Monroe's Doctrine." *New York Times Magazine*, September 9:46ff.

Smith, Peter H. (1985). "U.S.-Mexican Relations: The 1980s and Beyond," *Journal of Interamerican Studies and World Affairs* 27, 1:91–101.

Smith, Tony (1981). *The Pattern of Imperialism: The United States, Great Britain, and the Late-Industrializing World*. Boston: Little, Brown.

Sovetov, A. (1968). "The Present Stage in the Struggle Between Socialism and Imperialism." *International Affairs* (Moscow) 11, November.

Spanier, John W., ed. (1981). *Congress, the Presidency, and American Foreign Policy*. Elmsford, N.Y.: Pergamon Press.

Spanier, John, and Christopher C. Shoemaker (1984). *Patron-Client State Relationships*. New York: Praeger.

Spykman, Nicholas John (1942). *America's Strategy in World Politics*. New York: Harcourt Brace.

Stalin, J. V. (1974). *On the Opposition*. Peking: Foreign Languages.

Stavrianos, L. S. (1981). *Global Rift: The Third World Comes of Age*. New York: William Morrow.

Steel, Ronald (1967). *Pax Americana*. New York: Viking Press.

——— (1971/72). "A Sphere of Influence Policy?" *Foreign Policy* 5:107–18.

Steele, Jonathan, ed. (1974). *Eastern Europe Since Stalin*. New York: Crane, Russak.

Stein, Arthur A. (1984). "The Hegemon's Dilemma." *International Organization* 38, 2: 383–84.

Stein, Janice Gross (forthcoming). "Extended Deterrence in the Middle East: A Retrospective Analysis of American Strategy."

Steiner, Zara (1977). "The Foreign Office Under Sir Edward Grey," in F. H. Hinsley (ed.), *British Foreign Policy Under Sir Edward Grey*. London: Cambridge University Press: 22–69.

Stent, Angela (1985). "Soviet Policy Toward the German Democratic Republic," in Sarah M. Terry (ed.), *Soviet Policy in Eastern Europe*. New Haven: Yale University Press.

Stepan, Alfred (1981). "The United States and Latin America: Vital Interests and the Instruments of Power," in E. G. Ferris and J. K. Lincoln (eds.), *Latin American Foreign Policies: Global and Regional Dimensions.* Boulder, Colo.: Westview Press: 19–38.

Steward, Dick (1980). *Money, Marines, and Mission: Recent U.S. Latin American Policy.* Lanham, Md.: University Press of America.

Story, Dale (1982). "Trade Politics in the Third World: A Case Study of the Mexican GATT Decision." *International Organization* 36, 4:767–94.

Strachey, John (1960). *The End of Empire.* New York: Random House.

Street, James H. (1983). "Mexico's Development Dilemma." *Current History* 82, 488:410–14, 434.

———, and D. P. James, eds. (1979). *Technology Progress in Latin America.* Boulder, Colo.: Westview Press.

Stuart, Graham H., and James L. Tigner (1975). *Latin America and the United States,* 6th ed. Englewood Cliffs, N.J.: Prentice-Hall.

Suda, Zdenek (1984). "Central Europe—Lost and Forgotten?" *Kosmas* 2, 2:1–6.

Summers, Harry (1984). *On Strategy: The Vietnam War in Context.* Washington, D.C.: U.S. Government Printing Office for the Army War College.

Sweet, D. W. (1977). "Great Britain and Germany, 1905–11," in F. H. Hinsley (ed.), *British Foreign Policy Under Sir Edward Grey.* London: Cambridge University Press: 216–35.

Tajima, Takashi (1981). "China and South-East Asia: Strategic Interest and Policy Prospects." *Adelphi Papers* Winter, no. 172.

Talbott, Strobe (1978a). "A Display of Group-think." *Time,* June 26:31.

——— (1978b). "Comrade Fidel Wants You." *Time,* July 10:36–39.

Taylor, A. J. P. (1950). "Prelude to Fashoda: The Question of the Upper Nile, 1894–95." *Economic History Review* 65:52–80.

——— (1971). *The Struggle for the Mastery of Europe, 1848–1918.* New York: Oxford University Press: 467–74.

Terry, Sarah M., ed. (1984). *Soviet Policy in Eastern Europe.* New Haven: Yale University Press.

Thomas, Hugh (1971). *Cuba: The Pursuit of Freedom.* New York: Harper & Row.

——— (1977). *The Cuban Revolution.* New York: Harper & Row.

——— (1984). "Coping With Cuba," in Irving Louis Horowitz (ed.), *Cuban Communism,* 5th ed. New Brunswick, N.J., and London: Transaction Books: 775–89.

———, George A. Fauriol, and Juan Carlos Weiss (1984). *The Cuban Revolution: Twenty-Five Years Later.* Boulder, Colo.: Westview Press.

Thucydides (1982). *The Peloponnesian War.* Richard Crawley (trans.). New York: Random House.

Tilly, Charles, ed. (1975). *The Formation of National States in Western Europe.* Princeton, N.J.: Princeton University Press.

Toai, Van, and David Chanoff (1984). "Vietnam Parallels: Lest Managua Be Another Hanoi. . . ." *Wall Street Journal,* October 17.

Tocqueville, Alexis de (1945). *Democracy in America,* vol. 1. New York: Alfred A. Knopf.

Togliatti, Palmiro (1964). Cited in *New York Times,* September 1:2.

Touraine, Alain, et al. (1983). *Solidarity: Poland 1980–81.* Cambridge: Cambridge University Press.

Trilling, Lionel (1952). "Introduction," in George Orwell, *Homage to Catalonia.* New York and London: Harcourt Brace Jovanovich: v–xxiii.

Triska, Jan F. (1982). "Europe Realigned." *Stanford Magazine* 10, 3:22–27.

——— (1985). "Dominant Powers and Their Dependencies." *Kosmas* 3, 1:11–24.

————, and Paul M. Cocks (1977). *Political Development in Eastern Europe*. New York: Praeger.

————, and David Finley (1968). *Soviet Foreign Policy*. New York: Macmillan.

————, and Paul M. Johnson (1975). *Political Development and Political Change in Eastern Europe*. Denver: University of Denver Press.

Tsurutani, Taketsugu (1982). "Old Habits, New Times: Challenges to Japanese-American Security Relations." *International Security* 7, Fall: 175–87.

Tucker, Robert W. (1980/81). "The Purposes of American Power." *Foreign Affairs* 59, 2.

Turner, F. J. (1961). "The Significance of the Frontier in American History." *Frontier and Section: Selected Essays of Frederick Jackson Turner*. Englewood Cliffs, N.J.: Prentice-Hall.

Turner, Robert F. (1983). *The War Powers Resolution: Its Implementation in Theory and Practice*. Philadelphia: Foreign Policy Research Institute.

Ulam, Adam (1965). *The New Face of Soviet Totalitarianism*. New York: Praeger.

———— (1974). *Expansion and Coexistence*, revised ed. New York: Praeger.

*———— (1982). "Reflections on the Destiny of East Central Europe Since 1945," in Milorad M. Drachkovitch (ed.), *East Central Europe: Yesterday, Today, Tomorrow*. Stanford, Calif.: Hoover Institution Press: 3–18.

Ullman, Richard H. (1983). "At War with Nicaragua." *Foreign Affairs* 62, 1:39–58.

United Nations (1984). *Yearbook of International Trade Statistics*. New York: UN Statistical Office.

United Nations General Assembly (1960). *Official Records*. 15th session, agenda item 87, annexes: 8.

Valenta, Jiri (1979a). "The Bureaucratic Politics Paradigm and the Soviet Invasion of Czechoslovakia." *Political Science Quarterly* 94, 1: 55–76.

———— (1979b). *Soviet Intervention in Czechoslovakia*. Baltimore: Johns Hopkins University Press.

———— (1980). "From Prague to Kabul: The Soviet Style of Invasion." *International Security* Fall: 114–41.

———— (1984a). "Revolutionary Change, Soviet Intervention, and Normalization in East-Central Europe." *Comparative Politics* January: 127–51.

———— (1984b). "Soviet Policy Toward Hungary and Czechoslovakia," in Sarah M. Terry (ed.), *Soviet Policy in Eastern Europe*. New Haven: Yale University Press: 93–124.

*———— (1984c). "The Soviet Union and East Central Europe: Crisis, Intervention, and Normalization," in T. Rakowska-Harmstone (ed.), *Communism in Eastern Europe*. Bloomington: Indiana University Press: 329–59.

————, and Herbert Ellison (1986). *Grenada and Soviet/Cuban Policy: Internal Crisis and U.S./OECS Intervention*. Boulder, Colo.: Westview Press.

————, and William Potter, eds. (1984). *Soviet Decisionmaking for Security*. London: Allen & Unwin.

Vanous, Jan (1982). "East European Economic Slowdown." *Problems of Communism* 31, 4:1–19.

————, and Michael Marrese (1982). "Soviet Subsidies to Eastern Economies." *Wall Street Journal*, January 15.

Varas, Augusto (1984). "Ideology and Politics in Latin American–USSR Relations." *Problems of Communism* 33, 1:35–47.

Vardys, V. Stanley (1975). "The Problem of Nationality: Modernization and Baltic Nationalism." *Problems of Communism* 24, 5:32–48.

Villagran Kramer, Francisco (1982). "The Background to the Current Political Crisis in

Central America," in Richard E. Feinberg (ed.), *Central America: International Dimensions of the Crisis*. New York: Holmes & Meier: 15–35.

Vital, David (1967). *The Inequality of States: A Study of the Small Power in International Relations*. New York: Oxford University Press.

Vloyantes, John P. (1975). *Silk Glove Hegemony: Finnish-Soviet Relations, 1944–1974; A Case Study of the Theory of the Soft Sphere of Influence*. Kent, Ohio: Kent State University Press.

Wallerstein, Immanuel (1980). *The Modern World-System II: Mercantilism and the Consolidation of the European World-Economy, 1600–1750*. New York: Academic Press.

*——— (1982). "Socialist States: Mercantilist Strategies and Revolutionary Objectives," in Edward Friedman (ed.), *Ascent and Decline in the World System*. Beverly Hills: Sage Publications: 289–300.

Wall Street Journal (1981). June 8.

——— (1983). July 20.

Walter, Richard J. (1972). *The United States and Latin America*. New York: Seabury Press.

*Waltz, Kenneth N. (1959). *Man, the State, and War: A Theoretical Analysis*. New York: Columbia University Press.

——— (1967). *Foreign Policy and Democratic Politics: The American and British Experience*. Boston: Little, Brown.

Washington Times (1985). June 6:3D.

*Wasowski, S. (1983). "COMECON: The Recent Past and Perspectives for the 1980s," in Michael J. Sodaro and S. Wolchik (eds.), *Foreign and Domestic Policy in Eastern Europe in the 1980s*. New York: St. Martin's Press: 193–212.

Weber, Max (1978). *Economy and Society*, vol. 2. Berkeley: University of California Press.

Weinberger, Caspar W. (1984). "The Uses of Military Power." *New York Times*, November 29.

Wesson, Robert (1969). *Soviet Foreign Policy in Perspective*. Homewood, Ill.: Dorsey Press.

——— (1981). *The United States and Brazil: Limits of Influence*. New York: Praeger.

——— (1982a). *New Military Politics in Latin America*. New York: Praeger, and Stanford, Calif.: Hoover Institution Press.

——— (1982b). *U.S. Influence in Latin America in the 1980s*. New York: Praeger.

——— (1985). *The Russian Dilemma*, revised ed. New York: Praeger.

——— (1986). *Latin American Views of U.S. Policy*. New York: Praeger.

*Whetten, Lawrence L. (1982). "The Warsaw Pact as an Instrument for Inducing Political and Military Integration and Interdependency," in A. I. Broadhurst (ed.), *The Future of European Alliance Systems: NATO and the Warsaw Pact*. Boulder, Colo.: Westview Press: 237–66.

White, Richard Alan (1984). *The Morass: United States Intervention in Central America*. New York: Harper & Row.

White, Stephen (1978). "Communist Systems and the Iron Law of Pluralism." *British Journal of Political Science* 8, 1978:101–17.

Wiarda, Howard (1984). *In Search of Policy: The United States and Latin America*. Washington, D.C.: American Enterprise Institute.

Wight, M. (1949). *Power Politics*. London: Royal Institute of International Affairs.

——— (1977). *Systems of States*. Atlantic Highlands, N.J.: Humanities Press.

——— (1979). *Power Politics*. H. N. Bull and C. Holbraad (eds.). Harmondsworth: Penguin Books.

*Wiles, Peter J. (1982). "East Central Europe as an Active Element in the Soviet Empire," in Milorad M. Drachkovitch (ed.), *East Central Europe: Yesterday, Today, Tomorrow*. Stanford, Calif.: Hoover Institution Press: 81–105.

Willerton, John P. (1978). "Clientism in the Soviet Union." *Studies in Comparative Communism* Summer/Autumn: 159ff.

Windsor, Philip (1984). "Superpower Intervention," in Hedley Bull (ed.), *Intervention in World Politics*. Oxford: Clarendon Press.

Wit, Joel S. (1982). "American SLBM: Counterforce Options and Strategic Implications." *Survival* 24:163–74.

Witte, Sergi (1921). *The Memoirs of Count Witte*. Abraham Yarmolinsky (trans.). Garden City, N.Y.: Doubleday, Page.

Wolf, Charles, Jr. (1985). "The Costs of the Soviet Empire." *Science* 230, 429:997–1002.

Wolf, Eric R. (1982). *Europe and the People Without History*. Berkeley and Los Angeles: University of California Press.

Wolfe, Alan (1977). *The Limits of Legitimacy: Political Contradictions of Contemporary Capitalism*. New York: Free Press.

Wolff, Robert (1957). *The Balkans in Our Time*. Cambridge, Mass.: Harvard University Press.

Wright, Harrison M., ed. (1976). *The "New" Imperialism: Analysis of Late Nineteenth-Century Expansion*, 2nd ed. Lexington, Mass.: D. C. Heath.

Wyman, Donald L. (1978). "Dependence and Conflict in U.S.-Mexican Relations, 1920–1975," in R. L. Paarlberg (ed.), *Diplomatic Dispute: U.S. Conflict with Iran, Japan, and Mexico*. Cambridge, Mass.: Harvard Center for International Affairs: 85–141.

*Young, Oran (1968). "The Bases of International Bargaining," in his *Politics of Force*. Princeton, N.J.: Princeton University Press: 25–41.

——— (1982). "Regime Dynamics: The Rise and Fall of International Regimes." *International Organization* 36, 2:277–97.

Zeman, A. B. (1961). *The Breakup of the Habsburg Empire, 1914–1918*. Oxford: Oxford University Press.

Zimmerman, William (1972). "Hierarchical Regional Systems and the Politics of System Boundaries." *International Organization* 26, 1:18–36.

——— (1978). "Dependency Theory and the Soviet–East European Hierarchical Regional System: Initial Tests." *Slavic Review* 37, 4:604–23.

——— (1981). "Soviet–East European Relations in the 1980s and the Changing International System," in M. Bornstein, Z. Gitelman, and W. Zimmerman (eds.), *East-West Relations and the Future of Eastern Europe: Politics and Economics*. London: Allen & Unwin: 87–104.

——— (1984). "Soviet Relations with Yugoslavia and Romania," in Sarah M. Terry (ed.), *Soviet Policy in Eastern Europe*. New Haven: Yale University Press: 125–54.

Zimmern, A. (1939). *The League of Nations and the Rule of Law, 1918–1935*. London: Macmillan.

*Zwick, Peter (1983). *National Communism*. Boulder, Colo.: Westview Press.

Zylberg, J., and M. Monterichard (1982). "An Abortive Attempt to Change Foreign Policy: Chile 1970–73," in K. J. Holsti (ed.), *Why Nations Realign*. Boston and London: Allen & Unwin: 172–97.

Index

Act of Rio, 57
Adams, Henry, 37, 40
Afghanistan, 95, 213
Aggression, 221
Albania, 72
Alexander I, emperor of Russia, 34
Alliance for Progress, 59, 60, 203, 210, 227, 235
Alliance structure, American, 419–20
Annexation, 7
ANZUS Treaty, 133, 420
Arbatov, Georgy, 415
Arbenz, Jacobo, 58, 98, 273
Arms sales, 245, 246
Asymmetry of power, 106–7, 176, 214, 241, 440, 441
Atlantic Charter, 57
Australia, See Spheres of influence
Austria-Hungary: foreign policies, 304–5, 406; internal politics, 303–4
Austro-Russian competition in the Balkans, 402–3, 408

Balkan politics (pre-1914), 402
Balkan rivalries (pre-1914), 401
Bargaining model, See Power and exchange
Batista, Fulgencio, 98, 327, 328, 331, 337

Bay of Pigs, 58
Behavior control, 175, 195
Belloc, Hilaire, 120
Blaine, James G., 51
Bolívar, Simón, 35
Brezhnev, Leonid, 68, 73, 77, 204, 205, 264, 269, 412
Brezhnev doctrine, 180, 206, 216, 262, 264, 265, 268, 269. See also Limited sovereignty
Buffer zones, 91, 127, 128, 129; East Europe, 128, 244, 467; Latin America, 128
Bulgaria, 92

Camacho, Manuel Ávila, 353
Capitalism and socialism, economic dependency in, 449–53
Capitalist ideology, 119
Cardenas, Lázaro, 56, 306, 353
Carter, Jimmy, 63, 64, 268
Carter administration, 60, 229–30, 235, 251, 252, 258, 415
Castro, Fidel, 58, 306, 313, 314, 317, 319, 322, 323, 324, 328, 330, 331
Ceauşescu, Nicolae, 250, 304, 306, 308
Central American Common Market, 227
Churchill, Winston, 67
Cities, 195–97

Cleveland, Grover, 51, 52
Coercion, 174, 175, 176, 177, 180
Colonial disputes (1870–1914), 407–8
Colonial empires, European, 51, 108–9, 126–27. *See also* Dominant-subordinate relationships, European colonies
Colonial systems, 87–88
Committee for Defense of the Revolution (Cuba), 332, 333–34
Communist governments, East Europe, 412
Confederation of Mexican Workers, 357
Conference of Berlin (1884–85), 126, 402
Cordon sanitaire. See Buffer zones
Council for Mutual Economic Assistance (CMEA), 70, 72, 74, 75, 181, 210, 217, 301, 315, 323, 385–90, 391
Cuba, 52, 54–55, 58–59, 99, 257
Cuba, as socialist dependency, 318–20, 326, 451–52; Cuban elite–Soviet interests, 323–4; culture and education, 334–36; economy, 329–31; foreign and military politics, 337–40; influence and exploitation in economy, 320–22; mass organizations, 333–34; media, 333; militarization, 336–37; in political organization, 322–23; political system, 331–33; social progress, 327–29
Cuba, economic dependency of: capital, 315–16; debt, 316; energy, 316–17; exports, 314; production, 312–13; technology, 317; trade, 313–14; trade-partner concentration, 314–15
Cuban-Soviet Commission for Economic, Scientific and Technical Collaboration, 323
Czechoslovakia, 70, 73, 92, 95, 206, 246

Declaration of Havana, 56
Declaration of Liberated Europe, 68
Declaration on the Granting of Independence to Colonial Countries and Peoples, 457
Democracy, 425–26, 443, 444
Dependence, 6, 12, 207, 241; advantages of, 171–72; disadvantages of, 173–74
Dependencia, 207, 296, 297, 320, 321, 325, 326, 337, 339, 340, 451
Dependencies, bargaining profiles of, 190–93

Dependency, economic, 212, 449–53
Dependency literature. *See* Spheres of influence behavior, U.S.-USSR
Dependency relationships, 177, 452
Dependent development, 207, 209
Domestic politics, 425
Dominance, 440; advantages of, 171–72; disadvantages of, 172–74
Dominant powers: comparison, 3–6, 441–47; concept, 202; constraints on, 10–11; dilemmas of, 462–64; military intervention, 11
Dominant powers, strategies of, 8, 203–7, 443; costs, 209–10, 215; cultural penetration, 211; limitations, 213; military-political intervention, 210, 215; security, 209, 215, 216
Dominant-subordinate relationships, 456–58; definition, 105–7, 108; historical analogies, 169–71; patterns of, 188–93
Dominant-subordinate relationships, European colonies: boundaries, 111–12; coercion, 120; control, 109–10; cultural penetration, 117–20; geographical separation, 112–13; as peripheries, 115–16
Dominant-subordinate relationships, U.S.-Latin America, 110–23; sphere of influence boundaries, 112–17; U.S. cultural penetration, 118–20; U.S. forms of coercion, 121–22; U.S. informal influence, 110–11. *See also* Spheres of influence, U.S.–Latin America
Dominant-subordinate relationships, USSR–East Europe, 110–23; economic relations with dependents, 80–81; military relations with dependents, 79; political relations with dependents, 81; Soviet cultural penetration, 118–20; Soviet forms of coercion, 121–22; Soviet informal influence, 110–11; sphere of influence boundaries, 112–17. *See also* Spheres of influence, USSR–East Europe
Dominant-subordinate states: autonomous action, 107; compliance, 106–7; interaction, 105; penetrative action, 107; power asymmetry, 106–7. *See also* Asymmetry of power
Dominican Republic, 53–54, 59–60
Duarte, José Napoleón, 237

Dubček, Alexander, 277, 303
Dulles, John Foster, 57

East Europe, social change, 2–3, 453–56
East Germany, 72
East-West conflict, 212, 231
Economic systems, East Europe: competition, 373; crisis of economic structure, 374–75; dependence on Soviet economy, 379–83; growth, 374; income distribution, 378–79; indebtedness, 374–75; investment priorities, 373–74; uniformity, 373
Eisenhower administration, 58
El Salvador, 61
European Economic Community (EEC), 116–17
Expansionism: Russian, 64–65, 77–79; U.S., 50–51, 77–79

Fate control, 175, 189
Finland, 92
Finlandization, 216, 438
Foreign policy: in Aristotle, 146–47; in Bryce, 149; in Machiavelli, 147; in Montesquieu, 147–48; in Thucydides, 146; in Tocqueville, 148–49
Foreign policy in comparative literature: Japan, 151; U.S., 149–52, 228–31, 232; U.S.-USSR, 154–157; USSR, 152–54; West Europe, 150–52
Foreign policy, primacy of, 427–29
Free trade, 436
Frontiers, international, 127, 128–29

Gheorghiu-Dej, Gheorghe, 303
Gierek, Edward, 354, 356, 364
Global Development Policy (Mexico), 365
Gomułka, Władysław, 71, 304, 353
Gorbachev, Mikhail, 198
Gray areas, 124, 128. See also Spheres of restraint
Guatemala, 57–58
Guerrilla warfare, 61, 251–52

Haiti, 53–54, 55
Hawaii, 51, 53
Hegel, G. W. Friedrich, 4
Hegemonic systems, 85–86, 208, 211–12;

in contemporary politics, 462–65; vs. colonial systems, 87–89
Hegemonic systems, Great Britain and the Middle East: British hegemony, 88–89; military intervention, 89; recession to American interests, 89–90; revolutions, 90–91
Hegemonic systems, U.S. and Latin America: bureaucratic-authoritarian regimes, 100; economies and dictatorships, 97–98; industrialization and populism, 98–99; military intervention, 99; reality, 100–101
Hegemonic systems, USSR and East Europe, 91–96, 465–67; buffer states, 91; communist-party state, 91–92; economic obsolescence, 94–96; industrialization, 92–93; military intervention, 95; related to Western Europe, 468–69; uneven development, 96
Hegemony, 140–41, 425, 464
Hegemony, U.S., 219–22; as antirevolutionary power, 224–27; in Central America, 227, 232–38; in conflict with democracy, 229–31; in international economic systems, 222–24
Helsinki agreements, 129
Hobson, John A., 126
Honduras, 54
Hoxha, Enver, 302, 303, 306, 308
Hungary, 71–72, 92, 95

Ideology, 185–88, 242–43
Imperial systems, 195–96
Influence, 7, 141
Influenced states, 125, 130; economic dependency, 136; mutual relationships, 134; relationship with influencing power, 134–37, 142
Influencing powers, 125, 130, 132; behavior, 137–39; interaction, 139–40, 141; mutual relationship, 134–35, 137–38, 142, 143; relationship with influenced states, 134–36, 142, 143
Inter-American Treaty of Reciprocal Assistance, 57, 267
Interdependence, 6, 12, 207, 208
International order, 83–84, 134–37, 292
Intervention. See Military intervention

Interventionist behavior, 278–81
Interventionist policies, U.S., 226–27

Jaruzelski, Wojciech, 74
Johnson, Lyndon, 59, 60, 204, 220, 264, 267, 274
Johnson administration, 260

Kádár, János, 71
Karlovy Vary Conference of Communist and Workers' Parties, 205
Kellogg-Briand Pact, 267, 280
Kennedy, John F., 58, 203, 251, 267, 435
Kennedy administration, 260
Khrushchev, Nikita, 58, 71, 268, 304
Khrushchev doctrine, 269, 353
Kissinger, Henry, 410
Kuron, Jacek, 358

Lenin, Vladimir I., 35, 39, 65, 66, 126, 275, 457
Limited sovereignty, 267, 268, 269, 270. See also Brezhnev doctrine
Luttwak, Edward, 220

McKinley, William, 52, 62
Madariaga, Salvador de, 353
Madrid, Miguel de la, 356, 358
Maneuvers, military: U.S., 250, 253; USSR, 248
Market system, Latin America: dependence on U.S. economy, 381–83; debt, 378; economic potential, 377–78; income distribution, 378–79; U.S. regulation, 376–77
Marrese-Vanous method. See Wealth transfer
Marshall Plan, 69, 70, 465
Marxism-Leninism, 119, 291, 292
Mexico, 55
Mexico and Poland, bargaining relations with U.S. and USSR: bargaining profiles, 360–61; coercive opposition, 363; diversification, 362; ideology, 353; resources, 362; security, 368–69
Mexico and Poland, crisis 1970–80: constrained bargaining, 364–68; economy, 355; mass politics, 356–57; reforms, 356, 358–59

Mexico and Poland, similarities: 348–54
Middle East. See Hegemonic systems, Great Britain
Military assistance, 245
Military assistance, U.S., 246; Central America, 247; El Salvador, 251, 252; Guatemala, 251, 252; Honduras, 252–53
Military assistance, USSR, 246, 247
Military influence, use of: U.S., 257–58; USSR, 257–59
Military integration, U.S.–Latin America, 254
Military integration, USSR–East Europe, 249, 250
Military intervention, superpowers, 261–62; asymmetries, 282–84; costs, 432–36; in spheres of influence, 431; similarities, 263–70; in weaker states, 431–32
Military intervention, U.S., 81, 99, 100, 237, 303–4; in Cuba, 267; in the Dominican Republic, 263–64, 273, 274; in Grenada, 263–64, 274; in Guatemala, 263–64, 273; in light of national security, 270–74; in Mexico, 272, 273; in Nicaragua, 273
Military intervention, USSR, 81, 95, 303–4, 412; in Czechoslovakia, 263–64, 276–77; in Finland, 275; in Hungary, 263, 276; in light of national security, 270, 274; in Poland, 263, 268, 275, 277
Military relations, 183–84
Military relationships, U.S.–Central America, 244, 251, 255–57
Military relationships, USSR–East Europe, 246, 248, 255–57
Monism, 82, 211
Monroe Doctrine, 49–50, 53, 56, 57, 58, 63, 64, 180, 213, 217, 227, 243, 262, 264, 265–69, 281
Montevideo Declaration, 56, 267

Nagy, Imre, 275
National security, U.S., 63, 232–33
Nationalism, U.S., 51
Naval power, 114
New Economic Maneuver (Poland), 365
Nicaragua, 54, 55, 60, 61, 99, 257, 460
Nixon, Richard M., 58, 410, 435
Nixon doctrine, 435
Nonintervention, principle of, 56

North Atlantic Treaty Organization (NATO), 418, 465
Novotný, Antonín, 302
Nuclear revolution, 170
Nuclear war, avoidance of, 429–32, 437
Nuclear weapons, 121, 122, 178, 414, 418
Nutting, Wallace, 237

Olney, Richard, 52
Opportunity costs. *See* Wealth transfer
Ordaz, Gustavo Díaz, 353
Organization for Economic Cooperation and Development (OECD), 377
Organization of American States (OAS), 57, 58, 61, 133, 254, 267
Ottoman Empire, 401, 402, 408

Panama, 53, 59
Panama Canal Treaty, 268, 282
Pan-American Union, 57
Partido Comunista de Cuba, 332, 336
Partido Revolucionario Institucional (Mexico), 356, 357
Pax Britannica, 89
Peace of Westphalia, 86
Perón, Juan, 90, 98
Peurifoy, John, 58
Philippines, 52–53, 56
Platt Amendment, 52, 55, 267, 269, 270, 281, 282, 337
Pluralism, 82, 211
Poland, 71, 73–74, 92, 95
Poland and Mexico. *See* Mexico and Poland
Polish Corridor, 91
Polk, James, 50, 266
Portillo, José López, 354, 356
Potsdam Conference, 67
Power, 176, 241
Power and exchange, 176–78; model of (Blau), 175
Power, conditions of: coercion, 183–85; ideology, 185–88; indifference to benefits, 178–80; monopolization of rewards, 180–83
Power relationships, 241, 441
Public opinion, 425–56
Puerto Rico, 52

Rankeian axiom, 427

Rapacki Plan, 467
Raw materials, access to, 436–38
Reagan, Ronald, 198
Reagan administration, 60, 61, 63, 230–31, 234, 236, 237, 247, 252, 253, 415, 416, 418, 422
"Reagan Doctrine," 221
Regional relations, U.S.: economic, 290–91; ideology, 291–93; military, 289–90. *See also* Foreign policy, U.S.
Regional relations, USSR: economic, 290–91; ideology, 291–93; military, 289–90. *See also* Foreign policy, USSR
Restoration, policy of, 216
Roman Catholic Church, 118
Romania, 72, 92; military, 75, 250
Roosevelt, Franklin D., 56, 67
Roosevelt, Theodore, 53, 266, 280
Roosevelt Corollary, 55, 269, 270, 281, 282
Rusk, Dean, 204
Russell, Bertrand, 41
Russia, domestic crisis, 406–7

Saltwater colonialism, 112, 113
Salvadoran army, 252
Sandinistas, 61
San Martín, Ramón Grau, 337
Seely, John, 37
Sino-Soviet relations, 72, 413–14, 415
Solidarity, 74, 357
Somoza, Anastasio, 54, 98
South America, 56, 62, 63
Soviet-American rivalry in the Third World, 408–10
Soviet Johnson Doctrine, 11
Soviet strategic system, vulnerability of, 414–15
Soviet Union, encirclement of, 415–16
Sovietization, 68–69
Spheres of influence, 6, 47–49, 82–84, 142, 177, 447–49; by agreements, 130–31; associated with alliances, 132–33; Australia, 133; bargaining behavior in, 174–88; comparative analysis, 77–84; concept of, 125, 127, 132; in contemporary politics, 131, 134–40; European colonies, 126–27; evolution of, 193–99; intervention in, 431–32; justice and order in, 136–38; maintaining intern-

ational order, 134–37; power and dependence in, 174–77; recognition of, 132; term, first used, 126; by unilateral declaration, 129–30; Western Europe, 133. *See also* Dominant-subordinate relationships

Spheres of influence, history of: U.S., 49–64; USSR, 64–77

Spheres of influence, U.S.-USSR, comparison of: benefits, 26–28; complexities of, 28–32; in contemporary literature, 39–46; historical bases of, 33–39

Spheres of restraint, 127, 128, 129

Stalin, Joseph, 66, 67, 68, 70, 91, 178, 243, 244, 308

Strategic Defense Initiative, 418–19

Strategic resources, 178–79, 181

Strategists, 285

Strategy, 202

Strong, Josiah, 51

Subordinate regions: differences, 8–9; similarities, 9–10; strategies of, 11–12

Subordinate states, 458–62; concept of, 202; ideological loyalties, 287–88; interactions with hegemons, 288, 464; national sovereignty, 287; social change, 453–5

Subordinate states, bargaining power of, 461–62; control of resources, 179; debt repayments, 299–300; diversification, 181–83; economy, 298–99; ideology, 186–88; political resistance, 184–85; special relationships, 300. *See also* Power and exchange

Subordinate states, confrontational strategies of: doctrine, 307–8; economic development, 300; open defiance, 302–4; reduced vulnerability to economic sanctions, 305–7; social discontent, 301–2

Subordination, mechanisms of: economic control, 296–97; economic sanctions, 304–5; manipulation, 297–98; military coercion, 294–95, 303–4; political intervention, 296

Subsidization, 196–97

Superpowers, 188–90, 198

Taft administration, 53

Teheran Conference, 67

Teller Amendment, 52

Thayer, Alfred, 51

Tito, Joseph Broz, 306

Tocqueville, Alexis de, 35, 40, 148–49

Trotsky, Leon, 35

Trujillo, Rafael, 98

Truman, Harry S, 40

Truman Doctrine, 69, 70, 90, 465

Ubico, Jorge, 98

Ulbricht, Walter, 302

United Fruit Company, 57, 227, 273, 301

United Nations, Charter of, 133

U Thant, 263

Vargas, Getulio, 90, 98

Villa, Pancho, 273, 352

Walker, William, 266

War Powers Act, 228, 230

War Powers Resolution, 435

Warsaw Treaty, 72, 74, 75, 133, 246, 249, 250, 267, 275, 282, 465

Wealth transfer, 383–84; evaluation of, 390–99; opportunity costs, interpretation of, 386–89

Weinberger Doctrine, 435–36

Wilson, Woodrow, 39, 54, 62, 273, 425

Wilson Administration, 54

World policemen, 57, 67

Yalta Agreement, 2, 31, 67, 465, 466

Yugoslavia, 70, 75, 269

Zelaya, José Santos, 273

Contributors

Jan F. Triska is Professor of Political Science and Co-Chairman of the Program on International Relations at Stanford University. He was educated at Charles University Law School in Prague (J.U.D.), at Yale Law School (J.S.D.), and at Harvard University (PH.D., Department of Government). He has taught at Harvard, Cornell, the University of California, Berkeley, and Stanford. His most recent books include *The World of Superpowers* (with Robert North and Nobutaka Ike), 1985, and *Blue Collar Workers in Eastern Europe* (with Charles Gati, ed.), 1981.

David B. Abernethy is Professor of Political Science and Co-Chairman, International Relations Program, Stanford University.

Gabriel A. Almond is Emeritus Professor of Political Science, Stanford University.

Richard R. Fagen is Professor of Political Science and Gildred Professor of Latin American Studies, Stanford University.

David D. Finley is Professor of Political Science, Colorado College.

Michael I. Handel is Professor of International Relations, Hebrew University of Jerusalem, and Professor of National Security Affairs, U.S. Army War College, Carlisle Barracks, Pennsylvania.

Jeffrey L. Hughes is MacArthur Fellow, Department of Political Science, Stanford University.

Paul M. Johnson is Professor of Political Science, Florida State University.

Terry Karl is Assistant Professor of Government, Harvard University.

Paul Keal is M.A.I.R. Fellow, Department of International Relations, Research School of Pacific Studies, Australian National University, Canberra.

James R. Kurth is Professor of Political Science, Swarthmore College.

Richard Ned Lebow is Professor of Government and Director, Peace Studies Program, Cornell University.

Paul Marer is Professor of International Business and Management, School of Business, Indiana University.

Robert A. Packenham is Professor of Political Science, Stanford University.

Kazimierz Z. Poznanski is Associate Professor of Economics, Rensselaer Polytechnic Institute.

Condoleezza Rice is Assistant Professor of Political Science, Stanford University.

Jiri Valenta is Professor of Political Science and Director, East European and Strategic Studies, Graduate School of International Studies, University of Miami.

Robert Wesson is Emeritus Professor of Political Science, University of California, Santa Barbara, and Senior Research Fellow, Hoover Institution, Stanford University.